ENTREPRENEURSHIP

Starting, Developing, and Managing a New Enterprise

ENTREPRENEURSHIP

Starting, Developing, and Managing a New Enterprise

Third Edition

Robert D. Hisrich, Ph.D.
A. Malachi Mixon III Chair in Entrepreneurial Studies and Professor
The Weatherhead School of Management
Case Western Reserve University

Michael P. Peters, Ph.D.
Professor and Chair, Marketing Department
Boston College

IRWIN

Chicago • Bogota • Boston • Buenos Aires • Caracas
London • Madrid • Mexico City • Sydney • Toronto

IRWIN
Concerned About Our Environment

In recognition of the fact that our company is a large end-user of fragile yet replenishable resources, we at IRWIN can assure you that every effort is made to meet or exceed Environmental Protection Agency (EPA) recommendations and requirements for a "greener" workplace.

To preserve these natural assets, a number of environmental policies, both companywide and department-specific, have been implemented. From the use of 50% recycled paper in our textbooks to the printing of promotional materials with recycled stock and soy inks to our office paper recycling program, we are committed to reducing waste and replacing environmentally unsafe products with safer alternatives.

Senior sponsoring editor: *Craig Beytien*
Editorial coordinator: *Jennifer R. McBride*
Senior marketing manager: *Kurt Messersmith*
Project editor: *Karen J. Nelson*
Production manager: *Ann Cassady*
Designer: *Heidi J. Baughman*
Art coordinator: *Heather Burbridge*
Compositor: *Graphic Composition, Inc.*
Typeface: *10/12 Times Roman*
Printer: *R. R. Donnelley & Sons Company*

Library of Congress Cataloging-in-Publication Data

Hisrich, Robert D.
Entrepreneurship : starting developing, and managing a new enterprise / Robert D. Hisrich and Michael P. Peters.—3rd ed.
p. cm.
Includes bibliographical references and index.
ISBN 0-256-14147-9
1. New business enterprises—Management. 2. Entrepreneurship.
I. Peters, Michael P. II. Title.
HD62.5.H577 1995
658.4′21—dc20 94-9055
CIP

Printed in the United States of America
1 2 3 4 5 6 7 8 9 0 DO 1 0 9 8 7 6 5 4

To our wives, Tina and Debbie, and daughters Kary, Katy, Kelly, Christa and Kimberly, and their supportive entrepreneurial spirit.

Preface

Starting and operating a new business involves considerable risk and effort to overcome the inertia against creating something new. In creating and growing a new venture, the entrepreneur assumes the responsibility and risks for its development and survival, as well as enjoying the corresponding rewards. The fact that consumers, businesspeople, and government officials are interested in entrepreneurship is shown by the increasing research on the subject, the large number of college courses in entrepreneurship, the more than 2 million new enterprises started each year despite a 70 percent failure rate, the significant coverage and focus by the media, and the realization that this is an important topic for industrialized, developing, and once-controlled economies.

Who is the focus of all this attention—who is willing to accept all the risks and put forth the effort necessary to create a new venture? It may be a man or a woman, from an upper-class or lower-class background, a technologist or someone lacking technological sophistication, a college graduate or a high school dropout. The person may have been an inventor, manager, nurse, salesperson, engineer, student, teacher, homemaker, or retiree. It is someone able to juggle life between work, family, and civic responsibilities while meeting payroll.

To provide an understanding of this person and the entrepreneurial process, *Entrepreneurship* is divided into five major sections. **Part I—The Entrepreneurial Perspective**—introduces the entrepreneur and the entrepreneurial process from both a historical and a research perspective. The role and nature of entrepreneurship as a mechanism for creating new ventures and affecting economic development is presented, along with its career aspects and future direction. The characteristics and background of entrepreneurs are discussed, as well as some methods for individual self-assessment.

Part II—Starting a New Venture and Developing the Business—focuses on the elements in the entrepreneurial process. First, various aspects and models of creating the business are presented. Following an overview of the development and use of a business plan, a chapter is devoted to each of the plan's major components: the marketing plan, the financial plan, and the organizational plan.

One of the most difficult aspects of creating and establishing a new venture is the focus of **Part III—Financing a New Venture.** Following a general discussion of the alternative sources of capital, specific attention is given to two primary financing mechanisms: venture capital and public offerings.

Part IV—Managing the New Venture—presents material related to establishing, developing, and ending the venture. Particular attention is paid to managing the new venture both during early operations and during expansion. This part concludes with a discussion of the alternatives available to entrepreneurs for extricating themselves from ventures.

Part V—Special Issues for the Entrepreneur—deals with patents, trademarks, warranties, franchising, acquisition, intrapreneurship, and internationalizing the venture. A chapter is devoted to the very important concept of intrapreneurship—establishing entrepreneurship in an existing organization. The last chapter, "International Entrepreneurship: Opportunities and Problems," covers a topic of increasing importance in the hypercompetitive world environment. A comprehensive glossary concludes the book.

To make *Entrepreneurship* as meaningful as possible, each chapter begins with a profile of an entrepreneur whose career is especially relevant to the chapter material. Chapter objectives follow, and numerous examples occur throughout. Each chapter concludes with discussion questions, a list of key terms, and selected readings for further information.

Many people—students, business executives, entrepreneurs, professors, and publishing staff—have made this book possible. Of great assistance were the detailed and thoughtful comments of our reviewers: Nancy Bowman-Upton (Baylor University), Robert Brockhaus (St. Louis University), Alan Carsrud (University of Southern California), Karlin Conklin (University of Oregon), William Dwyer (Northeastern University), Fred Fry (Bradley University), Roger W. Hutt (Arizona State University West), Jack M. Kaplan (NYU Stern School of Business), Wayne Long (University of Calgary), Richard Judy (University of Wisconsin-Stevens Point), Roderick Powers (Iowa State University), Charles R. B. Stowe (Sam Houston State University), and J. William C. Tomlinson (University of British Columbia).

Particular thanks go to Bill Wetzel for helpful comments on Chapter 10, "Venture Capital" and to Lynn Moore for comments on Chapter 11, "Going Public." Special thanks are given to Barbara Bright, Brenda Harris, and Christa Peters for preparing the manuscript so competently, and to Catherine Brown, Erin Fogarty, and Alice Polterick for providing research material and editorial assistance for this edition.

We are deeply indebted to our spouses, Debbie and Tina, whose support and understanding helped bring this effort to fruition. It is to future entrepreneurs—our daughters, Christa, Kary, Katy, Kelly, and Kimberly and the generation they represent—that this book is particularly dedicated. May you always beg forgiveness rather than ask permission.

Robert D. Hisrich
Michael P. Peters

Contents in Brief

Contents

PART I

The Entrepreneurial Perspective

Chapter 1
Basis and Challenges of Entrepreneurship

Chapter 2
Self-Assessment and the Entrepreneurial Process

Chapter 3
Entrepreneurial Characteristics

Cases for Part I

CHAPTER

Basis and Challenges of Entrepreneurship

Chapter Objectives

1. To introduce the concept of entrepreneurship and its historical development.
2. To explain the entrepreneurial decision process.
3. To identify the basic types of start-up ventures.
4. To explain the role of entrepreneurship in economic development.
5. To discuss the future of entrepreneurship.

Ted Turner

Ted Turner, founder of Turner Broadcasting System, is an entrepreneur who loves living life on the edge. Who else would buy an unprofitable Metro-Goldwyn-Mayer film studio for $1.6 billion? Who else would bet on producing the Goodwill Games with U.S. versus Soviet athletes at a cost of about $50 million?

Robert Edward Turner III was born in 1938, and his boyhood was spent primarily in Savannah, Georgia. As a boy, he was an enthusiastic reader of books about heroes, from Horatio Hornblower to Alexander the Great.

Unsuccessful in playing any of the major sports, he turned to one that required no special physical attributes but relied on the ability to think, take chances, and compete—sailing. Turner became a fanatic sailor, using a method that earned him such nicknames as the Capsize Kid and Turnover Ted. He loved sailing's competitive frenzy.

Turner graduated from the second military school he attended and applied to Harvard for admission but was rejected. His father insisted that he attend an Ivy League college, so he went to Brown University to study Greek classics. Dismayed by this area of study, Turner's father eventually convinced him to change his major to economics. After two suspensions for infractions involving women, Turner was kicked out of Brown University for setting fire to his fraternity's homecoming float.

After a few years, Turner joined the family business. His father, R. E. Turner, Jr., was an ambitious businessman who had built a $1 million billboard business. However, in a short time, Turner's family disintegrated—his sister, Mary Jane, died, his parents were divorced, and his father killed himself.

Although his father's will left the Atlanta billboard company to Ted, a contract to sell the business had been signed before he died. Showing the deal-making ingenuity that has characterized his business activities, the young Turner convinced the buyers that, by shifting lease sites to another company he had inherited, he would be able to sabotage the company before the deal closed. The buyers backed down, and Turner's career moved forward. At the helm of the company, Turner began to expand, buying up billboard companies and radio stations. Since these constant acquisitions required huge outlays of cash and incurred debt, he learned to maintain a sufficient cash flow to cover payments.

In 1969, he took his company public with a merger that included a small Atlanta television station now called WTBS. In 1976, WTBS was the first station to become a network by beaming its signal to cable systems via satellite. By 1986, WTBS reached 36 million U.S. households and was cable television's most profitable advertising-supported network. The 1986 operating cash flow of the company was $70 million, and 1989 sales topped the $1 billion mark.

Turner did not sit back and watch the cash come in. He was, and is, always looking for ways to build his assets. Despite industry skepticism. Turner used the growing cash flow from WTBS to start the Cable News Network (CNN) in 1989. The 24-hour news channel was a success, winning praise from news professionals. This success enabled Turner to create another news network, Headline News. By 1986, the news networks were operating solidly in the black.

Turner's uncanny success in starting high-risk ventures is not accidental. A vigilant and relentless manager, Turner would often sleep on his office couch after working 18-hour days. Until autumn 1986, when Turner established a five-man management committee comprised of veteran TBS executives, he personally supervised company tasks and decisions. One person familiar with Turner's management style was surprised at the formation of the committee: "He [Turner] would never even let the five go out and have a beer together, let alone run the company."

Turner's talents extend beyond the corporate boardroom. A high risk taker, he won the America's cup race in 1977. In 1979, he won the Fastnet race off England's southwest coast, during which 156 competitors died in the violent seas.

In his own view, Turner is a quintessential achiever. He says, "I've got more awards than anybody—anybody my age. I've probably got more debt than anyone in the world. That's something, isn't it?" What makes him keep pushing for more?

Not satisfied with his accomplishments, Turner has established a visionary goal: to use his power and his network to influence world issues. He wants to concentrate on issues such as nuclear weapons, environmental abuse, and overpopulation. He speaks proudly of TBS specials, such as the one based on Martin Luther King, Jr. When asked if he would want to be president of the United States, Turner said, "The United States is only 5 percent of the world's population. I'm in global politics already."

Turner's view is both global and long term. In 1985, one CNN executive said, "Ted's mind is always 5 or 10 years down the road. Right now he's probably living in 1995." Turner's purchase of the MGM studio was motivated by rising licensing fees for old movies and television shows. Bill Bevins, TBS financial chief executive, projected that higher fees would lower operating profits from 40 percent of sales in 1985 to 10 percent in 1990. But at the end of 1989, gross profits were $631 million and sales were, as stated earlier, over $1 billion. Turner felt that the simple solution was either to increase buyer clout by taking over CBS or to acquire his own program library.

Turner's attempt to take over CBS in 1985 failed, costing him $23 million in lawyer and investment banker fees. But Turner, an undaunted optimist and aggressive competitor, views this attempted hostile takeover defeat as a triumph since CBS had to borrow heavily to acquire stock to stop the takeover, which Turner feels set CBS back 10 years.

Turner moved directly from this defeat to the acquisition of MGM. The 3,650-film library offered Turner Broadcasting a solution to rising licensing fees. About 1,000 of these films have enduring commercial value and will be aired on WTBS. Some analysts felt that the price paid—$1.6 billion—was too high, with the deal putting Turner heavily into debt. More debt for TBS resulted from Turner's decision to colorize about 10 percent of the films in this newly acquired library—at an average cost of $300,000 per film and a total cost of $22 million to $55 million.

Yet, despite these problems, people who know Turner well will not bet against him. He has an entrepreneurial spirit that thrives on these kinds of on-the-edge situations.

The saga of Ted Turner reflects that of many entrepreneurs in a variety of industries and various sized companies. The historical aspect of entrepreneurship, as well as the decision that Ted Turner and others have made to become entrepreneurs, is reflected in the following remarks of two successful entrepreneurs:

> Being an entrepreneur and creating a new business venture is analogous to raising children—it takes more time and effort than you ever imagine and it is extremely difficult and painful to get out of the situation. Thank goodness you cannot easily divorce yourself from either situation.
>
> When people ask me if I like being in business, I usually respond: On days when there are more sales than problems, I love it; on days when there are more problems than sales, I wonder why I do it. Basically, I am in business because it gives me a good feeling about myself. You learn a lot about your capabilities by putting yourself on the line. Running a successful business is not only a financial risk, it is an emotional risk as well. I get a lot of satisfaction from having dared it—done it—and been successful.

Do the profile of Ted Turner and these quotes fit your perception of the career of an entrepreneur? Both say a great deal about what it takes to start and operate a successful business. To understand this better, it is important to learn about the nature and development of entrepreneurship, the decision process involved in becoming an entrepreneur, and the role of entrepreneurship in the economic development of a country.

NATURE AND DEVELOPMENT OF ENTREPRENEURSHIP

Who is an entrepreneur? What is entrepreneurship? What is an entrepreneurial career path? These frequently asked questions reflect the increased national and international interest in the field. In spite of all this interest, a concise, universally accepted definition has not yet emerged. An overview of the development of the theory of entrepreneurship is illustrated in the development of the term itself (see Table 1–1). The word *entrepreneur* is French and, literally translated, means "between-taker" or "go-between."

TABLE 1–1 Development of Entrepreneurship Theory and Term *Entrepreneur*

Stems from French: means *between-taker* or *go-between.*

Middle Ages: actor (warlike action) and person in charge of large-scale production projects.

17th century: person bearing risks of profit (loss) in a fixed price contract with government.

1725: Richard Cantillon—person bearing risks is different from one supplying capital.

1797: Beaudeau—person bearing risks, planning, supervising, organizing, and owning.

1803: Jean Baptiste Say—separated profits of entrepreneur from profits of capital.

1876: Francis Walker—distinguished between those who supplied funds and received interest and those who received profit from managerial capabilities.

1934: Joseph Schumpeter—entrepreneur is an innovator and develops untried technology.

1961: David McClelland—entrepreneur is an energetic moderate risk taker.

1964: Peter Drucker—entrepreneur maximizes oportunities.

1975: Albert Shapero—entrepreneur takes initiative, organizes some social and economic mechanisms, and accepts risk of failure.

1980: Karl Vesper—entrepreneur seen differently by economists, pyschologists, business persons, and politicians.

1983: Gifford Pinchot—intrapreneur is an entrepreneur within an already established organization.

1985: Robert Hisrich—entrepreneur is the process of creating something different with value by devoting the necessary time and effort, assuming the accompanying financial, psychological, and social risks and receiving the resulting rewards of monetary and personal satisfaction.

Source: Robert D. Hisrich, "Entrepreneurship and Intrapreneurship: Methods for Creating New Companies That Have an Impact on the Economic Renaissance of an Area" in *Entrepreneurship, Intrapreneurship, and Venture Capital,* Robert D. Hisrich, ed (Lexington MA: Lexington Books, Inc., 1986), p 96.

Earliest Period

One early example of a go-between is Marco Polo, who attempted to establish trade routes to the Far East. As was the custom, he signed a contract with a money person (forerunner of today's capitalist) to sell his goods. A common contract during this time provided a loan to the merchant-adventurer at a 22.5 percent rate, including insurance. While the capitalist was a passive risk bearer, the merchant-adventurer took the active role in trading, bearing all the physical and emotional risks. Upon the successful completion of a journey by the merchant-adventurer, the capitalist took most of the profits (up to 75 percent), while the merchant-adventurer settled for the remaining 25 percent.

Middle Ages

In the Middle Ages, the term *entrepreneur* was used to describe both an actor and a person who managed large production projects. In such large production projects, this person did not take any risks, but merely managed the project using the resources provided. A typical entrepreneur in the Middle Ages was the cleric—the person in charge of great architectural works, such as castles and fortifications, public buildings, abbeys, and cathedrals.

17th Century

The connection of risk with entrepreneurship developed in the 17th century, with an entrepreneur being a person who entered into a contractual arrangement with the government to perform a service or to supply stipulated products. Since the contract price was fixed, any resulting profits or losses reflected the efforts of the entrepreneurs. One entrepreneur in this period was John Law, a Frenchman, who was allowed to establish a royal bank, which eventually evolved into an exclusive franchise to form a trading company in the New World—the Mississippi Company. Unfortunately, this monopoly on French trade led to Law's downfall when he attempted to push the company's stock price higher than the value of its assets; this eventually led to the collapse of the company.

Richard Cantillon, a noted economist and author in the 1700s, understood Law's mistake. Cantillon developed one of the early theories of the entrepreneur and is regarded by some as the founder of the term. He viewed the entrepreneur as a risk taker, observing that merchants, farmers, craftsmen, and other sole proprietors "buy at a certain price and sell at an uncertain price, therefore operating at a risk."[1]

18th Century

Finally, in the 18th century, the person with capital was differentiated from the one needing capital. In other words, the entrepreneur was distinguished from the capital provider (the present-day venture capitalist). One reason for this differentiation was the industrialization occurring throughout the world. Many of the inventions developed during this time were reactions to the changing world, as was the case with the inventions of Eli Whitney and Thomas Edison. Both Whitney and Edison were developing new technologies and were unable to finance their inventions themselves. While Whitney financed his cotton gin with expropriated British crown property, Edison raised capital from private sources to develop and experiment in the complex

---

[1] Robert F. Herbert and Albert H. Link, *The Entrepreneur—Mainstream Views and Radical Critiques* (New York: Praeger Publishers, 1982), p 17.

fields of electricity and chemistry. Both Edison and Whitney were capital users (entrepreneurs), not providers (venture capitalists). *In contrast*, a venture capitalist is a professional money manager who makes risk investments from a pool of equity capital to obtain a high rate of return on the investments.

19th and 20th Centuries

In the late 19th and early 20th centuries, entrepreneurs were frequently not distinguished from managers and were viewed mostly from an economic perspective:

> Briefly stated, the entrepreneur organizes and operates an enterprise for personal gain. He pays current prices for the materials consumed in the business, for the use of the land, for the personal services he employs, and for the capital he requires. He contributes his own initiative, skill and ingenuity in planning, organizing and administering the enterprise. He also assumes the chance of loss and gain consequent to unforseen and uncontrollable circumstances. The net residue of the annual receipts of the enterprise after all costs have been paid, he retains for himself.[2]

Andrew Carnegie is one of the best examples of this definition. Carnegie invented nothing, but instead adapted and developed new technology into products to achieve economic vitality. Carnegie, who descended from a poor Scottish family, made the American steel industry one of the wonders of the industrial world, primarily through his unremitting competitiveness, rather than his inventiveness or creativity.

In the middle of the 20th century, the notion of an **entrepreneur as an innovator** was established:

> The function of the entrepreneurs is to reform or revolutionize the pattern of production by exploiting an invention or, more generally, an untried technological possibility for producing a new commodity or producing an old one in a new way, opening a new source of supply of materials or a new outlet for products, by reorganizing a new industry. . . .[3]

The concept of innovation and newness is an integral part of entrepreneurship as indicated in this definition. Indeed, innovation, the act of introducing something new, is one of the most difficult tasks for the entrepreneur. It takes not only the ability to create and conceptualize but also the ability to understand all the forces at work in the environment. The newness can consist of anything from a new product to a new distribution system to a method for developing a new organizational structure. Edward Harriman, who reorganized the Ontario and Southern railroad through the Northern Pacific Trust, or John Pierpont Morgan, who developed his large banking house by reorganizing and financing the nation's industries, are examples of entrepreneurs fitting this definition. These organizational innovations are frequently as difficult to develop successfully as the more traditional technological innovations (transistors, computers, lasers) that are usually associated with the word.

---

[2]Richard T. Ely and Ralph H. Hess, *Outlines of Economics,* 6th ed (New York: Macmillan, 1937), p 488.

[3]Joseph Schumpeter, *Can Capitalism Survive?* (New York: Harper & Rowe, 1952), p 72.

This ability to innovate is an instinct that distinguishes human beings from other creatures. The instinct can be observed throughout history, from the Egyptians who designed and built great pyramids out of stone blocks weighing many tons each, to the Apollo lunar module, to laser beams. While the tools have changed with advances in science and technology, the ability to innovate has been present in every civilization.

ENTREPRENEUR DEFINITION

The concept of an entrepreneur is further refined when principles and terms from a business, managerial, and personal perspective are considered. In particular, aspects of entrepreneurship from a personal perspective have been explored in this century. This exploration is reflected in the following three definitions of an entrepreneur:

> In almost all of the definitions of entrepreneurship, there is agreement that we are talking about a kind of behavior that includes: (1) initiative taking, (2) the organizing and reorganizing of social and economic mechanisms to turn resources and situations to practical account, (3) the acceptance of risk or failure.[4]
>
> To an economist, an entrepreneur is one who brings resources, labor, materials, and other assets into combinations that make their value greater than before, and also one who introduces changes, innovations, and a new order. To a psychologist, such a person is typically driven by certain forces—need to obtain or attain something, to experiment, to accomplish, or perhaps to escape authority of others. . . . To one businessman, an entrepreneur appears as a threat, an aggressive competitor, whereas to another businessman the same entrepreneur may be an ally, a source of supply, a customer, or someone good to invest in. . . . The same person is seen by a capitalist philosopher as one who creates wealth for others as well, who finds better ways to utilize resources, and reduce waste, and who produces jobs others are glad to get.[5]
>
> Entrepreneurship is the dynamic process of creating incremental wealth. The wealth is created by individuals who assume the major risks in terms of equity, time, and/or career commitment or provide value for some product or service. The product or service may or may not be new or unique but value must somehow be infused by the entrepreneur by receiving and locating the necessary skills and resources.[6]

While each of these definitions views entrepreneurs from a slightly different perspective, each contains similar notions, such as newness, organizing, creating, wealth, and risk taking. Each definition is somewhat restrictive since entrepreneurs are found in all professions—education, medicine, research, law, architecture, engineering, social work, and distribution. Therefore, to include all types of entrepreneurial behavior, the following definition of entrepreneurship will be the foundation of this book:

---

[4] Albert Shapero, *Entrepreneurship and Economic Development* (Wisconsin: Project ISEED, LTD., The Center for Venture Management, Summer 1975), p 187.

[5] Karl Vesper, *New Venture Strategies* (Englewood Cliffs, NJ: Prentice-Hall, 1980), p 2.

[6] Robert C. Ronstadt, *Entrepreneurship* (Dover, MA: Lord Publishing Co., 1984), p 28.

> *Entrepreneurship* is the process of creating something different with value by devoting the necessary time and effort, assuming the accompanying financial, psychic, and social risks, and receiving the resulting rewards of monetary and personal satisfaction and independence.[7]

For the person who actually starts his or her own business, the experience is filled with enthusiasm, frustration, anxiety, and hard work. There is a high failure rate due to such things as poor sales, intense competition, lack of capital, or lack of managerial ability. The financial and emotional risk can also be very high. What, then, causes a person to make this difficult decision? The question can be best explored by looking at the decision process involved in becoming an entrepreneur.

THE ENTREPRENEURIAL DECISION PROCESS

Many individuals have difficulty bringing their ideas to the market and creating a new venture. Yet, entrepreneurship and the actual entrepreneurial decision have resulted in several million new businesses being started throughout the world, even in previously controlled economies such as those of China, Hungary, and Poland. While no one knows the exact number, in the United States (which leads the world in company formation) estimates indicate that from 1.1 to 1.9 million new companies have been formed each year in recent years.[8]

Indeed, millions of companies are formed despite recession, inflation, high interest rates, lack of infrastructure, economic uncertainty, and the fear of failure. Each of these companies is formed through a very personal human process that, although unique, has some characteristics common to all. Like all processes, the entrepreneurial decision entails a movement, *from* something *to* something—a movement from a present life-style to forming a new enterprise, as indicated in Table 1–2.

Change from Present Life-Style

The decision to leave a career or life-style is not an easy one. It takes a great deal of energy to change and to create something new. While individuals tend to start businesses in areas that are familiar, two work environments tend to be particularly good for spawning new enterprises: research and development, and marketing. While working in technology (research and development), individuals develop new product ideas or processes and often leave to form their own companies when these new ideas

---

[7]This definition is modified from the definition first developed for the woman entrepreneur. See: Robert D. Hisrich and Candida G. Brush, *The Woman Entrepreneur: Starting, Financing, and Managing a Successful New Business* (Lexington, MA: Lexington Books, 1985), p 18.

[8]This material is taken from an article by the author in Robert D. Hisrich, ed, *Entrepreneurship, Intrapreneurship, and Venture Capital: The Foundation of Economic Renaissance* (Lexington, MA: Lexington Books, 1986).

TABLE 1–2. Decisions for a Potential Entrepreneur

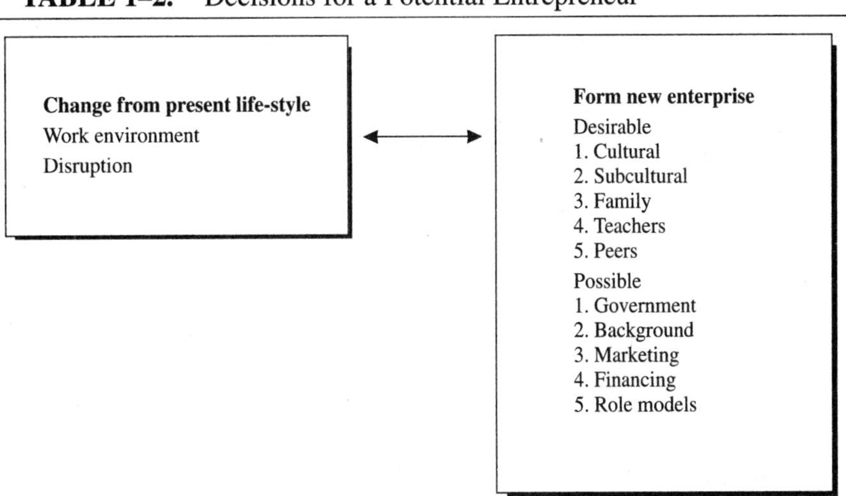

Source: Robert D. Hisrich, "Entrepreneurship and Intrapreneurship: Methods for Creating New Companies That Have an Impact on the Economic Renaissance of an Area" in *Entrepreneurship, Intrapreneurship, and Venture Capital,* Robert D. Hisrich, ed (Lexington Mass: Lexington Books, Inc., 1986), p 90.

are not accepted by their employers. Similarly, individuals in marketing have become familiar with the market and customers' unfilled wants and needs, and they frequently leave to start new enterprises to fill these needs.

Perhaps an even stronger incentive to overcome the inertia and leave a present life-style to create something new comes from a negative force—disruption. A significant number of companies are formed by people who have retired, who are relocated due to a move by the other member in a dual-career family, or who have been fired. There is probably no greater force than personal dislocation to galvanize a person's will to act. A study in one major city in the United States indicated that the number of new business listings in the Yellow Pages increased by 12 percent during a layoff period. Another cause of disruption that can result in company formation is someone's completion of an educational degree. For example, a student who is not promoted after receiving an MBA degree may become frustrated and decide to leave and start a new company.

What causes this personal disruption to result in a new company being formed as opposed to something else? The decision to start a new company occurs when an individual perceives that forming a new enterprise is both desirable and possible.

Desirability of New Venture Formation

The perception that starting a new company is desirable results from an individual's culture, subculture, family, teachers, and peers. A culture that values an individual who successfully creates a new business will spawn more company formations than one that does not. The American culture places a high value on being one's own boss, having individual opportunity, being a success, and making money—all aspects of entrepreneurship. Therefore, it is not surprising to find a high rate of company formation in the United States. On the other hand, in some countries successfully establishing a new business and making money are not as highly valued, and failure may be a disgrace. Countries with cultures that more closely emulate this attitude do not have as high a business formation rate.

No culture is totally for or against entrepreneurship. Many subcultures that shape value systems operate within a cultural framework. There are pockets of entrepreneurial subcultures in the United States. While the more widely recognized ones include Route 128 (Boston), Silicon Valley (California), and the North Carolina Triangle, some less-known but equally important entrepreneurial centers are Los Angeles, Indianapolis, Denver, Cleveland, and Austin. These subcultures support and even promote entrepreneurship—forming a new company—as one of the best occupations. No wonder more individuals actively plan new enterprises in these supportive environments.

There are variations within these subcultures (such as the Silicon Valley) caused by family traits. Studies of companies in a variety of industries throughout the United States and the world indicate that 50 to 72 percent of the founders of companies had fathers and/or mothers who valued independence. The independence achieved by company owners, professionals, artists, or farmers permeated their entire family life, giving encouragement and value to their children's company-formation activity.

Encouragement to form a company is further gained from teachers, who can significantly influence individuals regarding entrepreneurship as one possible career path. Schools with exciting courses in entrepreneurship and innovation tend to develop entrepreneurs and can actually drive the entrepreneurial environment in an economic area. For example, the number of entrepreneurship courses a person takes increases the probability of starting a venture. Both MIT and Harvard are located near Route 128; Stanford is in the Silicon Valley; the University of North Carolina, North Carolina State, and Duke are the points of the North Carolina Triangle; and Case Western Reserve University facilitates entrepreneurship in the Cleveland area. An area having a strong education base is almost always a prerequisite for entrepreneurial activity and company formation.

Finally, peers are very important in the decision to form a company. An area with an entrepreneurial pool and a meeting place where entrepreneurs and potential entrepreneurs can discuss ideas, problems, and solutions spawns more new companies than an area where these are not available.

Possibility of New Venture Formation

While the desire generated from the individual's culture, subculture, family, teachers, and peers needs to be present before any action is taken, the second necessary feature centers around this question: What makes it possible to form a new company? Several factors—government, background, marketing, role models, and finances—contribute to the creation of a new venture (see Table 1–2). The government contributes by providing the infrastructure to support a new venture. It is no wonder that more companies are formed in the United States, given the roads, communication and transportation systems, utilities, and economic stability compared with other countries. Even the U.S. tax rate for companies and individuals is better than in countries like Ireland or England. Countries that have a repressive tax rate, particularly for individuals, can suppress company formation since a significant monetary gain cannot be achieved, but the social, psychological, and financial risks are still present. The entrepreneur must also have the necessary background. A formal education and previous business experience give a potential entrepreneur the skills needed in forming and managing a new enterprise. While educational systems are important in providing the needed business knowledge, individuals will tend to be more successful in forming businesses in fields in which they have worked. Enterpreneurs are not born—they develop.

Marketing also plays a critical role in forming a new company. In addition to the presence of a market of sufficient size, there must also be a level of marketing know-how necessary to put together the best total package of product, price, distribution, and promotion needed for successful product launching. A company is more easily formed in an area where there is market demand rather than a push for technology.

A role model can be one of the most powerful influences in making company formation seem possible. To see someone else succeed makes it easier to picture yourself engaged in a similar activity—of course, even more successfully. A frequent comment of entrepreneurs when queried about their motivations for starting their new venture is: "If that person could do it, so can I!"

Finally, financial resources must be readily available. While most of the start-up money for any new company comes from personal savings, credit, friends, and relatives, there is often a need for additional seed (start-up) capital. Each new venture has a common trait—the need for seed and other types of risk capital. Risk-capital investors play an essential role in the development and growth of entrepreneurial activity. More new companies form when seed capital is readily available.

TYPES OF START-UPS

What types of start-ups result from this entrepreneurial decision process? One very useful classification system divides start-ups into three categories: life-style firms, foundation companies, and high-potential ventures. A **life-style firm** is privately held and usually achieves only modest growth due to the nature of the business, the objectives of the entrepreneur, and the limited money devoted to research and development. This type of firm may grow after several years to 30 or 40 employees and have annual revenues of about $2 million. A life-style firm exists primarily to support the owners and usually has little opportunity for significant growth and expansion.

The second type of start-up—the **foundation company**—is created from research and development and lays the foundation for a new industry. This firm can grow in 5 to 10 years from 40 to 400 employees and from $10 million to $20 million in yearly revenues. Since this type of start-up rarely goes public, it usually draws the interest of private investors only, not the venture-capital community.

The final type of start-up—the **high-potential venture**—is the one that receives the greatest investment interest and publicity. While the company may start out like a foundation company, its growth is far more rapid. After 5 to 10 years the company could employ around 500 employees with $20 to $30 million in revenue.

Given that the results of the decision-making process need to be perceived as desirable and possible for an individual to change from a present life-style to a radically new one, it is not surprising that the type and number of new business formations vary greatly throughout the United States. Some regions of the country have more support infrastructure and a more positive attitude toward new business creation. For example, seven of the nine census regions had increases in new corporations with the record total (163,051) up 1 percent from the previous high a year earlier. In this year, New England had the largest increase (4.6 percent) followed by the East North Center (up 4.3 percent), South Atlantic (up 3.8 percent), West South Central (up 3.5 percent) and East South Central (up 3.1 percent). The Pacific states declined 9 percent and the farm-belt states (West North Central region) 8.9 percent.

ROLE OF ENTREPRENEURSHIP IN ECONOMIC DEVELOPMENT

The role of entrepreneurship in economic development involves more than just increasing per capita output and income; it involves initiating and constituting change in the structure of business and society. This change is accompanied by growth and increased output, which allows more to be divided by the various participants. What in an area facilitates the needed change and development? One theory of economic growth depicts innovation as the key not only in developing new products (or services) for the market but also in stimulating investment interest in the new ventures being created. This new investment works on both the demand and the supply sides of the growth equation: The new capital created expands the capacity for growth (supply side), and the resultant new spending utilizes the new capacity and output (demand side).

In spite of the importance of investment and innovation in the economic development of an area, an adequate understanding of the **product-evolution process** is still lacking. This is the process through which innovation develops and commercializes through entrepreneurial activity, which in turn stimulates economic growth.

The product-evolution process is indicated in Figure 1–1 as a cornucopia, the traditional symbol of abundance. It begins with knowledge in science, thermodynamics, fluid mechanics, electronics, and technology and ends with products or services available for purchase in the marketplace.[9] The critical point in the product-evolution process is the intersection of knowledge and a recognized social need, which begins the product development phase. This point, called *iterative synthesis,* often fails to evolve into a marketable innovation.

---

[9]This process is discussed in Yao Tzu Li, David G. Jansson, and Ernest G. Cravelho, *Technological Innovation in Education and Industry* (New York: Van Nostrand Reinhold, 1980).

FIGURE 1–1 Product Evolution

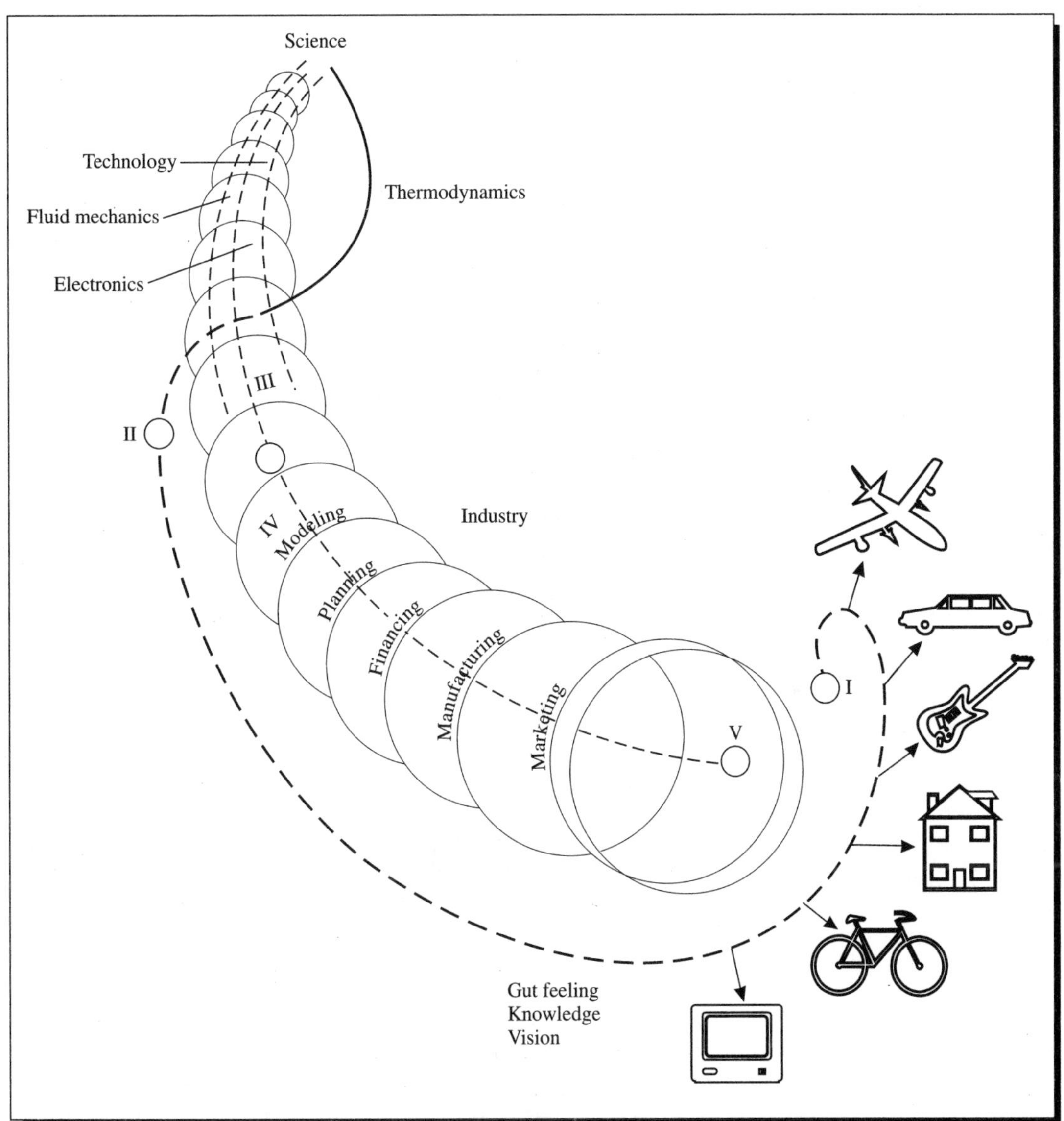

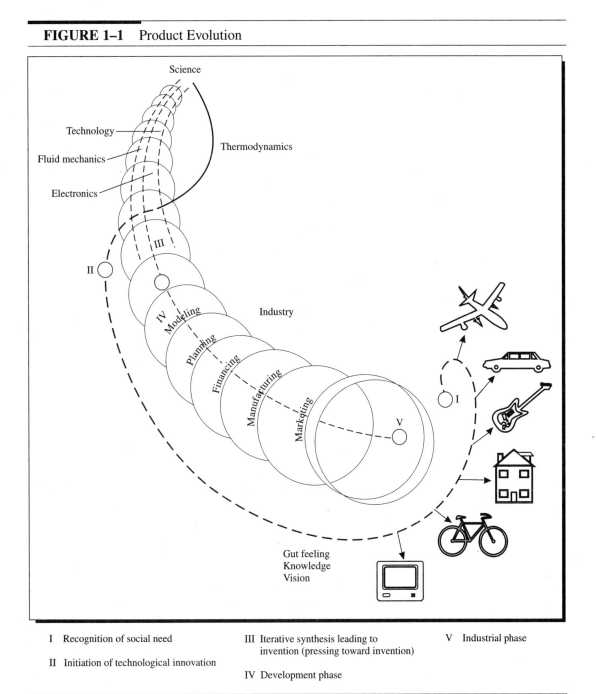

I Recognition of social need

II Initiation of technological innovation

III Iterative synthesis leading to invention (pressing toward invention)

IV Development phase

V Industrial phase

Source: Yao Tzu Li, David G. Jansson, and Ernest G. Cravelho, *Technology Innovation in Education and Industry* (New York: Von Nostrand Reinhold Company, 1980), p 27.

The innovation can, of course, be of varying degrees of uniqueness. Most innovations introduced on the market are **ordinary,** that is, with little uniqueness or technology. As expected, there are fewer **technological** and **breakthrough innovations,** with the number of actual innovations decreasing as the technology involved increases. Regardless of its level of uniqueness or technology, each innovation (particularly the latter two types) evolves and develops to commercialization through one of three mechanisms: the government, intrapreneurship, or entrepreneurship.

Government as an Innovator

The government is one method for commercializing the results of the interaction between a social need and technology. This is frequently called *technology transfer* and has been the focus of a significant amount of research effort. Despite all the effort, to date few inventions resulting from sound scientific government-sponsored research have reached (been transferred to) the commercial market. While most of the by-products from this scientific research have little application to any social need, the few products that do require significant modification to have market appeal. Though the government has the financial resources to successfully transfer the technology to the marketplace, it lacks the business skills, particularly marketing and distribution, necessary for successful commercialization. In addition, government bureaucracy and red tape often inhibit the necessary strategic business from being formed in a timely manner.

Intrapreneurship

Intrapreneurship (entrepreneurship within an existing business structure) can also bridge the gap between science and the marketplace. Existing businesses have the financial resources, business skills, and frequently the marketing and distribution system to successfully commercialize innovation. Yet, too often the bureaucratic structure, the emphasis on short-term profits, and a highly structured organization inhibit creativity and prevent new products and businesses from being developed. Corporations recognizing these inhibiting factors and the need for creativity and innovation have attempted to establish an intrapreneurial spirit in their organizations. In the present era of hypercompetition, the need for new products and the intrapreneurial spirit has become so great that more and more companies are developing an intrapreneurial environment, often in the form of strategic business units (SBUs). This topic is the focus of Chapter 17.

Entrepreneurship

Another method for bridging the gap between science and the marketplace is entrepreneurship. Many entrepreneurs have a difficult time bridging this gap and creating new ventures. They frequently lack managerial skills, marketing capability, or finances. Their inventions are frequently unrealistic, needing significant modification to be marketable. In addition, entrepreneurs frequently do not know how to interface with all the necessary entities, such as banks, suppliers, customers, venture capitalists, distributors, and advertising agencies.

Yet, in spite of all these difficulties, entrepreneurship is presently the most effective method for bridging the gap between science and the marketplace, creating new enterprises, and bringing new products and services to market. These entrepreneurial activities significantly affect the economy of an area by building the economic base and providing jobs. Given the significance of the impact on both the overall economy and the employment of an area, it is surprising that entrepreneurship has not become even more of a focal point in economic development.

THE FUTURE OF ENTREPRENEURSHIP

As evidenced by the many different definitions, the term *entrepreneurship* means different things to different people and can be viewed from different conceptual perspectives. However, in spite of the differences, there are some common aspects: risk taking, creativity, independence, and rewards. These commonalities will continue to be the driving force behind the notion of entrepreneurship in the future. One thing is clear—the future for entrepreneurship appears to be bright. We are living in the age of the entrepreneur, with entrepreneurship endorsed by educational institutions, governmental units, society, and corporations. Entrepreneurial education has never been so important in terms of courses and academic research. A total of 369 universities in the United States have at least one course in entrepreneurship. While most of these courses are in the business schools, 3 respondents have entrepreneurship courses in liberal arts colleges (Macalester, Mercer, and St. Thomas), 32 respondents have courses in engineering schools, and 17 respondents have courses in both the business and the engineering schools. Entrepreneurship courses are also in one department of home economics (Cal State) and one school of nursing (Northeastern University (Mass)). While the number of business schools offering at least one course in entrepreneurship increased from 210 in 1985 to 351 in 1991, a 67 percent increase, the number of engineering schools decreased from 39 in 1985 to 32, an 18 percent decrease. There are more courses in entrepreneurship at the undergraduate level than at the graduate level, as 37.6 percent of the sample offer undergraduate entrepreneurship courses, 23.7 percent offer graduate entrepreneurship courses, and 38.7 percent offer courses at both the graduate and undergraduate levels.[10]

A survey concerning entrepreneurship education in Europe also had interesting results. Many universities in the 24 countries surveyed had recently started a program in entrepreneurship. Most universities and associations in the countries did research on entrepreneurship, followed by training courses, and then education courses—

[10]These and other statistics on entrepreneurial education in the United States can be found in: Karl H. Vesper, "The State of Entrepreneurship Education," Chapter 2 in *Internationalizing Entrepreneurship Education and Training. Proceedings,* The Joint Entrepreneurship 1992 Conference. Dortmund, Germany. June 1992, pp 8–15.

courses for which degree credit was given. Very few of the sample were involved in the actual enterprise creation process where the university, faculty, and/or students shared in the sales and profits of the new venture.[11]

This increase in course offerings has been accompanied by an increase in academic research, endowed chairs in the area, entrepreneurship concentrations and majors, and centers of entrepreneurial activity. This trend will continue, supported by an increase in Ph.D. activity, which will in turn provide the needed faculty and research effort to support the future increases in course offerings, endowed positions, centers, and research efforts.

Various governments have also taken an increasing interest in promoting the growth of entrepreneurship. Individuals are encouraged to form new businesses and are provided such government support as tax incentives, buildings, roads, and a communication system—a strong government infrastructure—to facilitate this creation process. The encouragement by the federal and local governments should continue in the future as more lawmakers understand that new enterprises create jobs and increase the economic output in an area. Some local governments such as state governments in the United States are developing their own innovative industrial strategies for fostering entrepreneurial activity and the timely development of the technology of the area. The impact of this strategy is seen in the venture-capital industry, which is always sensitive to government regulations and policies. The current level and growth in venture-capital money have resulted from a lowering of the capital gains tax in 1978 from 49 percent to 28 percent in the United States and the institution of more relaxed rules regarding pension fund investment. Pension funds now contribute about 30 percent of the venture-capital money raised each year in the United States.

Society's support of entrepreneurship will also continue. This support is critical in providing both motivation and public support. Never before have entrepreneurs been so revered by the general populace. Entrepreneurial endeavors in the United States are considered honorable and even, in many cases, prestigious pursuits. A major factor in developing this societal approval is the media. The media has played and will continue to play a powerful and constructive role by reporting extensively on the general entrepreneurial spirit in the United States and highlighting specific success cases of this spirit in operation. Major articles in such prestigious newspapers as the *New York Times, The Wall Street Journal,* and the *Washington Post* have focused on the pioneer spirit of today's entrepreneurs, describing how this spirit benefits society by keeping the United States in the lead in technology. General business magazines such as *Barron's, Business Week, Forbes,* and *Fortune* have provided similar coverage by adding special columns on entrepreneurship and venturing. New magazines such as *Black Enterprise, Entrepreneur, Inc., Journal of Venturing,* and *Venture,* which focus on specific issues of the entrepreneurial process, starting new ventures, and small, growing businesses, have built solid and increasing circulation

---

[11] See: Robert D. Hisrich and Barra O'Cinneida, "Research Trends in Entrepreneurship: The Potential in Expanding Europe and Transatlantic Perspectives," *Proceedings,* 7th Nordic Conference on Small Business Research (June 1992), pp 1–9.

rates. Television on both a national and a local level has highlighted entrepreneurship by featuring specific individuals and issues involved in the entrepreneurial process. Not only have local stations covered regional occurrences, but nationally syndicated shows such as *The Today Show*, *Good Morning America*, and *20/20* have had special segments devoted to this phenomenon. This media coverage uplifts the image of the entrepreneur and growth companies, and focuses on their contributions to society.

Finally, large companies will continue to have an interest in their special form of entrepreneurship—intrapreneurship—in the future. These companies will be increasingly interested in capitalizing on their research and development in the increasingly competitive business environment. The largest 15 companies in the United States account for over 20 percent of the total U.S. research and development and over 40 percent of private-sector R&D. General Electric, for example, has created three $1 billion businesses internally in the last 15 years. Other companies will want to create more new businesses through intrapreneurship in the future, particularly in light of the hypercompetition and the need for globalization.

SUMMARY

The definition of an entrepreneur has evolved over time as the world's economic structure has changed and become more complex. From its beginnings in the Middle Ages, where it was used in relation to specific occupations, the notion of the "entrepreneur" has been refined and broadened to include concepts that are related to the person rather than the occupation. Risk taking, innovation, and creation of wealth are examples of the criteria that have been developed as the study of new business creations has evolved. In this text, entrepreneurship is defined as the process of creating something different with value by devoting the necessary time and effort; assuming the accompanying financial, psychic, and social risks; and receiving the resulting rewards of monetary and personal satisfaction and independence.

The decision to start an entrepreneurial venture consists of several sequential subdecisions:

1. The decision to leave a present career or life-style.
2. The decision that an entrepreneurial venture is desirable.
3. The decision that both external and internal factors make new venture creation possible.

While the decision-making process is applicable to each of the three types of start-up companies, the emphasis is certainly different. Because of their nature, a foundation company or a high-potential venture requires a more conscious effort to reach a defensible decision on these points than does a life-style firm.

There are both pushing and pulling influences active in the decision to leave a present career: the "push" of job dissatisfaction or even a layoff, and the "pull" toward entrepreneurship of seeing an unfilled need in the marketplace. Once the possibility of an entrepreneurial career is acknowledged, it is either accepted or rejected as a valid alternative. The desirability of starting one's own company is strongly influenced by culture, subculture, family, teachers, and peers. Any of these influences can function as a source of encouragement for entrepreneurship, with support ranging from government policies that favor business to strong personal role models of family or friends. Beyond the stage of seeing entrepreneurship as a "good idea," the potential entrepreneur must possess or acquire the necessary education, management skills, and financial resources for launching the venture.

The study of entrepreneurship has relevance today not only because it helps entrepreneurs better fulfill their personal needs but because of the economic contribution of the new ventures. More than increasing national income by creating new jobs, entrepreneurship acts as a positive force in economic growth by serving as the bridge between innovation and application. While the government gives great support to basic and applied research, it has not had great success in translating the technological innovations to products or services. While intrapreneurship offers the promise of a marriage of those research capabilities and business skills that one expects from a large corporation, the results so far in many companies have not been spectacular. This leaves the entrepreneur, who frequently lacks both technical and business skills, to serve as the major link in the process of innovation development, and economic growth and revitalization. The study of entrepreneurship and the education of potential entrepreneurs are essential parts of any attempt to strengthen this link so essential to a country's economic well-being.

QUESTIONS FOR DISCUSSION

1. Why study entrepreneurship?
2. Which definition of *entrepreneurship* best describes Ted Turner? Marco Polo? Your idea of what an entrepreneur is? List the strengths and weaknesses (as appropriate) of the various definitions highlighted in the text.
3. Give some reasons why an individual entrepreneur might succeed in bringing a product to the market where the government or a large corporation would fail.
4. Give some examples of each of the three types of start-up companies. Did any of your examples begin in one category and turn out to be something much smaller or larger than anticipated? How does the entrepreneur's vision for the future affect the decision to start the company?

KEY TERMS

breakthrough innovation
desirability of new venture formation
entrepreneur as an innovator
entrepreneurial decision process
entrepreneurship
foundation companies
government as an innovator

high-potential ventures
intrapreneurship
life-Style firm
ordinary innovation
possibility of new venture formation
product-evolution process
risk taking
technological innovation

SELECTED READINGS

Barrier, Michael. (1993). Business School, TQM, and You. *Nation's Business.* vol. 8 no. 7. pp 60–61.

More and more business schools are offering courses in entrepreneurship, preparing students to run their own businesses, as well as courses on small business management.

Benson, Gary L. (1993). Thoughts of an Entrepreneurial Chairholder Model Entrepreneurial Curriculum. *Journal of Applied Business Research.* vol. 9. no. 1. pp 140–146.

The model entrepreneurship curriculum at the undergraduate level would include courses on creativity, innovation, and product development; legal issues for entrepreneurship; and small business management.

Benson, Gary L. (1992). Teaching Entrepreneurship through the Classics. *Journal of Applied Business Research.* vol. 8. no 4, pp 135–140.

There are many lessons in entrepreneurship that can be learned from classical, renaissance, and industrial era authors. Books of particular value include Melville's *Moby Dick,* Machiavelli's *The Prince,* Plato's *Republic,* and Shakespeare's *King Lear.*

Bird, Barbara J., Hayward, David J., and Allen, David N. (1993). Conflicts in Commercialization of Knowledge: Perspectives from Science and Entrepreneurship. *Entrepreneurship: Theory and Practice.* vol. 17. no. 4. pp 57–77.

Faculty with entrepreneurial inclinations experience conflicts of interest and value. The study results indicate that the values and interests affect the relationships of the faculty member and his or her entrepreneurial activity.

Dulek, Ronald E. (1993). Models of Development & Business Schools and Business Communications. *Journal of Business Communications.* vol. 30. no. 3. pp 315–331.

Colleges of business develop by following a vertical model involving functional specialization or a horizontal model stressing breadth rather than depth. This latter model places more emphasis on such areas as leadership, communication, entrepreneurship, and strategy. The model adopted affects the curriculum and specifically the way the business communications course is taught.

Gartner, William B. (1993). Words Lead to Deeds: Towards an Organizational Emergence Vocabulary. *Journal of Business Venturing.* vol. 8. no. 3. pp 231–239.

The words used to describe and discuss entrepreneurship influence a person's ability to think about the topic and conduct research in the area.

Gartner, W. B. (January 1990). What Are We Talking About When We Talk About Entrepreneurship? *Journal of Business Venturing.* pp 15–28.

This research compares and contrasts the existing definitions of entrepreneurship proposed by practitioners and academics by using a "modified three-stage Delphi." In stage one, entrepreneurship definitions were collected from 44 participants, and these were analyzed and divided into 90 attributes. Stage two consisted of rating these 90 attributes followed by factor analyzation. This resulted in the authors identifying eight specific themes. In the final stage, these themes were evaluated through commentary, rankings, and ratings.

Gatewood, Elizabeth. (1993). The Expectancies in Public Sector Venture Assistance. *Entrepreneurship: Theory and Practice.* vol. 17. no. 2. pp 91–95.

Using the framework of expectancy theory, the way public sector assistance can positively influence venture creation through improving the entrepreneur's skills, abilities, and access to required resources is explained.

Hofer, Charles W., and Bygreve, William D. (1992). Researching Entrepreneurship. *Entrepreneurship: Theory and Practice.* vol. 16. no. 3. pp 91–100.

The nine important aspects of the entrepreneurial process have substantial implications for theory building and for the practice of researching entrepreneurship.

Kirchoff, Bruce B. (1991). Entrepreneurship's Contribution to Economics. *Entrepreneurship: Theory and Practice.* vol. 16. no. 2. pp 93–112.

Recent evidence of entrepreneurship's significant contribution to growth and development challenges general equilibrium theory and suggests that a new macro-theory that incorporates entrepreneurship is needed.

Mackenzie, Lynn Ryan. (1992). Fostering Entrepreneurship as a Rural Economic Development Strategy. *Economic Development Review.* vol. 10. no. 4. pp 38–44.

Rural communities must assess their strengths and weaknesses and develop a strategy for changing economic conditions through entrepreneurship and thereby move in a new economic direction.

McGrath, Rita Gunther, MacMillan, Jon C., Yang, Elena Ai-Yuang, and Tsai, William. Does Culture Endure or Is it Malleable? Issues for Entrepreneurial Economic Development. *Journal of Business Venturing.* vol. 7. no. 6. pp 441–458.

A study exploring the extent to which social interventions encourage entrepreneurship found that value structures related to individualism-collectivism and to attitudes toward the role of work were much more enduring than value structures related to acceptance of large differences in power and to risk.

Sage, Gary. (1993). Entrepreneurship as an Economic Development Strategy. *Economic Development Review.* vol. 2. no. 2. pp 66–67.

Since future economic development strategy needs to promote an environment that is conducive to new business formation and growth, six factors need to be particularly addressed that correlate well with the stimulation of new business.

Specht, Pamela Hammers. (1993). Munificence and Carrying Capacity of the Environment and Organization Formation. *Entrepreneurship: Theory and Practice.* vol. 17. no. 2. pp 77–86.

The areas of resource dependence and population ecology are combined to develop a model of the relationship between venture formation, environmental munificence, and carrying capacity.

Van de ven, Andrew H. (1993). The Development of an Infrastructure for Entrepreneurship. *Journal of Business Venturing.* vol. 8. no. 3. pp 211–230.

The infrastructure of institutional arrangements, resource endowments, pool of competent labor, and the necessary proprietary functions that an entrepreneurial community needs are examined, and the industry system that eventually emerges is discussed.

VanderWerf, Pieter A. (1993). A Model of Venture Creation in New Industries. *Entrepreneurship: Theory and Practice.* vol. 17. no. 2. pp 39–47.

Aspects of new industries make them particularly attractive to new venture creation. These ventures are typically created by individuals who know about the new area evolving.

CHAPTER

2

Self-Assessment and the Entrepreneurial Process

Chapter Objectives

1. To identify the general characteristics of an entrepreneur.
2. To explain the aspects of the entrepreneurial process.
3. To explain the differences between the entrepreneurial and managerial domains along five key business dimensions.
4. To discuss the aspects of an entrepreneurial career and an entrepreneur's education.

Frank Phillips

Frank Phillips, the first of nine children, was born November 28, 1873, in Greeley County, Nebraska, to Lucinda and Judge Lewis Franklin Phillips. The Phillipses were farmers in an area largely populated by Crow and Blackfoot Indians. In the summer of 1874, the family's Nebraska farm was ravaged by grasshoppers. Penniless, the family moved to Creston, Iowa, to start life over. As a young boy, Frank displayed an enterprising spirit. After he finished his assigned chores on the farm, he would hire himself out to area farmers, digging potatoes at 10 cents a day. Although the added work left Frank little time for playing games and other activities enjoyed by youngsters his age, he always had more pocket money than any of his friends.

On one of their family trips, young Frank spotted a town barber wearing flashy striped pants that were popular during the period. Frank recalls: "I made up my mind that I wanted to earn enough money so that I could afford to wear striped pants even on weekdays."

At the age of 14, Frank became a barber's apprentice. A hard-working, quick learner with an engaging personality, he was soon one of the city's most popular barbers and several years later bought his own barber shop. Since barber shops also served as informal town meeting places, Frank stocked cigars and other tobacco products and manufactured a hair tonic called "Mountain Sage." The items sold well, and the experience helped Frank develop a basic marketing principle he would later apply to his service station business—the value of catering to customers' wants and needs. This principle was later reflected in each Phillips gas station, which carried a complete line of automotive accessories and specialties. Frank Phillips also made the barbers who worked in his shop salesmen by giving them commissions on new customers. These efforts helped Frank Phillips become owner of all three barber shops in the town just 10 years after becoming an apprentice barber.

In 1897, Phillips married Jane Gibson, the daughter of a wealthy banker, sold his three barber shops, and began selling bonds in the New England states and the Chicago area for his father-in-law. On one trip in 1903, he learned about the possibilities of oil exploration in Indian territory. While Phillips, bankrolled by his father-in-law, organized the Anchor Oil and Gas Company in Bartlesville, Oklahoma, his younger brother sold shares of stock in the new company to increase operational revenues. Although the first three wells were unsuccessful, the fourth well, the Anna Anderson (which was to have been their last attempt if unsuccessful) was a huge gusher. Due to the success of the Anna Anderson and subsequent drilling projects, the Anchor Oil and Gas company prospered.

Frank and his brother sold their interest in Anchor Oil and Gas to turn their attention to new ventures, particularly in the banking industry. In 1906, they founded the Citizen's Bank and Trust with a capital investment of $50,000 and three years later purchased one of their rivals—the Bartlesville National Bank—and consolidated the two banks into the Bartlesville National Bank. During these early banking days, the Phillips brothers organized and promoted drilling ventures, most of which were sold or dissolved within a short time. As Frank was considering getting out of the oil business entirely and establishing a chain of banks throughout the Midwest, the United States entered World War I. Skyrocketing oil prices—from less than 40 cents a barrel to more than one dollar—changed Frank's perspective on the future of the oil industry. In the spring of 1917, 43-year old Frank Phillips and his brother consolidated all their individual oil holdings into the Phillips Petroleum Company. This consolidation gave the company assets of approximately $3 million, 27 employees, and an array of leases, producing wells, and equipment scattered throughout Oklahoma and Kansas.

Within a few years the new organization began to soar. A key to Phillips's early success was the company's ability to attract investors and obtain loans. Even though the oil business at that time was considered by many to be only slightly less risky than gambling, Phillips was able to convince investors (including conservative Eastern bankers) otherwise. Making frequent trips to Chicago and New York, he spent as much time in bankers' offices as in the oil fields. Phillips knew firsthand how bankers operated; he knew the information they required and the information they should not get. On several investor trips to his Oklahoma oil fields, Phillips would often "stage" a gusher (making sure oil would first spurt up) for the somewhat naive investors—a sight that rarely failed to impress these guests.

Needless to say, the Phillips Petroleum Company grew and prospered into one of the largest corporations in the oil industry. There are numerous reasons why Frank Phillips became a successful entrepreneur. Certainly, marrying into a wealthy family is one of them, as is luck. However, for Phillips to achieve what he did, he had to have something else: a vision of what he was and what would happen, an ability to sell himself and his ideas, a recognition of his own strengths and weaknesses, and the wherewithal to hire talent in areas in which he was lacking.

The various entrepreneurial events and stages in the life of Frank Phillips suggest several questions that each potential entrepreneur must answer. These are reflected in the following quotes of two successful entrepreneurs:

> My father started and operated his own business. He was so excited about the venture and provided such a strong role model I never even considered working for anyone else. He also said that you can't really make money or be satisfied unless you are your own boss.

> Why did I start my own business? Because I was a professional with experience and I wanted to be independent. Also, there was a market need for my product. There are times, however, I wonder why I did.

Like Frank Phillips, many other entrepreneurs and future entrepreneurs frequently ask themselves: Am I really an entrepreneur? Do I have what it takes to be a success? Do I have sufficient background and experience to start and manage a new venture? As enticing as the thought of starting and owning a business may be, the problems and pitfalls inherent in the process are as legendary as the success stories. The fact remains that more new business ventures fail than succeed. To be one of the few successful entrepreneurs requires more than just hard work and luck. It requires a hard, honest assessment both of the viability of the prospective business and, perhaps even more important, of one's own strength and weaknesses.

WHO SHOULD START HIS OR HER OWN BUSINESS?

Each day, thousands of individuals ask the difficult question, "Should I start my own business?" When queried, 85 percent of the populace said they would like to be in business for themselves. The driving force behind this desire to start a new venture is the desire to be one's own boss, to be independent. Since there is no definitive measurement developed that allows an individual to determine if he or she can be a successful entrepreneur, each individual needs to carefully appraise his or her situation through several different methods and self-assessment models. One way to determine if you have what it takes to be an entrepreneur is to fill out the questionnaire in Table 2–1 and check the answers at the end of this chapter. Keep in mind that the answers develop an average profile of an entrepreneur. There are many exceptions, and there is no such person as a typical entrepreneur.

According to the Small Business Administration, the creation of a new business is very risky. Over 1,000 small business firms, most less than five years old, fail each day. To help evaluate whether you have some of the abilities necessary to avoid this high failure rate and to be a successful entrepreneur, take the Entrepreneur Assessment Quiz in Table 2–2 before reading further. Note that this quiz has not been validated statistically. If you score well, however, you may have the ability to be a successful entrepreneur. If you do not, do not be discouraged. Many entrepreneurs believe that passion for the idea and the desire to succeed are the most important ingredients for success.

After you have completed this quiz in Table 2–2, count the number of Yes answers. Give yourself one point for each Yes. If you scored above 17 points, you have the drive to be an entrepreneur—the desire, energy, and adaptability to make a viable business venture a success. However, make sure any business venture you are contemplating is a good one.

If you scored from 13 to 17 points, your entrepreneurial drive is not as apparent. While you may definitely have the ability to be an entrepreneur, make sure that you can accept all the problems and headaches that accompany the joy of being your own boss.

TABLE 2–1 Characteristics of an Entrepreneur

1. An entrepreneur is most commonly the ______ child in the family.
   a. oldest   c. youngest
   b. middle   d. doesn't matter
2. An entrepreneur is most commonly:
   a. married   c. widowed
   b. single   d. divorced
3. An entrepreneur is most typically a:
   a. man   c. either
   b. woman
4. An individual usually begins his or her first significant entrepreneurial business enterprise at which age?
   a. teens   d. forties
   b. twenties   e. fifties
   c. thirties
5. Usually an individual's entrepreneurial tendency first appears evident in his or her:
   a. teens   d. forties
   b. twenties   e. fifties
   c. thirties
6. Typically, an entrepreneur has achieved the following educational attainment by the time the *first significant* business venture begins:
   a. less than high school   d. master's degree
   b. high school diploma   e. doctor's degree
   c. bachelor's degree
7. An entrepreneur's primary motivation for starting a business is:
   a. to make money   d. to create job security
   b. to be independent   e. to be powerful
   c. to be famous
8. The primary motivation for the entrepreneur's high ego and need for achievement is based upon a relationship with:
   a. spouse   c. father
   b. mother   d. children
9. To be successful in an entrepreneurial venture you need:
   a. money   d. a good idea
   b. luck   e. all of the above
   c. hard work
10. Entrepreneurs and venture capitalists:
    a. get along well   c. are cordial friends
    b. are the best of friends   d. are in conflict
11. A successful entrepreneur relies on which of the following for critical management advice?
    a. internal management team   c. financial sources
    b. external management professionals   d. no one
12. Entrepreneurs are best as:
    a. managers   c. planners
    b. venture capitalists   d. doers
13. Entrepreneurs are:
    a. high-risk-takers (big gamblers)   c. small-risk-takers (take few chances)
    b. moderate-risk-takers (realistic gamblers)   d. doesn't matter

TABLE 2–1 *(concluded)*

14. Entrepreneurs:
    a. are the life of a party
    b. are bores at a cocktail party
    c. will never go to parties
    d. just fit into the crowd at a party
15. Entrepreneurs tend to "fall in love" with:
    a. new ideas
    b. new employees
    c. new manufacturing ideas
    d. new financial plans
    e. all of the above
16. Entrepreneurs typically form:
    a. service businesses
    b. manufacturing companies
    c. financial companies
    d. construction companies
    e. a variety of ventures

Source: Reprinted with the permission of Lexington Books, an imprint of Macmillan Publishing Company from *The Woman Entrepreneur* by Robert D. Hisrich and Candida Brush. Copyright 1985 by Lexington Books.

If you scored below 13 points, your entrepreneurial drive is even less apparent. Even though most people say they want to be entrepreneurs, in reality many of them are actually better off working for someone else.

Regardless of your score, take time to develop and gain experience in your present position or your industrial area of interest while evaluating your real interests and desires before you actually become involved in the entrepreneurial process. Again, keep in mind that the quiz is not a scientifically validated indicator of entrepreneurial drive. Such an instrument has not yet been developed.

THE ENTREPRENEURIAL PROCESS

Perhaps the decision about whether to start your own business is best considered in light of an understanding of the entrepreneurial process.[1] The entrepreneurial process involves more than just problem solving in a typical management position. An entrepreneur must find, evaluate, and develop an opportunity by overcoming the strong forces that resist the creation of something new. The actual process itself has four distinct phases: (1) identify and evaluate the opportunity, (2) develop the business plan, (3) determine the resources required, and (4) manage the resulting enterprise created (see Table 2–3). While these phases proceed progressively, none is dealt with in isolation or is totally completed before work begins on factors in a sequential phase. For example, to successfully identify and evaluate an opportunity (phase 1), an entrepreneur must have in mind the type of business desired (phase 4).

[1] A developed version of this process can be found in Howard H. Stevenson, Michael J. Roberts, and H. Irving Grousbeck, *New Business Ventures and the Entrepreneur* (Homewood, IL: Richard D. Irwin, 1985), pp 16–23.

TABLE 2–2 Entrepreneur Assessment Quiz

1. Can you start a project and see it through to completion in spite of a myriad of obstacles? ___ Yes ___ No
2. Can you make a decision on a matter and then stick to the decision even when challenged? ___ Yes ___ No
3. Do you like to be in charge and be responsible? ___ Yes ___ No
4. Do other people you deal with respect and trust you? ___ Yes ___ No
5. Are you in good physical health? ___ Yes ___ No
6. Are you willing to work long hours with little immediate compensation? ___ Yes ___ No
7. Do you like meeting and dealing with people? ___ Yes ___ No
8. Can you communicate effectively and persuade people to go along with your dream? ___ Yes ___ No
9. Do others easily understand your concepts and ideas? ___ Yes ___ No
10. Have you had extensive experience in the type of business you wish to start? ___ Yes ___ No
11. Do you know the mechanics and forms of running a business (tax records, payroll records, income statements, balance sheets)? ___ Yes ___ No
12. Is there a need in your geographic area for the product or service you are intending to market? ___ Yes ___ No
13. Do you have skills in marketing and/or finance? ___ Yes ___ No
14. Are other firms in your indistrial classification doing well in your geographic area? ___ Yes ___ No
15. Do you have a location in mind for your business? ___ Yes ___ No
16. Do you have enough financial backing for the first year of operations? ___ Yes ___ No
17. Do you have enough money to fund the start-up of your business or have access to it through family or friends? ___ Yes ___ No
18. Do you know the suppliers necessary for your business to succeed? ___ Yes ___ No
19. Do you know individuals who have the talents and expertise you lack? ___ Yes ___ No
20. Do you really want to start this business more than anything else?___ Yes ___ No

Identifying and Evaluating the Opportunity

Identifying and evaluating a good opportunity is a most difficult task. Most good business opportunities do not suddenly appear but rather result from an entrepreneur being alert to possibilities or, in some cases, by establishing mechanisms to identify potential opportunities. For example, one entrepreneur asks at every cocktail party if anyone is using a product that does not adequately fulfill its intended purpose. This person is constantly looking for a need and opportunity to create a better product. Another entrepreneur always monitors the play and toys of her nieces and nephews. This is her way of looking for any unique toy product niche for a new venture.

TABLE 2–3 Aspects of the Entrepreneurial Process

Identify and Evaluate the Opportunity	*Develop Business Plan*	*Resources Required*	*Manage the Enterprise*
Creation and length of opportunity	Title Page Table of Contents	Existing resources of entrepreneur	Management style of structure
Real and perceived value of opportunity	Executive Summary	Resource gaps and available supplies	Key variables for success
Risk and returns of opportunity	1.0 Description of Business	Access to needed resources	Identify problems and potential problems
Opportunity versus personal skills and goals	2.0 Description of Industry 3.0 Marketing Plan		Implement control systems
Competitive situation	4.0 Financial Plan 5.0 Production Plan 6.0 Organization Plan 7.0 Operational Plan 8.0 Summary Appendices (Exhibits)		

Although most entrepreneurs do not have formal mechanisms for identifying business opportunities, some sources are often fruitful: consumers and business associates, members of the distribution system, and technical people. Often, consumers, such as business associates purchasing products to fit a certain life-style, are the best source of ideas for a new venture. How many times have you heard someone comment: "If only there was a product that would . . ." This comment occasionally results in the creation of a new business. One entrepreneur's evaluation of why so many business executives were complaining about the lack of good technical writing and word-processing services resulted in her creating her own business venture to fill this need. Her technical writing service grew to 10 employees in just two years.

As a result of their close contact with the end user, channel members of the distribution system also see product needs. One entrepreneur started a college bookstore after hearing all the students complain about the high cost of books and the lack of service provided by the only bookstore on campus. Many other entrepreneurs have identified business opportunities through a discussion with a retailer, wholesaler, or manufacturer's representative.

Finally, technically oriented individuals often conceptualize business opportunities when working on other projects. One entrepreneur's business resulted from seeing the application of a plastic resin compound in pallets while developing the resin application in another totally unrelated area—casket moldings.

Whether the opportunity is identified with the input from consumers, business associates, channel members, or technical people, each opportunity must be carefully screened and evaluated. This evaluation of the opportunity is perhaps the most critical element of the entrepreneurial process as it allows the entrepreneur to assess whether the specific product or service has the returns needed for the resources required. As indicated in Table 2–3, this evaluation process involves looking at the creation and length of the opportunity, its real and perceived value, its risks and returns, its fit with the personal skills and goals of the entrepreneur, and its differential advantage in its competitive environment.

It is important for the entrepreneur to understand the cause of the opportunity. Is it technological change, market shift, government regulation, or competition? These factors and the resulting opportunity have a different market size and time dimension.

The market size and the length of the **window of opportunity** are the primary bases for determining risks and rewards. The risks reflect the market, competition, technology, and amount of capital involved. The amount of capital forms the basis for the return and rewards. The methodology for evaluating risks and rewards, the focus of Chapters 7 and 9, frequently indicates that an opportunity does not offer either a financial or personal nonfinancial reward commensurate with the risks involved. The return and reward of the present opportunity needs to be viewed in light of any possible subsequent opportunities as well. One company, which delivered bark mulch to residential and commercial users for decoration around the base of trees and shrubs, added loam and shells to their product line. These products were sold to the same customer base using the same distribution (delivery) system. Similarly, follow-on products become very important for a company expanding or diversifying in a particular channel. A distribution channel such as K mart, Service Merchandise, or Target prefers to do business with multiproduct rather than single-product firms.

Finally, the opportunity must fit the personal skills and goals of the entrepreneur. It is particularly important that the entrepreneur be able to put forth the necessary time and effort required to make the venture succeed. Although many entrepreneurs feel that the desire can be developed along with the venture, typically it does not materialize, dooming the venture to failure. An entrepreneur must believe in the opportunity so much that the necessary sacrifices will be made so that the resulting organization will succeed.

Opportunity analysis, or what is frequently called an opportunity assessment plan, is *not* a business plan. Compared to a business plan, it should be shorter; focus on the opportunity, not the entire venture; and provide the basis to make the decision on whether to act on the opportunity.

Opportunity analysis includes the following: a description of the product or service; an assessment of the opportunity; an assessment of the entrepreneur and the team; specifications of all the activities and resources needed to translate the opportunity into a viable business venture; and the source of capital to finance the initial venture as well as its growth—first- and second-stage financing. The most difficult and most critical aspect of opportunity analysis is the assessment of the opportunity. This requires answering the following questions:

- What market need does it fill?
- What personal observations have you experienced or recorded with regard to that market need?
- What social condition underlies this market need?
- What market research data can be marshaled to describe this market need?
- What patents might be available to fulfill this need?
- What competition exists in this market? How would you describe the behavior of this competition?
- What does the international market look like?
- What does the international competition look like?
- Where is the money to be made in this activity?

Develop a Business Plan

A good **business plan** must be developed in order to exploit the opportunity defined. This is perhaps the most difficult phase of the entrepreneurial process. An entrepreneur usually has not prepared a business plan before and often does not have the resources available to do a good job. While the preparation of the business plan is covered in separate chapters (Chapters 5 to 8), it is important to understand the basic issues involved, and the three major sections of the plan (see Table 2–3). A good business plan is not only important in developing the opportunity but is also essential in determining the resources required, obtaining those resources, and successfully managing the resulting venture.

Resources Required

The resources needed for the opportunity must also be assessed. This process starts with an appraisal of the entrepreneur's present resources. Then, any resources that are critical must be distinguished from those that are just helpful. Care must be taken not to underestimate the amount and variety of resources needed. The downside risks associated with insufficient resources should also be assessed.

Acquiring the needed resources in a timely manner, while giving up as little control as possible, is the next, and quite difficult, step in the entrepreneurial process. An entrepreneur should strive to maintain as large an ownership position as possible, particularly in the start-up financing stage. As the business develops, more funds will probably be needed to finance the growth of the venture, requiring more ownership to be relinquished. Every entrepreneur should reluctantly give up an ownership position in the venture only after every other alternative has been explored. Not only must alternative suppliers of these resources be identified but also their needs and desires. By understanding resource supplier needs, the entrepreneur can structure a deal that enables the resources to be acquired at the lowest possible cost and loss of control.

Manage the Enterprise

After resources are acquired, the entrepreneur must employ them through implementation of the business plan. The operational problems of the growing enterprise must also be dealt with. This involves implementing a management style and structure, as well as determining the key variables for success (see Table 2–3). A control system must be identified so that any problem areas can be carefully monitored. Some entrepreneurs have difficulty managing and growing the venture they created—one difference between entrepreneurial and managerial decision making.

MANAGERIAL VERSUS ENTREPRENEURIAL DECISION MAKING

The difference between the entrepreneurial and managerial styles along five key business dimensions—strategic orientation, commitment to opportunity, commitment of resources, control of resources, and management structure—is summarized in Table 2–4.[2] Managerial styles are identified in the table under the heading Administrative Domain.

Strategic Orientation

The entrepreneur's strategic orientation depends on his or her perception of the opportunity. This orientation is most important when other opportunities have diminishing returns accompanied by rapid changes in technology, consumer economies, social values, or political rules. When the use of planning systems and measuring performance to control current resources is the strategic orientation, there is more pressure for the administrative (managerial) domain to be operant, as is the case with many large multinational organizations.

Commitment to Opportunity

In terms of the commitment to opportunity, the second key business dimension, the two domains vary greatly in terms of the length of this commitment. The entrepreneurial domain is pressured by the need for action, short decision windows, willingness to assume risk, and few decision constituencies, and has a short time span in terms of opportunity commitment. The administrative (managerial) domain is not only slow to act on an opportunity, but once action is taken the commitment is

[2]The differences are fully delineated in H. H. Stevenson and W. A. Sahlman, "Importance of Entrepreneurship in Economic Development," in *Entrepreneurship, Intrapreneurship, and Venture Capital,* ed Robert D. Hisrich (Lexington, MA: Lexington Books, 1986), pp 1–26.

TABLE 2–4 A Comparison of the Entrepreneurial and Administrative Domains

Entrepreneurial Domain Pressures toward this side		Key Business Dimension		*Administrative Domain* Pressures toward this side
Diminishing opportunity streams Rapidly changing: Technology Consumer economics Social values Political rules	Driven by perception of opportunity	Strategic orientation	Driven by resources currently controlled	Social contracts Performance measurement Social contracts Performance measurement criteria Planning systems and cycle
Action orientation Short decision windows Risk management Limited decision constituencies	Revolutionary with short duration	Commitment to opportunity	Evolutionary of long duration	Acknowledgment of multiple constituencies Negotiation of strategy Risk reduction Management of fit
Lack of predictable resource needs Lack of long-term control Social need for more opportunity per resource unit International pressure for more efficient resource use	Multistaged with minimal exposure at each stage	Commitment of resources	Single-staged with complete commitment upon decision	Personal risk reduction Incentive compensation Managerial turnover Capital allocation systems Formal planning systems
Increased resource Long resource life compared to need Risk of obsolescence Risk inherent in any new venture Inflexibility of permanent commitment to resources	Episodic use or rent of required resources	Control of resources	Ownership or employment of required resources	Power, status, and financial rewards Coordination Efficiency measures Inertia and cost of change Industry structures

TABLE 2–4 *(concluded)*

Coordination of key noncontrolled resources				Need for clearly defined authority and responsibility
Challenge to legitimacy of owners' control Employees desire for independence	Flat with multiple informal networks	Management structure	Formalized hierarchy	Organizational culture Reward systems Management theory

Source: Adapted from Howard H. Stevenson and William A. Sahlman, "Importance of Entrepreneurship in Economic Development," in *Entrepreneurship, Intrapreneurship, and Venture Capital: The Foundations of Economic Renaissance,* ed. Robert D. Hisrich (Lexington, MA: Lexington Books, 1986), pp 18–25.

usually for a long time span, too long in some instances. There are often no mechanisms set up in companies to stop and reevaluate an initial resource commitment once it is made—a major problem in the administrative (managerial) domain.

Commitment of Resources

An entrepreneur is used to having resources committed at periodic intervals, often based on certain tasks or objectives being reached. These resources, often acquired from others, are usually difficult to obtain, forcing the entrepreneur to achieve significant milestones using very few resources. This multistage commitment allows the resource providers (such as venture capitalists or private investors) to have as small an exposure as possible at each stage of business development and to constantly monitor the track record being established. Even though the funding may also be in stages in the administrative domain, the commitment of the resources is for the total amount needed. Administratively oriented individuals respond to the source of the rewards offered and receive personal rewards by effectively administering the resources under their control

Control of Resources

Control of the resources follows a similar pattern. Since the administrator (manager) is rewarded by effective resource administration, there is often a drive to own or accumulate as many resources as possible. The pressures of power, status, and financial rewards cause the administrator (manager) to avoid rental or other periodic use of the resource. The opposite is true for the entrepreneur who, under the pressures of limited resources, risk of obsolescence, need for flexibility, and the risks involved, strives to rent or otherwise achieve periodic use of the resources on an as-needed basis.

Management Structure

The final business dimension—management structure—also differs significantly between the two domains. In the administrative domain, the organizational structure is formalized and hierarchical in nature, reflecting the need for clearly defined lines of authority and responsibility based on management theory and the reward system. The entrepreneur, true to his or her desire for independence, employs a flat organizational structure with informal networks throughout.

ENTREPRENEURIAL CAREERS

What causes an individual to take all the social, psychological, and financial risks associated with starting a new venture? While there has been a somewhat limited focus on this aspect of entrepreneurship, since 1985 there has been an increased interest in entrepreneurial careers and education. This increased interest has been fostered by such factors as the recognition that small firms play a major role in job creation and innovation; an increased media coverage of entrepreneurs; an understanding that there are more entrepreneurs than those heralded in the media as thousands upon thousands of small, cottage companies are formed; the view that most large organizational structures do not provide an environment for self-actualization; the shift in employment, as women become increasingly more active in the workforce, and the number of families earning two incomes grow; and the formation of new ventures by female entrepreneurs at three times the rate of their male counterparts.

In spite of this increase, many people, particularly college students, do not consider entrepreneurship as a career. A conceptual model for understanding entrepreneurial careers, indicated in Table 2–5, views the career stages as dynamic ones, with each stage reflecting and interacting with other stages and events in the individual's life—past, present, and future. This **life-cycle approach** conceptualizes entrepreneurial careers in nine major categories: educational environment, the individual's personality, childhood family environment, employment history, adult development history, adult nonwork history, current work situation, the individual's current perspective, and the current family situation.[3]

While some have felt that entrepreneurs are less educated than the general population, this opinion has proven to be more myth than reality. Studies have found entrepreneurs overall and female entrepreneurs in particular to be far more educated than the general populace.[4] However, the types and quality of the education received

[3]Each of these categories is fully developed, particularly for the female entrepreneur, in D. D. Bowen and R. D. Hisrich, "The Female Entrepreneur: A Career Development Perspective," *Academy of Management Review* 2 (April 1986), pp 393–407; and J. D. Brodzinski, R. F. Sherer, and F. A. Wiebe, "Entrepreneur Career Selection and Gender: A Socialization Approach," *Journal of Small Business Management* 27 (March 1989), pp 37–43.

[4]See R. D. Hisrich and C. G. Brush, *The Woman Entrepreneur: Starting, Financing, and Managing a Successful New Business* (Lexington, MA: Lexington Books, 1986).

TABLE 2–5 A Framework for an Entrepreneur's Career Development

	← *TIME* →		
Life Space Areas	*Childhood*	*Earlier Adulthood*	*Present Adulthood*
Work/Occupation	Education and childhood work experience I	Employment history IV	Current work situation VII
Individual/ Personal	Childhood influences on personality, values, and interests II	Adult development history V	Individual's current perspective VIII
Nonwork/Family	Childhood family environment III	Adult family/nonwork history VI	Current family/ nonwork situation IX

Source: Adapted from Donald D. Bowen and Robert D. Hisrich, "The Female Entrepreneur: A Career Development Perspective," *The Academy of Management Review* II (April 1986). pp 393–407.

sometimes does not develop specific skills needed in the venture creation and management process. Sometimes women entrepreneurs have more of a disadvantage than male entrepreneurs in this respect, as they frequently major in nonbusiness and nonengineering disciplines.

Childhood influences have also been explored, particularly in terms of values and the individual's personality. The most frequently researched personality traits are the need for achievement, locus of control, risk taking, and gender identity. Since the personality traits are more thoroughly discussed in Chapter 3, it is sufficient here to indicate that few firm conclusions can be drawn from all the research regarding universal personality traits of entrepreneurs.

The research on the childhood family environment of the entrepreneur has had more definitive results. Entrepreneurs tend to have self-employed fathers, many of whom are also entrepreneurs. Many also have entrepreneurial mothers. The family, particularly the father or mother, plays an important role in establishing the desirability and credibility of entrepreneurship as a career path. As one entrepreneur said: "My father and mother always encouraged me to try new things and do everything very professionally. They wanted me to be the very best and have the freedom and independence of being my own boss."

Employment history also has an impact on entrepreneurial careers, in both a positive and negative sense. On the positive side, entrepreneurs tend to have a higher probability of success when the venture created is in their field of work experience. This increased success rate makes the providers of risk capital particularly concerned when this work experience is not present. Negative displacement (such as dissatisfaction with various aspects of one's job, being fired or demoted, being transferred to an undesirable location, or having one's spouse take a new position in a new geographic area) encourages entrepreneurship, not only in the United States but in other cultures as well.

Although no definitive research has been done on adult development history for entrepreneurs, it appears to also affect entrepreneurial careers. One's development history has somewhat more of an impact on women since they tend to start businesses at a later stage in life than men, usually after having experienced significantly more job frustration.

There is a similar lack of data on adult family/nonwork history. Although there is some information on the entrepreneurs' marital and family situations, the available data adds little to our understanding of entrepreneurial career paths.

The impact of the current work situation has received considerably more research attention. Entrepreneurs are known for their strong work values and aspirations, their long work days, and their dominant management style. Entrepreneurs tend to fall in love with the organization and will sacrifice almost anything in order for it to survive. This desire is reflected in the individual entrepreneur's current career perspective and family/nonwork situation. The new venture usually takes the highest priority in the entrepreneur's life and is the source of the entrepreneur's self-esteem.

ENTREPRENEURIAL EDUCATION AND TRAINING

While in college, few future entrepreneurs realize that they will pursue entrepreneurship as their major life goal. Even among the minority that do, relatively few individuals will start a business immediately after graduation, and even fewer will prepare for a new venture creation by working in a particular position or industry. This mandates that entrepreneurs continually supplement their education through books, trade journals, seminars, or taking courses in weak areas. Generally, skills that need to be acquired through seminars or courses include creativity, financing, control, opportunity identification, venture evaluation, and deal making.

Entrepreneurship education is a fast growing area in colleges and universities in the United States and Europe. While many universities offer at least one course in entrepreneurship at the graduate or undergraduate level, a few actually have a major or minor concentration in the area. Since the area is so new, the U.S. Department of Education has not yet separated entrepreneurship from small business, and the statistics associated with entrepreneurship are not as accurate as other educational statistics in more established educational areas.

While the courses in entrepreneurship vary by university, there is a great deal of commonality, particularly in the initial one or two courses in this field of study. These courses tend to reflect the overall objectives for a course in entrepreneurship. Sample course objectives, indicated in Table 2–6, tend to center around skill identification and assessment; understanding entrepreneurial decision making and the

TABLE 2–6 Overall Objectives for a Course in Entrepreneurship

- Understand the role of new and smaller firms in the economy
- Understand the relative strengths and weaknesses of different types of enterprises
- Know the general characteristics of an entrepreneurial process
- Assess the student's own entrepreneurial skills
- Understand the entrepreneurial process and the product planning and development process
- Know alternative methods for identifying and evaluating business opportunities and the factors that support and inhibit creativity
- Develop an ability to form, organize, and work in interdisciplinary teams
- Know the general correlates of success and failure in innovation and new venture creation
- Know the generic entry strategies for new venture creation
- Understand the aspects of creating and presenting a new venture business plan
- Know how to identify, evaluate, and obtain resources
- Know the essentials of:
  - Marketing planning
  - Financial planning
  - Operations planning
  - Organization planning
  - Venture launch planning
- Know how to manage and grow a new venture
- Know the managerial challenges and demands of a new venture launch
- Understand the role of entrepreneurship in existing organizations

Source: Robert D. Hisrich, "Toward An Organization Model for Entrepreneurial Education," *Proceedings*, International Entrepreneurship Conference, p 29.

entrepreneurial process; understanding the characteristics of entrepreneurs and their role in economic development on a domestic and, more recently, on an international basis; assessing opportunities and coming up with an idea for a new venture; writing and presenting a full-scale business plan; knowing how to obtain resources; managing and growing the enterprise; and understanding the role of entrepreneurship in an existing organization—intrapreneurship.

The skills required by entrepreneurs can be classified into three main areas: technical skills, business management skills, and personal entrepreneurial skills (see Table 2–7). Technical skills involve such things as writing, listening, oral presentations, organizing, coaching, being a team player, and technical know-how.

Business management skills include those areas involved in starting, developing, and managing any enterprise. Skills in decision making, marketing, management, financing, accounting, production, control, and negotiation are essential in launching and growing a new venture. The final skill area involves personal entrepreneurial

TABLE 2–7 Types of Skills Required in Entrepreneurship

Technical Skills
- Writing
- Oral Communication
- Monitoring Environment
- Technical Business Management
- Technology
- Interpersonal
- Listening
- Ability to Organize
- Network Building
- Management Style
- Coaching
- Being a Team Player

Business Management Skills
- Planning and Goal Setting
- Decision Making
- Human Relations
- Marketing
- Finance
- Accounting
- Management
- Control
- Negotiation
- Venture Launch
- Managing Growth

Personal Entrepreneurial Skills
- Inner Control/Disciplined
- Risk Taker
- Innovative
- Change Oriented
- Persistent
- Visionary Leader

Source: Robert D. Hisrich, "Toward An Organization Model for Entrepreneurial Education," *Proceedings,* International Entrepreneurship Conference, p 29.

skills. Some of these skills differentiate an entrepreneur from a manager. Skills included in this classification are inner control (discipline), risk taking, being innovative, being change oriented, being persistent, and being a visionary leader.

These skills and objectives form the basis of the modular approach to an entrepreneurship curriculum. By laying out modules, a course or sequence of courses can be developed, depending on the needs, interests, and resources at the particular university. This modular approach helps ensure that the most important areas of the field are covered in the courses offered, whether on a quarter or semester basis or involving one or a series of courses.

ENTREPRENEURIAL ETHICS

One aspect of entrepreneurship that has recently become more central to starting and growing a new venture, particularly in once-controlled economies, is the ethics and social responsibility of the entrepreneur. Does the entrepreneur understand and practice the going concern concept where customers are the focal point and are regularly dealt with in a fair manner? Does the entrepreneur understand the concept of giving back when good profit results are achieved? Generally, entrepreneurs in the U.S. view consumer relations, product quality, and employee relations as fundamental responsibilities of business ventures.[5] Entrepreneurs and their smaller businesses appear to have a better understanding of ethics and social responsibility issues than do larger businesses. Some internal and external factors impact the ethics of entrepreneurs and their smaller ventures differently than larger businesses.

The internal factors include different norms and pressures from the community and peers as well as differences in fear of punishment. External factors include the impact of trade organizations, churches, and competition. These internal and external factors sensitize the entrepreneur in terms of social responsibility and ethics.

SUMMARY

There is more to a successful business than a good idea; there must also be a good entrepreneur. Although the "ideal" entrepreneur cannot be profiled, there are certain trends and norms for a potential entrepreneur. Some of the characteristics and traits commonly found in successful entrepreneurs are examined in Table 2–2. In some respects, traits such as responsibility, tenacity, and the ability to handle ambiguity are more important to success than the product or service being offered.

The entrepreneurial process involves finding, evaluating, and developing opportunities for creating a new venture. Each step is important to the eventual success of the new firm, and each is closely related to the others. Before the opportunity identification stage can result in a meaningful search, the potential entrepreneur must have a general idea about the type of company desired. However, the resulting selection criteria employed cannot be too inflexible, or a valuable idea may be excluded.

There are both formal and informal mechanisms for identifying business opportunities. While formal mechanisms are generally found within a more established company, most entrepreneurs use informal sources for their ideas, such as being sensitive to the complaints and chance comments of friends and associates.

[5]For a discussion of the research and issues in ethics and social responsibility see: J. K. Thompson, H. L. Smith, and J. N. Hood, "Charitable Contributions by Small Businesses," *Journal of Small Business Management,* July 1993, pp 35–51; and N. Humphreys, D. P. Robin, R. E. Reidenbach, and D. L. Moak, "The Ethical Decision Making Process of Small Business Owner/Managers and Their Customers," *Journal of Small Business Management,* July 1993, pp 9–22.

Once the opportunity is identified, the evaluation process begins. Basic to the screening process is understanding the factors creating the opportunity—technology, market changes, competition, or changes in government regulations. From this base, the market size and time dimension associated with the idea can be estimated. It is important that the idea fit the personal skills and goals of the entrepreneur, as well as that the entrepreneur have a strong desire to see the opportunity brought to fruition. In the process of evaluating an opportunity, the required resources should be clearly defined and obtained at the lowest possible cost.

Managing a new venture differs in many ways from managing an existing operation particularly along five key dimensions: strategic orientation, commitment to opportunity, commitment of resources, control of resources, and management structure. The entrepreneurial venture presents the manager with a different set of circumstances than the corporate manager typically faces. A distinctly different set of skills needs to be developed, either through the entrepreneurial experience or education.

Just as there is no distinct entrepreneurial personality profile, there is no specific entrepreneurial career path. A life-cycle approach, focusing on the interaction of past, present, and future events in the individual's life, is more appropriate for the experiences of entrepreneurs than a more conventional time-line career path. Education, personality, childhood family life, employment history, adult development history, adult nonwork history, current work situation, current perspective, and current family situations affect the avenue through which an individual approaches entrepreneurship.

The education of potential entrepreneurs is a difficult task, complicated due to the absence of any clear career patterns. Many potential entrepreneurs are not educated in business or engineering schools; many do not know that they are going to be entrepreneurs in the future. The goal of an entrepreneurial education curriculum should be to provide a program addressing entrepreneurship at different levels: personal assessment, idea generation, opportunity assessment, developing a business plan, and the business skills needed at various stages in the life of an entrepreneurial venture.

QUESTIONS FOR DISCUSSION

1. Referring to the Entrepreneur Assessment Quiz in Table 2–2, divide the 20 questions into two groups: those that you think primarily reflect inherent personal characteristics that would be difficult or impossible for an adult to change, and those that you think are learned skills. Justify your choices. Why is each attribute important to the success of a new venture? List some attributes not on this list that are also important.
2. List five opportunities for a new business that have come to your attention recently. How were you made aware of these needs? List the sources of

Answers to Characteristics of an Entrepreneur Quiz (Table 2–1)

1. *Oldest.* While, indeed, entrepreneurs come from many different birth orders, there is a slight tendency for an entrepreneur to be the oldest child in the family, thereby having had time alone with parents without other siblings.

2. *Married.* While there has never been any statistical validation, most entrepreneurs are married when they start their first significant venture. The spouse plays an important support role.

3. *Man.* While men still outnumber women entrepreneurs in terms of actual numbers, women entrepreneurs are presently forming new ventures at two to three times the rate of men.

4. *Thirties.* While ventures may be started at any age, the first significant venture is usually started in the early 30s for men and late 30s for women.

5. *Teens.* An individual's ability to handle ambiguity, the drive for independence, and creativity (important characteristics for an entrepreneur) are evident early in life.

6. *Bachelor's degree.* While the Horatio Alger story is indeed still possible, most entrepreneurs are college educated, like most of the general populace in the United States. Women entrepreneurs are even more educated, with many having a master's degree. This education is particularly important in securing financing and starting technology-based ventures. While not as highly educated as those in the United States, entrepreneurs in foreign countries are at least as highly educated as the general populace.

7. *To be independent.* The need for independence (the inability to work for anyone else) is what drives the entrepreneur to take the risks to work all the hours necessary to create a new venture.

8. *Father.* Regardless of whether it is a love or a hate relationship, entrepreneurs report a strong parental relationship, particularly with the father. This strong father relationship is particularly important for women entrepreneurs.

9. *Luck.* Hard work, money, and a good idea are necessary but not sufficient for a successful venture. The venture formation by the entrepreneur is characterized also as being "lucky"—being in the right place at the right time.

10. *Are in conflict.* Venture capitalists and entrepreneurs have two different goals. The venture capitalist's goal is to make money and exit from the business within five years. The entrepreneur's goal is independence through survival of the organization.

11. *External management professionals.* This use of an external professional for advice often takes the form of a mentor or at least a good network system. The use of this individual(s) helps reduce the loneliness of being an entrepreneur.

12. *Doers.* Entrepreneurs take pride in creating and doing. They are definitely not managers and planners—the appropriate side of the entrepreneurial continuum. Rarely are they also good venture capitalists.

13. *Moderate risk takers.* The myth that entrepreneurs are high risk takers is nothing more than just that, a myth. The calculating decision to risk everything and perhaps fail reflects moderate risk taking.

14. *Just fit into a crowd.* Unless you knew that an individual was an entrepreneur there would be no way to distinguish an entrepreneur from a manager based on external physical appearance.

15. *All of the above. New* is an entrepreneurial magnet as it implies creativity and venture creation, the drive of every entrepreneur.

16. *Variety of ventures.* Entrepreneurs create a wide variety of ventures depending on their field of experience and backgrounds. Women entrepreneurs, however, do tend to concentrate in the service sector.

opportunities you have encountered in the last week or two. If your list is short, indicate how you could cultivate more sources.

3. List examples of new products or services that have resulted from the different sources of change discussed in the chapter.
4. As entrepreneurship becomes more popular and the education of entrepreneurs becomes more widespread, do you believe that a well-defined entrepreneurial career path will emerge? Support your answer.
5. Why do you think that some successful entrepreneurs have had difficulty in managing their companies beyond the start-up stage? How could entrepreneurial education help this problem?

KEY TERMS

administrative domain
business plan
entrepreneurial career
entrepreneurial domain
entrepreneurial process
life-cycle approach
opportunity identification
window of opportunity

SELECTED READINGS

Bellu, R. R. (1987). Entrepreneurs and managers: Are they different? In *Proceedings,* Babson Research Conference, pp 16–30.

This study, by using the Miner Sentence Completion Scales, Form-T, describes the differences among entrepreneurs and managers. An analysis of the results concludes that entrepreneurs tend to think that successful outcomes are attributable to internal causes and unsuccessful outcomes to unstable causes.

Bird, B. J. (1992). The operations of intentions in time: The emergence of the new venture. *Entrepreneurship: Theory and Practice.* vol. 17. no. 1. pp 11–20.

Entrepreneurial intention requires the individual's ability and willingness to sustain temporal tension—the stretch between a vision of what could be and current conditions. The other aspect of timing involves controlling or at least predicting the duration of the intervals in the venture creation process.

Bull, I., & Willard G. E. (1993). Towards a theory of entrepreneurship. *Journal of Business Venturing.* vol. 8. no. 3. pp 183–195.

Based on a summary of the current state of the development of the theory of entrepreneurship, an economic outcome approach to the study of entrepreneurship and a tentative theory of entrepreneurship are proposed.

Bull, I., & Winter, F. (1991). Community differences in business births and business growths. *Journal of Business Venturing.* vol. 6. no. 1. pp 29–43.

There is a positive correlation of entrepreneurship in a community with a large porportion of college graduates and a negative correlation when a large proportion of the population is over 65. There was also a weak correlation between community attitudes and the entrepreneurship measures used in the study.

Campbell, C. A. (1992). A decision theory model for entrepreneurial acts. *Entrepreneurship: Theory and Practice.* vol. 17. no. 1. pp 21–27.

Since the decision to become an entrepreneur is an alternative to wage labor, the entrepreneurial decision is at least partially attributable to economic motivation and can be characterized by a standard kind of decision model underpinned by the theory of utility maximization.

Covin, J. G., & Slevin, D. P. (1991). A conceptual model of entrepreneurship as firm behavior. *Entrepreneurship: Theory and Practice.* vol. 16. no. 1. pp 7–25.

The adoption of the proposed firm-behavior model of entrepreneurship uses behaviors not attributes to give meaning to the entrepreneurial process.

Cunningham, J. B., & L. J. (1991). Defining entrepreneurship. *Journal of Small Business Management.* vol. 29. no. 1. pp 45–61.

Several different schools of entrepreneurship are presented (the great person, psychological characteristics, classical management, leadership and intrapreneurship) useful for recognizing underlying values, responding to the future, and improving management.

Dumas, C. (1992). Integrating the daughter into family business management. *Entrepreneurship: Theory and Practice.* vol. 16. no. 4. pp 41–55.

The results of a study of founding fathers and daughters in 18 family-owned firms indicated that the daughter is often an untapped resource and may be particularly suited for working in collaboration with the founding father, giving both the opportunity to meet some vital needs.

Hood, J. N., & Young, J. E. (1993). Entrepreneurship's requisite areas of development: A survey of top executives in entrepreneurial firms. *Journal of Business Venturing.* vol. 8. no. 2. pp 115–135.

Based on information from 100 top executives in entrepreneurial firms, four broad areas of development were found to be necessary for effective entrepreneurships: content, skill and behavior, mentality, and personality.

Katz, J. B. (1993). The dynamics of organizational emergence: A contemporary group formation perspective. *Entrepreneurship: Theory and Practice.* vol. 17. no. 2. pp 97–101.

Such contributions from social psychology as role theory, theory, the minimal group paradigm, and the task group are important in understanding entrepreneurship and particularly the process of organizational emergence.

Katz, J. B. (1992). A psychological cognitive model of employment status choice. *Entrepreneurship: Theory and Practice.* vol. 17. no. 1. pp 29–37.

A psychological cognitive model of employment status using an individual's psychology in the form of values, decision-making processes, and social status insofar as it depends on personal history, and social context contributing to the decision process is proposed.

Mariotti, S. (1993). Entrepreneurship in the inner city. *Executive Speeches.* vol. 7. no. 3. pp 4–6.

Students at an inner city school have learned all the basic steps of starting and running a small business as well as the fundamentals of a market economy and have formed companies that have had more than $100,000 in sales in the last two years.

Miner, J., Norman R., & Brecker, J. S. (1992). Defining the inventor-entrepreneur in the context of established typologies. *Journal of Business Venturing.* vol. 7. no. 2. pp 103–113.

What is really indicative of inventor-entrepreneurship is a strong commitment to a company strategy of product development not a proclivity for taking out patents. These entrepreneurs develop an organization not as an end in itself but as a vehicle for invention and production of various products.

Stumpf, S. S., Roger, L. M., & Mullen, T. P. (1991). Developing entrepreneurial skills through the use of behavioral simulation. *Journal of Management Development.* vol. 10. no. 5. pp 32–45.

Behavioral simulation technology is appropriate for developing entrepreneurial skills as behavioral simulations create an appropriate teacher-learner environment to accomplish many of the learning objectives of entrepreneurship education.

Zahra, S. A. (1993). Environment, corporate entrepreneurship, and financial performance: A taxonomic approach. *Journal of Business Venturing.* vol. 8. no. 4. pp 319–340.

Four environmental settings (dynamic growth, hostile and rivalrous but technologically rich, hospitable product-driven growth, and static environment) were used to examine the relationship between a firm's external environment, corporate entrepreneurship, and financial performance.

CHAPTER

3

Entrepreneurial Characteristics

Chapter Objectives

1. To identify the key entrepreneurial feelings and motivations.
2. To identify key elements in an entrepreneur's background.
3. To discuss the importance of role models and support systems.
4. To identify the similarities and differences between male and female entrepreneurs.
5. To explain the differences between inventors and entrepreneurs.
6. To identify some general entrepreneur profiles.

Lillian Vernon Katz

Lillian Katz was born in Leipzig, Germany, in 1927 to parents she characterizes as hardworking and scrupulously honest. After living briefly in Holland, the family emigrated to the United States in 1937, when Lillian was 10 years old. She found the freedom of her New York City home exhilarating. The dominant figure in her early life was her father, a leather goods manufacturer, who instilled in Lillian the same characteristics of hard work and honesty that her mother possessed. He taught her that girls, no less than boys, could achieve any goal they wished in any field they chose. This paternal guidance gave his young daughter confidence in herself and her dreams.

In 1949, after majoring in psychology at New York University for two years, she married Sam Hochberg. Two years later, at 24, she was pregnant with her first child. They were living in a three-room apartment in Mount Vernon on Sam's $75 per week earnings. Feeling they would need an additional $50 per week to support the new baby, Lillian decided to open her own business. Her father's influence on her early life left her with no doubts about her ability to succeed. Because she did not want a 9-to-5 job but something that could be run from her own home, Lillian chose mail order after considering several alternatives.

Using $2,000 of wedding gift money, she launched her venture—Vernon Specialties Company—which offered personalized leather handbags and belts designed by Lillian and made by her father. Her concept for the business was to offer by mail something personalized that could not be readily found at an affordable price. An advertisement in the September 1951 issue of *Seventeen* magazine, costing $495, generated $16,000 in orders in six weeks for the fledgling company. The resulting profits were used to purchase more ads and buy more handbags and belts. Lillian worked during the day in a loft rented from her father and did the clerical work on her kitchen table at night. The line was soon expanded to include three colors of handbags and belts and personalized bookmarks costing $1. After the birth of her second son, David, she decided to include her own designs and Vernon Products was born.

Since the mid-1950s did not offer a positive environment for female entrepreneurs, Lillian confronted many obstacles. Some bankers would not even bother to talk to her, and neighbors felt she was not being a good mother because she left her sons with a nanny. However, Lillian overcame these problems, using her AT&T stock as collateral for bank loans and managing her business around her children's schedules. While the nanny did the cleaning, cooking, and laundry, Lillian did the shopping, ran the house, and joined in car pooling. There were times, however, when motherhood took second place, such as one Christmas when she sent her children to her mother's for the holidays due to a backlog of orders. While regretting this instance, Lillian accepts it as part of the cost of success: "I wasn't burdened with the guilt many working mothers have, because being a working mother seemed normal."

In 1956, Sam closed his retail store and turned it into a warehouse for the Vernon Specialties mail-order business. The manufacturing part of the business was worth around $1 million and the mail-order division around $1 million. While the business thrived, the marriage did not; Sam and Lillian were divorced after 20 years of marriage. Lillian chose to retain the mail-order business, a decision that later proved to have been an excellent one.

A year after her divorce, Lillian married Robbie Katz, a professional engineer and businessman who ran his own Lucite manufacturing business. With both her children in college, Lillian could begin to really devote herself to the company, which grew from $1 million in sales in 1970 to $137 million in sales by 1986—her 35th anniversary in business—to $155 million in 1989 to $137 million in 1992 and $190 million in 1993.

In developing the company from a million to a multimillion dollar business, Lillian found it necessary to hire professional managers—veterans of large corporate cultures—some of whom were unable to make the timely decisions required in the smaller company's fast-paced competitive situation. This opportunity allowed Lillian to identify both the entrepreneurial process through which the company began and grew and the management process necessary to help it continue to grow: "If I've learned anything over the past 35 years, it is the importance of drawing from the best qualities of both the entrepreneur and the professional manager. These are truly the left and right sides of the business brain, and they must harmonize in a healthy corporation."

With the day-to-day business operations in the hands of competent managers, Lillian concentrates on finding the best products for her catalog. In this search, she travels approximately 16 weeks each year, personally approving every item listed in the catalog. An item usually will not be carried unless someone she knows would like it or use it. Lillian was one of the first to handle goods from mainland China, going there in the 1970s.

Even with the time required for selecting the items in the catalog, Lillian still is personally involved in every aspect of the company's operation. She signs checks, reviews and helps write copy, and approves the catalog photos. The copy accompanying the catalog items is renowned in the industry.

Today, Lillian's sons, David and Fred, are both involved in the company's management. Fred is executive vice president and chief operating officer, and David is director of public affairs. The Lillian Vernon Corporation has grown from an initial investment of $2,000 to a publicly traded company with 1993 sales of $190 million. The company mailed 137 million catalogs in 1992 and received 4.3 million orders, with an average order size of $39. This increased in 1993 to 141 million catalogs mailed and 4.4 million orders received, with an average order size of $40. The company now includes the New Company, Inc., a wholesale division making brass items; Lillian Vernon International in Italy and Hong Kong; Lillian Vernon; The Store in New Rochelle, New York; and a state-of-the-art fully automated 454,000-square-foot fulfillment center, including 123,552 square feet of warehouse space and a mainframe computer used for inventory control.

Lillian Katz adamantly supports other entrepreneurial efforts. Many of the suppliers of her catalog items are owned by fellow entrepreneurs. In one speech, she urged the financial community to take a risk on an entrepreneur: "You are investing in potential, which can pay tremendous dividends." She sits on the board of several charities and foundations and is a member of the Women's Forum and the Committee of 200, groups of the brightest "fast-track" female executives in the country.

The success of the Lillian Vernon Corporation lies primarily in the dedication and hard work of its founder, Lillian Katz: "Hard work, long hours, and personal sacrifice are just some of the disciplines necessary to achieve this [success], but the end rewards are worth it!"

Lillian Katz exhibits one profile of an entrepreneur. Other entrepreneurs appearing in this book present different ones. Is there an exact entrepreneurial profile in terms of characteristics and background? This chapter addresses this question by looking at feelings about control, independence, and willingness to take risks; family, education, and occupational backgrounds; motivation; skills; male versus female entrepreneurs; entrepreneurs versus inventors; and general entrepreneurial profiles.

ENTREPRENEURIAL FEELINGS

Before considering the various characteristics and backgrounds of the typical entrepreneur, it should be emphasized that there are significant differences between individual entrepreneurs. There is really no such thing as a "true entrepreneurial profile." Entrepreneurs come from a variety of educational backgrounds, family situations, and work experiences. A potential entrepreneur may presently be a nurse, secretary, assembly line worker, salesperson, mechanic, homemaker, manager, or engineer. A potential entrepreneur can be male or female, of any race or nationality.

Locus of Control

One concern people have when considering forming a new venture is whether they will be able to sustain the drive and energy required not only to overcome the inertia in forming something new but also to manage the new enterprise and make it grow. Are you driven by an inner need to succeed and win? You can make an initial assessment by answering the 10 questions in Table 3–1. After answering these questions,

TABLE 3–1 Checklist for Feelings about Control

1. Do you often feel "That's just the way things are and there's nothing I can do about it"?	___ Yes	___ No
2. When things go right and are terrific for you, do you think "It's mostly luck!"?	___ Yes	___ No
3. Do you think you should go into business or do something with your time for pay because everything you read these days is urging you in that direction?	___ Yes	___ No
4. Do you know that if you decide to do something, you'll do it and nothing can stop you?	___ Yes	___ No
5. Even though it's scary to try something new, are you the kind who tries it?	___ Yes	___ No
6. Your friends, spouse, and mother tell you that it's foolish of you to want a career. Have you listened to them and stayed home all these years?	___ Yes	___ No
7. Do you think it's important for everyone to like you?	___ Yes	___ No
8. When you do a good job, is your pleasure in a job well done satisfaction enough?	___ Yes	___ No
9. If you want something, do you ask for it rather than wait for someone to notice you and "just give it to you"?	___ Yes	___ No
10. Even though people tell you "it can't be done," do you have to find out for yourself?	___ Yes	___ No

Source: Reprinted with the permission of Lexington Books, an imprint of Macmillan Publishing Company from *The Woman Entrepreneur* by Robert D. Hisrich and Candida G. Brush. ©1985 by Lexington Books, p. 6.

determine whether you are internally or externally driven by comparing your answers with the responses below. Answering Yes to questions 4, 5, 8, 9, and 10 indicates that you possess the internal control aspect of being an entrepreneur. Yes answers to questions 1, 2, 3, 6, and 7 indicate that you are more geared to external controls, which may inhibit your entrepreneurial tendencies and ability to sustain drive.

In evaluating these results and your internal-external control dimension, keep in mind that research is not conclusive about the role of locus of control in entrepreneurship. For example, only three of the nine research studies of Rotter's internality-externality (I-E) dimensions of entrepreneurs depicted them as having a sense of control over their lives, that is, being internals. One study indicated that entrepreneurial intentions were associated with internality, and another reported a positive correlation between career success and internality.[1] Two studies of entrepreneurs under

[1]For a review of these nine studies, see D. E. Jennings and C. P. Zietham, "Locus of Control: a Review and Directions for Entrepreneurial Research," *Proceedings* of the 43rd Annual Meeting of the Academy of Management, April 1983, pp 417–21. A discussion of the concept itself can be found in J. B. Rotter, "Generalized Expectancies for Internal versus External Control of Reinforcement," *Psychological Monographs* General and Applied Number 80 (1966).

TABLE 3–2 Checklist for Feelings about Independence

1. I hate to go shopping for clothes alone.	___ Yes	___ No
2. If my friends won't go to a movie I want to see, I'll go by myself.	___ Yes	___ No
3. I want to be financially independent.	___ Yes	___ No
4. I often need to ask other people's opinions before I decide on important things.	___ Yes	___ No
5. I'd rather have other people decide where to go on a social evening out.	___ Yes	___ No
6. When I know I'm in charge, I don't apologize, I just do what has to be done.	___ Yes	___ No
7. I'll speak up for an unpopular cause if I believe in it.	___ Yes	___ No
8. I'm afraid to be different.	___ Yes	___ No
9. I want the approval of others.	___ Yes	___ No
10. I usually wait for people to call me to go places, rather than intrude on them.	___ Yes	___ No

Source: Reprinted with the permission of Lexington Books, an imprint of Macmillan Publishing Company from *The Woman Entrepreneur* by Robert D. Hisrich and Candida G. Brush. ©1985 by Lexington Books, p. 7.

stress had mixed results—some entrepreneurs under stress shifted toward greater internality, while others shifted toward greater externality. Studies of 31 entrepreneurs in St. Louis indicated that more successful entrepreneurs were more internal, and entrepreneurs overall were more internal than the general populace but not more than male managers.[2] While internal beliefs appear to differentiate entrepreneurs from the general public, they do not differentiate entrepreneurs from managers; both have an internality tendency.

Feelings about Independence and Need for Achievement

Closely related to this feeling of control is the **need for independence.** An entrepreneur is generally the type of person who needs to do things in his or her own way and time and has a difficult time working for someone else. To evaluate your feelings on independence, answer the questions in Table 3–2. After completing the questions, compare your answers to those below. Yes answers to questions 1, 4, 5, 8, 9, and 10 indicate that you do not have a strong need for independence.

[2]See Robert H. Brockhaus, "Psychological and Environmental Factors Which Distinguish the Successful from the Unsuccessful Entrepreneur," *Proceedings* of the 40th Annual Meeting of the Academy of Management, August 1980, pp. 368–72; and Robert H. Brockhaus and W. R. Nord, "An Exploration of Factors Affecting the Entrepreneurial Decision: Personal Characteristics versus Environmental Conditions," *Proceedings* of the 40th Annual Meeting of the Academy of Management, August 1979, pp 364–68.

An even more controversial characteristic is the entrepreneur's **need for achievement.** McClelland's work on the need for achievement identified psychological characteristics present in entrepreneurs.[3] He specified three attributes from his overall theory of need for achievement (*n* Ach) as characteristics of entrepreneurs: (1) individual responsibility for solving problems, setting goals, and reaching these goals through their own efforts; (2) moderate risk taking as a function of skill, not chance; and (3) knowledge of results of decision/task accomplishment. McClelland's conclusion that a high *n* Ach leads individuals to engage in entrepreneurial behavior sparked several studies, the results of which are inconclusive; some studies report that there is a relationship between *n* Ach and entrepreneurs, while others do not. Perhaps a modification of McClelland's concept complete with a different set of measurements may result in a better understanding of the relationship between achievement and entrepreneurship.[4]

Risk Taking

Virtually all recent definitions of entrepreneurs mention a risk-taking component. Risk-taking, whether financial, social, or psychological, is a part of the entrepreneurial process. You can assess your risk-taking behavior by answering the questions in Table 3–3 and then comparing your responses to those below. If you answered Yes to questions 2, 5, and 9, you may need to develop a greater willingness to take risks. Many studies of risk taking in entrepreneurship have focused on the component of general risk-taking propensity. Since no conclusive causal relationships have been determined, it has not yet been empirically established that risk-taking propensity is a distinguishing characteristic of entrepreneurs. While this may be a function of the research instrument (Kogan-Wallach CDQ is the research instrument predominantly used), little can yet be concluded from the results of the empirical research on the risk-taking propensities of entrepreneurs of either sex.

ENTREPRENEUR BACKGROUND AND CHARACTERISTICS

Although many aspects of an entrepreneur's background have been explored, only a few have differentiated the entrepreneur from the general populace of managers. The background areas explored include childhood family environment, education, personal values, age, and work history.

---

[3]This is developed in three works of David McClelland: *The Achieving Society* (Princeton, NJ: Van Nostrand Publishing Co., 1961): "Business Drive and National Achievement," *Harvard Business Review* 40 (July–August 1962): pp 99–112; and "Achievement Motivation Can Be Developed," *Harvard Business Review* 43 (November–December 1965), pp 6–24.

[4]A good discussion of some alternative measurements is found in Alan L. Carsrud and Kenneth W. Olm, "The Success of Male And Female Entrepreneurs; A Comparative Analysis," in *Managing Take-Off in Fast Growth Firms,* Ray M. Smilor and Robert L. Kuhn, eds (New York: Praeger Publishers, 1986), pp. 147–62.

TABLE 3–3 Checklist for Willingness to Take Risks

1. Can you take risks with money, that is, invest, and not know the outcome?	___ Yes	___ No
2. Do you take an umbrella with you every time you travel? A hot water bottle? A thermometer?	___ Yes	___ No
3. If you're frightened of something, will you try to conquer the fear?	___ Yes	___ No
4. Do you like trying new food, new places, and totally new experiences?	___ Yes	___ No
5. Do you need to know the answer before you'll ask the question?	___ Yes	___ No
6. Have you taken a risk in the last six months?	___ Yes	___ No
7. Can you walk up to a total stranger and strike up a conversation?	___ Yes	___ No
8. Have you ever intentionally traveled an unfamiliar route?	___ Yes	___ No
9. Do you need to know that it's been done already before you're willing to try it?	___ Yes	___ No
10. Have you ever gone on a blind date?	___ Yes	___ No

Source: Reprinted with the permission of Lexington Books, an imprint of Macmillan Publishing Company from *The Woman Entrepreneur* by Robert D. Hisrich and Candida G. Brush. ©1985 by Lexington Books.

Childhood Family Environment

Specific research topics concerning the family environment of the entrepreneur include **birth order,** parents' occupation(s) and **social status,** and relationship with parents. The studies of birth order have had conflicting results since Henning and Jardim found that female executives tend to be the firstborn.[5] Being the firstborn or an only child is postulated to result in the child receiving special attention and thereby developing more self-confidence. For example, in a national sample of 408 female entrepreneurs, Hisrich and Brush found 50 percent to be firstborn.[6] However, in many studies of male and female entrepreneurs, the firstborn effect has not been present. Since the relationship to entrepreneurship has been only weakly demonstrated, further research on the firstborn effect is still needed to determine if it really does have an effect on an individual's becoming an entrepreneur.[7]

[5]M. Henning and A. Jardim, *The Managerial Woman* (Garden City NY: Anchor Press/Doubleday, 1977).

[6]Robert D. Hisrich and Candida G. Brush, "The Woman Entrepreneur: Management Skills and Business Problems," *Small Business Management* 22 (January 1984), pp. 30–37.

[7]For a review of some of this research, see C. J. Auster and D. Auster, "Factors Influencing Women's Choices of Nontraditional Careers." *Vocational Guidance Quarterly,* March 1981, pp 253–63; J. H. Chusmin, "Characteristics and Predictive Dimensions of Women Who Make Nontraditional Vocational Choices," *Personnel and Guidance Journal* 62 (September 1983), pp 43–47; and D. L. Sexton and C. A. Kent, "Female Executives and Entrepreneurs: A Preliminary Comparison," *Proceedings,* 1981 Conference on Entrepreneurship April 1981, pp 40–55.

In terms of the occupation of the entrepreneurs' parents, there is strong evidence that entrepreneurs tend to have self-employed or entrepreneurial fathers. Female entrepreneurs are as likely to report self-employment or entrepreneurial fathers as male entrepreneurs. Having a father who is self-employed provides a strong inspiration for the entrepreneur. The independent nature and flexibility of self-employment exemplified by the father is ingrained at an early age. As one entrepreneur stated, "My father was so consumed by the venture he started and provided such a strong example, it never occurred to me to go to work for anyone else." This feeling of independence is often further enforced by an entrepreneurial mother. Although the results are less consistent, female entrepreneurs appear to have more than their share of entrepreneurial mothers.

The overall parental relationship, regardless of whether they are entrepreneurs, is perhaps the most important aspect of the childhood family environment in establishing the desirability of entrepreneurial activity for the individual. Parents of entrepreneurs need to be supportive and encourage independence, achievement, and responsibility. This supportive relationship of the parents (particularly the father) appears to be most important for female entrepreneurs. Female entrepreneurs tend to grow up in middle- to upper-class environments, where families are likely to be relatively child-centered, and to be similar to their fathers in personality.[8]

Education

The educational level of the entrepreneur has also received significant research attention. While some may feel that entrepreneurs are less educated than the general population, research findings indicate that this clearly is not the case. Education was important in the upbringing of the entrepreneur. Its importance is reflected not only in the level of education obtained but in the fact that it continues to play a major role in helping to cope with problems entrepreneurs confront. Although a formal education is not necessary for starting a new business, as is reflected in the success of such high school dropouts as Andrew Carnegie, William Durant, Henry Ford, and William Lear, it does provide a good background, particularly when it is related to the field of the venture. In terms of type and quality of education, female entrepreneurs previously experienced some disadvantage. While nearly 70 percent of all women entrepreneurs have a college degree, many having graduate degrees, the most popular college majors are English, psychology, education, and sociology. Few have degrees in engineering, science, or math.[9] However, a mere count of the number of women in business and engineering schools indicates that the numbers have significantly increased. Both male and female entrepreneurs have cited an educational need in the areas of finance, strategic planning, marketing (particularly distribution), and management. The ability to deal with people and communicate clearly in the written and spoken word is also important in any entrepreneurial activity.

---

[8]See Robert D. Hisrich and Candida G. Brush, *The Woman Entrepreneur: Starting, Financing and Managing a Successful New Business* (Lexington, MA: Lexington Books, 1986).

[9]Hisrich and Brush, *The Woman Entrepreneur.*

Personal Values

Although there have many studies indicating that personal values are important for entrepreneurs, frequently these studies fail to indicate that entrepreneurs can be differentiated on these values from managers, unsuccessful entrepreneurs, or even the general populace. For example, while entrepreneurs tend to be effective leaders, this does not distinguish them from successful managers. While personal value scales for leadership as well as those scales for support, aggression, benevolence, conformity, creativity, veracity, and resource seeking are important for identifying entrepreneurs, they also identify successful individuals. Studies have shown that the entrepreneur has a different set of attitudes about the nature of the management process and business in general.[10] The nature of the enterprise, opportunism, institution, and individuality of the entrepreneur diverge significantly from the bureaucratic organization and the planning, rationality, and predictability of its managers. Perhaps all these traits, not individual ones, are encompassed in a winning image that allows the entrepreneur to create and enhance the new venture. In one study, *winning* emerged as the term best describing companies having an excellent reputation.[11] Five consensus characteristics found across consumer and leadership groups were superior quality in products; quality service to customers; flexibility—ability to adapt to changes in the marketplace; high-caliber management; and honesty and ethics in business practices. A successful entrepreneur is frequently characterized as a winner; winning is almost a prerequisite for his or her actually becoming one.

Age

The relationship of age to the entrepreneurial career process has also been carefully researched.[12] In evaluating these results, it is important to differentiate between entrepreneurial age (the age of the entrepreneur reflected in the experience) and chronological age. As discussed in the next section, entrepreneurial experience is one of the best predictors of success, particularly when the new venture is in the same field as previous business experience.

In terms of chronological age, most entrepreneurs initiate their entrepreneurial careers between the ages of 22 and 55. Although a career can be initiated before or after these years, it is not as likely because an entrepreneur requires experience, financial support, and a high energy level in order to successfully launch and manage a new venture. While an average age has little meaning, when appropriate training

[10] See, for example, Y. Gasse, *Entrepreneurial Characteristics and Practices* (Sherbrooke, Quebec: Rene Prumer Imprimeur, Inc., 1971).

[11] For a summary of the results of this study, see "To the Winners Belong the Spoils," *Marketing News* 20 (October 10, 1986), pp 1, 13.

[12] Much of this information is based on research findings in Robert C. Ronstadt, "Initial Venture Goals, Age, and the Decision to Start an Entrepreneurial Career," *Proceedings* of the 43rd Annual Meeting of the Academy of Management (August 1983), p 472; and Robert C. Ronstadt, "The Decision Not to Become an Entrepreneur." *Proceedings,* 1983 Conference on Entrepreneurship, April 1983, pp 192–212.

and preparation are present, earlier starts in an entrepreneurial career are better than later ones. Also, there are milestone years approximately every five years (25, 30, 35, 40, 45, and 50) when an individual is more inclined to start an entrepreneurial career. As one entrepreneur succinctly stated, "I felt it was now or never in terms of starting a new venture when I approached 30." Generally, male entrepreneurs tend to start their first significant venture in the early 30s, while women entrepreneurs tend to do so in their middle 30s.

Work History

Work history not only is a negative displacement in the decision to launch a new entrepreneurial venture, it also plays a role in the growth and eventual success of the new venture. While dissatisfaction with various aspects of one's job—lack of challenge, promotional opportunities, frustration, and boredom—often motivates the launching of a new venture (see Chapter 1), previous technical and industry experience is important once the decision to launch has been made. Experience in the following areas is particularly important: financing, such as bank financing and venture capital; superior product or service development for the market; manufacturing; development of distribution channels; and preparation of a marketing plan for market introduction.

As the venture becomes established and starts growing, managerial experience and skills become increasingly important. While most ventures start with managing one's own activities and those of a few part or full-time employees, as the number of employees increases along with the size, complexity, and geographical diversity of the business, the entrepreneur's managerial skills come more into play. This is particularly true when the new venture requires the addition of other managers.

In addition to managerial experience, entrepreneurial experience increases as the complexity of the venture increases. Most entrepreneurs indicate that their most significant venture was not their first one. Throughout their entrepreneurial careers, entrepreneurs are exposed to more "corridors" of new venture opportunities than individuals in other career paths.

MOTIVATION

What motivates an entrepreneur to take all the risks and launch a new venture, pursuing an entrepreneurial career against the overwhelming odds for success? Although many people are interested in starting a new venture and even have the background and financial resources to do so, few decide to actually start their own business. Individuals who are comfortable and secure in a job situation, have a family to support, prefer their present life-style and reasonably predictable leisure time often do not want to take the risks associated with venturing out alone.

While the motivations for venturing out alone vary greatly, the reason cited most frequently for becoming an entrepreneur is independence—not wanting to work for anyone else. This desire to be one's own boss is what drives both male and female entrepreneurs to accept all the social, psychological, and financial risks and to work the large number of hours needed to create and develop a successful new venture. Nothing less than this motivation would be enough to endure all the frustrations and hardships. Other motivating factors differ between male and female entrepreneurs. Money is the second reason for starting a new venture for men, while job satisfaction, achievement, opportunity, and money are the reasons in rank order for women. These second-order motivations reflect, in part, the work and family situation as well as the role model of the entrepreneur.

ROLE MODELS AND SUPPORT SYSTEMS

One of the most important factors influencing entrepreneurs in their career choice is **role models.**[13] Role models can be parents, brothers or sisters, other relatives, successful entrepreneurs in the community, or even nationally touted entrepreneurs. Successful entrepreneurs are viewed frequently as catalysts by potential entrepreneurs. As one person stated, "After evaluating Ted and his success as an entrepreneur, I knew I was much smarter and could do a better job. So, I started my own business."

Role models can also serve in a supportive capacity as mentors during and after the launch of a new venture. An entrepreneur needs a strong support and advisory system in every phase of the new venture. This support system is perhaps most crucial during the start-up phase as it provides information, advice, and guidance on such matters as organizational structure, obtaining needed financial resources, marketing, and market segments. Since entrepreneurship is a social role embedded in a social context, it is important that an entrepreneur establish connections to these support resources early in the new venture formation process.

As initial contacts and connections expand, they form a network with similar properties prevalent in a social network—density (extensiveness of ties between the two individuals) and centrality (the total distance of the entrepreneur to all other individuals and the total number of individuals in the network). The strength of the ties between the entrepreneur and any individual in the network is dependent on the frequency, level, and reciprocity of the relationship. The more frequent, in-depth, and mutually beneficial a relationship, the stronger and more durable the network between the entrepreneur and the individual.[14]

---

[13]The influence of role models on career choice is discussed in E. Almquist and S. Angust, "Role Model Influences on College Women's Career Aspirations," *Merrill-Palmer Quarterly* 17 (July 1971), pp 263–97; J. Strake and C. Granger, "Same-sex and Opposite-sex Teacher Model Influences on Science Career Commitment among High School Students," *Journal of Educational Psychology* 70 (April 1978), pp 180–86; Alam L. Carsrud, Connie Marie Gaglio, and Kenneth W. Olm, "Entrepreneurs-Mentors, Networks, and Successful New Venture Development; An Exploratory Study," *Proceedings,* 1986 Conference on Entrepreneurship, April 1986, pp 29–35; and Howard Aldrich, Ben Rosen, and William Woodward, "The Impact of Social Networks on Business Foundings and Profit; A Longitudinal Study," *Proceedings,* 1987 Conference on Entrepreneurship, April 1987, pp 154–68.

[14]A thoughtful development of the network concept can be found in Howard Aldrich and Catherine Zimmer, "Entrepreneurship through Social Networks," in *The Art and Science of Entrepreneurship* (Cambridge, MA; Ballinger Publishing Co., 1986), pp 3–24.

But how does an entrepreneur establish this needed support-system network? Although a network is usually not a formally organized, directly established structure, an informal network for moral and professional support still greatly benefits the entrepreneur.

Moral-Support Network

It is important for each entrepreneur to establish a **moral-support network** of family and friends—a cheering squad. This cheering squad plays a critical role during the many difficult and lonely times that occur throughout the entrepreneurial process. Most entrepreneurs indicate that their spouses are their biggest supporters. This support allows entrepreneurs to devote the excessive amounts of time necessary to the new venture.

Friends also play key roles in a moral-support network. Not only can friends provide advice that is often more honest than that received from other sources, but they also provide encouragement, understanding, and even assistance. Entrepreneurs can confide in friends without fear of criticism.

Finally, relatives (children, parents, grandparents, aunts, and uncles) can also be strong sources of moral support, particularly if they are also entrepreneurs. As one entrepreneur stated: "The total family support I received was the key to my success. Having an understanding cheering squad giving me encouragement allowed me to persist through the many difficulties and problems."

Professional-Support Network

In addition to moral encouragement, the entrepreneur needs advice and counsel throughout the establishment of the new venture. This advice can be obtained from a mentor, business associates, trade associations, or personal affiliations—different members of a **professional-support network.**

A mentor-protegee relationship is an excellent method for securing the needed professional advice as well as providing an additional source of moral support. Many entrepreneurs indicate that they have mentors. How do you find a mentor? This task sounds much more difficult than it really is. Since a mentor is a coach, a sounding board, and an advocate—someone with whom the entrepreneur can share both problems and successes—the individual selected needs to be an expert in the field. An entrepreneur can start the "mentor-finding process" by preparing a list of experts in various fields, such as in the fundamental business activities of finance, marketing, accounting, law, or management. These individuals can provide the practical "how-to" advice needed in the new venture. From this list, an individual who can offer the most assistance can be identified and start to become acquainted with the nature of the business. If the selected individual is willing to act as a mentor, he or she should be periodically apprised of the progress of the business so that a relationship can gradually develop.

Another good source of advice can be obtained through establishing a network of business associates. This group can be composed of self-employed individuals who have experienced starting a business; clients or buyers of the venture's product or service; experts such as consultants, lawyers, or accountants; and suppliers of the goods and services to the venture. Clients are a particularly important group to cultivate. This group represents the source of revenue to the venture and is the best source of word-of-mouth advertising. There is nothing better than word-of-mouth advertising from satisfied customers to help establish a winning business reputation and promote goodwill. Customers, excited about the entrepreneur's concern with the product or service fulfilling their need, provide valuable feedback on the present product or service as well as on new products or services being developed.

Suppliers are another important component in a professional-support network, as they help to establish credibility with creditors and customers. A new venture needs to establish a solid track record with suppliers in order to build a good relationship and ensure adequate availability of materials and other supplies. Suppliers can also provide good information on the nature and trends in the industry, as well as on competition.

Besides mentors and business associates, trade associations can provide an excellent mechanism for a professional-support network. Trade association members can be developed into a regional or national network and can be carefully cultivated to keep the new venture competitive. Trade associations keep up with new developments and can provide overall industry data.

Finally, personal affiliations of the entrepreneur can also be a valuable part of a professional-support network. Affiliations developed with individuals in hobbies, sporting events, clubs, civic involvements, and school alumni groups are excellent potential sources of referrals, advice, and information.

Each entrepreneur needs to establish both a moral- and a professional-support network, regardless of their final composition. These contacts provide confidence, support, advice, and information. As one entrepreneur stated: "In your own business, you are all alone. There is a definite need to establish support groups to share problems with and gain overall support for the new venture."

MALE VERSUS FEMALE ENTREPRENEURS

There has been a significant growth in female self-employment, with women now starting new ventures at three times the rate of men. Much is known about the characteristics of entrepreneurs, their motivations, backgrounds, families, educational background, occupational experiences, and the problems of both female and male entrepreneurs.

While the characteristics of both male and female entrepreneurs are, generally, very similar, in some respects female entrepreneurs possess very different motivations, business skill levels, and occupational backgrounds than their male counterparts.[15] Factors in the start-up process of a business for male entrepreneurs are also dissimilar to those of females, especially in such areas as support systems, sources of funds, and problems.[16] The major differences between male and female entrepreneurs are summarized in Table 3–4. As is indicated, men are often motivated by the drive to control their own destinies, to make things happen. This drive often stems from disagreements with their boss or a feeling that they can run things better. In contrast, women tend to be more motivated by the need for achievement arising from job frustration in not being allowed to perform and grow at the level at which they are capable.

Departure points and reasons for starting the business are similar for both men and women. Both generally have a strong interest and experience in the area of their venture. However, for men, the transition from a past occupation to the new venture is often facilitated when the new venture is an outgrowth of a present job, sideline, or hobby. Women, on the other hand, often leave a previous occupation with a high level of job frustration and enthusiasm for the new venture rather than experience, making the transition more difficult.

Start-up financing is another area where male and female entrepreneurs differ (see Table 3–4). While males often list investors, bank loans, or personal loans in addition to personal funds as sources of start-up capital, women usually rely solely on personal assets or savings. This points up a major problem for women entrepreneurs in obtaining financing and lines of credit.

Occupationally, there are also vast differences between male and female entrepreneurs. Although both groups tend to have experience in the field of their ventures, men more often are recognized specialists in their fields or have attained competence in a variety of business skills. In addition, their experience is often in manufacturing, finance, or technical areas. Most women, in contrast, usually have administrative experience, which is limited to the middle-management level, often in more service-related areas such as education, secretarial work, or retail sales.

In terms of personality, there are strong similarities between male and female entrepreneurs. Both tend to be energetic, goal-oriented, and independent. However, men are often more confident and less flexible and tolerant than women, which can result in very different management styles.

---

[15] An interesting comparison is found in Alan L. Carsrud and Kenneth W. Olm, "The Success of Male and Female Entrepreneurs: A Comparative Analysis," in *Managing Take-Off in Fast Growth Firms*, Ray M. Smitor and Robert L. Kuhn eds. (New York: Praeger Publishers, 1986), pp 147–62. For a summary of information on female entrepreneurs see: Candida B. Brush, "Research on Women Business Owners: Past Trends, A New Perspective, and Future Directions," *Entrepreneurship: Theory and Practice* 16, no. 4, pp 5–30.

[16] This material is also discussed in Robert D. Hisrich and Candida G. Brush, *The Woman Entrepreneur: Starting, Financing, and Managing a Successful New Business* (Lexington, MA; Lexington Books, 1986).

TABLE 3–4 Comparison Between Men and Women Entrepreneurs

Characteristic	*Male Entrepreneurs*	*Female Entrepreneurs*
Motivation	Achievement—strive to make things happen Personal independence—self-image as it relates to status through their role in the corporation is unimportant Job satisfaction arising from the desire to be in control	Achievement—accomplishment of a goal Independence—to do it alone Job satisfaction arising from previous job frustration
Departure point	Dissatisfaction with present job Sideline in college, sideline to present job, or outgrowth of present job Discharge or layoff Opportunity for acquisition	Job frustration Interest in and recognition of opportunity in the area Change in personal circumstances
Sources of funds	Personal assets and savings Bank financing Investors Loans from friends or family	Personal assets and savings Personal loans
Occupational background	Experience in line of work Recognized specialist or one who has gained a high level of achievement in the field Competent in a variety of business functions	Experience in area of business Middle-management or administrative-level experience in the field Service-related occupational background
Personality characteristics	Opinionated and persuasive Goal-oriented Innovative and idealistic High level of self-confidence Enthusiastic and energetic Must be own boss	Flexible and tolerant Goal-oriented Creative and realistic Medium level of self-confidence Enthusiastic and energetic Ability to deal with the social and economic environment
Background	Age when starting venture 25–35 Father was self-employed College educated—degree in business or technical area (usually engineering) Firstborn child	Age when starting venture 35–45 Father was self-employed College educated—degree in liberal arts Firstborn child
Support groups	Friends, professional acquaintances (lawyers, accountants) Business associates Spouse	Close friends Spouse Family Women's professional groups Trade associations
Type of business started	Manufacturing or construction	Service-related—educational services, consulting, or public relations

The backgrounds of male and female entrepreneurs tend to be similar, except that most women are a little older when they embark on their ventures (35–40 versus 25–35) and their educational backgrounds are different. Men often have studied in technical or business-related areas, while many women have a liberal arts education.

Support groups also provide a point of contrast between the two. Men usually list outside advisors (lawyers, accountants) as their most important supporters, with the spouse being second. Women list their spouses first, close friends second, and business associates third. Moreover, women usually rely heavily on a variety of sources for support and information, such as trade associations and women's groups, while men are not as likely to have as many outside supporters.

Finally, businesses started by male and female entrepreneurs differ in terms of the nature of the venture. While women are more likely to start a business in a service-related area—retail, public relations, educational services—men are more likely to enter manufacturing, construction, or high-technology fields. The result is often smaller female-owned businesses with lower net earnings. However, opportunities for women are greater than ever, with women starting businesses at a faster rate than men in the fastest growing area of the U.S. economy—the service area.

ENTREPRENEURS VERSUS INVENTORS

There is a great deal of confusion about the nature of an entrepreneur as opposed to an inventor and the similarities and differences between the two. An **inventor,** an individual who creates something for the first time, is a highly driven individual motivated by his or her own work and personal ideas. Besides being highly creative, an inventor tends to be well educated, with college or often postgraduate degrees; has family, education, and occupational experiences that contribute to creative development and free thinking; is a problem solver able to reduce complex problems to simple ones; has a very high level of self-confidence; is willing to take risks; and has the ability to tolerate ambiguity and uncertainty.[17] A typical inventor places a high premium on being an achiever, measuring achievement by the number of inventions developed and the number of patents granted. An inventor is not likely to view monetary benefits as a measure of success.

As indicated in this profile, an inventor differs considerably from an entrepreneur. While an entrepreneur falls in love with the organization (the new venture) and will do almost anything to ensure its survival and growth, an inventor falls in love with the invention and will only reluctantly modify the invention to make it more commercially feasible. The development of a new venture based on an inventor's work often requires the expertise of an entrepreneur—a team approach to new venture creation.

---

[17]This and other information on investors and the invention process can be found in Robert D. Hisrich, "The Inventor; A Potential Source for New Products," *The Mid-Atlantic Journal of Business* 24 (Winter 1985/86), pp 67–80.

GENERAL NONENTREPRENEURIAL PROFILES

In addition to inventors, there are several other personality types that have a difficult time in successfully creating and managing a new venture. These personality types have characteristics that can lead even the brightest entrepreneur with the best idea into bankruptcy, a concern of resource providers such as venture capitalists, bankers, suppliers, and customers. Eight of these personality types are profiled in Table 3–5: Shotgun Sam, Simplicity Sue, Prima Donna Paul, Ralph the Rookie, Meticulous Mary, Underdog Ed, Hidden Agenda Harry, and Inventor Irving. Each has certain flaws, such as lack of follow-through (Shotgun Sam), making everything much

TABLE 3–5 Eight Entrepreneurial Profiles

Profile	*Description*
Shotgun Sam	An entrepreneurial type who quickly identifies new promising business opportunities but rarely if ever follows through on the opportunity to create a successful new venture.
Simplicity Sue	An entrepreneurial type who always thinks everything is a lot simpler than it is to create a successful business through one or two easy solutions. Usually a great salesperson. This entrepreneur can make even the most improbable deal seem possible.
Prima Donna Paul	An entrepreneurial type so in love with his own idea that he feels everyone is out to take his idea and take advantage of him. This paranoia does not allow any trust to be established and help given.
Ralph the Rookie	An entrepreneurial type who is well grounded in theory but lacks real-world business experience.
Meticulous Mary	A perfectionist entrepreneurial type who is so used to having things under control that he or she cannot manage during a catastrophe and cannot handle periods of ambiguity and chaos.
Underdog Ed	An entrepreneurial type who is not comfortable with actually transforming the invention into a tangible business success. This entrepreneurial type likes to attend seminars and discuss problems but does not like putting things into action, so needs a strong managerial team.
Hidden Agenda Harry	An entrepreneur who does not have the right motives and objectives for developing and expediting a new enterprise.
Inventor Irving	An inventor more than an entrepreneur, who is more concerned about the invention itself rather than creating and expediting a business.

Source: "8 Demons of Entrepreneurship," *Success* (March 1986), pp 54–57.

simpler than it really is (Simplicity Sue), falling in love with the idea itself (Prima Donna Paul), lacking real world experience (Ralph the Rookie), being a perfectionist (Meticulous Mary), lacking the ability to put things into concrete action (Underdog Ed), lacking the right motives (Hidden Agenda Harry), and loving creating more than doing (Inventor Irving). While, in moderation, these tendencies pose no problems, an entrepreneur with an excess of any of these traits may need to modify it in order to have a higher probability in successfully launching a new venture.

SUMMARY

Is there something that differentiates an entrepreneur from the rest of the population? This chapter outlines the current thinking and research related to identifying the unique characteristics of a person who successfully launches a new venture. Developing an understanding of the characteristics and background of individuals starting new ventures is an important step in encouraging potential entrepreneurs and improving their probability of success.

A typical entrepreneurial profile in terms of experience and family background has been more clearly defined. Adult encouragement, the role model of successful entrepreneurial parents, and a supportive relationship that encourages independence and achievement are factors strongly linked with later entrepreneurial behavior. While there are personal characteristics and skills frequently present in successful entrepreneurs, such as leadership traits, creativity, opportunism, and intuition, so far no unique combination of traits, experiences, and acquired skills differentiates a successful entrepreneur from an unsuccessful one, or even from a manager.

The research clearly indicates that there are many variables involved in the decision to become an entrepreneur. There are many successful corporate business people who fit an entrepreneurial profile and yet choose to remain in their current careers. Perhaps these individuals lack an appropriate role model or support system. Seeing someone else challenge and overcome the risk in a venture start-up is frequently mentioned as a key influence in the entrepreneurial decision process. While an individual can act as an inspiration, a new venture is also in need of support from an individual or group providing information, advice, and guidance. There are many sources of support systems, starting with friends and family and moving into the wider circle of professional contacts, clients, and industry organizations.

Significant growth in the number of women employed outside the home has created a new field of research: Are female employees, managers, and entrepreneurs different from their male counterparts? It is clear that male and female entrepreneurs have much in common. While some of the background and personality characteristics are quite similar between the sexes, there are striking differences between them in terms of motivation, departure point, and business skills brought to the venture. The difference in type of business started can be attributed in large part to differences in education and work history.

In developing a unique description of an entrepreneur, there are several personality types that only appear to be entrepreneurial. One of these is the inventor, who can take on the role of an entrepreneur if a business is started around the product invented. Care needs to be taken to ensure that the business is not second in importance to the invention itself. Other problem character traits include a lack of tenacity, perfectionism, the tendency to oversimplify, and paranoia.

QUESTIONS FOR DISCUSSION

1. What is gained from analyzing the characteristics of an entrepreneur?
2. Recalling the definitions of entrepreneurship given in Chapter 1, what characteristics would you expect to find in a "typical" entrepreneur? Compare these with the characteristics described in this chapter.
3. Discuss why the research work on entrepreneurs, using standardized tests, has not led to conclusive results.
4. What factors present in our society could account for the differences between male and female entrepreneurs today? How do you think men and women entrepreneurs will differ in 10 years?

KEY TERMS

birth order
departure point
inventor
locus of control
moral-support network
motivation
need for achievement
need for independence
professional-support network
role models
social status
work history

SELECTED READINGS

Baumol, William J. (1993). Formal Entrepreneurship Theory in Economics. *Journal of Business Venturing*. vol. 8. no. 3. pp 197–210.

The role of entrepreneurship is explored in terms of the influences that determine the allocation of entrepreneurship and differences in the resulting contribution to production; the role of the entrepreneur in technology transfer and its importance for the economy; and the optional timing for the market introduction of an innovation.

Birley, Sue, and Westhead, Paul (1994). A Taxonomy of Business Start-Up Reasons and Their Impact on Firm Growth and Size. *Journal of Business Venturing.* vol. 9, no. 1., pp 7–32.

A study of 405 owner-managers in Great Britain identified seven owner-manager types. However, no relationship was found between these typologies and the subsequent growth and size of the business.

Brush, Candida B. (1992). Research on Women Business Owners: Past Trends, A New Perspective, and Future Directions. *Entrepreneurship: Theory and practice.* vol. 16, no. 4, pp 5–30.

A review of 57 articles indicates that there are more differences than similarities between male- and female-owned businesses. Women perceive their businesses as cooperative networks of relationships rather than as separate economic units, with the business being integrated into the women business owners' life.

Bygrave, William D. (1993). Theory Building in the Entrepreneurship Paradigm. *Journal of Business Venturing.* vol. 8, no. 3, pp 255–280.

The difficulties of representing the entrepreneurial process with mathematical models are discussed along with the possibility of using scientific chaos and chaotic zones in examining this phenomenon.

Enz, Cathy A., Dolinger, Marc J., and Daily, Catherine M. (1990). The Value Orientations of Minority and Non-Minority Small Business Owners. *Entrepreneurship: Theory and Practice.* vol. 15., no. 1. pp 23–35.

The results of a study of 252 small firms indicate that minority owners differ from nonminority owners in their value orientations and are also significantly different in the degree to which they perceive organizational value similarity with customers.

Fagenson, Ellen A., and Marcus, Eric C. (1991). Perceptions of Sex Role Stereotypic Characteristics of Entrepreneurs: Women's Evaluations. *Entrepreneurship Theory and Practice.* vol. 15, no. 4. pp 33–47.

A survey found that women in female-headed companies gave greater weight to feminine attributes than women who worked in companies headed by men. Regardless of the sex of the head of the company, the women assigned more weight to masculine attributes in their profile of a successful entrepreneur.

Fischer, Eileen M., Reuben, A. Rebecca, and Dyke, Lorreine S. (1993). A Theoretical Overview and Extension of Research on Sex, Gender, and Entrepreneurship. *Journal of Business Venturing.* vol. 8. no. 2, pp 151–168.

The review of prior findings on sex, gender, and entrepreneurship in light of liberal feminist theory and social feminist theory reveals mixed evidence of sex-based discrimination and meaningful socialized gender differences.

Gartner, William B., Bird, Barbara J., and Starr, Jennifer A. (1992). Acting As If: Differentiating Entrepreneurial from Organizational Behavior. *Entrepreneurship: Theory and Practice.* vol. 16. no. 3. pp 13–31.

Some relationships between entrepreneurship and organizational behavior are discussed, and the process of emergence is suggested as a useful metaphor for relating entrepreneurship to other disciplines.

Herron, Lanny, and Robinson, Richard B., Jr. (1993). A Structural Model of the Effects of Entrepreneurial Characteristics on Venture Performance. *Journal of Business Venturing.* vol. 8. no. 3. pp 281–294.

A structural causal model of entrepreneurial performance is derived from current economic, psychological, management, and entrepreneurial theory.

Hisrich, R. D. (1986). The Women Entrepreneur: Characteristics, Skills, Problems, and Prescriptions for Success. *The Art and Science of Entrepreneurship,* Cambridge, MA: Ballinger Publishing Co., pp 61–84.

The findings of a nationwide survey indicate the characteristics of women entrepreneurs, their degree of management and other business skills, and the problems they encounter in starting and operating a business. Prescriptions for success set forth include establishing a track record, continuing education, previous experience, ability to set priorities in personal responsibilities, development of a support system, and determination.

Hisrich, R. D., and Brush, C. G. (April 1985). Women and Minority Entrepreneurs; A Comparative Analysis. *Proceedings,* 1985 Conference on Entrepreneurship, pp 566–87.

Based on surveys, women and minority entrepreneurs are profiled and compared based on demographic composition and background of the entrepreneurs; the nature of their business ventures; the skills and personalities; and the problems encountered in starting and operating the business.

Hisrich, R. D., and O'Cinneide, B. (April 1986). The Irish Entrepreneur: Characteristics, Problems, and Future Success. *Proceedings,* 1986 Conference on Entrepreneurship, pp 66–81.

Based on the results of a mail survey and in-depth personal interviews, the Irish entrepreneur is profiled and recommendations made for helping present and future entrepreneurs in Ireland.

Kaish, Stanley, and Gilad, Benjamin (1991). Characteristics of Opportunities Search of Entrepreneurs vs. Executives: Sources, Interests, General Alertness. *Journal of Business Venturing.* vol. 6. no. 1, pp 45–61.

The results of a study of entrepreneurs and executives of a large financial company indicate that the entrepreneurs spent significantly more time in off-hours searching for information and paid special attention to the risk involved in new opportunities. Executives tended to focus on the economics of the opportunity. Differences between the two groups decreased as success and experience increased.

Kofs de Vries and Manfred, F. R. (1993). Doing a Maxwell: Or Why Not to Identify with the Aggressor. *European Management Journal.* vol. 2. no. 2, pp 169–174.

Using a clinical perspective, the life history of Robert Maxwell is discussed along with the factors causing his success and failure. Attention is focused on two particular concepts—reality testing and the use of defense mechanisms.

McGrath, Rita Gunther, MacMillan, Ian C., and Scheinberg, Sari. (1992). Elitists, Risk-Taking, and Rugged Individualists: An Exploratory Analysis of Cultural Differences Between Entrepreneurs and Non-Entrepreneurs. *Journal of Business Venturing.* vol. 7. no. 2, pp 115–135.

The findings of an investigation of entrepreneurs compared to nonentrepreneurs suggest that entrepreneurs have a persistent and characteristic value orientation irrespective of the values of their base culture. These values are high power distance, high individualism, low uncertainty avoidance, and high masculinity orientation.

Reynolds, Paul D. (1991). Sociology and Entrepreneurship: Concepts and Contributions. *Entrepreneurship: Theory and Practice.* vol. 16. no. 2, pp 47–70.

Sociology contributes the following to the understanding of entrepreneurship: (1) the development of societal conceptions concerning productive activities that are part of the entrepreneurial role, (2) attention to specific societal characteristics that affect entrepreneurship, and (3) attention to the impact of societal context on the decisions of individuals to pursue entrepreneurial options.

Sexton, D. L., and Bowman-Uptown, N. (1990). Female and Male Entrepreneurs; Psychological Characteristics and their Role in Gender-Related Discrimination. *Journal of Business Venturing.* vol. 5, no. 1, pp 29–36.

The findings of an experiment centered around gender-related managerial differences indicate that both sexes possess the required characteristics for effective managerial performance, making the negative attitudes existing towards women more myths than truths.

Spender, J. C. (1993). Some Frontier Activities Around Strategy Theorizing. *Journal of Management Studies.* vol. 30. no. 1, pp 11–30.

A review of previous works indicates that strategic management research has been mostly concerned with allocative entrepreneurship. Since creativity is the basic human response to the uncertainties of organizational and economic life, it needs to be studied as well.

Stewart, Alex. (1991). A Prospectus on the Anthropology of Entrepreneurship. *Entrepreneurship: Theory and Practice.* vol. 16. no. 2, pp 71–91.

Some themes in the anthropological findings can help develop the theory of entrepreneurship: the importance of the accumulation of knowledge and skills, the crucial role of informal methods in gaining access to resources, the spatial clustering of entrepreneurship, and the role of entrepreneurship in regional economic development.

Takyi-Asiedu, Stephen (1993). Some Socio-Cultural Factors Regarding Entrepreneurial Activity in Sub-Saharan Africa, *Journal of Business Venturing.* vol. 8. no. 2, pp 91–98.

The problems encountered in entrepreneurship development in Africa are caused in part by the lack of consideration of one important element—culture. Some cultural issues that retard entrepreneurial activity include power, distance, collectivism, and Confucian dynamism.

Johnson and Associates

The computer market was thriving. From 1988 to 1993, the worldwide software market was estimated to grow approximately 19 percent annually, from $25 billion in 1988 to a predicted $61 billion in 1993. The Johnson brothers, founders of Johnson and Associates, a software/consulting firm, didn't want to miss out on that opportunity.

They had formed Johnson and Associates in June of 1989 and had been in business for about six months. The firm specialized in computer software for small to medium-sized companies interested in using software on their personal computers for certain segments of their businesses.

So far, the firm had concentrated on three target markets for their products: health and racquet clubs, independent insurance agents, and wholesale produce distribution companies. The firm, located in Minneapolis, Minnesota, sold modifications of one primary product to all three markets. To date, however, their efforts had concentrated on the health club market. Initial plans were to cover the midwest states of Minnesota, Wisconsin, and Illinois, with the hope of national distribution in the future. In these three states there were about 1,400 fitness and health clubs and nationally there were about 22,000 fitness and health clubs.

There were four members in the firm: James and Michael Johnson (brothers), Steven Jackson, and Fred Wilson. Ever since their boyhood in Sioux Falls, South Dakota, James and Michael Johnson had talked about opening their own business. Their father, an accountant, always wished he had started his own accounting firm, but never had. Growing up hearing about their father's lost dream only made the Johnson boys more motivated to succeed.

James Johnson was two years older than Michael. He had always been a technology buff. He loved science and frequently won school prizes for his inventions. James was precise in his work, and a perfectionist in everything he did; that is, his room was always clean, his class notes were always perfect. Other than science and computer clubs, he didn't get involved in school activities. Aside from his brother, Michael, he had only a small group of friends. After high school, James had gone on to major in computer science at the University of Minnesota and finished second in his class. He worked as a computer programmer/analyst for two years before he and his brother started Johnson and Associates.

Michael Johnson, on the other hand, was the more charismatic of the boys. He was popular at school and spent most of his time on extracurricular activities such as football. It wasn't until the end of his second year at the University of Minnesota that he had definitely decided to major in business. He graduated six months before

Johnson and Associates was formed. During that time, he had worked as a consumer product salesman but had found that job unrewarding. He wanted to sell something that required more expertise. Johnson and Associates, he felt, would provide that opportunity.

Despite the differences between the Johnson brothers, they had remained good friends throughout high school and college. They felt their different personalities would complement each other in the computer business. James could take care of the technical aspects, while Michael could take care of marketing the product.

The two other members of the firm, Jackson and Wilson, had computer backgrounds. James Johnson had met Jackson in his computer classes at the University of Minnesota. Since college, Jackson has worked as a computer programmer for an insurance company. He had been instrumental in enabling the company to enter the information side of the insurance industry. He understood the needs of the insurance agent and contributed to the development of the company's insurance product.

Wilson was also from Sioux Falls and had known both the Johnson brothers since childhood and had played football with Michael in high school. He had attended a technical school for computer programming after high school and had spent the last two years working as a programmer for Republic Airlines.

All four men were healthy and energetic. They got along well for the most part, and they believed their abilities complemented each other and would permit them to make Johnson and Associates a success.

SOFTWARE AND PERSONAL COMPUTER INDUSTRY

Sales of computers in the United States in 1990 were expected to total $80 billion. Software expenditures were expected to rise from about 17 percent of total information technology expenditures in 1988 to some 20 percent in 1994.

Service and support, instruction, distribution, and establishment of a marketing presence were key components to the success of specialized software. Specifically, this software was expected to be accompanied by a service and support package and a tutorial package that could take the form of manuals, on-line instruction, or classroom lessons.

Software for business applications could be sold in computer stores, electronics stores, or by catalog. However, distribution of specialized software targeted to the national market depended on wooing computer retailers to carry the software on already crowded shelves. Eight major personal computer software vendors took up most of this space. Successful advertising to this market often required a budget in excess of $1 million, with almost all the money spent on print media and packaging.

There were also hundreds of small software vendors marketing their products to specialized customers. These companies relied heavily on trade journal advertising and personal selling to market their products.

Of these small software companies, those that had many products were more successful than those that depended on one product for their revenues. The major reason was competition. If a software company introduced a successful product, other companies soon developed software that could perform similar functions. This increased competition eventually resulted in declining profit margins for all of the companies.

Club-Kit. The first product Johnson and Associates developed, and the one they were currently trying to market, was a membership management program for health and fitness clubs. Club-Kit, as the program was named, provided a club with the capability to automate day-to-day operational tasks as well as develop sophisticated marketing information.

Price. The following table shows a breakdown of the Club-Kit cost system:

Direct Material Costs	
Personal computer	$2,000
Printer	1,200
Software	800
Total	$4,000

The total price for the system was originally set at $4,000. Of this amount $3,200 was a fixed cost for the hardware. Johnson and Associates set an initial price for their software package at $800.

The firm was currently considering two pricing strategies for Club-Kit. Since the cost of the software was actually $100, the table shows that there was a $700 profit margin for each disk sold. This $700 could be negotiable when selling the product. Alternatively, the firm could establish a set price of $800 for the software. Under this system, any reduction in price would be based on hardware selections made by the consumer. Two of the firm's members, Michael Johnson and Wilson, felt making their product price-flexible would be a good negotiating tool. James Johnson and Jackson, however, felt that the $700 profit margin should be maintained. Since all decisions were made by a "team" agreement, this issue was still on the drawing board. The two systems to date had sold for $4,000 each.

Distribution. The firm was considering how to distribute Club-Kit. They could sell the software themselves, sell through a manufacturer's agent, sell through retail outlets, or license the product to another firm. They had made two sales in the Minneapolis area so far, but both sales came about through friends who worked at the health clubs.

All four members agreed that they should sell the software themselves, specifically Michael Johnson and Jackson because they understood the product and would unquestionably work harder at selling than anyone else.

Promotion. No promotion on the product had been attempted to date. Advertising in trade journals and at trade shows has been mentioned, but no serious discussion or research had been conducted.

Through the first six months of operation, the firm's members had been primarily concentrating on developing the products and then later working with two health clubs who purchased the systems. Now that the two systems were up and working, they realized that a sound marketing program had to be developed and some decisions had to be made. Specifically: What should the marketing mix consist of? Should the service contract be a part of the price of the system? If so, how long should it last? What type of training should the firm offer?

Rock and Roll Bilge Pump

Rock and Roll Bilge Pump. The name alone should attract some interest in the product, owners Craig Peters and Burt Larson thought when they decided one year ago to market a new bilge pump for boats. Their product was innovative. It was the only bilge pump that didn't need batteries or electricity. It worked solely on the natural rocking motion of the waves.

Peters, who had invented the product, took care of manufacturing. Larson, who had over 20 years of experience as an advertising salesman, took care of marketing. So far, he had written retailers, distributors, and individual boat owners telling them about the product. He had also placed ads for the product in the leading trade magazines.

Positive publicity about the product had been generated and retailers had expressed interest in it. While sales had been slow in coming, Larson and Peters didn't think there was anything wrong with their current strategy. They just felt it was a matter of time before the Rock and Roll Bilge pump would catch on.

THE BOATING INDUSTRY

Pleasure boating began in the United States as a pastime for the rich, whose yachts decorated the coastal waterways from Bar Harbor, Maine, to Palm Beach, Florida. After World War II and the development of fiberglass, boating was popularized around the country, especially in the freshwater areas.

No matter how successful boating became as an inland pastime, it was still primarily a coastal business. The coastal states accounted for 52 percent of U.S. pleasure boats but more than 69 percent of marine dealer sales.

In addition, the bulk of money spent on boating was spent by people who owned larger boats. Sixty percent of the money was spent on boats ranging from 16 feet to 26 feet, even though these boats represented only 5 percent of the number of total boat sales.

Between 1975 and 1980, there was a 17.7 percent increase in the total number of pleasure boats in service. While boats under 16 feet in length represented the bulk of U.S. pleasure fleets, these smaller boats had increased only 11.5 percent from 1975 to 1980, well behind the 17.7 percent average rate of gain for all size segments.

Boats 16 to 26 feet, on the other hand, had experienced an incredible growth. There were 29 percent more new boats in this size range than in the smaller size group.

Growth in the 26- to 40-foot range had been a little under 15 percent. One reason for this was that boat owners had difficulty finding mooring spots for large boats. In contrast, launching spots for the under-26-foot pleasure boat could be found almost anywhere in the United States.

Beyond the 40-foot market, the absolute numbers were small, but the growth rates were high—160 percent above average. These owners were not sensitive to inhibitors such as cost, inflation, and interest rates.

Surveys and sales analyses showed that powerboaters usually entered and left the market as the spirit moved them. They were not as interested in boating per se as sailors were. One reason cited was the cost of fuel. Sailboat builders had to cope with interest and inflation problems, but the fuel situation was much less relevant for them than it was for powerboaters.

ROCK AND ROLL BILGE PUMP

In October of 1981, Craig Peters and Burt Larson formed a partnership to manufacture and market the bilge pump for boats.

Peters, 28, had grown up in Miami, Florida. An only child, he had started sailing with his parents, who were both marine biologists, when he was five. He fell in love with the ocean and spent as much of his time there as possible when he was growing up. His peers called him a loner because he spent most of his free time reading on his parents' boat. He did well in school and eventually received a college degree in engineering at a local university. Largely at his parents' urging, he took a job with Honeywell as an engineer. However, he soon decided he could not sit at a desk for the rest of his life and found himself back at the ocean—this time as a professional skipper of large yachts. He eventually married and moved to Newport, Rhode Island, where he had been stationed for the last 15 years.

In his spare time, Peter had invented the Rock and Roll Bilge Pump. After acquiring the necessary financing to manufacture the product, he had quit the skipper business, largely at the insistence of his wife, who did not like his long periods away from home. For the last year, Peters had worked full-time on the manufacturing aspect of the product.

Burt Larson, a man Peters had contacted about investing in the pump, had over 20 years of experience as an advertising salesman. He was originally from New York but had moved to the West Coast when he graduated from college. The urge to move closer to his family had brought him back to Newport, Rhode Island, about five years ago. His hobby was reading up on new inventions and investing in the ones he thought had a chance of becoming marketable products. To date, most of his investments had not been very successful. Even though he had no previous experience in the boating industry, he was sure the Rock and Roll Bilge Pump was a winner. He had initially been a silent investor in the project. However, as plans for the product progressed, Larson became more involved and more excited about the product. Since he wasn't that happy with his present advertising job, he eventually decided to make marketing the Rock and Roll Bilge Pump his full-time job.

The Product. The product's mode of operation was very simple. It worked on the natural action of waves, which rock a boat back and forth. Operating in a fashion similar to a hand pump, a weighted pendulum provided the priming needed to drive the pump. The rougher the water, the more motion from the pendulum and the more pumping was exerted. The bilge pump could flush out approximately 500 gallons of water per day.

The product's most distinctive feature was its ability to work automatically, without a conventional power system. It was the only pump on the market that would work on an unattended boat that had no conventional power system. This feature allowed boat owners to feel at ease while their boats were collecting water from leaks, rain, or rough water wash. The pump could also act as a backup to automatic electric pumps when battery drain was a problem.

Price. The pump was midrange within the competition in both feature and price. At the high end were the higher-priced automatics and industrial hand pumps. The lower end included the hand-operated mounted and portable pumps.

A suggested retail price of $49.50 was originally established. However, due to increased manufacturing costs, the price was recently raised to $60 per unit. This was still competitive with comparable automatic and hand pumps. The cost to marine retailers was originally set at $29.55 per unit, but due to the price increase was now $35.50. The shipping price was $2.50 F.O.B. manufacturer. A discount of $22.50 per unit, plus shipping costs, was offered if 10 or more units were ordered.

Manufacturing. Peters and Larson had established a small manufacturing facility outside of Chicago. The cost involved to set up the plant was $20,000: $10,000 in machinery investment and $10,000 in inventory.

As one size was suitable for boats ranging in length from 10 to 40 feet, the production process was standardized. Peters did all the manufacturing, assembling, and packaging of the product himself. Capacity was limited to approximately 100 units per week. However, production had halted completely for two months when Peters' wife was in the hospital.

Promotion. Since the beginning of the operations six months before, ads had been placed in several trade magazines. Form letters had been sent to retailers, distributors, and boat owners. Professionally designed flyers were responses to requests for information generated by the mail-order program.

Good local exposure had been achieved through participation in a local boat show. Reaction to the bilge pump was quite favorable from both boat owners and retailers.

Sail, a prestigious trade magazine, had recently written an editorial about the bilge pump which elaborated upon its distinctive features. Since the editorial amounted to an endorsement, Larson felt sure it would stimulate the reader's interest in the product.

So far, a total of $5,000 had been spent to promote the product. Larson had received approximately 50 requests for further product information and 30 sales from

EXHIBIT 1 Pro Forma Income Statement

Sales	*Year 1*	*Year 2*	*Year 3*
Volume	525	1,688	5,290
Selling price	$ 35.50	$ 39	$ 43
Variable expenses/unit	27	30	33
Dollar	18,638	65,832	227,470
Less variable expenses	14,175	50,640	174,570
Gross Margin:	$ 4,463	$ 15,192	$ 52,900
Less fixed expenses	31,650	35,595	48,635
Income (Loss) before Taxes	$(27,187)	$(20,403)	$ 4,265

the mail-order campaign. Five sales were generated from the boat show. While 12 units had been placed with various retailers as display models, there had been no sales.

Distribution. Little progress had been made in terms of establishing a distribution channel for the product. Limited production capacity was cited as the main deterrent. The partners felt that establishing a distribution channel would create a demand that Peters could not handle at the plant himself.

Financial Information. Exhibit 1 is a pro forma income statement that Larson had prepared for the next three years. The projections assumed that distribution efforts would begin in Illinois and then move into the Great Lakes states by the end of year two. The pro forma statement indicates that the bilge pump would lose $27,187 and $20,403 in years one and two, but would show a fair profit of $4,265 in year three.

Over the six months of operation, Larson had not concentrated on segmenting the boating industry. He had not determined a clearly defined target market and the appropriate distribution channels. Recently, he had broken down the categories of the boating population into the three segments and listed the pros and cons he felt were attached to each segment (see Exhibit 2). From this information, Larson had determined that the best market for the Rock and Roll Bilge Pump was weekend sailors who owned boats less than 30 feet in length. However, no analysis had been done of the potential market size and demand, the geographical location of that market, and the characteristics and buying habits of the end user.

Despite these problems, the partners felt they had made significant progress in achieving product awareness in the first year and felt optimistic about the future of the Rock and Roll Bilge Pump.

EXHIBIT 2 Alternative Markets

ALTERNATIVE MARKET 1—SAILBOATS

0–15 Feet

PRO

1. Usually do not come equipped with a pump
2. Large, growing market for day sailor
3. Appeal to energy-conscious consumer

CON

1. Some of these sailboats do not have an open cockpit or have no cockpit
2. These smaller boats are trailered or pulled from water when not in use
3. Rock and Roll pump is too expensive for buyer

16–26 Feet

PRO

1. Usually do not come equipped with a pump
2. Large use in ocean(s) where wave action is best
3. Large growing market
4. These boats stay moored
5. Owned by middle- to upper-income level people with disposable income
6. Energy-conscious consumer

CON

1. Sailboats in the upper end of this category tend to have an onboard electrical system and built-in bilge pump

27 Feet and above

PRO

1. High disposable income, may want to try gadget

CON

1. All boats in this class come equipped with automatic electric bilge pump
2. The larger boats may not feel the effect of wave motion sufficiently to operate pump

ALTERNATIVE MARKET 2—MOTOR BOATS

0–15 Feet

PRO

1. Pump works better in smaller boat
2. Expensive motors need protection from submersion
3. Large population of older, leaky wooden boats

CON

1. Usually are trailered
2. Cyclical market
3. Declining market
4. Price-sensitive market due to gas prices
5. Consumer not concerned with natural energy
6. Pump is too expensive for typical buyer

16 Feet and above

PRO

1. Owner typically has more disposable income
2. Relatively stable market
3. Stays moored

CON

1. These boats come equipped with electrical system and bilge pump
2. Consumer not concerned with natural energy

EXHIBIT 2 *(concluded)*

ALTERNATIVE MARKET 3—MANUAL POWERED BOATS
ALL LENGTHS

PRO

1. May be used for the boat left moored while the boat is being used for the day or weekend

CON

1. Owner is not interested in gadgets
2. Too expensive for buyer
3. These boats are trailered or pulled out of water

A. Monroe Lock and Security Systems

Ray Monroe was sitting back in his chair in his home office and was trying to understand why the new venture had not made him the rich man he thought he would be. A. Monroe Lock and Security Systems (AMLSS) had been established about two years ago and offered locksmithing services to residential and commercial customers as well as automobile owners in the greater Boston area. These services included lock rekeying, lock and deadbolt installation and repair, master key systems, emergency residential lockouts, foreign and domestic automobile lockouts, and window security locks. In addition, AMLSS was certified by the Commonwealth of Massachusetts to perform alarm installation and offered a full range of alarm products.

Financial results have been relatively poor, with losses of $4,000 in the first year and a profit of only about $2,500 in year two. Currently AMLSS's target market was three local communities in the Boston area with similar demographics (see Exhibit 1).

BACKGROUND

Ray Monroe was an only child with parents who were both successful entrepreneurs. Both his parents were now deceased, and he had received a rather nice inheritance that would satisfy any of his financial needs for the rest of his life. Ray had been educated at a local private high school and then at a small liberal arts college in Vermont. He was not a great student but seemed to always get by. His summers were usually spent at the college, taking summer courses.

Upon graduation his father had helped him get a job with a friend who owned a security and alarm manufacturing business in the western part of the state. Ray worked in various areas of the business learning a great deal about alarms and locks. After two and one-half years there, Ray decided that he'd prefer to be his own boss and using some of the inheritance of his parent's estate entered a special program to learn more about the locksmith business. His intent upon completion of the program was to start his own lock and security business. He felt from his prior experience and education that this market offered tremendous opportunities. Increased crime and residential house sales that often required new locks offered many opportunities to succeed in this business.

EXHIBIT 1 Demographic Profile of Present Market

Demographics	*Newton*	*Needham*	*Wellesley*
Total population	82,585	27,557	26,615
Total # households	29,455	10,160	8,472
percent family	67.4	74.5	75.6
percent nonfamily	32.6	25.5	24.4
Total # families	19,952	7,675	6,492
# Married-couple families	16,662	6,633	5,607
# Female-householder families	2,536	818	700
Median income per capita	$28,840	$27,935	$32,253
Education			
percent high school educated	91.7	94.4	95.4
percent college or higher educated	57.2	53.7	68.5
Labor Force			
percent of total population employed	70.1	67.1	63.9
percent of female population employed	62.7	57.2	54.9
Disability			
percent w/mobility or self-care dis. (16–64)	5	4.6	3.9
percent w/mobility or self-care dis. (65+)	24.7	28.2	21.1
Total # housing units	30,497	10,405	8,764
Median # of rooms	6.4	6.7	7.2
Total # of owner-occupied housing units	20,297	8,097	6,847
Total # of renter-occupied housing units	9,158	2,063	1,625
Total # of housing units authorized in permit issuing places (1991)	31	34	36
Retail industry—# of establishments (1987)	609	175	196
Service industry—# of establishments (1987)	1,106	343	490
Total # of lodging places	9	3	3

Ray did not want to offer alarm installations as part of his new venture since he felt that they were a lot of bother to install. He also knew that there were many large competitors already in the alarm market that would be able to offer products and service at much lower prices.

INDUSTRY STRUCTURE/COMPETITION

The locksmith industry was dominated by small operators, 60 percent of them consisting of an owner and one employee. Only about 20 percent of these firms had five or more employees.

Because of the low entry barriers, the number of small operators had grown dramatically in the past few years. Often, these businesses were operated out of the home, with no storefront, and concentrated mainly on the residential market. There were also a large number of family owned businesses that usually had a retail store and had been serving their communities for several generations of family members. The larger operators were the most sophisticated in terms of service and products and relied primarily on commercial accounts.

The Boston area was densely populated, with 160 locksmiths all advertising in the local yellow pages. In the three communities on which AMLSS concentrated, there were 37 other locksmiths.

PRESENT STRATEGY

Excluding alarms, Ray offered just about every locksmith service. His van was used to store these products and any necessary tools for servicing his clients. This company van was 10 years old with a few minor dents, but it ran quite well.

Ray had a beeper system and a cellular phone to respond to customer requests. After 5:00 P.M., however, Ray turned off the system and refused to take calls. During his operating hours he was able to respond to all requests fairly quickly even if he was not in the office, primarily because of the beeper and cellular phone. He had tried using an answering machine, but it did not allow him to respond to a customer fast enough, especially if he was at a job that kept him out of the office for a number of hours. He also knew that many job requests were emergencies and required quick response.

During the past year, Ray had decided to advertise in the yellow pages. He felt that with all the locksmiths listed in the yellow pages he needed to be at the top of the list, so he decided to use his middle name initial (for Arthur) to form A. Monroe Locksmith and Security Systems. The yellow pages ad seemed to help business and contributed to the $2,500 profit (see Exhibits 2 and 3 for billing and expenses).

EXHIBIT 2 A. Monroe Monthly Billings for Year Two

January	$ 800.01
February	1,660.85
March	1,877.26
April	1,048.62
May	459.19
June	904.12
July	940.10
August	1,069.37
September	1,564.64
October	1,762.19
November	3,047.37
December	1,200.80
TOTAL	16,334.52

EXHIBIT 3 Year Two Expenses

Business Expenses	
Selling expenses	$ 6,574
Memberships (Chambers Of Commerce and Associated Locksmiths of America)	790
Answering service	420
Telephone	600
Office expenses (materials/supplies)	950
Yellow pages	3,900
Other promotional expenses	600
Total expenses	$13,834

Ray spent a lot of his time in the office thinking of ways to increase his business, yet to this point nothing had been very successful. His understanding was that many of his competitors had found that the yellow pages were the most likely place for customers to find a locksmith. His ad identified the three communities, the service he offered, and a telephone number. In addition, he included that he was bonded and insured and a member of the Massachusetts Locksmith Association. Competitors typically stressed products and services, 24-hour emergency service, follow-up guarantee service, being bonded and insured, and a member in the locksmith association.

Time was running out on Ray, and he was trying to think of other businesses that he could start up. He would often question his decision to enter the locksmith business, but then he would quickly decide that since he didn't really need the money it wasn't a big deal. However, at some point he felt he should try to establish himself so he could settle down to a more routine life.

PART II

Starting a New Venture and Developing the Business

CHAPTER

The Business Idea

Chapter Objectives

1. To identify various sources of ideas for new ventures.
2. To discuss methods available for generating new venture ideas.
3. To discuss creativity and the techniques for creative problem solving.
4. To discuss the aspects of the product planning and development process.

Ken Olsen

In 1947, a young man with electrical engineering training from the Navy entered MIT and joined a student research team building MIT's first computer. Driven by a concept of computing radically different from that underlying the number-crunching ENIAC built by the University of Pennsylvania, this computer was to be interactive, small, and fast. The computer was designed with circuits that allowed quick response, so that the programmer would be able to carry on a primitive dialogue. Meeting with success, and showing himself to be a first-rate practical engineer, the student moved on to bigger projects. Landing a job on a liaison team with IBM, which was involved in manufacturing computers for MIT, he was shocked at the regimentation and production inefficiencies of the rapidly growing computer company. Knowing that he could do a better job on his own because of the management experience he had gained from being a Sunday school superintendent and backed by $70,000 in venture capital, the engineer founded his own company. Today that company has annual revenues of over $14 billion. The MIT engineer is indeed one of the most successful entrepreneurs in the history of American business. Kenneth Harry Olsen (known as Ken even to the secretaries) has taken Digital Equipment Corporation (DEC) farther, without acquisitions, than Henry Ford took Ford Motor Company, than Andrew Carnegie took U.S. Steel, than J. D. Rockefeller took Standard Oil. What are Ken's secrets?

First, he had a vision. An engineer by training and temperament, Ken knew what engineers (the customers) needed in a computer. At a time when computers were large mainframes housed in special centers, maintained by experts, and used to process large batches of data, he had a vision of a small, rugged, inexpensive machine that a user-engineer could apply to an endless variety of tasks. Working with a few friends from his lab days, Olsen introduced the PDP-1 in 1960—the world's first "small" computer.

Second, Olsen's engineering vision was integral to his management vision. Cheap and adaptable were the code words in the early years. He liked the freedom he found working in MIT's computer laboratory and worked to develop this openness in DEC. There was no organizational structure, no wall chart, just bands of engineers forming around products in the early years of the company. While pioneering new ground left room for unstructured growth into many niches, however, the technically more difficult projects were harder to support without more direction. To overcome this hurdle, Olsen reconsidered his management style (or lack thereof), thought about responsibility, and developed an organizational remedy practically unheard of in 1964. His plan was to make each of his senior people an entrepreneur within the company. Responsibility for a single product line—from development to sales—rested with one person. Each manager competed with other managers for the company's resources. Some engineers missed the looseness of early times and left, but those remaining enjoyed running their own operations, and DEC grew at a phenomenal rate.

While everyone was happy inventing computers, in 1979, the computer technology created by the managerial system again outgrew its structure. The chief engineers obtained approval to develop a new generation of super minicomputers, capable of automating entire companies. Could DEC marshal its many far-flung managers and manage the engineering disciplines required to support this multibillion dollar effort?

A challenge indeed. Once again, Olsen chose to remain faithful to his engineering vision. Feeling that the future in computers was in systems, networks, and computers talking to each other, Olsen felt the engineers were working on the right technology to be correctly positioned in the market. Five years were spent slowly dismantling the product line system and transforming DEC into a unified marketing organization. While no one was fired during this transformation, many long-time managers quit, unable to perform in the new system. Critics questioned whether the company could emerge healthy from such a struggle, suggesting that Olsen had succumbed to "founder's disease," unable to handle the demands of operating a mature company and unwilling to step down.

In spite of this pessimism, DEC survived and grew. Although putting the new centralized structure in place and having all new products use the same basic computing and communication methods were costly in terms of time and money, the company managed to leapfrog the competition in introducing networking capabilities. Company sales grew when the industry was mired in a slump, firmly entrenching DEC as number two in the computer industry. In the fiscal year ending July 1, 1989, revenues were $12.7 billion, versus $11.5 billion in 1988, with net income before taxes decreasing to $1.1 billion in 1989 from $1.3 billion in 1988. Then DEC experienced the same extreme downturn that enveloped the entire industry. The company lost $5.08/share on revenues of $13.91 billion in fiscal 1991, lost $22.39/share on revenues of $13.93 billion in fiscal 1992, and lost $1.93/share on revenues of $14.37 billion in fiscal 1993. The future does again appear brighter, with earnings of $0.80/share on revenues of $15.1 billion expected in fiscal 1994.

As was at the heart of Ken Olsen's success story, the starting point of being an entrepreneur and developing a new venture is the basic product or service being offered. This part of the new venture creation process is perhaps the most difficult to actualize. What is the origin of the new product or service idea that is so essential for an entrepreneur? It is usually internally generated through research and development, other sources of new ideas, or creative problem solving. A wide variety of techniques can be used to obtain the new product idea. Ken Olsen had his vision working on a government contract project while obtaining his Ph.D. degree. Fred Smith of Federal Express expressed his original idea in a paper he wrote to complete a college course. For others, such as Bob Reis of Final Technology, Inc., and Frank Perdue of Perdue Chickens, the idea came from work experience. No matter how it occurs, a sound idea for a new product (or service), properly evaluated, is essential to successfully launch a new venture.

SOURCES OF NEW IDEAS

As reflected in the stories of the millions of entrepreneurs throughout the world, there are many sources of ideas available. Some of the more useful sources are consumers, existing companies, distribution channels, the federal government, and research and development.

Consumers

Potential entrepreneurs should pay strict attention to what should be the focal point of the idea for a new product or service—the potential consumer. This attention can take the form of monitoring potential ideas and needs that are mentioned informally or of formally arranging for consumers to have an opportunity to express their opinions. Care needs to be taken to ensure that the idea or need is not just one person's but represents a large enough market to support a new venture.

Existing Companies

Potential entrepreneurs and intrepreneurs should also establish a formal method for monitoring and evaluating the products and services on the market. Frequently, this analysis uncovers ways to improve on these offerings, resulting in a new product that provides the basis for the formation of a new venture.

Distribution Channels

Members of the distribution channels are also excellent sources for new ideas. Because of their familiarity with the needs of the market, channel members frequently have suggestions for completely new products. These channel members can also be a source of help in marketing the entrepreneur's newly developed products. One found out from the sales clerks that the reason his hosiery was not selling was their color. Making the appropriate color changes allowed his company to become the leading supplier of nonbranded hosiery in that region of the United States.

Federal Government

The federal government can be helpful in finding and developing new product ideas in two ways. First, the files of the Patent Office contain numerous new product possibilities. Although the patents themselves may not be feasible new product introductions, they can frequently suggest other, more marketable, new product ideas. Several government agencies and publications are helpful in monitoring patent applications. The *Official Gazette,* published weekly by the U.S. Patent Office, summarizes each patent granted and lists all patents available for license or sale. Also, the Government Patents Board publishes lists of abstracts of thousands of government-owned patents. One good publication is the *Government-Owned Inventories Available for License.* Other government agencies, such as the Office of Technical Services, assist entrepreneurs in obtaining specific product information.

Second, new product ideas can come in response to government regulations. For example, the Occupational Safety and Health Act (OSHA), aimed at eliminating unsafe working conditions in industry, mandated that first-aid kits be in business establishments employing more than three people. The kit must contain specific items, depending on the company and the industry. The weatherproofed first-aid kit needed for a construction company, for example, is different than the one needed by a company manufacturing facial cream or a company in retail trade. In response to OSHA, both established and newly formed ventures marketed a wide variety of first-aid kits. One newly formed company—R&H Safety Sales Company—was successful in developing and selling first-aid kits that allowed companies (other than those in the construction industry) to comply with the act.

Research and Development

The largest source for new ideas is the entrepreneur's own "research and development," whether this is a more formal endeavor connected with one's current employment or an informal lab in the basement or garage. A more formal research and development department is often better equipped, enabling the entrepreneur to conceptualize, develop, and produce successful new product ideas. One research scientist in a Fortune 500 company developed a new plastic resin that became the basis of a new product—a plastic molded modular cup pallet—and a new venture—Arnolite Pallet Company, Inc.

METHODS FOR GENERATING IDEAS

Regardless of the wide variety of sources available, coming up with an idea to serve as the basis for a new venture is still frequently a problem. The entrepreneur can use several methods to help generate and test new ideas, including focus groups, brainstorming, and problem inventory analysis.

Focus Groups

Focus group interviews, or what is more commonly called focus groups, have been used in a variety of ways since the 1950s. A moderator leads a group of people through an open, in-depth discussion rather than simply asking questions to solicit participant response; the moderator focuses the discussion of the group on the new product area in either a directive or a nondirective manner. The group of from 8 to 14 participants is stimulated by comments from other group members in creatively conceptualizing and developing a new product idea to fulfill a market need. One company interested in the women's slipper market received its new product concept for a "warm and comfortable slipper that fits like an old shoe" from a focus group of 12 women from various socioeconomic backgrounds in the Boston area. The concept was developed into a new product and became an outstanding market success. The basis of the advertising message was formed by comments of focus groups members.

In addition to generating new ideas, the focus group is an excellent method for initially screening ideas and concepts. There are several procedures available to analyze and interpret the results more quantitatively. With the availability of such procedures, the focus group is a very useful method for generating new product ideas.[1]

Brainstorming

The brainstorming method for generating new product ideas is based on the fact that people can be stimulated to greater creativity by meeting with others and participating in organized group experiences. While most of the ideas generated from the group have no basis for further development, frequently one or two good ideas emerge. This has a greater chance to occur when the brainstorming effort focuses on a specific product or market area. When using this method, the following four general rules should be followed:

---

[1]For an in-depth presentation on focus group interviews in general and quantitative applications, see "Conference Focuses on Focus Groups: Guidelines, Reports, and "the Magic Plaque," *Marketing News,* May 21, 1976, p 8; Keith K. Cox, James B. Higginbotham, and John Burton, "Application of Focus Group Interviews in Marketing," *Journal of Marketing* 40 no. 1 (January 1976), pp 77–80; and Robert D. Hisrich and Michael P. Peters, "Focus Groups: An Innovative Marketing Research Technique," *Hospital and Health Service Administration* 27, no. 4 (July/August 1982), pp 8–21.

1. No criticism is allowed by anyone in the group—no negative comments.
2. Freewheeling is encouraged—the wilder the idea the better.
3. Quantity of ideas is desired—the greater the number of ideas, the more the likelihood of useful ideas emerging.
4. Combinations and improvements of ideas are encouraged—ideas of others can be used to produce still another new idea.

The brainstorming session should be fun, not work oriented, with no expert in the field present dominating or inhibiting the discussion.

A large commercial bank successfully used brainstorming to develop a journal that would provide quality information to their industrial clients. The brainstorming among executives focused on the characteristics of the market, the information content, the frequency of issue, and the promotional value of the journal for the bank. Once a general format and issue frequency were determined, focus groups of vice presidents of finance of Fortune 1000 firms in three cities—Boston, Chicago, and Dallas—discussed the new journal format and its relevancy and value to them.

Problem Inventory Analysis

Problem inventory analysis uses individuals in a manner analogous to focus groups to generate new product ideas. However, instead of generating new ideas themselves, consumers are provided with a list of problems for a general product category. They are then asked to identify and discuss products in this category that have the particular problem. This method is often very effective as it is easier to relate known products to suggested problems and arrive at a new product idea than to generate an entirely new product idea by itself. Problem inventory analysis can also be used to test a new product idea.

An example of this approach in the food industry is seen in Table 4–1. One of the most difficult aspects of this approach is developing an exhaustive list of problems, such as weight, taste, appearance, and cost. Once a complete list of problems is developed, individuals can usually associate products with each problem.

Results from product inventory analysis must be carefully evaluated as they may not actually reflect a new business opportunity. For example, General Food's introduction of a compact cereal box in response to the problem that the available boxes did not fit well on the shelf was not successful. The perceived problem of package size had little effect on actual purchasing behavior. To ensure the best results, problem inventory analysis should be used primarily to identify product ideas for further in-depth study.

CREATIVE PROBLEM SOLVING

Creativity is an important attribute of a successful entrepreneur. Unfortunately, creativity tends to decline with age, education, and lack of use. Creativity declines in stages—first when a person starts school, then in the teens, then at ages 30, 40, and

TABLE 4–1 Problem Inventory Analysis

Physiological	*Sensory*	*Activities*	*Buying Usage*	*Psychological/Social*
A. Weight fattening empty calories	A. Taste bitter bland salty	A. Meal planning forget get tired of it	A. Portability eat away from home take lunch	A. Serve to company would not serve to guests too much last-minute preparation
B. Hunger filling still hungry after eating	B. Appearance color unappetizing shape	B. Storage run out package would not fit	B. Portions not enough in package creates leftovers	B. Eating alone too much effort to cook for oneself depressing when prepared for just one
C. Thirst does not quench makes one thirsty	C. Consistency/ texture tough dry greasy	C. Preparation too much trouble too many pots and pans never turns out	C. Availability out of season not in supermarket	C. self-image made by a lazy cook not served by a good mother
D. Health indigestion bad for teeth keeps one awake acidity		D. Cooking burns sticks	D. Spoilage gets moldy goes sour	
		E. Cleaning makes a mess in oven smells in refrigerator	E. Cost expensive takes expensive ingredients	

Source: Edward M. Tauber, "Discovering New Product Opportunities with Problem Inventory Analysis." *Journal of Marketing* (January 1975). 69. Reprinted from *Journal of Marketing,* published by the American Marketing Association.

50. In addition, the latent creative potential of an individual can be stifled by perceptual, cultural, emotional, and organizational factors. Creativity can be unlocked and creative ideas and innovations generated by using any of the creative problem-solving techniques such as those in Table 4–2.[2]

[2] A discussion of each of these techniques can be found in Robert D. Hisrich and Michael P. Peters, *Marketing Decisions for New and Mature Products* (Columbus OH: Charles E. Merrill, 1984), pp 131–46; and Robert D. Hisrich, "Entrepreneurship and Intrapreneurship: Methods for Creating New Companies That Have an Impact on the Economic Renaissance of an Area," in *Entrepreneurship, Intrapreneurship, and Venture Capital* (Lexington, MA: Lexington Books, 1986), pp 77–104.

TABLE 4–2 Creativity and Problem-Solving Techniques

- Brainstorming
- Reverse brainstorming
- Synectics
- Gordon method
- Checklist method
- Free association
- Forced relationships
- Collective notebook method
- Heuristics
- Scientific method
- Kepner-Tregoe method
- Value analysis
- Attribute listing method
- Morphological analysis
- Matrix charting
- Sequence-attribute/modification matrix
- Inspired (big-dream) approach
- Parameter analysis

Brainstorming

The first technique—brainstorming—is probably the most well-known and widely used technique for both creative problem solving and idea generation. It is an unstructured process for generating all possible ideas about a problem within a limited time frame through the spontaneous contributions of participants. A good brainstorming session starts with a problem statement that is neither too broad (which would diversify ideas too greatly so that nothing specific would emerge) nor too narrow (which would tend to confine responses).[3] Once the problem statement is prepared, 6 to 12 individuals are selected so that a wide range of knowledge is represented. To avoid inhibiting responses, no group member should be a recognized expert in the field of the problem. All ideas, no matter how illogical, must be recorded, with participants not being allowed to criticize or evaluate during the brainstorming session.

Reverse Brainstorming

Reverse brainstorming is similar to brainstorming, except that criticism is allowed. In fact, the technique is based on finding fault by asking the question, "In how many ways can this idea fail?" Since the focus is on the negative, care must be taken to maintain the group's morale. Reverse brainstorming can be effectively used prior to

---

[3]For a discussion of this aspect, see Charles H. Clark, *Idea Management: How to Motivate Creativity and Innovation* (New York: ANA Com., 1980), p 47.

other creative techniques to stimulate innovative thinking.[4] The process most often involves the identification of everything wrong with an idea, followed by a discussion of ways to overcome these problems.

Synectics

Synectics is a creative process that forces individuals to solve problems through one of four analogy mechanisms: personal, direct, symbolic, and fantasy.[5] A group works through a two-step process, as indicated in Figure 4–1. The first step is to make the strange familiar. This involves, through generalizations or models, consciously reversing the order of things and putting the problem into a readily acceptable or familiar perspective, thereby eliminating the strangeness. Once the strangeness is eliminated, participants engage in the second step, making the familiar strange through personal, direct, or symbolic analogy, which ideally results in a unique solution being developed.

Gordon Method

The Gordon method, unlike many other creative problem-solving techniques, begins with group members not knowing the exact nature of the problem. This ensures that the solution is not clouded by preconceived ideas and habit patterns.[6] The entrepreneur starts by mentioning a general concept associated with the problem. The group responds by expressing a number of ideas. Then a concept is developed, followed by related concepts, through guidance by the entrepreneur. The actual problem is then revealed, enabling the group to make suggestions for implementation or refinement of the final solution.

Checklist Method

In the checklist method, a new idea is developed through a list of related issues or suggestions. The entrepreneur can use the list of questions or statements to guide the direction of developing entirely new ideas or concentrating on specific "idea" areas. The checklist may take any form and be of any length. One general checklist is[7]:

---

[4]For a discussion of this technique, see J. Geoffrey Rawlinson, *Creative Thinking and Brainstorming* (New York: John Wiley & Sons, 1981), pp 124 and 126; and W. E. Souder and R. W. Ziegler, "A Review of Creativity and Problem-Solving Techniques." *Research Management* 20 (July 1977), p 35.

[5]For a thorough discussion and application of this method, see W. J. Gordon, *Synectics: The Development of Creative Capacity* (New York: Harper & Row, 1961), pp 37–53.

[6]This method is discussed in J. W. Haefele, *Creativity and Innovation* (New York: Van Nostrand Reinhold, 1962), pp 145-47; Sidney J. Parnes and Harold F. Harding, *A Source Book for Creative Thinking* (New York: Charles Scribner's Sons, 1962), pp 307-23; and Souder and Ziegler, "Review of Techniques," pp 34–42.

[7]Alex F. Osborn, *Applied Imagination* (New York: The Scribner Book Companies, Inc., 1957), p 318.

FIGURE 4–1 Example of the Synectics Process

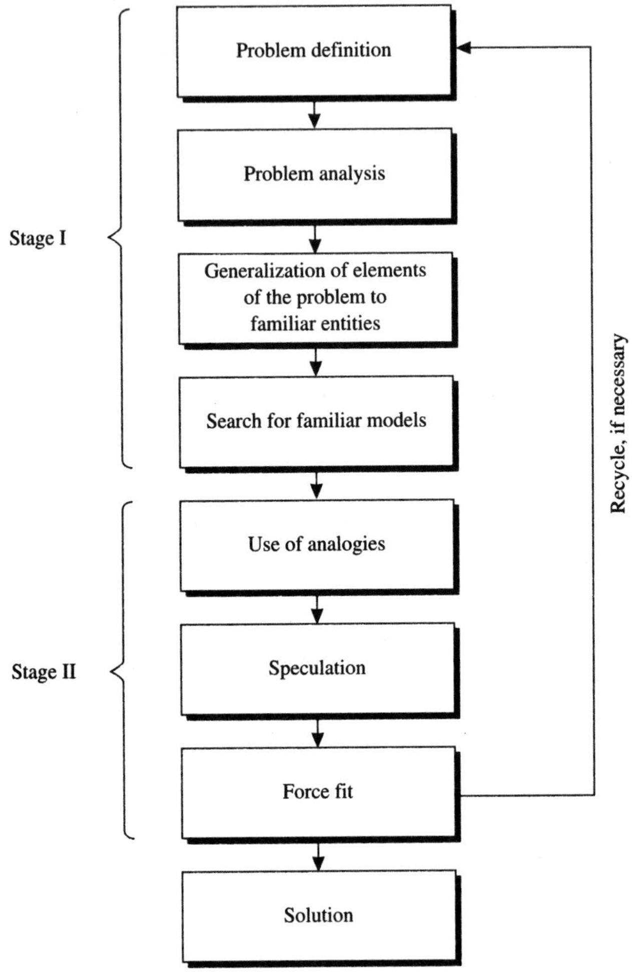

Source: William E. Souder and Robert W. Ziegler, "A Review of Creativity and Problem Solving Techniques," *Research Management,* July 1975, p 35.

- Put to other uses? New ways to use as is? Other uses if modified?
- Adapt? What else is like this? What other ideas does this suggest? Does past offer parallel? What could I copy? Whom could I emulate?
- Modify? New twist? Change meaning, color, motion, odor, form, shape? Other changes?
- Magnify? What to add? More time? Greater frequency? Stronger? Larger? Thicker? Extra value? Plus ingredient? Duplicate? Multiply? Exaggerate?

- Minify? What substitute? Smaller? Condensed? Miniature? Lower? Shorter? Lighter? Omit? Streamline? Split up? Understated?
- Substitute? Who else instead? What else instead? Other ingredient? Other material? Other process? Other power? Other place? Other approach? Other tone of voice?
- Rearrange? Interchange components? Other pattern? Other layout? Other sequence? Transpose cause and effect? Change pact? Change schedule?
- Reverse? Transpose positive and negative? How about opposites? Turn it backward? Turn it upside down? Reverse roles? Change shoes? Turn tables? Turn other cheek?
- Combine? How about a blend, an alloy, an assortment, an ensemble? Combine units? Combine purposes? Combine appeals? Combine ideas?

Free Association

One of the simplest, yet most effective methods that entrepreneurs can use to generate new ideas is free association. This technique is helpful in developing an entirely new slant to a problem. First, a word or phrase related to the problem is written down, then another and another, with each new word attempting to add something new to the ongoing thought processes, thereby creating a chain of ideas with a new product idea emerging.

Forced Relationships

Forced relationships, as the name implies, tries to force relationships among some product combinations. It is a technique that asks questions about objects or ideas in an effort to develop a new idea. The new combination and eventual concept is developed through a five-step process[8]:

1. Isolate the elements of the problem.
2. Find the relationships between these elements.
3. Record the relationships in an orderly form.
4. Analyze the resulting relationships to find ideas or patterns.
5. Develop new ideas from these patterns.

Table 4.3 illustrates this technique using paper and soap.

---

[8]Rawlinson, *Creative Thinking*, pp 52–59.

TABLE 4–3 Illustration of Forced Relationship Technique

Elements: Paper and Soap

Forms	*Relationship/ Combination*	*Idea/Pattern*
Adjective	Papery soap	Flakes
	Soapy paper	Wash and dry travel aid
Noun	Paper soaps	Tough paper impregnated with soap and usable for washing surfaces
Verb-correlates	Soaped papers	Booklets of soap leaves
	Soap "wets" paper	In coating and impregnation processes
	Soap "cleans" paper	Suggests wallpaper cleaner

Source: William E. Souder and Robert W. Ziegler, "A Review of Creativity and Problem Solving Techniques," *Research Management,* July 1975, p 37.

Collective Notebook Method

In the collective notebook method, a small notebook that easily fits in a shirt pocket is prepared. It includes a statement of the problem, blank pages, and any pertinent background data. Selected individuals consider the problem and its possible solutions, recording ideas at least once but preferably three times a day. At the end of a month, a list of the best ideas is developed, along with any suggestions.[9] This technique can also be used with a group of individuals who record their ideas, giving their notebooks to a central coordinator who synthesizes the data and summarizes all the material. The summary becomes the topic of a final creative focus group discussion by the group participants.

Heuristics

Heuristics relies on the entrepreneur's ability to discover through a progression of thoughts, insights, and learning. The technique is probably used more than imagined, simply because entrepreneurs frequently must settle for an estimated outcome of a decision rather than a certainty. One specific heuristic approach is called the heuristic

[9]For a thorough discussion of the collective notebook method, see J. W. Haefele, *Creativity and Innovation,* p 152.

ideation technique (HIT).[10] This involves locating all relevant concepts that could be associated with a given product area and generating a set of all possible combinations of ideas.

Scientific Method

The scientific method, widely used in various fields of inquiry, consists of principles and processes, conducting observations and experiments, and validating the hypothesis. The approach involves the entrepreneur defining the problem, analyzing the problem, gathering and analyzing data, developing and testing potential solutions, and choosing the best solution.

Value Analysis

The value analysis technique develops methods for maximizing value to the entrepreneur and the new venture.[11] To maximize value, the entrepreneur asks such questions as, "Can this part be of lesser quality, since it isn't a critical area for problems?" In a value analysis procedure, regularly scheduled times are established to develop, evaluate, and refine ideas.

Attribute Listing

Attribute listing is an idea-finding technique requiring the entrepreneur to list the attributes of an item or problem and then look at each from a variety of viewpoints. Through this process, originally unrelated objects can be brought together to form a new combination and possible new uses that better satisfy a need.[12]

Matrix Charting

Matrix charting is a systematic method of searching for new opportunities by listing important elements for the product area along two axes of a chart and then asking questions regarding each of these elements. The answers are recorded in the relevant

---

[10] See Edward M. Tauber, "HIT: Heuristic Ideation Technique," *Journal of Marketing,* January 1972, pp 58–70.

[11] For a discussion of value analysis and its application at General Electric, see "A Study on Applied Value Analysis," *Purchasing* 46 (June 8, 1959), pp 66–67.

[12] S. J. Parnes and H. F. Harding, eds., *A Source Book for Creative Thinking* (New York: Charles Scribner's Sons, 1962), p 308.

FIGURE 4–2 Illustration of Parameter Analysis

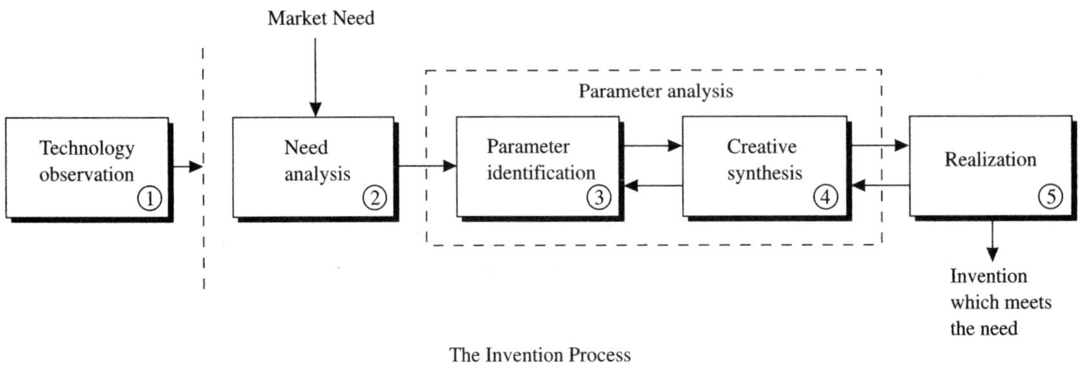

boxes of the matrix. Example questions that can elicit creative new product ideas include: What can it be used for? Where can it be used? Who can use it? When can it be used? How can it be used?

Big-Dream Approach

The big-dream approach to coming up with a new idea requires that the entrepreneur dream about the problem and its solution—thinking big. Every possibility should be recorded and investigated without regard to all the negatives involved or the resources required. In other words, ideas should be conceptualized without any constraints. This should continue until an idea is developed into a workable form.[13]

Parameter Analysis

A final method for developing new ideas—parameter analysis—involves two aspects—parameter identification and creative synthesis.[14] As is indicated in Figure 4–2, step one (parameter identification) involves analyzing variables in the situation to determine their relative importance. These variables become the focus of the investigation, with other variables being set aside. After the primary issues have been identified, the relationships between parameters that describe the underlying issues are examined. Through an evaluation of the parameters and relationships, a solution(s) is developed; this solution development is called *creative synthesis.*

[13]For a discussion of this approach, see M. O. Edwards, "Solving Problems Creatively," *Journal of Systems Management* 17, no. 1 (January–February 1966), pp 16–24.

[14]The procedure for parameter analysis is thoroughly discussed in Yao Tzu Li, David G. Jansson, and Ernest G. Cravalho, *Technological Innovation in Education and Industry* (New York: Reinhold Publishing Company, 1980), pp 26–49, 277-86.

FIGURE 4–3 The Product Planning and Development Process

Idea stage | Concept stage | Product development stage | Test marketing stage | Commercialization stage Product life cycle

Idea | Evaluate | Laboratory development | Evaluate | Pilot production run | Evaluate | Semicommercial plan trials | Evaluate

Introduction | Growth | Maturity | Decline

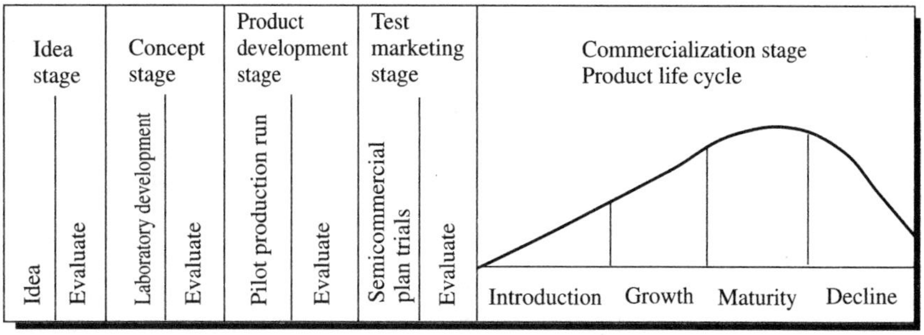

Source: Reprinted with the permission of Macmillan College Publishing Company from *Marketing Decisions for New and Mature Products,* 2/e by Robert Hisrich and Michael Peters, © 1991 by Macmillan College Publishing Company Inc. p. 165.

PRODUCT PLANNING AND DEVELOPMENT PROCESS

Once ideas emerge from idea sources or creative problem solving, they need further development and refinement into the final product or service to be offered. This refining process—the product planning and development process—is divided into five major stages: idea stage, concept stage, product development stage, test marketing stage, and commercialization (see Figure 4–3).[15]

Establishing Evaluation Criteria

As a new product idea evolves in the stages of the product planning and development process, criteria for evaluation need to be established. These criteria should be broad enough yet quantitative enough to screen the product carefully in all stages of development. Criteria should be developed to evaluate the new product in terms of market opportunity, competition, the marketing system, financial factors, and production factors.

A market opportunity in the form of a new or current need for the product idea must exist. The evaluation of adequate market demand is by far the most important criterion of a proposed new product idea. Assessment of the market opportunity and size needs to take into account such factors as the characteristics and attitudes of consumers or industries that may buy the product, the size of this potential market in dollars and units, the nature of the market with respect to its stage in the life cycle (growing or declining), and the share of the market the product could reasonably capture.

[15] For a detailed description of this process, see Robert D. Hisrich and Michael P. Peters, *Marketing Decisions for New and Mature Products* (Columbus OH: Charles E. Merrill Publishing, 1985), pp 157-78.

Current competing producers, prices, and marketing policies should also be evaluated, particularly in terms of their impact on the target market share of the proposed product. The new product should be able to compete successfully with products already on the market by having features that will meet or overcome current and anticipated competition. The new product should have some unique differential advantage based on an evaluation of all competitive products that could fill the same consumer needs.

The new product should be compatible with existing management capabilities and marketing strategies. The firm should be able to use its marketing experience and other expertise fully in this new product effort. For example, General Electric would have a far less difficult time adding a new kitchen appliance to its line than Procter & Gamble would. Several factors should be considered in evaluating the degree of fit: the degree of which the ability and time of the present sales force can be transferred to the new product, the ability to sell the new product through the company's established channels of distribution, and the ability to "piggy-back" the advertising and promotion required to introduce the new product.

The proposed product should also be able to be supported by and eventually contribute to the company's financial structure. This should be evaluated by estimating manufacturing cost per unit, sales and advertising expense per unit, and amount of capital and inventory required. The break-even point and the long-term profit outlook for the product also need to be determined.

Along with financial criteria, production or operation managers should determine how compatible the new product's production requirements are with existing plant, machinery, and personnel. If the new product idea cannot be integrated into existing manufacturing processes, not only is the new idea less positive, but new plant and production costs as well as amount of plant space must be determined if the new product is to be manufactured efficiently. All required materials needed in production of the product should be available and accessible in sufficient quantity.

In addition to establishing criteria for evaluating new product ideas, management should be concerned with formally evaluating an idea throughout its evolution. From the marketing perspective, three pretest marketing stages can be delineated in the product's evolutionary process: the idea stage, the concept stage, and the product development stage.

Idea Stage

Promising new product ideas should be identified and impractical ones eliminated in the **idea stage,** allowing maximum use of the company's resources. One evaluation method successfully used in this stage is the systematic market evaluation checklist, where each new product idea is expressed in terms of its chief values, merits, and benefits.[16] Consumers are presented with clusters of new product values to determine

[16] An example of the use and importance of this process is given in Louis Gedimen, "How to Screen New Product Ideas More Effectively," *Printer's Ink* 291, no. 4 (August 27, 1965), pp 63–64.

which, if any, new product alternatives should be pursued and which should be discarded. A company can quickly test many new product idea alternatives with this evaluation method; promising ideas can be further developed without wasting resources on ideas not compatible with the market's values.

It is also important for the company to determine the need for the new product as well as its value to the company. If there is no need for the suggested product, its development should not be continued. Similarly, the new product idea should not be developed if it does not have any benefit or value to the firm. In order to effectively determine the need for a new product, it is helpful to define the potential needs of the market in terms of timing, satisfaction, alternatives, benefits and risks, future expectations, price-versus-product performance features, market structure and size, and economic conditions. A form for helping in this need determination is indicated in Table 4–4. The factors indicated in this table should be evaluated not only in terms of the characteristics of the potential new product, but also in terms of the new product's competitive strength relative to each factor. This comparison with competitive products will indicate the proposed product's strengths and weaknesses.

The need determination should focus on the type of need, its timing, the users involved with trying the product, the importance of controllable marketing variables, the overall market structure, and the characteristics of the market. Each of these factors should be evaluated in terms of the characteristics of the new idea being considered and the aspects and capabilities of present methods for satisfying the particular need. This analysis will indicate the extent of the opportunity available.

In determining the value of the new product to the firm, financial scheduling, such as cash outflow, cash inflow, contribution to profit, and return on investment, needs to be evaluated in terms of other product ideas as well as investment alternatives. Using the form indicated in Table 4–5, the dollar amount of each of the considerations important to the new product idea should be determined as accurately as possible so that a quantitative evaluation can be made. These figures can then be revised as better information becomes available and the product continues to be developed.

Concept Stage

After a new product idea has been identified in the idea stage as having potential, it should be further developed and refined through interaction with consumers. In the **concept stage,** the refined product idea is tested to determine consumer acceptance without necessarily incurring the costs of manufacturing the physical product; that is, initial reactions to the concept are obtained from potential customers or members of the distribution channel if appropriate.[17] One method for measuring consumer acceptance is the conversational interview, in which selected respondents are exposed to statements that reflect the physical characteristics and attributes of the

[17] For a discussion of the importance and implementation of concept testing see A. R. Kroeger, "Test Marketing: The Concept and How It is Changing," *Media Scope,* December 1966, pp 63–68.

TABLE 4–4 Determining the Need of a New Product Idea

Factor	*Aspects*	*Competitive Capabilities*	*New Product Idea Capability*
Type of need			
Continuing need			
Declining need			
Emerging need			
Future need			
Timing of need			
Duration of need			
Frequency of need			
Demand cycle			
Position in life cycle			
Competing ways to satisfy need			
Doing without			
Using present way			
Modifying present way			
Perceived benefits/risks			
Utility to customer			
Appeal characteristics			
Customer tastes and preferences			
Buying motives			
Consumption habits			
Price vs. performance features			
Price–quantity relationship			
Demand elasticity			
Stability of price			
Stability of market			
Market size and potential			
Market growth			
Market trends			
Market development requirements			
Threats to market			
Availability of customer funds			
General economic conditions			
Economic trends			
Customer income			
Financing opportunities			

Source: Reprinted with the permission of Macmillan College Publishing Company from *Marketing Decisions for New and Mature Products* 2/e by Robert D. Hisrich and Michael P. Peters, © 1991 by Macmillan College Publishing Company, Inc. p. 190.

product idea. Where competing products exist, these statements can also compare the primary features of existing products. Favorable as well as unfavorable product features can be uncovered from analyzing consumers' responses, with favorable features being incorporated into the product.

Features, price, and promotion should be evaluated for both the concept being studied and for any major competing products to indicate any deficiencies or

TABLE 4–5 Determining the Value of a New Product Idea

Value Consideration	*Cost (in $)*
Cash outflow	
R&D costs	
Marketing costs	
Capital equipment costs	
Other costs	
Cash inflow	
Sales of new product	
Effect on additional sales of existing products	
Salvageable value	
Net cash flow	
Maximum exposure	
Time to maximum exposure	
Duration of exposure	
Total investment	
Maximum net cash in a single year	
Profit	
Profit from new product	
Profit affecting additional sales of existing products	
Fraction of total company profit	
Relative return	
Return on shareholder's equity (ROE)	
Return on investment (ROI)	
Cost of capital	
Present value (PV)	
Discounted cash flow (DCF)	
Return on assets employed (ROA)	
Return on sales	
Compared to other investments	
Compared to other product opportunities	
Compared to other investment opportunities	

Source: Reprinted with the permission of Macmillan College Publishing Company from *Marketing Decisions for New and Mature Products,* 2/e, by Robert D. Hisrich and Michael P. Peters. © 1991 by Macmillan College Publishing Company, Inc., p. 196.

benefits. By pointing out any major deficiencies in the product concept, research and development can be directed to develop a more marketable product, or the concept can be dropped from further consideration.

The relative advantages of the new product versus competitive products can be determined through questions. For example, how does the new concept compare with competitive products in terms of quality and reliability? Is the concept superior or deficient compared to products currently available in the market? What does this mean in terms of market opportunity for the firm? Similar evaluations should be done for each of the remaining aspects of the product, price, promotion, and distribution.

Product Development Stage

In the **product development stage,** consumer reaction to the physical product is determined. One tool frequently used in this stage is the consumer panel, in which a group of potential consumers is given product samples. Participants keep a record of their use of the product and comment on its virtues and deficiencies.

The panel of potential customers can also be given a sample of the product and one or more competitive products simultaneously. One test product may already be on the market; whereas, the other test product is new. Or both products can be new, with some significant variation between them. Then one of several methods, such as multiple brand comparisons, risk analysis, level of repeat purchases, or intensity of preference analysis, can be used to determine consumer preference.

Test Marketing Stage

While the results of the product development stage provide the basis of the final marketing plan, a market test can be done to increase the certainty of successful commercialization. This last step in the evaluation process—the **test marketing stage**—provides actual sales results, which indicate the acceptance level of consumers. Positive test results indicate the degree of probability of a successful product launch and company formation.

SUMMARY

The starting point for any successful new venture is the basic product or service to be offered. This idea can be either generated internally or externally through various techniques.

The possible sources of new ideas range from the comments of consumers to changes in government regulations. Monitoring the comments of acquaintances, evaluating the new products offered by competitors, becoming familiar with the ideas contained in previously granted patents, and becoming actively involved in research and development are also techniques for coming up with a good product idea. In addition, there are specific techniques entrepreneurs can use to generate ideas. For example, a better understanding of the consumer's true opinions can be gained from using a focus group. Another consumer-oriented approach is problem inventory analysis, through which consumers associate particular problems with specific products and then develop a new product that does not contain the identified faults.

Brainstorming, a technique useful in both idea generation and problem solving, stimulates creativity by allowing a small group of people to work together in an open, nonstructured environment. Other techniques useful in enhancing the creative process are checklists of related questions, free association, idea notebooks, and the "big-dream" approach. Some techniques are very structured, while others are designed to be more free-form. Each entrepreneur should know the techniques best suited to him or her and what other techniques are available if one approach does not work.

Once the idea or group of ideas is generated, the planning and developing process begins. If a large number of potential ideas have been uncovered, they must be screened or evaluated to determine their appropriateness for further development. Ideas showing the most potential are then moved through the concept stage, the product development stage, the test marketing stage, and finally into commercialization. The entrepreneur should constantly evaluate the idea throughout this process.

QUESTIONS FOR DISCUSSION

1. How would you go about monitoring and evaluating the new products being offered by existing companies? Is this a viable technique for generating new ideas? Why or why not?
2. Prepare a list of problems associated with the fast-food industry that could be used for a problem inventory analysis. How would the results generated by the analysis be of use to a potential fast-food entrepreneur?
3. Choose three problem-solving techniques and explain how each functions to overcome mental blocks.

KEY TERMS

attribute listing
big-dream approach
brainstorming
checklist method
collective notebook method
concept stage
creative problem solving
focus groups
forced relationships
free association
Gordon method
heuristics
idea stage
matrix charting
parameter analysis
problem inventory analysis
product development stage
product life cycle
product planning and development process
reverse brainstorming
scientific method
synectics
test marketing stage
value analysis

SELECTED READINGS

Brophy, David, & Shulman, Joel (1993). Financial Factors Which Stimulate Innovation. *Entrepreneurship: Theory and Practice.* vol. 17. no. 2. pp 61–75.

A model is proposed that suggests a relationship between the incidence and rate of innovation and the state of key financial factors grouped under two headings: investment valuation and financing.

Cooper, A. C., & Dunkelberg, C. (1986). Entrepreneurship and Paths to Business Ownership. *Strategic Management Journal.* vol 7, no. 1, pp 53–68.

Alternative paths to ownership are examined, including starting, purchasing, or inheriting a firm, as well as being promoted or brought in by existing owners. Data on 1,756 owner-managers is used to relate the path to ownership and the entrepreneur's background characteristics; motivations and attitudes; and previous careers, incubator origination, and processes of starting.

Daily, Catherine M., & Dalto, Dan R. (1993). Board of Directors Leadership and Structure: Control and Performance Implications. *Entrepreneurship: Theory and Practice.* vol. 17, no. 3. pp 65–81.

A study of 186 companies employing fewer than 500 people found that the very organizations the literature suggests might benefit most from independent governance structures are those that rely on them the least.

Dean, Thomas J., Meyer, G. Dale, & DeCastro, Julio (1993). Determinants of New Firm Formation in Manufacturing Industries: Industry Dynamics, Entry Barriers, and Organizational Inertia. *Entrepreneurship: Theory and Practice.* vol. 17, no. 2, pp 49–60.

This model of new-firm creation in manufacturing industries takes into account market dynamics, entry barriers, entrepreneurial constraints, and organizational inertia.

Hansen, Eric L., & Allen, Kathleen R. (1992). The Creation Corridor: Environmental Load and Pre-organization Information-Processing Ability. *Entrepreneurship: Theory and Practice.* vol. 17, no. 1, pp 57–65.

Entrepreneurs would appear to improve their ability to create new organizations when they establish preorganizational information—accessing and processing capabilities that are appropriate to their respective levels of environmental load.

Herron, Larry, & Sapienza, Harry J. (1992). The Entrepreneur and the Initiation of New Venture Launch. *Entrepreneurship: Theory and Practice.* vol. 17, no. 1, pp 49–55.

A structural model of the initiation of new venture creation is presented, linking psychological and behavioral concepts with those of organizational theory to explain the limitation of launch activities for new business enterprises.

Hisrich, Robert D. (1992). The Need For Marketing in Entrepreneurship. *Journal of Consumer Marketing.* vol. 9, no. 3, pp 43–47.

The importance of the relationship between marketing and entrepreneurship is discussed along with the commonalities of the two areas particularly in the new venture creation process.

Hornaday, Robert W. (1992). Thinking About Entrepreneurship: A Fuzzy Set Approach. *Journal of Small Business Management.* vol. 30, no. 4, pp 12–23.

A fuzzy set bounded by three dimensions—economic innovation, organization creation, and profit-seeking in the market sector—is used to develop a relatively complex but useful method of distinguishing the concept of entrepreneurship from other constructs.

Larson, Andrea, & Starr, Jennifer A. (1993). A Network Model of Organizational Formation. *Entrepreneurship: Theory and Practice.* vol. 17, no. 2, pp 5–15.

A network model of organization formation is presented that details three stages of entrepreneurial network activity used to secure the critical economic and noneconomic resources needed to start a business. These stages are: focusing on the essential dyads, converting dyadic ties to socioeconomics exchanges, and layering the exchanges with multiple exchange processes.

Learned, Kevin E. (1992). What Happened Before the Organization? A Model of Organization Formation. *Entrepreneurship: Theory and Practice.* vol. 17, no. 1, pp 39–48.

A model of organizational formation is proposed that suggests four dimensions in the founding process that culminate in a decision to found or not to found a new business venture: (1) propensity to found, (2) intent to found, (3) sense making, and (4) the decision.

Namon, John L., & Slevin, Dennis P. (1993). Entrepreneurship and the Concept of Fit: A Model and Empirical Tests. *Strategic Management Journal.* vol. 14, no. 2, pp 137–153.

A nominative model of fit is presented that determines the firm's fit with its environment based on the variables of entrepreneurial style, organizational structure, and mission strategy.

Schwenk, Charles R., & Shrader, Charles B. (1993). Effects of Formal Strategic Planning on Financial Performance in Small Firms: A Meta-Analysis. *Entrepreneurship: Theory and Practice.* vol. 17, no. 2, pp 53–64.

Strategic planning is a beneficial activity for small firms as it promotes longrange thinking, reduces the focus on operational details, and provides a structural means for identifying and evaluating strategic alternatives.

Shaver, Kelly G., & Scott, Linda R. (1991). Person, Process, Choice: The Psychology of New Venture Creation. *Entrepreneurship: Theory and Practice.* vol. 126, no. 2, pp 23–45.

A comprehensive psychological portrait of new venture creation is discussed that shows how an individual's cognitive representations of the world gets translated into action.

Starr, Jennifer A., & Fondas, Nanette (1992). A Model of Entrepreneurial Socialization and Organization Formation. *Entrepreneurship: Theory and Practice.* vol. 17, no. 1, pp 67–76.

The model describes ways in which entrepreneurs adapt their attitudes and behaviors in response to motivation, socializing agents, and contextual pressures in the entrepreneurial setting.

Terpstra, David E., & Olson, Philip D. (1993). Entrepreneurial Start-up and Growth: A Classification of Problems. *Entrepreneurship: Theory and Practice.* vol. 17, no. 3, pp 5–20.

A study of CEOs of 121 *Inc.* 500 firms found different types of dominant problems related to different stages of organizational development than was found in previous research.

Vos, Ed. (1992). Unlisted Businesses Are Not Financial Clones of Listed Businesses. *Entrepreneurship: Theory and Practice.* vol. 16, no. 4, pp 57–68.

A study of 209 unlisted companies compared to all of the publicly listed companies in New Zealand found that, even through the financial ratios between the two were correlated, the financial statements from the unlisted sector showed larger ranges and variability than those from the listed sector.

CHAPTER

5

The Business Plan

Chapter Objectives

1. To define what the business plan is, who prepares it, and who reads it.
2. To understand the scope and value of the business plan to investors, lenders, employees, suppliers, and customers.
3. To identify information needs and sources for business planning.
4. To present a comprehensive outline of an effective plan.
5. To present examples and a step-by-step explanation of the business plan.
6. To present helpful questions for the entrepreneur at each stage of the planning process.
7. To appreciate the importance of monitoring the business plan.
8. To understand the major reasons why business plans fail.

Joseph Wilson

The business plan, although often criticized for being "dreams of glory," is probably the single most important document to the entrepreneur at the start-up stage. Potential investors are not likely to consider investing in a new venture until the business plan has been completed. In addition, the business plan helps maintain a perspective for the entrepreneur of what needs to be accomplished. No one knows this better than Joe Wilson, founder of Ecomed Inc., a medical waste equipment manufacturer.[1]

After 13 years as an innovator and co-founder of Medical Safe Tec, a developer of mechanical and chemical infectious waste treatment for hospitals and laboratories, Joe Wilson decided he wanted a company of his own. A hard working and success driven man, Wilson came across an untapped market opportunity in the bio safety market. He recognized the growing fear of AIDS and the increasing problem of toxic waste washing ashore and causing the closing of many East Coast beaches. Safe disposal of such wastes had become an important priority for the medical profession, and Joe Wilson was determined to find a solution.

In 1990, Wilson designed a stand-alone 150 pound waste pulverizer that destroyed and decontaminated needles, syringes, glassware, tubes, vials, specimens, and bandages. The machine, the size of a dishwasher, retailed for about $4,000. With this innovative product, Wilson then launched Ecomed Inc. in 1990. Trying not to compete with large companies who manufactured large, expensive machines that targeted hospitals and health institutions, Wilson focused on the small user, such as doctors, biomedical research facilities, small laboratories, and penitentiaries. These potential customers had the same need as the hospitals but to a much smaller extent, and did not want to spend a large sum of money or have a bulky machine that took up too much space.

Wilson felt he was an engineer who could design and build new products but did not have a very strong business background and thus needed support in the planning and management of the operation. He felt he needed to step back and let someone with business experience assess the company and its opportunities, and then to-

[1]For more information on Ecomed Inc., see Bob Weinstein, "At Your Disposal," *Entrepreneur,* June 1993, pp 170–173; and Tom Barton, "ECOMED Makes Medical Waste Easy for the Little Guy," *Indianapolis Business Journal.* July 8–14, 1991, pp 10A–11A.

gether they could program the company's future direction. Wilson brought in David Haeberle to assist in the writing of the business plan and operations plan. Wilson and Haeberle spent months preparing the business plan, which provided the direction for the new venture, as well as an operations plan that provided the venture with a statement of how the business plan was to be accomplished. The business plan became an important factor in the venture finally receiving enough capital to begin manufacturing the new product.

In 1990 Ecomed was launched with a $45,000 bank loan, $7,000 of Wilson's savings, and $255,000 in seed money obtained from an investment group of 12 people. The funds were used to build nine prototype machines, to obtain patents, and to support marketing, promotion, and salaries. The business plan not only helped obtain the necesary capitalization but served management as an important guide in the early days of the start-up. By staying within the parameters of the plan, the entrepreneurs were able to remain focused on their strengths and were able to avoid the temptation of deviating from their goals and target market. The business plan thus served as an important control in management decision making.

In 1992, the company produced 567 units, which provided revenue of $1.4 million but also losses of about $250,000. These losses had been anticipated as part of the initial business plan, but both Wilson and Haeberle projected that by the year 1995 the business would achieve sales of 12,000 units, which would project to $27.2 million in sales and a profit of $4.3 million. The business plan also calls for Ecomed to remain a small lean company. Wilson feels that this will give him an advantage over larger companies that will be hindered by bureaucracy and large overhead.

Although the plan took significant time to prepare, it has allowed both Wilson and Haeberle to move ahead on a well-programmed and documented basis. Given that this industry could reach $1 billion by 1995, Wilson believes that the planning keeps the company on a targeted course and allows them to remain competitive as new players enter this very promising market.

PLANNING

Before beginning a discussion of the business plan, it is important for the reader to understand the different types of plans that may be part of any business operation. For any given organization, it is possible to find financial plans, marketing plans, human resource plans, production plans, and sales plans to name a few. Plans may be short-term or long-term, or they may be strategic or operational. Plans will also differ in scope depending on the type of business or the anticipated size of the start-up operation. Even though they may serve different functions, all of these plans have one important purpose: to provide guidance and structure to management in a rapidly changing market environment. Planning is not a one-time endeavor. Thus, the business plan is only the first phase of what will be a continuous effort in planning the operations and direction of a business.

WHAT IS THE BUSINESS PLAN?

The business plan is a written document prepared by the entrepreneur that describes all the relevant external and internal elements involved in starting a new venture. It is often an integration of functional plans such as marketing, finance, manufacturing, and human resources. It also addresses both short-term and long-term decision making for the first three years of operation. Thus, the business plan—or, as it is sometimes referred to, the game plan or road map—answers the questions, Where am I now? Where am I going? How will I get there? Potential investors, suppliers, and even customers will request or require a business plan.

If we think of the business plan as a road map, we might better understand its significance. Let's suppose you were trying to decide whether to drive from Boston to Los Angeles (mission or goal) in a motor home. There are a number of possible routes, each requiring different time frames and costs. Like the entrepreneur, the traveler must make some important decisions and gather information before preparing the plan.

The travel plan would consider external factors such as emergency car repair, weather conditions, road conditions, sights to see, available campgrounds, and so on. These factors are basically uncontrollable by the traveler but must be considered in the plan, just as the entrepreneur would consider external factors such as new regulations, competition, social changes, changes in consumer needs, or new technology.

On the other hand, the traveler does have some idea of how much money is available, how much time he or she has, and the choices of highways, roads, campgrounds, sights, and so forth. Similarly, the entrepreneur has some control over manufacturing, marketing, and personnel in the new venture.

The traveler should consider all of these factors in determining what roads to take, what campgrounds to stay in, how much time to spend in selected locations, how much time and money to allow for vehicle maintenance, who will drive, and so on. Thus, the travel plan responds to the three questions, Where am I now? Where am I going? and How do I get there? Then the traveler in our example—or the entrepreneur, the subject of our book—will be able to determine how much money will be needed from existing sources or new sources to achieve the plan.

We saw in the opening example of this chapter how Joe Wilson of Ecomed used the business plan to address these questions. The functional elements of the business plan are discussed here but are also represented as separate chapters in this book.

WHO SHOULD WRITE THE PLAN?

The business plan should be prepared by the entrepreneur; however, he or she may consult with many other sources in its preparation. Lawyers, accountants, marketing consultants, and engineers are useful in the preparation of the plan. We saw in the opening scenerio how Joe Wilson went out and actually hired an associate who would not only be employed as a manager but would be able to offer some expert advice in the preparation of the initial business plan. Some of the above sources can be found through services offered by the Small Business Administration (SBA), Service Core of Retired Executives (SCORE), Small Business Development Centers (SBDC), universities, and friends or relatives. When there is doubt, the entrepreneur should consult with the sources being considered to ascertain their availability, scope of expertise, and fees. In the Ecomed example, Joe Wilson, the founder of the new venture, decided to hire someone who could not only assist in the preparation of the business plan but also become an important part of the management team to operate the business.

To help determine whether to hire a consultant or to make use of other resources, the entrepreneur can make an objective assessment of his or her own skills. Figure 5–1 is an illustration of a rating to determine what skills are lacking and by how much. For example, a sales engineer recently designed a new machine that allows a user to send a 10-second personalized message in a greeting card. A primary concern was how best to market the machine: as a promotional tool a firm could use for its distributors, suppliers, shareholders, or employees or as a retail product for end users. This entrepreneur, in assessing his skills, rated himself as excellent in product design and sales, good in organizing, and only fair or poor in the remaining skills. Through such an assessment, the entrepreneur can identify what skills are needed and from where they can be obtained.

SCOPE AND VALUE OF THE BUSINESS PLAN—WHO READS THE PLAN?

The business plan may be read by employees, investors, bankers, venture capitalists, suppliers, customers, advisors, and consultants. Since each of these segments will read the plan for different purposes, it must be comprehensive enough to address all

FIGURE 5–1 Skills Assessment

Skills	*Excellent*	*Good*	*Fair*	*Poor*
Accounting/taxes				
Planning				
Forecasting				
Marketing research				
Sales				
People management				
Product design				
Legal issues				
Organizing				

their issues and concerns. In some ways, the business plan must try to satisfy the needs of everyone; whereas, in the actual marketplace the entrepreneur's product will be trying to meet the needs of selected groups of customers.

However, there are probably three perspectives that need to be considered when preparing the plan. First is the perspective of the entrepreneur, who understands better than anyone the creativity and technology involved in the new venture. The entrepreneur must be able to clearly articulate what the venture is all about. Secondly is the marketing perspective. Too often, an entrepreneur will only consider the product or technology and not consider whether someone would buy it. Entrepreneurs must try to consider their business through the eyes of their customer. This customer orientation is discussed further in Chapter 6. The third perspective is that of the investor. The entrepreneur should try to view his or her business through the eyes of the investor. Sound financial projections are required; if the entrepreneur does not have the skills to prepare this information, then outside sources can be of assistance.[2]

The depth and detail in the business plan depend on the size and scope of the proposed new venture. An entrepreneur planning to market a new portable computer will need a quite comprehensive business plan, largely because of the nature of the product and market. On the other hand, an entrepreneur who plans to open a retail video store will not need the comprehensive coverage required by a new computer manufacturer. Thus, differences in the scope of the business plan may depend on whether the new venture is a service, involves manufacturing, or is a consumer good or industrial product. The size of the market, competition, and potential growth may also affect the scope of the business plan.

The business plan is valuable to the entrepreneur, potential investors, or even for the review of new personnel, who are trying to familiarize themselves with the venture and its goals and objectives. The business plan is important to these people because:

- It helps determine the viability of the venture in a designated market.
- It provides guidance to the entrepreneur in organizing his or her planning activities.
- It serves as an important tool in helping to obtain financing.

Potential investors are very particular about what should be included in the business plan. Even if some of the information is based on assumptions, the thinking process required to complete the plan is a valuable experience for the entrepreneur since it forces him or her to assess such things as cash flow and cash requirements. In addition, the thinking process takes the entrepreneur into the future, leading him or her to consider important issues that could impede the road to success.

The process also provides a self-assessment of the entrepreneur. Usually, he or she feels that the new venture is assured of success. However, the planning process forces the entrepreneur to bring objectivity to the idea and reflect on such questions

[2]Donald F. Kuratko and Arnold Cirtin, "Developing A Business Plan for Your Clients," *The National Public Accountant,* January 1990, pp 24–27.

as, Does the idea make sense? Will it work? Who is my customer? Does it satisfy customer needs? What kind of protection can I get against imitation by competitors? Can I manage such a business? Whom will I compete with? This self-evaluation is similar to role-playing, requiring the entrepreneur to think through various scenarios and consider obstacles that might prevent the venture from succeeding. The process allows the entrepreneur to plan ways to avoid such obstacles. It may even be possible that, after preparing the business plan, the entrepreneur realizes the obstacles cannot be avoided or overcome. Hence the venture may be terminated while still on paper. Although this certainly is not the most desirable conclusion, it would be much better to terminate the business endeavor before investing further time and money.

INFORMATION NEEDS

Before committing time and energy to preparing a business plan, the entrepreneur should do a quick feasibility study of the business concept to see if there are any possible barriers to success. The information, which can be obtained from many sources, should focus on marketing, finance, and production. Before beginning the feasibility study, the entrepreneur should clearly define the goals and objectives of the venture. These goals help define what needs to be done and how it will be accomplished. These goals and objectives also provide a framework for the business plan, marketing plan, and financial plan.

Goals and objectives that are too general or not feasible make the business plan difficult to control and implement. An example illustrates this point.

Jim McCurry and Gary Kusin had a great concept: a retail store that would sell computer software and video games to the home market rather than the business market. At the time of their brainstorm, they discovered that there were no retailers trying to meet the needs of this target market. Thus, their idea was a virtually untapped market niche.[3]

The plan they prepared was weak and overly optimistic in terms of reaching any of their goals. Fortunately for them, Gary was able to turn to an old family friend, Ross Perot, for advice on their business plan. Ross shot holes in their sloppily written business plan but imparted new learning for these entrepreneurs as to what was a good plan. For example, they had planned to open 12 stores in the first month, with many other openings scheduled throughout the year and across the country. They had no idea how or where these stores would be opened. With their newfound supporter and partner Ross Perot, who liked the business concept and was willing to guarantee their $3 million line of credit with a bank for one-third equity, the two entrepreneurs restructured their plan and began pursuit of more reasonable goals. Their first store

[3]Bob Weinstein, "Soft Sell," *Entrepreneur,* July 1993, pp 143–47.

was opened in Dallas in 1983. They christened their company Babbage's, after the 19th century mathematician, Charles Babbage, who was credited with designing the first computing machine. Today, the 259-store chain ranks among the leaders in consumer software, with about $209 million in sales.

The preceding example illustrates the lack of feasible business goals and a clear understanding of how these goals would be achieved. These two entrepreneurs were lucky to have a connection with someone who could provide them with direction. Not all entrepreneurs are as fortunate. The important lesson is that the business plan cannot be taken lightly and that it must reflect reasonable goals.

We can compare the above example with Joe Wilson and Ecomed Inc. For his start-up, Wilson had clearly defined goals that he translated into specific, successful marketing strategies. For example, Wilson's goal of producing 567 units with the invested capital allowed him to focus on his target market and control growth and costs. From this plan, losses in the early stages were minimized.

Market Information

One of the initial important elements of information needed by the entrepreneur is the market potential for the product or service. In order to ascertain the size of the market, it is first necessary for the entrepreneur to define the market. For example, is the product most likely to be purchased by men or women, high income or low income, rural or urban, highly educated or less educated, and so on. A well-defined target market will make it easier to project market size and subsequent market goals for the new venture. For example, an entrepreneur has developed a unique training aid for golfers. This product allows the user to practice in the basement or garage during the off-season. The product will determine distance, slice, or hook of a drive. The product would thus appeal to a well-defined market: avid golfers who are interested in improving their score.

To assess the total market potential, the entrepreneur should consider trade associations, government reports, and published studies (see Figure 5–8 for examples of secondary sources). In some instances, this information is readily available.[4] In our example above, the entrepreneur should be able to estimate the size of the market from secondary data. Golf magazines and associations would provide information on the golf market by geographic area. Other demographic information about this market is also likely to be available. Information from golf stores or from pro shops regarding training aids would also be helpful. Contacting a few of these stores to discuss training aids could provide valuable insights for the business plan. From this, the entrepreneur would be able to determine an approximate size of market.

---

[4]For more information on issues and questions relating to market information needs, see Michael P. Peters, "The Role of Planning in the Marketing of New Products." *Planning Review,* November 1980, pp 24–28.

Operations Information Needs

The relevance of a feasibility study of the manufacturing operations depends on the nature of the business. Most of the information needed can be obtained through direct contact with the appropriate source. The entrepreneur may need information on the following:

- Location—The company's location and its accessibility to customers, suppliers, and distributors need to be determined.
- Manufacturing operations—Basic machine and assembly operations need to be identified, as well as whether any of these operations would be subcontracted and by whom.
- Raw materials—The raw materials needed and suppliers' names, addresses, and costs should be determined.
- Equipment—The equipment needed should be listed and whether it will be purchased or leased.
- Labor skills—Each unique skill needed, the number of personnel in each skill, pay rate, and an assessment of where and how these skills will be obtained should be determined.
- Space—The total amount of space needed should be determined, including whether the space will be owned or leased.
- Overhead—Each item needed to support manufacturing, such as tools, supplies, utilities, salaries, and so on, should be determined.

Most of the above information will be incorporated directly into the business plan. Each item may require some research but is deemed necessary by those who will assess the business plan and consider funding the proposal.

Financial Information Needs

Before preparing the business plan, the entrepreneur must have a complete evaluation of the profitability of the venture. The assessment will primarily tell potential investors if the business will be profitable, how much money will be needed to launch the business and meet short-term financial needs, and how this money will be obtained (i.e., stock, debt, etc.).

There are traditionally three areas of financial information that will be needed to ascertain the feasibility of the new venture: (1) expected sales and expense figures for at least the first three years, (2) cash flow figures for the first three years, and (3) current balance sheet figures and pro forma balance sheets for the next three years.

Determination of the expected sales and expense figures for each of the first 12 months and each subsequent year is based on the market information discussed earlier. Each expense item should be identified and given on a monthly basis for the year. Estimates of cash flow consider the ability of the new venture to meet expenses at designated times of the year. The cash flow forecast should identify the beginning cash, expected accounts receivable and other receipts, and all disbursements on a monthly basis for the entire year.

Current balance sheet figures provide the financial conditions of the business at any particular time. They identify the assets of the business, the liabilities (what is owed), and the investment made by the owner or other partners.

WRITING THE BUSINESS PLAN

The business plan could take more than 200 hours to prepare, depending on the experience and knowledge of the entrepreneur. It should be comprehensive enough to give any potential investor a complete picture of the new venture and will help the entrepreneur clarify his or her thinking about the business.

Many entrepreneurs incorrectly estimate the length of time that an effective plan will take to prepare. Once the process has begun, however, the entrepreneur will realize that it is invaluable in sorting out the business functions of a new venture.

The outline for a business plan is illustrated in Figure 5–2. Each of the items in the outline is detailed in the following paragraphs of this chapter. Key questions in each section are also appropriately detailed.[5]

Introductory Page

This is the title or cover page, which provides a brief summary of the business plan's contents. The introductory page should contain the following:

- The name and address of the company.
- The name of the entrepreneur(s) and a telephone number.
- A paragraph describing the company and the nature of the business.
- The amount of financing needed. The entrepreneur may offer a package, that is, stock, debt, and so on. However, many venture capitalists prefer to structure this package in their own way.
- A statement of the confidentiality of the report. This is for security purposes and is important for the entrepreneur.

---

[5]For additional material, see *Business Plan for Small Manufacturers,* 2nd ed. (Lexington, MA: Haley Publications, 1985).

FIGURE 5–2 Outline of a Business Plan

I. Introductory Page
   A. Name and address of business
   B. Name(s) and address(es) of principals
   C. Nature of business
   D. Statement of financing needed
   E. Statement of confidentiality of report

II. Executive Summary—Three to four pages summarizing the complete business plan

III. Industry Analysis
   A. Future outlook and trends
   B. Analysis of competitors
   C. Market segmentation
   D. Industry forecasts

IV. Description of Venture
   A. Product(s)
   B. Service(s)
   C. Size of business
   D. Office equipment and personnel
   E. Background of entrepreneurs

V. Production Plan
   A. Manufacturing process (amount subcontracted)
   B. Physical plant
   C. Machinery and equipment
   D. Names of suppliers of raw materials

VI. Marketing Plan
   A. Pricing
   B. Distribution
   C. Promotion
   D. Product forecasts
   E. Controls

VII. Organizational Plan
   A. Form of ownership
   B. Identification of partners or principal shareholders
   C. Authority of principals
   D. Management-team background
   E. Roles and responsibilities of members of organization

VIII. Assessment of Risk
   A. Evaluate weakness of business
   B. New technologies
   C. Contingency plans

IX. Financial Plan
   A. Pro forma income statement
   B. Cash flow projections
   C. Pro forma balance sheet
   D. Break-even analysis
   E. Sources and applications of funds

X. Appendix (contains backup material)
   A. Letters
   B. Market research data
   C. Leases or contracts
   D. Price lists from suppliers

This title page sets out the basic concept that the entrepreneur is attempting to develop. Investors consider it important because they can determine the amount of investment needed without having to read through the entire plan. An illustration of this page can be found in Figure 5–3.

Executive Summary

This section of the business plan is prepared after the total plan is written. About three to four pages in length, the executive summary should stimulate the interest of the potential investor. The investor uses the summary to determine if the entire business plan is worth reading. Thus, it would highlight in a concise and convincing manner the key points in the business plan, that is, the nature of the venture, financing needed, market potential, and support as to why it will succeed.

Industry Analysis

It is important to put the new venture in a proper context. In particular, the potential investor, while assessing the venture on a number of criteria, needs to know which industry the entrepreneur will be competing in. Discussion of the industry outlook, including future trends and historical achievements, should be included. The entrepreneur should also provide insight on new product developments in this industry.

FIGURE 5–3 Sample Introductory Page

KC CLEANING SERVICE
OAK KNOLL ROAD
BOSTON, MA 02167
(617) 969-0100

Co-owners: Kimberly Peters, Christa Peters

Description of Business:

This business will provide cleaning service on a contract basis to small and medium-sized businesses. Services include cleaning of floors, carpets, draperies, and windows, and regular sweeping, dusting, and washing. Contracts will be for one year and will specify the specific services and scheduling for completion of services.

Financing:

Initial financial requested is a $100,000 loan to be paid off over 6 years. This debt will cover office space, office equipment and supplies, two leased vans, advertising, and selling costs.

This report is confidential and is the property of the co-owners listed above. It is intended only for use by the persons to whom it is transmitted and any reproduction or divulgence of any of its contents without the prior written consent of the company is prohibited.

Competitive analysis is also an important part of this section. Each major competitor should be identified, with appropriate strengths and weaknesses described, particularly as to how they might affect the new venture's potential success in the market.

Who is the customer? The market should be segmented and the target market for the entrepreneur identified. Most new ventures are likely to compete effectively in only one or a few of the market segments. This strategy may be a function of the competition, who may be more vulnerable in one or a few segments of the total market.

Any forecasts made by the industry or by the government should be noted. A high-growth market may be viewed more favorably by the potential investor. Some key questions the entrepreneur should consider are described in Figure 5–4.

Description of Venture

The new venture should be described in detail in this section of the business plan. This will enable the investor to ascertain the size and scope of the business. Key elements are the product(s) or service(s), the location and size of the business, the personnel and office equipment that will be needed, the background of the entrepreneur(s), and the history of the venture. Figure 5–5 summarizes some of the important questions the entrepreneur needs to answer when preparing this section of the business plan.

Location of any business may be vital to its success, particularly if the business is retail or involves a service. Thus, the emphasis on location in the business plan is a function of the type of business. In assessing the building or space the business will occupy, the entrepreneur may need to evaluate such factors as parking, access from roadways to facility, access to customers, suppliers, or distributors, delivery rates, and town regulations or zoning laws. An enlarged local map may help give the location some perspective with regard to roads, highways, access, and so forth.

Recently, an entrepreneur considered opening a new doughnut shop at a location diagonally across from a small shopping mall on a heavily traveled road. Traffic

FIGURE 5–4 Critical Issues for Industry Analysis

1. What are total industry sales over the past five years?
2. What is anticipated growth in this industry?
3. How many new firms have entered this industry in the past three years?
4. What new products have been recently introduced in this industry?
5. Who are the nearest competitors?
6. How will your business operation be better than this?
7. Are each of your major competitors' sales growing, declining, or steady?
8. What are the strengths and weaknesses of each of your competitors?
9. What is the profile of your customers?
10. How does your customer profile differ from that of your competition?

counts indicated a large potential customer base if people would stop for coffee and so forth on their way to work. After enlarging a local map, the entrepreneur noted that the morning flow of traffic required drivers to make a left turn into the doughnut shop, crossing the outbound lane. Unfortunately, the roadway was divided by a concrete center strip with no break to allow for a left-hand turn. The only possibility for entry into the shop required the customer to drive down about 400 yards and make a U-turn. It would also be difficult for the customer to get back on the roadway traveling in the right direction. Since the town was unwilling to open the road, the entrepreneur eliminated this site from any further consideration.

This simple assessment of the location, market, and so on saved the entrepreneur from a potential disaster. Maps that locate customers, competitors, and even alternative locations for a building or site can be helpful in this evaluation. Some of the important questions that might be asked by an entrepreneur are as follows:

- How much space is needed?
- Should I buy or lease the building?
- What is the cost per square foot?
- Is the site zoned for commercial use?
- What town restrictions exist for signs, parking, and so forth?
- Is renovation of the building necessary?
- Is the facility accessible to traffic?
- Is there adequate parking?
- Will the existing facility have room for expansion?
- What is the economic, demographic profile of the area?
- Is there an adequate labor pool available?
- What are local taxes?
- Are sewage, electricity, and plumbing adequate?

FIGURE 5–5 Describing the Venture

1. What are your product(s) and/or service(s)?
2. Describe the product(s) and/or service(s), including patent, copyright, or trademark status.
3. Where will the business be located?
4. Is your building new? Old? In need of renovations? (If renovation needed, state costs.)
5. Is the building leased or owned? (State the terms.)
6. Why is this building and location right for your business?
7. What additional skills or personnel will be needed to operate the business?
8. What office equipment will be needed?
9. Will equipment be purchased or leased?
10. What is your business background?
11. What management experience do you have?
12. Describe personal data such as education, age, special abilities, and interests.
13. What are your reasons for going into business?
14. Why will you be successful in this venture?
15. What development work has been completed to date?

If the building or site decision involves legal issues such as a lease or requires town variances, the entrepreneur should hire a lawyer. Problems relating to regulations and leases can be avoided easily, but under no circumstances should the entrepreneur try to negotiate with the town or a landlord without good legal advice.

Production Plan

If the new venture is a manufacturing operation, a production plan is necessary. This plan should describe the complete manufacturing process. If some or all of the manufacturing process is to be subcontracted, the plan should describe the subcontractor(s), including location, reasons for selection, costs, and any contracts that have been completed. If the manufacturing is to be carried out in whole or in part by the entrepreneur, he or she will need to describe the physical plant layout; the machinery and equipment needed to perform the manufacturing operations; raw materials and suppliers' names, addresses, and terms; costs of manufacturing; and any future capital equipment needs. In a manufacturing operation, the discussion of these items will be important to any potential investor in assessing financial needs.

If the venture is not a manufacturing operation but a retail store or service, this section would be titled "merchandising plan" and the purchasing of merchandise, inventory control system, and storage needs should be described. Figure 5–6 summarizes some of the key questions for this section of the business plan.

Marketing Plan

The marketing plan (discussed in detail in Chapter 6) is an important part of the business plan since it describes how the product(s) or service(s) will be distributed, priced, and promoted. Specific forecasts for product(s) or service(s) are indicated in order to project profitability of the venture. The budget and appropriate controls needed for marketing strategy decisions are also discussed in detail in Chapter 6.

Potential investors regard the marketing plan as critical to the success of the new venture. Thus, the entrepreneur should make every effort to prepare as comprehensive and detailed a plan as possible, so that investors can be clear as to what the goals of the venture are and what strategies are to be implemented to effectively achieve these goals. Marketing planning will be an annual requirement (with careful monitoring and changes made on a weekly or monthly basis) for the entrepreneur and should be regarded as the road map for short-term decision making.

Organizational Plan

This section of the business plan should describe the venture's form of ownership, that is, proprietorship, partnership, or corporation. If the venture is a partnership, the terms of the partnership should be included. If the venture is a corporation, it is important to detail the shares of stock authorized, share options, names, and addresses and résumés of the directors and officers of the corporation. It is also helpful to provide an organization chart indicating the line of authority and the responsibilities of the members of the organization. Alternative forms of organization and discussion of the various layouts of an organization are discussed further in Chapter 8.

Figure 5–7 summarizes some of the key questions the entrepreneur needs to answer in preparing this section of the business plan. This information provides the potential investor with a clear understanding of who controls the organization and how other members will interact in performing their management functions.

Assessment of Risk

Every new venture will be faced with some potential hazards, given the particular industry and competitive environment. It is important to the entrepreneur to recognize the potential risks and prepare an effective strategy to deal with them. Major

FIGURE 5–6 Production Plan

1. Will you be responsible for all or part of the manufacturing operation?
2. If some manufacturing is subcontracted, who will be the subcontractor(s)? (Give names and addresses.)
3. Why were these subcontractors selected?
4. What are the costs of the subcontracted manufacturing? (Include copies of any written contracts.)
5. What will be the layout of the production process? (Illustrate steps if possible.)
6. What equipment will be needed immediately for manufacturing?
7. What raw materials will be needed for manufacturing?
8. Who are the suppliers of new materials and appropriate costs?
9. What are the costs of manufacturing the product?
10. What are the future capital equipment needs of the venture?

If a Retail Operation or Service:

1. From whom will merchandise be purchased?
2. How will the inventory control system operate?
3. What are storage needs of the venture and how will they be promoted?

FIGURE 5–7 Organization Structure

1. What is the form of ownership of the organization?
2. If a partnership, who are the partners and what are the terms of agreement?
3. If incorporated, who are the principal shareholders and how much stock do they own?
4. What type and how many shares of voting or nonvoting stock have been issued?
5. Who are members of the board of directors? (Give names, addresses, and résumés.)
6. Who has check-signing authority or control?
7. Who is each member of the management team and what is her or his background?
8. What are the roles and responsibilities of each member of the management team?
9. What are the salaries, bonuses, or other forms of payment for each member of the management team?

risks for a new venture could result from a competitor's reaction; weaknesses in the marketing, production, or management team; and new advances in technology that might render the new product obsolete. Even if these factors present no risks to the new venture, the business plan should discuss why that is the case.

It is also useful for the entrepreneur to provide alternative strategies should any of the above risk factors occur. These contingency plans and strategies illustrate to the potential investor that the entrepreneur is sensitive to important risks and is prepared should any occur.

Financial Plan

The financial plan is discussed further in Chapter 7. This, like the marketing, production, and organization plans, is an important part of the business plan. It determines the potential investment commitment needed for the new venture and indicates whether the business plan is economically feasible.

Generally, three financial areas are discussed in this section of the business plan. First, the entrepreneur should summarize the forecasted sales and the appropriate expenses for at least the first three years, with the first year's projections provided monthly. The form for displaying this information is illustrated in Chapter 7. It includes the forecasted sales, cost of goods sold, and the general and administrative expenses. Net profit after taxes can then be projected by estimating income taxes.

The second major area of financial information needed is cash flow figures for three years, with the first year's projections provided monthly. Since bills have to be paid at different times of the year, it is important to determine the demands on cash on a monthly basis, especially in the first year. Remember that sales may be irregular, and receipts from customers may also be spread out, thus necessitating the borrowing of short-term capital to meet fixed expenses such as salaries and utilities. A form for projecting the cash flow needs for a 12-month period can be found in Chapter 7.

The last financial item needed in this section of the business plan is the projected balance sheet. This shows the financial condition of the business at a specific time. It summarizes the assets of a business, its liabilities (what is owed), the investment of the entrepreneur and any partners, and retained earnings (or cumulative losses). A form for the balance sheet and more detailed explanations of the items included are discussed further in Chapter 7. Any assumptions considered for the balance sheet or any other item in the financial plan should be listed for the benefit of the potential investor.

Appendix

The appendix of the business plan generally contains any backup material that is not necessary in the text of the document. Reference to any of the documents in the appendix should be made in the plan itself.

Letters from customers, distributors, or subcontractors are examples of information that should be included in the appendix. Any documentation of information, that is, secondary data or primary research data used to support plan decisions, should also be included. Leases, contracts, or any other types of agreement that have been initiated may also be included in the appendix. Last price lists from suppliers and competitors may be added.

USING AND IMPLEMENTING THE BUSINESS PLAN

The business plan is designed to guide the entrepreneur through the first year of operations. It is important that the implementation of the strategy contain control points to ascertain progress and to initiate contingency plans if necessary. Some of the controls necessary in manufacturing, marketing, financing, and the organization are discussed in subsequent chapters. Most important to the entrepreneur is that the business plan not end up in a drawer somewhere once the financing has been attained and the business launched.

There has been a tendency among many entrepreneurs to avoid planning. The reason often given is that planning is dull or boring and is something used only by large companies. This may be an excuse; perhaps the real truth is that some entrepreneurs are afraid to plan.[6] Planning is an important part of any business operation. Without good planning, the entrepreneur is likely to pay an enormous price. All one has to do is consider the planning done by suppliers, customers, competitors, and banks to realize that it is important for the entrepreneur. It is also important to realize that without good planning the employees will not understand the company's goals and how they are expected to perform in their jobs.

Bankers are the first to admit that few business failures result from a lack of cash but, instead, fail because of the entrepreneur's inability to plan effectively. Intelligent planning is not a difficult or impossible exercise for the inexperienced entrepreneur. With the proper commitment and support from many outside resources, such as those shown in Figure 5–8, the entrepreneur can prepare an effective business plan.

In addition, the entrepreneur can enhance effective implementation of the business plan by developing a schedule to measure progress and to institute contingency plans. These frequent readings or control procedures will be discussed further below.

Measuring Plan Progress

During the introductory phases of the start-up, the entrepreneur should determine the points at which decisions should be made as to whether the goals or objectives are on schedule. Typically, the business plan projections will be made on a 12-month

---

[6] Bruce G. Posner, "Real Entrepreneurs Don't Plan," *Inc,* November 1985, pp 129–35.

FIGURE 5–8 Sources of Information

- Small Business Administration
- Department of Commerce
- Federal information centers
- Bureau of Census
- State and municipal governments
- Banks
- Chambers of Commerce
- Trade associations
- Trade journals
- Libraries
- Universities and community colleges

schedule. However, the entrepreneur cannot wait 12 months to see if the plan has been successfully achieved. Instead, on a frequent basis (i.e., the beginning of each month), the entrepreneur should check the profit and loss statement, cash flow projections, and information on inventory, production, quality, sales, collection of accounts receivable, and disbursements for the previous month. This feedback should be simple but be able to provide key members of the organization with current information in time to correct any major deviations from the goals and objectives outlined. A brief description of each of these control elements is given below:

- Inventory control—By controlling inventory, the firm can ensure maximum service to the customer. The faster the firm gets back its investment in raw materials and finished goods, the faster capital can be reinvested to meet additional customer needs.
- Production control—Compare the cost figures estimated in the business plan against day-to-day operation costs. This will help to control machine time, worker hours, process time, delay time, and downtime cost.
- Quality control—This will depend on the type of production system but is designed to make sure that the product performs satisfactorily.
- Sales control—Information on units, dollars, specific products sold, price of sales, meeting of delivery dates, and credit terms are all useful to get a good perspective of the sales of the new venture. In addition, an effective collection system for accounts receivable should be set up to avoid aging of accounts and bad debts.
- Disbursements—The new venture should also control the amount of money paid out. All bills should be reviewed to determine how much is being disbursed and for what purpose.

Updating the Plan

The most effective business plan can become out of date if conditions change. Environmental factors such as the economy, customers, new technology, or competition and internal factors such as the loss or addition of key employees can all change the direction of the business plan. Thus, it is important to be sensitive to changes in the company, industry, and market. If these changes are likely to affect the business plan, the entrepreneur should determine what revisions are needed. In this manner, the entrepreneur can maintain reasonable targets and goals and keep the new venture on a course that will increase its probability of success.

WHY SOME BUSINESS PLANS FAIL

Generally, a poorly prepared business plan can be blamed on one or more of the following factors:

- Goals set by the entrepreneur are unreasonable.
- Goals are not measurable.
- The entrepreneur has not made a total commitment to the business or to the family.
- The entrepreneur has no experience in the planned business.
- The entrepreneur has no sense of potential threats or weaknesses to the business.
- No customer need was established for the purposed product or service.

Setting goals requires the entrepreneur to be well-informed about the type of business and the competitive environment. Goals should be specific and not so mundane as to lack any basis of control. For example, the entrepreneur may target a specific market share, units sold, or revenue. These goals are measurable and can be monitored over time.

In addition, the entrepreneur who has not made a total commitment to the business or to his or her family will not be able to meet the demands of a new venture. For example, it is difficult to operate a new venture on a part-time basis while still holding onto a full-time position. And it is also difficult to operate a business without an understanding from family members as to the time and resources that will be needed. Lenders or investors will not be favorably inclined toward a venture that does not have full-time commitment. Moreover, lenders or investors will expect the entrepreneur to make a significant financial commitment to the business even if it means a second mortgage or a depletion of savings.

Generally, a lack of experience will result in failure unless the entrepreneur can either attain the necessary knowledge or team up with someone who already has it. For example, an entrepreneur trying to start a new restaurant without any experience or knowledge of the restaurant business would be disastrous.

The entrepreneur should also document customer needs before preparing the plan. Customer needs can be identified from direct experience, letters from customers, or from marketing research. A clear understanding of these needs and how the entrepreneur's business will effectively meet them is vital to the success of the new venture.

SUMMARY

This chapter has established the scope and value of the business plan and outlined the steps in its preparation. The business plan may be read by employees, investors, lenders, suppliers, customers, and consultants. The scope of the plan will depend on the size and the specific industry for which the venture is intended.

The business plan is essential in launching a new venture. The results of many hours of preparation will represent a comprehensive, written, and well-organized document that will serve as a guide to the entrepreneur and as an instrument to raise necessary capital and financing.

Before beginning the business plan, the entrepreneur will need information on the market, manufacturing operations, and financial estimations. This information should be evaluated based on the goals and objectives of the new culture. These goals and objectives provide a framework for a controlling business plan.

The chapter provides a comprehensive discussion and outline of a typical business plan. Each key element in the plan is discussed and examples are provided. Control decisions are presented to ensure the effective implementation of the business plan. In addition, some insights as to why business plans fail are discussed.

QUESTIONS FOR DISCUSSION

1. Why is a business plan so important to the entrepreneur? To the investor?
2. What kind of information should be provided in the industry analysis of the business plan? Where can the entrepreneur get information on any specific industry?
3. What are some examples of potential hazards that should be evaluated in the risk-assessment section of the business plan? How would they differ for a service, manufacturer, or retailer?
4. What is the purpose of the financial plan to the potential investor? What kinds of financial information will be needed? Why?
5. Why is it necessary to update the business plan? What specific factors can enhance the need to update it?
6. Why do some business plans fail?

KEY TERMS

assessment of risk
business plan
description of venture
financial plan
industry analysis
marketing plan
organizational plan
production plan

SELECTED READINGS

Business Plan for Small Manufacturers. (1980). Small Business Administration, Office of Management Assistance. Washington, DC: U.S. Printing Office.

A brief working aid for the entrepreneur in manufacturing who needs a business plan. Asks the entrepreneur questions and provides space to write in information. Completion of the working aid can become the basis for the business plan.

Job, D. D. (1985). *Developing a Business Plan.* 2nd ed. Lexington, MA: Haley Publications.

A step-by-step guide on how to prepare a business plan written by an entrepreneur with significant experience with new ventures. Provides detailed explanations of each step in the plan preparation.

Kuratko, D. F., and A. Cirtin. (January 1990). Developing your business plan for your clients. *The National Public Accountant,* pp 24–27.

Because of the continued growth in new venture launches, the accountant is playing an important role in providing assistance in the preparation of the financial analysis for the business plan.

Larson, E. (February 1987). The best-laid plans. *Inc.* 9, no. 2, pp 60–64.

Criticizes the business plan as a document that every entrepreneur needs to get started, yet no one really follows. Provides many examples of entrepreneurs who simply did not follow their original plans.

Richman, T. (February 1988). Anatomy of a start-up: drive-in movies. *Inc.* 10, no. 2, pp 42–49.

Takes the reader through the preparation of a business plan for a new venture, drive-through video kiosks. Includes description of executive summary, key personnel, competitive analysis, financial analysis, and marketing strategy.

Washes, L. (January 1989). The business plan that gets the loan. *Working Woman,* pp 82–85.

Provides an interesting inside view of the preparation and implementation of a business plan. Describes how two women met to discuss their dream business, researched the industry, and settled on a fine jewelry and artwork shop that needed a $30,000 loan, which the business plan helped attain.

CHAPTER

The Marketing Plan

Chapter Objectives

1. To explain the marketing system and its key components.
2. To understand the differences between business planning, strategic planning, and market planning.
3. To describe the role of marketing research in determining marketing strategy for the marketing plan.
4. To define the steps in preparing the marketing plan.
5. To illustrate different creative strategies that may be used to differentiate or position the new venture's products or services.

Michael S. Dell

Some experts might argue that organizing and launching a business is the easiest part of getting started but that sustaining the business is the most difficult and most challenging. As we've seen in earlier chapters, businesses fail at an alarming rate, yet too often we blame lack of finances or poor management for the demise. A closer look will often reveal that the real problems relate to marketing issues such as identifying the customer, defining the right product and service to meet customer needs, pricing, distribution, and promotion.

Because the entrepreneur must anticipate these issues both in the short run and the future, it is important for him or her to develop and prepare a marketing plan. Planning, as discussed in the previous chapter, spans a wide range of activities and is intended to formally detail the business activities, strategies, responsibilities, budgets, and controls to meet specific, designated goals.

No one knows this better than Michael S. Dell. Now in his late twenties, Michael Dell is the upstart in the very competitive micro-computer market, where many of the more established firms have had difficulties or failed. He has been described as the most innovative and creative person in marketing computers in the last decade and able to achieve success in a market that others have thought impossible.[1]

Michael always had entrepreneurial tendencies. At age 12, he started a nationwide mail-order stamp auction, which netted him his first $2,000. Even though his parents wanted him to be a doctor, Michael always knew, especially after extending his knowledge of computers at the University of Texas at Austin, that he would someday own his own computer business.

Fed up with sales people in electronics stores who lacked knowledge, Dell dropped out of school in 1984 at age 19 and took $1,000 of savings to launch PCs Limited, soon renamed Dell Computer Corporation. His business idea was to use innovative mail-order marketing to reach his customers. It was here that Dell faced his first hurdle: where to find a source of machines. Initially, he decided to buy IBM computers on the gray market because IBM would not allow their dealers to sell PCs to anyone intending to resell them. However, this was not sufficient to

[1] See the following for a comprehensive history of Michael S. Dell. S. A. Forest, & C. Arnst, "The Education of Michael Dell," *Business Week,* March 22, 1993, pp 82–88; A. Alper, "Dell Withdraws $200M Stock Offering," *Computerworld,* March 1, 1993, p 20; M. Fitzgerald, "Dell Trying to Get Back on Track," *Computerworld,* August 23, 1993, p 155.

meet his customers' needs, so Dell again resorted to his creativity, realizing that many dealers often carried a large inventory of hardware, much of which they could not sell. Dell knocked on the doors of these retailers and offered to buy their surplus at cost. He then modified the PCs with graphics cards and hard disks and sold them by direct marketing.

By 1985, the company, with the help of 40 employees, was assembling its own PCs by buying off-the-shelf components. In 1986, he hired E. Lee Walker and made him president and chief operating officer. Whereas Michael Dell was basically a shy person, Walker was an aggressive venture capitalist who had excellent financial and managerial experience. Walker became Dell's mentor and helped him gain the confidence he needed to run the business. This experience was also supplemented with the hiring of Morton H. Meyerson, former president of Electronic Data Systems Corporation, who helped Dell make the jump from a fast-growing medium-sized firm to a mature large one.

In 1988, Dell Computer went public and raised $31.1 million of much needed capital. Dell, however, still retained more than 75 percent ownership of the company. In 1991, his company received the number one ranking by J. D. Power & Associates for customer satisfaction. Although Dell faced some problems in a second public offering that was withdrawn, his firm grew by 126 percent in 1993 with sales of $2 billion, making Dell Computer the fourth largest PC maker in the United States behind IBM, Apple, and Compaq.

The above story reveals an intriguing yet simple marketing approach: Eliminate dealers and distributors and work hard to meet customer needs through quality service. His marketing plan was simple yet aggressive in trying to position the company as a lower priced assemble-to-order direct-response business. This aggressiveness was demonstrated by Dell's use of comparative ads that tossed barbs at Compaq, one of the firm's major competitors. Compaq's subsequent lawsuit that claimed these comparisons were not between similar models led to a settlement in 1991.

Dell's future will not be easy, as other firms begin to follow suit with direct-marketing strategies. Recent problems with product quality in the notebook line plus matching by competitors of price and convenience will represent an important marketing challenge for the company. Compaq recently began a direct-marketing campaign, as have many of the low-priced electronics superstores. The tight money market may also create cash problems for Dell, particularly given that the stock has not rebounded after poor fourth quarter earnings. However, in spite of these factors, Michael Dell seems ready to face the challenge. He insists that the competitors are now playing the game in his ball park and that with his marketing experience in direct marketing the company will continue to grow.

As can be seen from the Dell Computer example, there are many creative alternatives to marketing a product or service. The entrepreneur must assess the needs of the target market, estimate the size of the market, and then implement a strategy that effectively positions the product or service in a competitive environment. The positioning strategy, as described in the marketing section of the business plan, is critical in determining the resources needed to launch the business.

The marketing plan represents a significant element in the business plan for a new venture. Marketing planning should be an annual activity that focuses on implementing decisions related to the marketing-mix variables (product, price, distribution, and promotion). Like the annual budgeting cycle, market planning has also become an annual activity and should be incorporated by all entrepreneurs, regardless of the size or type of the business. These marketing plans must be monitored frequently, especially in the early stages of start-up, in order to determine if the business is "on plan." If not "on plan," changes in the marketing mix or even in the goals and objectives may be warranted.

As part of the business plan, the marketing plan section should focus on strategies for the first three years of the new venture. The first year's goals and strategies will be the most comprehensive, with monthly projections. For years two and three, the entrepreneur will need to project market results based on longer-term strategic goals of the new venture. Each year the entrepreneur should prepare an annual marketing plan before any decisions are made regarding production/manufacturing, personnel changes, or financial resources needed. This process is often referred to as an operational plan, since it contains specific objectives and strategies for short-term results. It becomes the basis for planning other aspects of the business. This chapter will focus on the short-term aspects of the marketing plan, while realizing that the entrepreneur will need to also provide market projections for years two and three as part of the business plan.

Information for developing the marketing plan may necessitate conducting some marketing research. Marketing research involves the gathering of information in order to determine such information as who will buy the product or service, what is the size of the potential market, what price should be charged, the most appropriate distribution channel, and what is the most effective promotion strategy to inform and reach potential customers. The market research that is conducted does not have to be very sophisticated since most entrepreneurs have limited resources. Suggestions on how to conduct market research are discussed below.

MARKET RESEARCH

Information will be very important to the entrepreneur in the early stages of the new venture. There is some evidence to indicate that the use of market information can affect performance; thus, it is necessary for the entrepreneur to consider conducting some level of market research.[2]

Market research begins with a definition of objectives or purpose. This is often the most difficult step since many entrepreneurs lack knowledge or experience in

[2]M. P. Peters & C. Brush, "The Impact of Market Information Scanning Practices on the Performance of New Service and Manufacturing Ventures." 1993 Babson College Entrepreneurial Research Conference, Houston Texas.

marketing and often don't even know what they want to accomplish from a research study. This, however, is the very reason why marketing research can be so meaningful to the entrepreneur.[3]

Step One: Defining the Purpose or Objectives

The most effective way to begin is for the entrepreneur to sit down and make a list of the most glaring gaps in his or her marketing plan. For example, the entrepreneur may think there is a market for his or her product but is not sure who the customer will be or even if the product is appropriate in its present form. Thus, one objective would be to ask people what they think of the product or service and if they would buy it, and to collect some background demographics and attitudes of these individuals. This would satisfy the objective or problem that the entrepreneur defined above. Other objectives may be to determine the following:

- How much potential customers would be willing to pay for the product or service.
- Where potential customers would prefer to purchase the product or service.
- Where the customer would expect to hear about or learn about such a product or service.

Step Two: Gathering Data—Secondary Sources

The most obvious source of information for the entrepreneur is data that already exists, or secondary data. This is usually found in trade magazines, libraries, government agencies, and universities. A search in a library will often reveal published information on the industry, competitors, trends in consumer tastes and preferences, innovations in the market, and even specific information about strategies now being employed by competitors already in the market. Commercial data may also be available but the cost may be prohibitive to the entrepreneur. However, business libraries may subscribe to some of these commercial services. Before considering any additional sources of information, the entrepreneur should exhaust all secondary sources of information.

Step Three: Gathering Information—Primary Sources

Information that is new is primary data. Gathering primary data involves a data collection procedure such as observation, interviewing, focus groups, or experimentation, and a data collection instrument, such as a questionnaire.

Observation is the simplest approach. The entrepreneur might observe potential customers and record some aspect of their buying behavior. Interviewing or

[3]W. R. Dillon, T. J. Madden, & N. H. Firtle, *Essentials of Marketing Research,* (Homewood, IL: Richard D. Irwin, Inc., 1993), p 7.

surveying is the most common approach used to gather market information. It is more expensive than observation but is more likely to generate more meaningful information. Interviews would be conducted in person, by telephone or through the mail. Each of these methods offers advantages and disadvantages to the entrepreneur and should be evaluated accordingly.[4] Table 6–1 provides comparisons of each of these three methods of data collection.

The questionnaire, or data collection instrument, used by the entrepreneur should include questions specifically designed to fulfill one or more of the objectives the entrepreneur listed earlier. Questions should be designed so they are clear and concise, do not bias the respondent, and are easy to answer. Support in the design of questionnaires can often be attained through Small Business Development Centers, members of SCORE, or students in marketing research classes at a local college or university. Since the instrument is important in the research process, it is recommended that the entrepreneur seek assistance if he or she has no experience in designing questionnaires.

Focus groups are a more informal method for gathering more in-depth information. A focus group is a sample of 10 to 12 potential customers, who are invited to participate in a discussion relating to the entrepreneur's research objectives. The focus group will discuss issues in an informal, more open format, enabling the entrepreneur to ascertain certain information. For example, an entrepreneur was recently interested in whether consumers would be willing to sit in front of a computer at a kiosk in a shopping mall and design their own greeting card. A focus group of a cross section of people was formed so the entrepreneur could learn about card buying, pricing, and the public's interest in designing their own cards, including the message. It was found from the focus group that individuals felt uncomfortable sitting in front of a computer in a mall and would not be willing to pay a premium price for such a benefit. This information became important in the marketing plan for this new venture. Focus groups should be led by an experienced monitor or someone other than the entrepreneur. Often this is a good project for students at a college or university in a marketing research class.

Experimentation involves control over specific variables in the research process. Typically, this process would require a laboratory setting where the experimenter could control and investigate the effects of defined variables. But given the needs of most new ventures, this method would not be very appropriate at this point.

Step Four: Analyzing and Interpreting the Results

Depending on the size of the sample, the entrepreneur can either hand tabulate the results or enter them on a computer. In either case, the results should be evaluated and interpreted in response to the research objectives that were specified in the first step of the research process. Often, summarizing the answers to questions will give some preliminary insights. Then data can be cross tabulated in order to provide more

---

[4]Dillon et al., *Essentials of Marketing Research,* pp 152–175.

TABLE 6–1 A Comparison of Survey Methods

	Characteristics of Methods				
Method	*Costs*	*Flexibility*	*Response Rate*	*Speed*	*Depth*
Telephone	Can be inexpensive, depending on telephone distance and length of interview. For local research, probably the least expensive.	Some flexibility possible to clarify or explain questions.	Good response rate possible (possible 80 percent) depending on not-at-homes or refusals.	Fastest method of obtaining information Can contact many respondents in a short period.	Least detail possible because of 8–10 minute time limitation. Also limited open-ended questions.
Mail	Can be very inexpensive, depending on number of units mailed and weight of mailing.	No flexibility since questionnaire self-administered. Instrument needs to be self-explanatory, or data will be invalid.	Poorest response rate since respondent has choice of whether to complete questionnaire.	Slowest method because of time required to mail and wait for respondents to complete questionnaire and then return to researcher.	Some depth possible since respondent completes questionnaire at his or her leisure.
Personal	Most expensive of these techniques. Requires face-to-face contact, which is time-consuming per interview.	Most flexible of all methods because of face-to-face contact. Can also record facial expressions or emotion.	The most effective response rate because of face-to-face contact.	Somewhat slow because of dead time needed for travel between interviews.	Most detail possible because of extensive use of open-ended questions.

focused results. For example, the entrepreneur may want to compare the results to questions by different age groups, sex, occupation, location, and so on. Continuing this fine-tuning can provide valuable insights.

UNDERSTANDING THE MARKETING PLAN

Once the entrepreneur has gathered all the necessary information, he or she can sit down to prepare the marketing plan. The marketing plan, like any other type of plan, may be compared to a road map used to guide a traveler. It is designed to provide answers to three basic questions:[5]

[5]R. D. Hisrich & M. P. Peters, *Marketing Decisions for New and Mature Products,* 2nd ed. (New York, NY: Macmillan, 1991), pp 63–78.

1) *Where have we been?* When used as a stand-alone document (operational plan) this would imply some background on the company, its strengths and weaknesses, some background on the competition, and a discussion of the opportunities and threats in the marketplace. When the marketing plan is integrated as part of the business plan, this segment would focus on some history of the marketplace, marketing strengths and weaknesses of the firm, and market opportunities and threats.
2) *Where do we want to go (short term)?* This question primarily addresses the marketing objectives and goals of the new venture in the next 12 months. In the initial business plan, the objectives and goals often go beyond the first year because of the need to project profits and cash needs for the first three years.
3) *How do we get there?* This question discusses the specific marketing strategy that will be implemented, when it will occur, and who will be responsible for the monitoring of activities. The answers to these questions are generally determined from the marketing research carried out before the planning process is begun. Budgets will also be determined and used in the income and cash flow projections.

Management should understand that the marketing plan is a guide for implementing marketing decision making and not a generalized, superficial document. When entrepreneurs do not take the appropriate time to develop a marketing plan they usually have misunderstood the meaning of the marketing plan and what it can and cannot accomplish. Table 6–2 illustrates some of the things that the marketing plan can and cannot do.

The mere organization of the thinking process involved in preparing a marketing plan can be helpful to the entrepreneur because, to develop the plan, it is necessary to formally document and describe as many marketing details as possible that will be part of the decision process during the next year. This process will enable the entrepreneur to not only understand and recognize the critical issues but to be prepared in the event that any change in the environment occurs.

CHARACTERISTICS OF A MARKETING PLAN

The marketing plan should be designed to meet certain criteria. Some of the important characteristics that must be incorporated in an effective marketing plan are as follows:

- It should provide a strategy for accomplishing the company mission or goal.
- It should be based on facts and valid assumptions. Some of the facts needed are illustrated in Table 6–3.
- It must provide for the use of existing resources. Allocation of all equipment, financial resources, and human resource must be described.
- An appropriate organization must be described to implement the marketing plan.
- It should provide for continuity so that each annual marketing plan can build on it, successfully meeting longer-term goals and objectives.

TABLE 6–2 What Market Planning Can and Cannot Do

Can Do	*Cannot Do*
• It will enhance the firm's ability to integrate all marketing activities so as to maximize efforts toward achieving the corporate goals and objectives.	• It will not provide a crystal ball that will enable management to predict the future with extreme precision.
• It will minimize the effects of surprise from sudden changes in the environment.	• It will not prevent management from making mistakes.
• It establishes a benchmark for all levels of the organization.	• It will not provide guidelines for every major decision. Judgment by management at the appropriate time will still be critical.
• It can enhance management's ability to manage since guidelines and expectations are clearly designated and agreed to by many members of the marketing organization.	• It will not go through the year without some modification as the environment changes.

TABLE 6–3 Facts Needed for Market Planning

- Who are the users, where are they located, how much do they buy, who do they buy from, and why?
- How have promotion and advertising been employed and which approach has been more effective?
- What are the pricing changes in the market, who has initiated these changes, and why?
- What are the market's attitudes concerning competitive products?
- What channels of distribution supply consumers, and how do they function?
- Who are the competitors, where are they located, what advantages/disadvantages do they have?
- What marketing techniques are used by the most successful competitors? By the least successful?
- What are the overall objectives of the company for next year and five years hence?
- What are the company's strengths? Weaknesses?
- What are one's production capabilities by product?

- It should be simple and short. A voluminous plan will be placed in a desk drawer and likely never used. However, the plan should not be so short that details of how to accomplish a goal are excluded.
- The success of the plan may depend on its flexibility. Changes, if necessary, should be incorporated by including "what if" scenarios and appropriate responding strategies.
- It should specify performance criteria that will be monitored and controlled. For example, the entrepreneur may establish an annual performance criterion of 10 percent of market share in a designated geographic area. To attain this goal, certain expectations should be made at given time periods (i.e., at the end of three months we should have a 5 percent share of market). If the goal is not attained, new strategy or performance standards may be established.

It is clear from the preceding discussion that the market plan is not intended to be written and then put aside. It is intended to be a valuable document, referred to often and providing guidelines for the entrepreneur during the next time period.

Since the term *marketing plan* denotes the significance of marketing, it is important to understand the marketing system. The marketing system identifies the major interacting components, both internally and externally to the firm, that enable the firm to successfully provide products and/or services to the marketplace. Figure 6–1 provides a summary of the components that comprise the marketing system.[6]

As can be seen from Figure 6–1, the environment (external and internal) plays a very important role in developing the market plan. Thus, some research on these variables would be a good starting point for the entrepreneur before preparing the market plan. This analysis can begin with data obtained from secondary sources discussed in the marketing research section above. These environmental variables are described below. From these descriptions it is often easy to determine where the data may be found.

ENVIRONMENTAL ANALYSIS

Environmental analysis attempts to give the entrepreneur extensive insight as to the current market conditions as well as the possible impact of external environmental factors that are uncontrollable by the entrepreneur. These variables play an important role in convincing potential investors not only that the entrepreneur is aware of these trends but that he or she considers these factors in projecting sales for the new venture. Some of these environmental variables that describe the industry and or market conditions that could impact the new venture are as follows:

- *Economy*—The entrepreneur should consider trends in GNP, unemployment by geographic area, disposable income, and so on. This data is readily available from government or municipal agencies.

---

[6]P. Kotler & G. Armstrong, *Principles of Marketing,* 6th ed. (Englewood Cliffs: NJ: Prentice-Hall, 1994) pp 66–90.

FIGURE 6–1 The Marketing System

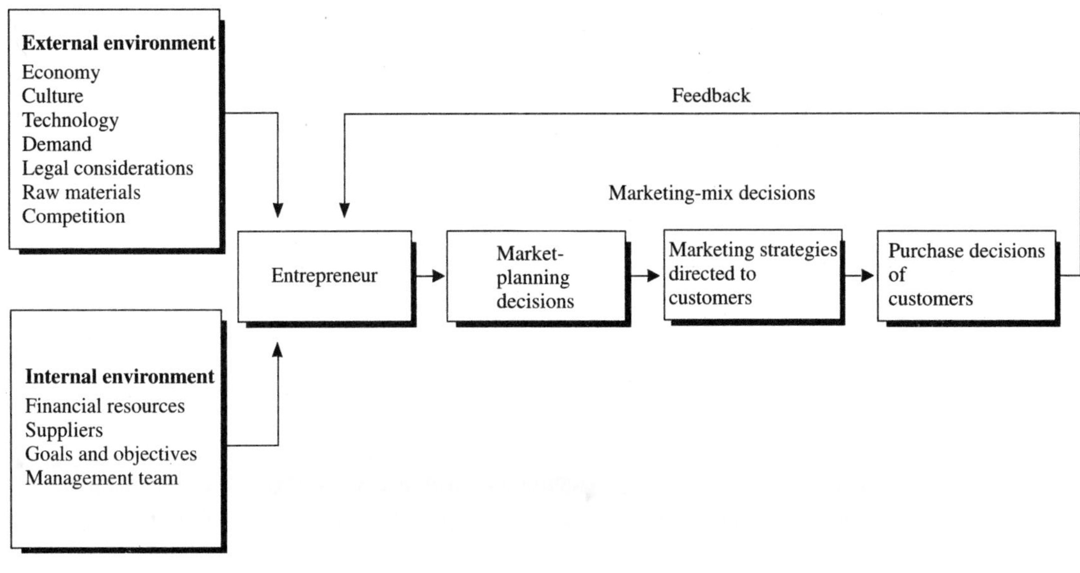

- *Culture*—An evaluation of cultural changes may consider shifts in the population by demographics, for example, the impact of the baby boomers or the growing elderly population. Shifts in attitudes, such as buy American, or trends in safety, health, nutrition, and concern for the environment may all have an impact on the entrepreneur's market plan. This information can also be found in magazines, newspapers, or trade journals.
- *Technology*—Advances in technology are difficult to predict. However, the entrepreneur should consider potential technological developments determined from resources committed by major industries or the U.S. government. Being in a market that is rapidly changing due to technological development will require the entrepreneur to make careful short-term marketing decisions as well as being prepared with contingency plans given any new technological developments that may affect his or her product or service. Often, trade associations and even trade conferences have speakers who discuss this variable.
- *Industry demand*—Demand as it relates to the industry is often available from published sources. Knowledge of whether the market is growing or declining, the number of new competitors, and possible changes in consumer needs are all important issues in trying to ascertain the potential business that might be achieved by the new venture. The demand for the entrepreneur's product or service will require some additional marketing research that will be discussed later in this chapter.

- *Legal concerns*—There are many important legal issues in starting a new venture; they are discussed in Chapter 11. The entrepreneur should be prepared for any future legislation that may affect the product or service, channel of distribution, price, or promotion strategy. New legislation, such as the deregulation of prices, restrictions on media advertising (i.e., ban on cigarette ads, or requirements for advertising to children), and safety regulations affecting the product or packaging are a few examples of legal restrictions that can affect any marketing program. This information will often be monitored in industry journals or by trade associations.
- *Competition*—Most entrepreneurs generally face potential threats from larger corporations. The entrepreneur must be prepared for these threats and should be aware of who the competitors are and what their strengths and weaknesses are so that an effective marketing plan can be implemented. Most competitors should be easily identified from experience, trade journal articles or advertisements, or even the yellow pages.
- *Raw materials*—Some assessment of the availability of raw materials may be necessary in situations where the raw materials are limited or access to suppliers may be difficult. Trends regarding shortages are often published in the trade journals.

All of the above external factors are generally uncontrollable. However, as indicated, an awareness and assessment of these factors using some of the sources identified can provide strong support in developing the appropriate marketing strategy.

In addition to the above factors, there are internal environmental factors that are more controllable by the entrepreneur but can also affect the preparation of the marketing plan and implementation of an effective marketing strategy. Some of the major internal variables are as follows:

- *Financial resources*—The financial plan, discussed in the next chapter, should outline the financial needs for the new venture. Any marketing plan or strategy should consider the availability of financial resources as well as the amount of funds needed to meet the goals and objectives stated in the plan.
- *Management team*—It is extremely important in any organization to make appropriate assignments of responsibilities for the implementation of the marketing plan. In some cases the availability of a certain expertise may be uncontrollable (i.e., a shortage of certain types of technical managers). In any event, the entrepreneur must build an effective management team and assign the responsibilities to implement the marketing plan.
- *Suppliers*—The suppliers used are generally based on a number of factors, such as price, delivery time, quality, management assistance, and so on. In some cases, where raw materials are scarce or there are only a few suppliers of a particular raw material or part, the entrepreneur has little control over the decision. Since the price of supplies, delivery time, and so on are likely to impact many marketing decisions, it is important to incorporate these factors into the marketing plan.

- *Company mission*—As indicated in Chapter 5, every new venture should define the nature of its business. This statement that helps to define the company's mission basically describes the nature of the business and what the entrepreneur hopes to accomplish with that business. This mission statement or business definition will guide the firm through long-term decision making.

THE MARKETING MIX

The above environmental variables will provide much important information in deciding on what will be the most effective marketing strategy to be outlined in the marketing plan. The actual short-term marketing decisions in the marketing plan will consist of four important marketing variables: product or service, pricing, distribution, and promotion. These four factors are referred to as the *marketing mix.* Each variable will be described in detail in the strategy or action plan section of the marketing plan discussed later in this chapter. Although flexibility may be an important consideration, the entrepreneur needs a strong base to provide direction for the day-to-day marketing decisions. Some of the critical decisions in each area are described in Table 6–4.

STEPS IN PREPARING THE MARKETING PLAN

Figure 6–2 illustrates the various stages involved in preparing the marketing plan. Each of these stages, when followed, will complete the necessary information to formally prepare the marketing plan. Each of the steps is outlined and discussed, using examples to assist the reader in fully understanding the necessary information and procedure for preparing the marketing plan.[7]

Defining the Business Situation

The business situation is a review of where the company has been. It responds to the first of the three questions mentioned earlier in this chapter. It also considers many of the factors that were defined in the environmental analysis section above.

To fully respond to this question, the entrepreneur should provide a review of past performance of the product and the company. If this is a new venture, the background will be more personal, describing how the product or service was developed and why (i.e., consumer needs that will be satisfied). If the plan is being written in any subsequent years of the new venture other than pre–start-up, it would contain information on present market conditions and performance of the company's goods and services. Any future opportunities or prospects should also be included in this section of the plan.

---

[7]D. R. Lehmann & R. S. Winer. *Analysis for Marketing Planning,* 2nd ed. (Homewood IL: Richard D. Irwin, 1991), p 7.

TABLE 6–4 Critical Decisions for Marketing Mix

Marketing Mix Variable	*Critical Decisions*
Product	Quality of components or materials, style, features, options, brand name, packaging, sizes, service availability, and warranties
Price	Quality image, list price, quantity, discounts, allowances for quick payment, credit terms, and payment period
Channels of Distribution	Use of wholesalers and/or retailers, type of wholesalers or retailers, how many, length of channel, geographic coverage, inventory, and transportation
Promotion	Media alternatives, message, media budget, role of personal selling, sales promotion, (displays, coupons, etc.), and media interest in publicity

Industry analysis should begin with a review of secondary sources at the library. Trade magazines, government publications, or published articles may be useful in determining how attractive the industry is for the entrepreneur. Information on size of market, growth rate, source and availability of suppliers, threat of innovation or new technology, regulations, new entries, and effects of economic conditions should be documented before the marketing strategy is determined. Video Van, a new start-up venture wants to deliver and pick up videotapes at a price competitive with most video clubs or stores. Thus, this section of the plan would describe the video industry and trends that would support the need for this service.

In this section of the marketing plan, the entrepreneur should also provide a detailed assessment of the competitive environment. Each competitor should be identified, along with their location, size, market share, sales, profits, strengths, and weaknesses. In evaluating such things as their ability to develop new products, management ability, manufacturing capabilities and financial capabilities, these factors could be rated by the entrepreneur as excellent, good, fair, or poor. This analysis will provide evidence for the entrepreneur's marketing strategy.

Defining the Target Market/Opportunities and Threats

From the marketing research done earlier, the entrepreneur should have a good idea of who the customer or the target market will be. This target market will usually represent one or more segments of the entire market. Thus, it is important even before beginning the research to understand what market segmentation is before determining the appropriate target market.

Market segmentation is the process of dividing the market into smaller homogeneous groups. Market segmentation allows the entrepreneur to more effectively

FIGURE 6–2 Sample Flow Chart for a Marketing Plan

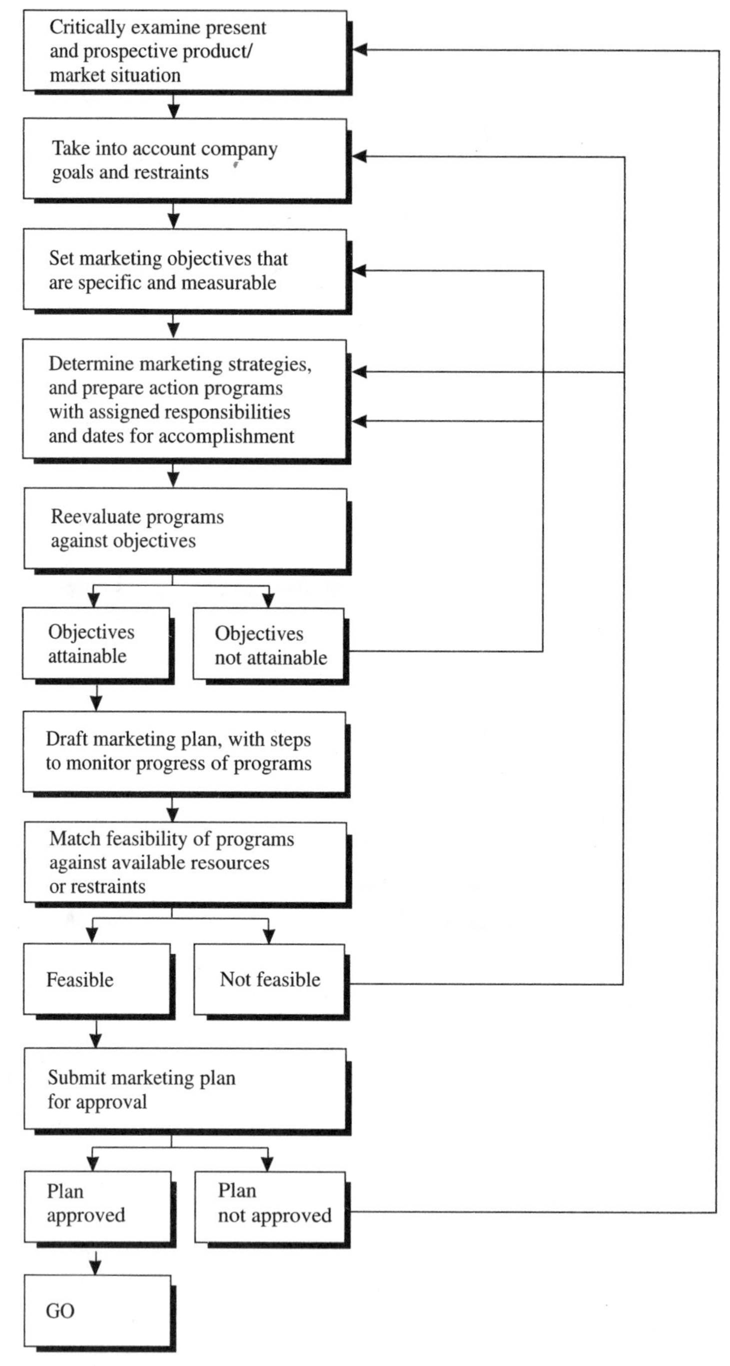

From David S. Hopkins, *The Marketing Plan* (New York: The Conference Board, 1981), p 17.

respond to the needs of more homogeneous consumers. Otherwise, the entrepreneur would have to identify a product or service that would meet the needs of everyone in the marketplace.

Henry Ford's vision was to manufacture a single product (one color, one style, one size, etc.) for the mass market. His Model T was produced in large numbers on assembly lines, enabling the firm to reduce costs through specialization of labor and materials. Although his strategy was unique, any successful mass market strategy employed today would be unlikely.

In 1986, Paul Firestone of Reebok discovered that many consumers who bought running shoes were not athletes. They bought the shoe for comfort and style. Firestone then developed a marketing plan targeted directly to this segment.

The process of segmenting and targeting customers by the entrepreneur should proceed as follows:[8]

1. Decide what general market or industry you wish to pursue.
2. Divide the market into smaller groups based on characteristics of the customer or buying situations. Consumer characteristics could be one or more of the following:
   a) Geography (i.e., state, country, city, region).
   b) Demographics (i.e., age, sex, occupation, education, income, race, etc.).
   c) Psychographic (i.e., personality, lifestyle, etc.).

   Buying situations that might be considered in segmenting the market are as follows:
   a) Desired benefits (i.e., product features).
   b) Usage (i.e., rate of use).
   c) Buying conditions (i.e., time available, product purpose, etc.).
   d) Awareness or buying intention (i.e., familiarity of product, willingness to buy, etc.).
3. Select segment or segments to target.
4. Develop marketing plan integrating product, price, distribution, and promotion.

Let's assume that an entrepreneur has developed a unique liquid cleaner that can clean a restaurant grill at operating temperatures; remove grease from household appliances; clean whitewall tires, bumpers, upholstery, and engines; and clean boats. At least four markets could be identified from its uses: restaurants, households, automobiles, and boats. Each of the markets is then segmented on the basis of the variables discussed above. The entrepreneur finds that in the restaurant market there is little competition, the product's advantages are most evident, and massive marketing resources are not necessary for entry. On this basis, the entrepreneur chooses the restaurant market. This market is then segmented by state, by type of restaurant (i.e.,

---

[8] Kotler and Armstrong, *Principles of Marketing* pp 234–263.

fast-food, family, etc.), and whether the restaurant is part of a hospital, school, company, etc. Each of these segments is evaluated, and the entrepreneur chooses to initially target independent family restaurants in a four-state region.

This market offers the greatest opportunity because no other product exists that can perform grill cleaning at operating temperature and without damage to the grill. The threats in this market include ease of entry and potential imitation by major competitors—in fact, a number of large firms such as Colgate-Palmolive and Procter & Gamble may be interested in the market. However, regardless of the threats, the greatest opportunity is presented in the restaurant grill cleaning segment. This becomes the target market.

Considering Strengths and Weaknesses

It is important for the entrepreneur to consider its strengths and weaknesses in the target market. For example, referring to the liquid grill cleaner, its primary strength in its market is clearly its unique application: It can be used on a hot operating grill with no discernible odor. Other strengths might relate to the fact that the company has experience in the restaurant business and understands the customer.

Weaknesses would relate to the production capacity limited by space and equipment. In addition, the company lacks a strong distribution system for the product and would have to depend on manufacturers' representatives. Lack of cash to support a heavy promotional effort could also be identified as a weakness.

Establishing Goals and Objectives

Before marketing strategy decisions can be outlined, the entrepreneur must establish realistic and specific goals and objectives. These marketing goals and objectives should describe where the company is going and should specify such things as market share, profits, sales (by territory and region), market penetration, number of distributors, awareness level, new product launching, pricing policy, sales promotion, and advertising support.

For example, the entrepreneur of a new frozen diet product may determine the following objectives for the first year: 10 percent market penetration, 60 percent of market sampled, distribution in 75 percent of the market. All of these goals must be considered reasonable and feasible given the business situation described earlier.

All of the above goals were quantifiable and could be measured for control purposes. However, not all goals and objectives must be quantified. It is possible for a firm to establish such goals or objectives as complete research of customer attitudes toward product, set up sales training program, improve packaging, change name of product, or find new distributor. It is a good idea to limit the number of goals or objectives to between six and eight. Too many goals make control and monitoring difficult. Obviously, these goals should represent key areas to ensure marketing success.

Defining Marketing Strategy and Action Programs

Once the marketing goals and objectives are established, the entrepreneur can begin to develop the marketing strategy or action plan to achieve them. These strategy and action decisions respond to the question, How do we get there? As indicated earlier, these decisions reflect on the marketing mix variables. Some of the possible decisions that would be made for each variable are discussed below.

- *Product or Service*—This element of the marketing mix indicates a description of the product or service to be marketed in the new venture. This product or service definition may consider more than the physical characteristics. For example, Dell Computer's product is computers, which is not distinctive from many other existing competitors. What makes the product(s) distinctive is the fact that they are assembled from off-the-shelf components and that they are marketed using direct marketing techniques promising quick delivery and low prices. Thus, the product is more than its physical components. It involves packaging, the brand name, price, warranty, image, service, delivery time, features, and style. When considering market strategy, the entrepreneur will need to consider all or some of these issues, keeping in mind the goal of satisfying customer needs.
- *Pricing*—One of the more difficult decisions in this section of the marketing plan is determining the appropriate price for the product or service. A product with quality, expensive components will require a high price to maintain the proper image. The entrepreneur will also have to consider many other factors, such as costs, discounts, freight, and markups. The problem in estimating price is often associated with the difficult task of estimating costs, since they are often reflected in demand, which in itself is difficult to project. Marketing research can often assist the entrepreneur in determining a reasonable price that consumers would be willing to pay.
- *Distribution*—This factor provides utility to the consumer, that is, it makes a product convenient to purchase. This variable must also be consistent with other marketing mix variables. For example, a high-quality product will not only carry a high price but also should be distributed in outlets with a quality image.

There are many options for the entrepreneur to consider in distributing the product. Issues such as type of channel, number of intermediaries, and location of channel members should be described in this section of the marketing plan. In a new venture, it may be appropriate because of the costs in starting the venture to consider direct mail or telemarketing as a means of distributing the product or service.

The recent success of direct-marketing techniques can be attributed to changes in the American household. The growth in dual income families, the increased interest in time saving, and the acceptance of this method contributed significantly to its success. The percentage of households where there are children under 18 and a working mother has increased from about 25 percent in 1960 to over 64 percent today.[9]

---

[9]E. Kotite, "Who Will Buy?" *Entrepreneur,* February 1991, p 92.

Single men and women have also grown in importance as direct-marketing customers. Marriages are occurring later and single people are achieving successful professional careers that carry with them good salaries and an interest in time-saving ways to shop for such products as clothing, furniture, household accessories, electronics, gifts, and entertainment products, to name a few. Mail order catalog shopping has been one of the fastest growing segments of retailing in the past few years and has led to many successful mail order businesses, such as L.L. Bean, The Sharper Image, J Crew, Victoria's Secret, Lillian Vernon, and Harriet Carter. Each of these catalogs appeals to unique market segments and tries to meet their needs with fast response, good prices, and quality merchandise.

Direct mail marketing is one of the simplest and lowest in entry costs for an entrepreneur to launch.[10] All you need is a good mailing list, a catalog or brochure with products described, and a toll free number for customers. With the growth and expansion in computer technology, mailing lists are not only inexpensive, they can be directed to a very narrowly defined target market. Mailing lists can be easily purchased at very reasonable costs from mailing list brokers, who are listed in the yellow pages.

Direct marketing techniques are not a guarantee for success. The entrepreneur should evaluate all possible options for distribution before making a decision in the marketing plan. Marketing research as well as networking among business associates and friends can often provide helpful insights.

- *Promotion*—It is usually necessary for the entrepreneur to inform potential consumers about the product's availability or to educate the consumer, using advertising media such as print, radio, or television. Usually television is too expensive unless the entrepreneur considers cable television a viable outlet. A local service or retail company such as a pet store may find that using community cable stations is the most cost-effective method to reach customers. Larger markets can be reached using direct mail, trade magazines, or newspapers. The entrepreneur should carefully evaluate each alternative media, considering not just costs but the effectiveness of such media in meeting the market objectives mentioned earlier in the marketing plan.

It is also possible to make use of publicity as a means of introduction to the market. Unique or creative marketing ideas are often of special interest to the media. Local newspapers or trade magazines will often write articles about new start-ups. A public relations strategy that sends news releases to these media can often result in free advertising.[11] Entrepreneurs should consider these outlets in conjunction with any other promotional methods.

All of these marketing mix variables will be described in detail in the marketing strategy or action plan section of the marketing plan. As indicated earlier, it is

---

[10] E. Roman, "More for Your Money," *Inc,* September 1992, pp 113–116.

[11] B. Solomon, "Tricks of the Trade," *Entrepreneur,* November 1993, pp 144–149.

important that the marketing strategy and action programs be specific and detailed enough to guide the entrepreneur through the next year. Examples of a poor and good marketing strategy are as follows:

- Poor strategy—We will increase sales for our product by lowering the price.
- Good strategy—We will increase sales for our product by 6 to 8 percent by (1) lowering the price 10 percent, (2) attending an important trade show in New York City, and (3) conducting a mailing to 5,000 potential customers throughout the United States.

Designating Responsibility for Implementation

Writing the marketing plan is only the beginning of the marketing process. The plan must be implemented effectively in order to meet all of the desired goals and objectives. Someone must take the responsibility for implementing each of the strategy and action decisions made in the marketing plan. Typically, the entrepreneur will assume this responsibility since he or she will be interested in the control and monitoring of the venture.

Budgeting the Marketing Strategy

Effective planning decisions must also consider the costs involved in the implementation of these decisions. If the entrepreneur has followed the procedure of detailing the strategy and action programs to meet the desired goals and objectives, costs should be reasonably clear. If assumptions are necessary, they should be clearly stated so that anyone else who reviews the written marketing plan (i.e., a venture-capital firm) will understand these implications.

This budgeting of marketing action and strategy decisions will also be useful in preparing the financial plan. Details of how to develop a financial plan are discussed in Chapter 7.

Monitoring Progress of Marketing Actions

Generally, monitoring of the plan involves tracking specific results of the marketing effort. Sales data by product, territory, sales rep, and outlet are a few of the specific results that should be monitored. What is monitored is dependent on the specific goals and objectives outlined earlier in the marketing plan. Any "weak" signals from the monitoring process will provide the entrepreneur with the opportunity to redirect or modify the existing marketing effort to allow the firm to achieve its initial goals and objectives.

Table 6–5 summarizes the outline for a typical marketing plan. Variations of this outline will depend on the market and the nature of the product, as well as the general company mission.

Coordination of the Planning Process

For a new venture, the management team must coordinate the planning process. Since many of the members of the team may lack expertise in market planning, this presents problems in its effective completion. In many cases, the entrepreneur may be the only person involved in preparing the market plan, especially if it is a new venture. In this case, coordination may not be an issue. However, the entrepreneur may still lack the understanding and experience for preparing a market plan. In this instance, the entrepreneur should seek help from any available sources, such as the SBA, Small Business Development Centers, universities, marketing consultants, and even textbooks.

Implementation of the Market Plan

The marketing plan is meant to be a commitment by the entrepreneur to a specific strategy. It is not a formality that serves as a superficial document to outside financial supporters or suppliers. It is meant to be a formal vehicle for answering the three questions posed earlier in this chapter and a commitment to make adjustments as needed or dictated by market conditions

CONTINGENCY PLANNING

Generally, the entrepreneur does not have the time to consider many alternative plans of action should the initial plan fail. However, as stated earlier, it is important for the entrepreneur to be flexible and prepared to make adjustments where necessary. It is unlikely that any marketing plan will succeed exactly as planned.

TABLE 6–5 Outline for a Marketing Plan

- Situation Analysis
  - Background
  - Opportunities and threats
  - Strengths and weaknesses
- Objectives and goals
- Marketing strategy and action programs
- Budgets
- Controls

WHY SOME PLANS FAIL

Marketing plans are ineffective or fail in meeting marketing goals for different reasons. In fact, failure may also be considered a matter of degree since some goals may be met and others missed completely. The overall failure of the plan will be judged by management and may depend on the mere solvency of the organization. Some of the reasons for failure can be avoided if the entrepreneur is careful in preparing the marketing plan. Some of the more common reasons for failure that can be controlled are as follows:

- Lack of a real plan—The marketing plan is superficial and lacks detail and substance, especially regarding goals and objectives.
- Lack of an adequate situation analysis—It is invaluable to know where you are and where you have been, before deciding where you want to go. Careful analysis of the environment can result in reasonable goals and objectives.
- Unrealistic goals—This generally results because of a lack of understanding of the situation.
- Unanticipated competitive moves, product deficiencies, and acts of God—With a good situation analysis, as well as an effective monitoring process, competitive decisions can be assessed and predicted with some degree of accuracy. Deficiencies in the product often result from rushing the product to the market. For an act of God such as an oil spill, flood, hurricane, war, and so on, the entrepreneur has no control.

SUMMARY

Marketing planning is a critical element in ensuring the long-term success of any entrepreneurial effort. The marketing plan designates the response to three questions: Where have we been? Where are we going? How do we get there?

To be able to respond effectively to these questions, it is generally necessary for the entrepreneur to conduct some marketing research. This research may involve secondary sources or a primary data collection process. Information from the research will be very important in determining the marketing mix factors or the marketing strategy to be implemented in the marketing plan.

The marketing plan entails a number of major steps. First, it is important to conduct a situation analysis to assess the question "Where have we been?" Market segments must be defined and opportunities identified. This will help the entrepreneur determine a profile of the customer. Goals and objectives must be established. These goals and objectives must be realistic and detailed (quantified if possible). Next, the marketing strategy and action programs must be defined. Again, these should be detailed so that the entrepreneur clearly understands how the venture is going to get where it wants to go.

The marketing strategy section or action plan describes how to achieve the goals and objectives already defined. There may be alternative marketing approaches that could be used to achieve these defined goals. The use of creative strategies such as direct marketing may give the entrepreneur a more effective entry into the market.

The action programs should also be assigned to someone to ensure their implementation. If the plan has been detailed, the entrepreneur should be able to assign some costs and budgets for implementing the marketing plan. During the year, the marketing plan will be monitored in order to discern the success of the action programs. Any "weak" signals will provide the entrepreneur with the opportunity to modify the plan and/or develop a contingency plan.

Careful scrutiny of the marketing plan can enhance its success. However, many plans fail, not because of poor management or poor product, but because the plan was not specific or had inadequate situation analysis, unrealistic goals, or did not anticipate competitive moves, product deficiencies, and acts of God.

QUESTIONS FOR DISCUSSION

1. Although the external environment is considered "uncontrollable," the entrepreneur can prepare him- or herself by conducting an environmental analysis. Explain how this would be done for a manufacturer entering the baby disposable market (i.e., diapers, clothes, bibs, etc.).
2. Marketing research data may be collected from either secondary or primary sources. Discuss the differences in these sources, using specific examples.
3. What are the major characteristics of an effective marketing plan?
4. One of the important elements of the marketing plan is the goals and objectives. Give some examples of goals and objectives that might be in a marketing plan. How would you monitor these goals?
5. Why do some marketing plans fail?

KEY TERMS

marketing system
marketing mix
market plan
target market
marketing goal and objectives
situation analysis

SELECTED READINGS

Huffman, F. (July 1993). Guerilla Guru. *Entrepreneur,* pp 74–79.
Highlights of an interview with Jay Conrad Levinson, the author of *Guerilla Marketing.* His new book focuses on the role of marketing in a new venture.

Lehmann, D. R., & Winer, R. S. (1991). *Analysis for Marketing Planning.* Homewood, IL: Richard D. Irwin Inc.

Covers most of the aspects of the marketing plan in detail. Although in the business plan some of the aspects outlined would be premature for an entrepreneur, the book will be useful as a guide for someone with a limited background in marketing.

Makens, C. (1986). *The Marketing Plan Workbook.* Englewood Cliffs NJ: Prentice-Hall.

Provides a step-by-step procedure for preparing a marketing plan. Ready-to-use worksheets for each market planning function enable the user to identify what information is needed and how to complete every phase of the planning process.

Peters, M. P. (November 1980). The role of planning in the marketing of new products. *Planning Review,* pp 24–7.

Discusses the significance of planning as a means of ensuring the success of a new product. Planning for new products is divided into two catagories: market develoment planning—exploiting existing or new markets—and technological development planning—improving the utilization of the firm's existing scientific and production skills or acquiring new skills.

Roman, E. (September 1992). More for your money. *Inc.,* pp 113–116.

A good how-to article for anyone interested in direct marketing. The author reinforces the need for marketing and a marketing orientation. Direct marketing is reccommended as an alternative, creative way to meet the needs of your customer.

Washer, L. (October 1992). Marketing 101: Finding Your First Customer. *Working Woman,* pp 53–54, 65.

Emphasizes the importance of defining the target market in the marketing plan. Defining the target market is the first step before developing a strategy for tapping that segment.

Welles, E. O. (August 1993). Virtual realities. *Inc.,* pp 50–58.

Paul Farrow, an entrepreneur, describes the creative process he used to market his kayaks. Beginning with market research to determine what the customer wanted, he built a fast growing, single-employee business using strategic alliances and a concentration on marketing value to the customer.

CHAPTER

7

The Financial Plan

Chapter Objectives

1. To understand why positive profits can still result in a negative cash flow.
2. To learn how to prepare monthly pro forma cash flow and income statements for the first year of operation.
3. To understand the preparation of the pro forma balance sheet at the end of the first year of operation.
4. To learn the purpose and preparation of the pro forma sources and applications of funds at the end of the first year.
5. To explain the application and calculation of the break-even point for the new venture.

Scott A. Beck

One of the important characteristics of a successful entrepreneur is the ability to spot or identify an opportunity and then, with effective marketing and financial planning, turn that opportunity into a major financial success. Scott A. Beck, a somewhat shy yet precocious entrepreneur, has been able to achieve this success not once but twice, with Blockbuster Video and more recently with Boston Chicken.[1]

Scott's familiarity with starting a business was homegrown since his father was also a successful entrepreneur who, along with several partners, founded Waste Management Inc. in the 1960s. As a youngster growing up on the south side of Chicago, he worked summers and had many opportunities to talk shop with his father and the partners. Scott always displayed a good business sense and was described as being a real risk taker when it came to financial decisions. In fact, while taking a break from his studies at Southern Methodist University, he visited one of his father's partners and began dabbling in the silver futures.

His love for financial deals seemed to keep him from his college studies, and he didn't graduate until 1989. By that time in his life he had been an independent investment advisor selling real estate limited partnerships and a Merrill Lynch & Co. leveraged buyout fund. Always looking for deals, in 1985 he spotted Blockbuster Video. He persuaded his father to invest and, armed with a comprehensive financial plan, launched franchises in Detroit, Chicago, Minneapolis, and Atlanta. In 1989, the parent company purchased Beck's 104 units for $120 million in stock, and Beck became Blockbuster's vice chairman and chief operating officer.

In 1991, Saad Nadhim, a former franchise partner, spoke to Beck about a new chicken franchise called Boston Chicken. Although not initially enthused, Scott and two other partners finally warmed up to the opportunity and invested about $24 million to take control of the business.

Boston Chicken, founded in 1985, struggled initially because of financial and management weaknesses. The chain had been formed at an opportune time because of the growing concern about nutrition and health. As a more nutritional alternative to fast food burgers or fried chicken the company was viewed by Beck and his

[1]See Richard A. Melcher, "Does Scott Beck have another winning recipe?" *Business Week,* December 13, 1993, p 100; Milford Hewitt, "Boston Chicken Shares Soar on Wings of IPO," *Nation's Restaurant News,* November 22, 1993, p 1, 100; and William Power, "Heard on the Street," *Wall Street Journal,* January 27, 1994, p c2.

partners as a company with a good future. Beck and his team expanded the chain aggressively in large doses rather than one or two units at a time. This strategy put serious drains on cash and required some creative financial planning.

In 1992 with the extensive drain on cash due to the expansion, the company struggled financially, losing $5.8 million on revenues of $8.3 million. However, with continued efforts at expansion (175 units), in 1993 Beck and his partners finally turned a profit of $1.6 million on revenues of $42.5 million. Beck was still not satisfied and felt that it was necessary to raise more money for further expansion through a public offering.

On November 9, 1993, Boston Chicken went public and quickly became the most successful first-day stock price increase of any new issue in any industry over the past two years. The initial public offering price was $20, which by the close of the day had climbed to $48.50. On that day the company sold 1.9 million shares, which was 11 percent of the 16.8 million shares outstanding (mostly held by Beck and other company executives).

Beck and his partners have continued their aggressive expansion strategy and project 450 stores by the end of 1994. Increased competition from KFC and others will make this goal a difficult challenge. In addition, the effect on cash flow and on the balance sheet will be important as they try to meet these optimistic goals.

The financial plan provides the entrepreneur with a complete picture of how much and when funds are coming into the organization, where funds are going, how much cash is available, and the projected financial position of the firm. It provides the short-term basis for budgeting control and helps prevent one of the most common problems for new ventures—lack of cash. Even in the case of Scott Beck's two endeavors described above, financial planning was a critical element in expansion success.

The financial plan must explain to any potential investor how the entrepreneur plans to meet all financial obligations and maintain its liquidity in order to either pay off debt or provide a good return on investment. In general, the financial plan will need three years of projected financial data to satisfy any outside investors. The first year should reflect monthly data.

This chapter discusses each of the major financial items that should be included in the financial plan: pro forma income statements, break-even analysis, pro forma cash flow, pro forma balance sheets, and pro forma sources and applications of funds. Decisions about how to manage and control assets, cash, inventory and so on are discussed as part of Chapter 12 on managing the venture in its early stages of existence.

PRO FORMA INCOME STATEMENTS

The marketing plan discussed in the previous chapter provides an estimate of sales for the next 12 months. Since sales is the major source of revenue and since other operational activities and expenses relate to sales volume, it is usually the first item that must be defined.

Figure 7–1 summarizes all of the profit data during the first year of operations for MPP Plastics. This company makes plastic moldings for such customers as hard goods manufacturers, toy manufacturers, and appliance manufacturers. As can be seen from the pro forma income statement in Figure 7–1, the company begins to earn a profit in the fourth month. Cost of goods sold fluctuates because of the higher costs incurred for materials and labor in order to meet the sales demands in a particular month.

In preparing the pro forma income statement, sales by month must be calculated first. Marketing research, industry sales, and some trial experience might provide the basis for these figures. Forecasting techniques such as survey of buyers' intentions, composite of sales force opinions, expert opinions, or time series may be used to project sales.[2] As would be expected, it will take a while for any new venture to build up sales. The costs for achieving these increases can be disproportionately higher in some months, depending on the given situation in any particular period.

The pro forma income statements also provide projections of all operating expenses for each of the months during the first year. Each of the expenses should be listed and carefully assessed to make sure that any increases in expenses are added in the appropriate month.[3] For example, selling expenses, such as travel, commissions, entertainment and so on, should be expected to increase somewhat as territories are expanded and as new salespeople or representatives are hired by the firm. Selling expenses as a percentage of sales may also be expected to be higher initially since more sales calls will have to be made to generate each sale, particularly when the firm is an unknown.

Salaries and wages for the company should reflect the number of personnel employed as well as their role in the organization (see the organization plan in the next chapter). As new personnel are hired to support the increased business, the costs will need to be included in the pro forma statement. In January, for example, a new secretary is added to the staff. Other increases in salaries and wages may also reflect raises in salary.

The entrepreneur should also consider the need to increase insurance, attend special trade shows, or add space for warehousing. All of these are reflected in the pro forma statement in Figure 7–1. Insurance for liability, medical, and so on is increased in November and again in May. These charges can be determined easily from an insurance company and reflect the status of the operations at that time. In February, an important trade show increases the advertising budget significantly. Any unusual expenses such as the trade show should be flagged and explained at the bottom of the pro forma statement.

In February of the first year, the company incurs additional debt to finance inventory and additional space, which is added in May. Although no charges are reflected in this statement, any additional equipment that will be needed (i.e., new machinery, cars, trucks, etc.) should also be reflected by additional depreciation expenses in the month incurred.

---

[2]Douglas J. Dalrymple and Leonard J. Parsons, *Marketing Management: Strategy and Cases,* 5th ed. (New York: John Wiley & Sons, 1990), pp 241–55.

[3]See E. A. Helfert, *Techniques of Financial Analysis,* 7th ed. (Homewood, IL: Richard D. Irwin, Inc., 1991), pp 135–165.

FIGURE 7–1

MPP PLASTICS, INC.
Pro Forma Income Statement
First Year by Month (000s)

	July	Aug	Sept	Oct	Nov	Dec	Jan	Feb	Mar	Apr	May	June
Sales	40.0	50.0	60.0	80.0	80.0	80.0	90.0	95.0	95.0	100.0	110.0	115.0
Less: cost of goods sold	26.0	34.0	40.0	54.0	50.0	50.0	58.0	61.0	60.0	64.0	72.0	76.0
Gross profit	14.0	16.0	20.0	26.0	30.0	30.0	32.0	34.0	35.0	36.0	38.0	39.0
Operating expenses												
Selling expenses	3.0	4.1	4.6	6.0	6.0	6.0	7.5	7.8	7.8	8.3	9.0	9.5
Advertising	1.5	1.8	1.9	2.5	2.5	2.5	3.0	7.0*	3.0	3.5	4.0	4.5
Salaries and wages	6.5	6.5	6.8	6.8	6.8	6.8	8.0	8.0	8.0	8.3	9.5	10.0
Office supplies	0.6	0.6	0.7	0.8	0.8	0.8	0.9	1.0	1.0	1.2	1.4	1.5
Rent	2.0	2.0	2.0	2.0	2.0	2.0	2.0	2.0	2.0	2.0	3.0	3.0
Utilities	0.3	0.3	0.4	0.4	0.6	0.6	0.7	0.7	0.7	0.8	0.9	1.1
Insurance	0.2	0.2	0.2	0.2	0.3	0.3	0.3	0.3	0.3	0.3	0.6	0.6
Taxes	1.1	1.1	1.2	1.2	1.2	1.2	1.6	1.6	1.6	1.7	1.9	2.0
Interest	1.2	1.2	1.2	1.2	1.2	1.2	1.2	1.5	1.5	1.5	1.5	1.5
Depreciation	3.3	3.3	3.3	3.3	3.3	3.3	3.3	3.3	3.3	3.3	3.3	3.3
Miscellaneous	0.1	0.1	0.1	0.1	0.1	0.1	0.1	0.2	0.2	0.2	0.2	0.2
Total operating expenses	19.8	21.1	22.4	24.5	24.8	24.8	28.6	33.4	29.4	31.1	35.3	37.2
Profit (loss) before taxes	(5.8)	(5.2)	(2.4)	1.5	5.2	5.2	3.4	0.6	5.6	4.9	2.7	1.8
Taxes	0	0	0	0.75	2.6	2.6	1.7	0.3	2.8	2.45	1.35	0.9
Net profit (loss)	(5.8)	(5.2)	(2.4)	0.75	2.6	2.6	1.7	0.3	2.8	2.45	1.35	0.9

*Trade show

In addition to the monthly pro forma income statement for the first year, projections should be made for years 2 and 3. Generally, investors prefer to see three years of income projections. Year 1 totals have already been calculated in Figure 7–1. Figure 7–2 illustrates the yearly totals of income statement items for each of the three years. For the first year, the percent of sales is calculated. This percentage can then be used as a guide in determining the projected expenses for years 2 and 3.

In year 3, the firm expects to significantly increase its profits as compared to the first year. In some instances, the entrepreneur may find that the new venture does not begin to earn a profit until sometime in year 2 or 3. This often depends on the nature of the business and start-up costs. For example, a service-oriented business may take less time to reach a profitable stage than a high-technology company or one that requires a large investment in capital goods and equipment, which will take longer to recover.

In projecting the operating expenses for years 2 and 3, it is helpful to first look at those expenses that will likely remain stable over time. Items like depreciation, utilities, rent, insurance, and interest can be more easily determined if you know the

FIGURE 7–2

MPP PLASTICS, INC.
Pro Forma Income Statement
Three-Year Summary (dollars in thousands)

		Year 1	*Year 2*	*Year 3*
Sales	100%	995.0	1450.0	2250.0
Less: COGS	64.8%	645.0	942.5	1460.0
Gross profit	35.2%	350.0	507.5	790.0
Operating expenses				
Selling expenses	8.0%	79.6	116.0	180.0
Advertising	3.8%	37.7	72.5	90.0
Salaries, wages	9.2%	92.0	134.0	208.0
Supplies	1.1%	11.3	16.5	25.6
Rent	2.6%	26.0	37.9	58.8
Utilities	0.8%	7.5	11.5	16.5
Insurance	0.4%	3.8	4.5	9.5
Taxes	1.8%	17.4	25.4	39.4
Interest	1.6%	15.9	15.5	14.9
Depreciation		39.6	39.6	39.6
Miscellaneous	0.2%	1.7	2.2	2.7
Total operating expenses	33.4%	332.5	475.6	685.0
Profit (loss) before taxes	1.8%	17.5	31.9	105.0
Taxes	0.9%	8.75	15.95	52.5
Net profit (loss)	0.9%	8.75	15.95	52.5

forecasted sales for years 2 and 3. Selling expenses, advertising, salaries and wages, and taxes may be represented as a percentage of the projected net sales. When calculating the projected operating expenses, it is most important to be conservative for initial planning purposes. A reasonable profit that is earned with conservative estimates lends credibility to the potential success of the new venture.

BREAK-EVEN ANALYSIS

In the initial stages of the new venture, it is helpful for the entrepreneur to know when a profit may be achieved. This will provide further insight into the financial potential for the start-up business. Break-even analysis is a useful technique for determining how many units must be sold or how much sales volume must be achieved in order to break even.

We already know from the projections in Figure 7–1 that MPP Plastics will begin to earn a profit in the fourth month. However, this is not the break-even point since the firm has obligations for the remainder of the year that must be met, regardless of

FIGURE 7–3 Determining the Break-Even Formula

By definition, break-even is where	
Total Revenue (TR)	= Total Costs (TC)
(TR)	= Selling Price (SP) × Quantity (Q)
and (TC)	= Total Fixed Costs (TFC)* + Total Variable Costs (TVC)†
Thus: SP × Q = TFC + TVC	
Where TVC	= Variable Costs/Unit (VC/Unit)‡ × Quantity (Q)
Thus SP × Q = TFC + (VC/Unit	= TFC × Q)
(SP × Q) − (VC/Unit × Q)	
Q (SP − VC/Unit)	= TFC
Q	$= \dfrac{\text{TFC}}{\text{SP} - \text{VC/Unit}}$

*Fixed costs are those costs that, without change in present productive capacity, are not affected by changes in volume of output.
†Variable costs are those that are affected in total by changes in volume of output.
‡The variable cost per unit is all those costs attributable to producing one unit. This cost is constant within defined ranges of production.

the number of units sold. These obligations, or fixed costs, must be covered by sales volume in order for a company to break even. Thus, break-even is that volume of sales at which the business will neither make a profit nor incur a loss.

The break-even sales point indicates to the entrepreneur the volume of sales needed to cover total variable and fixed expenses. Sales in excess of the break-even point will result in a profit as long as the selling price remains above the costs necessary to produce each unit (variable cost).[4]

The break-even formula is derived in Figure 7–3 and is given as

$$\text{B/E (Q)} = \frac{\text{TFC}}{\text{SP} - \text{VC/unit (marginal contribution)}}$$

As long as the selling price is greater than the variable costs per unit, some contribution can be made to cover fixed costs. Eventually, these contributions will be sufficient to pay all fixed costs, at which point the firm has reached break-even.

The major weakness in calculating the break-even lies in determining whether a cost is fixed or variable. For new ventures these determinations will require some judgment. However, it is reasonable to expect such costs as depreciation, salaries and wages, rent, and insurance to be fixed. Materials, selling expenses such as commissions, and direct labor are most likely to be variable costs. The variable costs per unit can usually be determined by allocating the direct labor, materials, and other expenses that are incurred with the production of a single unit.

Thus, if we determine that the firm has fixed costs of $250,000, variable costs per unit of $4.50, and a selling price of $10.00, the break-even will be as follows

[4]See Eric Berkowitz, Roger Kerin, and William Rudelius, *Marketing*, 3rd ed. (Homewood IL: Richard D. Irwin, Inc. 1994), pp 366–68.

$$\text{B/E} = \frac{\text{TFC}}{\text{SP} - \text{VC/unit}}$$

$$= \frac{\$250{,}000}{\$10.00 - \$4.50}$$

$$= \frac{250{,}000}{5.50}$$

$$= 45{,}454 \text{ units}$$

Any units beyond 45,454 that are sold by the above firm will result in a profit of $5.50 per unit. Sales below 45,454 units will result in a loss to the firm. In those instances where the firm produces more than one product, break-even may be calculated for each product. Fixed costs would have to be allocated to each product or determined by weighting the costs as a function of the sales projections. Thus, it might be assumed that 40 percent of the sales are for product X; hence, 40 percent of total fixed costs would be allocated to that product. If the entrepreneur feels that a product requires more advertising, overhead, or other fixed costs, this should be included in the calculations.

One of the unique aspects of break-even is that it can be graphically displayed, as in Figure 7–4. In addition, the entrepreneur can try different states of nature (i.e., different selling prices, different fixed costs and/or variable costs) to ascertain the impact on break-even and subsequent profits.

PRO FORMA CASH FLOW

Cash flow is not the same as profit. Profit is the result of subtracting expenses from sales; whereas, cash flow results from the difference between actual cash receipts and cash payments. Cash flows only when actual payments are received or made. Sales may not be regarded as cash because a sale may be incurred but payment may not be made for 30 days. In addition, not all bills are paid immediately. On the other hand, cash payments to reduce the principal on a loan do not constitute a business expense but do constitute a reduction of cash. Also, depreciation on capital assets is an expense, which reduces profits, not a cash outlay.

As stated earlier, one of the major problems that new ventures face is cash flow. On many occasions, profitable firms fail because of lack of cash. Thus, using profit as a measure of success for a new venture may be deceiving if there is a significant negative cash flow.

It is important for the entrepreneur to make monthly projections of cash flow similar to the monthly projections made for profits. The numbers in the cash flow projections are constituted from the pro forma income statement, with modifications made to account for the expected timing of the changes in cash. If disbursements are greater than receipts in any time period, the entrepreneur must either borrow funds or must have cash in a bank account to cover the higher disbursements. Large positive

FIGURE 7–4 Graphic Illustration of Break-Even

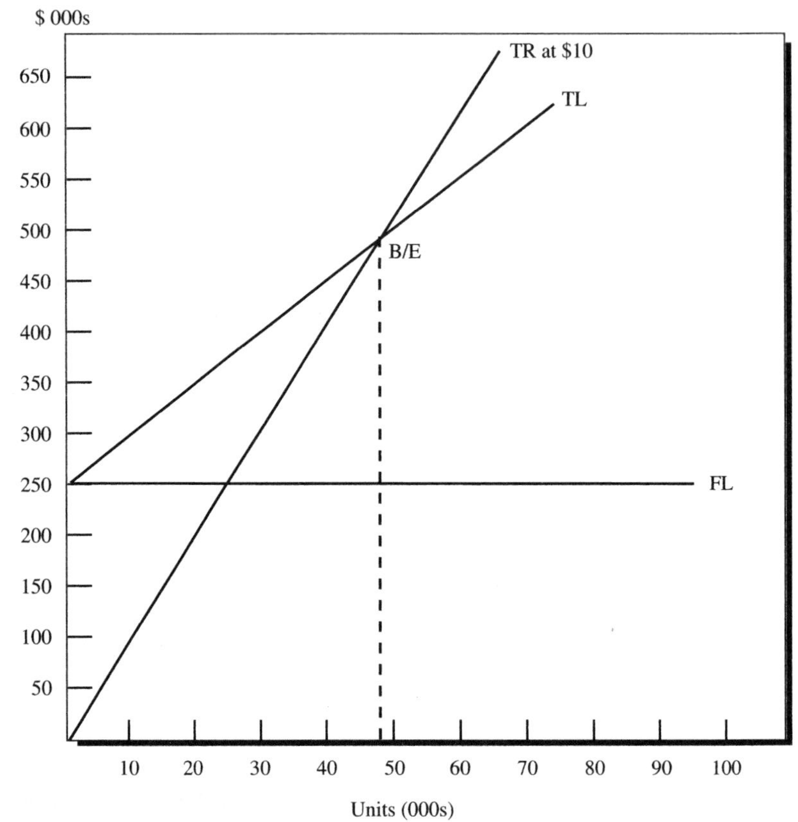

cash flows in any time period may need to be invested in short-term sources or deposited in a bank in order to cover future time periods when disbursements are greater than receipts. Usually the first few months of the start-up will require external cash (debt) in order to cover the cash outlays. As the business succeeds and cash receipts accumulate, the entrepreneur can support negative cash periods.

Figure 7–5 illustrates the pro forma cash flow over the first 12 months for MPP Plastics. As can be seen, there is a negative cash flow based on receipts less disbursements for the first four months of operation. The likelihood of incurring negative cash flows is very high for any new venture, but the amounts and length of time before cash flows become positive will vary, depending on the nature of the business. Chapter 12 discusses how the entrepreneur can manage cash flow in the early years of a new venture. In this chapter, we will focus on how to project cash flow before the venture is launched.

FIGURE 7–5

MPP PLASTICS, INC.
Pro Forma Cash Flow
First Year by Month (000s)

	July	*Aug*	*Sept*	*Oct*	*Nov*	*Dec*	*Jan*	*Feb*	*Mar*	*Apr*	*May*	*June*
Receipts												
Sales	24.0	46.0	56.0	72.0	80.0	80.0	86.0	93.0	95.0	98.0	106.0	113.0
Disbursements												
Equipment	100.0	100.0	40.0	0	0	0	0	0	0	0	0	0
Cost of goods	20.8	32.4	40.8	51.2	50.8	50.0	55.4	61.4	60.2	63.2	70.4	75.2
Selling expenses	1.5	3.55	5.35	5.3	6.0	6.0	6.75	7.65	7.8	8.05	8.55	9.25
Salaries	6.5	6.5	6.8	6.8	6.8	6.8	8.0	8.0	8.0	8.3	9.5	10.0
Advertising	1.5	1.8	1.9	2.5	2.5	2.5	3.0	7.0	3.0	3.5	4.0	4.5
Office supplies	0.3	0.6	0.65	0.75	0.8	0.8	0.85	0.95	1.0	1.1	1.3	1.45
Rent	2.0	2.0	2.0	2.0	2.0	2.0	2.0	2.0	2.0	2.0	3.0	3.0
Utilities	0.3	0.3	0.4	0.4	0.6	0.6	0.7	0.7	0.7	0.8	0.9	1.1
Insurance	0.8	0.8	0.8	0	0.4	0	0	0.5	0	0	0	0
Taxes	0.8	0.8	0.9	1.8	0.9	0.9	2.2	1.3	1.3	2.3	1.5	1.6
Loan principal and interest	2.6	2.6	2.6	2.6	2.6	2.6	2.6	2.9	2.9	2.9	2.9	2.9
Total disbursements	137.1	151.35	112.2	73.35	73.4	72.2	81.5	92.4	86.9	92.15	102.05	109.0
Cash flow	(113.1)	(105.35)	(46.2)	(1.35)	6.6	7.8	4.5	0.6	8.1	5.85	3.95	4.0
Beginning balance	275.0	161.9	56.55	10.35	9.0	15.6	23.4	27.9	28.5	36.6	42.45	46.4
Ending balance	161.9	56.55	10.35	9.0	15.6	23.4	27.9	28.5	36.6	42.45	46.4	50.5

The most difficult problem with projecting cash flows is determining the exact monthly receipts and disbursements. Some assumptions are necessary and should be conservative so that enough funds can be maintained to cover the negative cash months. In this firm, it is anticipated that 60 percent of each month's sales will be received in cash, with the remaining 40 percent paid in the subsequent month. Thus, in August 60 percent of the August sales are received in cash and 40 percent of the July sales, giving a total of $46,000. Similar assumptions can be made for other disbursements. For example, from experience it is expected that 80 percent of the cost of goods will be a cash outlay in the month incurred. The remaining 20 percent is paid in the next month. Additional outlays will be made for materials to maintain an inventory.

Using conservative estimates, cash flows can be determined for each month. These cash flows will also assist the entrepreneur in determining how much money he or she will need to borrow. For this firm, $225,000 was borrowed from a bank and

$50,000 from the personal savings of the two entrepreneurs. By the end of the year, the cash balance reaches $50,400 as sales build up and cash receipts exceed cash disbursements. This cash surplus can be used to repay any debt, be invested in highly liquid assets as a buffer in case of negative cash months, or can be used to purchase any new capital equipment.

It is most important for the entrepreneur to remember that the pro forma cash flow, like the income statement, is based on best estimates. As the venture begins, it may be necessary to revise cash flow projections to ensure that their accuracy will protect the firm from any impending disaster. The estimates or projections should include any assumptions so that potential investors will understand how and from where the numbers were generated.[5]

In the case of both the pro forma income statement and the pro forma cash flow, it is sometimes useful to provide several scenarios, each based on different levels of success of the business. These scenarios and projections serve not only the purpose of generating pro forma income and cash flow statements but, more important, familiarize the entrepreneur with the factors affecting the operations.

PRO FORMA BALANCE SHEET

The entrepreneur should also prepare a projected balance sheet depicting the condition of the business at the end of the first year. The balance sheet will require the use of the pro forma income and cash flow statements to help justify some of the figures.[6]

The pro forma balance sheet reflects the position of the business at the end of the first year. It summarizes the assets, liabilities, and net worth of the entrepreneurs.

Every business transaction affects the balance sheet, but because of the time and expense, as well as need, it is common to prepare balance sheets at periodic intervals (i.e., quarterly or annually). Thus, the balance sheet is a picture of the business at a certain moment and does not cover a period of time.

Figure 7–6 depicts the balance sheet for MPP Plastics. As can be seen, the total assets equal the sum of the liabilities and owner's equity. Each of the categories is explained below:

- *Assets*—These represent everything of value that is owned by the business. Value is not necessarily meant to imply the cost of replacement or what its market value would be but is the actual cost or amount expended for the asset. The assets are categorized as current or fixed. Current assets include cash and anything else that is expected to be converted into cash or consumed in the operation of the business during a period of one year or less. Fixed assets are those that are tangible and will be used over a long period of time.

---

[5]See Clyde P. Stickney, *Financial Statement Analysis: A Strategic Perspective* (New York: Harcourt Brace Jovanovich, 1990), pp 275–90.

[6]Helfert, *Techniques of Financial Analysis,* pp 135–65.

FIGURE 7–6

MPP PLASTICS, INC.
Pro Forma Balance Sheet
End of First Year

Assets		
Current assets		
Cash	$ 50,400	
Accounts receivable	46,000	
Merchandise inventory	10,450	
Supplies	1,200	
Total current assets		$108,050
Fixed assets		
Equipment	240,000	
Less depreciation	39,600	
Total fixed assets		200,400
Total assets		$308,450
Liabilities and Owner's Equity		
Current liabilities		
Accounts payable	$ 23,700	
Current portion of long-term debt	16,800	
Total current liabilities		$ 40,500
Long-term liabilities		
Notes payable		209,200
Total liabilities		249,700
Owner's equity		
C. Peters, capital	25,000	
K. Peters, capital	25,000	
Retained earnings	8,750	
Total owners' equity		58,750
Total liabilities and owner's equity		$308,450

These current assets are often dominated by receivables or money that is owed to the new venture from customers. Management of these receivables is important to the cash flow of the business since the longer it takes for customers to pay their bills the more stress is placed on the cash needs of the venture. A more detailed discussion of management of the receivables is presented in Chapter 12.

- *Liabilities*—These accounts represent everything owed to creditors. Some of these amounts may be due within a year (current liabilities), and others may be long-term debts, such as the loan taken by MPP Plastics to purchase equipment and support cash flow. Although prompt payment of what is owed (Payables) establishes good credit ratings and a good relationship with suppliers, it is often necessary to delay payments of bills in order to more effectively manage cash flow. Ideally, any business owner wants bills to be paid on time by suppliers so that he or she can pay any bills owed on time. Unfortunately, during recessions many firms hold back payment of their bills in order to better manage cash flow. The problem with this strategy is that while the entrepreneur may think that slower payment of bills will generate better cash flow, he or she may find that their customers are thinking the same thing, with the result that no one gains any cash advantage. More discussion of these issues are in Chapter 12.

- *Owner Equity*—This amount represents the excess of all assets over all liabilities. It represents the net worth of the business. The $50,000 that was invested into the business by the two entrepreneurs is included in the owner equity or net worth section of the balance sheet. Any profit from the business will also be included in the net worth as retained earnings. Thus, all revenue increases assets and owner equity, and all expenses decrease owner equity and either increase liabilities or decrease assets.

PRO FORMA SOURCES AND APPLICATIONS OF FUNDS

The pro forma sources and applications of funds statement illustrates the disposition of earnings from operations and from other financing. Its purpose is to show how net income was used to increase assets or to pay off debt.

It is often difficult for the entrepreneur to understand how the net income for the year was disposed of and the effect of the movement of cash through the business. Questions often asked are: Where did the cash come from? How was the cash used? What happened to asset items during the period?

Figure 7–7 shows the pro forma sources and applications of funds for MPP Plastics, Inc., after the first year of operation. Many of the funds were obtained from personal funds or loans. Since, at the end of the first year, a profit was earned, it too would be added to the sources of funds. Depreciation is added back because it does not represent an out-of-pocket expense. Thus, typical sources of funds are from operations, new investments, long-term borrowing, and sale of assets. The major uses or applications of funds are to increase assets, retire long-term liabilities, reduce owner or stockholder's equity, and pay dividends. The sources and applications of funds statement emphasizes the interrelationship of these items to working capital. The statement helps the entrepreneur as well as investors to better understand the financial well-being of the company as well as the effectiveness of the financial management policies of the company.

SUMMARY

Several financial projection techniques were discussed in this chapter. Each of the planning tools is designed to provide the entrepreneur with a clear picture of where funds come from, how they are disbursed, the amount of cash available, and the general financial well-being of the new venture.

FIGURE 7–7

MPP PLASTICS, INC.
Pro Forma Sources and Applications of Cash
End of First Year

Sources of funds		
Mortgage loan	150,000	
Term loan	75,000	
Personal funds	50,000	
Net income from operations	8,750	
Add depreciation	39,600	
Total funds provided		$323,350
Applications of funds		
Purchase of equipment	240,000	
Inventory	10,450	
Loan repayment	16,800	
Total funds expended		267,250
Net increase in working capital		56,100
		$323,350

The pro forma income statement provides a sales estimate in the first year (monthly basis) and projects operating expenses each month. The break-even point can be determined from projected income. This measures the point where total revenue equals total cost.

Cash flow is not the same as profit. It reflects the difference between cash actually received and cash disbursements. Some cash disbursements are not operating expenses (i.e., repayment of loan principal), and likewise some operating expenses are not a cash disbursement (i.e., depreciation expense). Many new ventures fail because of a lack of cash, even when the venture is profitable.

The pro forma balance sheet reflects the condition of the business at the end of a particular period. It summarizes the assets, liabilities, and net worth of the firm.

The pro forma sources and applications of funds help the entrepreneur to understand how the net income for the year was disposed of and the effect of the movement of cash through the business. It emphasizes the interrelationship of assets, liabilities, and stockholder's equity to working capital.

QUESTIONS FOR DISCUSSION

1. What are the major differences between the pro forma income statement and pro forma cash flow?
2. Experience indicates that many new profitable ventures fail. Explain.
3. What is break-even? What assumptions are made in break-even analysis? What is the effect of an increase in selling price on break-even?

4. Explain the purpose of the pro forma balance sheet. How does the balance sheet reflect each transaction made by the business?
5. When should the sources and applications of funds be completed? What is the net increase in working capital?

KEY TERMS

pro forma income	**break-even**
pro forma cash flow	**assets**
pro forma balance sheet	**liabilities**
pro forma sources and applications of funds	**owner's equity**

SELECTED READINGS

Evanson, D. R. (September 1993). Take care. *Entrepreneur,* pp 92–7.

Insurance premiums can be a major cash drain for the new venture. Yet the entrepreneur must have, at minimum, appropriate workers' compensation, liability, and casualty insurance coverage. This article explains how buying wisely can ease any cash drain in the early stages of the new venture.

Frankston, F. M. (January 1981). A simplified approach to financial planning. *Journal of Small Business Management,* pp 7–15.

Most ventures in their financial planning overlook the financial resources plan or projection of the balance sheet at year end. An excellent example is presented starting with the profit plan, cash flow plan, and projected balance sheet.

Jones, S., Cohen, M. B., & Coppola, V. V. (1988). *Coopers & Lybrand Guide to Growing Your Business.* New York: John Wiley & Sons, pp 155–210.

A valuable reference for a start-up venture. One section focuses on financial planning and provides a step-by-step explanation of the issues related to pro forma statements and projections. A case study is used to explain how to prepare these statements.

Kriss, E. (January 1993). How to survive the end of inflation. *Inc.,* pp 66–70.

Financial planning during a no-growth economy can be very difficult. This author believes we are entering a period of deflation and offers planning suggestions on capital expenditures, compensation plans, financing receivables, and long-term contracts.

Laitinen, E. K. (July 1992). Prediction of failure of a newly founded firm. *Journal of Business Venturing,* pp 323–40.

This is a study that looks at financial variables that are likely to contribute to the failure of a new venture. Included are 20 failed and 20 non-failed firms that are analyzed. Specific financial variables and ratios were found to be the best predictors of failure.

Rich, S. R., & Gumpert, D. (January 1987). Closely watched trends. *Inc.,* pp 94–6.

Describes nine key indicators to help the entrepreneur monitor financial activities before they result in serious problems. Problems like cash on hand, rising expenses, lengthening receivables, and so on are discussed.

Sahlman, W. A. The financial perspective: what should entrepreneurs know. in Sahlman, W. A., & Stevenson, H. H. (1992). *The Entrepreneurial Venture.* Boston: Harvard Business School Publications, pp 323–47.

This reading describes financing as a thinking process that involves cash, risk, and value. Fundamental financial conepts are discussed in relation to important decsion making for the entrepreneur.

CHAPTER

8

The Organizational Plan

Chapter Objectives

1. To understand the importance of the management team's ability and commitment to the new venture.
2. To understand the differences in production, sales, and marketing-oriented organizations.
3. To learn how to prepare a job analysis, job description, and job specification.
4. To advise the entrepreneur on the purpose and use of a board of directors or board of advisors.
5. To understand the legal and tax advantages and disadvantages of a proprietorship, partnership, limited liability company, and corporation.
6. To explain the S corporation as an alternative form of incorporation.

Starbucks

Building a strong, lasting organization requires careful planning and strategy. No one knows this better than Howard Schultz. In 1987, he purchased a floundering company, Starbucks, for $250,000 that sold whole coffee beans at retail. In order to transform this business, Schultz initiated an organization plan that focused on a quality work force. His intent at the time of purchase was to build a local business into a national retail company, and to do so he needed loyal employees who took pride in their work and would carry this positive attitude to the customer.[1]

At the core of Schultz's vision was a very generous and comprehensive employee benefits package that included health care, stock options, training, career counseling, and product discounts for all employees full- or part-time. Since most retailers experience high turnover, Schultz focused his plan on low turnover and loyalty. His unique plan was based on the concept that employees would work harder and more intelligently if they had a stake in their success. From 1987 to 1993, Starbucks expanded to 156 stores with about 2,000 employees, averaging $700,000 a week in sales.

From the beginning, Schultz saw the important connection between Starbucks's growth and his ambitious organizational employee benefits plan. With more than half of the employees working 20 hours per week, designing the plan was difficult because of higher insurance and training costs, especially since it was rare for any organization to support its part-time staff to this extent. However, in spite of the extensive range of benefits, the costs only represented one-quarter of the company's labor costs. With 25 hours of classroom training included for every new employee, Starbucks has achieved a lower turnover and higher loyalty.

The plan initially led to a doubling of the company's losses to $1.2 million. By 1991 however, sales increased 84 percent, and the company earned its first profits. For the 1993 fiscal year, the company had sales of $90 million and is expected to grow even more extensively with 90 new stores targeted for 1994.

The organization that Schultz has put into place has also enhanced marketing creativity, with new promotions and products and ways to save money for the company. As Schultz describes it, the unique organization plan with all of the employee

[1]Matt Rothman, "Into the Black," *Inc.*, January 1993, 59–65.

benefits acts as a glue that binds workers to the company, enhancing loyalty and, more importantly, encouraging effective customer service, which over time has contributed to high growth and profits.

DEVELOPING THE MANAGEMENT TEAM

We can see from the Starbucks example the importance of employees, and their loyalty and commitment to the organization. Also significant to potential investors is the management team and its ability and commitment to the new venture. It's clear from the Starbucks example that without the creativity and vision of Schultz, the venture would have likely continued its demise, as was the case under the previous owners.

Investors will usually demand that the management team not attempt to operate the business as a sideline or part-time while employed full-time elsewhere. It is expected that the management team be prepared to operate the business full-time and at a modest salary. It is unacceptable for the entrepreneurs to try to draw a large salary out of the new venture, and investors may perceive any attempt to do so as a lack in psychological commitment to the business.

Generally, the design of the initial organization will be simple. In fact, the entrepreneur may find that he or she performs all of the functions of the organization alone. This is a common problem and a significant reason for many failures. The entrepreneur sometimes thinks that he or she can do everything and is unwilling to give up responsibility to others or even include others in the management team. In most cases when this occurs, the entrepreneur will have difficulty making the transition from a start-up to a growing well-managed business.[2] Regardless of whether there is one or more individuals involved in the start-up, as the work load increases the organizational structure will need to expand to include additional employees with defined roles in the organization. Effective interviewing and hiring procedures will need to be implemented to insure that new employees will effectively grow and mature with the new venture. Personnel issues such as these are discussed in more detail in Chapter 12, which addresses some of the important management decisions in the early stages of an organization's life. A job analysis that may be included in the initial business plan submitted to investors is discussed below.

For many new ventures, predominantly part-time employees may be hired, raising important issues of commitment and loyalty that Schultz was able to successfully overcome with some creativity in his organization. However, regardless of the number of actual personnel involved in running the venture, the organization must identify the major activities required to operate it effectively.

---

[2]Mark Stevens, "Unlocking the Mysteries of Business Survival," *Dun & Bradstreet Reports,* November/December 1990, pp 48–49.

The design of the organization will be the entrepreneur's formal and explicit indication to the members of the organization as to what is expected of them. Typically, these expectations can be grouped into the following five areas:[3]

- *Organization structure*—This defines members' jobs and the communication and relationship these jobs have with each other. These relationships are depicted in an organization chart.
- *Planning, measurement, and evaluation schemes*—All organization activities should reflect the goals and objectives that underlie the venture's existence. The entrepreneur must spell out how these goals will be achieved (plans), how they will be measured, and how they will be evaluated.
- *Rewards*—Members of an organization will require rewards in the form of promotions, bonuses, praise, and so on. The entrepreneur or other key managers will need to be responsible for these rewards.
- *Selection criteria*—The entrepreneur will need to determine a set of guidelines for selecting individuals for each position.
- *Training*—Training, on or off the job, must be specified. This training may be in the form of formal education or learning skills.

The organization's design can be very simple, that is, one in which the entrepreneur performs all of the tasks (usually indicative of start-up) or more complex, in which other employees are hired to perform specific tasks. As the organization becomes larger and more complex, the preceding areas of expectation become more relevant and necessary.

Figure 8–1 illustrates two stages of development in an organization. In Stage 1 in this example, the new venture is operated by basically one person, the entrepreneur. This organizational chart reflects the activities of the firm in production, marketing/sales, and administration. Initially, the entrepreneur may manage all of these functions. At this stage, there is no need for submanagers; the owner deals with everyone involved in the business and all aspects of the operation. In this example, the president manages production, which may be subcontracted; marketing and sales (possible use of agents or reps); and all administrative tasks, such as bookkeeping, purchasing, and shipping. Planning, measurement and evaluation, rewards selection criteria, and training would not yet be critical in the organization.

As the business expands, the organization may be more appropriately described by Stage 2. Here, submanagers are hired to coordinate, organize, and control various aspects of the business. In the example in Figure 8–1, the production manager is responsible for quality control and assembly of the finished product by the subcontractor. The marketing manager develops promotion and advertising strategy and coordinates the efforts of the expanding rep organization. The administrative manager then assumes the responsibility for all administrative tasks in the business operation. Here the elements of measurement, evaluation, rewards, selection, and training become apparent.

---

[3] J. W. Lorsch, "Organization Design: A Situational Perspective," in *Perspectives on Behavior in Organizations,* 2nd ed., eds. J. R. Hackman, E. E. Lawler III, and L. W. Porter (New York: McGraw-Hill, 1983), pp 439–47.

FIGURE 8–1 Stages in Organizational Design

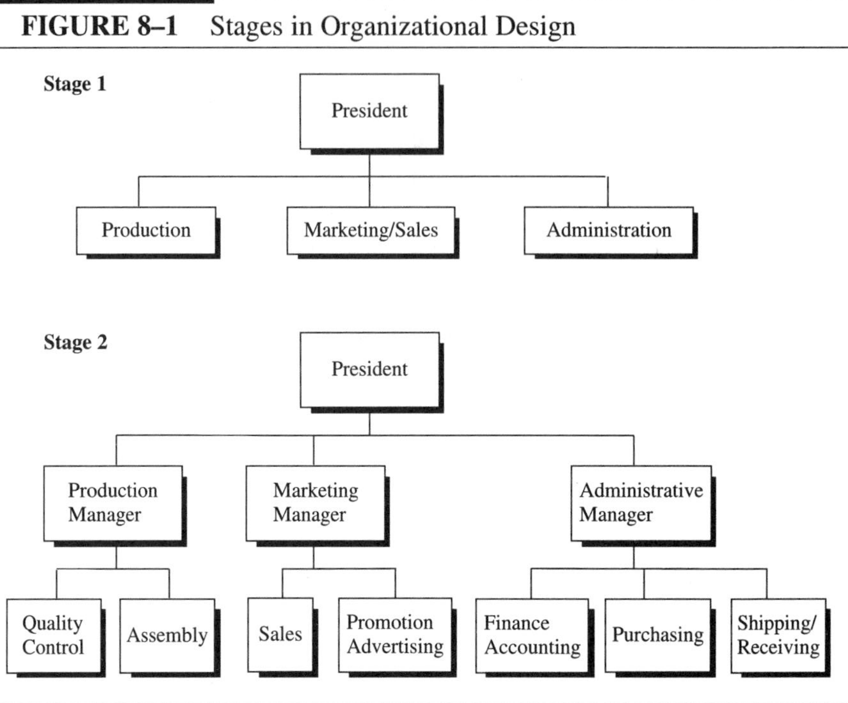

A third stage may exist when the firm achieves a much larger size (i.e., 1,000 employees). The activities below each manager in Stage 2 would then be represented by a third level of managers (i.e., quality control manager).

As the organization evolves, the manager or entrepreneur's decision roles also become critical for an effective organization. As entrepreneur, the manager's primary concern is to adapt to changes in the environment and seek new ideas. When a new idea is found, the entrepreneur will need to initiate development either under his or her own supervision (Stage 1 in Figure 8–1) or by delegating the responsibility to someone else in the organization (Stage 2 in Figure 8–1). In addition to the role of adaptor, the manager will also need to respond to pressures such as an unsatisfied customer, a supplier reneging on a contract, or a key employee threatening to quit. Much of the entrepreneur's time in the start-up will be spent "putting out fires."

Another role for the entrepreneur is that of allocator of resources. The manager must decide who gets what. This involves the delegation of budgets and responsibilities. The allocation of resources can be a very complex and difficult process for the entrepreneur since one decision can significantly affect other decisions. The final decision role is that of negotiator. Negotiations of contracts, salaries, prices of raw materials, and so on are an integral part of the manager's job and since he or she can be the only person with the appropriate authority, it is a necessary area of decision making.[4]

[4]H. Mintzberg, The Manager's Job: Folklore and Fact. In *Perspectives on Behavior in Organizations,* 2nd ed., eds. J. R. Hackman, E. E. Lawler III, and L. W. Porter (New York: McGraw-Hill, 1983), pp 5–15.

MARKETING-ORIENTED ORGANIZATION

Many entrepreneurs lack understanding of the role of marketing in the organization. Because of insufficient knowledge, the entrepreneur often ignores marketing and focuses on manufacturing and sales. The entrepreneur may believe that marketing is selling and that the key objective of the firm is to sell as much product as possible in order to meet income and/or cash flow needs. This philosophy may lead to serious problems in competitive markets where consumers will select those products that are more likely to satisfy their specific needs. The transition of development by a firm into a marketing-oriented organization may evolve as follows:[5]

- *Production orientation*—Here management concentrates on producing as much as possible since they assume that their product is better than that of their competitors and that they can sell all that is produced.
- *Sales orientation*—In this situation, the entrepreneur focuses on sales techniques and hard-sell approaches to persuade the consumer to buy the product.
- *Marketing orientation*—This philosophy focuses on the consumer's needs and wants. Management's objective is to determine these needs and develop and deliver products that will effectively meet them.

The entrepreneur often confuses selling and marketing. Selling focuses on the needs of the seller, and marketing focuses on the needs of the buyer.[6] Figure 8–2 illustrates the organizational structure differences between production, selling, and marketing organizations. In the production orientation organization, there is no marketing activity outlined. In the selling orientation organization, marketing is confused with sales. Any marketing research or promotion is performed by the sales manager. As the firm becomes marketing-oriented, all of the marketing functions, including sales, report to a higher-level marketing manager or vice president.

BUILDING THE SUCCESSFUL ORGANIZATION

Before writing the organization plan, it will be helpful for the entrepreneur to prepare a job analysis. The job analysis will serve as a guide in determining hiring procedures, training, performance appraisals, compensation programs, and job descriptions and specifications. In a very small venture, this process would be simple, but as the size and complexity of the venture change, the process becomes more complex.

The best place to begin the job analysis is with the tasks or jobs that need to be performed to make the venture viable. The entrepreneur should prepare a list of necessary tasks and skills. Once a list is completed, the entrepreneur should

[5]E. Berkowitz, R. Kerin, S. Hartley and W. Rudelius, *Marketing,* 4th ed. (Burr Ridge, IL 1994), p 53.

[6]T. Levitt, "Marketing Myopia," *Harvard Business Review,* July–August 1960, pp 45–56.

FIGURE 8–2 Production, Selling, and Marketing Organizations

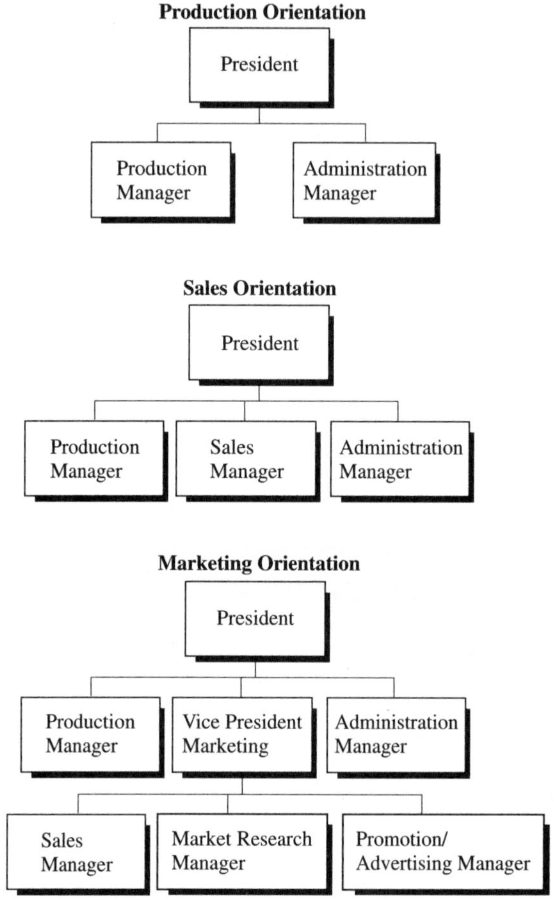

determine how many positions will be necessary to accomplish these needs and what type of person or persons would be ideal. Decisions on where to advertise for employees, how they will be trained, who will train them, how they will be evaluated, and how they will be compensated are important in the early organizational planning for the new venture.

Perhaps the most important issues in the business plan are the job descriptions and specifications, discussed in detail below. Many of the other decisions, such as hiring procedures, training, performance appraisals, benefits, and so on, can be summarized in a personnel manual that does not need to be part of the business plan. However, the entrepreneur should consider these issues and may at some point find

FIGURE 8–3 Example of Job Description

Sales Manager: Responsible for hiring, training, coordinating, and supervising all sales representatives, internal and external to the firm. Monitor sales by territory in the four-state market area. Call on key accounts in market area once every two weeks to provide sales promotion and merchandising support. Prepare annual sales plan for firm, including sales forecasts and goals by territory.

it necessary to hire a consultant to assist him or her in the preparation of such a manual.[7] These topics are discussed in more detail in Chapter 12 regarding the management of a growing organization.

JOB DESCRIPTIONS

The entrepreneur should clarify the roles of employees by preparing job descriptions. These job descriptions should specify the details of the work that is to be performed and any special conditions or skills involved in performing the job.[8] Job descriptions must contain information on what tasks are to be performed, the importance of each task, and the time required for each task. A job description communicates to candidates for employment what will be expected of them. It should be written in clear, direct, simple language. Figure 8–3 is an example of a job description for a sales manager.

It should be noted, however, that the entrepreneur may need to also list necessary behavioral traits in a job description. Dave Weignand, president and founder of Advanced Network Design, a telecommunications firm, begins with the job description that includes the activities needed in the job, but he then itemizes the behaviors necessary to execute those activities. These behaviors can then be incorporated as questions in the interviewing process. For example, a sales manager's position may require him or her to build confidence in others who face rejection from potential clients and have difficulty making appointments. The only way to determine whether someone fits this requirement will be through careful questioning in an interview.[9]

The entrepreneur with no prior experience may find it difficult to write job descriptions. As stated earlier, the most effective method when no direct experience exists is to first outline the needs and objectives of the new venture and then work backward to determine the specific activities that will be needed to achieve these goals and objectives. These activities can then be categorized into areas of responsibility, that is, marketing, production, administration, and so on, and job descriptions may then be prepared. As the venture grows, these job descriptions may be upgraded or modified to meet the goals and objectives of the firm.

---

[7] E. S. Ellman, How to Write a Personnel Manual. *Inc Special Reports,* Stacey Lewis, ed. (1989), pp 66–68.

[8] P. Grant, "What Use is a Job Description?" *Personnel Journal,* February 1988, pp 45-53.

[9] Ellyn E. Spragins, "Hiring Without the Guesswork," *Inc,* February 1992, pp 80–87.

JOB SPECIFICATIONS

Job specifications should also be clear to the potential employee. The skills and abilities needed to perform the job must be outlined, including prior experience and education requirements. For example, the sales manager position in Figure 8–3 may require three to five years of sales experience, a bachelor's degree in business, experience in sales training, management experience, writing skills, and communication skills.

It is also important for the entrepreneur to stipulate how much travel will be necessary and how much effort will be devoted to developing new business. Reporting responsibilities should also be outlined. Will the sales manager report to the vice president, CEO, or some other designated individual in the new venture? All of this information will help prevent conflicts, misunderstandings, and communication breakdowns in the organization. Time spent deciding on these specifications and requirements before hiring will save the entrepreneur from personnel problems in the long run.

THE ROLE OF A BOARD OF DIRECTORS

An entrepreneur may find it necessary in its organization plan to establish a board of directors or board of advisors. The board of directors may serve a number of functions: (1) improving the company's image, (2) developing longer-term marketing plans for expansion, (3) supporting day-to-day activities, or (4) developing a network of information sources for the entrepreneurs. Each function or combination of functions may be a formal part of the organization, with assigned responsibility to the directors depending on the needs of the new venture. A board of advisors would be more loosely tied to the organization and would serve the venture only in an advisory capacity for some of the functions or activities mentioned above.

Although it is most common to see a board of directors appointed after a venture has been launched, there may be provisions to include a board as part of the initial business plan. In this case, the board would represent an important part of the management team and the organization plan when the entrepreneur seeks funding for the new venture. Typically, this board would assist the entrepreneur in day-to-day decision making for either financial remuneration or, more likely, for stock or ownership in the business. Since a board's involvement has been shown to be positively related to financial performance, an entrepreneur can only benefit from its existence.[10]

The external board of directors with diverse backgrounds and expertise can be instrumental in providing objectivity to a new venture. Ideally, the board should consist of five to seven members with limited terms to allow for a continuous infusion

[10]William Q. Judge, Jr., and Carl P. Zeithaml, "Institutional and Strategic Choice Perspectives on Board Involvement in the Strategic Decision Process," *Academy of Management Journal,* October 1992, pp 766–94.

of new ideas from different people. The members of the board would be selected on their basis of willingness to serve, their expertise, and their commitment to supporting the entrepreneur.

Board performance (especially for the board of directors) needs to be regularly evaluated by the entrepreneurs. It's the chair's responsibility to provide an appraisal of each board member. In order to provide this appraisal, the chair (and or founders) should have a written description of the responsibilities and expectations of each member.

As business becomes more involved in global markets, there will be many changes in the governance of a board of directors. It appears that these changes are leading to greater efficiency in the functions of board members as well as greater accountability for its decisions.

In 1992, Wemco Inc., a family owned company, sold an estimated $85 million of neckties, thanks in part to its board of directors. Conflicts and bickering between two brothers had led to loss of business from two of their biggest customers, May Department Stores and Rich's Department Stores. The two brothers agreed on one thing and that was to appoint a board of directors to help govern the business as well as to resolve disputes within the family. The twelve directors, of which eight are not family, have led to a revamping of the organization for specific management functions, with the overall board helping in long-term strategy issues.[11]

LEGAL FORMS OF BUSINESS

There are three basic legal forms of business formation and one new form that is gaining acceptance. The three basic legal forms are (1) proprietorship, (2) partnership, and (3) corporation, with variations particularly in partnerships and corporations. The new form of business formation is the limited liability company, which is now possible in most states. The typical corporation form is known as a C corporation. Figure 8–4 describes the legal factors involved in each of these with the differences in the limited partnership, and S Corporation noted where appropriate. These three basic legal forms of business are compared with regard to ownership, liability, start-up costs, continuity, transferability of interest, capital requirement, management control, distribution of profits, and attractiveness for raising capital. The limited liability company (LLC) is discussed separately after the comparisons of the three basic legal forms of business.

It is very important that the entrepreneur carefully evaluate the pros and cons of the various legal forms of organizing the new venture. This decision must be made prior to the submission of a business plan and request for venture capital.

---

[11] Claire Poole, "Family Ties," *Forbes,* April 26, 1993, pp 124–26.

FIGURE 8–4 Factors in Three Forms of Business Formation

Factors	*Proprietorship*	*Partnership*	*Corporation*
Ownership	Individual	No limitation on number of partners.	No limitation on number of stockholders.
Liability of owners	Individual liable for business liabilities	In general partnership, individuals all liable for business liabilities. In limited partnership, partners are liable for amount of capital contribution.	Amount of capital contribution is limit of shareholder liability.
Costs of starting business	None other than filing fees for trade name	Partnership agreement, legal costs and minor filing fees for trade name. Limited partnership requires more comprehensive agreement, hence higher costs.	Created only by statute. Articles of incorporation, filing fees, taxes, and fees for states in which corporation registers to do business.
Continuity of business	Death dissolves the business	Death or withdrawal of one partner terminates partnership unless partnership agreement stipulates otherwise. In limited partnership, death or withdrawal of one of limited partners has no effect on continuity. Limited partner can withdraw capital after six months after notice is provided.	Greatest form of continuity. Death or withdrawal of owner(s) will not affect legal existence of business.
Transferability of interest	Complete freedom to sell or transfer any part of business	General partner can transfer his/her interest only with consent of all other general partners. Limited partner can sell interest without consent of general partners.	Most flexible. Stockholders can sell or buy stock at will. Some stock transfers may be restricted by agreement. In S Corporation, stock may be transferred only to an individual.

FIGURE 8–4 *(concluded)*

Factors	*Proprietorship*	*Partnership*	*Corporation*
Capital requirements	Capital raised only by loan or increased contribution by proprietor	Loans or new contributions by partners require a change in partnership agreement.	New capital raised by sale of stock or bonds or by borrowing (debt) in name of corporation. In S Corporation, only one class of stock and limited to 35 shareholders.
Management control	Proprietor makes all decisions and can act immediately	All partners have equal control and majority rules. In limited partnership, only the general partners have control of the business.	Majority stockholder(s) have most control from legal point of view. Day-to-day control in hands of management who may or may not be major stockholders.
Distribution of profits and losses	Proprietor responsible and receives all profits and losses.	Depends on partnership agreement and investment by partners.	Shareholders can share in profits by receipt of dividends.
Attractiveness for raising capital	Depends on capability of proprietor and success of business.	Depends on capability of partners and success of business.	With limited liability for owners, more attractive as an investment opportunity.

The evaluation process requires the entrepreneur to determine the priority of each of the factors mentioned in Figure 8–4 as well as the tax factors discussed later in this chapter. These factors will vary in importance, depending on the type of new business.

In addition to these factors, it is also necessary to consider some intangibles. These various types of organizational structures reflect an image to suppliers, existing clients, and prospective customers. For example, suppliers may prefer to deal with profit-making organizations rather than nonprofit companies. This attitude may be reflected in the perceived impressions that nonprofit firms are slow in paying their bills. Customers may sometimes prefer to do business with a corporation. Because of their continuity and ownership advantages, they are sometimes viewed as a more stable type of business. As a customer, it may be desirable to have assurance that the firm will be in business for a long time.

The variations of organizational structure as well as the advantages and disadvantages are numerous and can be quite confusing to the entrepreneur. In the next section of this chapter, some of the confusion is clarified and will assist the entrepreneur in making these important decisions.

Ownership

In the proprietorship, the owner is the individual who starts the business. He or she has full responsibility for the operations. In a partnership, there may be some general partnership owners and some limited partnership owners. In the corporation, ownership is reflected by ownership of shares of stock. Other than the S Corporations, where the maximum number of shareholders is 35, there is no limit as to the number of shareholders who may own stock.

Liability of Owners

This is one of the most critical reasons for establishing a corporation rather than any other form of business. The proprietor and general partners are liable for all aspects of the business. Since the corporation is an entity or legal "person," which is taxable and absorbs liability, the owners are liable only for the amount of their investment. In the case of a proprietorship or regular partnership, no distinction is made between the business entity and the owner(s). Then, to satisfy any outstanding debts of the business, creditors may seize any assets the owners have outside the business.

In a partnership, usually the general partners share the amount of personal liability equally, regardless of their capital contributions, unless there is a specific agreement to the contrary. The only protection for the partners is insurance against liability suits and each putting his or her assets in someone else's name. The government may disallow the latter action if it feels this was done to defraud creditors.

In a limited partnership, the limited partners are liable only for the amount of their capital contributions. This amount, by law, must be registered at a local courthouse, thus making this information public.

Costs of Starting Business

The more complex the organization, the more expensive it is to start. The least expensive is the proprietorship, where the only costs incurred may be for filing for a business or trade name. In a partnership, in addition to filing a trade name, a partnership agreement is needed. This agreement requires legal advice and should explicitly convey all the responsibilities, rights, and duties of the parties involved. A limited partnership may be somewhat more complex than a general partnership because it must comply strictly with statutory requirements.

The corporation can be created only by statute. This generally means that before the corporation may be legally formed, the owners are required to (1) register the name and articles of incorporation and (2) meet the state statutory requirements (some states are more lenient than others). In complying with these requirements, the corporation will likely incur filing fees, an organization tax, and fees for doing business in each state. Legal advice is necessary to meet all the statutory requirements.

Continuity of Business

One of the main concerns of a new venture is what happens if one of the entrepreneurs (or the only entrepreneur) dies or withdraws from the business. Continuity differs significantly for each of the forms of business. In a sole proprietorship, the death of the owner results in the termination of the business. Sole proprietorships are thus not perpetual, and there is no time limit on how long they may exist.

The partnership varies, depending on whether it is a limited or a general partnership and on the partnership agreement. In a limited partnership, the death or withdrawal of a limited partner (who can withdraw capital six months after giving notice to other partners) has no effect on the existence of the partnership. A limited partner may be replaced, depending on the partnership agreement. If a general partner in a limited partnership dies or withdraws, the limited partnership is terminated unless the partnership agreement specifies otherwise, or all partners agree to continue.

In a partnership, the death or withdrawal of one of the partners results in termination of the partnership. However, this rule can be overcome by the partnership agreement. Usually the partnership will buy out the deceased or withdrawn partner's share at a predetermined price based on some appraised value. Another option is that a member of the deceased's family may take over as a partner and share in profits accordingly. Life insurance owned by the partnership is a good solution for protecting the interests of the partnership, along with carefully outlining contingencies in the partnership agreement.

The corporation has the most continuity of all of the forms of business. Death or withdrawal has no impact on the continuation of the business. Only in a closely held corporation, where all the shares are held by a few people, may there be some problems trying to find a market for the shares. Usually, the corporate charter requires that the corporation or the remaining shareholders purchase the shares. In a public corporation this, of course, would not be an issue.

Transferability of Interest

There can be mixed feelings as to whether the transfer of interest in a business is desirable. In some cases, the entrepreneur(s) may prefer to evaluate and assess any new owners prior to giving them a share of the business. On the other hand, it is also desirable to be able to sell one's interest whenever one wishes. Each of the forms of business offers different advantages as to the transferability of interest.

In the sole proprietorship, the entrepreneur has the right to sell or transfer any assets in the business. The limited partnership provides for more flexibility than the partnership regarding transfer of interest. In the limited partnership, the limited partners can sell their interests at any time without consent of the general partners. The person to whom the limited partner sells, however, can have only the same rights as the previous owner. A general partner in either a limited partnership or partnership cannot sell any interest in the business unless there is some provision for doing so in the partnership agreement. Usually the remaining partners will have the right of refusal of any new partner, even if the partnership agreement allows for transfer of interest.

The corporation has the most freedom in terms of selling one's interest in the business. Shareholders may transfer their shares at any time without consent from the other shareholders. The disadvantage of this right is that it can affect the ownership control of a corporation through election of a board of directors. Shareholders' agreements may provide some limitations on the ease of transferring interest, usually by giving the existing shareholders or corporation the option of purchasing the stock at a specific price or at the agreed-on price. Thus, they sometimes can have the right of first refusal. In the S Corporation, the transfer of interest can occur only as long as the buyer is an individual.

Capital Requirements

The need for capital during the early months of the new venture can become one of the most critical factors in keeping a new venture alive. As was discussed in Chapter 7, the lack of cash flow and need for pro formas emphasize the likely need for capital in the early stages of the new venture. The opportunities and ability of the new venture to raise capital will vary, depending on the form of business.

For a proprietorship, any new capital can come only from loans by any number of sources or by additional personal contributions by the entrepreneur. In borrowing money from a bank, the entrepreneur in this form of business may need collateral to support the loan. Often, an entrepreneur will take a second mortgage on his or her home as a source of capital. Any borrowing from an outside investor may require giving up some of the equity in the proprietorship. Whatever the source, the responsibility for payment is in the hands of the entrepreneur, and failure to make payments can result in foreclosure and liquidation of the business. However, even with these risks the proprietorship is not likely to need large sums of money, as might be the case for a partnership or corporation.

In the partnership, loans may be obtained from banks but will likely require a change in the partnership agreement. Additional funds contributed by each of the partners will also require a new partnership agreement. As in the proprietorship, the entrepreneurs are liable for payment of any new bank loans.

In the corporation, new capital can be raised in a number of ways. The alternatives are greater than in any of the legal forms of business. Stock may be sold as either voting or nonvoting. Nonvoting stock will of course protect the power of the existing major stockholders. Bonds may also be sold by the corporation. This alternative would be more difficult for the new venture since a high bond rating will likely occur only after the business has been successful over time. Money may also be borrowed in the name of the corporation. As stated earlier, this protects the personal liability of the entrepreneurs.

Management Control

In any new venture, the entrepreneur(s) will want to retain as much control as possible over the business. Each of the forms of business offers different opportunities and problems as to control and responsibility for making business decisions.

In the proprietorship, the entrepreneur has the most control and flexibility in making business decisions. Since the entrepreneur is the single owner of the venture, he or she will be responsible and have sole authority over all business decisions.

The partnership can present problems over control of business decisions if the partnership agreement is not concise regarding this issue. Usually in a partnership, the majority rules unless the partnership agreement states otherwise. It is most important that the partners are friendly toward one another and that delicate or sensitive decision areas of the business are spelled out in the partnership agreement.

The limited partnership offers a compromise between the partnership and the corporation. In this type of organization, we can see some of the separation of ownership and control. The limited partners in the venture have no control over business decisions. As soon as the limited partner is given some control over business decisions, he or she then assumes personal liability and can no longer be considered a limited partner.

Control of day-to-day business in a corporation is in the hands of management, who may or may not be major stockholders. Control over major long-term decisions, however, may require a vote of the major stockholders. Thus, control is separated based on the types of business decisions. In a new venture, there is a strong likelihood that the entrepreneurs who are major stockholders will be managing the day-to-day activities of the business. As the corporation increases in size, the separation of management and control becomes more probable.

Stockholders in the corporation can indirectly affect the operation of the business by electing someone to the board of directors who reflects their personal business philosophies. These board members, through appointment of top management, then affect the operation and control of the day-to-day management of the business.

Distribution of Profits and Losses

Proprietors receive all distributions of profits from the business. As discussed earlier, they are also personally responsible for all losses. Some of the profits may be used to pay back the entrepreneur for any personal capital contributions that are made to keep the business operating.

In the partnership, the distribution of profits and losses depends on the partnership agreement. It is likely that the sharing of profits and losses will be a function of the partners' investments. However, this can vary, depending on the agreement. As in the proprietorship, the partners may assume liability. The limited partnership provides an alternative that protects against personal liability but may reduce shares of any profits.

Corporations distribute profits through dividends to stockholders. These distributions are not likely to absorb all of the profits that may be retained by the corporation for future investment or capital needs of the business. Losses by the corporation will often result in no dividends. These losses will then be covered by retained earnings or through other financial means discussed earlier.

Attractiveness for Raising Capital

In both the proprietorship and the partnership, the ability of the entrepreneurs to raise capital depends on the success of the business and the personal capability of the entrepreneur. These two forms are the least attractive for raising capital, primarily because of the problem of personal liability. Any large amounts of capital needed in these forms of business should be given serious consideration.

The corporation, because of its advantages regarding personal liability, is the most attractive form of business for raising capital. Shares of stock, bonds, and/or debt are all opportunities for raising capital with limited liability. The more attractive the corporation, the easier it will be to raise capital.

TAX ATTRIBUTES OF FORMS OF BUSINESS

The tax advantages and disadvantages of each of the forms of business differ significantly. Some of the major differences are discussed below. There are many minor differences that, in total, can be important to the entrepreneur. If the entrepreneur has any doubt about these advantages, he or she should get outside advice. Figure 8–5 provides a summary of some of the major tax advantages of these forms of business. These are discussed further below.

Tax Issues for Proprietorship

For the proprietorship, the IRS treats the business as the individual owner. All income appears on the owner's return as personal income. Thus, the proprietorship is not regarded by the IRS as a separate tax entity. As can be seen in Figure 8–5, this treatment of taxes affects the taxable year, distribution of profits to owners, organization costs, capital gains, capital losses, and medical benefits. Each of these is treated as if it is incurred by the individual owner and not the business.

The proprietorship has some tax advantages when compared to the corporation. First, there is no double tax when profits are distributed to the owner. Another advantage is that there is no capital stock tax or penalty for retained earnings in the business. Again, these advantages exist because the proprietorship is not recognized as a separate tax entity; all profits and losses are a part of the entrepreneur's tax return.

FIGURE 8–5 Tax Attributes of Various Legal Forms of Business

Attributes	*Proprietorship*	*Partnership*	*Corporation*
Taxable year	Usually a calendar year.	Usually calendar year, but other dates may be used.	Any year end can be used at beginning. Any changes require changes in incorporation.
Distribution of profits to owners	All income appears on owner's return.	Partnership agreement may have special allocation of income. Partners pay tax on their pro rata shares of income on individual return even if income not immediately distributed.	No income is allocated to stockholders.
Organization costs	Not amortizable.	Amortizable over 60 months.	Amortizable over 60 months.
Dividends received	$100 dividend exclusion for single return and $200 on joint return.	Dividend exclusion of partnership passes to partner (conduit).	80% or more of dividend received may be deducted (after 12/31/86).
Capital gains	Taxed at individual level. A deduction is allowed for long-term capital gains.	Capital gain to partnership will be taxed as a capital gain to the partner (conduit).	Taxed at corporate level. After July 1, 1987 the maximum rate will be 34%.
Capital losses	Carried forward indefinitely.	Capital losses can be used to offset other income. Carried forward indefinitely (conduit).	Carry back three years and carry over five years as short-term capital loss offsetting only capital gains.
Initial organization	Commencement of business results in no additional tax for individual.	Contributions of property to a partnership not taxed.	Acquisition of stock for cash entails no immediate taxes. Transfer of property in exchange for stock may be taxable if stock value greater than contributed property.
Limitations on losses deductible by owners	Amount at risk may be deducted except for real estate activities.	Partnership investment plus share of recourse liability if any. At-risk rules may apply except for real estate partnership.	No losses allowed except on sale of stock or liquidation of corporation. In S Corporation, shareholders' investment to corporation is deductible.

FIGURE 8–5 *(concluded)*

Attributes	*Proprietorship*	*Partnership*	*Corporation*
Medical benefits	Itemized deductions for medical expenses in excess of percentage of adjusted gross income on individual's return. No deduction for insurance premium.	Cost of partners' benefits not deductible to business as an expense. Possible deduction at partner level.	Cost of employee-shareholder coverage deductible as business expense if designed for benefit of employee.
Retirement benefits	Limitations and restrictions basically same as regular corporations.	Same as for corporations.	Limitations on benefits from defined benefit plans—lesser of $90,000 or 100% of compensation. Limitations on contributions to defined contribution plans—lesser of $30,000 or 25% of compensation (15% of aggregate for profit-sharing plans).

Tax Issues for Partnership

The partnership's tax advantages and disadvantages are very similar to those of the proprietorship, especially regarding income distributions, dividends, and capital gains and losses. Limited partnerships can provide some unique tax advantages since the limited partner can share in the profits without being responsible for any liability beyond his or her investment.

Both the partnership and proprietorship are organizational forms that serve as nontaxable conduits of income and deductions. These forms of business do have a legal identity distinct from the partners or owners, but this identity is only for accounting reporting.

It is especially important for partnerships to report income since this serves as the basis for determining the share of each partner. The income is distributed based on the partnership agreement. The owners then report their share as personal income and pay taxes based on this amount.

Tax Issues for Corporation

Since the corporation is recognized by the IRS as a separate tax entity, it has the advantage of being able to take many deductions and expenses that are not available to the proprietorship or partnership. The disadvantage is that the distribution of dividends is taxed twice, as income of the corporation and as income of the stockholder.

This double taxation can be avoided if the income is distributed to the entrepreneur(s) in the form of salary. Bonuses, incentives, profit sharing, and so on, are thus allowable ways to distribute income of the corporation as long as the compensation is reasonable in amount and payment was for services rendered.

The corporate tax may be lower than the individual rate; although, with the new tax laws effective in 1987, these advantages may be lessened. The entrepreneur is best advised to consider the tax pros and cons and to decide on that basis. Projected earnings may be used to calculate the actual taxes under each form of business in order to identify the one that provides the best tax advantage. Remember, tax advantages should be balanced by liability responsibility in the respective form of business.

S CORPORATION

The S Corporation combines the tax advantages of the partnership and the corporation. It is designed so that venture income is declared as personal income on a pro rata basis by the shareholders. In fact, the shareholders benefit from all of the income and the deductions of the business. In order to be an S Corporation, the venture must meet the following qualifications:[12]

- Must be a domestic corporation.
- Cannot be a subsidiary of another corporation.
- Can have only one class of stock.
- Must have 35 shareholders or less.
- Shareholders must be individuals, estates, or certain types of trusts.
- No shareholder can be an alien.

If all of the above requirements are met, then a corporation may elect S Corporation status. This election must have the unanimous consent of the shareholders. If the election of an S Corporation is made during the year, any shareholders prior to the election in that year who have surrendered their shares must also consent to the S Corporation status. This rule is designed to prevent gains or losses in that taxable year from being allocated to nonconsenting shareholders. If the decision to elect S Corporation status is made after the 15th of the third month of the taxable year, it does not become effective until the following taxable year.

Advantages of an S Corporation

The S Corporation offers the entrepreneur some distinct advantages over the typical corporation, or C corporation. However, there are also disadvantages.[13] In those instances when the disadvantages are great, the entrepreneur should elect C corporation form. Some of the advantages of the S Corporation are as follows:

[12] S. Jones, M. B. Cohen, & V. V. Coppola, *Growing Your Business* (New York: John Wiley & Sons, 1988), pp 106–12.

[13] I. L. Blackman, "Pro's and Con's of S Corporations." *National Petroleum News,* November 1988, p 72.

- Capital gains or losses from the corporation are treated as personal income or losses by the shareholders on a pro rata basis (determined by number of shares of stock held). The corporation is thus not taxed.
- Shareholders retain limited liability protection of C Corporation.
- It is not subject to a minimum tax, as is the C Corporation.
- Stock may be transferred to low-income-bracket family members (children must be 14 years or over).
- Stock may be voting or nonvoting.
- This form of business may use the cash method of accounting.
- Corporate long-term capital gains and losses are deductible directly by the shareholders to offset other personal capital gains or losses.

Disadvantages of an S Corporation

Although the advantages appear to be favorable for the entrepreneur, this form of business is not appropriate for everyone. The disadvantages of the S Corporation are as follows:

- There are stringent requirements to qualify for this form of business.
- If the corporation earns less than $100,000, then the C Corporation would have a lower tax.
- The S Corporation may not deduct most fringe benefits for shareholders.
- The S Corporation must adopt a calendar year for tax purposes.
- Only one class of stock is permitted for this form of business (common stock).
- The net loss of the S Corporation is limited to the shareholder's stock plus loans to the business.

The Tax Reform Act of 1986 added some provisions that affect the allocation of stock to lower-tax-bracket family members and the disposition of assets sold within a 10-year period after the election of an S Corporation. With the new tax laws and changing rates, owners need to compare alternative forms before election. This should be done with the advice of a tax attorney, since once a decision is made, it is difficult to change again.

State laws regarding the S Corporation vary from state to state. This inconsistency reinforces the need to review all options carefully before deciding on the corporate form.

THE LIMITED LIABILITY COMPANY

Until recently, the recognized forms of business organization were proprietorships, partnerships (general or limited), and corporations (C or S). A new entity is the limited liability company (LLC), which can offer similar advantages as the S Corporation but with more liberal tax rules under Subchapter K.[14] This business form is a partnership-corporation hybrid that has the following distinctive characteristics:

- Whereas the corporation has shareholders and partnerships have partners, the LLC has members.
- No shares of stock are issued, and each member owns an interest in the business as designated by the articles of organization, which is similar to the articles of incorporation or certificates of partnership.
- Liability does not extend beyond the member's capital contribution to the business. Thus, there is no unlimited liability, which can be detrimental in a proprietorship or general partnership.
- Members may transfer their interest only with the unanimous written consent of the remaining members.
- The standard acceptable term of an LLC is 30 years. Dissolution is also likely when one of the members dies, the business goes bankrupt, or all members choose to dissolve the business.

Based on the above characteristics, it appears that the LLC is similar to an S Corporation. There are, however, major distinctions, particularly related to eligibility restrictions. Entrepreneurs should consult an attorney before making a final decision. Differences with the limited partnership are mainly a result of the fact that the limited partnership must have at least one general partner who has unlimited liability for partnership debts. In the LLC, every member has limited liability.

The growth and acceptability of the LLC will depend on how many states enact LLC statutes and, of course, whether the Federal Government decides to place restrictions on eligibility for such an organization.

THE ORGANIZATION AND USE OF ADVISORS

The entrepreneur will usually need to use outside advisors, such as accountants, bankers, lawyers, advertising agencies, and market researchers. These advisors can become an important part of the organization and thus will need to be managed just like any other permanent part of it.

The relationship of the entrepreneur and outside advisors can be enhanced by seeking out the best advisors and involving them thoroughly and at an early stage. Advisors should be assessed or interviewed just as if they were being hired for a permanent position. References should be checked and questions asked to ascertain the quality of service as well as compatibility with the management team.[15]

---

[14] L. Witner & K. Simons, "Tax Aspects of Limited Liability Companies," *The CPA Journal,* August 1993, pp 22–32.

[15] H. H. Stevenson & W. A. Sahlman, "How Small Companies Should Handle Advisors," *Harvard Business Review,* March–April 1988, pp 28–34.

Hiring and managing outside experts can be effectively accomplished by considering these advisors as advice suppliers. Just as no manager would buy raw materials or supplies without knowledge of their cost and quality, the same approval can be used for advisors. Entrepreneurs should ask these advisors about fees, credentials, references, and so on before hiring them.

Even after the advisors have been hired, the entrepreneur should question their advice. Why is the advice being given? Make sure you understand the decision and its potential implications. There are many good sources of advisors, such as the SBA, other small businesses, chambers of commerce, universities, friends, and relatives. Careful evaluation of the entrepreneur's needs and the competency of the advisor can make advisors a valuable asset to the organization of a new venture.

SUMMARY

The organization plan for the entrepreneur requires some major decisions that could affect long-term effectiveness and profitability. It is important to begin the new venture with a strong management team that is committed to the goals of the new venture. The management team must be able to work together effectively toward these ends. With pressures from competition, it is important to have an effective organization with clearly defined roles and job descriptions. Decisions are needed on hiring procedures, training, supervising, compensation, evaluation of performance, and so on.

A board of directors or board of advisors can provide important management support for the entrepreneurs in starting and managing the new venture. It may be appropriate to include a board in the initial business plan in order to enhance the credibility of the entrepreneurs as well as provide valuable expertise. Selecting the board should be done carefully, with the intent to select members that will take their roles seriously and provide the kind of support welcomed and necessary during the critical start-up and early stages of the new venture.

Once the structure and roles of the members of the organization are defined, the entrepreneur(s) must decide on the legal form of business. The three major legal forms of business are the proprietorship, partnership, and corporation. Each differs significantly and should be evaluated carefully before a decision is made. This chapter provides considerable insight and comparisons regarding these forms of business to assist the entrepreneur in this decision.

The S corporation and the limited liability company are alternative forms of a business that are gaining popularity. Each of these allows the entrepreneur to retain the protection from personal liability provided by a corporation but retain the tax advantages of a partnership. There are important advantages as well as disadvantages of these forms of business, and entrepreneurs should carefully weigh both before deciding.

Advisors will also be necessary in the new venture. Outside advisors should be evaluated as if they were to be hired as permanent members of the organization. Information on their fees and referrals can help determine the best choices.

QUESTIONS FOR DISCUSSION

1. What role does the management team play in the assessment and evaluation of the new venture by potential investors? What criteria are used by the investors to evaluate the new venture?
2. The new venture is likely, over time, to develop into a larger organization that will require major changes in the organizational structure. Describe these changes. What effect does marketing orientation, as opposed to a sales or production orientation, have on the new venture's organization?
3. What are some of the key advantages of the limited partnership over the partnership form of organization?
4. What effect does death or sale of one's interest by an entrepreneur have on each of the three major forms of business?
5. What is meant by the statement that the proprietorship and partnership are nontaxable conduits of income and deductions? How does this differ from the corporation?
6. What is an S corporation and how does it differ from a regular corporation?

KEY TERMS

C corporation
corporation
job descriptions
job specifications
marketing-oriented organization
proprietorship
partnership
S corporation

SELECTED READINGS

Barrett W. (June 21, 1993). Ozzie & Harriet, L.P. *Forbes,* pp 196–97.
To many entrepreneurs, the limited partnership are gaining popularity as an attractive way to run a family business. H & H Bagels, with annual sales of $5.5 million, has a unique organization with the founder as a general partner and members of the family as limited partners to protect their liability. The founder has, however, created a wholly owned corporation to serve as the general partner, thus protecting the founder's personal assets.

Dun & Bradstreet, Inc. (1989). *The Challenges of Managing a Small Business.*
Provides an interesting overview of many of the important issues an entrepreneur will face in organizing and managing the new venture. Ten challenges are discussed, including knowing your business, managing people, and coping with regulations and paperwork.

Grant, P. C. (February 1988). What use is a job description? *Personnel Journal,* pp 45–53.
Job descriptions are the building blocks to a successful new venture organization. This article provides some important insight as to why the job description is important and how

to write one. Discusses the importance of the job analysis, which should be implemented on a regular basis once the new venture has become established.

Hanks, S. H. (February 1990). The organization life cycle: Integrating content and process. *Journal of Small Business Strategy,* pp 1–11.

As the venture evolves, it moves through life-cycle stages, which results in differing problems. This article summarizes the critical issues and strategies an entrepreneur will face in trying to develop an effective organization.

Hyatt, J. (March 1990). How to hire employees. *Inc.,* pp 106–8.

Thomas Melohn, president and co-owner of North American Tool & Die Inc., shares his hiring process, which has cut turnover from 27 percent to less than 4 percent and virtually eliminated absenteeism. His process is based on the importance of first establishing a set of values and then finding people that have these values.

O'Connell, F. J. (January 1991). Boosting your benefits. *Entrepreneur,* pp 26–28.

A very practical discussion of legal and tax issues related to benefits that may be offered to employees. Includes a brief discussion of medical insurance, group-term life insurance, disability insurance, employee assistance programs, and retirement plans.

Witner, L., and K. Simons. (August 1993). Tax aspects of limited liability companies. *The CPA Journal,* pp 22–32.

This article provides a good summary of the pros and cons of a limited liability company by comparing it with other forms of business. Discussed are the implications of formation, tax regulations, limited liability, continuity of life, transfer of ownership, and centralized management. Also identified are the states with existing statues that presently allow an LLC and those with pending legislation.

Voice Concepts

DESCRIPTION OF COMPANY

Voice Concepts is a new company, formed to market and sell the "talking chip," or message maker. The organization is a partnership consisting of two businesspeople from Washington D.C. (Tom and Christa Tonis) and two from New Hampshire (Paul and Kim Russo). All believe that their knowledge of and experience in the retail market will pave the way for the message maker to be successful and profitable in the United States.

Omega Products of America is a subsidiary of a Japanese manufacturer. This product was their second attempt at the U.S. market. The first product was a chip that was used in music cards and books. This product met with great price resistance amongst distributors and was eventually dropped. So with a new technology and a strategy of finding an exclusive marketing and distribution partner, Omega was set to embark on its second market entry.

Omega's objective was to sell the machine and the chips to someone like Voice Concepts who would take the marketing responsibility for the product. Voice Concepts, in return, was interested in exclusive rights to the U.S. market. Both, of course, also needed to consider potential profits and risks. Final specification of the contract was still in negotiation. The founders of Voice Concepts all felt that a lease arrangement for the machines, with a purchase option, would be the most acceptable strategy to the retailer. The Russos had in fact conducted some preliminary research and found that for similarly priced products a lease for $500 per year would be acceptable. After the first year, the retailer would have the option of purchasing the machine for $800 and after the second year for $350. They believed that Omega might even be willing to drop their prices on the machines by another 20 percent if the Tonises and Russos could convince them there was a good market opportunity here, especially for the chips, which were the most important element in the business operation.

PRODUCT

The product is a combination of a machine and a computer chip that records an individual's voice message. Once the message is recorded on the chip, it can be inserted into a blank greeting card. When the chip is pressed by the receiver of the card it is activated to play back the recorded message an extended number of times.

There is an enhanced value to the "talking chip" over prerecorded or written messages because it can be personalized. It is believed that people will pay more for the card because it is an extension of themselves; it contains their voice and emotion expressed in their language. A Polaroid photo option is going to be combined with the "talking chip" to further personalize the card if the customer desires. Retail prices are set at $10 for the "talking chip" card and $15 for the "talking chip" photo card.

After exploring many different applications and uses for its "talking chip," the company believes that the retail market will be the most successful for the product introduction. Although Voice Concepts feels it should target the souvenir and novelty item segments of the retail market initially, it also believes there are many other possible applications for this product. This market, which includes all age groups, will be reached by the use of kiosks in tourist areas such as Fanueil Hall in Boston, theme parks such as Walt Disney World in Orlando, and large shopping malls.

SOUVENIR/NOVELTY INDUSTRY

The souvenir and novelty industry is a highly fragmented market that is experiencing rapid growth. The exact size of this market is difficult to ascertain since anything that has the name of a location on it could be construed as a souvenir, and what is defined as a "novelty" item is also quite ambiguous. An annual survey conducted in 1992 by *Souvenirs and Novelties,* a bimonthly trade publication, estimates annual sales volume at $1.4 billion. This figure represents a consolidation of information collected from many sources including press releases, published surveys, phone contacts, trade shows, and reader service card information. Although 439 businesses were included in the survey, many attractions and outlets were not.

It has been determined that the theme park per capita spending is higher than spending at zoos, museums, and other educational attractions. Additionally, consumers seem to becoming more price sensitive and are increasingly looking to spend less than $10 for a souvenir.

GREETING CARD INDUSTRY

The greeting card industry is a $3.7 billion market that is dominated by three major players. Hallmark, American Greetings, and Gibson Greetings are all well-established greeting card companies with extensive distribution channels. These three companies command a combined market share of 85 percent. The remaining 15 percent market share is fragmented among an estimated 500 players.

The greeting card industry has begun to refocus its efforts away from traditional holiday cards and concentrate more on alternative products that are purchased and sent for no specific occasion or are personalized by the sender to reflect some specific occasion. Greeting card companies have found tremendous growth in this segment and have responded to consumer needs with many types of cards.

OPPORTUNITIES

The fastest growing type of greeting card is the alternative or nonoccasion card. American Greetings's research found that alternative cards appeal to the baby boomers, ages 25–44. The card from Voice Concepts falls into this category and would suggest an opportunity to enter this nontraditional segment. The souvenir/novelty industry has very low capital requirement barriers, thus offering easy market entry.

THREATS

Since Voice Concepts' product is not a technological innovation, once the product is introduced it is very likely that competitors will be able to reproduce the technology and enter the marketplace. To counter this situation, Voice Concepts must capture a significant market share immediately when the product enters the market. Because the product will have a relatively low repeat-purchase rate, continued expansion into new markets or changes in the use of the product must be planned.

PRODUCT POSITIONING AND STRATEGY

Voice Concepts' "talking chip" product will be initially positioned as a "souvenir" item from a tourist location. The "talking chip" can be purchased alone, or combined with a Polaroid picture. The product can be kept as a souvenir for oneself or sent to a friend or loved one as a greeting.

The product will be distributed primarily through independent retail outlets located at resort and tourist areas. The "talking chip" can use a name that better fits this positioning and will inform consumers of what the product does. Possible names include "Sight and Sound Souvenirs" or "The Memory Maker."

DISTRIBUTION

Specialty leasing, such as kiosks, is a relatively new method emerging in the retail industry. It involves the use of free-standing kiosks or pushcarts as supplemental tenants in a mall or retail area. This leasing allows retail merchants to capture increased traffic and achieve their own goals for maximum profit. It also gives the developer an added profit, usually based on the level of sales achieved by the merchant. Presentation of the kiosk must be in line with the specifications provided by the developer, and every aspect of the kiosk and the product must be approved.

TARGET MARKET

Using the number of annual visitors as a criteria for selecting markets, Voice Concepts has chosen three locations for the initial product introduction: Fanueil Hall Marketplace in Boston (14 million annual visitors), the Mall area in Washington, D.C. (19 million annual visitors), and Walt Disney World in Orlando (25 million annual visitors). Larger New England shopping malls will also be targeted for potential locations on a per kiosk basis. Voice Concepts sales forecast is based on the assumption that the kiosk operators will generate sales from .2 percent of the visitors to the tourist location. Exhibit 1 shows the number of tourists to each destination and an estimated sales forecast.

PRICING

The current suggested retail price of $10 for the "talking chip" and $15 for the chip and a Polaroid may cause a problem for Voice Concepts. Cards are generally in the range of $1 to $5. To combat this initial "price shock," the company will have to differentiate their product from a basic card. Additionally, profit margin analysis has shown that the margins are significantly below the norm (50 percent) for kiosk retailers, making decreases in the price structure from Omega integral to the success of the product.

The current price structure of the chip/card is as follows:

Price to Voice Concepts from Omega	$6.50
Price to Retailers	$9.12
Price to End Consumers	$9.95

EXHIBIT 1 Sales Forecast

Location	*Visitors*	*Sales (.2%)*
Fanueil Hall, Boston	14 million	28,000
The Mall, D.C.	19 million	38,000
Disney World, Orlando	25 million	50,000
Estimated annual sales		116,000

The following profit margin analysis, based on Fanueil Hall kiosk rental information, illustrates that this price structure does not provide the retailers with enough of a margin to operate profitably. To simply increase the retailers' margin by decreasing Voice Concepts' margin would result in negative earnings for Voice Concepts. Combining these facts with the fact that the retail price cannot be increased, based on findings from research and the focus group, makes it clear that Omega must reduce the price to Voice Concepts and either lower their profits or reduce their costs of manufacturing.

Given the total price to the kiosk operators of $9.12 ($8.12 for each chip and $1.00 for each card) and a suggested selling price of $9.95, the margin is only $.83 per sale. To cover estimated rental costs of $320 per month and salary expenses of $700 per week, the kiosk operator will have to sell 1,229 units per week to merely break even.

As part of their lease agreement, the kiosk operator will have to pay 10 percent on all additional sales over $1,500 per week, making the break-even point even higher. More units will have to be sold to cover the extra 10 percent variable cost. This point illustrates a fundamental problem in the cost structure: The kiosk operator makes a profit of $.83 per unit and yet will have to pay 10 percent of the sales price ($.995) to Fanueil Hall, resulting in a $.17 loss per unit sold on all sales over $1,500 per week.

Research has indicated that consumers will not be willing to spend more than the $10/$15 suggested retail price. Working with this $10 ceiling and allowing the kiosk operators to make a 50 percent profit, the cost per unit (card and chip) should be $6.67. However, reducing the cost to the kiosks to $6.67 will reduce Voice Concepts' profit margin to $.17 per unit of 3 percent, based on a card plus chip cost from Omega of $6.50. Voice Concepts must negotiate a lower price from Omega to achieve a 40 percent margin for the company and allow for a 50 percent margin to the kiosk operators (see Exhibit 2). Omega's cost for the chip was estimated by the Tonises and Russos to be below $2.00; therefore, a price of $4.76 to Voice Concepts would seem to be a reasonable solution. In the past, Omega has been open to these kinds of changes when given strong market evidence to support changes.

EXHIBIT 2 Price Structure

	Chip	*Chip and Photo*
Price to end consumer	$10.00	$15.00
Cost to retailer	$6.67	$10.00
Cost to Voice Concepts	$4.76	$7.14

FINANCING

The Russos will work out of their homes for the first year in order to reduce overhead expenses. Omega also agreed that for the first year Voice Concepts would not have to pay for machines or chips until they were sold to a retailer. Thus, Voice Concepts would not have to obtain business loans or venture capital to finance the start-up. Additional inventories will be maintained by Omega at their West Coast warehouse after being imported from Japan. Orders will be delivered to the retailer. Retailers will need to make an initial investment of $1,100 for the machine to record the messages on the "talking chip." Voice Concepts hopefully will be able to offer, as described earlier, the leasing program with the option to purchase in order to reduce the start-up costs and make the venture more attractive to retailers.

The Beach Carrier

Mary Ricci has a new product concept, The Beach Carrier, that she is ready to bring to market. Ricci is creative, optimistic, enthusiastic, flexible, and motivated. She is willing to put substantial time into developing and bringing The Beach Carrier to market. Although she lacks capital, Ricci is unwilling to license or sell the pattern to a manufacturer; she is determined to maintain control and ownership of the product throughout the introduction and market penetration phases. Ricci believes there is a significant amount of money to be made and refuses to sell her product concept for a flat fee.

THE PRODUCT

The Beach Carrier is a bag large enough to carry everything needed for a day at the beach, including a chair. When empty, the bag can be folded down to a 12-by-12 square for easy storage. The bag's 36-inch by 36-inch size, adjustable padded shoulder strap, and various sized pockets make it ideal for use in carrying chairs and other items to the beach or other outdoor activities, such as concerts, picnics, and barbecues. The bag can also be used to transport items, such as ski boots, that are difficult to carry. Manufactured in a lightweight, tear-resistant, fade-proof fabric that dries quickly, the bag will be available in a variety of fluorescent and conservative colors.

COMPETITION

There are currently no manufacturers producing a novelty bag similar to The Beach Carrier, but the product is easily duplicated. Ricci's success could bring new entrants with substantial manufacturing and distribution capabilities into the market.

MARKETING RESEARCH

Ricci commissioned a consulting company to perform a feasibility study for the product, which included a demographic profile, cost estimates, packaging recommendations and a patent search. The patent search revealed two products they felt Ricci's product would infringe on. Both products, however, were chairs that could be disassembled into tote bags; Ricci's product is not a chair, nor would a chair be sold in conjunction with the product.

A focus group was used to determine potential consumer response. Results of the focus group indicated that several features of the product should be modified. For example, the material was perceived as durable; however, the fluorescent color was see-through and considered "trendy," lessening the perceived quality of the bag. The size also represented an issue, as the bag was perceived as much larger than it had to be.

MARKET POTENTIAL

People who use suntan and sunscreen products have been identified as the primary target market for The Beach Carrier. Research indicates that 43.9 percent of the adult U.S. population, or 77,293,000 people, use suntan and sunscreen products. Of these, 57.8 percent are female. Assuming that women are the primary purchasers of beach bags, the potential market is estimated at 44,675,000. Beach bags are replaced every three years. The primary market for suntan and sunscreen products is described in Exhibit 1. The marketing share objectives for the first year of The Beach Carrier's sales have been determined based on the following assumptions:

- People who use suntan and sunscreen products represent the market for The Beach Carrier.
- Most men do not buy beach bags; consider women only (57.8 percent of population).
- Women buy new beach bags every three years on average, i.e., one-third will buy a new bag this year.

Based on these assumptions, the unit sales needed to achieve market share objectives of 1 percent, 2 percent and 5 percent of the total market during the first year of The Beach Carrier's sales, are shown in Exhibit 2. Ricci is targeting 1 percent of this potential market. Regional market share objectives can be developed from the same data as seen in Exhibit 3A and 3B.

STRATEGY

Ricci investigated several methods of marketing The Beach Carrier, including selling it in upscale (i.e., Bloomingdale's) or discount (i.e., Wal-Mart) stores, licensing the product concept to a manufacturer, selling the idea for a flat fee, selling the bag to corporations for use as a promotional item, and setting up a mail-order operation. Ricci believes that the mail-order option, while requiring the most effort, will provide higher margins, lower risk, and the overall best fit with Ricci's strengths and weaknesses, her market penetration objectives, and her limited financial resources.

The mail-order sales strategy will be implemented nationally using a regional rollout, following a seasonal demand pattern. With three month intervals between rollout phases, national market exposure will be achieved within 12 months.

EXHIBIT 1

Segment	*Percentage of Total Users of Suntan/Sunscreen Products*
Age 18–44	66.9%
High school graduate	40.2%
Employed full–time	60.5%
No child in household	54.5%
Household income of $30,000+	55.3%

EXHIBIT 2

	Population	*Sunscreen Users*	*Replace Bag This Year*
Total adults	176,250,000	77,293,000	25,764,333
Females	92,184,000	44,671,000	14,890,333

Market Share	*1%*	*2%*	*5%*
Total adults	257,643	515,287	1,288,217
Females	148,903	297,807	744,517

EXHIBIT 3A

	Population	*Sunscreen Users*	*Women*	*Replace Bag This Year*
Northeast	37,366,000	17,165,000	9,921,370	3,307,123
Midwest	43,426,000	19,630,000	11,346,140	3,782,047
South	60,402,000	23,980,000	13,860,440	4,620,147
West	35,057,000	16,518,000	9,547,404	3,182,468
Total	176,251,000	77,293,000	44,675,354	14,891,785

EXHIBIT 3B

	1%	*2%*	*5%*
Northeast	33,071	66,142	165,356
Midwest	37,820	75,641	189,102
South	46,201	92,403	231,007
West	31,825	63,649	159,123
Total	148,917	297,835	744,588

PROMOTION

The product will be promoted in novelty and general interest mail-order catalogs and special interest magazines that appeal to beachgoers and boat owners.

PRICING

The costs of manufacturing have been estimated at $6.50 per unit for material, zippers, Velcro, and so on. The costs for assembly and packaging have been estimated at $3.50 per unit, bringing the total manufacturing cost to $10.00. After analyzing competitive products and focus group results, a mail-order price in the $12.99 to $14.99 range has been established.

DISTRIBUTION

The product will be manufactured at a local New England factory, drop-shipped to a storage facility, and shipped via UPS to the consumer. Initially, inventory can be carried at no cost in Ricci's house or garage.

FINANCING

A $30,000 small business loan is the minimum amount Ricci needs to fund her fixed costs for the first phase of the rollout for the mail-order program. Marketing the product through traditional retail channels would require approximately $250,000 for advertising and other selling costs associated with a new product introduction.

BREAK-EVEN ANALYSIS

Break-even analysis was performed at three mail-order prices, as seen in Exhibit 4. Based on this analysis, Ricci must meet only one-fourth of her target sales goal, or one-quarter of 1 percent of the total market, in order to break even in the first year.

EXHIBIT 4

Unit Variable Cost		*Unit Price*	*Contribution*
Materials	$ 6.50	$12.99	$2.99
Assembly	3.00	$13.99	$3.99
Packaging	0.50	$14.99	$4.99
Total Unit VC	$10.00		

Fixed Costs	*Northeast*	*Midwest*	*South*	*West*	*Total*
Advertising	$25,000	$25,000	$25,000	$25,000	$100,000
Warehousing	266	305	372	256	1,199
General S&A	2,500	2,500	2,500	2,500	10,000
Total Fixed Costs	$27,766	$27,805	$27,872	$27,756	$111,199
Break-Even Units					
@$12.99	9,286	9,299	9,322	9,283	37,190
% of total market	0.28%	0.25%	0.20%	0.29%	0.25%
@$13.99	6,959	6,969	6,985	6,956	27,869
% of total market	0.21%	0.18%	0.15%	0.22%	0.19%
@$14.99	5,564	5,572	5,586	5,562	22,284
% of total market	0.17%	0.15%	0.12%	0.17%	0.15%

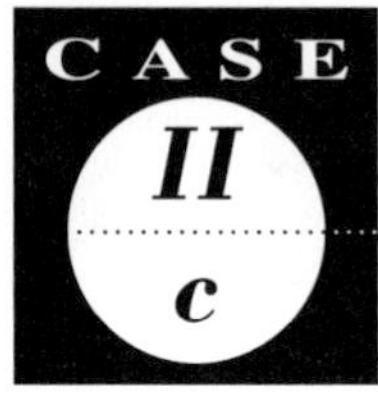

Insta-Lite

Insta-Lite, a product that eliminates the need for kindling when starting wood fires, was conceived and developed by George Bradley. With the increased amount of wood being burned, Bradley felt there was a strong need for a product that acted the same as kindling but had none of its drawbacks.

Insta-Lite, in his opinion, did that. Bradley initially intended to manufacture, market, and sell the product himself. Since his primary business was in construction, and his resources were limited, Bradley planned to manufacture Insta-Lite initially on a part-time basis in his garage and later consider an automated process. The operation was not capital-intensive. It consisted of nothing more than the raw materials, a mixing vat and funnels, free storage and workspace in his garage, and the use of a pick-up truck through his construction business.

Bradley's long-range goal was to attain mass distribution through major retail and grocery outlets. However, he felt that the only way to achieve this goal would be to first successfully sell the product in local wood stove stores. That way, he could build working capital to finance future expansion and mass distribution, and he could generate proof of demand for the product to major retail outlets. Bradley felt secure that his goals were reachable, but first he needed to develop a plan to get his product to the market.

THE PRODUCT CONCEPT

At its most basic level, Insta-Lite was a substitute for kindling. The need fulfilled by kindling substitutes was not a functional deficiency but rather a convenience deficiency. Kindling is an excellent fire-starting aid, but it has many undesirable features. For instance, it is not always available, it can be very costly (up to $5 per bushel in some areas), it is bulky and difficult to store, it attracts dust and insects, and it is cumbersome to carry.

Bradley felt the ideal kindling substitute should start fires at least as well as kindling yet incorporate improvements that eliminate these problems. He wanted to produce a product that was easy to transport and store, was clean and had no dust or insect problems, and was readily and conveniently available.

Insta-Lite was the result of these efforts. Consisting of a liquid combination of petroleum distillates and pine scent, it was packaged in one-quart plastic containers weighing approximately 18 pounds each.

The procedure for using the product in a fireplace was to place a log, split side up, on a newspaper and apply Insta-Lite. After the liquid soaked in for a few minutes, the log was then placed, split side down, on the grate. A crumpled newspaper was placed under the grate and lit. The burning newspaper lit the Insta-Lite-soaked log and produced a flame immediately. Each quart of Insta-Lite yielded eight fire starts.

Insta-Lite had to be used with care, however. It was toxic and required adequate ventilation. In addition, it could never be applied directly to an open flame and had to be stored away from children in a cool, dry place.

THE WOOD-BURNING INDUSTRY IN NEW ENGLAND

According to recent surveys, the number of homes burning wood in New England was on the increase. In the winter of 1983-84, there was more than a 30 percent increase in the number of cords of wood burned compared to the 1981–82 season.

Massachusetts, in particular, showed one of the highest percentage increases, and, according to studies, there was no evidence of this trend slowing down. In the winter of 1983–84, Massachusetts residents burned over 2 million cords of wood—the equivalent of what all of New England burned in 1981. Exhibit 1 shows a

EXHIBIT 1 Wood Burned in Massachusetts: Winter 1983–84

County	*Total Households*	*Households Burning Wood*	*Cords Burned*	*Households with Wood Stoves or Furnaces*	*Percent Increase in 1983 Alone*
Barnstable	82,936	N/A	84,668	N/A	N/A
Berkshire	147,530	35,300	95,261	18,000	36
Bristol	341,549	N/A	120,373	N/A	N/A
Dukes	5,890	N/A	9,889	N/A	N/A
Essex	671,993	252,000	430,004	97,600	60
Franklin	40,535	23,600	44,668	20,600	18
Hampden	344,163	70,200	162,818	30,900	10
Hampshire	120,819	36,900	82,372	19,000	17
Middlesex	982,486	412,916	541,272	84,000	21
Nantucket	4,333	N/A	1,963	N/A	N/A
Norfolk	529,083	N/A	203,041	N/A	N/A
Plymouth	420,083	N/A	168,373	N/A	N/A
Suffolk	447,969	97,400	90,600	1,400	0
Worchester	393,844	184,400	271,414	87,700	12
Southeastern Massachusetts counties (grouped)	N/A	383,600	N/A	161,700	N/A
Total	4,533,213	1,501,043	2,306,716	520,900	21

breakdown of wood-burning households by Massachusetts counties. Of the 2.3 million cords of wood burned in Massachusetts that year, two-thirds were burned in wood stoves or furnaces. The remaining one-third was burned in fireplaces. Exhibit 2 illustrates this point.

The same surveys also showed that more than one-half of those using wood stoves began doing so within the last four years. The increased interest in wood was attributed to the rising cost of fuel prices.

In contrast, from 1981–83, wood burned in fireplaces declined by 15 percent, suggesting that consumers were becoming more aware of the greater efficiency of wood stoves.

This trend toward wood stoves had significant consequences for Insta-Lite because, in its present form, Insta-Lite could not be used in stoves or furnaces. This limitation was not as significant if the individuals with wood stoves and furnaces burned wood continuously. That is, even though they bought a greater percentage of wood, they would actually have a relatively low number of fire starts.

The use of Insta-Lite would be most affected in those situations where the wood stove served as a supplemental heating source, where the rate of starts was high. Such might be the case, for example, for a working family that kept the thermostat at 58 degrees during the day when no one was home and started the wood stove fire each night. Data were not available on such usage categories for stove owners.

MARKET POTENTIAL FOR INSTA-LITE

The numbers presented in the preceding studies served as the basis for quantifying the market potential for Insta-Lite in Bradley's target market, the three neighboring Massachusetts counties of Essex, Middlesex, and Suffolk (see Exhibit 3).

The market potential for each county was computed by multiplying the number of households that burned wood in fireplaces by both an upper limit of 90 and a lower limit of 20 fire starts per season. This resulted in the total number of fire starts during the season for each county. Then, the total starts for each county were divided by eight to determine the market potential in quarts for Insta-Lite. (One quart of Insta-Lite yielded eight fire starts.)

EXHIBIT 2 Fuel Wood Burned by Type of Household

	Number of Cords	*Percent*
Homeowner stoves/furnaces	1,395,563	60.5%
Homeowner fireplaces	634,347	27.5
Renters	184,537	8.0
Second homes	92,269	4.0

EXHIBIT 3 Market Potential for Insta-Lite 30 Percent Market Penetration

		Number of Fire Starts		*Number of Quarts*	
County	*Total Number of Fireplaces*	*Upper Limit*	*Lower Limit*	*Upper Limit*	*Lower Limit*
Essex	160,000	14,400,000	3,200,000	1,800,000	400,000
Middlesex	330,333	29,729,970	6,606,660	3,716,246	825,833
Suffolk	96,000	8,640,000	1,920,000	1,080,000	240,000
Total	586,333	52,769,970	11,726,660	6,596,246	1,465,833

Retail Channel Interviews

Paralleling the increase in the amount of wood being burned was an increase in the number of retail outlets specializing in sales and service of wood, wood-burning equipment, and related items. In addition, home centers, hardware stores, and other related outlets had expanded their alternative-energy product lines.

To determine the appropriate marketing strategy for Insta-Lite, Bradley conducted telephone interviews with several local managers of wood stove stores, fireplace accessory stores, and wood dealers selected from the yellow pages. He described the product concept in general terms and asked the respondents (1) whether or not they saw a need for such a product, (2) if they knew of any similar product, and (3) what would be required for them to carry such a product.

Wood stove stores. Four wood-burning stove stores were contacted. Each manager reported that the manufacturers of wood-burning stoves did not recommend the use of liquid fire-starting aids and that their use would invalidate the warranties of most major stove manufacturers. Specific laws required stove manufacturers to warn the consumer in the product labeling and in the operator's manual against using chemicals. This warning included such products as Dura-Flame logs.

One of the major dangers associated with the use of chemicals was the potential for flash fires. A second danger was the buildup of creosote, a tarlike substance, in the chimney or pipes. If this happened, the creosote would heat when a fire was started and flakes of wood would stick to it. These deposits could eventually choke off the chimney or result in a chimney fire.

Another store manager was enthusiastic about the product concept but thought liquid was the wrong way to go. Instead, in the near future he was planning to carry a product called Fire-Up. Fire-Up consisted of small, heat-sealed plastic bags filled with paraffin-impregnated kerosene. He felt this product would be safer and neater because it was encapsulated. He also liked the fact that the manufacturer supplied a display for the product.

Two stores carried another competitive product, Kindle-All, also a paraffin-based product, for $2. Both reported having no success in selling the product. These managers were not interested in such products due to their low profit margin. Stoves had high prices and high profit margins.

An interesting feature of Kindle-All was that it was endorsed by Jotul, a major wood stove manufacturer. One manager said this was a key to success with such products because a package could be given away with each stove purchased. He also mentioned that the Wood Stove Directory, which listed the names and addresses of all the major manufacturers, could be purchased in his store.

Firewood dealers. Six firewood dealers were contacted. They were mixed in their reaction. Two of the six, who delivered to the inner city, saw a need for such a product concept. Suburban dealers, however, felt that where kindling was both free and plentiful there would be no demand for such a product. The other two respondents indicated that they might be interested in handling such a product.

Fireplace accessory stores. Four stores were contacted. One said they had carried Kindle-All with no success. Two of the four expressed concern for product safety and were not willing to accept liability for damage that might result from misuse of the product.

Competition

As discovered from the retail channel interviews, Insta-Lite faced a considerable amount of competition. A competitive matrix is presented in Exhibit 4. There were seven products considered to be in the same product class, but all were paraffin-based. In addition, there was one product that sold as a gift item with a high selling price of $10. There were also two nonconsumable products not thought to be comparable to Insta-Lite. Finally, there was kindling itself.

Paraffin-based products were cleaner and easier to use than Insta-Lite. The user need only drop a pellet or pouch into the stove or hearth. There was no need to spread newspaper and pour liquid on the logs. Insta-Lite, however, started a roaring fire faster.

Price

Bradley felt that a price of $1 per quart to distributors and a price of $1.89 to consumers was competitive.

Financial Analysis

Exhibit 5 presents the figures associated with the garage operation. Bradley assumed that the maximum production capacity would be 2,600 cases annually. The variable cost per unit was projected at .482 and fixed costs at $10,000 annually.

EXHIBIT 4 Competitive Matrix

Brand	*Product Use/Form*	*Cost/Fire*	*Manufacturer/ Distributor*
Fire-Up*	Heat sealed plastic pouch containing paraffin and kerosene. Throw individual packet in fire. One box = 3″ × 4″ × 2″	19.5¢ (10 in a box, $1.95/box)	Rights owned by Webster Industries Nova Scotia; developed by U.S. Stove Company
Flame-On*	Pellets, paraffin-based	24.8¢ (6 pack, $1.49)	Falcon Marketing International P.O. Box 2249 Redwood City, CA
Fire-Wick*	Similar to Fire-Up	11.3¢ (15 per box, $1.69)	Coughlin Products Inc. 1011 Clifton Ave Clifton, NJ 01013
Kindle-All*	Wood chippings coated in paraffin	22.7¢ (enough for 30 fires, $2.95)	Kristia Associates Portland, ME
Adirondack Fire Starters*	Small paper cups filled with paraffin	6.5¢–12.9¢ (20 in a bag—use 1 or 2, $1.29/bag)	Community Workshop Inc. 21 Thomson Ave Glens Falls, NY 12801
Fire Starters*	White substance impregnated with alcohol	24.3¢ (24 boxes/case, $20.50/ case, 8–10 in box)	Hubbard Coal Company 431 Stephenson Hwy.
Piney Woods Products	Pine sticks coated, treated, shrink-packed	35.9¢ (Key—1 ft. in diameter, 167 sticks, 4–6 to start fire, $10/K ea.)	Piney Woods Products P.O. Box 7219 Beaumont, TX
Unknown	Cast iron well in fire brick-red kerosene in well and leave entire brick in fire	Unknown	Sundials and Mores New Ipswitch, NH
Wonderwood*	Paraffin-coated logs	16¢	Unknown
Cape Cod lighter	Metal product which can be filled with kerosene and placed in the stove or hearth	Unknown	Unknown
Kindling wood	Organic—by-product of firewood—falls from trees	0–50¢ 0–$5 per bushel	Some wood dealers, readily available
Insta-Lite	Petroleum distillate—soak wood, use newspaper and start fire similar to charcoal lighter	23.6¢ 1 qt. 6–8 fires	Tom Forsyth Melrose, MA

EXHIBIT 4 *(concluded)*

Brand	*Key Features/ Benefits*	*Where Used*	*Comments*
Fire-Up*	Encapsulated, easy heat, clean, enough BTUs for 15 minutes	Wood-burning stoves, fireplaces, all fires	Provide display, need no kindling or paper
Flame-On*	Easy to light, self-contained, clean heat	Wood stove, fireplaces, all fires	Povide display, need no kindling or paper
Fire-Wick*	Encapsulated, easy heat, clean	Wood stoves, barbecues, all fires	Tend to break, not as clean as Fire-Up, advertised as "Safer than fluids, no flare-ups." Need no kindling or paper
Kindle-All*	Safe, easy, patent pending	Wood stoves, fireplaces, hibachis, barbecues, campfires	Endorsed by Jotul Stoves, widely available in MA outlets, no kindling or paper
Adirondack Fire Starters*	Encapsulated, easy, clean	All fires	Made by sheltered workshop. Sold in Home Center Stores. Sales reported high. Provide a display from shipping box
Fire Starters*	Not that easy to use	Fireplaces	Imported from Ireland
Piney Woods Products	Decorator packaging to display in front of living-room hearth	Fireplaces, wood stoves	Gift item
Unknown	Reusable, refillable	Wood stoves, fireplaces	Patent pending
Wonderwood*	Safe, semidurable	Wood stoves, fireplaces	—
Cape Cod lighter	Reusable, refillable	Stove, hearth	—
Kindling wood	Free to many, safe, available	Stove, fireplace, camp fires, all fires	—
Insta-Lite	No kindling needed, odorless, colorless, possibly faster than paraffin-coated products	Fireplaces	Cannot be used in wood stoves

*Products classified as similar to Insta-Lite

EXHIBIT 5 Garage Operations*

Production capacity: 50 cases per week; 2,600 annually

Variable Costs per Quart:			*Fixed Costs (Annualized):*	
Package		.160	Telephone	$1,600
Carton		.030	Travel/delivery	6,400
Label/cap		.050		
Labeling		.014	Misc. selling	2,000
Ingredients		.225		
Total		.482	Total	$10,000
(12 quarts per case)			Variable cost per case	$5.78
Selling price per case—	Wholesale			$12.00
	Direct			$22.68
Break-even quantity—	Wholesale		10,000/6.22 =	1,608 cases
	Direct		10,000/16.9 =	592 cases

*Assumptions:
No cost for rent
No salary paid to Bradley
No legal fees
All accounting and collections done by Bradley
No provision for product liability insurance
No escalation on material prices
Travel/delivery estimated at $0.20 per mile
No allocation for promotion

Exhibit 6 presents the figures associated with a subcontracted automated filling process. The minimum production order was 1,665 cases. The variable cost per unit was projected at $0.572 and fixed costs at $40,000 annually.

Revenues. Assuming a 30 percent market penetration (see Exhibit 2) and a wholesale price for Insta-Lite of $1, Bradley's total revenue would be $442,250 at the lower limit and $1,990,125 at the upper limit of fire starts. Selling Insta-Lite directly to the consumer at a price of $1.89 would place the value of the business at $835,853 at the lower limit and $3,761,336 at the upper limit.

Based on the above analysis, Bradley had to decide whether to go ahead with the product as developed, and if so, what his marketing strategy should be.

EXHIBIT 6 Subcontracted Automated Filling*

Production Capacity: Minimum order of 1,665 cases

Variable Costs per Quart:		*Fixed Costs (Annualized):*	
Package	0.16	Telephone	$1,200
Packaging (labor)	0.09	Salaries	29,000
Carton	0.033	Travel	4,500
Label/cap	0.05	Accounting	1,800
Labeling	0.014	Legal fees	1,500
Ingredients	0.225	Insurance	2,000
Total	0.572	Total	$40,000
Variable cost per case			$6.86
Selling price per case—	Wholesale		$12.00
	Direct		$22.68
Break-even quantity—	Wholesale	40,000/5.14 =	7,782 cases
	Direct	40,000/15.82=	2,528 cases

*Assumptions:
No cost for rent
No escalation on material prices
No allocation for promotion

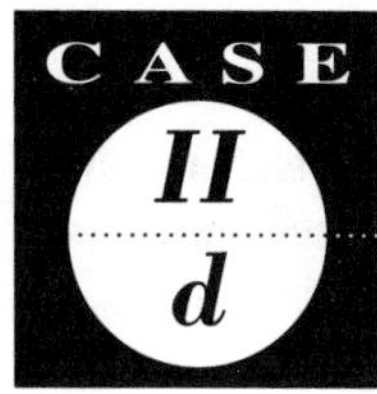

Salad Seasons

Early in 1985, Tom Mitchell, the owner and founder of Salad Seasons, came up with an idea for frozen salad kits. He had heard several suppliers and retailers talk about how fresh salad ingredients were difficult to preserve and sometimes were wasted because they were not sold right away. Mitchell considered that one option was to add preservatives to the ingredients but felt that concerned consumers would dismiss the idea. Then he thought about freezing salads. He felt that the advantages of a frozen salad kit with individually packaged ingredients included a longer shelf life and easy handling.

His fresh salads had been doing reasonably well in the San Francisco area, which was currently his only geographic market. Mitchell was aware of his opportunities: Consumers were spending more of their disposable income eating out, fast-food sales were growing, and consumers were more health conscious. None of his competitors were selling frozen salad kits, and he felt the kit could meet the consumer needs by being reasonably priced, ready to eat, and free of preservatives. He wanted to position the product in the high-quality market. He also wanted to expand his geographic market to include selected retail and food accounts in the Chicago and Washington, D.C., areas.

Mitchell's major concern was that he had limited financial resources. He was sure his concept would catch on but needed to analyze his financial situation.

THE SALAD INDUSTRY

The prepared salad market is roughly $500 million. Salads can accompany most meals and therefore can compete in the foodservice industry for the consumer's dollar. The major segments within the growing $175 billion retail food market are commercial/contract, institutional/internal, and military.

COMPETITION

There are several competitors in the prepared salad market. Sales for the two largest firms account for 40 percent of the $500 million. Most of their volume comes from inexpensively priced macaroni, potato, and cole slaw salads. They both have strong positions in the foodservice and retail markets and offer a full line of fresh salads. Distribution occurs mainly through brokers and food distributors.

ENVIRONMENTAL ANALYSIS

Salad Seasons's target market is the 25- to 40-age group. This group tends to have single adults or two-income-earners who devote less time to the kitchen and consider convenience to be important. They are generally more health conscious, which suggests a ready market for prepared foods such as salads.

Capital costs are low at Salad Seasons because the physical plant is not highly technical. Their technology is easily movable, and so good economies of scale should be possible. However, because competitors could easily imitate the product, Salad Seasons had to penetrate the market quickly.

FINANCIAL CONSIDERATIONS

In 1984, Salad Seasons had invested $100,000 in capital to start the business. Mitchell was concerned about the cash flow situation, especially since they experienced a negative cash flow from operations of $75,000 in 1985, following the opening of the business. This loss was due primarily to start-up costs. To accommodate their frozen salad line, they planned to invest $1 million in 1988 for a new plant where they could process meats and increase freezer capacity.

SALES PROJECTIONS

When Mitchell began selling the frozen kits in mid-1986, they achieved a great deal of acceptance in the San Francisco area. The food distributors and retail food stores especially liked the product's long shelf life. It was expected that the line would eventually grow to account for 75 percent of total sales in the market, up from 50 percent in 1986. Total sales were expected to grow 200 percent in 1987. After 1987, the rate of sales was expected to decrease to 15 percent per year due to gradual saturation and imitation by competitors. Mitchell hoped to be able to maintain the 15 percent growth rate for the near future with the expectation that Salad Seasons would be established with the national accounts by 1988.

Sales in 1986 were $2 million. The average price per unit was $1.75 and was expected to remain the same over the next four years. The average variable cost per unit was $1.20, also expected to remain about the same over the next few years. Fixed costs were projected to rise due to additional hires, promotional efforts, and expansion into the new plant.

	1986	*1987*	*1988*	*1989*
Total fixed costs ($)	$700,000	$1.3 million	$2 million	$2 million
Depreciation ($)	$3,000	$5,000	$105,000	$105,000

The required rate of return on the investment was estimated to be about 10 percent to account for the risk associated with the venture, and the tax rate was 46 percent.

Tom Mitchell needed to know what his sales had to be in order to break even. He also wanted to know if his cash flow situation allowed for future capital expenditures, and he was anxious to get a handle on his return on investment. How should he proceed?

Gourmet to Go

INTRODUCTION

Today, many households have two incomes. At the end of the day the questions arise, "Who will cook?" or even "What do I cook?" Time is limited. After a long day at work, few people want to face the lines at the grocery store. Often the choice is to eat out. But the expense of dining out or the boredom of fast food soon becomes unappealing. Pizza or fast-food delivery solves the problem of going out but does not always satisfy the need for nutritious, high-quality meals. Some people prefer a home-cooked meal, especially without the hassle of grocery shopping, menu planning, and time-consuming preparation.

Jan Jones is one of those people. She is a hard-working professional who would like to come home to a home-cooked meal. She would not mind fixing it herself but, once at home, making an extra trip to the store is a major hassle. Jones thought it would be great to have the meal planned and all the ingredients at her fingertips. She thought of other people in her situation and realized there might be a market need for this kind of service. After thinking about the types of meals that could be marketed, Jones discussed the plan with her colleagues at work. The enthusiastic response led her to believe she had a good idea. After months of marketing research, menu planning, and financial projections, Jones was ready to launch her new business. The following is the business plan for Gourmet to Go.

EXECUTIVE SUMMARY

Gourmet to Go is a new concept in grocery marketing. The product is a combination of menu planning and grocery delivery; a complete package of groceries and recipes for a week's meals are delivered to a customer's door. The target market is young urban professionals—two-income households in which individuals have limited leisure time, high disposable income, and a willingness to pay for services.

The objective is to develop a customer base of 400 households by the end of the third year after start-up. This level of operation will produce a net income of about $100,000 per year and provide a solid base for market penetration in the future.

The objective will be achieved by creating an awareness of the product through an intense promotional campaign at start-up, and by providing customers first-class service and premium-quality goods.

The capital requirement to achieve objectives is $199,800. Jones will invest $143,000 and will manage and own the business. The remainder of the capital will be financed through bank loans.

PRODUCT

The product consists of meal-planning and grocery-shopping services. It offers a limited selection of preplanned five-dinner packages delivered directly to the customer.

The criteria for the meal packages will be balanced nutrition, easy preparation, and premium quality. To ensure the nutritional requirement, Gourmet to Go will hire a nutritionist as a consultant. Nutritional information will be included with each order. The most efficient method for preparing the overall meal will be presented. Meals will be limited to recipes requiring no more than 20 minutes to prepare. Premium-quality ingredients will be a selling feature. The customer should feel that he or she is getting better-quality ingredients than could be obtained from the grocery store.

MANUFACTURING AND PACKAGING

Since the customer will not be shopping on the premises, Gourmet to Go will require only a warehouse-type space for the groceries. The store location or decor will be unimportant in attracting business. There will be fewer inventory expenses since the customer will not be choosing among various brands. Only premium brands will be offered.

It will be important to establish a reliable connection with a distributor for high-quality produce and to maintain freshness for delivery to the customer.

As orders are processed, the dinners will be assembled. Meats will be wrapped and ready for the home freezer. All ingredients will be labeled according to the dinner to which they belong. The groceries will be sorted and bagged according to storage requirements: freezer, refrigerator, and shelf. Everything possible will be done to minimize the customer's task. Included in the packaging will be the nutritional information and preparation instructions.

Customers will be given the option of selecting their own meals from the monthly menu list or opting for a weekly selection from the company.

FUTURE GROWTH

Various options will be explored to expand the business. Some customers may prefer a three- or four-meal plan if they eat out more often or travel frequently. Another possibility might be the "last-minute gourmet," that is, they can call any evening for one meal only.

Increasing the customer base will increase future sales. Expansion of Gourmet to Go can include branches in other locations or even future franchising in other cities. With expansion and success, Gourmet to Go might be a prime target for a larger food company to buy out.

INDUSTRY

The Gourmet to Go concept is a new idea with its own market niche. The closest competitors would be grocery stores and restaurants with delivery services.

Of the 45 grocery stores in Tulsa, only one offers a delivery service. It is a higher-priced store and will deliver for $4, regardless of order size. However, it offers no assistance in meal planning.

A number of pizza chains will deliver pizza as well as fried chicken. There is also a new service that will pick up and deliver orders from various restaurants. However, Gourmet to Go would not be in direct competition with these services because the meals available from them are either of a fast-food type or far more expensive than a Gourmet to Go meal.

SALES PREDICTION

The market segment will be two-income households with an income of at least $40,000 per year. In Tulsa, this will cover an area of 14 tracts in the southeast section of the city. The area includes 16,600 households that meet the target requirements of income with an age range of 25 to 45 years. By the end of the third year, a customer base of 400 households will be developed (2.3 percent of the target market). At a growth rate of 2.73 percent a year, the target market of households should increase over three years to 18,000.

MARKETING

Distribution

The product will be delivered directly to the customer.

Sales Strategy

Advertising will include newspaper ads, radio spots, and direct mail brochures. All three will be used during normal operations, but an intense campaign will precede start-up. A series of "teaser" newspaper ads will be run prior to start-up, announcing a revolution in grocery shopping. At start-up, the newspaper ads will have evolved into actually introducing the product and radio spots will begin as well. A heavy advertising schedule will be during the first four weeks of business. After start-up, a direct mailing will detail the description of the service and a menu plan.

Newspaper ads aimed at the target markets will be placed in entertainment and business sections. Radio spots will be geared to stations most appealing to the target market. Since the product is new, it may be possible to do interviews with newspapers and obtain free publicity.

Sales promotions will offer large discounts to first-time customers. These promotions will continue for the first six months of operations.

The service will be priced at $10 per week for delivery and planning, with the groceries priced at full retail level. According to the phone survey, most people who were interested in the service would be willing to pay the weekly service charge.

FINANCIAL

Various financial statements are indicated in Exhibits 1 through 8.

MANAGEMENT

The management will consist of the owner/manager. Other employees will be delivery clerks and order clerks. It is anticipated that after the business grows, an operations manager might be added to supervise the employees.

EXHIBIT 1 Sources and Uses of Funds

Sources of Funds	
Jan Jones (personal funds)	$143,086
Bank loans for computer and vehicles*	56,700
Total sources	$199,786
Uses of Funds	
Computer, peripherals, and software	$ 20,700
Food lockers and freezers	10,000
Delivery vehicles	36,000
Phone system	1,000
Miscellaneous furniture and fixtures	3,000
Start-up expenses†	41,900
Working capital‡	87,186
Total uses	$199,786

*Total for initial three-year period. Computer and one delivery van will be acquired prior to start-up, one delivery van will be added six months after start-up, and another will be added 18 months after start-up. Financing will be handled simultaneously with procurement.

‡See detail, following.

†To cover negative cash flow over first 1½ years of operation. (See pro forma cash flow statements.)

EXHIBIT 2 Start-Up Expenses

Ad campaign		
Ad agency*	$ 2,000	
Brochures†	5,000	
Radio spots‡	5,600	
Newspaper ads§	5,000	
Total		$17,600
Prestart-up salaries**		14,300
Nutritionist consulting		5,000
Miscellaneous consulting (legal, etc.)		1,000
Prestart-up rent and deposits		3,000
Prestart-up utilities and miscellaneous supplies		1,000
		$41,900

*40 hrs. @ $50/hr
†20,000 brochures; printing, development, etc. @ $0.25/ea
‡4 weeks intense campaign: 20 spots/week (30 seconds); $70/spot
§50 ads at an average of $100/ad
**Jan Jones @ 3 months; clerks, two @ 2 weeks

EXHIBIT 3 Capital Equipment List

Computers:		
Apple, MacIntosh Office System		
3 work stations	$ 7,500	
Laser printer	7,000	
Hard disk	2,400	
Networking	1,800	
Software	2,000	
Total		$20,700
Delivery vans, Chevrolet Astro		36,000
Food lockers and freezers		10,000
Phone system (AT&T)		1,000
Furniture and fixtures		3,000
		$70,700

EXHIBIT 4 Pro Forma Income Statement

	Year 1											
	Mo. 1	*Mo. 2*	*Mo. 3*	*Mo. 4*	*Mo. 5*	*Mo. 6*	*Mo. 7*	*Mo. 8*	*Mo. 9*	*Mo. 10*	*Mo. 11*	*Mo. 12*
Sales[(1)]	2,150	3,225	5,375	10,750	16,125	19,320	21,500	23,650	25,800	27,950	30,100	32,250
Less: Cost of goods sold[(2)]	1,376	2,064	3,440	6,880	10,320	12,384	13,760	15,136	16,512	17,888	19,264	20,640
Gross Profit	774	1,161	1,935	3,870	5,805	6,936	7,740	8,514	9,288	10,062	10,836	11,610
Less:												
Operating expenses												
Salaries and wages[(3)]	6,400	6,400	6,400	6,400	6,400	6,400	8,300	8,300	8,300	8,300	8,300	8,300
Operating supplies	300	300	300	300	300	300	300	300	300	300	300	300
Repairs and maintenance	200	200	200	200	200	200	200	200	200	200	200	200
Advertising and promotion[(4)]	110	160	270	540	810	970	1,080	1,180	1,290	1,400	1,500	1,610
Bad debts	50	50	50	50	50	50	50	50	50	50	50	50
Rent[(5)]	1,330	1,330	1,330	1,330	1,330	1,330	1,330	1,330	1,330	1,330	1,330	1,330
Utilities	1,000	1,000	1,000	1,000	1,000	1,000	1,000	1,000	1,000	1,000	1,000	1,000
Insurance	400	400	400	400	400	400	400	400	400	400	400	400
General office	100	100	100	100	100	100	100	100	100	100	100	100
Licenses	100	0	0	0	0	0	0	0	0	0	0	0
Interest[(6)]	340	340	340	340	340	340	465	465	465	465	465	465
Depreciation[(7)]	790	790	790	790	790	790	790	790	790	790	790	790
Total operating expenses	11,120	11,070	11,180	11,450	11,720	11,880	14,015	14,115	14,225	14,335	14,435	14,545
Profit (loss) before taxes	(10,346)	(9,909)	(9,245)	(7,580)	(5,915)	(4,944)	(6,275)	(5,601)	(4,937)	(4,273)	(3,599)	(2,935)
Less: Taxes	0	0	0	0	0	0	0	0	0	0	0	0
Net profit (loss)	(10,346)	(9,909)	(9,245)	(7,580)	(5,915)	(4,944)	(6,275)	(5,601)	(4,937)	(4,273)	(3,599)	(2,935)

(1) Sales—per Action Plan; see Exhibit 1 for detail. Average unit sale is $40.00 for groceries plus $10.00 per week for delivery (Exhibit 2), making the monthly unit sales per household (2 people) $215.00.

(2) Cost of Goods Sold—80% of retail grocery price, or $32.00 per household per week ($138.00/month household). (80% an average margin on groceries—*Progressive Grocer;* April 1984; p. 94.)

(3) Salaries and Wages: Ms. Jones's salary will be $4,500/month. Order clerks will be paid $1,000/month, and delivery clerks will be paid $900/month. One additional order clerk and delivery clerk each will be added once sales reach 100 households, and again at 200 households. Salaries will escalate at 6%/year.

(4) Advertising and Promotion: The grocery industry standard is 1% of sales. However, "Dinner Kits" being a new business will require more than that level; 5% of sales is used in this plan. (Special prestart-up advertising is covered with other start-up expenses.)

(5) Rent—2,000/ft.^{2} @ $8.00/ft.^{2}; 1,333 $1/month; escalate at 6%/year.

(6) Interest—Loans on computer ($10,000), and delivery vehicles ($12,000 ea.) at 12.5%/year. (Delivery vehicles will be added with delivery clerks.) (Debt service—based on three-year amortization of loans with payments of ⅓ at the end of each of three years.)

(7) Depreciation—All equipment will be depreciated per ACRS Schedules: vehicles and computers—3 years; furniture and fixtures—10 years.

EXHIBIT 5 Pro Forma Income Statement

	Year 2				*Year 3*			
	Q 1	*Q 2*	*Q 3*	*Q 4*	*Q 1*	*Q 2*	*Q 3*	*Q 4*
Sales[1]	112,875	129,000	161,000	193,500	209,625	225,750	241,875	258,000
Less: Cost of goods sold[2]	72,240	82,560	103,200	123,840	134,160	144,800	154,800	165,120
Gross Profit	40,635	46,440	57,800	69,660	75,465	80,950	87,075	92,880
Less:								
Operating expenses								
Salaries and wages[3]	24,900	32,700	32,700	38,400	40,800	40,800	40,800	40,800
Operating supplies	900	900	900	900	900	900	900	900
Repairs and maintenance	600	600	600	600	600	600	600	600
Advertising and promotion[4]	5,640	6,540	8,060	9,680	10,480	11,290	12,090	12,900
Bad debts	150	150	150	150	150	150	150	150
Rent[5]	4,230	4,230	4,230	4,230	4,480	4,480	4,480	4,480
Utilities	3,000	3,000	3,000	3,000	3,000	3,000	3,000	3,000
Insurance	1,200	1,200	1,200	1,200	1,200	1,200	1,200	1,200
General office	300	300	300	300	300	300	300	300
Licenses	0	0	0	0	0	0	0	0
Interest[6]	1,431	1,431	1,306	1,306	965	840	715	715
Depreciation[7]	3,900	3,900	3,900	3,900	4,230	4,230	4,230	4,230
Total operating expenses	46,251	54,951	56,346	63,666	67,105	67,790	68,465	69,275
Profit (loss) before taxes	(5,616)	(8,511)	1,454	5,994	8,360	13,160	18,610	23,605
Less: Taxes	0	0	0	0	0			
Net profit (loss)	(5,616)	(8,511)	1,454	5,994	8,360	13,160	18,610	23,605

[1]Sales—per Action Plan; see Exhibit 1 for detail. Average unit sale is $40.00 for groceries plus $10.00 per week for delivery (Exhibit 2), making the monthly unit sales per household (2 people) $215.00.

[2]Cost of Goods Sold—80% of retail grocery price, or $32.00 per household per week ($138.00/month household). (80% an average margin on groceries—*Progressive Grocer;* April 1984; p. 94.)

[3]Salaries and Wages: Ms. Jones's salary will be $4,500/month. Order clerks will be paid $1,000/month, and delivery clerks will be paid $900/month. One additonal order clerk and delivery clerk each will be added once sales reach 100 households, and again at 200 households. Salaries will escalate at 6%/year.

[4]Advertising and Promotion: The grocery industry standard is 1% of sales. However, "Dinner Kits" being a new business will require more than that level; 5% of sales is used in this plan. (Special prestart-up advertising is covered with other start-up expenses.)

[5]Rent—2,000ft² @ $8.00/ft.²; 1,333 $/month; escalate at 6%/year.

[6]Interest—Loans on computer ($10,000), and delivery vehicles ($12,000 ea.) at 12.5%/year. (Delivery vehicles will be added with delivery clerks.) (Debt service—based on three-year amortization of loans with payments of ⅓ at the end of each of three years.)

[7]Depreciation—All equipment will be depreciated per ACRS Schedules: vehicles and computers—3 years; furniture and fixtures—10 years.

EXHIBIT 6 Pro Forma Cash Flow Statement

	Year 1												
	Mo. 1	*Mo. 2*	*Mo. 3*	*Mo. 4*	*Mo. 5*	*Mo. 6*	*Mo. 7*	*Mo. 8*	*Mo. 9*	*Mo. 10*	*Mo. 11*	*Mo. 12*	*Total*
Cash receipts													
Sales	2,150	3,225	5,375	10,750	16,125	19,350	21,500	23,650	25,800	27,950	30,100	32,250	218,225
Other													
Total cash receipts	2,150	3,225	5,375	10,750	16,125	19,350	21,500	23,650	25,800	27,950	30,100	32,250	218,225
Cash disbursements													
Cost of goods sold	1,376	2,064	3,440	6,880	10,320	12,384	13,760	15,136	16,512	17,888	19,264	20,640	139,664
Salaries and wages	6,400	6,400	6,400	6,400	6,400	6,400	8,300	8,300	8,300	8,300	8,300	8,300	88,200
Operational supplies	300	300	300	300	300	300	300	300	300	300	300	300	3,600
Repairs and maintenance	200	200	200	200	200	200	200	200	200	200	200	200	2,400
Advertising and promotion	110	160	270	540	810	970	1,080	1,180	1,290	1,400	1,500	1,610	10,920
Bad debts	50	50	50	50	50	50	50	50	50	50	50	50	600
Rent	1,330	1,330	1,330	1,330	1,330	1,330	1,330	1,330	1,330	1,330	1,330	1,330	15,960
Utilities	1,000	1,000	1,000	1,000	1,000	1,000	1,000	1,000	1,000	1,000	1,000	1,000	12,000
Insurance	400	400	400	400	400	400	400	400	400	400	400	400	4,600
General office	100	100	100	100	100	100	100	100	100	100	100	100	1,200
Licenses	100	0	0	0	0	0	0	0	0	0	0	0	100
Interest	340	340	340	340	340	340	465	465	465	465	465	465	4,830
Debt service (principle)	0	0	0	0	0	0	0	0	0	0	0	10,900	10,900
Total cash disbursements	11,706	12,344	13,830	17,540	21,250	23,474	26,985	28,461	29,947	31,433	32,909	45,295	295,174
Net cash flow	(9,556)	(9,119)	(8,455)	(6,790)	(5,125)	(4,124)	(5,485)	(4,811)	(4,147)	(3,483)	(2,809)	(13,045)	(76,949)

EXHIBIT 7 Pro Forma Cash Flow Statement

	Year 2				*Year 3*			
	Q 1	*Q 2*	*Q 3*	*Q 4*	*Q 1*	*Q 2*	*Q 3*	*Q 4*
Cash receipts								
Sales	112,875	129,000	161,000	193,500	209,625	225,750	241,875	258,000
Other								
Total cash receipts	112,875	129,000	161,000	193,500	209,625	225,750	241,875	258,000
Cash disbursements								
Cost of goods sold	72,240	82,560	103,200	123,840	134,160	144,480	154,800	165,120
Salaries and wages	24,900	32,700	32,700	38,400	40,800	40,800	40,800	40,800
Operational supplies	900	900	900	900	900	900	900	900
Repairs and maintenance	600	600	600	600	600	600	600	600
Advertising and promotion	5,640	6,450	8,060	9,680	10,480	11,290	12,090	12,900
Bad debts	150	150	150	150	150	150	150	150
Rent	4,230	4,230	4,230	4,230	4,480	4,480	4,480	4,480
Utilities	3,000	3,000	3,000	3,000	3,000	3,000	3,000	3,000
Insurance	1,200	1,200	1,200	1,200	1,200	1,200	1,200	1,200
General office	300	300	300	300	300	300	300	300
Licenses	0	0	0	0	0	0	0	0
Interest	1,431	1,431	1,306	1,306	965	840	715	715
Debt service (principle)	0	4,000	0	10,900	4,000	4,000	0	10,900
Total cash disbursements	114,591	137,521	155,646	194,506	201,035	212,040	219,035	241,065
Net cash flow	(1,716)	(8,521)	5,354	(1,006)	8,590	13,710	22,840	16,935

EXHIBIT 8 Pro Forma Balance Sheets

End of:	Yr 1	Yr 2	Yr 3		Yr 1	Yr 2	Yr 3
	Assets				*Liabilities*		
Current assets				Accounts payable	10,320	17,200	25,800
Cash	2,000	3,000	4,000	Notes payable	0	0	0
Accounts receivable	16,125	26,833	40,313	Total current liabilities	10,320	17,200	25,800
Inventory	10,320	17,200	25,800	Long-term liabilities			
Supplies	300	300	300	Bank loans payable	33,800	30,900	12,000
Prepaid expenses	1,330	1,330	1,330	Personal loans payable	0	0	0
Total current assets	30,075	48,663	71,743	Total long-term liabilities	33,800	30,900	12,000
Fixed assets				Total liabilities	44,120	48,100	37,800
Furniture and fixtures	12,600	11,200	9,800	Owner's equity			
Vehicles	18,000	17,880	4,440	Paid-in capital	110,744	52,882	0
Equipment	18,630	16,560	14,490	Retained earnings	(75,559)	(6,679)	63,735
Total fixed assets	49,230	45,640	28,730	Total owner's equity	35,185	46,203	63,735
Total assets	79,305	94,303	100,473	Total liabilities and equity	79,305	94,303	101,535

PART III

Financing a New Venture

CHAPTER

9

Sources of Capital

Chapter Objectives

1. To identify the types of financing available.
2. To understand the role of commercial banks in financing new ventures, the types of loans available, and bank lending decisions.
3. To discuss Small Business Administrative (SBA) loans.
4. To understand the aspects of research and development limited partnerships.
5. To discuss government grants, particularly small business innovation research grants.
6. To understand the role of private placement as a source of funds.

Walt Disney

Where does an entrepreneur get the funds to turn his or her dreams into reality? While funds come from a variety of sources, in the case of Walt Disney, it all started with a clandestine paper route.

Born in Chicago and raised on a small farm in Missouri, Walt Disney moved to Kansas City with his family when he was 10 years old. He and his brother worked without pay delivering newspapers for their father's circulation franchise. Whenever Walt found a new customer, he bypassed his father, buying the additional papers directly from the newspaper office, thereby establishing his own route. With the profits from this private venture, he was able to satisfy his sweet tooth without the knowledge of his parents, who forbade candy in their home.

From this beginning, Disney's entrepreneurial career branched out. As a teenager, he lied about his age and joined the Red Cross to serve in World War I, following his revered older brother, Roy. After he arrived in France with the last of the volunteers, his age quickly became a detriment. Duped by his comrades into picking up a bar bill larger than his first paycheck (which he had yet to receive), Walt was forced to sell his boots on the black market, swearing he would never be conned again. He learned to play a good game of poker, and started a con game of his own—"doctoring" German steel helmets he collected from the battlefield to look as though the previous owner had been shot in the head. He sold them as "genuine war souvenirs" to soldiers passing through the Red Cross station. Walt amassed what he considered to be a small fortune, which he sent home to his mother for safekeeping.

On returning home at the end of the war, Walt tried to fulfill his childhood dream of being a newspaper cartoonist. Although displaying artistic talent, he could not draw the negative, satirical cartoons wanted by the papers. Discouraged by the cold reception in Chicago, Walt moved to Kansas City with his brother Roy, who found him a job illustrating advertisements and catalogs for a client of one of the local banks. Since it was only a short-term job, after the Christmas rush Walt Disney was again unemployed and bothering his brother. Teaming up with a more skilled artist he had met on his first job, Walt Disney convinced a local publisher that his low-budget throwaway paper would be greatly improved by adding illustrated advertisements. Won over by Disney's charm, the publisher allowed the two artists to use a spare room (actually, a bathroom) as their studio. Using $250 from Walt's wartime earnings, Walt purchased enough equipment and supplies to start the business.

Always on the alert for more business opportunities, Walt contracted the service to other printers in town. Before long, "Iwerks & Disney" moved into a real office, and the two had enough money to attend the local movie house, where they were fascinated with the cartoon features. Responding to an advertisement for a cartoonist for the Kansas City Film Ad Company, Disney tried to sell the services of the partnership. When he was informed that the job was available to him alone, he gave his half of the partnership to Iwerks and walked away from the illustration business.

Quickly becoming the star of the artistic staff, Disney stayed with the Film Ad Company for only a short time, before founding his own production company, Laugh-O-Gram Films, Inc. In an attempt to raise capital in order to branch out from advertising, Disney sold shares in his company to a number of local citizens. With the $15,000 in capital, he created two cartoon shorts based on fairy tales, which were distributed nationally. Even though both were extremely popular, Disney did not receive any payments and was soon broke. However, he managed to save a camera and a copy of his most original work, "Alice's Wonderland," from the creditors. After raising some money by taking news photographs for the local papers, Disney headed west to Hollywood to start anew.

Even though the story becomes more complicated and the money raised much larger, the theme remains the same. Using his copy of "Alice's Wonderland" and the two fairy tale shorts to demonstrate his talent, Disney relied on charm, old contacts, and family for financial support: a Laugh-O-Gram client agreed to finance the production of several short "Alice" adventures; his brother Roy helped with the business deals; and some of his old Kansas City supporters renewed their contributions. Disney Productions went through cycles of feast and famine brought about by the founder's drive for perfection. When Disney got his way, the products were outstanding but expensive, and the two Disney brothers often found themselves over their heads in dealing with the motion picture industry. Just when they thought they had a hit, ideas were stolen, profits were not accounted for, and their whole world seemed to be on the verge of collapse. Then, miraculously, a new idea would appear and the studio would flourish again. It was during this time that Disney Productions added sound and color to their increasingly popular short cartoons, which increased both their artistic impact and their cost. Although its name was known worldwide, Disney Productions found it difficult to turn a profit.

The turning point in terms of profit was the production of a full-length cartoon feature: *Snow White and the Seven Dwarfs.* Premiering in 1937, it was a costly box office success. With a production budget of nearly 10 times that of a "live" feature, the cartoon would have ruined the company had it been a failure. Fortunately, it became one of the most successful motion pictures in history. From the profits, Walt Disney started working on three new features and expanded the plan and facilities. The new movies, *Pinocchio, Bambi,* and *Fantasia,* were each completed well over budget, and were not initially successful in the American market. To make matters worse, the outbreak of World War II just as these films were being released destroyed the profitable European market. With construction debts increasing, the only financing alternative appeared to be going public—selling stock. In April 1940, 755,000 units of common stock and preferred shares were sold, raising nearly $8 million in capital, once again saving the company.

However, being a public corporation was not the ultimate salvation for Disney Productions. Walt Disney, like many typical entrepreneurs, was used to running the company by controlling everything to the tiniest detail and did not like relegating any responsibilities and duties to the shareholders. Growing weary of cartooning and movies, Walt turned his attention to another dream—an amusement park. Roy, however, did not see this as a money-maker, and convinced the board of directors and several bankers to turn down Walt's request for money. Desperate for the cash to fulfill his fantasy, Walt Disney turned to a different source of capital: television. Although television was the newest entertainment rage, Disney Productions had avoided it, viewing it as too demeaning. Since all other sources of revenue were blocked, Disney agreed to a joint venture with ABC, the newest and smallest of the broadcasting companies. In return for $5 million in financing for the park, Disney agreed to put Mickey Mouse on TV. Things have not been the same since, for ABC, Disney Productions, or the American public.

As was the case throughout Walt Disney's entrepreneurial career, one of the most critical problems confronted by each entrepreneur is securing financing for the venture. While this is a problem throughout the life of the enterprise, it is particularly acute at start-up. From the entrepreneur's perspective, the longer the venture can operate without outside capital, the lower the cost of the capital in terms of interest rates or equity loss in the company. If an amount of money were invested in a company after three years, following a track record of sales and profit, a stated equity position would obtain maybe about 10 percent. In contrast, the same amount of capital invested earlier in the history of the company might obtain a 30 percent equity position. From the perspective of the provider of the funds, a potential investment opportunity needs to have an appropriate risk/return ratio. A higher return is expected when there is a greater risk involved. An investor will seek to maximize return for a given level of risk or minimize risk for a given level of return. This chapter describes some common (as well as some not so common) sources of capital and the conditions under which the money is obtained. As was the case with Walt Disney, different sources of capital are generally used at different times in the life of the venture.

AN OVERVIEW

For the entrepreneur, financing can be reviewed from the perspective of debt versus equity or internal versus external sources of funds.

Debt or Equity Financing

Generally, financing can be one of two types: debt financing or equity financing. Debt financing is a financing method involving an interest-bearing instrument, usually called a loan, the payment for which is only indirectly related to the sales and profits of the new venture. Typically, debt financing (also called asset-based financing) requires that some asset (such as a car, house, machine, or land) be available as collateral.

Debt financing requires the entrepreneur to pay back the amount of funds borrowed plus a fee expressed in terms of the interest rate and sometimes points for being able to use the money. If the financing is short-term (less than one year), the money is used to provide working capital to finance inventory, accounts receivable, or the operation of the business. The funds are typically repaid from the resulting sales and profits during this year's time period. Long-term debt (lasting more than one year) is frequently used to purchase some asset such as a piece of machinery, land, or a building with part of the value of the asset (usually up to about 50 percent to 80 percent of the total value) being used as collateral for the long-term loan. Particularly when interest rates are low, debt (as opposed to equity financing) has the advantage of allowing the entrepreneur to retain a large ownership portion in the venture and have a greater return on the equity. However, care must be taken that the debt is not so great that regular interest payments become difficult if not impossible to make, and growth and development are inhibited sometimes to the extent that bankruptcy results.

Equity financing, on the other hand, typically does not require collateral and offers the investor some form of ownership position in the venture. The investor shares in the profits of the venture, as well as any disposition of its assets on a pro rata basis. Key factors favoring the use of one type of financing over another are the availability of funds, the assets of the venture, and the prevailing interest rates. Usually, an entrepreneur meets financial needs by employing a combination of debt and equity financing.

Internal or External Funds

From another perspective, there are two types of funds available: internal or external funds. The type of funds most frequently employed is internally generated funds. Internally generated funds can come from several sources within the company: profits, sale of assets, reduction in working capital, extended payment terms, and accounts receivable. In every new venture, the start-up years usually involve plowing all the profits back into the venture; even outside equity investors expect no payback in these early years. Sometimes, the needed funds can be obtained by selling little-used assets. Assets, whenever possible, should be on a rental basis (preferably a lease with an option to buy) not an ownership basis, as long as there is not a high level of inflation and the terms are favorable to conserve cash, particularly during the start-up phase of the company's operation.

Another short-term, internal source of funds can be obtained by reducing short-term assets: inventory, cash, and other working-capital items. Sometimes, an entrepreneur can generate the needed cash for a short 30 to 60 days through extended payment terms from suppliers. While care must be taken to ensure good supplier relations and continuous sources of supply, taking a few extra days before paying the bills can also generate needed short-term funds. A final method for internally generating funds is by collecting bills (accounts receivable) more quickly. Care should be taken not to irritate key accounts when implementing this practice, as certain customers have unalterable payment practices. Mass merchandisers, for example, pay their bills to supplying companies in 60 to 90 days, regardless of a supplying company's accounts receivable policy, the size of the company, or the discount for prompt payment offered. If a company wants this mass merchandiser to carry its product, it will have to abide by this payment schedule.

The other general category of funds is those external to the firm. Alternative sources of external financing need to be evaluated on three bases: the length of time the funds are available, the costs involved, and the amount of company control lost. In selecting the best of the various sources of funds," from one's self to government programs, these sources need to be evaluated along these three dimensions (see Table 9–1). The more frequently used sources of funds (commercial banks, the Small Business Administration [SBA] loans, R&D limited partnerships, government grants, and private placement) indicated in the table are discussed in depth below.

COMMERCIAL BANKS

Commercial banks are by far the most frequently used source of short-term funds by the entrepreneur. The funds provided are in the form of debt financing and as such require some tangible guaranty or collateral—some asset with value. This collateral can be in the form of business assets (land, equipment, or the building of the venture), personal assets (the entrepreneur's house, car, land, stock, or bonds), or the assets of a cosigner of the note, who will guarantee that the loan will be repaid.

Types of Bank Loans

There are several types of bank loans available. To ensure a reasonable expectation of repayment, these loans are based on the assets or the cash flow of the venture. The asset base for loans include accounts receivable, inventory, equipment, or real estate.

Accounts receivable loans. Accounts receivable provide a good basis for a loan, especially if the customer base is well-known and creditworthy. On determination of the creditworthiness of the customer base, a bank may finance up to 80 percent of the value of the accounts receivable. When customers such as the government are involved, an entrepreneur can develop a factoring arrangement whereby the factor (the bank) actually "buys" the accounts receivable at a value below the face value of the sale and collects the money directly from the account. In this case, if any of the receivables are not collectible, the factor sustains the loss, not the business. The cost of factoring the accounts receivable is of course higher than the cost of securing a loan against the accounts receivable without factoring being involved, since the bank

TABLE 9–1 Alternative Sources of Financing

	Length of Time		*Cost*				*Control*	
Source of Financing	*Short-Term*	*Long-Term*	*Fixed Rate Debt*	*Floating Rate Debt*	*Percent of Profits*	*Equity*	*Covenants*	*Voting Rights*
Self		X				X	X	X
Family and friends	X	X	X	X		X	X	X
Suppliers and trade credit	X				X			
Commercial banks	X		X	X			X	
Asset-based lenders		X	X	X			X	
Institutions and insurance companies		X	X	X	X		X	
Pension funds		X			X	X	X	
Venture capital		X				X	X	X
Private equity placements						X	X	X
Public equity offerings					X	X		X
Government programs		X						

has more risk when factoring. The costs of factoring involve both the interest charge on the amount of money advanced until the time the accounts receivable are collected, the commission covering the actual collection, and protection against possible uncollectible accounts.

Inventory loans. Inventory is another of the firm's assets that is often a basis for a loan, particularly when the inventory is very liquid, that is, can be sold easily. Usually, the finished goods inventory can be financed to up to 50 percent of its value. Trust receipts are a unique type of inventory loan used to finance floor plans of retailers, such as automobile and appliance dealers. In trust receipts, the bank advances a large percentage of the invoice price of the goods and is paid on a pro rata basis as the inventory is sold.

Equipment loans. Equipment can be used to secure longer-term financing, from 3 to 10 years. Equipment financing can be of several types: financing the purchase of new equipment, financing used equipment already owned by the company, sale-leaseback financing, or lease financing. When new equipment is being purchased or presently owned equipment is used as collateral, usually from 50 to 80 percent of the value of the equipment can be financed, depending on its salability. Given the entrepreneur's propensity to rent versus own, sale-leaseback or lease financing of equipment is widely used. In the sale-leaseback arrangement, the entrepreneur "sells" the equipment to a lender and then leases it back for the life of the equipment to ensure its continued use. In lease financing, the company acquires the use of the equipment through a small down payment and a guarantee to make a specified number of payments over a period of time. The total amount paid is the selling price plus the finance charges.

Real estate loans. Real estate is also frequently used in asset-based financing. This mortgage financing is usually easily obtained to finance a company's land, plant, or building, usually up to 75 percent of its value.

Cash Flow Financing

The other type of debt financing frequently provided by commercial banks and other financial institutions is cash flow financing. These *conventional bank loans* include lines of credit, installment loans, straight commercial loans, long-term loans, and character loans. Lines of credit financing are perhaps the form of cash flow financing most frequently used by entrepreneurs. In arranging for a line of credit to be used as needed, the company pays a "commitment fee" at the start to ensure that the commercial bank will make the loan when requested and then pays interest on any outstanding funds borrowed from the bank. Frequently, the loan must be repaid on a periodic basis at least until it is reduced to a certain agreed-upon level.

Installment loans. Installment loans can also be obtained by a going venture with a track record of sales and profits. These short-term funds are frequently used to cover working capital needs for a period of time, such as when seasonal financing is needed. These loans are usually for 30 to 40 days.

Straight commercial loan. A hybrid of the installment loan is the straight commercial loan by which funds are advanced to the company for 30 to 90 days. These self-liquidating loans are frequently used for seasonal financing and building up inventories.

Long-term loans. When a longer time period for use of the money is required, long-term loans are used. These loans (usually only available to strong, more mature companies) can make funds available for up to 10 years. The debt incurred is usually repaid according to a fixed interest and principal schedule; although, the principal can sometimes start being repaid in the second or third year of the loan.

Character loan. When the business itself does not have the assets to support a loan, the entrepreneur may need a character (personal) loan. These loans frequently must have the assets of the entrepreneur or other individual pledged or the loan cosigned by another individual. Assets that are frequently pledged include cars, homes, land, and securities. One entrepreneur's father pledged a $50,000 certificate of deposit as collateral for his son's $40,000 loan. In extremely rare instances, the entrepreneur can obtain money on an unsecured basis for a short time when a high credit standing has been established.

Bank Lending Decisions

One problem for the entrepreneur is how to successfully secure a loan from the bank. Due to previous bad loan decisions by banks, particularly in some depressed areas of the country, banks are very cautious in lending money since they cannot afford to incur more bad loans. Regardless of the area of the world, commercial loan decisions are made only after the loan officer and loan review committee do a careful review of the borrower and the financial track record of the business. These decisions are based on both quantifiable information and subjective judgments.[1]

The bank lending decisions can be summarized as the five Cs of lending: Character, Capacity, Capital, Collateral, and Conditions. Past financial statements (balance sheets and income statements) are reviewed in terms of key profitability and credit ratios, inventory turnover, aging of accounts receivable, the entrepreneur's capital invested, and commitment to the business, which were indicated in Chapter 4. Future projections on market size, sales, and profitability are also evaluated to determine the ability to repay the loan and the margin surrounding that ability. Several questions are usually raised regarding this ability. Does the entrepreneur expect to be carried by the loan for an extended period of time? If problems occur, is the entrepreneur committed enough to spend the effort necessary to make the business a success? Does the business have a unique differential advantage in a growth market? What are the downside risks? Is there protection (such as life insurance on key personnel and insurance on the plant and equipment) against disasters?

While the answers to these questions and the analysis of the company's records allow the loan officer to assess the quantitative aspects of the loan decision, the intuitive factors, particularly the first two Cs—Character and Capacity—are also taken into account. This part of the loan decision—the gut feeling—is the most difficult part of the decision to assess. The entrepreneur must present his or her capabilities and the prospects for the company in a way that elicits a positive response—the loan being given. This intuitive part of the loan decision becomes even more important when there is little or no track record, limited experience in financial management, a nonproprietary product or service (one not protected by a patent or license), or few assets available.

Some of the concerns of the loan officer and the loan committee can be reduced by providing a good loan application. While the specific loan application format of each bank differs to some extent, generally the application format is a "Mini" business plan consisting of an executive summary, business description, owner/manager profiles, business projections, financial statements, amount and use of the loan, and repayment schedule. This information provides the loan officer and loan committee with the two most important pieces of information: the creditworthiness of the individual and the venture and the ability of the venture to make enough sales and profit to repay the loan and the interest. The entrepreneur should evaluate several alternative banks, select one, call for an appointment, and then carefully present the case

---

[1]For a discussion of bank lending decisions, see A. D. Jankowicz & R. D. Hisrich, "Institution in Small Business Lending Decisions," *Journal of Small Business Management,* July 1987, pp. 45–52; N. C. Churchill & V. L. Lewis, "Bank Lending to New and Growing Enterprises," *Journal of Business Venturing,* Spring 1986, pp. 193–206; R. T. Justis, "Starting a Small Business: An Investigation of the Borrowing Procedure," *Journal of Small Business Management,* October 1982, pp. 22–31; and L. Fertuck, "Survey of Small Business Lending Practices," *Journal of Small Business Management,* October 1982, pp. 42–48.

for the loan to the loan officer. Presenting a positive business image and following the established procedure are important in obtaining the needed funds from a commercial bank.

Regardless of the type of commercial bank loan, the entrepreneur should generally borrow the maximum amount, as long as the prevailing interest rates and the terms, conditions, and restrictions of the loan are satisfactory. Care must be taken to ensure that the venture will generate enough cash flow to repay the interest and principal on the loan in a timely manner. The entrepreneur should evaluate the track record and lending procedures of several banks in the area to secure the money needed on the most favorable terms available. This "bank shopping procedure" will provide the needed funds at the most favorable rates and positively impact the financial returns of the venture.

SMALL BUSINESS ADMINISTRATION LOANS

Frequently, an entrepreneur is missing the necessary track record, assets, or some other ingredient to obtain a commercial bank loan. This problem can stem from a lack of communication and differences in objectives between the entrepreneur and the banker. For example, the entrepreneur frequently emphasizes the top line—sales—while the bank loan officer emphasizes the bottom line—profit. Although sales are important, the entrepreneur should be careful to make a balanced presentation, emphasizing both sales and profit.

When differences cannot be resolved or there are other factors causing the entrepreneur to be unable to secure a regular commercial bank loan, an alternative is a Small Business Administration (SBA) Guaranty Loan. In this loan, the SBA guarantees that 80 percent of the amount loaned to the entrepreneur's business will be repaid to the bank by the SBA—the U.S. Government—if the company cannot make payment. This guarantee allows the bank to make a loan that has a higher risk than loans it would otherwise make. The process for securing such a loan is outlined in Table 9–2. This procedure is the same as the one used for securing a regular loan, except that government forms and documentation are also required. Usually, some banks in a city will specialize in these loans; these banks are better able to assist the entrepreneur in filling out the appropriate forms correctly, minimizing the time involved in the government's processing, and approving (or disapproving) the loan.

Both long- and short-term loans can be guaranteed by the SBA. If the collateral is of a lasting nature, such as land and buildings, a maximum loan period of 15 years on existing buildings and 20 years on new construction can be obtained. If the loan is for inventory, machinery, equipment, or working capital, a maximum loan period of 10 years is available, although the usual time is 5 years. Once the application has been correctly filled out with all the required supporting materials, it is generally processed within 15 days if no backlog exists. If an SBA Guaranty Loan is granted, it has additional reporting requirements beyond those that exist with a conventional commercial bank loan. Since there is typically no difference in the interest rates charged between a conventional bank loan and an SBA guaranteed loan, a

TABLE 9–2 SBA Loan Application Procedure

1. Assemble the information outlined below.
2. Take it to your bank and ask your banker to review the information and loan proposal. (It will be necessary for you to locate a bank that is willing to participate with SBA and make the loan since direct loan funds from SBA are quite limited and an unreliable source of financing.)
3. If the bank is willing to participate, ask the bank to forward the information to us for our review, along with their comments.

INFORMATION NEEDED FOR LOAN REVIEW

1. Brief résumé of business.
2. Brief résumé of management, setting forth prior business experience, technical training, education, age, health, etc.
3. Itemized use of loan proceeds:

Working capital	$____________
Land	$____________
Building	$____________
Furniture and fixtures	$____________
Machinery and equipment	$____________
Automotive equipment	$____________
Other	$____________
Total	$____________

4. Current business balance sheet and profit/loss statement.
5. Year-ending balance sheets and profit/loss statements for the last three years or, if the business has been in existence less than three years, furnish the financial statements for each year it has been in operation. (Copies of the financial statements submitted with the income tax returns are adequate.)
6. If the business is not in existence but is proposed, furnish a projected balance sheet of the business showing its proposed assets, liabilities, and net worth upon commencement of operations, together with projected annual operating statements for the first three years of operation.
7. Furnish a separate personal balance sheet showing all assets owned and liabilities owed outside of the business.

The above information is what a loan officer will need to properly analyze your loan proposal.

commercial bank loan is usually better, as it has fewer reporting requirements and allows the entrepreneur to establish a good banking relationship based on the merits of the business. Such a relationship will be valuable as the venture grows and matures and more bank financing is needed.

RESEARCH AND DEVELOPMENT LIMITED PARTNERSHIPS

Research and development limited partnerships are another possible source of funds for entrepreneurs in high-technology areas. Instead of using debt from lenders, equity from owners, or cash from internal operations, this method of financing provides funds from investors looking for tax shelters. A typical R&D partnership arrangement is established between a sponsoring company developing the technology with funds being provided by a limited partnership. R&D limited partnerships are good alternatives for funding, particularly for small entrepreneurial companies lacking access to capital markets. They are particularly good when the project involves a high degree of risk and significant expense in doing the basic research and development. In research and development limited partnerships, these risks, as well as the ensuing rewards, are shared.

Major Elements

The three major components of any R&D limited partnership are the contract, the sponsoring company, and the limited partnership. The contract specifies the agreement between the sponsoring company and the limited partnership, whereby the sponsoring company agrees to use the funds provided to do the proposed research and development that hopefully will result in a marketable technology for the partnership. The sponsoring company does not guarantee results, but rather performs the work on a best-effort basis, being compensated by the partnership on either a fixed-fee or cost-plus arrangement. The typical contract has several key features. The first is that the liability for any loss incurred is borne by the limited partners. Second, there are some tax advantages to both the limited partnership and the sponsoring company. This tax deduction is based on two tax authorizations: Section 174 of the Internal Revenue Code and the *Snow vs. Commissioner* case of 1974. Section 174 allows a taxpayer to deduct R&D costs as incurred expenses rather than have these costs capitalized as part of the final cost of the product. This regulation was supported by the U. S. Supreme Court ruling in *Snow vs. Commissioner,* which said that it was sufficient for the taxpayer to incur the expenses of research and development in connection with a trade or business in order to treat the investment as an expense versus a cost. Limited partners may deduct their investments in the R&D contract under Section 174 in the year their investments are made. Depending on the tax bracket of the limited partner (the higher the bracket the more significant the effect), this deduction significantly increases the rate of return of the investment in the limited partnership, thereby increasing the compensation for the high risk involved.

The second component involved in this contract is the limited partners. Like the stockholders of a corporation, the *limited partners* have limited liability but differ in not being a total taxable entity. Income and loss from the partnership are allocated to each individual's tax return. Consequently, any tax benefits of the losses in the early stages of the R&D limited partnership are passed directly to the limited partners, offsetting other income and reducing the partners' total taxable incomes. When the technology is successfully developed in later years, the partners share in the profits. In some instances, these profits for tax purposes are at the lower capital gains tax rate versus the ordinary income rate.

The final component—the sponsoring company—acts as the *general partner* developing the technology. The sponsoring company usually has the base technology but needs to secure limited partners to further develop and modify it for commercial success. It is this base technology that the company is offering to the partnership in exchange for money. The sponsoring company usually retains the rights to use this base technology to develop other products and the right to use the developed technology in the future for a license fee. Otherwise, a cross-licensing agreement is established, whereby the partnership allows the company to use the technology for developing other products.

Procedure

An R&D limited partnership generally goes through three stages: the funding stage, the development stage, and the exit stage. In the funding stage, a contract is established between the sponsoring company and limited partners, and the money is invested for the proposed research and development effort. All the terms and conditions of ownership, as well as the scope of the research, are carefully documented.

In the development stage, the sponsoring company performs the actual research, using the funds from the limited partners. If the technology is subsequently successfully developed, the exit stage commences, in which the sponsoring company and the limited partners commercially reap the benefits of the effort. There are three basic types of arrangements for doing this: equity partnerships, royalty partnerships, and joint ventures.

In the typical equity partnership arrangement, the sponsoring company and the limited partners form a new, jointly owned corporation. Based on the formula established in the original agreement, the limited partners' interest can be transferred to equity in the new corporation on a tax-free basis. An alternative is to incorporate the R&D limited partnership itself and then either merge it into the sponsoring company or continue as a new entity.

An alternative exit to the equity partnership arrangement is a royalty partnership. In this situation, a royalty based on the sale of the products developed from the technology is paid by the sponsoring company to the R&D limited partnership. The royalty rates typically range from 6 to 10 percent of gross sales and often decrease at certain established sales levels. Frequently, an upper limit, or cap, is placed on the cumulative royalties paid.

A final exit arrangement is through a joint venture. Here the sponsoring company and the partners form a joint venture to manufacture and market the products developed from the technology. Usually, the agreement allows the company to buy out the partnership interest in the joint venture at a specified time or when a specified volume of sales and profit have been reached.

Benefits and Costs

As with any financing arrangement, the entrepreneur must carefully assess the appropriateness of establishing an R&D limited partnership in terms of the benefits and costs involved. Among the several benefits is that an R&D limited partnership provides the needed funds with a minimum amount of equity dilution, while reducing the risks involved. In addition, an increase in business and financial planning occurs. Finally, the sponsoring company's financial statements are strengthened through the attraction of outside capital.

There are some costs to be considered in this financial arrangement. First, there are the time and money involved. An R&D limited partnership frequently takes a minimum of six months to establish (if it's established at all) and $50,000 in professional fees. These can increase to a year and $400,000 in costs for a major effort. And the track record is not as good; most R&D limited partnerships offered are unsuccessful. Second, the restrictions placed on the technology can be substantial. To give up the technology developed as a by-product of the primary effort may be too high a price to pay for the funds. Third, the exit from the partnership may be too complex and involve too much fiduciary responsibility. Finally, typically an R&D limited partnership is more expensive to establish than are conventional financing arrangements. These costs and benefits need to be carefully evaluated in light of other financial alternatives available before a research and development limited partnership is chosen as the funding vehicle.

Examples

In spite of the many costs involved, there are numerous examples of successful R&D limited partnerships. Syntex Corporation raised $23.5 million in an R&D limited partnership to develop five medical diagnostic products. Genetech was so successful in developing human growth hormone and gamma Interferon products from its first $55 million R&D limited partnership that it raised $32 million through a second one six months later to develop a tissue-type plasminogen activator. Trilogy

Limited raised $55 million to develop a high-performance computer. And the list goes on. Indeed, R&D limited partnerships offer one financial alternative to fund the development of a venture's technology.

GOVERNMENT GRANTS

Sometimes the entrepreneur can obtain federal grant money to develop and launch an innovative idea. A program of particular interest designed for the small business is the Small Business Innovation Research (SBIR) grant program, created in 1982 as a part of the Small Business Innovation Development Act. The act requires that all federal agencies with R&D budgets in excess of $100 million award a portion of their R&D funds to small businesses through the SBIR grants program. This act not only provides an opportunity for small businesses to obtain research and development money but provides a uniform method by which each participating agency solicits, evaluates, and selects the research proposals for funding. In the first year of the SBIR program, 730 projects were awarded Phase I grants totaling more than $40 million. While the amount of money available varies each year, it is usually not less than this amount.

Eleven federal agencies are involved in the program (see Table 9–3). Each agency develops topics and publishes solicitations describing the R&D topic it will fund. Small businesses submit proposals directly to each agency using the format required in the specific solicitation; the format is somewhat standardized, regardless of the agency. Each agency, using its established evaluation criteria, evaluates each proposal on a competitive basis and makes awards through a contract, grant, or cooperative agreement.

The SBIR grant program has three phases (see Table 9–4). Phase I awards are up to $50,000 for six months of feasibility-related experimental or theoretical research. The objective of this research is to determine the technical feasibility of the research

TABLE 9–3 Federal Agencies Participating in Small Business Innovation Research Program

- Department of Defense (DOD)
- National Aeronautics and Space Administration (NASA)
- Department of Energy (DOE)
- Health and Human Services (HHS)
- National Science Foundation (NSF)
- U.S. Department of Agriculture (USDA)
- Department of Transportation (DOT)
- Nuclear Regulatory Commission (NRC)
- Environmental Protection Agency (EPA)
- Department of Interior (DOI)
- Department of Education (DOED)

TABLE 9–4 Three Phases of Funding in the SBIR Program

Phase I	*Phase II*	*Phase III*
SBIR funds (Idea stage)	SBIR funds (Product stage)	Private-sector funds (Business stage)

effort and assess the quality of the company's performance through a relatively small monetary commitment. Successful projects are then considered for further federal funding support in Phase II.

Phase II is the principal R&D effort for those projects most promising at the end of Phase I. Phase II awards are up to $500,000 for 24 months of further research and development. The money is to be used to develop prototype products or services. A small business receiving a Phase II award has demonstrated good research results in Phase I, developed a proposal of sound scientific and technical merit, and obtained a commitment for follow-on private-sector financing in Phase III for commercialization.

Phase III does not involve any direct funding from the SBIR program. Funds from the private sector or regular government procurement contracts are needed to commercialize the developed technologies in Phase III.

Procedure

Applying for an SBIR grant is a straightforward procedure. The government agencies participating (those listed in Table 9–3) publish solicitations describing the areas of research they will fund. Each of these annual solicitations contains documentation on the agency's R&D objectives, proposal format, due dates, deadlines, and selection and evaluation criteria. The second step involves the submission of the proposal by a company or individual. The proposal—25 pages maximum—follows the standard proposal format. Each agency screens the proposals it receives. Those passing the screen are evaluated by knowledgeable scientists or engineers on a technological basis. Finally, awards are granted to those projects that have the best potential for commercialization. Any patent rights, research data, technical data, and software generated in the research are owned by the company or individual not by the government.

The SBIR grant program is one viable alternative for obtaining funds for a technically based entrepreneurial company that is independently owned and operated and employs 500 or fewer individuals. Not only can the company have any organization structure (corporation, partnership, sole proprietorship), it need not even be formally established before the award is granted.

PRIVATE PLACEMENT

A final source of funds for the entrepreneur is private investors, who may be family and friends or wealthy individuals. Individuals who handle their own sizeable investments frequently use advisors, such as accountants, technical experts, financial planners, or lawyers, in making their investment decisions.

Type of Investors

An investor usually takes an equity position in the company and can influence the nature and direction of the business to a certain extent and may be involved to some degree in the business operation. The degree of involvement in the direction or the day-to-day operations of the venture is an important point for the entrepreneur to consider in selecting an investor. While some investors want to be actively involved in the business, others desire at least an advisory role in the direction and operation of the venture and want to share in its profits. Still others are more passive in nature, desiring no active involvement in the venture at all. Generally this more passive investor is primarily interested in recovering his or her investment plus a good rate of return.

Private Offerings

A formalized approach for obtaining funds from private investors is through a private offering. A private offering is different from a public offering or going public (the focus of Chapter 11) in several ways. Public offerings involve a great deal of time and expense, in part to fulfill the numerous regulations and requirements involved. The process of registering the securities with the Securities and Exchange Commission (SEC) is an arduous task requiring a significant number of reporting procedures once the firm has gone public. Since this process was established primarily to protect unsophisticated investors, a private offering is faster and less costly when a limited number of sophisticated investors are involved who have the necessary business acumen and ability to absorb risk. These sophisticated investors still need access to material information about the company and its management. What constitutes material information? Who is a sophisticated investor? How many is a limited number? Answers to these questions are provided in Regulation D.

Regulation D

Regulation D contains: (1) a number of broad provisions designed to simplify private offerings, (2) general definitions of what constitutes a private offering, and (3) specific operating rules—Rule 504, Rule 505, and Rule 506. Regulation D requires the issuer of a private offering to file five copies of Form D with the Securities and

Exchange Commission (SEC) 15 days after the first sale, every six months thereafter, and 30 days after the final sale. Also, it provides rules governing the notices of sale and the payment of any commissions involved.

The entrepreneur issuing the private offering carries the burden of proving that the exemptions granted have been met. This involves completing the necessary documentation and research. For example, the degree of sophistication of each potential investor needs to be thoroughly investigated and documented. Each offering memorandum presented to an investor needs to be numbered and must contain instructions that the document should not be reproduced or disclosed to any other individual. The date that the investor (or the designated representative) reviews the company's information—its books and records—as well as the date(s) of any discussion between the company and the investor should also be recorded. At the close of the offering, the offering company needs to verify and note that no persons other than those recorded were contacted regarding the securities. The book documenting all the specifics of the offering needs to be placed in the company's permanent file. The general procedures of Regulation D are further broadened by the three Rules—504, 505, and 506.

Rule 504 provides the first exemption to a company seeking to raise a small amount of capital from numerous investors. Under Rule 504, a company can sell up to $500,000 of securities to any number of investors, regardless of their sophistication, in any 12-month period. While there is no specific form of disclosure required, the issuing company cannot engage in any general solicitation or advertising. Some states do not allow investors to resell their shares unless the security is registered.

Rule 505 changes both the investors and the dollar amount of the offering. This rule permits the sale of $5 million of unregistered securities in the private offering in any 12-month period. These securities can be sold to any 35 investors and to an unlimited number of accredited investors. This eliminates the need for the sophistication test and disclosure requirements called for by Rule 504.

What constitutes an "accredited investor?" Accredited investors include: (1) institutional investors (banks, insurance companies, investment companies, employee benefit plans containing over $5 million in assets, tax-exempt organizations with endowment funds of over $25 million, and private business development companies), (2) investors who purchase over $150,000 of the issuer's securities, (3) investors whose net worth is $1 million or more at the time of sale, (4) investors with incomes in excess of $200,000 in each of the last two years, and (5) directors, executive officers, and general partners of the issuing company.

Companies eligible to issue under Rule 505 have been expanded to include oil and gas companies, partnerships, and non-North American companies. Like Rule 504, Rule 505 permits no general advertising or solicitation through public media. When only accredited investors are involved, no disclosure is required under Rule 505 (similar to the issuance under Rule 504). However, if the issuance involves any unaccredited investors, additional information must be disclosed. Regardless of the amount of the offering, two-year financial statements for the two most recent years must be available unless such a disclosure requires "undue effort and expense." When this occurs for any issuing company other than a limited partnership, a balance sheet as of 120 days prior to the offering can be used instead. All companies selling private-placement securities to both accredited and unaccredited investors must furnish appropriate company information to both and allow any questions to be asked prior to the sale. Rule 506 goes one step further than Rule 505 by allowing an issuing company to sell an unlimited number of securities to 35 investors and an unlimited number of accredited investors and relatives of issuers. As is the case with each of the other rules, no general advertising or solicitation through public media can be involved.

In securing any outside funding, the entrepreneur must take great care to disclose all information as accurately as possible. Investors generally have no problem with the company as long as its operations continue successfully and the success is reflected in the valuation. But if the business turns sour, both investors and regulators scrutinize the company's disclosures in minute detail to determine if any technical or securities law violations occurred. When any violation of security law is discovered, management and sometimes the company's principal equity holders can be held liable as a corporation and as individuals. When this occurs, the individual is no longer shielded by the corporation and is open to significant liability and potential lawsuits. Lawsuits under securities law by damaged investors have almost no statute of limitations, as the time does not begin until the person harmed discovers or should reasonably be expected to discover the improper disclosure. The suit may be brought in federal court in any jurisdiction in which the defendant is found or lives or transacts business. An individual can file suit as a single plaintiff or as a class action on behalf of all persons similarly affected. Courts have awarded large attorney's fees as well as settlements when any security law violation occurs. Given the number of law suits and the litigious nature of U.S. society, the entrepreneur needs to be extremely careful to make sure that any and all disclosures are accurate. If this is not enough of an incentive, it should be kept in mind that the SEC can take administrative, civil, or criminal action as well, without any individual lawsuit involved. This action can result in fine, imprisonment, or the restoration of the monies involved.

BOOTSTRAP FINANCING

Even when capital is available in the form of debt or equity, an entrepreneur needs to make sure that the capital is really needed. An alternative to acquiring outside capital that should be considered is bootstrap financing.[2] This approach is particularly important at start-up and early years of the venture when capital from debt financing (i.e. in terms of higher interest rates) or from equity financing (i.e. in terms of loss of ownership) is more expensive.

[2] Bootstrap financing is discussed in Anne Murphy, "Capital Punishment," *Inc.*, November 1993, pp 38–42 and Michael P. Cronin, "Paradise Lost," *Inc.*, November 1993, pp 48–53.

In addition to the monetary costs, outside capital has other costs as well. First, it takes time—usually between three to six months—to raise outside capital or to find out that there is no outside capital available. During this time, the entrepreneur may not be paying enough attention to such important areas as marketing, sales, product development, and operating costs. When a business needs capital, it is usually when it can least afford the time to raise it. One company's CEO spent so much time raising capital that sales and marketing were neglected to such an extent that the forecasted sales and profit figures on the pro forma income statements were not met for the first three years following the capital infusion. This led to investor concern and irritation—which required more of the CEO's time.

Second, outside capital often decreases a firm's drive to make money. One successful manager would never hire a person as one of his commission salespeople if they "looked too prosperous." He felt that if a person was not hungry, he or she would not push as hard to sell. The same concept could be applied to outside funded companies that may have the tendency to substitute outside capital for income while overlooking the need for increased sales and cost controls.

Third, the availability of capital increases the impulse to spend. It can cause a company to hire more staff before they are needed and to move into costlier, more elaborate facilities. A company can easily forget the basic axiom of venture creation: staying lean and mean. Some examples of companies successfully growing by staying lean and mean and using internal capital instead of outside capital are indicated in Table 9–5. Each of these ten companies in different business areas had start-up capital ranging from $0 to $1,500. From this small capital base, the founders grew their companies to sales ranging from $2.8 million to $38 million by employing bootstrap financing and staying lean and mean.

Fourth, outside capital can decrease the company's flexibility. This can hamper the direction, the drive, and the creativity of the entrepreneur founder. Unsophisticated investors are particularly a problem, as they often object to a company moving away from the focus and direction outlined in the business plan that attracted their investment. This attitude can encumber a company to such an extent that the needed change cannot be implemented or else is implemented very slowly after a great deal of time and effort has been spent in consensus building. This can substantially demoralize the entrepreneur founder who likes the freedom of not working for someone else.

Finally, outside capital may cause more disruption and problems in the venture than was present without it. Capital is not provided without the expectation of a return—sometimes before the business should be giving one. Also, particularly if certain equity investors are involved, the entrepreneur founder is under pressure to continuously grow the company so that an initial public offering can be as soon as possible. This emphasis on short-term performance can be at the expense of the long-term success of the company.

In spite of these potential problems, an entrepreneur founder at times needs some equity funding, particularly to finance growth, which would be too slow or not at all if internal sources of funds were used. These problems and successes of the compa-

TABLE 9–5 Examples of Bootstrap Financing

The Company (Location, Year Founded, Business Description)	*The Founder(s)*	*$$ Started With*	*Numbers Now (1993 PROJECTIONS)*	*Key Early Capital Sources*	*Number of Months Before First Paycheck*
CROSSCOUNTRY COURIER Bismarck, N. D.; founded 1979 Provides courier and delivery services.	**Dewey Tietz.** Formerly a manager of an equipment manufacturer.	$1,500	**$4.8** million in sales **$240,000** in pretax profits **104** employees	Personal savings	12; first salary $8,400/year.
BUCKEYE BEANS & HERBS Spokane, WA.; founded 1983 Manufactures specialty foods.	**Jill and Doug Smith.** She's a potter who started Buckeye as a Christmas project; he formerly sold real estate.	$1,000	**$6.3** million in sales **$800,000** in pretax profits **35** employees	Suppliers	36 (Doug) and 60 (Jill); Jill kept her pottery business on the side.
CIVCO MEDICAL INSTRUMENTS Kalona, IA; founded 1982 Manufactures medical accessories.	**Victor J. Wedel.** Formerly chief technologist, University of Iowa.	$ 100	**$3.2** million in sales **$800,000** in pretax profits **35** employees	Bank loan	36; she worked full-time, he worked part-time on the side. First salary $8,000/year.
CLEAR IMAGE Orem, UT; founded 1980 Produces and duplicates videos.	Kelly M. Thayer. Formerly a shoe salesman.	$ 600	**$9** million in sales **$810,000** in pretax profits **90** employees	Unemployment check after being laid off from a department store	36; lived off his wife's income from the same store that fired him. First salary $900/month.
EXECUTRAIN Atlanta; founded 1984 Provides and franchises software training.	**David and Kim Deutsch (with Mike Addison and Mike Moss).** David had an M.B.A.; Kim, working toward hers, submitted the ExecuTrain business plan for a course. The class gave it an F.	$ 500	**$15** million in sales* **$3.5** million in pretax profits* **101** employees* (*not including franchises)	20 credit cards, small loans from family, customer financing	12; two of the partners kept day jobs. Took expenses in year two.

DAYDOTS LABEL Fort Worth; Founded 1985 Manufactures self-adhesive labels.	**Mike Milliorn.** Formerly a salesman for a printing company.	$ 0	**$4.6** million in sales **$690,000** in pretax profits **42** employees	Bank loan	60, but kept his printing job while running the business. First salary $40,000/year.
SPECTRUM ASSOCIATES Woburn, MA.; founded 1987 Provides software products and services.	**John Nugent and Tony Baudanza.** Formerly customer-service managers at a venture-backed software company.	$ 0	**$38** million in sales **$5.7** million in pretax profits **115** employees	Customers who prepaid	4; first salary $30,000/year each.
VICTORIAN PAPERS Kansas City, Mo.; founded 1987 Sells greeting cards and gifts wholesale, retail, and through catalogs.	**Melissa and Randy Rolston.** Randy worked for an ad agency and then started one. Melissa was a former freelance illustrator and at-home mom.	$ 0	**$3.5** million in sales **$420,000** in pretax profits **56** employees	Savings, suppliers, credit cards	Almost 0; drew cash for expenses. Salary still is not fixed; comes from profits, varies from month to month.
METROGRAPHICS PRINTING & COMPUTER SERVICES Fairchild, N. J.; Founded 1987 Distributes printing and computer services.	**Andrew Duke, Jeff Bernstein, and Patrick Veltri.** Duke was a big-company veteran.	$ 100 each	**$2.5** million in sales **$2,000,000** in pretax profits **12** employees	Suppliers	6; then expenses only for the next 6. Partners still work on commission.
NORTHWORD PRESS Minocqua, WI.; founded 1984 Publishes nature books and tapes.	**Tom and Pat Klein.** He was a nonprofit administrator; she quit her job in a frame shop to start the company.	$ 600	**$7.6** million in sales **$700,000**-plus in pretax profits **45** employees	Prepaying customers; cash flow from first book. *Loan Magic;* one angel	Almost 0; drew $12,000 in each of the first two years. $24,000 in the following two.

Source: Anne Murphy, "Capital Punishment," *Inc.*, November 1993, pp 41–42.

nies grown through internal sources of funds should serve as a warning. Outside capital should only be sought after all possible internal sources of funds have been explored. And when outside funds are needed and obtained, the entrepreneur should not forget to stay intimately involved with the basics of the business.

SUMMARY

All business ventures require capital. While capital is needed throughout the life of a business, the new entrepreneur faces significant difficulties in acquiring capital for start-up. An entrepreneur should first explore all methods of internal financing. These methods include using profits, selling unused assets, reducing working capital, obtaining credit from suppliers, and collecting accounts receivable promptly. After all internal sources have been exhausted, the entrepreneur may find it necessary to seek additional funds through external financing. External financing can be in the form of debt or equity. When considering external financing, the entrepreneur needs to consider the length of time, cost, and amount of control of each alternative financial arrangement.

Commercial bank loans are the most frequently used source of short-term external debt financing. This source of funding requires collateral, which may be asset-based or may take the form of cash flow financing. In either case, banks tend to be cautious about lending, particularly if they have had a recent history of bad loan decisions. They carefully weigh the five Cs of lending: Character, Capacity, Capital, Collateral, and Condition. Not every entrepreneur will qualify under the bank's careful scrutiny. When this occurs, an alternative for an entrepreneur is the SBA Guaranty Loan. The SBA guarantees 80 percent of the loan, allowing banks to lend money to businesses that might otherwise be refused.

A special method of raising capital for high-technology firms is a research and development (R&D) limited partnership. A contract is formed between a sponsoring company and a limited partnership. The partnership bears the risk of the research, receiving some tax advantages and sharing in future profits, including a fee to use the research in developing any future products. The entrepreneur has the advantage of acquiring needed funds for a minimum amount of equity dilution while reducing his own risk in the venture. However, setting up an R&D limited partnership is expensive, and the time factor (at least six months) may be too long for some ventures. Restrictions placed upon the technology as well as the complexities of exiting the partnership need careful evaluation.

Government grants are another alternative available to small businesses through the SBIR program. Businesses can apply for grants from 11 agencies. Phase I awards carry a stipend of up to $50,000 for six months of initial research. The most promising Phase I projects may qualify for Phase II support of up to $500,000 for 24 months of research.

Finally, the entrepreneur can seek private funding. Individual investors frequently require an equity position in the company and some degree of control. A less expensive and less complicated alternative to a public offering of stock is found in a private offering. By following the procedures of Regulation D and three specific rules—504, 505, and 506—an entrepreneur can sell private securities. When making a private offering, the entrepreneur must exercise care in accurately disclosing information and adhering precisely to the requirements of the SEC. Securities violations can lead to lawsuits against individuals as well as the corporation.

The entrepreneur needs to consider all possible sources of capital and select the one that will provide the needed funds with minimal cost and loss of control. Usually, different sources of funds are used at various stages in the growth and development of the venture, as occurred in the case of Walt Disney, a successful entrepreneur indeed.

QUESTIONS FOR DISCUSSION

1. Why is it important for an entrepreneur to generate financing internally as much as possible rather than depending entirely on external financing? How does the entrepreneur accomplish this?
2. In order to retain as much control as possible in your company, what sources of capital would you first investigate? Refer to Table 9–1.
3. Which of the commercial bank loans described in this chapter might be available for starting up a new business?
4. Under what circumstances would you form an R&D limited partnership rather than using other funding sources? How might this create problems for you once your research is successful, and how might you solve those problems?
5. Describe the process you would follow to pursue an SBIR grant. Would this be a good avenue for an individual with a great idea but no funds or company? Why or why not?
6. What criteria must be adhered to in obtaining funds through a private offering?

KEY TERMS

asset base for loans
conventional bank loans
debt financing
equity financing
general partner
internal funds
limited partners
private offerings
private placement
Regulation D
research and development limited partnerships
Small Business Innovation Research (SBIR) grants

SELECTED READINGS

Arnold, J. L. (1985). Exempt offerings: Going public privately. *Harvard Business Review,* 63, no. 1, pp 16–18+.

Due to recent policy and regulatory changes, smaller companies can now enjoy many benefits of going public without having to endure the legal, accounting, and other demands of registering securities. The author explains the concept of an exempt offering selling securities to small groups of qualified investors and offers advice for assessing situations under which offerings make the most sense.

Auken, Howerd E., & Carter, R. B. (April 1989). Acquisition of capital by small business. *Journal of Small Business Management* 27, no. 2, pp 1–9.

Concentrates on the financing characteristics of many small businesses and their success rates due to capital acquisition. The specific sources of equity and debt capital are examined, as well as different experiences of capitalization and size of debt relative to equity, and certain lending requirements imposed by lenders on new businesses requesting start-up funds.

Brophy, David J., and Chambers, Brian R. (1991). The growth capital symposium: an intervention into the market for growth capital. *Proceedings,* Conference on Entrepreneurship, pp 422–434.

Concerned with the origins of high-technology ventures in terms of their owners and capital structure. Data from five studies shed light on who starts new high-tech ventures, where they get their capital, what they give up versus gain, what happens when they are turned down for venture financing, and where they find capital for expansion.

Bruno, A. V., & Tyebjee, T. T. (1984). The entrepreneur's search for capital. *Proceedings,* 1984 Conference on Entrepreneurship, pp 18–31.

A study of the results of a program that brings entrepreneurs and investors together compared to the results of a control population not in the program indicates that entrepreneurial firms in a program have a higher probability of getting funds and a higher rate of survivorship.

Carter, Richard B., and Van Auken, Howard E. (1990). Personal equity investment and small business financial difficulties. *Entrepreneurship Theory and Practice* 15, no. 2, pp 51–60.

The data analyzed from 132 entrepreneurial firms identified a significant negative relation between first-year financial difficulties and the percent of start-up capital represented by the entrepreneurs' personal funds.

Chatigeat, T., Balsmeier, Phillip W., and Stanley, Thomas O. (1991). Fueling Asian Immigrants' Entrepreneurship: A Source of Capital. *Journal of Small Business Management* 29, no. 3, pp 50–61.

The successful establishment of new ventures by immigrants has been the result of support networks that provide, among other things, capital loaned through informal financial markets known as Rotating Saving and Credit Societies (RSCS). The societies employ three methods to gather and dispense funds and have good assurance of being repaid due to the extensive peer pressure operating.

Churchill, N. C., & Lewis, V. L. (April 1985). Bank lending to new and growing enterprises. *Proceedings,* 1985 Conference on Entrepreneurship, pp 338–357.

Based on an examination of individual accounts representing large and small borrowers and companies of different ages, the results found no significant differences in profitability to the bank for loans to small businesses of different sizes.

Davidson, Wallace N., and Dutia, Dipa. (1991). Debt, liquidity, and profitability: problems in small firms. *Entrepreneurship Theory and Practice* 16, no. 1, pp 53–64.

Data from 86,000 firms in 343 industries indicates that small firms have lower current and quick ratios than large firms. Small firms are sometimes forced to finance growth with debt rather than internally generated equity, causing lower profitability.

Dunkelberg, W. C., & Cooper, A. C. (April 1983). Financing the start of a small enterprise. *Proceedings,* 1983 Conference on Entrepreneurship, pp 369–381.

An examination of patterns of financing for 1,805 small firms indicated that: (1) both primary and secondary sources of funds were considered, with personal savings being the most important source; and (2) patterns of financing varied according to how ownership was achieved, years of ownership, initial size of firm, and industry classification.

Freear, J., & Wetzel, W. E., Jr. (1988) Equity Financing for new technology-based firms. In *Proceedings,* 1983 Conference on Entrepreneurship, pp 347–367.

CEOs of technology-based ventures completed questionnaires on their firm's financial history indicating how new technology-based ventures go about raising equity capital.

Goldstein, J. (April 1984). Undercapitalization is a winning entrepreneurial strategy. *Proceedings,* 1984 Conference on Entrepreneurship, pp 409–413.

Failure of a new small business is commonly attributed to a lack of capital. The author advances the proposition that the opposite is true—that lack of capital could be a prime cause of the success of a venture. Using anecdotal material, the author develops the "One-Tenth Financing Principle," discusses areas of operation where having less capital could be of benefit to the venture, and points out some advantages to starting on a small scale and growing slowly.

Harrison, Richard T., & Mason, Colin M. (1991). Informal venture capital in the U.K. and the U.S.A. *Proceedings,* 1991 Conference on Entrepreneurship, pp 469–481.

When comparing informal investors in the U.S.A. and U.K., these two groups were similar in terms of demographics. U.K. informal investors invest less, operate more independently, have higher rates of return and capital gain expectations, and are less satisfied overall with the performance of their portfolio than their U.S. counterparts.

MacMillan, I. C., Kulow, D. M., & Khoylian, R. (1988) Venture capitalists' involvement in their investments: extent and performance. *Proceedings,* 1988 Conference on Entrepreneurship, pp 303–323.

Examines how venture capitalists are involved in management decisions and also how this involvement affects the venture in regards to performance.

McMullen, W. E., Long, R., & Tapp, J. (April 1984). Entrepreneurial share transaction strategies. *Proceedings,* 1984 Conference on Entrepreneurship, pp 32–42.

Share capital is a strategic resource that is available for inducing commitments to the development of new ventures. An interview study of 28 Canadian entrepreneurs was undertaken to determine changing patterns of equity distribution from the point of incorporation forward.

Oystein, Fredriksen, Olofsson, Christer, and Wahlbin, Clas. (1991). The role of venture capital in the development of portfolio firms. *Proceedings,* Conference on Entrepreneurship, pp 435–444.

The results of a study of 59 portfolio companies of venture capital firms indicate that the development of the companies was not related to the influence exerted by the venture capital firm.

CHAPTER

10

Venture Capital

Chapter Objectives

1. To explain the three basic stages of venture funding.
2. To discuss the three risk-capital markets.
3. To discuss the informal risk-capital market.
4. To discuss the nature of the venture-capital industry and the venture-capital decision process.
5. To explain all aspects of valuing your company.
6. To identify several valuation approaches.
7. To explain how to structure a deal.

Frederick W. Smith

Who would think that an entrepreneur with a $10 million inheritance would need more capital to get his company off the ground? The business world is filled with stories of companies, large and small, that started in a garage with an initial investment of a few hundred dollars. But none of those companies needed a nationwide distribution system in place, complete with a fleet of airplanes and trucks, before accepting its first order. And, none of those garage start-ups grew up to be Federal Express.

Frederick W. Smith, a Memphis native whose father made his fortune after founding a bus company, conceived the idea for his air cargo company while an economics student at Yale in the 1960s. The professor of one of Smith's classes was a staunch supporter of the current system of air freight handling, whereby the cargo packages literally hitched rides in any unused space on a passenger flight. Fred Smith saw things differently and, in a paper, described the concept of a freight-only airline, which would fly all packages to one central point, where they would be distributed and flown out again to their destinations. This operation could take place at night, when the airports were less crowded, and with proper logistical control, the packages could be delivered the next day. Whether it was the novelty of the idea, the fact that it went against the professor's theories, or the fact that it was written in one night and was turned in late, the first public display of Smith's grand idea earned him a C.

It was more than just a novel idea for a term paper, though. Smith had seen how the technological base of the country was changing. More companies were becoming involved in the production and use of small, expensive items such as computers, and Smith was convinced they could use his air cargo idea to control their inventory costs. Overnight delivery from a single distribution center to anywhere in the country could satisfy customers' needs without a company needing a duplicate investment in inventory stored in regional warehouses. Smith even thought of the Federal Reserve bank as a potential customer, with vast quantities of checks that had to be delivered to all parts of the country every day. But the Vietnam War and a family history of patriotic service intervened. Smith joined the Marine Corps and was sent to Vietnam, first as a platoon leader and then as a pilot.

After nearly four years of service and 200 ground support missions as a pilot, he left Vietnam, ready to start building something. He went to work with his stepfather, managing a struggling aircraft modification and overhaul shop. Difficulty in getting parts to the shop in Little Rock, Arkansas, revived his interest in the air cargo concept. He commissioned two feasibility studies, both of which returned favorable results based on a high initial investment. The key to this company would be the ability to serve a large segment of the business community from the very beginning, and the key to the required level of service was cash. Full of optimism, Smith went to Chicago and New York, confident that he would be returning with basket loads of investment checks. Progress turned out to be slower than he'd anticipated, but through his boundless energy, belief in his idea, and technical knowledge of the air freight field, he was finally able to get enthusiastic backing (and $5 million in capital) from New Court Securities, a Manhattan-based, Rothschild-backed venture-capital investment bank. This helped the rest of the financing fall into place. Five other institutions, including General Dynamics and Citicorp Venture Capital, Ltd., got involved, and Smith went back to Memphis with $72 million. This was the largest venture-capital start-up deal in the history of American business.

Federal Express first took to the skies in April of 1973, carrying 18 packages the first night. Volume picked up rapidly and service was expanded—it looked as though Federal Express was a true overnight success. Smith's understanding of a market need had been accurate, but he had not counted on OPEC causing a massive inflation of fuel costs just as his company was getting started. By mid-1974, the company was losing more than $1 million a month. His investors were not willing to keep the company going, and his relatives were suing him for mismanaging the family fortune (nearly $10 million of Smith money was invested). But Smith never lost faith in his idea, and finally won enough converts in the investment community to keep the doors open long enough to straighten out the pricing problems caused by OPEC. After losing $27 million in the first two years, Federal Express turned a profit of $3.6 million in 1976.

The development and growth of Federal Express was tightly regulated. Due to old laws designed to protect the early pioneers of the passenger airline industry, Smith was required to obtain approval for operating any aircraft with a payload in excess of 7,500 pounds. Since the major airlines—the giants of industry—were not ready to share the cargo market, he was not able to obtain this needed approval and had to operate a fleet of small Falcon jets instead. While this worked well at start-up, by 1977 his operation had reached the capacity of these smaller planes. Since they were already flying several planes on the most active routes, it did not make sense to buy more Falcons. Smith took his salesmanship to Washington and, with the help of a grass-roots Federal Express employee effort, was able to obtain legislation creating a new class of all-cargo carriers. This gave Smith the operating latitude he needed.

Although Smith had the approval to operate large jets, he needed to find a way to purchase them. The corporate balance sheet of the company was still a mess from early losses, and the long-suffering early investors needed some reward.

Smith took his company public on April 12, 1978, raising enough money to purchase used Boeing 727s from ailing passenger airlines. The investors were indeed richly rewarded, with General Dynamics watching their $5 million grow to more than $40 million by the time Federal Express was first traded on the New York Stock Exchange in December 1978.

The company continued to perform since its public offering, growing from revenue per share of $5.5 million in 1978 to over $153 million in 1994 in steady upward progression except for one year, 1992, where revenue/share dropped to $139 million from previous year sales of $143 million. Similarly, the stock price, and therefore return to shareholders, continued to rise with the stock having a 20:3 price earnings ratio in the $70/share range in 1994.

FINANCING THE BUSINESS

In evaluating the appropriateness of venture-capital financing, an entrepreneur must determine the amount and the timing of the funds required, as well as the projected company sales and growth rates. Conventional small businesses and privately held middle-market companies tend to have a more difficult time obtaining external equity capital, especially from the venture-capital industry. Venture-capital firms like to invest in high-potential ventures like Fred Smith's Federal Express. The three basic stages of funding as the business develops are indicated in Table 10–1. The funding problems, as well as the cost of the funds, differ in each stage. **Early-stage financing** is usually the most difficult and costly to obtain. Two types of financing occur during this stage: seed capital and start-up. Seed capital, the most difficult financing to obtain through outside funds, is usually a relatively small amount of funds needed to prove concepts and finance feasibility studies. Since venture capitalists usually have a minimum funding level of $400,000 and higher, they are rarely involved in this type of funding except in the case of a high-technology venture proposed by an entrepreneur with a successful track record needing a significant amount of capital. The second type of funding in this early-stage category is start-up financing. As the name implies, start-up financing is involved in developing and testing some initial products to determine if commercial sales are feasible. These funds are also difficult to obtain.

Expansion or **development financing** (the second basic financing type) is easier to obtain than early-stage financing. Venture capitalists play an active role in providing funds here. As the firm develops in each stage, the funds for expansion are less costly. Generally, funds in the second stage are used as working capital to support initial growth. In the third stage, the company is at break-even or a positive profit level and uses the funds for major sales expansion. Funds in the fourth stage are usually used as bridge financing in the interim period as the company prepares to go public.

TABLE 10–1 Stages of Business Development Funding

Early-Stage Financing	
• Seed capital	Relatively small amounts to prove concepts and finance feasibility studies
• Start-up	Product development and initial marketing, but with no commercial sales yet; funding to actually get company operations started
Expansion or Development Financing	
• Second stage	Working capital for initial growth phase, but no clear profitability or cash flow yet
• Third stage	Major expansion for company with rapid sales growth, at break-even or positive profit levels but still private company
• Fourth stage	Bridge financing to prepare company for public offering
Acquisitions and Leveraged Buyout Financing	
• Traditional acquisitions	Assuming ownership and control of another company
• Leveraged buyouts (LBOs)	Management of a company acquiring company control by buying out the present owners
• Going private	Some of the owners/managers of a company buying all the outstanding stock, making the company privately held again

Acquisition or **leveraged buyout financing** is more specific in nature. It is issued for such activities as traditional acquisitions, leveraged buyouts (management buying out the present owners), and going private (a publicly held firm buying out existing stockholders, thereby becoming a private company).

There are three **risk-capital markets** involved in financing stages of a firm's growth. These are the **informal risk-capital market,** the **venture-capital market,** and the **public-equity market.** Each can play a role in the financing needed for a firm to grow. While all three risk-capital markets can be a source of funds for stage-one financing, the public-equity market is available only for high-potential ventures, particularly when high technology is involved. Recently, some biotechnology companies raised their first-stage financing through the public-equity market, as investors were excited about the potential prospects and returns in this high-interest area. Similar funding occurred in the areas of oceanography and fuel alternatives when they were "hot areas." Venture-capital firms also provide some first-stage funding. However, the venture must require a minimum level of capital set by the firm—$400,000 and up. As discussed later in this chapter, a venture-capital company establishes this minimum level of investment since the due diligence in evaluating a deal and the effort in monitoring one once the funds are committed is about the same for a $100,000 as for a $1 million investment. By far the best source of funds for first-stage financing is the informal risk-capital market—the third type of risk-capital market.

INFORMAL RISK-CAPITAL MARKET

The informal risk-capital market is by far the most misunderstood and inefficient type of risk capital since it is composed of a virtually invisible group of wealthy investors—often called "**business angels**"—who are looking for equity-type investment opportunities in a wide variety of entrepreneurial ventures. Typically investing anywhere from $10,000 to $500,000, these angels provide the funds needed in all stages of financing, but particularly start-up (first-stage) financing. Firms funded from the informal risk-capital market frequently raise second- and third-round financing from professional venture-capital firms or the public-equity market.

Despite being misunderstood by and virtually inaccessible to many entrepreneurs, the informal investment market contains the largest pool of risk capital in the United States, about $50 billion compared to the professional venture-capital market with a pool of about $35 billion. Although there is no verification of the size of this pool of money or of the total amount of financing provided by these business angels, some related statistics provide indications. A 1980 survey of a sample of issuers of private placements by corporations, reported to the Securities and Exchange Commission under Rule 146, found that 87 percent of those buying these issues were individual investors or personal trusts, with $74,000 as the average amount invested.[1] Private placements filed under Rule 145 average over $1 billion per year. Another indication is found on examination of the filings under Regulation D—the regulation exempting certain private and limited offerings from the registration requirements of the Securities Act of 1933 discussed in Chapter 11. In its first year, over 7,200 filings, worth $15.5 billion, were made under Regulation D. Corporations accounted for 43 percent of the value ($6.7 billion), or 32 percent of the total number of offerings (2,304). Corporations filing limited offerings (under $500,000) raised $220 million, an average of $200,000 per firm. The typical corporate issuers tended to be small, with fewer than 10 stockholders, revenues and assets less than $500,000, stockholders' equity of $50,000 or less, and five or fewer employees.[2]

Similar results were found in an examination of the funds raised by small technology-based firms prior to making initial public offerings. The study revealed that unaffiliated individuals (the informal investment market) accounted for 15 percent of these funds, while venture capitalists accounted for only 12 to 15 percent. During the start-up year, unaffiliated individuals provided 17 percent of the external capital.[3]

---

[1] *Report of the Use of the Rule 146 Exemption in Capital Formation.* Directorate of Economic Policy Analysis, Securities and Exchange Commission. Washington, DC, 1983.

[2] *An Analysis of Regulation D.* Report by the Directorate of Economic and Policy Analysis, Securities and Exchange Commission, Washington, DC, 1984.

[3] Charles River Associates, Inc., *An Analysis of Capital Market Imperfections,* National Bureau of Standards, Washington, DC, February, 1976.

Similar results were found in a study of angels in New England. The 133 individual investors studied reported risk-capital investments totaling over $16 million in 320 ventures between 1976 and 1980. These investors averaged one deal every two years, with an average size of $50,000. Although 36 percent of these investments averaged less than $10,000, 24 percent averaged over $50,000. While 40 percent of these investments were start-ups, 80 percent involved ventures less than five years old.[4]

The size and number of these investors have increased dramatically, due in part to the rapid accumulation of wealth in various sectors of the economy. In 1986, the Federal Reserve Board estimated that there were 1.6 million millionaires in the United States. In 1993, millionaires ranged in net worth up to $8.325 billion, according to the *Forbes* annual survey of the 400 wealthiest people in America. The Forbes 400 represented a combined net worth of approximately $328 billion in 1993. These individuals are just a few of the numerous individuals and families with substantial means. One study of consumer finances found that the net worth of 1.3 million U.S. families was over $1 million.[5] These families, representing about 2 percent of the population, accumulated most of their wealth from earnings, not inheritance. These research findings indicate that about 311,000 families have invested over $151 billion in nonpublic businesses in which they have no management interest. Each year, over 100,000 individual investors finance between 30,000 and 50,000 firms, with a total dollar investment of between $7 billion and $10 billion. What are the characteristics of these angels and why do they invest this amount of money?

The characteristics of these informal investors, or angels, are indicated in Table 10–2. They tend to be well educated, with many having graduate degrees. While they will finance firms anywhere in the United States (and a few in other parts of the world), most of the firms receiving investment are within one day's travel. They will make one to two deals each year, with individual firm investments ranging from $10,000 to $500,000, the average being $175,000. If the opportunity is right, angels might well invest from $500,000 to $1 million. In some cases, angels will join with other angels, usually from a common circle of friends, to finance larger deals.

Is there a preference in the type of ventures in which they invest? While angels invest in every type of investment opportunity, from a small retail store to a large oil exploration operation, generally they prefer manufacturing, of both industrial and consumer products; energy; service; and retail/wholesale trade. The returns expected decrease as the number of years the firm has been in business increases, from a median five-year capital gain of 10 times for start-ups to 3 times for established firms over five years old. These investing angels are more patient in their investment

[4]W. E. Wetzel, Jr., "Entrepreneurs, Angels, and Economic Renaissance," in R. D. Hisrich, ed., *Entrepreneurship, Intrapreneurship, and Venture Capital* (Lexington, MA: Lexington Books, 1986), pp 119–40. Other information on angels and their investments can be found in W. E. Wetzel, Jr., "Angels and Informal Risk Capital," *Sloan Management Review* 24 (Summer 1983), pp 23–24, and W. E. Wetzel, Jr., "The Informal Venture Capital Market: Aspects of Scale and Market Efficiency," *Journal of Business Venturing,* Fall 1987, pp 299–314.

[5]R. B. Avery & G. E. Elliehausen, "Financial Characteristics of High Income Families," *Federal Reserve Bulletin.* Washington, DC, March 1986.

TABLE 10–2 Characteristics of Informal Investors

Demographic Patterns and Relationships
- Well educated with many having graduate degrees
- Will finance firms anywhere in United States
- Most firms financed within one-day's travel
- Majority expect to play an active role in ventures financed
- Have clusters of 9–12 other investors

Investment Record
- Range of investment: $10,000–$500,000
- Average investment: $175,000
- One to two deals each year

Venture Preference
- Most financings in start-ups or ventures less than five years old
- Most interest in financing:
  - Manufacturing—industrial/commercial products
  - Manufacturing—consumer products
  - Energy/natural resources
  - Services
  - Retail/wholesale trade

Risk/Reward Expectations
- Median 5-year capital gains of 10 times for start-ups
- Median 5-year capital gains of 6 times for firms under 1 year old
- Median 5-year capital gains of 5 times for firms 1–5 years old
- Median 5-year capital gains of 3 times for established firms over 5 years old

Reasons for Rejecting Proposals
- Risk/return ratio not adequate
- Inadequate management team
- Not interested in proposed business area
- Unable to agree on price
- Principals not sufficiently committed
- Unfamiliar with area of business

horizons, having no problem with a 7-to-10 year time period before cashing out, in contrast to the more predominant 5-year time horizon in the formal venture-capital industry. Investment opportunities are rejected when there is an inadequate risk/return ratio, an inadequate management team, a lack of interest in the business area, or when the principals are not sufficiently committed to the venture.

Where do these angel investors generally find their deals? Deals are found through referrals by business associates, friends, active personal research, investment bankers, and business brokers (see Table 10–3). However, even though these **referrals sources** provide some deals, most angel investors are not satisfied with the number and type of investment referrals. As indicated in Figure 10–1, 51 percent of the investors surveyed were either partially or totally dissatisfied with their referral systems and indicated that at least moderate improvement is needed.

One method for improving this referral process has been successful at the Massachusetts Institute of Technology (MIT) and the University of Tulsa. Each of these universities has a sort of a computer dating service for money—a computerized

TABLE 10–3 Referral Sources for Deals of Angels

	Frequency of Classification		
	Frequent Source	*Occasional Source*	*Not a Source*
Business associates	62	37	18
Friends	59	44	15
Active personal search	46	29	36
Investment bankers	17	28	66
Business brokers	12	36	62
Commercial bankers	9	30	68
Other	7	5	46
Attorneys	3	50	55
Accountants	2	41	66

Source: W. E. Wetzel, Jr., Venture Capital Network, Inc: An Experiment in Capital Formation. *Proceedings,* 1984 Conference on Entrepreneurship, April 1984, p 114.

FIGURE 10–1 Angels' Satisfaction with Referral Sources

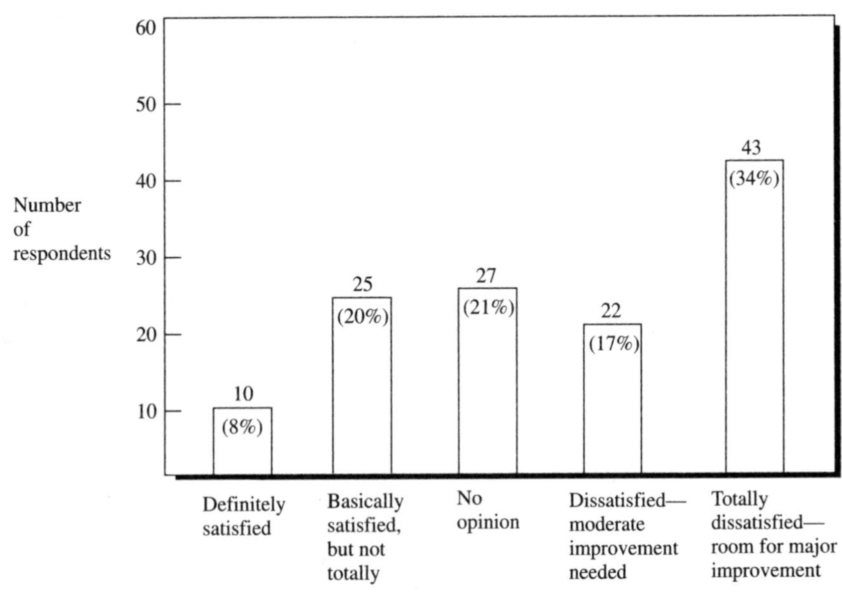

Source: W. E. Wetzel, Jr., Venture Capital Network, Inc: An Experiment in Capital Formation, *Proceedings,* 1984 Conference on Entrepreneurship, April 1984, p 115.

system that matches entrepreneurs with investing angels on a confidential basis. The two institutions also make this resource available to affiliated universities. Entrepreneurs enter the system—the Venture Capital Network (VCN) at MIT and the Venture Capital Exchange (VCE) at the University of Tulsa—by filling out questionnaires on their business and funding needs. These requests are matched with the investors on each system who have indicated an interest in the entrepreneur's area of business. After reviewing the information provided by the entrepreneur (the answers to the questions and supporting material), the investor decides whether to be identified to him or her so that more in-depth discussion between the two parties can take place. The Securities and Exchange Commission's rules and regulations prohibit the systems from advising either the investor or entrepreneur or from having any involvement in the final negotiations between the two parties. Both the VCE and VCN have linked entrepreneurs to their investment capital in a wide variety of companies.[6]

VENTURE CAPITAL

The important and little-understood area of venture capital will be discussed in terms of its nature, the venture-capital industry in the United States, and the venture-capital process.

Nature of Venture Capital

Venture capital is one of the least-understood areas in entrepreneurship. Some think that venture capitalists do the early-stage financing of relatively small, rapidly growing technology companies. While true, this is a narrow definition; it is better to view venture capital more broadly as a professionally managed pool of equity capital. Frequently, the **equity pool** is formed from the resources of wealthy limited partners. Other principal investors in venture-capital limited partnerships are pension funds, endowment funds, and other institutions, including foreign investors. The pool is managed by a general partner—the venture-capital firm—in exchange for a percentage of the gain realized on the investment and a fee. The investments are in early-stage deals as well as second- and third-stage deals and leveraged buyouts. In fact, venture capital can best be characterized as a long-term investment discipline, usually over a five-year period, in the creation of early-stage companies, the expansion and revitalization of existing businesses, and the financing of leveraged buyouts of existing divisions of major corporations or privately owned businesses. In each investment, the venture capitalist takes an **equity participation** through stock,

[6]D. C. Foss, "Venture Capital Network: The First Six Months of the Experiment," *Proceedings,* Babson Entrepreneurial Research Conference, Philadelphia, April 1985, pp 314–24.

warrants, and/or convertible securities and has an active involvement in the monitoring of each portfolio company bringing investment, financing planning, and business skills to the firm.[7]

Overview of the Venture-Capital Industry

While the role of venture capital was instrumental throughout the industrialization of the United States, it did not become institutionalized until after World War II. Before World War II, venture investment activity was a monopoly of wealthy individuals, investment banking syndicates, and a few family organizations with a professional manager. The first step toward institutionalizing the venture-capital industry began in 1946 with the formation of the American Research and Development Corporation (ARD) in Boston. The ARD was a small pool of capital from individuals and institutions put together by General Georges Doriot to make active investments in selected emerging businesses. One of its best investments was in Digital Equipment Corporation.

The next major development in institutionalizing the venture-capital industry was the Small Business Investment Company Act of 1958. This act married private capital with government funds to be used by professionally managed small business investment companies (SBICs) to infuse capital into start-up and growing small businesses. With the tax advantages, government funds for leverage, and a private capital company, SBICs were the start of the now formal venture-capital industry. The 1960s saw a significant expansion of SBICs with approximately 585 SBIC licenses approved, involving more than $205 million in private capital. Many of these early SBICs failed due to inexperienced portfolio managers, unreasonable expectations, focus on short-term profitability, and an excess of government regulations. These early failures caused the SBIC program to be restructured, eliminating some of the unnecessary government regulations and increasing the amount of capitalization needed. There are approximately 360 SBICs operating today, of which 130 are minority small business investment companies (MESBICs) funding minority enterprises (see Table 10–4).

During the late 1960s, small **private venture-capital firms** emerged.[8] The private venture-capital companies were usually formed as limited partnerships, with the venture-capital company acting as the general partner, receiving a management fee and a percentage of the profits earned on any single deal. The limited partners supplied the funding. The limited partners were frequently institutional investors such

[7]Aspects of venture capital are discussed in J. Timmons & W. D. Bygrave, "Venture Capital's Role in Financing Innovation for Economic Growth," *Journal of Business Venturing* 1, Spring 1986, pp 161–76; R. B. Robinson, Jr., "Emerging Strategies in the Venture Capital Industry," *Journal of Business Venturing* 2, Winter 1987, pp 53–78; and H. H. Stevenson, D. F. Muzyka, & J. A. Timmons, "Venture Capital in Transition: A Monte Carlo Simulation of Changes in Investment Patterns," *Journal of Business Venturing* 2, Winter 1987, pp 103–22.

[8]For the role of SBICs, see Farrell K. Slower, "Growth Looms for SBICs," *Venture* (October 1985), 46–47, and M. H. Fleischer, "The SBIC 100—More Deals for the Bucks," *Venture* (October 1985), 50–54.

TABLE 10–4 Overview of Venture-Capital Market

	Private Venture-Capital Firms	Small Business Investment Companies (SBICs)	Corporate/Industrial Venture Capitalists
Estimated number	200	360 (230 SBICs) (130 MESBICs)	100 in business with 20–30 active (Exxon, G.E., Monsanto, 3M, Allstate Insurance, Xerox, Citicorp, First Chicago Corporation)
Principal objectives and motives	Capital gains 25%–40% compounded after tax per year; 5–10 times original investment in 5–10 years	Capital gains same range as private	Capital gains same range as SBICs: Investment in cutting-edge technology and new market acquisition

as insurance companies, endowment funds, bank trust departments, pension funds, and wealthy individuals and families. There are about 200 private venture-capital firms today.

The third type of venture-capital firm also developed during this time: the venture-capital division of major corporations. These firms, of which there are approximately 100, are usually associated with banks and insurance companies, although companies such as 3M, Monsanto, and Xerox are also involved. Corporate venture-capital firms are more prone to invest in windows on technology or new market acquisition than are private venture-capital firms or SBICs. Some of these corporate venture-capital firms have had very disappointing results, causing some corporations to invest in independent, professionally managed venture-capital funds instead of managing their own fund.

In response to the need for economic development, a fourth type of venture-capital firm has emerged: the **state-sponsored venture-capital fund.** These state-sponsored funds have a variety of formats. While the size and investment thrust vary from state to state, from $2.2 million in Colorado to $42 million in Michigan, each fund typically is required to invest a certain percentage of capital in companies in the particular state. Generally, the funds professionally managed by the private sector, outside the states' bureaucracy and political processes, have performed better.

There has been significant growth in the venture-capital industry in both size and number of firms. The number of venture-capital firms peaked in 1989, at which time 674 firms managed an average $51 million in capital (Figure 10–2). In 1992, there were 617 firms managing an average of $50.4 million in capital. The total pools of

FIGURE 10–2 Number and Size of U.S. Venture Capital Firms

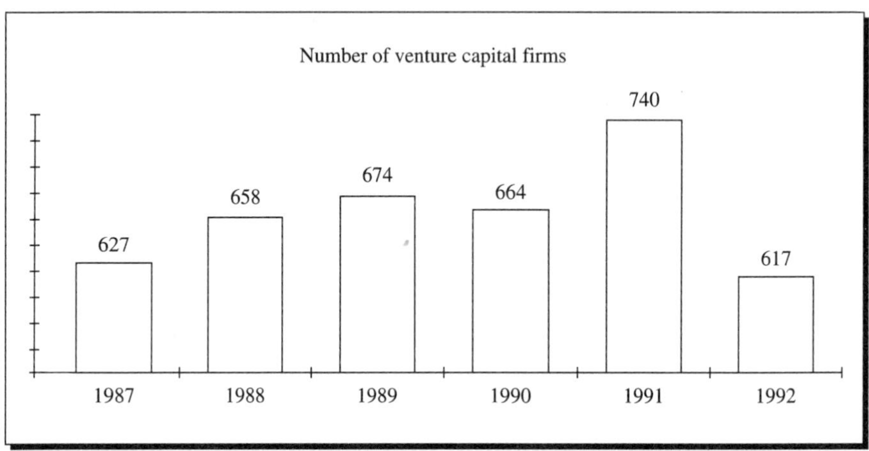

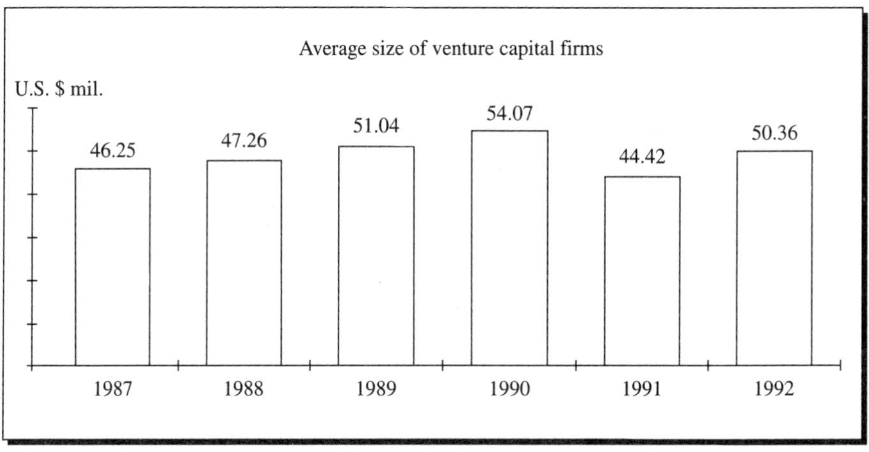

Source: Venture Economics

venture capital peaked in 1990 at $35.9 billion. In 1992, that total was $31.07 billion. The total amount of venture capital actually disbursed to portfolio companies peaked in 1997, when $3.977 billion went to 1,737 companies. Both the total amount of capital disbursed and the number of companies decreased until 1992, when total capital disbursements jumped 87 percent, from $1.358 billion in 1991 to $2.543 billion in 1992. Similarly, the number of companies receiving these funds increased from 792 in 1991 to 1,087 in 1992, a 37 percent increase. Most venture capital is generated by institutional investors. Figure 10–3 depicts the sources of capital.

FIGURE 10–3 Source-Distribution of New Funds

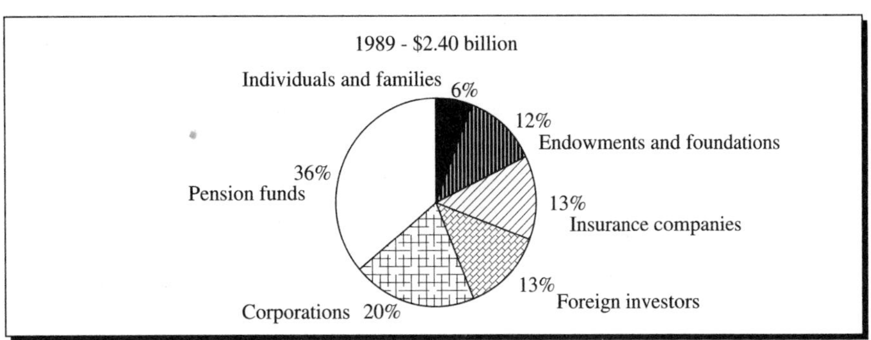

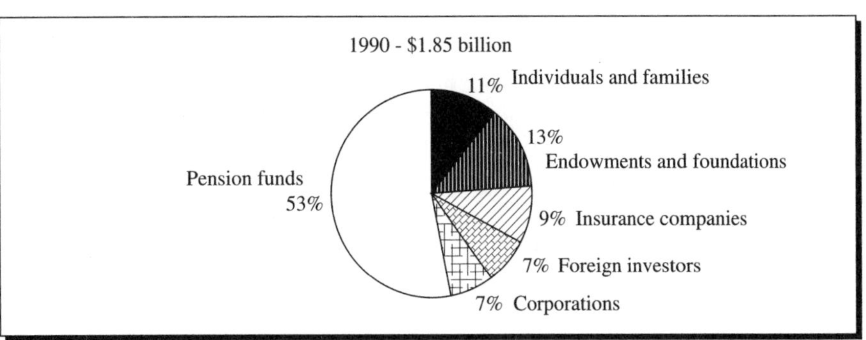

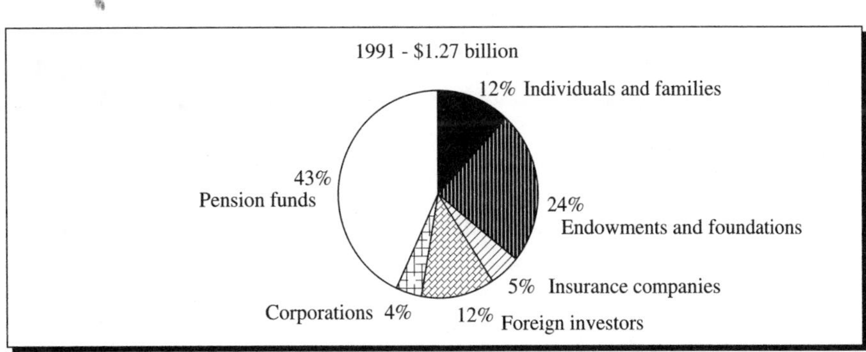

Source: Venture Economics

Pension funds continue to contribute the most. Since 1978 when 32 percent of the new funds in the venture-capital industry were supplied by families and individuals, there has been an obvious shift in the sources of these funds. In 1986, there was a change in capital gains tax codes to attempt to stimulate the private investor source. From Figure 10–3, it is clear that pension funds, insurance companies, and endowments dominate despite the tax change.[9]

This growth in funds and the change in their sources have affected the structure of the venture-capital industry. Venture-capital firms can be classified into groups of small, medium, large, and super (extra-large) funds. Each fund, regardless of its size, tends to specialize in its portfolio companies by investment stage, degree of technology, type of product, and geographic region. In 1978, the $2.9 billion in venture capital was managed primarily by private venture firms (45 percent, followed by corporate venture-capital firms (34 percent) and others, including SBICs (21 percent). By 1992, 93 percent of funds ($28.99 billion) were managed by 515 independent firms (i.e., independent public and private firms, family groups, and some SBICs) or 83 percent of all firms. This left $2.046 billion of capital managed by 102 (17 percent) corporate industrial or corporate financial groups. The larger firms (those managing over $100 million) managed more of the venture-capital funds. Seventy venture-capital firms controlled 57 percent of the total pool of funds under management, while 193 firms managed only 2.4 percent of these funds.

The industry-investment preferences by venture-capital firms have changed over time. While the consumer and medical/health segments accounted for only 14 percent of the investment dollars in 1978–80, their total increased to 25 percent in 1990–92 (See Figure 10–4). Energy related investments commanded 9 percent of the 1978–89 total funds. In 1990–92, this same sector declined to less than 1 percent of the total funds. Although the biotechnology segment had been heralded as receiving so much venture-capital attention, the amounts invested have been moderate, increasing from 7 percent in 1987–89 to 9 percent in 1992. It appears that the venture-capital industry is shifting toward lower-technology investments across a wide variety of industries.

As would be expected, there is a significant difference in the size of the various types of venture-capital firms. In 1992, 11 percent of the venture-capital firms controlled over half of the total assets. Even though the number of these mega-fund firms has decreased from 90 in 1991 to 70 in 1992, the average amount of capital each of these firms manages increased from $216 million to $253 million.

Finally, venture-capital funds tend to raise capital in particular geographic regions. In 1991, California, Massachusetts, and New York received 63 percent of all new disbursements. In the first six months of 1993, however, there seemed to be a regional shift. The Southeastern states' investment totals ranked the region third,

---

[9]For a discussion of this change in investors and the impact of the 1986 change in capital gains tax on the venture capital industry, see W. D. Bygrave, and J. M. Shulman, "Capital Gains Tax: Bane or Boom for Venture Capital?" *Proceedings,* Babson Research Conference, April 1988, pp 324–38; and T. Soja and J. E. Reyes, *Investment Benchmarks: Venture Capital* (Needham, MA: Venture Economics, 1990).

FIGURE 10–4 U.S. Venture-Capital Investment by Industry Sector

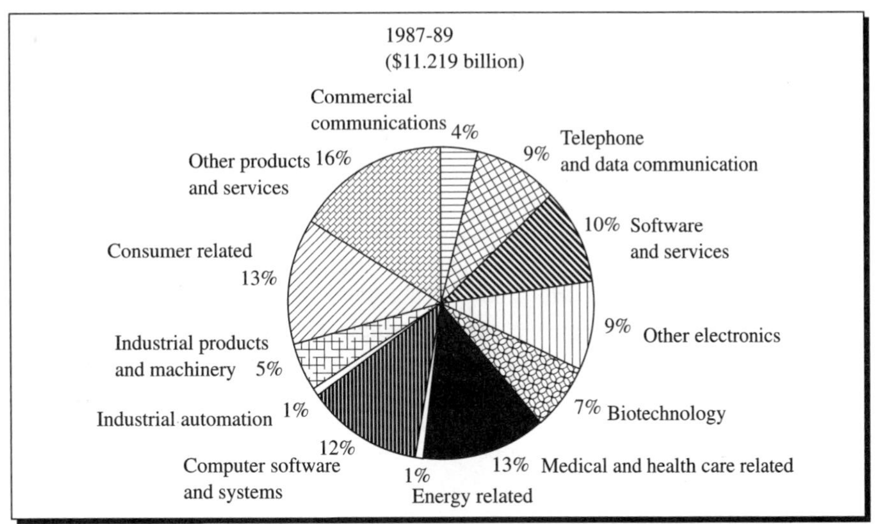

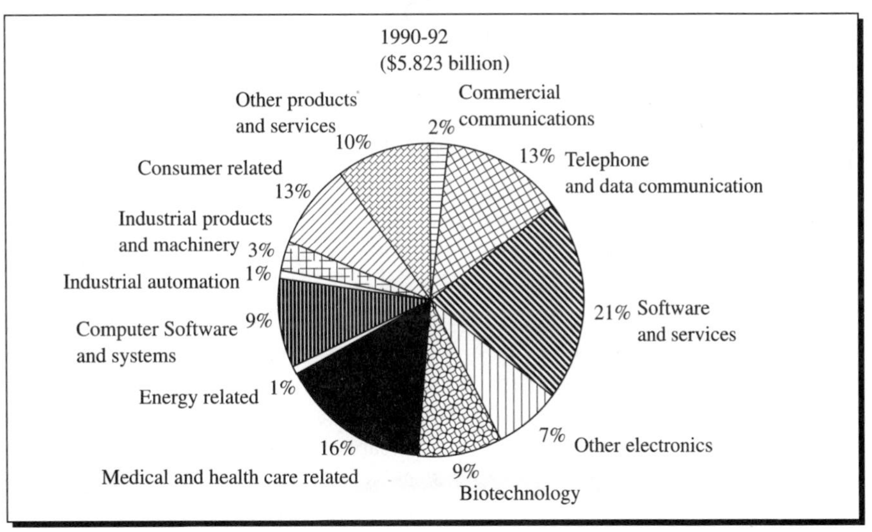

Source: Venture Economics

displacing the Midwest. Ranked 19th in 1992, Connecticut replaced New Jersey as the third highest state for capital disbursed. Similarly, Tennessee moved from 24th with $14 million to 5th with $70 million disbursed.

Venture-Capital Process

To be in a position to secure the needed funds, the entrepreneur needs to understand the philosophy and objectives of a venture-capital firm, as well as the venture-capital process. An overview of venture capitalists in terms of the evaluation criteria and process, portfolio, and deal pricing is given in Table 10–5. The objective of a venture-capital firm is to generate long-term capital appreciation through debt and equity investments, typically in young, high-growth ventures. To achieve this objective, the venture capitalist is willing to make any changes or modifications necessary in the business investment. Since the objective of the entrepreneur is the survival of the business, the objectives of the two are frequently at odds, particularly when problems are encountered.

The portfolio objective in terms of return criteria and risk involved of typical venture-capital firms is shown in Figure 10–5. Since there is more risk involved in financing a business earlier in its development, more return is expected from early-stage financing (50 percent ROI) than from acquisitions or leveraged buyouts (30 percent ROI), the late stage in development. The significant risk involved and the pressure that venture-capital firms feel from their investors (limited partners) to make safer investments with higher rates of return have caused these firms to invest even greater amounts of their funds in later stages of financing. In these late-stage investments, there are lower risks, faster returns, less managerial assistance needed, and fewer deals to be evaluated. As is indicated in Figure 10–6, 22 percent of venture-capital investments in 1990 were in seed, start-up, or other early-stage ventures. By 1992, the percentage amount decreased to 24 percent. Even with this decrease, the absolute amount increased from $529 million in 1990 to $619 million in 1992.

Another change has occurred in the amount invested in present portfolio companies versus new ones. The 22 percent invested in new companies in 1989 decreased to 7 percent in 1990. Again, the investment strategy can reduce the risks and increase the return for the venture capitalists.

In most cases, the venture capitalist does not seek control of a company and would rather have the firm at more risk than him- or herself. Once the decision to invest is made, the venture capitalist will do anything necessary to support the management team so that the business and the investment prosper. While venture capitalists expect a seat on the board of directors, the management team is expected to direct and run the daily operations of the company. A venture capitalist will support the management team with investment dollars, financial skills, planning, and expertise in any specific area needed.

Since the venture-capital investment in the company is for a long time (typically five years or more), it is important that there is mutual trust and understanding between the entrepreneur and the venture capitalist. There should be no surprises in the firm's performance. Both good and bad news should be shared, with the objective of

TABLE 10–5 Venture Capitalists

Evaluation Criteria
- Strong management team
- Unique opportunity
- Appropriate return in terms of capital appreciation

Evaluation Process
- Initial screening
- Initial agreement of terms
- Due diligence (industry, market, players)
- Go or no-go decision
- Document deal and close
- Monitor deal

Venture Portfolio Goal
- 20% early stage—50–60% ROI
- 40% development financing—40% ROI
- 40% acquisitions and leverage buyouts—30% ROI

Typical Venture Portfolio of 10 Deals
- 4 belly-up
- 3 walking wounded (or living dead)
- 2 hits
- 1 home run

Factors in Pricing a Deal
- Return
- Amount of money needed now and later
- Quality of deal
- Quality of team
- Amount entrepreneur is investing
- Prospects of company in future
- Upside potential
- Downside potential
- Liquidity
- Exit avenues

Guiding "Rules" of Venture Capitalists
- It costs more than you think
- It takes longer than you have planned
- Anything you think won't happen, will

taking the necessary action to allow the company to grow and develop in the long run. The venture capitalist should be available to the entrepreneur to discuss problems and develop strategic plans.

In making an investment, the venture capitalist uses three general criteria. First, the company must have a **strong management team,** with the individuals having solid experience and background, commitment to the company, capabilities in their specific areas of expertise, the ability to meet challenges, and the flexibility to scramble whenever necessary. A venture capitalist would rather invest in a first-rate management team and a second-rate product than the reverse. The management team's commitment should be reflected in dollars invested in the company. While the amount is somewhat important, more important is the size of this investment relative to their ability to invest. The commitment of the management team should be backed by the support of the family, particularly the spouse, of each key team player. A positive family environment and spousal support allow team members to spend the 60 to 70 hours per week necessary to start up the company. One successful venture capitalist makes it a point to have dinner with the entrepreneur and spouse and even visit the entrepreneur's home before making an investment decision. This individual said, "I find it difficult to believe an entrepreneur can successfully run and manage a business and put in the necessary time when the home environment is running amok."

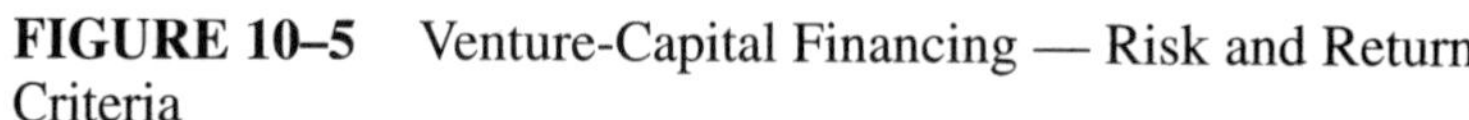

FIGURE 10–5 Venture-Capital Financing — Risk and Return Criteria

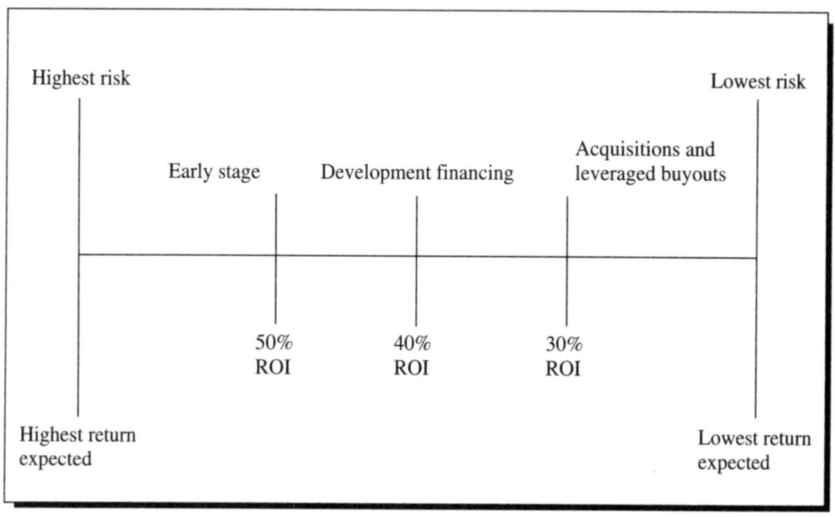

The second criterion is that the **product/market opportunity** must be unique, having a differential advantage in a growing market. Having a unique market niche is essential since the product or service must be able to compete and grow over the five-year investment period. This uniqueness needs to be carefully spelled out in the marketing portion of the business plan and is even more favorably viewed when it can be protected by a patent or a trade secret.

The final criterion for investment is that the business opportunity must have significant capital appreciation. The exact amount of capital appreciation varies, depending on such factors as the size of the deal, the stage of development of the company, the upside potential, the downside risks, and the available exits. The venture capitalist typically expects a 40 to 60 percent return on investment in most situations.

The venture-capital process implementing these criteria is both an art and a science.[10] The art part consists of the venture capitalist's intuition, gut feeling, and the creative thinking involved in the process. The science part is the systematic approach and data gathering involved in the assessment; this requires both analysis and discipline.

---

[10]For a thorough discussion of the venture-capital process, see A. D. Silver, "The Venture Capital Process," *Venture,* December 1983, pp 86–9; B. Davis, "Role of Venture Capital in the Economic Renaissance of an Area," in R. D. Hisrich, ed. *Entrepreneurship, Intrapreneurship, and Venture Capital* (Lexington, MA: Lexington Books, 1986), pp 107–18; M. Gorman & W. Sahlman, "What Do Venture Capitalists Do?" *Proceedings,* Babson Research Conference, April 1986, pp 414–36; and Robert D. Hisrich & A. D. Jankowicz, "Intuition in Venture Capital Decisions: An Exploratory Study Using a New Technique," *Journal of Business Venturing* 5 (January 1990), pp 49–63.

FIGURE 10–6 U.S. Venture-Capital Investment by Stage

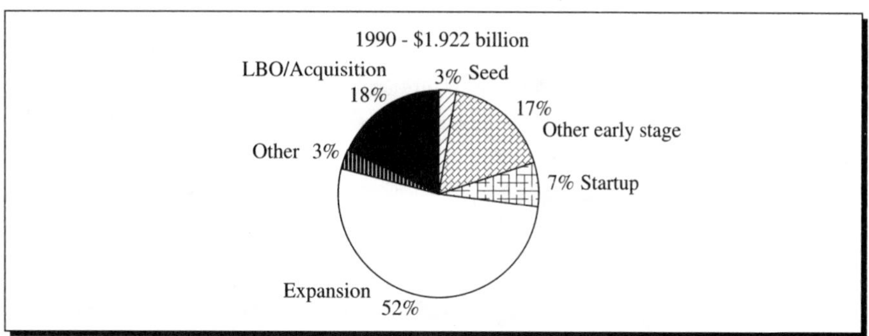

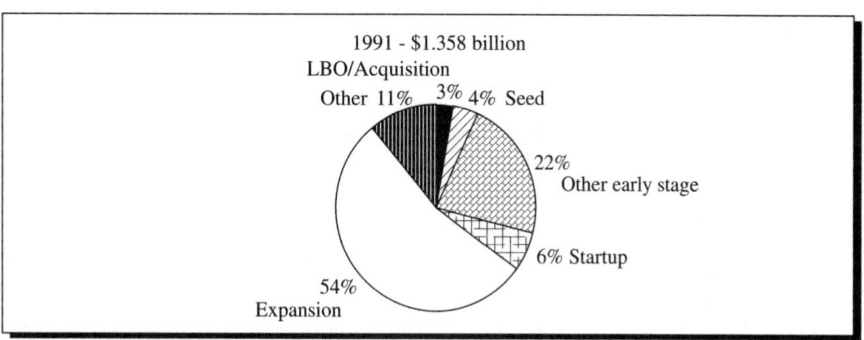

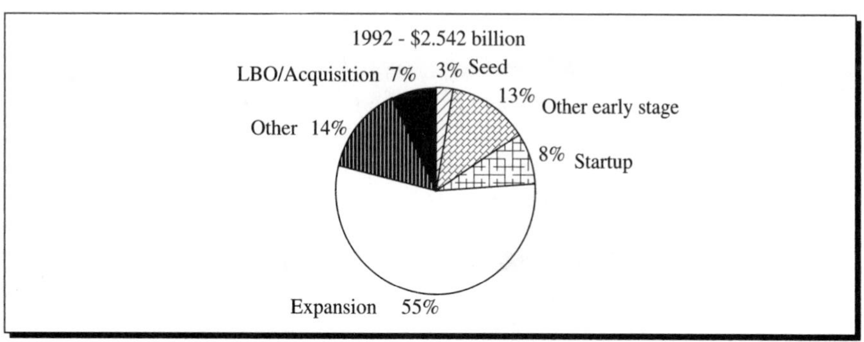

Source: Venture Economics

The process starts with the investment objectives and philosophy of the venture-capital firm. The firm must decide on the composition of its portfolio mix, including the number of start-ups, expansion companies, and management buyouts; the types of industries; the geographic region for investment; and any product or industry specializations.

The venture-capital process can be broken down into four primary stages: preliminary screening, agreement on principal terms, due diligence, and final approval. The **preliminary screening** begins with the receipt of the business plan. A good business plan is essential in the venture-capital process. Most venture capitalists will not even talk to an entrepreneur who doesn't have one. As the starting point, the business plan must have a clear-cut mission and clearly stated objectives, which are supported by an in-depth industry and market analysis and pro forma income statements. The executive summary is the most important part of this business plan as it is used for initial screening in this preliminary evaluation. Many business plans are never evaluated beyond the executive summary. When evaluating the business, the venture capitalist first determines if he or she has seen the deal or similar deals before. The investor then determines if the proposal fits his or her long-term policy and short-term cash needs in order to develop an appropriate portfolio balance. In this preliminary screening, the venture capitalist investigates the economy of the industry and evaluates whether he or she has the appropriate knowledge and ability to invest in that industry. The investor reviews the numbers presented to determine if the business can reasonably deliver the ROI required. In addition, the credentials and capability of the management team are evaluated to determine if they can carry out the plan presented.

The second stage is the agreement on principal terms between the entrepreneur and the venture capitalist. The venture capitalist wants a basic understanding of the principal terms of the deal at this stage of the process before making the major commitment of time and effort involved in the due diligence process.

The third stage—detailed review and **due diligence**—is by far the longest, involving anywhere from one to three months. There is a detailed review of the company's history, the business plan, the résumés of the individuals, their financial history, and target market customers. The upside potential and downside risk are assessed. There is a thorough evaluation of the markets, industry, financial analysis, customers, and management.

In the last stage—final approval—a comprehensive, internal investment memorandum is prepared. This document reviews the venture capitalist's findings and details the investment terms and conditions of the investment transaction. This information is used to prepare the formal legal documents that both the entrepreneur and venture capitalist will sign to conclude the transaction.[11]

[11] A discussion of some of the important sectors in this decision process can be found in I. MacMillan, L. Zemann, and Subba Narasimba, "Criteria Distinguishing Successful from Unsuccessful Ventures in the Venture Screening Process," *Journal of Business Venturing* 2, Spring 1987, pp 123–38; J. B. Roure and M. A. Meidique, "Linking Prefunding Factors and High-Technology Venture Success," *Journal of Business Venturing* 1, Fall 1986, pp 295–306; and E. H. Buttner and B. Rosen, "Funding New Business Ventures: Are Decision Makers against Women Entrepreneurs?" *Journal of Business Venturing* 4, Winter 1987, pp 249–62.

Locating Venture Capitalists

One of the most critical decisions for the entrepreneur is selecting which venture-capital firm to approach. Since venture capitalists tend to specialize either geographically by industry (manufacturing industrial products or consumer products, high-technology or service) or by size and type of investment, the entrepreneur should approach only those who may have an interest in the investment opportunity. Where do you find this venture capitalist?

While venture capitalists are located throughout the United States, there are several traditional centers of concentration: Boston, Chicago, New York, and San Francisco. More recently, several new centers have emerged: Atlanta, Dallas, Los Angeles, and Washington, D.C.[12] An entrepreneur should carefully research the names and addresses of prospective venture-capital firms that might have an interest in the particular investment opportunity. Accountants and lawyers are good sources for introductions to prospective venture capitalists. There are also regional and national venture-capital associations. These associations will frequently send the entrepreneur a directory listing their members, the types of businesses their members invest in, and any investment restrictions for a nominal fee or none at all.

Approaching a Venture Capitalist

The entrepreneur should approach a venture capitalist in a professional business manner. Since venture capitalists receive hundreds of inquiries and are frequently out of the office working with portfolio companies or investigating potential investment opportunities, it is important to begin the relationship positively. The entrepreneur should call any potential venture capitalist to ensure that the business is in an area of the individual's investment interest. Then the business plan should be sent along with a short professional letter.

Since venture capitalists receive many more plans than they are capable of funding, they screen out as many plans as possible. They tend to focus and put more time and effort on those plans that were referred. In fact, one venture-capital group said that 80 percent of their investments over the last five years were in referred companies. Consequently, it is well worth the entrepreneur's time to seek out an introduction to the venture capitalist. Typically this can be obtained from an executive of a portfolio company, an accountant, lawyer, banker, or business school professor.

The entrepreneur should be aware of some basic rules of thumb before implementing the actual approach (more detailed guidelines are presented in Table 10–6). First, take great care in selecting the right venture capitalist to approach. Venture capitalists tend to specialize in certain industries and will rarely invest in a business

[12] A complete listing of venture capital firms in the United States and throughout the world can be found in *Venture's Guide to International Venture Capital* (New York: Simon and Schuster, 1985); and E. S. Pratt, *Guide to Venture Capital Sources* (Wellesley, MA: Capital Publishing Corporation, 1988).

TABLE 10–6 Guidelines for Dealing with Venture Capitalists

- Carefully determine the venture capitalist to approach for funding the particular type of deal. Screen and target the approach. Venture capitalists do not like deals that have been excessively "shopped."
- Once a discussion is started with a venture capitalist, do not discuss the deal with other venture capitalists. Working several deals in parallel can create problems unless the venture capitalists are working together. Time and resource limitations may require a cautious simultaneous approach to several funding sources.
- It is better to approach a venture capitalist through an intermediary who is respected and has a preexisting relationship with the venture capitalist. Limit and carefully define the role and compensation of the intermediary.
- The entrepreneur or manager, not an intermediary, should lead the discussions with the venture capitalist. Do not bring a lawyer, accountant, or other advisors to the first meeting. Since there are no negotiations during this first meeting, it is a chance for the venture capitalist to get to know the entrepreneur without interference from others.
- Be very careful about what is projected or promised. The entrepreneur will probably be held accountable for these projections in the pricing, deal structure, or compensation.
- Disclose any significant problems or negative situations in this initial meeting. Trust is a fundamental part of the long-term relationship with the venture capitalist; subsequent discovery by the venture capitalist of an undisclosed problem will cause a loss of confidence and probably prevent a deal.
- Reach a flexible, reasonable understanding with the venture capitalist regarding the timing of a response to the proposal and the accomplishment of the various steps in the financing transaction. Patience is needed, as the process is complex and time-consuming. Too much pressure for a rapid decision can cause problems with the venture capitalist.
- Do not sell the project on the basis that other venture capitalists have committed themselves. Most venture capitalists are independent and take pride in their own decision making.
- Be careful about glib statements such as "There is no competition for this product," or "There is nothing like this technology available today." These statements can indicate a lack of homework, or that a perfect product has been designed for a nonexistent market.
- Do not indicate an inordinate concern for salary, benefits, or other forms of current compensation. Dollars are precious in a new venture. The venture capitalist wants the entrepreneur committed to an equity appreciation similar to that of the venture capitalist.
- Eliminate to the extent possible any use of new dollars to take care of past problems such as payment of past debts or deferred salaries of management. New dollars of the venture capitalist are for growth, to move the business forward.

outside these areas, regardless of the merits of the business proposal and plan. Second, venture capitalists tend to know each other, particularly in a specific region of the country. When a large amount of money is involved, they will invest in the deal together, with one venture-capital firm taking the lead. Since this degree of familiarity is present, a venture-capital firm will probably find out if others have seen your business plan. Therefore it is not advised to shop around among venture capitalists, as even a good business plan can quickly become "shopworn." Third, when meeting the venture capitalist, particularly for the first time, bring only one or two key members of the management team. A venture capitalist is betting on your management team and its track record, not on outside experts. Any experts can be called in as needed.

Finally, be sure to develop a brief and well-thought-out oral presentation. This should cover the company's business, the uniqueness of the product or service, the prospects for growth, the major factors behind achieving the sales and profit objectives, the backgrounds and track records of the key managers, the amount of financing required, and the returns anticipated. The first presentation is critical. As one venture capitalist stated, "I need to sense a competency, a capability, a chemistry within the first half hour of our initial meeting. The entrepreneur needs to look me in the eye and present his story clearly and logically. If a chemistry does not start to develop, I start looking for reasons not to do the deal."

Following a favorable initial meeting, the venture capitalist will do some preliminary investigation of the plan. If favorable, another meeting between the management team and venture capitalist will be scheduled. This meeting is also critical, as both parties will ask questions in order to assess the other and to determine if a good working relationship can be established and if a feeling of trust and confidence is evolving. During this mutual evaluation, the entrepreneur should be careful not to be too inflexible about the amount of company equity he or she is willing to share. If the entrepreneur is too inflexible, the venture capitalist might end negotiations. The next step in the venture-capital process is establishing an initial agreement of terms. If turned down by one venture capitalist, do not become discouraged. Select the next most probable candidate and repeat the procedure. One study found that a significant number of companies denied funding by one venture capitalist were able to obtain funds from other outside sources, including other venture capitalists.[13]

VALUING YOUR COMPANY

A problem confronting the entrepreneur when obtaining outside equity funds, whether from the informal investor market (the angels) or the formal venture-capital industry, is determining a value for the company. This valuation is at the core of

---

[13] A. V. Bruno & T. T. Tyebjee, "The One That Got Away: A Study of Ventures Rejected by Venture Capitalists," *Proceedings,* 1983 Babson Research Conference, Wellesley, MA, 1983, pp 289–306.

the entrepreneur's major concern and anxiety—how much ownership is an investor entitled to for funding the venture? The amount of ownership should be determined by first considering the factors in valuation.

Factors in Valuation

Although they may vary depending on the situation, there are eight factors the entrepreneur should consider when valuing the venture. The first factor, and the starting point in any valuation, is the nature and history of the business. The characteristics of the specific venture and the industry in which it operates are fundamental in every evaluation process. The history of the company from its inception provides information on the strength and diversity of the company's operations, the risks involved, and the company's ability to withstand any adverse conditions.

Valuation must also consider the outlook of the economy in general as well as that of the particular industry. This, the second factor, involves an examination of the financial data of the venture compared to that of other companies in the industry. Management's capability now and in the future, as well as the future market for the company's products, is assessed. Will these markets grow, decline, or stabilize, and in what economic conditions?

The third factor is the book value (net value) of the stock and the overall financial condition of the business. The book value (often called owner's equity) is the acquisition cost (less accumulated depreciation) minus liabilities. Frequently, the book value is not a good indication of fair market value, as balance sheet items are almost always carried at cost, not market value. The value of plant and equipment, for example, carried on the books at cost less depreciation may be low due to the use of an accelerated depreciation method or other market factors, making the assets more valuable than indicated in the book value figures. Land, particularly, is usually reflected lower than fair market value. For valuation, the balance sheet must be adjusted to reflect the higher values of the assets, particularly land, so that a more realistic company worth is determined. A good valuation should also value operating and nonoperating assets separately and then combine the two into the total fair market value. A thorough valuation includes comparative annual balance sheets and profit and loss statements for the past three years when available.

Even though book value develops the benchmark, the future earning capacity of the company, the fourth factor, is the most important factor in valuation. Previous years' earnings are generally not simply averaged but weighted, with the most recent earnings receiving the highest weighting, reflecting their importance. Income by product line should be analyzed to judge future profitability and value. Special attention should be paid to depreciation, nonrecurring expenses, officers' salaries, rental expense, and historical trends.

A fifth valuation factor is the dividend-paying capacity of the venture. Since the entrepreneur in a new venture typically pays little if any dividends, it is the future capacity to pay dividends rather than actual dividend payments made that is important. The dividend-paying capacity should be capitalized.

An assessment of goodwill and other intangibles of the venture is the sixth valuation factor. Frequently, these intangible assets cannot be valued without reference to the tangible assets of the venture.

The seventh factor in valuation involves assessing the previous sale of stock. Previous stock sales better represent future sales if the sales are recent. Motives regarding the new sale (if other than arriving at a fair price) and any change in economic or financial conditions during the intermittent period should be considered.

The final valuation factor is the market price of stocks of companies engaged in the same or similar lines of business. This factor is used in the specific valuation method discussed later in this section. The critical issue is the degree of similarity between the publicly traded company and the one being valued.

General Valuation Approaches

There are several valuation approaches that can be used in valuing the venture. One of the most widely used approaches assesses comparable publicly held companies and the prices of these companies' securities. This search for a similar going concern is both an art and a science. First, the company must be classified in an industry, since companies in the same industry share similar markets, problems, economies, and potential for sales and earnings. The review of all publicly traded companies in this industry classification should evaluate size, amount of diversity, dividends, leverage, and growth potential until the most similar company is identified. This method is often inaccurate as it is very difficult to find a truly comparable company. When a large privately held company is involved, better results are usually obtained, as the relative sales price of this company is generally related to the stock price of a publicly held company in the same industry in the given time period.

A second widely used valuation approach is the **present value of future cash flow.** This method adjusts the value of the cash flow of the business for the time value of money and the business and economic risks. Since only cash (or cash equivalents) can be used in reinvestment, this valuation approach generally gives more accurate results than profits. In using this method, the sales and earnings are projected back to the time of the valuation decision when shares of the company are offered for sale. The period between the valuation and sale dates is determined. The potential dividend payout and the expected price-earning ratio or liquidation value at the end of the period must be calculated. Finally, a rate of return needed by investors must be established, less a discount rate for failure to meet these expectations.

Another valuation method, used only for insurance purposes or in very unique circumstances, is **replacement value.** This method is used, for example, when there is a unique asset involved that the buyer really wants. The valuation of the venture is based on the amount of money it would take to replace (or reproduce) that asset or another important asset or system of the venture.

The **book value** approach uses the adjusted book value or net tangible asset value to determine the firm's worth. Adjusted book value is obtained by making the necessary adjustments to the stated book value by taking into account any depreciation (or appreciation) of plant and equipment and real estate, as well as needed adjustments to inventory resulting from the accounting methods employed. The following basic procedure can be used:

Book value	$______
Add (or subtract) any adjustments such as appreciation or depreciation to arrive at figure on next line—the fair market value	______
Fair market value (the sale value of the company's assets)	______
Subtract all intangibles that cannot be sold, such as goodwill	______
Adjusted book value	______

Being simple to calculate, the book valuation approach is particularly good in a relatively new business, in businesses where the sole owner has died or is disabled, and in businesses with speculative or highly unstable earnings.

The **earnings approach** is the most widely used method of valuing a company, as it provides the potential investor with the best estimate of the probable return on investment. The potential earnings are calculated by weighting the most recent operating year's earnings after they have been adjusted for any extraordinary expenses that would not have normally occurred in the operations of a publicly traded company. Then an appropriate price-earnings multiple is selected based on norms of the industry and the investment risk. A higher multiple will be used for a high-risk business and a lower multiple for a low-risk business. For example, a low-risk business in an industry with a seven times earnings multiple would be valued at $4.2 million if the weighted average earnings over the past three years was $0.6 million (7 times $0.6 million).

An extension of this approach is the **factor approach,** where three major factors are used to determine value: earnings, dividend-paying capacity, and book value. Appropriate weights for the particular company being valued are developed and multiplied by the capitalized value, resulting in an overall weighted valuation. An example is indicated below.

Approach (in 000s)	*Capitalized Value*	*Weight*	*Weighted Value*
Earnings: $40 × 10	$400	0.4	$160
Dividends: $15 × 20	300	0.4	120
Book value: $600 × 0.4	240	0.2	48
Average			328
10% discount			33
Per share value			$295

A final valuation approach that gives the lowest value of the business is **liquidation value.** Liquidation value is often difficult to obtain, particularly when cost and losses must be estimated for selling the inventory, terminating employees, collecting accounts receivable, selling assets, and other closing-down activities. Nevertheless, it is also good for an investor to obtain a downside risk value in appraising a company.

General Valuation Method

One approach an entrepreneur can use to determine how much of his or her company a venture capitalist will want for a given amount of investment can be calculated using the formula below.

$$\text{Venture capitalist ownership(\%)} = \frac{\text{VC \$investment} \times \text{VC investment multiple desired}}{\text{Company's projected profits in year 5} \times \text{Price earnings multiple of comparable company}}$$

For example, a company needing $500,000 of venture-capital money, anticipating profits of $650,000, where the venture capitalist wants an investment multiple of 5 times and the price earnings multiple of a similar company is 12, would have to give up 32 percent of the company to obtain the needed funds as calculated below.

$$\frac{\$500{,}000 \times 5}{\$650{,}000 \times 12} = 32\%$$

A more accurate method for determining this percentage is given in Table 10–7. The step-by-step approach takes into account the time value of money in determining the appropriate investor's share. The following hypothetical example uses this step-by-step procedure in determining the investor's share. H&B Associates, a start-up

TABLE 10–7 Steps in Valuing Your Business and Determining Investors' Share

1. Estimate the earnings after taxes based on sales in the fifth year.
2. Determine an appropriate earnings multiple based on what similar companies are selling for in terms of their current earnings.
3. Determine the required rate of return.
4. Determine the funding needed.
5. Calculate, using the following formulas.

$$\text{Present value} = \frac{\text{Future valuation}}{(1 + i)^n}$$

where:

future valuation = total estimated value of company in 5 years
i = required rate of return
n = number of years

$$\text{Investors' share} = \frac{\text{Initial funding}}{\text{Present value}}$$

manufacturing company, estimates it will earn $1 million after taxes on sales of $10 million. The company needs $800,000 now to reach that goal in five years. A similar company in the same industry is selling at 15 times earnings. A venture-capital firm, Davis Venture Partners, is interested in investing in the deal and requires a 50 percent compound rate of return on investment. What percentage of the company will have to be given up to obtain the needed capital?

$$\text{Present Value} = \frac{\$1{,}000{,}000 \times 15 \text{ times earning multiple}}{(1 + 0.50)^5}$$

$$= \$1{,}975{,}000$$

$$\frac{\$800{,}000}{\$1{,}975{,}000} = 41\% \text{ will have to be given up}$$

DEAL STRUCTURE

In addition to valuating the company and determining the percentage of the company that may have to be given up to obtain funding, a critical concern for the entrepreneur is the nature of the deal—the terms of the transaction between the entrepreneur and the funding source.[14] In order to make the venture look as attractive as possible to potential sources of funds, the entrepreneur must understand the needs of the investors as well as his or her own needs. The needs of the funding sources include the rate of return required, the acceptable level of risk, the timing and form of return, the amount of control desired, and the perception of the risks involved in the particular funding opportunity. While certain investors are willing to bear a significant amount of risk to obtain a significant rate of return, others want less risk and are willing to settle for less return. Still other investors are more concerned about the amount of influence and control they will be able to exert once the investment has been made.

The entrepreneur's needs revolve around similar concerns, such as degree and mechanisms of control, amount of financing needed, and the goals for the particular firm. Before negotiating the terms and structure of the deal with the venture capitalist, the entrepreneur should assess the relative importance of these concerns in order to make appropriate trade offers if needed. Since the final deal structure reflects the circumstances involved as well as what is in vogue at the time, both the venture capitalist and entrepreneur should feel comfortable with it. A good working relationship needs to be established to ease any differences that might arise later. This open, honest relationship will be needed to deal with problems that will occur with the growth of the company.

---

[14]For a discussion of some problems with venture capital deals, see "Why Smart Companies Are Saying No to Venture Capitalists," *Inc.*, August 1984, pp. 65–75.

SUMMARY

In financing a business, the entrepreneur determines the amount and timing of needed funds. In the first stage, seed or start-up capital is the most difficult to obtain, with the most likely source being the informal risk-capital market (angels). These investors are wealthy individuals who average one or two deals per year, ranging from $10,000 to $500,000. Generally, they find their deals through referrals.

Although venture capital may be used in the first stage, it is primarily used in the second or third stage to provide working capital for growth or expansion. Venture capital is broadly defined as a professionally managed pool of equity capital. Since 1958, small business investment companies (SBICs) have combined private capital and government funds to finance the growth and start-up of small businesses. Private venture-capital firms have developed since the 1960s, with limited partners supplying the funding. At the same time, venture-capital divisions operating within major corporations began appearing. More recently, some states have begun to sponsor venture-capital funds to foster economic development.

To achieve the venture capitalist's primary goal of generating long-term capital appreciation through investments in business, three criteria must be met. First, the company must have strong management. Second, the product/marketing opportunity must be unique. Third, the capital appreciation must be significant, offering a 40 to 60 percent return on investment.

The process of obtaining venture capital includes preliminary screening, agreement on principal terms, due diligence, and final approval. Through a referral, entrepreneurs need to approach a potential venture capitalist with a professional business plan and a good oral presentation. After a successful initial presentation, the entrepreneur and investor agree on principal terms before the due diligence process is begun. This stage involves a detailed analysis of the markets, industry, and finances and can take one to three months. The final stage requires a comprehensive documentation of the details of the transaction.

The problem of placing value on the company is of concern to the entrepreneur. The determination of how much ownership the investor is entitled to for funding the venture can be made through the valuation process. Eight factors can be used as a basis for valuation: the nature and history of the business, the economic outlook, book value, future earnings, dividend-paying capacity, intangible assets, sales of stock, and market price of stocks of similar companies. Numerous valuation approaches can also be used. These include assessment of comparable publicly held companies, present value of future cash flow, replacement value, book value, earnings approach, factor approach, and liquidation value. A formula to determine the percentage of ownership a venture capitalist will want is the venture capitalist's investment times the multiple desired divided by the company's projected profits in year five times the price earnings multiple of a comparable company.

In the end, the entrepreneur and investor must agree on the terms of the transaction, known as the deal. In negotiation, the entrepreneur should assess his or her own priorities in order to prioritize offers if needed. If care is taken in structuring the deal, both the entrepreneur and investor will maintain a satisfactory relationship while achieving their goals through the business' growth and development.

QUESTIONS FOR DISCUSSION

1. As an entrepreneur seeking venture capital, what factors would you take into account before approaching a venture-capital company?
2. Why would an entrepreneur look for an "angel" rather than approach a venture-capital company?
3. Given the angel's dissatisfaction with referral sources, what other methods might facilitate investment referrals?
4. Why is it important for the entrepreneur to establish a high degree of trust with the potential investor?
5. Study Table 10–7. What conclusions can you make regarding the investor's required percentage of ownership?

KEY TERMS

acquisition financing
book value
business angels
deal structure
development financing
due diligence
early-stage financing
earnings approach
equity participation
equity pool
factor approach
factors in valuation
general valuation method
informal risk-capital market
leveraged buyout financing
liquidation value
preliminary screening
present value of future cash flow
private venture-capital firms
product/market opportunity
public-equity market
referral sources
replacement value
risk-capital markets
SBIC firms
state-sponsored venture-capital fund
strong management team
venture-capital process
venture-capital market

SELECTED READINGS

Brophy, D. J., Amonsen, E., & Bontrager, P. (April 1982). Analysis of structuring and pricing of venture capital investment proposals. *Proceedings,* 1982 Conference on Entrepreneurship, pp 358–95.

Illustrates the use of a computerized simulation model that incorporates sensitivity analysis and probability estimation to aid the negotiation parties in easily and effectively analyzing alternative financing structures from their own and others' points of views.

Bruno, A. V., & Tyebjee, T. T. (April 1983). The one that got away: A study of ventures rejected by venture capitalists. *Proceedings,* 1983 Conference on Entrepreneurship, pp 289–306.

Investigated entrepreneurs who were denied venture-capital financing at some point in the firm's history. A profile is created of denied entrepreneurs by examining characteristics common to the firm denied. It also examines the perceptions of denied entrepreneurs regarding the venture-capital industry. Examines, where possible, the effects of denial on the firm and therefore on the innovation process.

Fried, V. H., & Hisrich, R. D. (Fall 1988). Venture capital research: Past, present, and future. *Entrepreneurship: Theory and Practice* 13 no. 1, pp 15–28.

Since 1980, venture capital has become an important source of funding for entrepreneurs. For this reason, it has also emerged as an area of research activity and academic interest. This paper surveys the current efforts being made in this field of research and suggests ideas for further research about venture capital. A model of the venture capital process is derived, and advice is given to improve the methodology of future research.

Gorman, M., & Sahlman, W. A. (April 1986). What do venture capitalists do? *Proceedings,* 1986 Conference on Entrepreneurship, pp 414–36.

Sheds light on the relationship between the venture capitalists and their portfolio companies. Among the general areas covered are: (1) how much time venture capitalists spend with their portfolio companies, (2) the roles venture capitalists play in their portfolio companies, and (3) what happens to the relationship between venture capitalists and the portfolio company during hard times.

Gorman, M., & Sahlman, W. A. (July 1989). What do venture capitalists do? *Journal of Business Venturing* 4, no. 4, pp 231–48.

Gives the results of a survey used to show the relationship between venture capitalists and their particular portfolio companies. Portfolio companies generally helped to raise additional funding, but strategic analysis and recruiting a management team were also performed. The most frequently mentioned cause of failure was attributed to the senior management of the venture.

Goslin, L. N., & Barge, B. (April 1986). Entrepreneurial qualities considered in venture capital Support. *Proceedings,* 1986 Conference on Entrepreneurship, pp 366–79.

Analyzes the responses to a survey sent to three groups of venture-capital firms. The survey focused on identifying the entrepreneurial qualities that the venture capitalists considered critical to a favorable decision to support the start-up activity. Results show that the significant factor leading to funding is the management team, followed in importance by the product, and then other factors.

Gupta, U. (1986). Hands on venture capital. *Venture* 8, no. 1, pp 44–50.

Highlights New Enterprise Associates, a venture-capital firm with a strong emphasis on managing the companies in which they invest. The current relationship between venture capitalists and entrepreneurs is investigated.

Harper, C. P., & Rose, L. C. (1983). Accuracy of appraisers and appraisal methods of closely held companies. *Entrepreneurship: Theory and Practice* 17, no. 3, pp 21–33.

The results of a study valuing 258 closely held firms indicates that valuation estimates are sensitive to both the methodology used and the background of the appraiser making the valuation. The best valuation estimates come from a combination of methodologies.

Hisrich, R. D., & Jankowicz, A. D. (January 1990). Intuition in venture capital decisions: An exploratory study using a new technique. *Journal of Business Venturing* 5, no. 1, pp 49–63.

Discusses a study that used the repertory grid to examine the intuition involved in entrepreneurial decision making. Investment decisions can be grouped into one of three areas: management, unique opportunity, and appropriate return. Despite the general trends listed, it was shown by cluster analysis that each venture capitalist had a different way of structuring the institution needed for an investment decision.

Landstrom, H. (1993). Informal risk capital in Sweden and some international comparisons. *Journal of Business Venturing* 8, no. 6, pp 525–542.

The informal risk-capital market is described, and the informal investor is profiled in terms of the investor demographics, investment activity, portfolio characteristics, and the relationship with the portfolio company.

MacMillan, I. C., Siegel, R., & Subba Narasimba, P. N. (April 1985). Criteria used by venture capitalists to evaluate new venture proposals. *Proceedings,* 1985 Conference on Entrepreneurship, pp 126–41.

Presents the results of a questionnaire administered to 100 venture capitalists attempting to determine the most important criteria they use to decide on funding new ventures. These clusters of venture capitalists are identified: those who carefully assess the competitive and implementation risks, those who seek easy bail-out, and those who deliberately keep as many options open as possible.

Sandberg, W. R., Schweiger, D. M., & Hofer, C. W. (1987). Determining venture capitalists' decision criteria: The use of verbal protocols. *Proceedings,* Babson Research Conference, pp 392–407.

Describes how the use of verbal protocols can help us understand more about venture capitalists and their criteria for decision making in new ventures.

Thompson, J. K., Smith, H. L., & Hood, J. (1983). Charitable contributions by small businesses. *Journal of Small Business Management* 31, no. 3, pp 35–51.

Based on an investigation of charitable contributions and their decisions in small business, the findings suggest the typical small business has few formal policies and yet donates $4,000 per year and 160 hours of employee time to charitable causes.

Timmons, J. A., & Bygrave, W. D. (1986). Venture capital's role in financing innovation for economic growth. *Journal of Business Venturing* 1, no. 2, pp 161–76.

Surveyed venture-capital firms in an attempt to determine the flow of venture capital from 1967 through 1982 and to identify any differences between "highly innovative" technological ventures and "least-innovative" ventures. Indicates that the "capital" in venture capital is the least important factor in fostering technological innovation; rather the management skills of the venture capitalist in nurturing the entrepreneur accelerated the emergence of highly innovative technologies.

Tyebjee, T. T., & Bruno, A. V. (1981). Venture capital decision making: Preliminary results from three empirical studies. *Proceedings,* 1981 Conference on Entrepreneurship, pp 281–320.

Has two objectives: the first is to review the available material and literature on venture-capital decision making and its impact on entrepreneurship and, second, to elucidate a research methodology concerned with several of the important topics. Preliminary results of these studies by the author are presented.

Waldron, D., & Hubbard, C. M. (1991). Valuation methods and estimates in relationship to investing versus consulting. *Entrepreneurship: Theory and Practice* 16, no. 1, pp 43–52.

Eight investors and ten consultants evaluated a small avionics firm. While there was little convergence on the values assigned on either a within-group or between-group basis, the actual buyer paid more that the highest value assigned.

Wetzel, W. E., Jr. (1987). The informal venture capital market aspects of scale and market efficiency. *Proceedings,* Babson Research Conference, pp 412–28.

Discusses how the informal venture market is disabled since many investors do not fully understand venture financing. Presents an example of how to increase the efficiency of the venture-capital market.

CHAPTER

11

Going Public

Chapter Objectives

1. To identify the advantages and disadvantages of going public.
2. To identify some alternatives to going public.
3. To discuss the timing of going public and underwriter selection.
4. To explain the registration statement and timetable for going public.
5. To discuss the legal issues of going public and blue sky qualifications.
6. To discuss some important issues for a venture after going public.

Sam Walton

Sam Walton, the Wal-Mart magnate, has been frequently identified as the richest man in America. He is well known for his marketing strategy of introducing discount stores to the smaller cities and towns ignored by the other chains, but that is not the only foundation for his success. In large part, the growth of his company and the concurrent growth of his personal wealth can be directly attributed to his judicious use of the equity markets.

Walton got his start in retailing in 1940 as a salesman and management trainee at J.C. Penney. He was one of the best shirt salesmen in the organization, but he knew that it was just a training ground for his real calling as a store owner. In 1945, along with his brother Bud, he began operating a Ben Franklin five-and-dime store in Newport, Arkansas. After five successful years, they moved to a store in Bentonville, Arkansas, where Sam lived until his death. The Walton brothers began expanding, buying other variety stores in the area. Utilizing all of his knowledge about sales, Sam set up his own buying office and applied advertising and other marketing principles to his group of stores that others thought were applicable only to bigger ventures. Moving into the 1960s, the Waltons owned enough stores to be the most successful Ben Franklin franchisees in the country.

A new concept was developing in the retail business in the early 60s: discounting. When Gibson's, a Texas-based discounter, opened a store in Fayetteville, where the Waltons had a variety store, Sam decided to try an experiment. Starting with a single department, his discounting attempt soon enveloped a complete store. Despite Walton's success with this experiment, and the growing threat of discounting to the local variety stores, the Ben Franklin executives were not receptive to changing the positioning of their chain. Sam decided to strike out on his own. After a brief tour around the country in search of new ideas, he developed a plan to begin operating his own discount stores in towns with a population of less than 25,000. The first Wal-Mart was opened in Rogers, Arkansas, in 1962.

Sam's profits dictated the growth rate of his business. This make-do-with-what-you-have philosophy carried over to the new Wal-Mart stores. To open the first store, Sam and Bud pooled all their available resources and planned the size and location of the store based on that amount of capital. There was no room in the tight budget for fancy displays or large offices if they were to offer quality merchandise at competitive prices in small towns. Evidently, the pipe-rack displays and bare floors were only a minor inconvenience to the shoppers, because Wal-Mart was a success from the start.

Early in the development of the Wal-Mart concept, Sam realized the vital role of distribution in determining profitability. He knew he needed the same low-cost, efficient delivery methods used by his larger counterparts. Rather than build warehouses to serve existing outlets, he clustered his expansion outlets around existing distribution points. At this point, Sam considered a public offering of stock. In 1970, after eight years in the discount store business, there were about 30 Wal-Mart Discount City stores. It became apparent to Walton that he needed his own warehouse to be able to buy in the volume necessary to support new openings. Yet he did not feel that the company could afford to incur the heavy debt burden needed. In the midst of a boom in new issues and on the strength of his impressive growth record, Walton sold a small part of his business to the public for $3.3 million. This cash helped pay for a $5 million distribution center, big enough to serve 80 to 100 stores.

With his distribution center in place, Sam was ready to grow. Two years later, with 512 stores and $678 million in sales, Wal-Mart was listed on the New York Stock Exchange. Original investors who paid $16.50 a share now have shares worth over $900. Sam tapped the public equity market several additional times when he needed to expand or upgrade his system, managing to keep his overall capital costs well below those of his competitors with his careful planning and tight budgeting. This helped sales, earnings, and dividends continue to grow. In 1987, sales were $15,879 million with earnings of $.28 and a dividend of $.03. This increased in a progressive fashion to $55,484 million with earnings of $.87 and a dividend of $.105 and is projected to reach $67,500 million in 1983 and $82,750 in 1994 with earnings of $1.03 and $1.23, respectively. Of course, one of the more recent significant challenges to the company has been filling Sam Walton's shoes upon his death. The successor, Wal-Mart president and CEO, David Glass, will have to provide clear direction and leadership as the company wrestles with a new set of problems relating to compound annual growth, communications, merchandise selection and sourcing flexibility, and a tendency for a more impersonal, bureaucratic organization resulting from its larger size.

Sam Walton judiciously decided when to use the public equity market for money to finance the expansion of his business—Wal-Mart. The decision to "go public"—a phrase used to describe the transformation of a closely held corporation into one where the general public has proprietary interest—should be carefully thought out. To some entrepreneurs, going public is the ultimate rite, signaling entry into the most exclusive legitimate business community. But before doing so there are several issues the entrepreneur must carefully address, as Sam Walton did. These include assessing the advantages and disadvantages of going public, evaluating the alternatives to going public, determining the timing of doing so, selecting the underwriter, preparing the registration statement and timetable, and understanding the blue sky qualifications and the resulting reporting requirements.

ADVANTAGES AND DISADVANTAGES

Going public occurs when the entrepreneur and other equity owners of the venture offer and sell some part of the company to the public through a registration statement filed with the Securities and Exchange Commission (SEC) pursuant to the Securities Act of 1933. The resulting capital infusion to the company and the large numbers of stockholders and outstanding shares of stock provide the company with financial resources for its business plan and a relatively liquid investment vehicle for the public investors. Consequently, the company will theoretically have greater access to capital markets in the future and a more objective picture of the public's perception of the value of the business. However, given the reporting requirements, the large number of stockholders, and the costs involved, the entrepreneur must carefully evaluate the advantages and disadvantages of going public before initiating the process. A list of the advantages and disadvantages is given in Table 11–1.

Advantages

There are four primary advantages of going public: obtaining a new equity capital, obtaining value and transferability of the organization's assets, enhancing ability to obtain future funds, and acquiring prestige. Whether it be first-stage, second-stage, or third-stage financing, a venture is in constant need of capital to finance its start-up and growth. The new capital provides the needed working capital, plant and equipment, or inventories and supplies necessary for the venture's growth and survival. Going public is often the best way to obtain this needed capital on the best possible terms.

TABLE 11–1 Advantages and Disadvantages of Going Public

Advantages
- Obtaining capital with less dilution to founders
- Enhanced ability to borrow
- Enhanced ability to raise equity
- Liquidity and valuation
- Prestige
- Personal wealth

Disadvantages
- Expense
- Disclosure of information
- Pressures to maintain growth pattern
- Loss of control

Going public also provides a mechanism for valuing the company and allowing this value to be easily transferred among parties. Many family-owned or other privately held companies may need to go public so that the value of the company can be disseminated among the second and third generations. Venture capitalists view going public as the most beneficial way to attain the liquidity necessary to exit a company with the best possible return on their earlier-stage funding. Other investors, as well, can more easily liquidate their investment since the company's stock takes on value and transferability. Because of this liquidity, the value of a publicly traded security frequently is higher than shares of one that is not publicly traded. In addition, publicly traded companies often find it easier to acquire other companies by using their securities in the transactions.

The third primary advantage is that publicly traded companies usually find it easier to raise additional capital, particularly debt. Money can be borrowed more easily and on more favorable terms when there is value attached to a company and that value is more easily transferred. Not only debt financing but future equity capital is more easily obtained when a company establishes a track record of increasing stock value.

A final advantage, prestige, occurs because a publicly traded company is more widely known. This prestige can facilitate obtaining good suppliers as well as other support services.

Disadvantages

While the advantages of going public are significant for a new venture, they must be carefully weighed against the numerous disadvantages. There is a tendency today for entrepreneurs to keep their companies private, even in times of a hot stock market.[1] For example, only 17 of 1987's 500 fastest growing companies took advantage of good stock market conditions and went public. Why did so many of these companies avoid the supposed gold rush of an **initial public offering (IPO)?**

One of the major reasons is the public exposure and potential loss of control of a publicly traded company. To stay on the cutting edge of technology, companies frequently need to sacrifice short-term profits for long-term innovation. This can require reinvesting in technology that in itself may not produce any bottom-line results, even in the long run. Making long-term decisions is increasingly difficult in publicly traded companies where sales/profit evaluations indicate the capability of management as reflected in the value of the stock. The evaluation mechanism accompanying publicly traded companies can partially affect decision making; and when enough shares are sold to the public, the company can lose control of decision making. This loss of control can eventually result in the company being acquired by an unfriendly tender offer, as was discussed in Chapter 4.

---

[1]J. Kotkin, "What I Do in Private Is My Business," *Inc.*, November 1986, pp 66–81.

Some of the most troublesome aspects of being public are the loss of flexibility and increased administrative burdens that result. The company must make decisions in light of the fiduciary duties owed to the public shareholder, and it is obliged to disclose to the public all material information regarding the company, its operations, and its management. One publicly traded company had to retain a more expensive investment banker than would have been required by a privately held company in order to obtain an "appropriate" fairness opinion in a desired merger. The investment banker increased the expenses of the merger by $150,000, in addition to causing a three-month delay in the merger proceedings. Also, the management of a publicly traded company spends a significant amount of additional time addressing queries from shareholders, press, and financial analysts.

If all these disadvantages have not caused the entrepreneur to look for alternative financing rather than an IPO, the expenses involved may. The major expenses of going public include accounting fees, legal fees, underwriter's fees, registration and blue sky filing fees, and printing costs. The accounting fees involved in going public vary greatly, depending in part on the size of the company, the availability of previously audited financial statements, and the complexity of the company's operations.

Generally, the costs of going public (undertaking an IPO) are $300,000 to $600,000, although they can be much greater when significant complexities are involved. Additional reporting, accounting, legal, and printing expenses can run anywhere from $50,000 to $250,000 per year, depending on the company's past practices in the areas of accounting and shareholder communications. In addition to the SEC reports that must be filed, a proxy statement and other materials must be submitted to the SEC for review before distribution to the stockholders. These materials contain certain disclosures concerning management, its compensation, and transactions with the company, as well as the items to be voted on at the meeting. Public companies must also submit an annual report to the shareholders containing the audited financial information for the prior fiscal year and a discussion of any business developments. The preparation and distribution of the proxy materials and annual report are some of the more significant items of additional expense incurred by a company after it is public.

Accounting fees for an initial public offering fluctuate widely but are typically $50,000 to $100,000. Fees are at the lower end of this range if the accounting firm has regularly audited the company over the past several years. They are at the higher end of the range if the company has had no prior audits or if it engages a new accounting firm. The accounting fee covers the preparation of financial statements, the response to SEC queries, and the preparation of "cold comfort" letters for the underwriters described later in this chapter.

Legal fees will also vary significantly, typically ranging from $60,000 to $175,000. These fees generally cover preparing corporate documents, preparing and clearing the registration statement, negotiating the final underwriting agreement, and closing the sale of the securities to these underwriters. Frequently, additional legal fees are involved in a company going public. This so-called housekeeping work can be extensive, particularly if a major reorganization is involved. A public company also pays legal fees for the work involved with the National Association of Securities Dealers, Inc. (NASD) and the state blue sky filings. The legal fees for NASD and state blue sky filings range from $8,000 to $30,000, depending on the size of the offering and the number of states in which the securities will be offered.

The underwriters' fees include a cash discount (or commission), which usually ranges from 7 to 10 percent of the public offering price of the new issue. In some IPOs, the underwriters can also require other compensation, such as warrants to purchase stock, reimbursement for some expenses—most typically legal fees—and the right of first refusal on any future offerings. The NASD regulates the maximum amount of the underwriter's compensation and reviews the actual amount for fairness before the offering can take place. Similarly, any underwriter's compensation is also reviewed in blue sky filings.

There are other expenses in the form of SEC, NASD, and state blue sky registration fees. Of these, the SEC registration fee is quite small: one-fiftieth of 1 percent of the maximum aggregate public offering price of the security. For example, the SEC fee would be $4,000 on a $20 million offering. The minimum fee is $100. Regardless of the amount, the SEC fee must be paid by certified or cashier's check. The NASD filing fee is also small in relation to the size of the offering: $100 plus one-hundredth of 1 percent of the maximum public offering price. In the above example of a $20 million offering, this would be $2,100. The maximum NASD fee is $5,100. The amount of the state blue sky fees depends entirely on the number of states in which the offering is registered. If the initial public offering is registered in all states, the total blue sky filing fees can be more than $15,000, depending on the size of the offering.

The final major expense—printing costs—typically ranges from $50,000 to $200,000. The registration statement and prospectus discussed later in this chapter account for the largest portion of these expenses. The exact amount of expenses varies, depending on the length of the prospectus, the use of color or black and white photographs, the number of proofs and corrections, and the number printed. It is important for the company to use a good printer because accuracy and speed are required in the printing of the prospectus and other offering documents.

THE ALTERNATIVES TO GOING PUBLIC

Since most of the alternatives to going public were presented in Chapter 9, only the most widely used ones will be briefly discussed here. The two most commonly used alternatives are private placements and bank loans. A private placement of securities, particularly with institutional investors—insurance companies, investment companies, or pension funds—is one way to obtain the needed funds with minimum effort. These funds are frequently in the form of intermediate or long-term debt, often carrying a floating interest rate, or preferred stock with specific dividend requirements. In addition, most private placement transactions also carry certain **restrictive covenants.** These covenants are not intended to hamper the operations of the venture but to protect the investor and allow the investment to be profitably liquidated at a later date. The **liquidation covenant** usually contains a provision allowing the investor to require registration of a sale or other disposition of its securities at any time. The entrepreneur must evaluate whether this or any of the other covenants impose too many restrictions on the successful operation of the company before selecting private placement as an alternative source of funds.

To qualify for a private placement under the Securities and Exchange Act of 1933, a company must have a limited number of investors, each of whom has enough sophistication in financial and business matters to be capable of evaluating the risks and merits of the investment. This requires that the investors have available all the information that would be included in a registration statement. In addition, the investors have to agree to hold the securities for a specified period following the purchase. As a rule of thumb, equity securities for a specified private placement will be sold at 20 to 30 percent less than the company might receive for the same securities in a public offering.

In addition to private placement, a bank loan is a viable alternative to going public. Bank loans are a common way to raise additional funds. However, this additional capital is in the form of debt, not equity, and therefore often must have some collateral of the company or the guaranty of the entrepreneur behind it. This collateral is typically in the form of contracts, accounts receivable, machinery, inventory, land, or buildings—some tangible asset. Even when some assets are available for collateral, bank loans are typically made on a short-, or at best, medium-term basis. The interest, which is usually at a floating rate, must also be considered when evaluating this alternative source of funds. The repayment schedule and rigidity of this financial alternative may preclude its use.

Other debt financing can be obtained from nonbank lenders, such as equipment leasing companies, mortgage bankers, trade suppliers, or inventory and accounts receivable financing companies. This money has either fixed or fluctuating interest rates and established payment periods similar to bank loans. Usually these loans offer the entrepreneur a greater degree of flexibility than bank loans, although not nearly as much as equity capital.

TIMING OF GOING PUBLIC AND UNDERWRITER SELECTION

Probably the two most critical issues in a successful public offering are the timing of the offering and the firms involved—the underwriting team. An entrepreneur should seek advice from several financial advisors as well as other entrepreneurs who are familiar with the process.

Timing

Am I ready to go public? This is the critical question that entrepreneurs must ask themselves before launching this effort. In answering this question, the entrepreneur should evaluate several critical factors.

First, is the company large enough? While it is not possible to establish rigid minimum size standards that must be met before an entrepreneur can go public, large New York investment banking firms prefer at least a 500,000 share offering at a minimum $10 per share. This means that the company would have to have a past offering value of at least $12.5 million in order to support this $5 million offering, given that the company is willing to sell shares representing not more than 40 percent of the total number of shares outstanding after the offering is completed. This company valuation will be obtained only with significant sales and earnings performance or solid prospects for future growth and earnings.

Second, what is the amount of the company's earnings, and how strong is its financial performance? Not only is this performance the basis of the company valuation previously discussed, but it also determines both if a company can successfully go public and the type of firm willing to underwrite the offering. While the exact criteria vary from year to year, reflecting the market conditions, generally a company must have at least one year of good earnings and sales before its stock offering will be acceptable to the market. Larger underwriting firms have more stringent criteria, some as high as sales of $15 to $20 million, $1 million or more net income, and a 30 to 50 percent annual growth rate.

Third, are the market conditions favorable for an initial public offering? Underlying the sales and earnings, as well as the size of the offering, is the prevailing general market condition. Market conditions affect both the initial price that the entrepreneur will receive for the stock and the aftermarket—the price performance of the stock after its initial sale. Some market conditions are more favorable for IPOs than others. Unless there is such an urgent need for money that delay is impossible, the entrepreneur should attempt to take his or her company public in the most favorable market conditions.

Fourth, how urgently is the money needed? As previously indicated, the entrepreneur must carefully appraise both the urgency of the need for new money and the availability of outside capital from other sources. Since the sale of common stock decreases the ownership position of the entrepreneur and other equity owners involved in the start-up, the longer the time before going public, given profits and sales growth, the less percentage of equity the entrepreneur will have to give up per dollar invested.

Finally, what are the needs and desires of the present owners? Sometimes the present owners lack confidence in the future viability and growth prospects of the business or they have a need for liquidity. Going public is frequently the only method for present stockholders to obtain the cash needed. This occurs particularly when venture-capital money is involved. The goal of the typical venture capitalist is to liquidate the investment within 5 to 10 years.

Underwriter Selection

Once the entrepreneur has determined that the timing for going public is favorable, he or she must carefully select a **managing underwriter,** who will take the lead in forming the **underwriting syndicate.** The underwriter is of critical importance in establishing the initial price for the stock of the company; supporting the stock in the aftermarket so that the price stabilizes and, one hopes, rises; and creating a strong following among security analysis.

Although most public offerings are conducted by a syndicate of underwriters, the entrepreneur needs to select only the lead or managing underwriter(s). The managing underwriters will then develop the strongest possible syndicate of underwriters for the initial public offering. An entrepreneur should ideally develop a relationship with several potential managing underwriters (investment bankers) at least one year before going public. Frequently, this occurs during the first- or second-round financing, where the advice of an investment banker helps structure the initial financial arrangements to position the company to go public later.

Since selecting the investment banker is a major factor in the success of the public offering, the entrepreneur should approach one through a mutual contact. Commercial banks, attorneys specializing in securities work, major accounting firms, providers of the initial financing, or prominent members of the company's board of directors can usually provide the needed suggestions and introductions. Since the relationship will be ongoing, not ending with the completion of the offering, the entrepreneur should employ several criteria in the selection process. These include reputation, distribution capability, advisory services, experience, and cost.

An initial public offering rarely involves a well-known company; hence, the managing underwriter needs a good reputation to develop a strong syndicate team and provide confidence to both individual and institutional investors. This confidence and respect in financial circles of the managing underwriter helps sell the public offering and supports the stock in the aftermarket.

The success of the offering is also a function of the underwriter's distribution capability. An entrepreneur wants the stock of his or her company distributed to as wide and varied a base as possible. Since each investment banking form has a different client base, the entrepreneur should compare client bases of possible managing underwriters. Is the client base strongly institutional, individual investors, or balanced between the two? Is the base more internationally or domestically oriented? Are the investors long-term or speculators? What is the geographic distribution—local, regional, or nationwide? A strong managing underwriter and syndicate with a quality client base will help the stock sell well and perform well in the aftermarket.

Some underwriters are better able than others to provide financial advisory services. While this factor is not as important as the previous two in selecting an underwriter, financial counsel is frequently needed before and after the IPO. An entrepreneur should address such questions as: Can the underwriter provide sound financial advice? Has the underwriter given good financial counsel to previous clients? Can it render assistance in obtaining future public or private financing? The answers to these questions will indicate the degree of ability among various possible managing underwriters.

As reflected in the previous questions, the experience of the investment banking firm is important. The chosen firm should have experience in underwriting issues of companies in the same or at least very similar industries. This experience will give the managing underwriter credibility, the capability to explain the company to the investing public, and the ability to price the IPO accurately.

The final factor to be considered in the choice of a managing underwriter is cost. As was discussed previously, going public is a very costly proposition. And, as indicated in Table 11–2, costs do vary greatly among underwriters. This table reflects the highest price obtained by underwriters for taking lower-quality deals public. The average gross spread as a percentage of the offering was around 10 percent. Costs associated with various possible managing underwriters must be carefully weighed against the other four factors. At this stage, the entrepreneur should not try to cut corners, given the stakes involved in a successful initial public offering.

REGISTRATION STATEMENT AND TIMETABLE

Once the managing underwriter has been selected, a planning meeting is set that includes company officials responsible for preparing the registration statement, the company's independent accountants and lawyers, and the underwriters and their counsel. At this important meeting, frequently called the "all hands" meeting, a timetable is prepared, indicating dates for each step in the registration process. This timetable establishes the effective date of the registration, which determines the date of the final financial statements to be included. The company's end of the year, when regular audited financial statements are routinely prepared, is taken into account to avoid any possible extra accounting and legal work. The timetable should indicate the

TABLE 11–2 Costs of Underwriters

The Most Expensive Underwriters
(These underwriters exacted the highest price for taking lower-quality deals public)

*Underwriter**	*Average Total Expense as Percent of Offering†*	*Average Gross Spread as Percent of Offering‡*	*Average Size of Offering*	*Total Number of Deals*
1. Vanderbilt Securities Inc.	29.1%	10.0%	$468,590	7
2. Alpine Securities Corp.	27.2	14.4	260,000	5
3. Western Capital and Securities Inc.	25.4	13.2	481,600	5
4. Patten Securities Corp.	22.7	10.0	1,027,125	9
5. Stuart-James Co.	20.9	10.0	2,201,875	8
6. Rooney, Pace Inc.	20.1	9.9	4,349,600	7
7. Steinberg & Lyman Investment Bankers	19.8	10.0	3,565,500	5
8. Blinder, Robinson & Co.	19.5	10.0	2,428,571	7
9. D. H. Blair & Co.	18.5	9.9	4,772,065	17
10. Dillon Securities Inc.	18.5	10.2	851,820	5

*Includes only underwriters that completed five or more IPOs
†Average total expenses include legal, accounting, and printing fees that don't go to the underwriter; it also includes nonaccountable expenses that do go to the underwriter
‡Average gross spread includes underwriting fees, management fees, and selling concessions to the underwriter
Source: Securities Data Co., Venture

individual responsible for preparing the various parts of the registration and offering statement. Problems often arise in an initial public offering when the timetable is not carefully developed and agreed to by all parties involved.

After preliminary preparation has been completed, the first public offering normally requires six to eight weeks to prepare, print, and file the registration statement with the SEC. Once the registration statement has been filed, the SEC generally takes four to eight weeks to declare the registration effective. Delays frequently occur in this process during the heavy periods of market activity, during peak seasons such as March when the SEC is reviewing a large number of proxy statements, when the company's attorney is not familiar with federal or state regulations, when a complete and full disclosure is resisted by the company, or when the managing underwriter is inexperienced.

In reviewing the registration statement, the SEC is charged with attempting to ensure only that the document makes a **full and fair disclosure** of the material reported. The SEC has no authority to withhold approval of or require any changes in the terms of an offering that it deems unfair or inequitable, so long as all material information concerning the company and the offering are fully disclosed. The NASD will review each offering, principally to determine the fairness of the underwriting compensation and its compliance with NASD bylaw requirements.

While certain states will review an application for registration in the same manner as the SEC (i.e., solely concerned with full and fair disclosure), others review it to determine whether the offering is "fair, just, and equitable" to the investors in its state. These states actually have the authority to reject an offering on the basis of the perceived merits. Some of the matters the blue sky examiners focus on most often are the percentage of ownership retained by the promoters and the amount of capital invested by them for those shares (the amount of "cheap stock" outstanding); the underwriting compensation; the existence of transactions between the officers, directors, or other promoters of the enterprise and the issuer itself (i.e., loans or sales to management and other sorts of self-dealing); and the financial performance and stability of the issuer. Once the effective date has been established by the SEC, the underwriters will immediately offer the shares to the public.

An example summary of the key dates for an initial public offering for KeKaKa Corporation is given in Table 11–3. The company's fiscal year ends March 31, and audited financial statements have been prepared for each prior year of the company's existence. This year's audited financial statements are being prepared in the usual timely manner.

The registration statement itself consists primarily of two parts; the **prospectus** (a legal offering document normally prepared as a brochure or booklet for distribution to prospective buyers) and the **registration statement** (supplemental information to the prospectus, which is available for public inspection at the office of the SEC). Both parts of the registration statement are governed principally by the Securities and Exchange Act of 1933 (the "1933 Act"), a federal statute requiring the registration of securities to be offered to the public. This act also requires that the prospectus be furnished to the purchaser at or before the making of any written offer or the actual confirmation of a sale. Specific SEC forms set forth the informational

TABLE 11–3 Summary of Key Dates for KeKaKa Corporation

All hands meeting	May 15
First draft of S-1 distributed	June 15
All hands meeting	June 22
All hands meeting	July 1
Registration filing date	July 15
Public offering effective	September 8
Closing of offering	September 17

requirements for a registration. Most initial public offerings will use **form S–1** or, in the case of smaller offerings, **form S–18.** The appropriate form to be used depends on the company's business; the amount of public information already available on the company; the type of security to be offered; the company's size and past financial performance; and, in some instances, the proposed type of purchasers.

The Prospectus

This part of the registration statement is almost always written in a highly stylized narrative form as it is the selling document of the company. While the exact format is left up to the company, the information must be presented in an organized, logical sequence and an easy-to-read, understandable manner in order to obtain SEC approval. Some of the most common sections of a prospectus include the cover page, prospectus summary, the company, risk factors, use of proceeds, dividend policy, capitalization, dilution, selected financial data, the business, management and owners, type of stock, underwriter information, and the actual financial statements.

The cover page includes such information as company name, type and number of shares to be sold, a distribution table, date of prospectus, managing underwriter(s), and syndicate of underwriters involved. There is a preliminary prospectus and then a final prospectus once approval by the SEC is granted. The cover page of a preliminary prospectus booklet and the final prospectus booklet are shown in Tables 11–4 and 11–5, respectively. The preliminary prospectus is used by the underwriters to solicit investor interest in the offering while the registration is pending. The final prospectus contains all of the changes and additions required by the SEC and blue sky examiners and the information concerning the price at which the securities will be sold. The final prospectus must be delivered with or prior to the written confirmation of purchase orders from investors participating in the offering.

The prospectus starts with a table of contents and summary. The prospectus summary highlights the important features of the offering, similar to the executive summary of a business plan discussed previously.

A brief introduction of the company follows, which describes the nature of the business, the company's history, major products, and location.

TABLE 11–4 Preliminary Prospectus

Information contained herein is subject to completion or amendment. A registration statement relating to these securities has been filed with the Securities and Exchange Commission. These securities may not be sold nor may offers to buy be accepted prior to the time the registration statement becomes effective. This prospectus shall not constitute an offer to sell or the solicitation of an offer to buy nor shall there be any sale of these securities in any State in which such offer, solicitation or sale would be unlawful prior to registration or qualification under the securities laws of any such State.

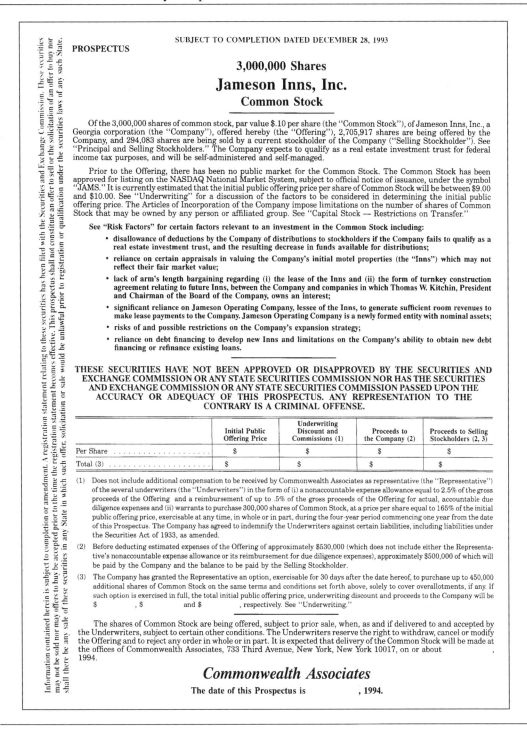

SUBJECT TO COMPLETION DATED DECEMBER 28, 1993

PROSPECTUS

3,000,000 Shares

Jameson Inns, Inc.

Common Stock

Of the 3,000,000 shares of common stock, par value $.10 per share (the "Common Stock"), of Jameson Inns, Inc., a Georgia corporation (the "Company"), offered hereby (the "Offering"), 2,705,917 shares are being offered by the Company, and 294,083 shares are being sold by a current stockholder of the Company ("Selling Stockholder"). See "Principal and Selling Stockholders." The Company expects to qualify as a real estate investment trust for federal income tax purposes, and will be self-administered and self-managed.

Prior to the Offering, there has been no public market for the Common Stock. The Common Stock has been approved for listing on the NASDAQ National Market System, subject to official notice of issuance, under the symbol "JAMS." It is currently estimated that the initial public offering price per share of Common Stock will be between $9.00 and $10.00. See "Underwriting" for a discussion of the factors to be considered in determining the initial public offering price. The Articles of Incorporation of the Company impose limitations on the number of shares of Common Stock that may be owned by any person or affiliated group. See "Capital Stock — Restrictions on Transfer."

See "Risk Factors" for certain factors relevant to an investment in the Common Stock including:

- **disallowance of deductions by the Company of distributions to stockholders if the Company fails to qualify as a real estate investment trust, and the resulting decrease in funds available for distributions;**
- **reliance on certain appraisals in valuing the Company's initial motel properties (the "Inns") which may not reflect their fair market value;**
- **lack of arm's length bargaining regarding (i) the lease of the Inns and (ii) the form of turnkey construction agreement relating to future Inns, between the Company and companies in which Thomas W. Kitchin, President and Chairman of the Board of the Company, owns an interest;**
- **significant reliance on Jameson Operating Company, lessee of the Inns, to generate sufficient room revenues to make lease payments to the Company. Jameson Operating Company is a newly formed entity with nominal assets;**
- **risks of and possible restrictions on the Company's expansion strategy;**
- **reliance on debt financing to develop new Inns and limitations on the Company's ability to obtain new debt financing or refinance existing loans.**

THESE SECURITIES HAVE NOT BEEN APPROVED OR DISAPPROVED BY THE SECURITIES AND EXCHANGE COMMISSION OR ANY STATE SECURITIES COMMISSION NOR HAS THE SECURITIES AND EXCHANGE COMMISSION OR ANY STATE SECURITIES COMMISSION PASSED UPON THE ACCURACY OR ADEQUACY OF THIS PROSPECTUS. ANY REPRESENTATION TO THE CONTRARY IS A CRIMINAL OFFENSE.

	Initial Public Offering Price	Underwriting Discount and Commissions (1)	Proceeds to the Company (2)	Proceeds to Selling Stockholders (2, 3)
Per Share	$	$	$	$
Total (3)	$	$	$	$

(1) Does not include additional compensation to be received by Commonwealth Associates as representative (the "Representative") of the several underwriters (the "Underwriters") in the form of (i) a nonaccountable expense allowance equal to 2.5% of the gross proceeds of the Offering and a reimbursement of up to .5% of the gross proceeds of the Offering for actual, accountable due diligence expenses and (ii) warrants to purchase 300,000 shares of Common Stock, at a price per share equal to 165% of the initial public offering price, exercisable at any time, in whole or in part, during the four-year period commencing one year from the date of this Prospectus. The Company has agreed to indemnify the Underwriters against certain liabilities, including liabilities under the Securities Act of 1933, as amended.

(2) Before deducting estimated expenses of the Offering of approximately $530,000 (which does not include either the Representative's nonaccountable expense allowance or its reimbursement for due diligence expenses), approximately $500,000 of which will be paid by the Company and the balance to be paid by the Selling Stockholder.

(3) The Company has granted the Representative an option, exercisable for 30 days after the date hereof, to purchase up to 450,000 additional shares of Common Stock on the same terms and conditions set forth above, solely to cover overallotments, if any. If such option is exercised in full, the total initial public offering price, underwriting discount and proceeds to the Company will be $, $ and $, respectively. See "Underwriting."

The shares of Common Stock are being offered, subject to prior sale, when, as and if delivered to and accepted by the Underwriters, subject to certain other conditions. The Underwriters reserve the right to withdraw, cancel or modify the Offering and to reject any order in whole or in part. It is expected that delivery of the Common Stock will be made at the offices of Commonwealth Associates, 733 Third Avenue, New York, New York 10017, on or about   , 1994.

Commonwealth Associates

The date of this Prospectus is   , 1994.

PROSPECTUS

2,600,000 Shares

Jameson Inns, Inc.

Common Stock

Jameson Inns, Inc., a Georgia corporation (the "Company"), hereby offers (the "Offering") 2,600,000 shares of common stock, par value $.10 per share (the "Common Stock"). The Company expects to qualify as a real estate investment trust ("REIT") for federal income tax purposes, and will be self-administered and self-managed.

Prior to the Offering, there has been no public market for the Common Stock. The Common Stock has been approved for listing on the NASDAQ National Market System under the symbol "JAMS." See "Underwriting" for a discussion of the factors considered in determining the initial public offering price. The Articles of Incorporation of the Company impose limitations on the number of shares of Common Stock that may be owned by any person or affiliated group. See "Capital Stock — Restrictions on Transfer."

See "Risk Factors" for certain factors relevant to an investment in the Common Stock including:

- **disallowance of deductions by the Company of distributions to stockholders if the Company fails to qualify as a real estate investment trust, and the resulting decrease in funds available for distributions;**
- **reliance on certain appraisals in valuing the Company's initial motel properties (the "Inns") which may not reflect their fair market value;**
- **material benefits to be received by Mr. Kitchin and other affiliates of the Company;**
- **lack of arm's length bargaining regarding (i) the lease of the Inns and (ii) the form of turnkey construction agreement relating to future Inns, between the Company and companies in which Thomas W. Kitchin, President and Chairman of the Board of the Company, owns an interest;**
- **significant reliance on Jameson Operating Company, lessee of the Inns, to generate sufficient room revenues to make lease payments to the Company. Jameson Operating Company is a newly formed entity with nominal assets;**
- **risks of and possible restrictions on the Company's expansion strategy;**
- **reliance on debt financing to develop new Inns and limitations on the Company's ability to obtain new debt financing or refinance existing loans.**

THESE SECURITIES HAVE NOT BEEN APPROVED OR DISAPPROVED BY THE SECURITIES AND EXCHANGE COMMISSION OR ANY STATE SECURITIES COMMISSION NOR HAS THE SECURITIES AND EXCHANGE COMMISSION OR ANY STATE SECURITIES COMMISSION PASSED UPON THE ACCURACY OR ADEQUACY OF THIS PROSPECTUS. ANY REPRESENTATION TO THE CONTRARY IS A CRIMINAL OFFENSE.

	Initial Public Offering Price	Underwriting Discount and Commissions (1)	Proceeds to the Company (1,2,3)
Per Share	$9.00	$.72	$8.28
Total (3)	$23,400,000	$1,872,000	$21,528,000

(1) Does not include additional compensation to be received by Commonwealth Associates as representative (the "Representative") of the several underwriters (the "Underwriters") in the form of (i) a nonaccountable expense allowance equal to 2% of the gross proceeds of the Offering and a reimbursement of up to .5% of the gross proceeds of the Offering for actual, accountable due diligence expenses and (ii) warrants to purchase 260,000 shares of Common Stock, at a price per share equal to 165% of the initial public offering price, exercisable at any time, in whole or in part, during the four-year period commencing one year from the date of this Prospectus. The Company has agreed to indemnify the Underwriters against certain liabilities, including liabilities under the Securities Act of 1933, as amended.

(2) Before deducting estimated expenses of the Offering of approximately $900,000 (which does not include either the Representative's nonaccountable expense allowance or its reimbursement for due diligence expenses).

(3) The Company has granted the Representative an option, exercisable for 30 days after the date hereof, to purchase up to 390,000 additional shares of Common Stock on the same terms and conditions set forth above, solely to cover overallotments, if any. If such option is exercised in full, the total initial public offering price, underwriting discount and proceeds to the Company will be $26,910,000, $2,152,800 and $24,757,200, respectively. See "Underwriting."

The shares of Common Stock are being offered, subject to prior sale, when, as and if delivered to and accepted by the Underwriters, subject to certain other conditions. The Underwriters reserve the right to withdraw, cancel or modify the Offering and to reject any order in whole or in part. It is expected that delivery of the Common Stock will be made at the offices of Commonwealth Associates, 733 Third Avenue, New York, New York 10017, on or about February 3, 1994.

Commonwealth Associates

The date of this Prospectus is January 26, 1994.

Then a discussion of the risk factors involved is presented. Such issues as a history of operating losses, a short track record, the importance of certain key individuals, dependence on certain customers, significant level of competition, or lack of market uncertainty are presented so that the purchaser is aware of the speculative nature of the offering and the degree of risk involved in purchasing.

The next section—use of proceeds—needs to be carefully prepared, as the actual use of the proceeds must be reported to the SEC following the offering. This section is of great interest to potential purchasers, as it indicates the reason(s) the company is going public and its future direction.

The dividend policy section details the company's dividend history and any restrictions on future dividends. Of course, most entrepreneurial companies have not paid any dividends but have retained their earnings to finance future growth.

The capitalization section indicates the overall capital structure of the company both before and after the public offering.

Whenever there is significant disparity between the offering price of the shares and the price paid for shares by officers, directors, or founding stockholders, a dilution section is necessary in the prospectus. This section describes the dilution, or decrease, of the purchaser's equity interest that will occur.

Form S–1 requires that the prospectus contain, at the end, selected financial data for each of the last five years of company operation to highlight significant trends in the company's financial condition. This analysis of the results of the company's operations and their impact on the financial conditions of the company covers at least the last three years of operation. It provides information that potential purchasers can use to assess the company's cash flow from internal and external sources.

The next section—the business—is the largest in the prospectus. It provides information on the company, its industry, and its products, such as historical development of the company; principal products, markets, and distribution methods; new products being developed; sources and availability of raw materials; backlog orders; export sales; number of employees; and nature of any patents, trademarks, licenses, franchises, and physical property owned.

Following the business section is a discussion of management and security holders. The section covers background information, ages, business experience, total remuneration, and stock holdings of directors, nominated directors, and executive officers. Also any stockholder (not in the above categories) who beneficially owns more than 5 percent of the company must be indicated.

The description of capital stock section, as the name implies, describes the par and stated value of the stock being offered, dividend rights, voting rights, liquidity, and transferability if more than one class of stock exists.

Following this, the underwriter information section explains the plans for distributing the stock offering, such as the amount of securities to be purchased by each underwriting participant involved, the underwriters' obligations, and the indemnification of the company.

The prospectus part of the registration statement concludes with the actual financial statements. Form S–1 requires audited balance sheets for the last two fiscal years, audited income statements and statements of retained earnings for last three fiscal years, and unaudited interim financial statements as of within 135 days of the date the registration statement becomes effective. It is this requirement that makes it so important to pick a date for going public in light of year-end operations and to develop a good timetable to avoid the time and costs of preparing additional interim statements.

Part II

This section of Form S–1 contains specific documentation of the issue in an item-and-answer format, including such exhibits as the articles of incorporation, the underwriting agreements, company bylaws, stock option and pension plans, and contracts. Other items presented include indemnification of directors and officers, any sale of unregistered securities within the past three years, and expenses related to going public.

Form S–18

In April 1979, the SEC adopted a simplified form of the registration statement—Form S–18—for companies planning to register no more than $7.5 million of securities. This form was designed to make going public easier and less expensive by requiring less vigorous reporting requirements. Form S–18 requires less detailed descriptions of the business, officers, directors, and legal proceedings; requires no industry segment information; allows financial statements to be prepared in accordance with generally accepted accounting practices rather than under the guidelines of Regulation S-X; and requires an audited balance sheet at the end of the last fiscal year (rather than the last two years) and audited change in financial positions and stockholders equity for the last two years (rather than the last three years). While Form S–18 can be filed for review with the SEC's Division of Corporation Finance in Washington, D.C., as are all S–1 forms, it can also be filed with the SEC's regional office.

Procedure

Once the preliminary prospectus is filed, it can be distributed to the underwriting group. This preliminary prospectus is called a **red herring,** because a statement printed in red ink appears on the front cover. The red herring for Jameson Inns, Inc., is shown in Table 11–4.

The registration statements are then reviewed by the SEC to determine if adequate disclosures have been made. Some deficiencies are almost always found and are communicated to the company either by telephone or a **deficiency letter.** This preliminary prospectus contains all the information contained in the final prospectus except that which is not known until shortly before the effective date: offering price, underwriters' commission, and amount of proceeds. These items are filed through a **pricing amendment** and appear in the final prospectus (see Table 11–5). To see the difference between a red herring and a final prospectus, compare the two Jameson Inns, Inc., documents shown in Table 11–4 and Table 11–5. This time, usually around a month between the initial filing of the registration statement and its effective date, is called the waiting period, during which time the underwriting syndicate is formed and briefed.

LEGAL ISSUES AND BLUE SKY QUALIFICATIONS

In addition to all the legal issues surrounding the actual preparation and filing of the prospectus, there are several other important legal concerns. Perhaps the one that is of the most concern to the entrepreneur is the **quiet period**—the period of time from when the decision to go public is made to 90 days following the date of its becoming effective. Care must be taken during this period regarding any new information about the company or key personnel. Any publicity effort designed to create a favorable attitude about the securities to be offered is illegal. The guidelines established by the SEC regarding the information that can and cannot be released should be understood not only by the entrepreneur but by everyone in the company as well. All press releases and other printed material should be cleared with the attorneys involved as well as the underwriter. The entrepreneur and key personnel must curtail speaking engagements and television appearances to avoid any possible problematic response to interviewer or audience questions. One entrepreneur whose company was in the process of going public had to postpone a guest appearance on the "Today Show," during which she was to discuss "Women Entrepreneurs," a video scheduled for release after the quiet period was over.

Blue Sky Qualifications

The securities of the company going public must also be qualified under the **blue sky laws** of each state in which the securities will be offered, unless the state has an exemption from the qualification requirements. These blue sky laws cause additional delays and costs to the company going public, as was discussed earlier in this chapter. Many states allow their state securities administrators to prevent the offering from being sold in the state on such substantive grounds as past stock issuances, too much dilution, or too much compensation to the underwriter, even though all required disclosures have been met and clearance has been granted by the SEC.

It is the responsibility of the managing underwriter to determine the states and the number of securities that will be sold in each. The number of securities to be qualified in each state and the offering price are important, as the blue sky laws and qualification fees in many states vary, depending on the number and price. Only after the company has qualified in a particular state and the overall registration statement has been cleared by the SEC can the underwriters sell the number of shares that have been allowed in that particular state. Most states require the company to file sales reports following the offering so that the number of sales sold in the state can be determined and any additional fees assessed if necessary.

AFTER GOING PUBLIC

After the initial public offering has been sold, there are still some areas of concern to the entrepreneur. These include aftermarket support, relationship with the financial community, and reporting requirements.

Aftermarket Support

Once the stock has been issued, the underwriting firm and the entrepreneur should monitor its price, particularly in the initial weeks following its offering. Generally, the managing underwriting firm will be the principal market marker in the company's stock and will be ready to purchase or sell stock in the interdealer market. To stabilize the market, preventing the price from going below the initial public offering price, this underwriter may enter bids to buy the stock in the early stages following the offers—giving **aftermarket support.** This support is important in allowing the stock not to be adversely affected by a precipitous drop in price.

Relationship with the Financial Community

Once a company has gone public, the financial community will take a greater interest in it. An entrepreneur will need an increasing portion of time to develop a good relationship with this community. The relationship established has a significant effect on the market interest and therefore the price of the company's stock. Since many investors rely on analysts and brokers for investment advice, the entrepreneur should attempt to meet these individuals as much as possible. Regular appearances before societies of security analysts should be a part of establishing this relationship, as well as public disclosures through formal press releases. Frequently, it is best to designate one person in the company to be the information officer, ensuring that the press, public, and security analysts are dealt with in a friendly, efficient manner. There is nothing worse than a company not responding in a timely manner to information requests from security brokers and analysts, the trade, the press, and the general public.

Reporting Requirements

As discussed at the beginning of this chapter, one of the negative aspects of going public is the new reporting requirements. One of the first requirements is the filing of a Form SR sales report, which the company must do within 10 days after the end of the first three-month period following the effective date of the registration. This report includes information on the amount of securities sold and still to be sold, and on the proceeds obtained by the company and their use. A final Form SR sales report must be filed within 10 days of the completion or termination of the offering.

The company must file annual reports on Form 10–K, quarterly reports on Form 10–Q, and specific transaction reports on Form 8–K. The information in Form 10–K on the business, management, and company assets is similar to that in Form S–1 of the registration statement. Of course, audited financial statements are required.

The quarterly report on Form 10–Q contains primarily the unaudited financial information for the most recently completed fiscal quarter. No 10–Q is required for the fourth fiscal quarter.

A Form 8–K report must be filed within 15 days of such events as the acquisition or disposition of significant assets by the company outside the ordinary course of the business, the resignation or dismissal of the company's independent public accountants, or a change in control of the company.

The company must also follow the proxy solicitation requirements regarding holding a meeting or obtaining the written consent of security holders. The timing and type of materials involved are detailed in the Securities and Exchange Act of 1933.

These are but a few of the reporting requirements required of public companies. All the requirements must be carefully observed since even inadvertent mistakes can have negative consequences on the company. Of course the reports must be filed on time.

SUMMARY

Going public—the transformation of a closely held corporation to one where the general public has proprietary interest—is indeed arduous. An entrepreneur must carefully assess whether the company is ready to go public as well as whether the advantages outweigh the disadvantages. In assessing readiness, the entrepreneur must take into account the size of the company, earnings and performance, market conditions, urgency of monetary need, and the desires of the current owners. The entrepreneur needs to consider the primary advantages of going public—new capital, liquidity and valuation, enhanced ability to obtain funds, and prestige—along with the disadvantages—expense, disclosure of information, loss of control, and pressure to maintain growth.

Once the decision is made to proceed, a managing investment banking firm must be selected and the registration statement prepared. The expertise of the investment banker is a major factor in the success of the public offering. In selecting an investment banker, the entrepreneur should employ the following criteria: reputation, distribution capability, advisory services, experience, and cost. To prepare for the registration date, the entrepreneur must organize an "all hands" meeting of company officials, the company's independent accountants and lawyers, and the underwriters and their counsel. A timetable must be established for the effective date of registration and for the preparation of necessary financial documents, including the preliminary and final prospectus. Following the registration and review of the SEC, the entrepreneur must carefully observe the 90-day quiet period and qualify under the blue sky laws of each state in which the securities will be offered.

After the initial public offering, the entrepreneur needs to maintain a good relationship with the financial community and to adhere strictly to the reporting requirements of public companies. The decision to go public requires much planning and consideration. Going public, indeed, is not for every entrepreneurial venture.

QUESTIONS FOR DISCUSSION

1. Explain the major reasons you might not wish to go public, even if your entrepreneurial venture met the general criteria for a public offering. If possible, give examples.
2. Why is going public often the best way to increase the growth of a successful privately held company?
3. You have decided to go public with your company and you need to choose an investment banker. Three possibilities have been suggested by your board of directors. Firm A has the best reputation and overall experience but also has the highest cost. Firm B has excellent distribution capability but has not handled any companies similar to yours. Firm C has the lowest cost but is unlikely to distribute beyond the local area. Explain your choice of A, B, or C and discuss under what circumstances you might choose the others.
4. In preparing a prospectus for the SEC, how would you use the help of management staff in areas other than accounting and finance?
5. Why do you think the SEC imposes a quiet period on companies that have decided to go public?

KEY TERMS

aftermarket support
blue sky laws
deficiency letter
Form S–1
Form S–18
full and fair disclosure
going public
initial public offering (IPO)
liquidation covenant
managing underwriter
pricing amendment
prospectus
quiet period
red herring
registration statement
reporting requirements
restrictive covenant
underwriting syndicate

SELECTED READINGS

Burden, R. S., Copeland, J. E., Jr., Hermanson, R. S., & Wat, L. (1984). Going public—What it involves, *Journal of Accountancy* 157, no. 3, pp 63–76.

Lists advantage and disadvantage of going public, examines some characteristics of companies making the decision to go public, describes the general process required, and gives pointers on selecting an underwriter.

Cuday, M. J. (1984). Going wrong by going public. *Fortune* 110, no. 13, pp 173–76.

Questions the real motives of an entrepreneur's decision to go public, raises several drawbacks to offering publicly traded stock, and uses author's experience as an example of ways to avoid the cash flow problems often seen as the "push" toward going public.

Hansen, R. S., & Pinkerton, J. M. (June 1984). Direct equity financing: A resolution of a paradox. *Journal of Financing* 37, no. 3, pp 651–65.

When raising new equity capital, managers have historically rejected the direct-offer method, favoring instead the apparently more costly underwritten public issue. Provides a resolution for this equity financing paradox by demonstrating empirically that firms that engage in direct offers do so because their specific situation offers a cost advantage and not because direct offers are themselves a more efficient method of equity financing.

Johnson, J. J., & Miller, R. E. (1985). Going public: Information for small business. *Journal of Small Business Management* 23, pp 38–44.

Examines new public equity offerings from the standpoint of the issuer. Methods, characteristics, and options related to public offerings are presented. Discussions with investment bankers were conducted in order to present a description of how offering methods are matched to businesses.

Ruhnka, J. C. (October 1985). Raising equity capital through limited offerings: Criteria for choice of exemptions. *Journal of Small Business Management* 23, no. 4, pp 45–53.

Provides criteria for planning exempt stock offerings, clarifying the relationship between financial and legal requirements. Planning guidelines are provided to be used in coordinating (a) the timing and size of offerings with the stage-wise development of a venture, and (b) the resulting financial requirements with the regulatory framework for exemption.

Steven, A. (March 1985). A lunge into the fishbowl. *Nation's Business* 73, no 3, pp 77–78.

Summarizes the results of a survey of CEOs of companies that had recently gone public. The main points discussed are: (1) selection of underwriting firm, (2) handling the loss of autonomy, and (3) administrative burdens imposed by SEC regulations.

Sutton, D. P., & Post, T. (1986). The cost of going public. *Venture* 8, no. 4, pp 30–40.

What entrepreneurs pay to go public is determined by their industry group, the size of the offering, the underwriter that supports them, the quality of their company, and general market conditions. This article reviews these different components, giving case studies for both successful and unsuccessful initial public offerings.

Trostel, A., & Nichol, M. (1982). Privately-held and publicly-held companies: A comparison of strategic choices and management process. *Academy of Management Journal* 25, pp 47–62.

Describes the development of a theory relating differences between privately held and publicly held companies to differences in their strategies and management processes. The existence of differences implies that, in developing strategies, the traditional analysis of strengths and weaknesses in comparison to competitors, as well as analysis of opportunities and threats in the environment, should include the factor of form of ownership.

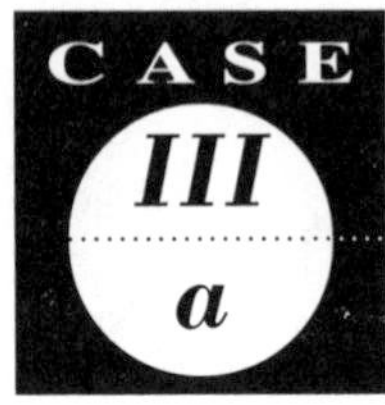

Nature's Way

Dr. Eric Swanson, a long-time chemical engineer, was close to coming up with a product he was sure would sell. Nature's Way, as he called it, would be the first talcum powder deodorant to appear on the market. Swanson, who had been working on the product for years, perceived Nature's Way to be a response to three problems with current deodorant and antiperspirant products on the market: discomfort in application (cold, wet, or sticky), staining of clothing, and possible irritation to the user's skin caused by the amount of chemicals in the products. According to Swanson, Nature's Way was superior to these products for the following reasons:

- The talcum powder had a dry, soft, warm application.
- It did not stain clothing.
- It was formulated from all-natural ingredients.
- It did not mask odor or inhibit perspiration, but rather it interacted biologically to prevent body odor.

Although the product was finally near completion, Swanson was out of funds, and several concerns were hampering his ability to acquire additional funding:

- The product had not been tested.
- The product did not stop wetness.
- There were no other talcum-based products on the market.
- The application method had not been finalized.
- Production requirements and methods had not been specified and/or developed.

Swanson had invested all of his own funds and had borrowed $10,000 from his brother. He had also approached his bank for a $5,000 loan but was rejected for the concerns just mentioned. Swanson knew he needed to find solutions to these problems, but he needed further capital before he could proceed. He also needed to formulate a specific strategy to get his product to the market. The following outlines the information he had obtained on the market so far.

INDUSTRY BACKGROUND

Nature's Way Deodorant would compete in the deodorant and antiperspirant category of the health and beauty aid consumer product market. Individuals used these products as protection against the effects of perspiration: body odor (deodorants) and wetness (antiperspirants). Existing products came in the following forms: aerosol, roll-on, liquid pump spray or squeeze bottle, pad, stick/solid, or cream.

Deodorants contain ingredients considered safe by the Food and Drug Administration (FDA) and as such are not regulated. Antiperspirants, however, use aluminum chlorohydrate, which is regulated by the FDA. These products must get FDA approval.

In 1984, the U.S. deodorant and antiperspirant market represented $700 million in retail sales, with an estimated unit volume of 330 million. Demand was well established, with over 88 percent of the total U.S. adult population aged 18 years and older reporting usage between 7 and 14 times a week. There was slight seasonal and geographic difference in usage, with a 15 to 20 percent higher volume reported during the warmer seasons of the year.

COMPETITION

The total product offerings of the top four manufacturers (Gillette, Bristol-Myers, Procter & Gamble, and Carter Wallace) exceeded 200. While no single brand had more than a 13 percent market share, the top 13 brands accounted for almost 97 percent, or $682 million of total retail sales. This left a retail market of $23 million for the remaining nonmajor competition.

The major manufacturers all followed a strategy of offering broad product lines, with a minimum of two sizes within each line. This allowed the consumer a wide range of product choices carrying a single manufacturer's identity. This benefited manufacturers because it increased volume potential, it allowed for increased exposure because their products controlled a larger share of the retailer's shelf space, and it increased the impact of brand advertising and promotion.

Promotion was used as a means of reinforcing brand loyalty and influencing uncommitted users. Approximately 14.3 percent of total retail sales, or $100 million, was spent on advertising. The major competitors spent approximately 94 percent of those advertising dollars on television. Nonmajor brands spent a little less, 82 percent of their advertising dollars, on television.

Promotional discounting was used heavily, from the manufacturer to the retailer and from the retailer to the customer. Retailers were heavily supported with promotional materials, such as shelf talkers, displays, and window dressings. Customers could take advantage of product discounts, store coupons, and new-product samples. Couponing was used frequently as an inducement to sample a new product and was less common for the established product lines.

Exhibit 1 shows the range of pricing among major competitors in the deodorant and antiperspirant market.

NATURE'S WAY

Distribution

Dr. Swanson had three distribution alternatives: the natural or health food industry, mass distribution, or direct selling.

EXHIBIT 1 Pricing among Major Brand Competitors by Product Type (1984 data)

Product Type		*Price Range (99%)*
Aerosols	4 oz. size	$2.16–$2.64
	6 oz. size	2.92– 3.84
Roll-ons	1½ oz. size	1.67– 2.07
	2½ oz. size	2.46– 3.02
Stick/solids	2 oz. size	1.83– 2.31
	2½ oz. size	1.95– 2.43

Health food industry. Products in the health food industry, which were marketed in health food stores and similar outlets, ranged from appliances for food preparation to pure water.

The number of health food retail outlets in this market was approximately 30,000 in 1984, with 9,000 companies controlling all of the outlets. Some companies operated outlets throughout the United States, while most companies that had more than one store usually confined their activities to major cities and contiguous areas. The approximate total market value in 1984 was $2.4 billion. See Exhibit 2 for specific data on this market.

Approximately 5 percent of the 155 million adult population in the United States regularly used or purchased products from health food stores in 1981.

To find out about the typical natural food consumer, Swanson conducted interviews with some retailers and analyzed information from trade magazines. He came up with the following profile:

> 25 to 35 years of age; a 60:40 ratio of females to males; white; sophisticated/astute; ecologically concerned; 50 percent earn $20,000 or more; middle- to upper-class appearance.

A survey about deodorant and antiperspirant products being carried by health food stores in one metropolitan area revealed that approximately 10 to 15 brands were available, priced at $2.50 to $3.00. Generally, only one size was offered, there were no aerosol sprays, and most were sold in unattractive, earth-tone packages.

Mass market. The deodorant and antiperspirant market was segmented on the basis of product type such as aerosol, roll-on, or solid/stick. Because of recent environmental concerns, consumers were buying fewer aerosol products, resulting in an increased market share for roll-ons and solid/stick forms.

While the same percentage of males used deodorants as females, females tended to use deodorant or antiperspirant more often, and household members often shared it.

Common distribution channels available to the mass market were:

Wholesale—Retailer expects a gross margin of 40 percent.
Distributor (takes possession of goods)—Requires a 25 percent margin.
Manufacturer's Representative—Requires 5 to 10 percent commission on manufacturer's selling price.

EXHIBIT 2 Health Industry Market

Year	*Sales (in Billions)*	*Percent Change*
1980	$0.86	
1981	1.03	+20
1982	1.44	+40
1983	1.77	+23
1984	2.40	+36

Major Segments	*Percent of Total (1984)*
Vitamin supplements	36
Groceries	10
Herb and herb spices	10
Body care	8
All others	36

Body Care Segment	*Sales (000s)*
1980	$ 42
1981	49
1982	76
1983	115
1984	182

Categories of the Body Care Segment	*Percent*
Hair care	30
Skin care	33
Soaps and cleaners	22
Personal care (includes deodorants)	15

Direct selling. In 1984, consumers purchased $9 billion of merchandise through direct selling companies. In 1981, sales were $6 billion.

Over 60 percent of all dollar sales were related to cosmetic items, and most sales were made through a personal visit to a purchaser's home.

Products sold directly carried a higher retail price. The convenience and social atmosphere associated with this type of purchase allowed for a 10 percent premium over standard retail prices. Approximately 90 percent of all direct salespeople worked part-time, earning their incomes through commission (25 to 35 percent) or purchasing goods at wholesale and selling them for a profit.

Dr. Swanson had determined that he would need $5,000 in additional funding to finalize the product. He would then need to persuade investors that his product was marketable in order to raise additional financing to get it to the market. Next, he needed to put the above information in a proposal—a proposal that investors could not resist.

The Winslow Clock Company

For the third time, Dr. Winslow sat up in bed, flipped on the light, and reached for the Winslow Clocks business plan. Maybe reading through it again would calm his growing fears. As he flipped through the pages, he recalled again all the years of thinking, tinkering, and discovery that had gone into the development of his alarm clock. How could something he spent so much time and energy on be wrong? It was such a good idea, this "throwable" alarm clock—millions of Americans would want to get this kind of revenge on their daily call to the rat race. And, in its final design, it contained all kinds of computer-age technology. Surely, the investors tomorrow will love it!

What had happened to his confidence? He had been sure enough to invest all of his savings in the clock's development. What a time to get second thoughts! Didn't he use the best technical help available to design the clock and plan the production and marketing? Maybe that was his problem—too much dependence on "experts." Being a practicing psychiatrist, he considered himself a good judge of character and motivation, but maybe his obsession with his clock had clouded his perception. Should he take more time to personally study the different production and marketing scenarios? He didn't have any more time, if he wanted to get production started in time to hit the Christmas season. Should he wait another year, or risk going to market at a slow time of year, or . . . ?

The more he thought, the more the doubts and worries grew. He had to put a stop to this pointless mental exercise. The business plan he held in his hands was what he had to sell tomorrow at the meeting, so he better have confidence in it. If things went badly, then he could think about changing things. For now, he would read over the business plan for the Winslow Clock Company (which follows) just once more, concentrating on the favorable arguments his business "experts" had made.

SUMMARY

The attached five-year business plan for Winslow Clocks is based primarily on the estimated potential of the company's first product, an alarm clock designed and patented by Dr. Michael Winslow, a psychiatrist by profession. He expected the sales and profits generated by this product to reach $8.5 million and $1.5 million, respectively, within three years, which would provide sufficient resources to enable the company to expand its line into related products now under consideration.

History of the Product

Under development for 10 years, the concept for the clock stems from Dr. Winslow's thought that it would be fun to have the liberty to "get back at" the alarm that so readily awakens everyone each morning. The "fun" part—and what makes the alarm unique—is that you throw it to turn it off.

Development of the microchip and related technology in recent years has made the design of such a clock possible at reasonable cost. The technical assistance on the clock was provided by students at the MIT Innovation Center under the direction of its director. The business and marketing planning for the clock was done with the help of Boston College M.B.A. candidates at the Small Business Development Center under the direction of its faculty associate.

In addition, Dr. Winslow has contracted with a number of professional consultants in the areas of product design, product engineering, marketing and advertising, production, legal matters, and accounting.

Market Acceptance

Early reaction from such major retailers as Bloomingdale's and Hammacher Schlemmer in New York has been very positive, supporting the fact that the targeted levels of sales are achievable.

The U.S. clock market itself has demonstrated its acceptance of new ideas. For example, from 1984 to 1985 the overall growth in U.S. factory production of alarm clocks grew at the rage of 7 percent, from 14.9 million to 16.0 million units, while the newer, battery-operated quartz alarm clock segment grew at the rate of 29 percent, from 4.7 to 6.1 million units.[1]

Thus, in what might otherwise be considered a mature market, new design and technology are eagerly sought by retailers and customers anxious to provide or find a refreshing selection of alternatives. The company's projected level of sales in its first year represents less than 1 percent of this growing segment of the U.S. clock market.

Competition

Although several major manufacturers account for most clock sales (with Japanese manufacturers dominating the sale of quartz movements), there is nevertheless a significant annual volume attributable to smaller specialty designers, most of whom purchase the clock movements on an OEM (original equipment manufacturer) basis from the larger producers and concentrate on unique housing designs.

---

[1] *Merchandising Magazine,* Gralla Publications, 7th Annual Housewares Issue, January 1982, p 24.

Seiko, the company supplying the movement for Dr. Winslow's clock, has made impressive strides in the United States in the last four years by increasing their annual OEM business from 400,000 to 2 million units. Besides selling their own Seiko and Picco brands, they are developing a reputable supplier business. This strategy allows Seiko to enjoy some of the profit opportunity created by an expanded market without all of the marketing costs and risks.

In addition, a number of large retailers contract with the major manufacturers for private-label production. This somewhat fragmented structure has created profitable opportunities for products designed for niches within the large clock market.

The question arises, If the product is attractive enough to create a niche in the market, how soon will it have competition? The concept of a "throwable" alarm and several components designed specifically for the product are patented. In addition, it would require some time and expense for potential competitors to develop the impact switch and the microchip used in Dr. Winslow's clock.

Financial Projections: Opportunities and Risks

Financial projections for the first five years of the company are summarized below. (Sales are based only on the first product, to be introduced in 1986.)

	1986	*1987*	*1988*	*1989*	*1990*
Unit sales (000s)	50	150	200	150	125
Selling price	$42.50	$42.50	$42.50	$40.00	$40.00
Net sales (000s)	$2,125	$6,375	$8,500	$6,000	$5,000
Net profit (000s)	$ 333	$ 823*	$1,503	$ 781	$ 496
Profit ratio	16.0%	13.0%	17.7%	13.0%	10.0%

*Assuming $650,000 term loan (plus interest) paid back in December.

Because components and subassemblies would be purchased rather than manufactured by the company, and then assembled and shipped by an outside contractor, the capital investment required is minimal, estimated at less than $50,000, primarily for tooling. Another $50,000 for start-up expenses, prototypes, and preproduction operating expenses would also be required in the first two months of 1986.

By March, however, the commitment increases. Due to the company's lack of credit history, all indications are that suppliers will require letters of credit accompanying the $814,000 in parts orders placed between March and September of 1986, when shipments are expected to begin. In addition, operating expenses between March and October are forecast at $176,000.

Given the projected level of sales in the first two years, the company is seeking equity capital of $600,000 as early as possible in 1986. An additional term loan of approximately $650,000 would be needed by June to carry financing and operating costs through year end.

It should be emphasized that, while this combined cash injection of $1.2 million is at apparent risk for at least the six to eight months prior to the beginning of shipments (and of course, beyond), two factors diminish this risk. First, the initial selling effort in the spring of 1986 to secure orders for the Christmas season should provide a clear indication of market acceptance by the end of April. The long lead time required to order components then becomes a positive factor. Orders for 40,000 of the first season's production of 50,000 units could be cancelled (with no penalty a month in advance on standard items such as the clock movement). This alone would save almost $730,000. In addition, many operating expenses could be curtailed accordingly and alternative marketing plans put into place. (Direct mail-order marketing, for example, is an approach that will be explored from the beginning anyway, and in a downside case certainly would be a viable alternative.)

The second factor that diminishes the risk is that low fixed costs allow the break-even point to be projected at 16,000 units, which should be achieved in October, the second month of actual shipments.

According to its projected cash flow, the company should be able to repay its term loan in full within 18 months. From that point on it can fund its continuing operations from the generated working capital.

Return on investment is calculated at 19, 33, and 37 percent in the first three years, respectively, and return on net worth at 34, 46, and 45 percent. Net present value for the original investors would be $1.7 million, based on five years of net cash flow and not including the salable value of the firm or its continuing earning power after that time. Payback is expected in one and one-half years, based on the forecast of sales and profits. Specific financial details are found in Exhibits 1 through 7.

EXHIBIT 1

WINSLOW CLOCKS
Pro Forma Income Statements
5-Year Projection

	1986	*1987*	*1988*	*1989*	*1990*
Unit sales	50,000	150,000	200,000	150,000	125,000
Price	$42.50	$42.50	$42.50	$40.00	$40.00
Net sales (000s)	$2,125	$6,375	$8,500	$6,000	$5,000
Bad debt allowance (2%)	43	128	170	120	100
Adjusted net sales	2,082	6,247	8,330	5,880	4,900
Cost of goods sold	1,093	3,253	4,630	3,655	3,267
Gross margin	989	2,994	3,700	2,225	1,633
Operating costs	323	552	695	663	642
E.B.I.T	666	2,442	3,005	1,562	991
Taxes (50%)	333	1,221	1,502	781	495
Net income	$ 333	$1,221	$1,503	$ 781	496

EXHIBIT 2

WINSLOW CLOCKS
Pro Forma Balance Sheet
As of December 31 ($000s)

	1985	*1986*	*1987*	*1988*	*1989*	*1990*
Assets						
Cash	5	203	256	1,019	2,722	3,539
Accounts receivable	—	1,345	2,044	2,726	1,924	1,283
Inventory						
Finished goods	—	73	44	48	53	58
Work-in-process	—	106	—	78	—	—
Raw materials	55	—	141	155	171	188
Net fixed assets	40	36	32	29	26	24
Total assets	100	1,763	2,517	4,055	4,896	5,092
Liabilities						
Accounts payable	40	50	141	155	171	181
Accrued liabilities	—	—	560	581	626	309
Est'd tax liability	—	70	—	—	—	—
Short-term debt	—	650	—	—	—	—
Long-term debt	—	—	—	—	—	—
Common stock	—	600	600	600	600	600
Paid-in capital (M. Winslow)	60	60	60	60	60	60
Retained earnings	—	333	1,156	2,659	3,439	3,935
Total liabilities	100	1,763	2,517	4,055	4,896	5,092

INDUSTRY INFORMATION

The clock market in the United States has been growing at between 8 and 10 percent per year, with significantly higher growth (three times the industry average) recorded in the segments where innovative design or a technological change has been offered. The recent introduction of battery-operated quartz mechanisms combined with sleek styling to create lightweight, portable, wireless clocks has led to at least a 25 percent annual growth rate for decorative or kitchen wall clocks and to almost a 29 percent increase for alarm clocks.

There are clocks in most households; clocks comprise an enduring and important retail gift category; and, as with many items that are so inherently useful they might be considered a household necessity, the greater the opportunity to differentiate the product, the greater the ability to segment the market by appealing to consumers through unique designs, fashioned to suit a wide variety of tastes and income levels.

A handful of major competitors are the dominant force in the industry and often not only sell their own brands but make private-label brands for large retailers as well. (Seiko, for example, produces the private-label quartz alarm clocks for both

EXHIBIT 3

WINSLOW CLOCKS
*Statement of Sources and Uses of Funds**
Year Ended December 31 (000s)

	1986	*1987*	*1988*	*1989*	*1990*
Sources					
Funds provided by operations					
Net income after taxes	333	823	1,503	780	496
Plus depreciation	4	4	3	3	2
Inc.—accounts payable	10	91	14	16	17
Inc.—accrued liabilities	—	560	21	45	—
Inc.—taxes payable	70				
Inc.—common stock	600	—	—	—	—
Inc.—short-term debt	650				
Dec.—accounts receivable	—			802	641
Dec.—inventories				57	—
Total sources	1,667	1,478	1,541	1,703	1,156
Uses					
Inc.—cash	198	53	763	1,703	817
Inc.—accounts receivable	1,345	699	682	—	—
Inc.—inventories	124	6	96	—	22
Dec.—accrued liabilities	—	—	—	—	317
Dec.—taxes payable	—	70	—	—	—
Dec.—short-term debt	—	640	—	—	—
Total uses	1,667	1,478	1,541	1,703	1,156

*Based on pro forma balance sheets and income statements.

EXHIBIT 4 Break-Even Quantity Calculation

1. Contribution margin per unit is estimated to be $20.81 in 1986 and 1987. (See unit sales, cost, margin analysis.)
2. Fixed costs for unit sales in the first year of 50,000 units are estimated to be $332,910, including $10,200 paid for prototype development in 1985. Break-even quantity would be $332,910/20.81 = 16,000 units.
3. Based on the expected seasonality of sales in the first year of selling, the break-even point should be reached in mid-October 1986, in the second full month of product shipments.

EXHIBIT 5 Financial Data Backup

Unit Sales, Cost, Margin Analysis	
Retail suggested list	$85.00
Dealer margin	42.50
Mfr. selling price (dealer cost)	42.50
Cost of goods sold*	14.60
Gross margin	$27.90
*Other variable costs**	
Warranty	.05
Quality control allowance	.29
Shipping & handling contribution	.20
Co-op advertising allowance	2.13
Selling commissions	4.25
Designer/developer fee	.17
Subtotal variable costs	7.09
Net margin	$20.81
Note: Total cost of goods	$21.69

*Backup detail provided.

J. C. Penney and Sears.) As a result, clock movements are inexpensive and readily available, which in turn spawns a significant opportunity for a number of smaller companies to specialize in unique designs—from the very inexpensive to one-of-a-kind collector's items.

Clocks are sold through a variety of retail outlets, from mass merchandisers to department and specialty stores, to furniture and interior design stores, to jewelry stores and shops that deal exclusively in clocks—all the way to museum gift stores.

Catalog sales are also an important means of reaching the clock consumer. Furthermore, within a department store clocks can be found in such diverse departments as gifts, luggage, electronics, fine collectibles, furniture, or jewelry, occasionally even in a clock department.

This diversity of product as well as placement makes the clock market a natural arena for independent sales representatives to operate. This fact, in turn, simplifies to some extent the problems that the smaller producers face in trying to get their product to the national marketplace without incurring a disproportionate expense for the hiring, training, and support of a sales force.

It is apparent, then, that the market for clocks has ample room for product differentiation. Dr. Winslow's clock, we believe, presents an exciting opportunity to capitalize on a segment of this significant market.

THE PRODUCT: PRESENT AND FUTURE

The product will first be described and then discussed in terms of its future potential.

EXHIBIT 6 Financial Data Backup

Cost of Goods Sold Analysis		
Item		
Movement*	$2.77	$ 3.87
(and circuit board)	$1.10	
Chip (production model)		$ .79
Capacitors (3)		.30
Impact switch		1.03
Battery holder		.20
Photo transistor		.30
Ball		.87
Molded sphere		.20
Velcro®		.07
Molded cube (housing)		2.00
Batteries		.95
Face, crystal, hands, etc.		.60
Board		.40
Board assembly		1.00
Feet		.05
Speaker, lamp, socket		1.08
Assembly		.50
Product subtotal		$14.21
Package (inc. inside corrugated)		.24
Printed inserts		.05
Portion (1/6) master carton		.10
Package subtotal		$14.60

Note: Tooling not amortized in these calculations because first production run estimated to be 10K units; all other costs listed here based on runs of 100K. Tooling at this point treated as a capital expenditure, and listed under fixed costs.
*Add $0.30 premium per unit for air shipments.

Product Description

The battery-operated quartz alarm clock consists of two basic parts. The first is a lightweight black foam ball, approximately 4½ inches in diameter, which contains the "brains" of the clock—a microchip, circuit board, impact switch, small batteries, and the audio device for the alarm—all held inside a plastic capsule, which is secured by a Velcro® closure within the larger foam ball. The second part of the clock is the quartz movement, housed in a handsomely styled cube of molded plastic.

What makes the clock functionally unique is that the alarm is turned off by throwing the ball. Great care was taken to use materials that have virtually no chance of damaging the wall or any other object. The specifically designed impact switch is sensitive enough that even a light impact will stop the alarm. On the other hand, a throw of considerable force will not disturb the contents of the inner capsule. Two insurance companies specializing in product liability testing have

EXHIBIT 7 Critical Risks and Problems

Listed below are those areas of particular concern and importance to the Management.

1. *Timing* will play a critical role in the success of this venure. The key variables are:
   - product readiness
   - financing
   - approach to the marketplace
   - production, from delivery of components to assembly, inventorying, and shipping procedures
2. *Projections* used are "best" estimates and all financial needs and operating costs have been based on what is considered to be the most likely volume of sales achievable. Because selling activities will begin early in 1986, reaction from the marketplace should be clear by late spring. Decisions can still be made to cut back—or to gear up—for the 1986 season.

   The first commitment to Seiko for 10,000 units (cost of $4.17 each) will have been made by mid-March, and estimates for the entire year will be in their production plan by then. While cutbacks can be made as late as a month in advance, increased production might be a problem since it would bump into Seiko's heaviest production season.
3. *Financing* would be another major consideration if sales were much in excess of expectations, particularly because we must assume that early orders are going to require an accompanying letter of credit. For this and other reasons, the marketing plan is meant to guard against some of these problems and is specifically geared to reach up-scale stores and catalogs who will commit early to carry the "limited production" of the first year.
4. *Ironing out production* and assembly problems will be of major importance in June and July. Although the process is not complex, it will be totally new, and the production rate is currently scheduled at 5,000 units in July and 10,000 in August in order to meet anticipated shipping requirements in September, and to build minimal inventory requirements. For these reasons, selection of an experienced production manager will be critical.

been consulted. They both feel the product is safe and free enough from liability risk that they have quoted Winslow Clocks the minimum premium for liability insurance.

Several achievements have made the clock technologically possible. There is no need for an electrical connection between the clock base and the ball because an ultrasound device signals the alarm to go off. A receiver in the inner capsule "reads" the signal and triggers the humorous crescendo of the alarm; upon "advice" from the impact switch, a satisfying tone of demise is produced when the alarm hits the wall. In addition, a timing device has been built into the circuitry that automatically shuts off the alarm after one minute if the ball is not thrown.

The overall design and finish of the clock is clean and sophisticated to eliminate any sense of gimmickry that might lessen the perceived value of the clock. This elegant styling and the sophisticated electronics, combined with both the psychological satisfaction and the sense of fun and playfulness inherent in being able to throw one's alarm clock, should appeal to a significant cross section of consumers, from executives to athletes. The product has a strong appeal to retailers as well, who, in the words of a Bloomingdale's executive, look for "something refreshing and new to pull people into the stores."

Technical specifications of the product are as follows:

Dimensions:	Base—4½″ × 4½″ × 4½″
	Ball—4½″ diameter
Color:	Model A—white clock housing with black face, charcoal ball, white, yellow, and red hands
	Model B—black housing with other colors in Model A
Accuracy of movement:	± 20 seconds per month
Hands:	Luminescent minute and hour hands
Foam ball:	35 ppi Crest Foam

Future Potential

The new technological innovations that have emerged during development of this first product have significance for the future of the company as well. First, extensions of the basic concept are possible in a variety of clocks with other features. Obvious examples are clock radios and snooze-alarms. In addition, as production quantities increase, specialty designs for the premium market become possible at reasonable cost.

A family of related products such as posters, a wall-mountable target, and other clocks, all dealing with the frustration people feel with time, alarm clocks, and schedules, are natural offshoots of the throwable alarm, and their development is currently being explored.

MARKETING PLAN AND STRATEGY

Given the clock's unique function, design, and appeal, the first year's marketing plan will focus on placing the clock in upscale department stores, clock specialty stores, and catalogs that reach upper-middle and upper-income executives and families. The early strategy is to keep the clock out of the mass market and discounters' trade, instead making it readily available to consumers more interested in its characteristics and uniqueness than its suggested list price of $85.

The sales, cost, and margin analysis are based on the assumption that the suggested list price of $85 and dealer price of $42.50 will be held constant for three years. The goal is to introduce the product with a large enough margin for the dealer in the higher-end retail and catalog business to make an adequate return and to allow the company to recapture its fixed costs as quickly as possible.

While the suggested list and dealer price at this time are expected to remain the same in the second and third years, part of the strategy will be to refine the production and assembly costs, negotiate volume discounts with suppliers, and devise other cost-saving measures in order to offer more marketing support to the expanded dealer base without sacrificing profitability. If necessary, cost-saving measures will be adopted that will make it possible to lower the price dramatically as a strategy of defense against competitors in years three and four of the product's life.

Sales Tactics

The principals of the firm will contact potential buyers directly at first, beginning in early 1986 when there are still budgets available for merchandise for the 1986 Christmas season. 1986 sales are planned at 50,000 units, on a first-come, first-served basis, unless a retailer will commit for a guaranteed order prior to June 1.

A sales rep organization will also be retained to continue these early sales efforts and to expand distribution after the first season. A commission averaging 10 percent of the dealer price per unit has been incorporated into the cost of sales to cover the activities of these sales reps.

In addition, an experienced, full-time, in-house sales manager will coordinate the selling and promotional activities of the independent rep organization. Other responsibilities of the sales manager will include (1) making direct contact with buyers, (2) making direct contact with sales reps and evaluating their performance, (3) coordinating the marketing support and promotional activities of the sales rep force, and (4) developing other possible avenues for marketing the company's products—the direct marketing approach referred to earlier is an obvious example.

Advertising and Publicity

A publicity campaign aimed at generating interest in the clock's development, in its state-of-the-art technology, and in its founder's concept of "functional fun" will be launched in early fall of 1986. This publicity and accompanying new product announcements will be targeted at the "executive toy" purchaser.

In addition, a print ad campaign slated for the 1986 Christmas retail market and a cooperative advertising plan to help participating dealers is expected to aid sell-through in the clock's first major season on the market.

Expanded advertising marketing support for the second season will include attendance at trade shows (notably the Consumer Electronics Show, the National Hardwares Show, and at least one of the major gift shows); an in-store promotion plan highlighted by a 90-second video spot designed and produced by a Clio-award-winning studio based in Cambridge, Massachusetts; continuation of the co-op advertising plan; and an overall advertising budget slated at 5 percent of anticipated sales for the year.

OPERATIONS MANAGEMENT

Having all assembly and subassembly operations handled by independent contractors, with final shipment from the final point of assembly, keeps the need for office, production staff, and overhead to a minimum.

While Dr. Winslow will oversee all operations, his regular staff will supervise the critical functions of marketing and business development, administration (including office management, billing, accounts receivable and payable, etc.), and production management (the control of all facets of outside assembly and vendor supplies and relations).

Marketing and business developing (including sales in the initial stages) would be managed by Ms. Kristen Jones, who has 15 years of experience in marketing and finance in both domestic and international operations for Polaroid Corporation. She has an M.B.A. from Boston College and a B.A. from Brown University.

The production management area (including product engineering) is currently handled in an advisory capacity by several consultants, including Mr. Steve Canon (see enclosed profile). As the company approaches actual production (now slated for June/July 1986 start-up), a full-time production manager will be hired. Several candidates are presently being considered for this position.

Strong relationships with highly responsible subcontractors have already been established. These include Seiko, for the precision quartz movement and related technology; Rogers Foam in Somerville, Massachusetts, for the ball; Aerodyne Control Corporation in Farmingdale, New York, for the switch; and Santin Engineering in Beverly, Massachusetts, for the plastic molding.

The assembly operation, including packaging and shipment to fulfill sales orders, will also be handled by an outside contractor in the Boston area. Several companies are being considered and will be quoting on the specifications early in 1986. A decision is expected to be made by the beginning of February. The possibility of an assembly operation outside the United States will be investigated as a cost-saving measure once production is being handled efficiently here.

The administration position will have the responsibility for handling all office functions, including billing, receivables, credit, payables, and so on. Two candidates are now being considered. It will be important to fill this function as soon as possible, even if it is on a part-time basis for the first few months. The candidates are available for such a schedule, if necessary.

Other critical areas that are now and will continue to be handled by consultants are advertising (including sales promotion and publicity)—Bill Barlow—and product design—John Edwards.

MANAGEMENT

Dr. Michael Winslow is the inventor of the clock and founder and president of the company. His profession is psychiatric medicine and he is currently practicing at the Boston Evening Medical Center in Boston, Massachusetts, and at the Matthew

Thornton Health Plan in Nashua, New Hampshire, in addition to maintaining his private practice. Dr. Winslow earned his undergraduate B.S. degree at the University of Michigan and his medical degree at Boston University Medical School.

It was while he was a resident in psychiatry that he conceived of the idea for the clock. He first pursued the concept as a hobby, trying to find a way to throw the clock without damaging either it or the surface it hit. Within the last two years, as it became apparent that it would be possible to create and produce such a clock for a reasonable cost, further development of the idea became another full-time occupation for Dr. Winslow.

Though he is a man of great energy, part of Dr. Winslow's success in bringing the product from the initial concept to the prototype stage lies in his effectiveness in finding and utilizing the outside resources he has needed. He has also had enough confidence in—and received enough encouragement about—the ultimate marketability of the product that he has invested his own savings in development costs, a sum of approximately $60,000 to date.

Because his profession is very important to him, Dr. Winslow intends to continue his private medical practice. But he will also serve as president of Winslow Clocks, hiring professional managers to run the day-to-day operations for him and using consultants in those aspects of the business where a particular expertise is needed.

Kristen Jones, following a year at the Museum of Fine Arts, Boston, as an assistant to the Head of Research, joined Polaroid Corporation, Cambridge, Massachusetts, where her experience and responsibilities grew over a broad range of marketing and finance assignments.

In the years that Polaroid's International Division grew from $30 million to $350 million in annual sales, she was responsible for sales planning and forecasting for all its amateur photographic products; later, as a financial analyst, her job was to assess the company's 130 distributor markets around the world for potential as profitable wholly owned subsidiaries, as well as to carry out new product profitability analyses.

She then joined the domestic marketing division, where her assignments ranged from sales administration to marketing manager in charge of a test program to assess the potential of selling the company's instant movie system on a direct basis. In her last position as national merchandising manager, she created and managed the merchandising programs to support the national sales efforts for all consumer products.

In February of 1982, she took advantage of the company's voluntary severance program to complete work on her Master's degree in business administration at Boston College. Ms. Jones earned her B.A. degree at Brown University in Providence, Rhode Island.

Steve Canon is a consultant, teacher, and businessman whose broad range of experience covers many aspects of new product design, development, and marketing.

He presently has over 35 products of his own on the market and also teaches marketing and business law at the Rhode Island School of Design. In addition, he is publishing a book in the spring of 1986, dealing with invention, product development, and marketing.

Among his numerous accomplishments, he has taught product design at Harvard, Yale, Princeton, and the Rhode Island School of Design; he has won awards, including two from Ford Motor Company for innovative product development; and he has appeared on television talk shows, both as guest and host, discussing product marketing.

While his primary contributions to Winslow Clocks are in the fields of product development and manufacturing/production, his knowledge of new product introductions has been very helpful in a number of other areas as well.

Bill Barlow has been president and creative director of Bill Barlow Advertising since 1978. Prior to establishing his own company, Barlow was director of advertising for Bose Corporation in Framingham, Massachusetts, a national sales promotion manager and creative director at Polaroid Corporation, and a creative supervisor for New York Telephone in New York City.

In four years on his own, Barlow has built an impressive list of clients and has won numerous awards and honors for excellence in advertising. His current list of clients includes Polaroid Corporation, Hewlett-Packard, Digital Equipment, Atari, Bose, and Anaconda-Ericsson Telecommunications.

He will be responsible for advertising, promotional support materials, and publicity for Winslow Clocks.

John Edwards is the founder of Edwards Design Associates, Inc., which specializes in industrial design, product development, and graphic design. For the past seven years, this company has provided an integrated approach to the design of both products and the packaging and collateral materials to support the product.

Among its clients, primarily in the consumer products and financial fields, are Polaroid, Bose, Revlon, Chaps, Helena Rubinstein, Avco, Putnam Funds, Franklin Spots, and Hallmark.

Edwards has a B.S. degree in mechanical engineering from Worcester Polytechnic Institute, and an M.S. degree in industrial design from the Illinois Institute of Technology.

In addition to designing Dr. Winslow's product, Edwards has also provided invaluable help in finding sources for the manufacture of several components, for injection molding and for packaging.

Rug Bug Corporation

A. L. Young has come a long way with his latest invention, the Rug Bug, a motorized wheelchair made especially for children. His lightweight, relatively inexpensive model has no direct competition in a field dominated by companies that produce scaled-down versions of adult models, inappropriate for the needs of children. A working prototype has been built, office space and manufacturing capacity contracted, and an initial sales force recruited. The only piece lacking is enough capital to produce the first 200 units. A business plan has been drawn up describing the product, its manufacture, and the marketing plan. After several fruitless months seeking financing, Young was contacted by a group of investors who had seen a summary of his proposal. Feeling that this might be his only chance, Young has contacted you for advice on how to present his plan. He has sent you the following copy of his business plan and a list of questions. What recommendations would you make?

Young's questions:

1. I'm not much of a writer—do you think my descriptions of the product, competition, marketing, and so forth are adequate? Could it be improved easily without additional outside information (my meeting is in two days!)?
2. The pro forma income and cash flow statements were developed from a model I found in a book. Did I leave anything out?
3. I think $150,000 is a good amount to ask for—big enough to show we are serious about creating a growing business, but not large enough to scare them away. Are they going to want to know what I plan to do with every penny? What should I do if they are only willing to invest less?
4. I really don't know what to expect from these investors. I have my own idea of how much of the company I want to give up for the $150,000, but I don't know what they would consider reasonable. Can you give me any suggestions?

The Rug Bug Corporation was established on October 23, 1985, by Mr. and Mrs. A. L. Young as a Delaware corporation. The sole purpose of the corporation is to manufacture and distribute a revolutionary, motorized wheelchair, designed for children under the age of 10. The Rug Bug motorized wheelchair will retail for approximately one half the cost of any other motorized wheelchair for this age group. It will weigh almost 50 percent less than the standard motorized wheel chair. The unique design of the Rug Bug accounts for the differences in the retail cost and weight of the chair. In addition, the Rug Bug has numerous safety features, which are offered on no other motorized wheelchair available. These three features—cost, weight, and safety—allow the Rug Bug to fill a special niche in the market for motorized wheelchairs for children. It is an appropriate time to introduce this product in light of the current trend in the medical field to recommend the use of motorized chairs for children. Recently, the medical profession determined that the spatial relations and sense of movement offered via a motorized chair provide a handicapped child with sensory experiences normal for young children. The target market for this product will be greatly increased due to this philosophical change. In order to establish the company, the Rug Bug Corporation will need $150,000. This will finance the production of the molds for various parts, the manufacture of 200 units (of which 190 will be sold), and initial marketing efforts. In addition, the company will use the funds for product liability insurance, legal fees, and continued research/development.

DESCRIPTION OF THE BUSINESS

The Rug Bug Corporation is primarily a manufacturing and distribution company in the start-up phase of operation. The inventor's initial research led to the development of a prototype. Marketing research shows the Rug Bug to be the only vacuum-molded, plastic, motorized wheelchair with safety features available today. The owners of the Rug Bug Corporation believe the company will be successful because of low production costs, reasonable retail costs, safety factors, low weight, and visual appeal. The use of motorized chairs by the target age group has been limited, primarily for two reasons: (1) The current cost of motorized wheelchairs for children ranges from $3,000 to $8,000. It has been difficult to justify such an investment for a chair since a child's growth is typically rapid, therefore limiting the time the chair can be utilized. The Rug Bug will retail for $1,850. This is a significant price differential, especially for a chair that offers additional features such as safety control; (2) In previous years, the medical community considered muscle use to be the primary concern in a handicapped child's development. They are recently shifting away from that stance, with many now emphasizing the development of spatial skills, spatial relations, and sense of movement—all areas that the motorized chair can help strengthen.

DESCRIPTION OF THE PRODUCT

The Rug Bug is a vacuum-molded plastic body wheelchair powered by a rechargeable battery. The 25-pound chair has the following safety features as standard equipment:

1. A pressure-sensitive bumper strip surrounding the vehicle allows the unit to move away from any obstruction it might encounter.
2. Dual front antennae extending upward prevent the chair from moving under low objects, such as a coffee table.

3. In the case of a confrontation with an uneven surface, an electric eye located under the front of the chair will deactivate power in that direction. The power remains operative in other directions, allowing the occupant to move away from the potential hazard.
4. A hand-held remote control unit enables an adult to take over control of the chair from the occupant.
5. A variable speed control is built into the unit beyond reach of the occupant. As the ability of the occupant to maneuver the chair increases, so may the speed.
6. Though built with a very low center of gravity, the chair is designed with a roll bar.

The computerized control panel defines the Rug Bug as a technical machine; however, in appearance, the Rug Bug is more similar to a currently popular battery-operated riding toy. The visual appeal immediately distinguishes the Rug Bug from any other motorized wheelchair on the market today.

MARKETING COMPONENT

1. *Market Size*—According to the Frost and Sullivan Report No. 1468, the market for supplies and services for rehabilitation will increase to $1.36 billion in 1990 from $774.5 million in 1985. This figure includes exercise equipment increasing to $477.4 million (1990) from $302.6 million (1985) and manual powered wheelchairs and carts and scooters increasing to $362.4 million (1990) from $197.4 million (1985). Powered wheelchairs will have 24 percent of the market in 1990 ($86.9 million) versus 17 percent of the market in 1985 ($33.6 million). According to the U.S. government report, Youth and Children Coordinate for Kids, there are 668,340 orthopedically impaired children and children with cerebral palsy, ages two to seven, in this country, who might have need of a motorized wheelchair. This figure does not reflect any other potential users in this age bracket, such as the muscular dystrophy population.
2. *Competition*—Everest and Jennings is the industry leader in motorized wheelchairs, with 1983 sales of $158 million. The company's business has grown steadily in spite of charges that the company's chairs were not as good as they were in the 1950s. Poor design caused some faltering, and the frequency of breakdowns resulted in repairs that took months. Although the Veterans Administration spends more than $7 million a year for wheelchairs, performance standards are still being refined, and there are no federal wheelchair regulations. Most of Everest and Jennings's chairs are still manual, but their power market is growing. Currently, this company lists motorized wheelchairs for children, ranging in cost from $3,000 to $8,000 per unit. No other company has been found that offers a motorized wheelchair for less. It is significant to note that none of Everest and Jennings's chairs have safety features. These steel-frame

motorized wheelchairs weigh approximately 50 pounds per unit. Following a 1978 accident that left her a paraplegic, M. Hamilton formed Motion Designs to make a lightweight wheelchair when Everest and Jennings indicated no interest in the project. Overall, the wheelchair has not been modified essentially since its inception in 1933, except, of course, by wheelchair sports enthusiasts. However, some 25,000 people every year suffer auto, motorcycle, and swimming accidents that put them into wheelchairs, and the disabled today are generally much more mobile and independent than their earlier counterparts. Motion Designs introduced its first rigid but lightweight chairs in 1980 and in 1982 produced the Quickie-2, a 24-pound foldable chair. Finally, Everest and Jennings brought out its own line of lightweight sports and everyday chairs, which put pressure on the new competitors to keep up. Motion Designs responded by making its chair completely modular, with interchangeable accessories. Users can adjust or mix the parts to attain a perfect fit. The newest entry into the market is a motorized stand-up wheelchair, retailing for $8,000.

3. *Distribution*—Since there are distinct and different methods for purchasing wheelchairs, Rug Bug will establish two different distribution systems. A direct system, initially employing individuals connected with the company, will call on hospitals, the Veterans Administration, Shriners, and organizations connected with the care and development of handicapped children. Of the initial 200 products, 190 will be sold in these outlets in order to generate sales without paying retail markups. This will also give the product good exposure. Manufacturers' representatives will make direct sales for subsequent production runs. A 15 percent commission on the selling price will be paid on all direct sales. After the initial 190 units have been sold (with 10 units being kept for demonstration purposes), the company will add a retail distribution system. Several retail outlets will be used in each of the major markets, including drugstores, bicycle shops, and medical supply stores. Drugstores accounted for $117.6 million in wheelchair sales in 1983 and are an important outlet for the company. Bicycle shops, while not usually a source for the purchase of wheelchairs, are an important outlet, as they will provide any service needed in addition to sales. Company-authorized service outlets will be established in each market for ease of repair, an aspect the consumer should appreciate. Retail margins will be 30 percent off the established retail selling price of $1,850.
4. *Price*—The company will sell the product to the stores for $1,850, which includes a retail markup of 30 percent of the established retail selling price. This price will position the product favorably against competition and allow for significant growth in market share as well as profit.
5. *Promotion*—Quality brochures describing the product and its characteristics will be developed and distributed as point-of-purchase sale materials in the retail outlets as well as in all hospitals, clinics, and other organizations working with handicapped children. In addition, sales material, including a price list indicating markups and return per square foot of selling space required, will be developed for use in the company's direct sales effort.

EXHIBIT 1

THE RUG BUG CORPORATION
Pro Forma Income Statement
First Year, by Month
1987/1988

	May 87	*June 87*	*July 87*	*Aug 87*	*Sept 87*	*Oct 87*
Sales	0	0	0	$37,000	$55,500	$55,500
Less: Cost of goods sold	0	0	0	8,710	13,066	13,066
Commission	0	0	0	5,550	8,325	9,325
Gross profit	0	0	0	$22,740	$34,109	$34,109
Operating expenses						
President salary	$ 2,000	$ 2,000	$ 2,000	$ 2,000	$ 2,000	$ 2,000
Secretary salary	0	0	0	0	0	1,167
Employee insurance	42	42	42	42	42	42
Product liability insurance				763	1,145	1,145
Research and development	0	0	0	1,819	2,729	2,729
Advertising/printing	417	417	417	417	417	417
Travel expenses	625	625	625	625	625	625
Organization expenses	850	850	850	850	850	850
Total operating expenses	$ 3,934	$ 3,934	$ 3,934	$ 6,516	$ 7,807	$ 8,974
Profit (loss) before tax	(3,934)	(3,934)	(3,934)	16,223	26,302	25,135
Taxes	(1,574)	(1,574)	(1,574)	6,489	10,521	10,054
Net profit (loss)	$(2,360)	$(2,360)	$(2,360)	$ 9,734	$15,781	$15,081
Quantity sold	0	0	0	20	30	30
Price	1,850	1,850	1,850	1,850	1,850	1,850
DL–DM–MAGF cost	436	436	436	436	436	436
Commission percent	15	15	15	15	15	15
Tax rate	40	40	40	40	40	40

(1) President salary at $24,000 per year
(2) Secretary salary begins on the 6th month
(3) Product liability is proportionate to quantity sold
(4) Organization expenses (registration fee, legal fee, etc.) are amortized over the first year

Nov 87	*Dec 87*	*Jan 88*	*Feb 88*	*Mar 88*	*Apr 88*	*Total*
$74,000	$74,000	$74,000	$74,000	$92,500	$92,500	$629,000
17,421	17,421	17,421	17,421	21,776	21,776	148,077
11,100	11,100	11,100	13,875	13,875	13,875	94,350
$45,479	$45,479	$45,479	$45,479	$56,849	$56,849	$386,573
$ 2,000	$ 2,000	$ 2,000	$ 2,000	$ 2,000	$ 2,000	$ 24,000
1,167	1,167	1,167	1,167	1,167	1,167	8,169
42	42	42	42	42	38	500
3,638	3,638	3,638	3,638	4,548	4,548	30,926
1,526	1,526	1,526	1,526	1,908	1,908	12,973
417	417	417	417	413	417	5,000
625	625	625	625	625	625	7,500
850	850	850	850	850	850	10,200
$10,266	$10,266	$10,266	$10,266	$11,553	$11,553	$ 99,269
35,214	35,214	35,214	35,214	45,296	45,296	287,304
14,085	14,085	14,085	14,085	18,119	18,119	114,922
$21,128	$21,128	$21,128	$21,128	$27,178	$27,178	$172,382
40	40	40	40	50	50	340
1,850	1,850	1,850	1,850	1,850	1,850	
436	436	436	436	436	436	
15	15	15	15	15	15	
40	40	40	40	40	40	

LOCATION OF THE BUSINESS

The office section of the Rug Bug will be located at Barn Bicycle on East 61st Street, Tulsa, Oklahoma. The molded plastic body will be manufactured and the product assembled at the Inter-Ocean Oil Company, located at 2630 Mohawk Boulevard, Tulsa, Oklahoma. The Rug Bug Corporation will not be charged for usage of either facility, although it will pay for utilities and telephones at both.

MANAGEMENT/OPERATIONS

Al Young, inventor, will serve as the president of Rug Bug Corporation. In addition, Young will concentrate on the research/development section of operations. Mr. Young's past experience with electronics and computers fits well with the needs of the company. His ability to transform a concept into a viable product is shown through the prototype that Rug Bug currently has in existence.

Wayne Dunn and Dwaine Farrill will continue to operate in the marketing component of the company. Their extensive knowledge of and profound belief in the product make both Dunn and Farrill ideal people to initially market it on a commissioned basis.

Linda Bryant will initially serve as the unpaid controller of the company. Ms. Bryant will serve as single signatory on the banking account and prepare and monitor monthly financial reports. She has served as a cash management officer at The Fourth National Bank of Tulsa for over two years and is currently its director of business development.

FINANCIAL INFORMATION

To ramp up, the Rug Bug Corporation needs $150,000. The funds will be used to develop the molds for various parts, manufacture 200 units (of which 190 will be sold), start the initial marketing effort, and pay employee salaries, product liability insurance, legal fees, and other expenses of the organization (see Exhibit 1). The company will achieve significant sales and profits starting in the first year, as indicated in the various pro forma income statements (see Exhibits 1 to 3). The pro forma income cash flow statements (Exhibits 4 to 6) and balance sheets (Exhibits 7 to 9) further indicate the tremendous growth and profit potential.

EXHIBIT 2

THE RUG BUG CORPORATION
Pro Forma Income Statement
Second Year, by Quarter
1988/1989

	Qtr 1	*Qtr 2*	*Qtr 3*	*Qtr 4*	*Total*
Sales—Direct	$555,000	$1,110,000	$2,220,000	$3,330,000	$7,215,000
—Retail	194,250	388,500	582,750	777,000	1,942,500
Total sales	749,250	1,498,500	2,802,750	4,107,000	9,157,500
Cost of goods sold—Direct	130,656	261,312	522,624	783,936	1,698,528
—Retail	65,328	130,656	195,984	261,312	653,280
Commission—Direct	83,250	166,500	333,000	499,500	1,082,250
—Retail	29,138	58,275	87,413	116,550	291,375
Gross profit	$440,879	$ 881,757	$1,663,730	$2,445,702	$5,432,067
Operating expenses					
President salary	$ 7,200	$ 7,200	$ 7,200	$ 7,200	$ 28,800
Secretary salary	3,500	3,500	3,500	3,500	14,000
VP—Finance salary			12,500	12,500	25,000
Employee insurance	125	125	125	125	500
Product liability insurance	7,425	14,050	25,092	36,133	82,700
Research and development	35,270	70,541	133,098	195,656	434,565
Advertising/printing	2,500	2,500	2,500	2,500	10,000
Travel expenses	1,875	1,875	1,875	1,875	7,500
Accounting services	2,500	2,500	2,500	2,500	10,000
Depreciation—computer	750	750	750	750	3,000
Bad debt expense	5,828	11,655	17,483	23,310	58,275
Total operating expenses	$ 57,895	$ 99,791	$ 185,890	$ 259,489	$ 603,065
Profit (loss) before tax	382,983	781,966	1,477,839	2,186,213	4,829,002
Taxes	153,193	312,787	591,136	874,485	1,931,601
Net profit (loss)	$229,790	$ 469,180	$ 886,704	$1,311,728	$2,897,401
Quantity sold—Direct	300	600	1,200	1,800	3,900
—Retail	150	300	450	600	1,500
Price—Direct	1,850	1,850	1,850	1,850	
—Retail	1,295	1,295	1,295	1,295	
DL–DM–MAFG cost	436	436	436	436	
Commission percent	15	15	15	15	
Tax rate	40	40	40	40	

(1) Product liability insurance = ($7500 − 6% tax)/5400 − $3200
(2) Personal computer depreciated at straight line over a 5-year life with no salvage value
(3) Bad debt expense provision at 3% of retail sales
(4) Taxes (federal and state) provided at 40%

EXHIBIT 3

THE RUG BUG CORPORATION
Pro Forma Income Statement
Third Year, by Quarter
1989/1990

	Qtr 1	*Qtr 2*	*Qtr 3*	*Qtr 4*	*Total*
Sales—Direct	3,700,000	5,550,000	7,400,000	9,250,000	25,900,000
—Retail	1,554,000	2,331,000	3,108,000	3,885,000	10,878,000
Total sales	5,254,000	7,881,000	10,508,000	13,135,000	36,778,000
Cost of goods sold—Direct	$ 871,040	$1,306,560	$1,742,080	$2,177,600	$6,097,280
—Retail	522,624	783,936	1,045,248	1,306,560	3,658,368
Commission—Direct	555,000	832,500	1,110,000	1,387,500	3,885,000
—Retail	233,100	349,650	466,200	582,750	1,631,700
Gross profit	$3,072,236	$4,608,354	$6,144,472	$7,680,590	$21,505,652
Operating expenses					
President salary	$ 8,640	$ 8,640	$ 8,640	$ 8,640	$ 34,560
Secretary salary	3,500	3,500	3,500	3,500	14,000
VP—Finance salary	15,000	15,000	15,000	15,000	60,000
Employee insurance	125	125	125	125	500
Research and development	245,779	368,668	491,558	614,447	1,720,452
Product liability insurance	31,086	46,229	61,371	76,514	215,200
Advertising printing	3,125	3,125	3,125	3,125	12,500
Travel expenses	1,875	1,875	1,875	1,875	7,500
Accounting services	2,500	2,500	2,500	2,500	10,000
Depreciation—computer	750	750	750	750	3,000
Bad debt expense	66,600	99,900	133,200	166,500	466,200
Total operating expenses	$ 378,980	$ 550,312	$ 721,644	$ 892,976	$ 2,543,912
Profit (loss) before tax	2,693,256	4,058,042	5,422,828	6,787,614	18,961,740
Taxes	1,077,303	1,623,217	2,169,131	2,715,045	7,584,696
Net profit (loss)	$1,615,954	$2,434,825	$3,253,697	$4,072,568	$11,377,044
Quantity sold—Direct	2,000	3,000	4,000	5,000	14,000
—Retail	1,200	1,800	2,400	3,000	8,400
Price—Direct	1,850	1,850	1,850	1,850	
—Retail	1,295	1,295	1,295	1,295	
DL–DM–MAFG cost	436	436	436	436	
Discount percent	30	30	30	30	
Commission percent	15	15	15	15	
Tax rate	40	40	40	40	

(1) Product liability insurance = ($200,000 − 6% tax) − $3200

EXHIBIT 4

THE RUG BUG CORPORATION
Pro Forma Cash Flow Statement
First Year, by Month
1987/1988

	May 87	*June 87*	*July 87*	*Aug 87*	*Sept 87*	*Oct 87*
Cash receipts						
Sales	0	0	0	$37,000	$55,500	$55,500
Others	$75,000	$75,000	$ 0	$ 0		
Total cash receipts	$75,000	$75,000	0	$37,000	$55,500	$55,500
Cash disbursements						
Salaries						
President	$ 2,000	$ 2,000	$ 2,000	$ 2,000	$ 2,000	$ 2,000
Secretary						1,167
Employee insurance	100	150	250			
Product liability insurance	12,973					
Research and development	0	0	0	1,819	2,729	2,729
Advertising	2,500	1,500	1,000			
Travel expense	3,750	2,250	1,500			
Organization fees	5,100	3,060	2,040			
Commissions				5,500	8,325	8,325
Inventory	17,421	26,131	43,552			
Total disbursements	$43,844	$35,091	$50,342	$ 9,369	$13,054	$14,221
Net cash flow	31,156	39,909	(50,342)	27,631	42,446	41,279
Cumulative cash flow	31,156	71,065	20,723	48,354	90,800	

(*continues on page 342*)

EXHIBIT 4 *(concluded)*

THE RUG BUG CORPORATION
Pro Forma Cash Flow Statement
First Year, by Month
1987/1988

Nov 87	Dec 87	Jan 88	Feb 88	Mar 88	Apr 88
$74,000	$74,000	$74,000	$74,000	$92,500	$92,500
$74,000	$74,000	$74,000	$74,000	$92,500	$92,500
2,000	2,000	2,000	2,000	2,000	2,000
1,167	1,167	1,167	1,167	1,167	1,167
638	3,638	3,638	3,638	4,548	4,548
11,100	11,100	11,100	11,100	13,875	13,875
10,900	10,900	21,800	21,800	65,400	65,400
$28,805	$28,805	$39,705	$39,705	86,990	$86,990
45,195	45,195	34,295	34,295	5,510	5,510
45,195	90,390	124,685	158,980	164,490	170,000

EXHIBIT 5

THE RUG BUG CORPORATION
Pro Forma Cash Flow Statement
Second Year, by Quarter
1988/1989

	Qtr 1	*Qtr 2*	*Qtr 3*	*Qtr 4*	*Total*
Cash receipts					
Sales	$680,615	$1,424,038	$2,722,460	$4,020,883	$8,847,996
Others					
Total cash receipts	$680,615	$1,424,038	$2,722,460	$4,020,883	$8,847,996
Cash disbursements	$7,200	$7,200	$7,200	$7,200	$28,800
Salaries					
President					
Secretary	3,500	3,500	3,500	3,500	14,000
VP—Finance			12,500	12,500	25,000
Employee insurance	125	125	125	125	500
Research and development	35,270	70,541	133,098	195,636	434,565
Product liability insurance	82,700				82,700
Advertising	1,250	1,250	1,250	1,250	5,000
Travel expenses	1,875	1,875	1,875	1,875	7,500
Accounting services	2,500	2,500	2,500	2,500	10,000
Commissions	102,092	213,606	408,369	603,132	1,327,199
Inventory cost	327,000	610,400	937,400	1,308,000	3,182,800
Taxes	114,922				114,922
Personal computer	15,000				15,000
Total cash disbursements	$693,434	$ 910,997	$1,507,817	$2,135,738	$5,247,986
Net cash flow	(12,819)	513,041	1,214,643	1,885,145	3,600,010
Cumulative cash flow	(12,819)	500,222	1,714,865	3,600,010	
Units produced	750	1,400	2,150	3,000	7,300
Unit cost	436	436	436	436	

EXHIBIT 6

THE RUG BUG CORPORATION
Pro Forma Cash Flow Statement
Third Year, by Quarter
1989/1990

	Qtr 1	*Qtr 2*	*Qtr 3*	*Qtr 4*	*Total*
Cash receipts					
Sales	$4,956,150	$7,559,840	$10,163,530	$12,767,220	$35,446,740
Others					
Total cash receipts	$4,956,150	$7,559,840	$10,163,530	$12,767,220	$35,446,740
Cash disbursements					
Salaries					
President	$ 8,640	$ 8,640	$ 8,640	$ 8,640	$ 34,560
Secretary	3,500	3,500	3,500	3,500	14,000
VP—Finance	12,500	12,500	15,000	15,000	55,000
Employee insurance	125	125	125	125	500
Research and development	245,779	368,668	491,558	614,447	1,720,452
Product liability insurance	30,743	46,114	61,486	76,857	215,200
Advertising	1,250	1,250	1,250	1,250	5,000
Travel expenses	3,750	3,750	3,750	3,750	15,000
Accounting services	2,500	2,500	2,500	2,500	10,000
Commissions	743,423	1,133,976	1,524,530	1,915,083	5,317,011
Inventory cost	1,831,200	2,528,800	3,313,600	3,749,600	11,423,200
Taxes	1,931,601				1,931,601
Total cash disbursements	$4,815,010	$4,109,823	$5,425,938	$6,390,752	$20,741,524
Net cash flow	141,140	3,450,017	4,737,592	6,376,468	14,705,216
Cumulative cash flow	141,140	3,591,156	8,328,748	14,705,216	
Units produced	4,200	5,800	7,600	8,600	26,200
Unit cost	436	436	436	436	

EXHIBIT 7

THE RUG BUG CORPORATION
Pro Forma Balance Sheet
As of 4/30/88

Cash	$302,079
Inventory	135,225
Accounts receivable	0
Total assets	$437,304
Commissions payable	0
Taxes payable	114,922
Retained earnings	172,382
Common stock	150,000
	$437,304

EXHIBIT 8

THE RUG BUG CORPORATION
Pro Forma Balance Sheet
As of 4/30/89

Cash	$3,902,089
Computer	12,000
Inventory	1,017,145
Accounts receivable	259,000
Total assets	$5,190,234
Commissions payable	38,850
Taxes payable	1,931,601
Retained earnings	3,069,783
Common stock	150,000
	$5,190,234

EXHIBIT 9

THE RUG BUG CORPORATION
Pro Forma Balance Sheet
As of 4/30/90

Cash	$18,607,305
Computer	9,000
Inventory	1,541,938
Accounts receivable	1,259,000
Total assets	$21,453,243
Commissions payable	195,250
Taxes payable	7,584,696
Retained earnings	13,523,297
Contributed capital	150,000
	$21,453,243

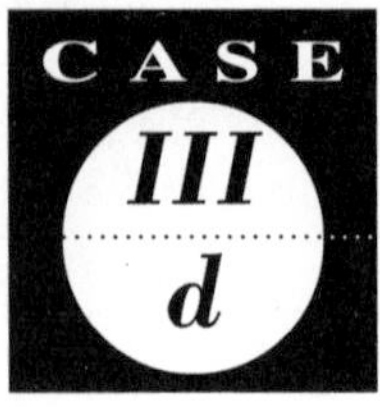

Nature Bros. Ltd.

Background

It was Thanksgiving Day 1976 that Dale Morris remembers as the "public debut" of his creation, a new seasoned salt mix. Although he was a salesman by temperament and career, his hobby was cooking. Having experimented with both traditional home cooking and more exotic gourmet cooking, Morris had developed an appreciation for many herbs and spices. He had also done a lot of reading about the health hazards of the typical American diet. When his mother learned that she had high blood pressure, Morris decided it was time for some action. He created a low-salt seasoning mix, based on a nutritive yeast extract, that could be used to replace salt in most cases. This Thanksgiving dinner, prepared for 25 family members and friends, would be his final testing ground. He used his mix in all the recipes except the pumpkin pie—everything from the turkey and dressing to the vegetables and even the rolls. As the meal progressed, the verdict was unanimously in favor of his secret ingredient, although he had a hard time convincing them that it was his invention and that it was only 10 percent salt. Everyone wanted a sample to try at home.

Over the next two years, Morris perfected his product. Experiments in new uses led to "tasting parties" for friends and neighbors, and the holiday season found the Morris's kitchen transformed into a miniature assembly line producing gift-wrapped bottles of the mix. Morris became something of a celebrity in his small town, but it wasn't until the Ladies' Mission Society at his church approached him with the idea of allowing them to sell his mix as a fund-raiser that he realized the possibilities of his creation. His kitchen-scale operation could support the sales effort of the church women for a short time, but if he wanted to take advantage of a truly marketable product, he would have to make other arrangements.

Morris agreed to "test-market" his product through the church group while he looked for ways to expand and commercialize his operation. The charity sale was a huge success (the best the women had ever done) and, based on this success, Morris moved to create his own company. Naming his product "Nature Bros. Old Fashioned Seasoning," he incorporated the company in 1978 as Nature Bros. Ltd. Morris used most of his savings to develop and register the trademarks, packaging, and displays for his product. He researched the cost of manufacturing and bottling his product in large quantities and concluded that he just didn't have the cash to get started. His first attempts to raise money, in the form of a personal bank loan, were unsuccessful, and he was forced to abandon the project.

For several years he concentrated on his career, becoming a regional vice-president of the insurance company he worked for. He continued to make "Nature Bros. Seasoning" in small batches, mainly for his mother and business associates. These users eventually enabled Morris to get financial support for his company. To raise $65,000 to lease manufacturing equipment and building space, he sold stock to his mother and to two other regional vice-presidents of the insurance company. For their contributions, each became owners of 15 percent of Nature Bros. Ltd. The process of getting the product to the retail market began in August of 1985, and the first grocery store sales started in March of 1986.

The initial marketing plan was fairly simple—get the product in the hands of the consumer. Morris personally visited the managers of individual supermarkets, both chains and independents, and convinced many to allow a tasting demonstration booth to be set up in their stores. These demonstrations proved as popular as the first Thanksgiving dinner trial nearly 10 years earlier. Dale Morris's product was a hit, and in a short time he was able to contract with food brokerage firms to place his product in stores in a 10-state region.

PRESENT SITUATION

As indicated in the balance sheet (see Exhibit 1), more capital is needed to support the current markets and expand both markets and products. Two new products are being developed: a salt-free version of the original product and an MSG-based flavor enhancer that will compete with Accent. Morris worked with a business consultant in drawing up a business plan to describe his company, its future growth, and its capital needs. Portions of this plan are included below.

OVERALL PROJECTIONS

The first section discusses the objectives and sales projections for 1987 and 1988 (Exhibits 2 and 3). The resulting pro forma income statements for 1987 to 1991 are in Exhibits 4 and 5.

1987 OBJECTIVES

The company's objectives for 1987 are to stabilize its existing markets and to achieve a 10 percent market share in the category of seasoned salt, a 20 percent market share in salt substitutes, and a 10 percent market share in MSG products. Although the original product contains less than 10 percent salt, the company has developed a salt-free product to compete with other such products, such as the one shown in the advertisement in Exhibit 6. The dollar volume for the seasoned salt

EXHIBIT 1

NATURE BROS. LTD.
Balance Sheet
As of September 30, 1986

Unaudited	
Current assets	
110 Cash—American Bank	$ 527.11
112 Cash—Bank of Okla-Pryor	31.86
115 Cash on hand	24.95
120 Accounts receivable	21,512.75
125 Employee advances	327.37
140 Inventory—Shipping	940.43
141 Inventory—Raw materials	1,082.29
142 Inventory—Work-in-progress	803.70
143 Inventory—Packaging	4,548.41
144 Inventory—Promotional	2,114,95
Total current assets	$31,913.82
Fixed assets	
160 Leasehold improvements	$ 2,402.25
165 Fixtures and furniture	1,222.46
167 Equipment	18,768.21
169 Office equipment	.00
170 1986 Lincoln town car	15,000.00
180 Less: Accumulated depreciation	(7,800.01)
181 Less: Amortization	(502.50)
Total fixed assets	$29,090.41
Other assets	
193 Organizational cost	$ 4,083.36
194 Prepaid interest	2,849.69
195 Utility deposits	.00
Total fixed and other assets	$36,023.46
Total assets	$67,937.28
Current liabilities	
205 Accounts payable	$15,239.41
210 Note payable-premium finances	88.26
220 Federal tax withheld	150.00
225 F.I.C.A. tax withheld	937.92
230 State tax withheld	266.49
231 State and federal employment taxes	230.92
Total current liabilities	$16,913.00
Long-term liabilities	
245 Note payable—All fill	$ 2,734.86
246 Note payable—American Bank	23,740.00
247 Note payable—Sikeston Leasing	15,126.66
Total long-term liabilities	$41,601.52
Total liabilities	$58,514.52

EXHIBIT 1 *(concluded)*

NATURE BROS. LTD.
Balance Sheet
As of September 30, 1986

Capital account	
290 Original capital stock	$ 1,000.00
291 Additional paid-in capital	$41,580.00
292 Treasury stock	(70.00)
295 Retained earnings	(3,819.71)
298 Net profit or loss	(29,267.53)
Total owner's equity account	$ 9,422.76
Total liabilities and equity	$67,937.28

category in the seven markets the company is in will amount to $3,965,942 in 1987. In 1986, sales of the company in the Oklahoma market were 11 percent of the total sales for that market for the eight-month period that the company was operational. Since these sales were accomplished with absolutely no advertising, the company can be even more successful in the future in all seven current markets with a fully developed and funded advertising campaign. The marketing approach will include advertisements in the print media, with ads on "food day" offering cents-off coupons. This program will take place in all seven markets, while stores will continue to use floor displays for demonstrations. Near 100 percent warehouse penetration should be achieved in 1987 in these markets.

The goal for the category of salt substitutes for 1987 is 20 percent of market share. This larger market share can be achieved since there is only one main competitor—Mrs. Dash—and the company is already outselling that product in Oklahoma. The company's product is superior in all respects and has a retail price advantage of 10 to 20 cents per can over Mrs. Dash. In addition, the company's product is much more versatile than Mrs. Dash; aggressive marketing and advertising will emphasize the tremendous variety of usage, the great taste, and the health benefits of the products. The informal consumer surveys at demonstrations indicated that consumers prefer Nature Bros. to Mrs. Dash by a wide margin.

A new product, which is already developed, will be added during this time. Called "Enhance," it is also a dry-mixed, noncooked, low-overhead, high-profit food product. Its category—MSG products—has a dollar volume of $978,545 in these markets. This category includes only one main competitor—Accent—made by Pet Inc. Accent has not been heavily advertised, and it is a one-line product with little initial name recognition. The company's new product will have a 30 to 40 cent per can retail price advantage to help achieve a 10 percent share of this category. In

EXHIBIT 2 1987 Sales Projection

Category	*Seasoned Salt*	*Salt Substitute*	*MSG*
Our Product	*Old Fashioned Seasoning*	*Salt-Free Old Fashioned Seasoning*	*Enhance*
Existing markets # 1			
Oklahoma	$ 550,922	$ 357,819	$118,889
Nebraska	399,630	302,769	100,958
Springfield	254,310	192,671	64,017
Arkansas	217,980	165,147	54,871
Houston	835,590	633,064	210,342
Dallas	1,162,560	880,785	292,649
Albuquerque	544,950	412,868	137,179
	$3,965,942	$2,945,123	$978,545
Market share (%)	× 10%	× 20%	× 10%
1st year sales	$ 396,594	$ 589,024	$ 97,854
		396,594	
		589,024	
		97,854	
Total 1st year sales volume		$1,083,472	

summary, 1987 will be spent solidifying the company's present market positions, which make up 10.7 percent of the total U.S. grocery market, resulting in a 1987 sales volume of $1,083,472.

1988 OBJECTIVES

The company intends to open eight new markets in 1988: Los Angeles, Phoenix, Portland, Sacramento, Salt Lake City, San Francisco, Seattle, and Spokane. These new markets make up 17.1 percent of grocery store sales, according to the *Progressive Grocer's Marketing Guidebook,* the industry standard. In the category of seasoned salt, these markets have a dollar volume of $7,609,443 a year. Salt substitutes sell at a volume of $5,032,014, and the MSG category $1,642,764. With proper advertising, the company's shares forecast in our current markets will also be realized.

A 10 percent penetration of the seasoned salt category is a very conservative projection considering the strong health consciousness on the West Coast. The products will be introduced in shippers, used in store demonstrations, and supported with media advertising to achieve at least a 10 percent market share. This would result in sales of $760,943 in that category.

EXHIBIT 3 1988 Sales Projection

Category	*Seasoned Salt*	*Salt Substitute*	*MSG*
Our Product	*Old Fashioned Seasoning*	*Salt-Free Old Fashioned Seasoning*	*Enhance*
Existing markets # 1			
Oklahoma	$ 578,468	$ 375,709	$ 124,889
Nebraska	489,473	317,908	105,675
Springfield MO	311,483	202,305	67,248
Arkansas	266,985	173,404	57,641
Houston	1,023,443	664,716	220,957
Dallas	1,423,921	942,822	307,419
Albuquerque	667,463	433,510	144,103
Existing markets total	$4,761,236	$3,110,374	$1,027,932
Market share	× 15%	× 25%	× 15%
Existing markets $ volume	$ 714,185	$ 775,593	$ 154,189
New markets:			
Los Angeles	$2,892,339	$1,878,544	$ 624,444
Phoenix	622,965	404,609	134,495
Portland	578,647	375,709	124,888
Sacramento	845,453	549,113	182,530
Salt Lake	578,647	375,708	124,888
San Francisco	1,156,935	751,419	249,777
Seattle	578,647	375,708	124,888
Spokane	355,980	231,206	76,854
New markets total	$7,609,443	$5,032,014	$1,642,764
Market share	× 10%	× 20%	× 10%
New markets $ volume	$ 760,943	$1,006,420	$ 164,276
New markets $ total	760,943	1,006,420	164,276
Existing markets $ total +	714,185	777,593	154,189
Total volume	$1,475,128	$1,784,013	$ 318,465

Old Fashioned Seasoning sales	$1,475,128
Salt-Free Old Fashioned Seasoning sales	1,784,013
Enhance sales (a new product)	318,465
Total 1988 sales	$3,557,606

A 20 percent penetration is targeted in the salt-free category. With aggressive marketing, price advantage at retail, and better packaging, the company will be well positioned against the lower-quality products of our competitors. With the dollar volume of this category at $5,032,014, a conservative estimate of our share would be $1,006,420.

In the category of MSG, a 10 percent share will be achieved. The main competitor in this category does very little advertising. Again, attractive packaging, aggressive marketing, high quality, and a retail price advantage of 30 to 40 cents per unit

EXHIBIT 4 1987 Pro Forma Totals

	1987	*Percent*
Sales	$1,083,472	100%
Cost of goods		
Packaging	129,444	11.9
Ingredients	175,668	16.2
Plant labor	35,580	3.2
Freight in	24,036	2.2
Shipping materials	924	.08
Total cost of goods sold	365,004	33.68
Gross profit	718,468	66.31
Operating expenses		
President's salary	43,200	
Sales manager	30,000	
Secretary	14,400	
Employee benefits	2,400	
Insurance	1,992	
Rent	3,000	
Utilities	1,800	
Phone	7,200	
Office supplies	1,200	
Postage	1,200	
Car lease	5,640	
Professional services	3,000	
Travel and entertainment	24,000	
Freight out	59,088	5.4
Advertising	216,684	20.0
Promotion	12,036	1.1
Brokerage	54,168	5.0
Incentives	7,500	.6
Cash discounts	21,660	2.0
Total expenses	510,168	47.0
Cash flow		
Taxes	207,648	19.1
Net profit before debt service	155,736	14.3

will enable the company to realize a 10 percent market penetration. This share of the West Coast markets will generate sales of $164,276. Total sales of all three products in these eight new markets will be around $1,931,639.

The company plans to continue to solidify the markets previously established through couponing, co-op advertising, quality promotions, and word-of-mouth advertising. Market share in these original markets should increase by another 5 percent in 1988.

The dollar volume of the seasoned salt category in 1988 should be around $4,761,236, and our market share at 15 percent would amount to $714,185. The dollar volume for the salt substitute category would be $3,110,374, giving sales at

EXHIBIT 5

NATURE BROS. LTD.
Pro Forma Income Statement
1988–1991

	1988	*1989*	*1990*	*1991*
Sales	$3,557,606	$6,136,224	$10,089,863	$18,506,302
Cost of goods				
Packaging	423,355	730,210	1,200,693	2,202,249
Ingredients	572,774	987,932	1,624,467	2,979,514
Plant labor	37,359	48,826	60,867	63,910
Freight in	72,930	125,793	206,842	379,379
Shipping materials	2,960	4,908	8,071	14,805
Total cost of goods sold	$1,106,575	$1,897,618	$3,100,240	$5,639,858
Percent of sales	31.36%	31.41%	30.90%	30.65%
Gross profit	2,451,031	4,238,606	6,988,923	12,866,444
Operating expense				
President's salary	43,200	51,840	62,208	74,649
Sales manager	30,000	36,000	39,000	45,000
Sales rep	25,000	30,000	34,000	38,000
Sales rep		25,000	30,000	34,000
Sales rep			26,000	30,000
Sales rep				28,000
Secretary	16,000	18,000	20,000	22,000
Secretary				15,000
Employee benefits	2,400	4,000	10,000	15,000
Insurance	3,000	4,000	5,000	5,000
Rent	3,600	3,600	3,600	3,600
Utilities	2,400	3,000	3,500	4,500
Phone	12,000	14,000	15,000	18,000
Office supplies	2,000	2,500	3,000	5,000
Postage	2,000	2,500	3,000	4,000
Car lease	5,640	5,640	5,640	5,640
Car lease	3,600	3,600	4,000	4,000
Car lease		3,600	3,600	4,000
Car lease			4,000	4,000
Professional services	6,000	8,000	8,000	10,000
Travel and entertainment	48,000	72,000	96,000	120,000
New equipment	4,000	14,000	14,000	24,000
Freight out	197,269	334,424	549,897	1,000,859
Advertising	711,521	1,227,244	2,017,972	3,701,260
Promotion	40,000	68,112	111,997	205,419
Brokerage	177,880	306,811	504,493	925,315
Incentives	24,547	42,399	69,680	205,419
Cash discounts	71,152	122,724	201,792	370,126
Total expenses	$1,431,209	$2,402,994	$3,845,192	$6,921,787
Cash flow before taxes	1,019,822	1,835,612	3,845,192	6,921,787
Taxes	209,063	458,903	785,932	1,486,164
Net profit before debt service	$810,759	$1,376,709	$2,357,799	$4,458,493
Percent of sales	22.78%	22.43%	23.36%	24.09%

EXHIBIT 6 Competitive Advertisement

Source: *Tulsa World,* June 17, 1987.

25 percent of $775,593. In the MSG category, a 15 percent market share of the $1,027,932 volume would give sales of $154,189. The company's total sales for the existing markets in 1988 will be in excess of $1,643,967.

The totals for 1988 sales of Nature Bros. Old Fashioned Seasoning will be $1,475,128. Nature Bros. Salt-Free volume should be $1,784,013. The sales of Enhance, our MSG product, should be $318,465. This will give us a total sales volume of $3,557,606 for all three products in 1988.

FINANCIAL NEEDS AND PROJECTIONS

In this plan, Morris indicated a need for $100,000 equity infusion to expand sales, increase markets, and add new products. The money would be used to secure warehouse stocking space, do cooperative print advertising, give point-of-purchase display allowances, and pay operating expenses.

NEW PRODUCT DEVELOPMENT

The company plans to continue an ongoing research and development program to introduce new and winning products. Four products are already developed that will be highly marketable and easily produced. Personnel are dedicated to building a large and profitable company and attracting quality brokers. The next new product targets a different market segment but can be brought on-line for about $25,000 by using our existing machinery, types of containers, and display pieces. A highly respected broker felt that the product would be a big success. The broker previously represented the only major producer of a similar product, Pet Inc., which had sales of $4.36 million in 1985. The company can achieve at least a 10 percent market share with this product in the first year. The company's product will be at least equal in quality and offer a 17 percent price advantage to the consumer, while still making an excellent profit.

Another new product would require slightly different equipment. This product would be initially produced by a private-label manufacturer. The product would be established before any major machinery was purchased. Many large companies use private-label manufacturers, or co-packers, as they are called in the trade. Consumer tests at demonstrations and food shows have indicated that each of these products will be strong.

PLANT AND EQUIPMENT

The company's plant is located in a nearly new metal building in Rose, Oklahoma. The lease on the building limits payments to no more than $300 per month for the next seven years. The new computer-controlled filling equipment will be paid off in two months, and the seaming equipment is leased from the company's container manufacturer for only $1 per year. The company has the capability of producing about 300,000 units a month with an additional $15,000 investment for an automatic conveyer system and a bigger product mixer. This production level would require two additional plant personnel, working one shift with no overtime. The company could double this production if needed with the addition of another shift. One of the main advantages of the company's business is the very small overhead required to produce the products. The company can generate enough product to reach sales of approximately $4 million a year while maintaining a production payroll of only $37,000 a year.

To meet the previously outlined production goals, the company will need to purchase another filling machine in 1988. This machine will be capable of filling two cans at once with an overall speed of 75 cans per minute, which would increase capacity to 720,000 units a month. A higher-speed seaming machine will also need to be purchased. The filling machine would cost approximately $22,000; a rebuilt seamer would cost $25,000, a new one, $50,000. With the addition of these two machines, the company would have a capacity of 1,020,000 units per month on one shift.

By 1989, the company will have to decide whether to continue the lease or to buy the property where located and expand the facilities. The property has plenty of land for expansion for the next five years. The company has the flexibility to produce other types of products with the same equipment and can react quickly to changes in customer preferences and modify its production line to meet such demands as needed.

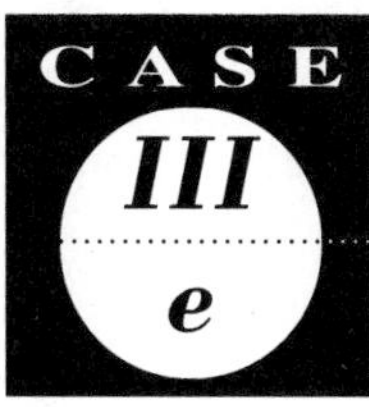

Fastcom Technologies, Inc.

The management team of Fastcom Technologies, Inc., has developed a plan to outmaneuver some big players in communications, including MCI and Federal Express, with the new product SmartFax. John R. Goram, CEO and president of Fastcom Technologies, Inc., has successfully launched five manufacturing companies and feels that SmartFax will make Fastcom Technologies a winner.

SmartFax will take advantage of the existing market of personal computer users. It offers this market a component to use with their existing systems at a price that is attractive compared to other options for transmitting documents. Through SmartFax, a personal computer can transmit a paper document over a telephone line without the time-consuming manual input. On the receiving end, SmartFax reproduces a duplicate of the document.

Major communication companies feel the need to speed up paper communications. R&D departments are focusing on the development of electronic mail. The communications industry has been experimenting with and investing in one system after another, from those using phone lines to personal computers. Can Fastcom Technologies beat its competitors and fill the market need?

According to Frederick W. Smith, Chairman of Federal Express, "We know we're headed in the right direction ('Zapmail') in terms of the market. . . . It's just a matter of when."[1] But less than a month after that statement appeared, Federal Express discontinued its Zapmail service with a $340 million pretax write-off.

What seemed like a great idea just has not produced the expected results. Federal Express discovered that they were competing with *themselves* in trying to convert managers to the Zapmail service. Their own overnight delivery system seemed adequate to most of their customers, who could not see the value in paying a premium for same-day service. On the other hand, MCI, with hopes to tap into the segment of personal computer users, discovered that most PCs were not equipped to communicate with other PCs. Despite advanced communication systems and communication technology, the old method of communication (the U.S. Postal Service) is still doing well. In 1985, the U.S. Postal Service grossed $27.7 billion.

So why does Goram think his SmartFax will succeed where others have failed or have had limited and disappointing successes? Can the following business plan convince the potential investor? Will the idea actually work in the marketplace? Following are some portions of the company's business plan.

[1] M. Schrage, "Electronic mail catching on," *Tulsa World,* October 19, 1986, pp 42–43.

EXECUTIVE SUMMARY

Fastcom Technologies, Inc. (FCT) is an electronics company founded in Oklahoma in 1985. The management team consists of four key managers involved in everyday business operations, two special advisors on the board of directors, and other individuals bringing in needed expertise.

FCT's first product, SmartFax, is a personal computer peripheral that will transmit the contents of a paper document over a telephone line to a similar device. SmartFax automatically reads the document, eliminating the need for time-consuming manual input. A duplicate of the document is reproduced at the receiving end.

SmartFax provides the speed associated with electronic mail and facsimile transfer services, preserves the integrity of the "paper" office, and, at $2,500 per unit, costs less than a low-end facsimile machine or laser printer. No personal computer peripheral and no facsimile machine currently on the market has this capacity.

SmartFax will be marketed through four distribution channels: personal computer original equipment manufacturers (OEMs), personal computer retail chains, value-added resellers (VARs), and direct sales to special accounts. Direct competition between Smartfax and facsimile machines will be avoided by moving the product through one of these channels, personal computer distribution channels.

On the basis of projections that facsimile machine annual sales will double to 500,000 units by 1989, SmartFax sales should be strong. Three percent market share obtainment (15,000 units per year), will generate an income of about $4.3 million.

FCT obtained initial financing of $250,000 from TDM Computer Products in Tulsa, Oklahoma. These monies were used from March 1986 through September 1986 to establish offices, pay rent and utilities, pay development and support personnel, and purchase office supplies, furniture, fixtures, electronic components, and electronic laboratory equipment. Prototype I was in operation in June 1986. A $73,000 loan from the Tulsa Economic Development Corporation was used to complete Prototype II development by November 1, 1986. A $500,000 loan will be obtained in February 1987 to purchase manufacturing facilities and equipment.

A $500,000 stock issue in October–November 1986 will be used to complete product development. Prototype III will be ready for production in March 1987. A $1.8 million stock issue in March 1987 will pay for overhead, salaries, subcontracted manufacturing processes, and manufacturing parts inventories. This money will also provide a cash buffer to cover accounts receivable for 30 to 45 days following product shipment.

Projected gross revenue is $19.5 million by the end of 1989, with projected income after tax being $3.0 million. Using a 10 times earnings multiple, Fastcom Technologies, Inc., will have an estimated market value of $30 million by the end of 1989.

THE PRODUCT

Product Description

SmartFax is a personal computer peripheral that transmits the contents of a paper document over a telephone modem to another PC or to a facsimile machine.

To be more specific, a PC equipped with SmartFax:

- Senses or "reads" the image printed on the document.
- Stores that information into PC memory.
- Compresses the information into a package that can be transmitted efficiently.
- Sends the information through a modem over ordinary telephone lines to another PC or to a facsimile machine.

On the receiving end, a PC equipped with SmartFax:

- Receives the coded message over a standard telephone modem.
- Decodes the information, expanding it into usable data.
- Displays or prints the information in its original form.
- Magnetically stores the information onto a computer disk.

On the receiving end, a facsimile machine:

- Receives the SmartFax transmitted message.
- Prints the information in its original form.

SmartFax is an attractive 3 inch by 14 inch by 14 inch unit incorporated easily into the desktop personal computer workstation. A personal computer peripheral, SmartFax has three components:

1. A *program* that simplifies the document transfer process for the user while providing automatic, unattended transmission during low-rate, long-distance telephone usage hours. Fully menu-driven, the software guides the novice user through the steps required to use the document reader, dial the other party, and successfully transmit the data. Additional features allow images to be conveniently stored and retrieved from a disk-based computer data base. A memory-resident program, SmartFax may be activated with special keystrokes without terminating other computer operations.
2. A *document reader* capable of scanning any length document from 4 to 8.5 inches wide. The high-resolution scan (1,728 × 2,340 dots per page), taking approximately four seconds to complete, creates an excellent quality display and single-color printed document. In fact, reader capabilities exceed by several times the output resolution available with most monitors and printers used today. These capabilities make SmartFax compatible with the newer, high-resolution personal computer monitors and laser printers that will be released over the next two to three years.
3. A *printed circuit board* that works with most IBM-PC, XT, or AT-compatible personal computers. The board established industry standards. Installed easily into an open slot inside the computer, the board contains patentable circuit

designs and proprietary software used to compress, process, and store the information/image. Compressing the data up to 48 times, the circuit board reduces data file size for rapid transmission and compact storage. The sophisticated video interface to the monitor can "paint" a full screen in one second. An optional 9,600 bit per second modem for telephone transmission is available.

SmartFax provides a number of capabilities not currently available:

- Convenient use requiring minimal orientation.
- Long-term storage and retrieval.
- Rapid screen display (painting).
- Compatibility with personal computer workstations.
- Ability to convert paper documents into electronically coded information that can be used with other personal computer applications such as word processors or spreadsheets.
- Substantial cost savings.

Although Japanese facsimile machine manufacturers are adding computer capabilities to make their machines more "intelligent," their stand-alone design precludes the device from becoming a personal computer peripheral.

Until now the optical character reader (OCR) market has been limited to a few companies that could afford expensive units. SmartFax, though, will offer *automated text and document input* to the 15 million personal computers being used by businesses today, revolutionizing computer productivity.

Manufacturing and Packaging

Manufacturing costs will be approximately $830 per unit for the first few thousand units. Variable costs should decrease soon to around $690 per unit. Further cost reductions will be possible at higher production volumes than are projected. At $690 per unit, there is a gross margin of about 43 percent.

The following components will be made by others: circuit board, scanner, and scanner case. The CEP/memory/video/PBX board and the imager board will be made and stuffed by a "board house" with the necessary manufacturing and testing equipment. The company will have to pay set-up charges, including a large fee for developing the necessary test equipment.

The drive mechanism and drive electronics (the scanner) will be made by a company that specializes in this type of mechanism. That company and FCT will jointly design the unit. They will agree on a schedule of delivery, which may result in a fairly large amount of inventory being kept on hand.

The scanner cases must be bought in large quantities. Initially, a metal case similar to the IBM PC main unit case will be used. Later, a molded plastic case will be designed. The cost for this is between $20,000 and $75,000, depending on whether vacuum or injection molding is required.

Even though all the main subcomponents are manufactured out-of-house, final assembly, testing, rework, quality control, and shipping make up a substantial operation. This will eventually require about 20 to 25 people working in an assembly plant that has about 10,000 square feet of floor space. One assembler will be able to assemble 10 units a day. One tester will be able to test 30 units a day. One rework technician will be able to rework two units a day. The reject rate at this point should be about 5 percent. One quality control technician will be able to do final tests on about 20 units a day. One shipper will be able to handle about 40 units a day.

The building should be able to accommodate about 16,000 units a year. Starting with a staff sufficient to build 3,000 units a year, the company plans to increase the production capabilities to 6,000 units and then to 12,000.

While all the set-up costs for production will be incurred before we release the product, hiring all the necessary people can be postponed until after the first contract is obtained. Assemblers can be trained in six weeks, and quality control and test personnel can be trained in eight weeks.

An experienced manufacturing manager will be hired in the first quarter of 1987. The person will have successfully managed an operation producing a similar product for placement in similar distribution channels.

Future Growth

Recently, electronic component manufacturers have made a number of dramatic breakthroughs in "chip" technology. Capitalizing on the newest, proven technology, FCT's engineers have used many of these chips in SmartFax, which has reduced costs and enhanced performance.

After the basic SmartFax unit has been developed, the company will design a number of hardware and software upgrades to enhance the product. These include optical character recognition capabilities, integration with a high-speed thermal printer, gray-scale differentiation for reproducing photographs, larger-capacity document readers, video camera interfacing, printer drivers for a number of common printers, higher-resolution output for laser printers, color capabilities, and a large-scale document server compatible with laser devices and PC networks.

INDUSTRY

Background

SmartFax offers improved speed, greater convenience, and better quality results than higher-priced facsimile devices. The document reader is attractive and small enough to place on top of the PC. In contrast to facsimile machines, SmartFax can catalog and store scanned documents in a computerized database. It can also retrieve documents quickly and conveniently.

Users will find the menu-driven operating software easy to learn and use. As an additional plus, the software does not interfere with other work being done on the PC.

With the addition of upgraded software, SmartFax can also be used for desktop publishing and for character recognition applications.

SmartFax is being developed, in part, under a contract with Telex Computer Products. Portions of the software are being written in cooperation with the Center for Microcomputer Applications at The University of Tulsa.

SmartFax fills a business need for the immediate and direct exchange of documents between locations. It holds a unique position in the document exchange market, as it integrates facsimile capabilities with personal computers. A strong market for document exchange has already been developed and is growing. Personal computer marketing channels are well-defined, accessible, and receptive to new enhancements, especially in the field of office automation. The advantages of integrating these two markets are an existing customer base, existing distribution channels to sell through, easily perceived product value, and easily understood features and benefits.

SmartFax appeals to many different types of businesses, as indicated by the broad base of customers using Federal Express and facsimile machines. Strongest demand will be from businesses operating in multiple locations or dealing with documents they do not create. SmartFax is particularly attractive in situations where accuracy is important and the form of the document has intrinsic value; for example, signatures, graphs, charts, designs, stamps, bids, proposals, price lists, invoices, freight bills, accounting statements, affidavits, contracts, copy, proofs, rush orders, quotes, purchase orders, or handwritten notes.

Competition

FCT will face no direct competition upon market entry. Because significant competitive pressure should exist by the end of the first year, the company will have to establish itself in the market by creating strong identity and penetrating the distribution system. The release of new hardware and software enhancements will help keep the company ahead of the competition.

Competition will not be coming from the current facsimile machine makers, which are all Japanese, or the few document-scanner makers already in the market. Instead, competition will develop from new sources. This will give about six to eight months' lead time before a competitive product appears from companies already making and marketing PC peripherals and computer manufacturers.

As a new class of personal computer peripheral, SmartFax has no direct competitor. Indirectly, SmartFax will compete with the facsimile machine market. Companies with high volume requirements for facsimile transfer, for example, may decide to purchase a dedicated, stand-alone facsimile machine rather than a PC peripheral. Although corporate uses for SmartFax and for facsimile machines have some overlap, the marketing and distribution channels differ substantially. Facsimile machines are sold through office equipment supply companies to office services or administrative personnel, much as typewriters and copy machines are sold. In contrast, SmartFax will sell through computer supply companies to management information services (MIS) personnel, much as personal computers and laser printers are sold.

At $2,500, SmartFax costs no more than low-end facsimile units, placing it in an extremely competitive price position. The purchases of $2,000 to $3,000 laser printers indicate that companies are willing to purchase PC peripherals in this price range.

Eager to expand their computer services and areas of control, MIS managers command larger budgets and generally wield greater influence than office service or administrative personnel. They are in a better position to purchase telecommunications equipment than office services personnel. MIS managers will see SmartFax as an opportunity to offer additional capabilities for their PC clients, expand and control company telecommunications functions, and enhance their presence throughout the organization.

Professionals, small-business owners, and individual personal computers will be a secondary target market.

Sales Projections

Over 200,000 stand-alone facsimile machines will be sold in the United States in 1986, and growth rates will be as high as 40 percent per year through 1989, reaching 1 million units being sold by 1990. If, as conservatively projected, annual sales of facsimile machines double to 500,000 units by 1989, about 100,000 personal computer peripheral facsimile devices (similar to SmartFax) will be sold—roughly 20 percent of the facsimile machine market. If FCT commands only 15 percent of the PC peripheral FAX-device market (3 percent of the total FAX market), or 15,000 units per year, they will make a respectable profit: $3.0 million from only one of the markets the company is addressing.

Within the next couple of years, technical advances will lower component prices. This will enable the company to lower the price to $1,000 to $1,500, substantially below facsimile machines. Marketing studies indicate that when this occurs, the demand for the product will increase dramatically, perhaps by a factor of 5 to 10 times.

MARKETING

Distribution Channels

In the tradition of other personal computer peripherals, SmartFax will be sold through multiple distribution channels:

- Original equipment manufacturers (OEMs) who manufacture personal computers (IBM, Telex, Compaq, Zenith, etc.).
- Personal computer retail chains who sell computers to large businesses, small businesses, local government facilities, and individual end users (Tandy, ComputerLand, BusinessLand, etc.).
- Value added resellers (VARs) who customize PC equipment and software for vertical markets (e.g., attorneys, doctors, and CPAs).
- FCT direct sales to the government.
- FCT special account sales directly to large telecommunications companies (Federal Express, Purolator, etc.) and to third-party board manufacturers (AST, Quadram, Hercules, etc.).

With a large outside sales and service force, OEMs have a unique opportunity to reach MIS managers in large organizations. Already, OEMs are aggressively selling their personal computer lines to complement their larger computer installations. As a result, in 1986 personal computers comprised nearly one-third of the mainframe computer workstations. The OEM representatives are also supplying large companies and government installations with stand-alone PC workstations to replace expensive and inflexible dedicated word processors. In addition, many financial analysts, engineers, and other professionals are purchasing PCs to enhance their capabilities.

The OEMs will account for a large share of FCT's market. Two OEM options will be available: manufacturing license or component sales agreement. FCT has already established a licensing agreement (joint manufacturing rights) with TDM Computer Products. In addition, they will discuss sales with IBM, Digital Equipment Corporation, Data General, Honeywell, and WANG.

The OEM sales will be enhanced with distribution through large computer retail chains, VARs, and direct special sales. Diversifying the distribution channels will guard against becoming too dependent on one outlet. Today, in addition to servicing a busy walk-in trade, large computer retail chains such as ComputerLand, BusinessLand, Tandy, MicroAge, Entre, and the Bell Operating Companies employ over 1,500 outside sales professionals who call on companies and government offices of all sizes. Projections indicate that by 1989 there will be 7,200 computer stores in the United States, accounting for $16 billion in sales, a growth rate of 25 percent per year. Today, of the nearly 3,500 computer specialty stores in the United States, about half are affiliated with a major chain.

In addition to walk-in traffic and outside sales, retailers and some OEMs also distribute products through VARs, who sell customized PC systems to a vertical market: physicians, attorneys, insurance companies, government offices, and so forth. The VAR creates a unique personal computer system by adding hardware and/or software to the basic PC. The "turnkey" systems are easy to use and meet specific needs of professions or businesses.

FCT will also sell directly to large accounts such as telecommunications companies (Federal Express, Purolator, etc.), third-party PC board manufacturers (AST, Quadram, Hercules, etc.), and government installations.

FINANCIAL PROJECTIONS

In March 1986, FCT entered into a development contract with TDM Computer Products in Tulsa, Oklahoma. In exchange for manufacturing rights to SmartFax (for a $30 royalty per unit), Telex provided a $250,000 interest-free loan with no payback for the first two years. In March 1988, Fastcom begins a 50-month payback at a 10 percent rate of interest.

These monies were used from March 1986 through September 1986 to establish offices, to pay rent and utilities, to pay development and support personnel, and to purchase office supplies, furniture, fixtures, electronic components, and electronic laboratory equipment.

In October 1986, Fastcom received a $73,000 loan from the Tulsa Economic Development Corporation. These monies were used from October through November 1986 to complete the first prototype and pay administrative overhead. Payback beings April 1, 1987, with three equal monthly payments.

Beginning in October 1986, Fastcom will generate additional capital by selling stock to major investors. Legal counsel advises that this can be done without registering the stock.

A total of $500,000 of stock will be issued in October-November 1986, which will be used to complete product development.

A $1.8 million stock issue in March 1987 will pay for overhead, salaries, subcontracted manufacturing processes, and manufacturing parts inventories. This money will also provide a cash buffer to cover sales accounts receivable for 30 to 45 days following product shipment.

A loan application submitted in the latter part of 1986 will provide $500,000 for purchasing manufacturing facilities and equipment, beginning February 1987.

Since gross revenue will be $3.4 million and total expenses will be $4.1 million in 1987, FCT will incur no income tax liabilities. By the end of 1988, projected gross income is $2.5 million. With a valuation of 10 times earnings (earnings multiplier), FCT will have an established market value of $16.5 million at the end of 1988 (see Exhibit 1).

- *Current Shareholders*—As of September 1, 1986, 59 shareholders held 2,767,950 shares of Fastcom Technologies, Inc., stock. John R. Goram, the largest shareholder, controls 21 percent of the issued shares. The largest four shareholders control approximately 50.5 percent of the issued shares.
- *Stock Options for TDM*—At TDM Computer Product's option, the $250,000 loan may be converted into 250,000 shares at $1.00 per share (in blocks of 50,000 shares). If more than 2.5 million shares have been issued at the time TDM exercises its option, TDM can purchase 10 percent of the shares issued and thus obtain a 10 percent ownership position.
- *Stock Options for Employees and Consultants*—332,500 shares have been allocated for employee and consultant stock options to pay for bonuses and for services rendered.

EXHIBIT 1 Financial Summary

	Invest Loan	*Unit Sales*	*Price*	*Gross Revenue*	*COG*
Factor	1.00	1.00	1.00		1.00
1986					
1st qtr.					
2nd qtr.	$ 200,000	0	0	0	0
3rd qtr.	123,000	0	0	0	0
4th qtr.	400,000	0	0	0	0
1986 total	$ 723,000	0	0	0	0
1987					
1st qtr.	2,400,000	0	0	0	0
2nd qtr.	0	0	0	0	0
3rd qtr.	0	750	1,663	423,938	633,873
4th qtr.	0	1,300	1,654	1,553,938	1,035,373
1987 total	$2,400,000	$ 2,050	$3,316	$ 1,977,875	$ 1,669,246
1988					
1st qtr.	0	2,500	1,324	2,544,400	1,739,763
2nd qtr.	0	2,700	1,322	3,398,400	1,882,364
3rd qtr.	0	2,900	1,321	3,658,400	2,013,364
4th qtr.	0	3,100	1,319	3,918,400	2,152,311
1988 total	0	$11,200	$5,286	$13,519,600	$ 7,787,802
1989					
1st qtr.	0	3,500	1,325	4,276,320	2,414,311
2nd qtr.	0	3,700	1,330	4,733,880	2,550,606
3rd qtr.	0	4,000	1,333	5,060,080	2,750,759
4th qtr.	0	4,300	1,336	5,472,080	2,955,206
1989 total	0	$15,500	$5,324	$19,542,360	$10,670,883

- *Unissued Shares*—On August 14, 1986, the stockholders authorized the issuance of an additional 2.5 million shares to complete product development and to capitalize the company's production and sales operation during 1987.

On August 26, 1986, FCT entered into a royalty agreement with Vision Phone, Inc. In exchange for technology, patents, copyrights, and know-how, FCT agreed to pay Vision Phone $1.00 per unit sold, not to exceed a total of $150,000.

- *Sales Volume Sensitivity Analysis*—Cash flow is relatively insensitive to a sales volume variance of 90 to 120 percent of projected sales. If sales are at 90 percent, the company will reach our projected break-even point in the first quarter

Net Revenue	*Expenses*	*Income*	*After-Tax Income*	*Customer Cash Flow*
	1.00		0.34	
0	$ 114,441	$ (114,441)	$ (114,441)	$ 85,559
0	111,350	(111,350)	(111,350)	97,209
0	111,350	(111,350)	(111,350)	97,209
0	270,637	(270,637)	(270,637)	226,573
	$ 496,428	$ (496,428)	$ (496,428)	
0	724,689	(724,689)	(724,689)	1,901,883
0	806,049	(806,049)	(806,049)	1,095,834
(209,935)	461,179	(691,115)	(691,115)	404,720
518,565	499,679	18,885	12,464	417,184
$ 308,630	$2,511,597	$(2,202,967)	$(2,209,388)	
804,637	738,530	66,106	43,630	460,814
1,516,036	748,386	767,651	506,649	967,464
1,645,036	863,113	781,924	516,070	1,483,533
1,766,089	874,474	891,615	588,466	2,071,999
$5,731,798	$3,224,503	$2,507,295	$ 1,654,815	
1,862,009	936,178	925,831	611,048	2,683,048
2,183,274	1,211,703	971,571	641,237	3,324,285
2,309,321	1,115,218	1,194,104	788,108	4,112,393
2,516,874	1,011,924	1,504,950	993,267	5,105,660
$8,871,477	$4,275,021	$4,596,456	$ 3,033,661	

of 1988; and in the first quarter of 1988, the lowest cumulative cash will be $28,500. If sales volume reaches 120 percent of projected sales, the company will reach the projected break-even point in the fourth quarter of 1987, and the lowest cumulative cash will be $489,000 in the third quarter of 1987.

However, if sales drop to 80 percent of projections with no price increase, an additional $415,000 of capital must be raised to support goods in inventory until the 4th quarter of 1989 (see Exhibit 2).

EXHIBIT 2 Sensitivity Analysis ($000)

	Percent Variance from Plan				
Sales volume	*80%*	*90%*	*100%*	*110%*	*120%*
Break-even point					
Gross operating income	2Q 88	2Q 88	4Q 88	4Q 87	4Q 87
Cumulative cash flow at end of 1987	$28	$226	$417	$562	$707
Point of lowest cumulative cash	1Q 88	1Q 88	3Q 87	3Q 87	3Q 87
	($415)	$37	$405	$447	$489
Company value, 4Q 1989 @10 × at earnings	$4,500	$17,400	$30,300	$43,200	$56,100
Conclusion: The financial plan is relatively insensitive to sales variances between 85 and 120%. If sales projections drop by more than 15%, an additional $400,000 investment may be required to avoid reductions in marketing and future product development.					
Break-even point					
Gross operating income	4Q 87	4Q 87	4Q 87	2Q 88	2Q 88
Cumulative cash flow at end of 1987	$681	$549	$447	$257	$90
Point of lowest cumulative cash	3Q 87	3Q 87	3Q 87	1Q 88	1Q 88
	$531	$468	$405	$149	($192)
Company value, 4Q 1989 @10 × at earnings	$44,400	$37,400	$30,300	$23,300	$16,300
Conclusion: A price increase of $200 will be necessary if COG increases by more than 15% (result in $300,000 minimum cash flow).					

MANAGEMENT

FCT's management team includes four key managers.

President and CEO John R. Goram reports to the board of directors. Goram has overall responsibility for marketing, economic studies, product selection, finance, staffing, plant construction, and start-up. He has successfully launched five manufacturing companies, including the Great Plains Natural Food Company in Kansas City. He received a B.S. degree in chemistry from the University of Kansas and pursued his doctoral studies in anthropology at UCLA, where he taught economic development and anthropology.

L. John Krasmat is vice president of finance. He owns an equipment sales and service business, AMS Equipment, Ltd., in Tulsa. He is experienced in purchasing, sales, service, financial management, inventory control, personnel management, and customer relations. He received his B.A. degree in sociology and completed his course work for a Master's degree in industrial psychology at the University of Tulsa.

Terry L. Toley is engineering manager and vice president of operations. Toley has extensive experience with both hardware and software computer development. He was senior engineer for new automation product development at C-E Natco Research and Development. He received his B.S. degree in computer science and his Master's degree in chemical instrumentation from Eastern New Mexico University.

James D. Renningham, manager of product planning and development and vice president of marketing, comes to FCT with 17 years experience in marketing, software development, engineering, and finance. He has a B.A. degree in economics and computer science from Oklahoma State University.

In addition to the four key managers, FCT employs a number of consultants and subcontractors.

PART IV

Managing the New Venture

Chapter 12
Managing During Early Operations

Chapter 13
Managing Growth and Expansion

Chapter 14
Ending the Venture

Cases for Part IV

CHAPTER

12

Managing During Early Operations

Chapter Objectives

1. To describe the important procedures for financial control during the early stages of the new venture's operation.
2. To understand the differences between the accrual and cash method of accounting.
3. To discuss the important issues in managing cash, expenses, assets, debt, profits, and taxes.
4. To describe simplified methods for efficient record keeping.
5. To understand the problems that can result from rapid growth of the new venture.
6. To illustrate control processes for marketing and sales plans.
7. To understand how to effectively promote the new venture through publicity and advertising.

Gordon Crane

The early years of existence are critical to the entrepreneur in shaping the new venture's future direction and potential success. As a venture grows and enjoys success, it is likely that competitive pressures will intensify, further straining financial resources. Entrepreneurs must evaluate and select competitive strategies that will allow their new venture to successfully penetrate defined markets. Often, an early strategy will be developed with limited financial and human resources, no reputation, and unfavorable odds. Yet the entrepreneur will continue to seek opportunities and ways of competing that are unique or innovative in this market. Long-term success will likely depend on the decisions the entrepreneur makes during the early years of operation.

One entrepreneur who has been able to make all the right decisions during the early years of a new venture is Gordon Crane, founder of Apple & Eve Inc., a producer of natural fruit juices. He has not only been able to grow the new venture, but he has done so in a very competitive market.[1]

After graduating from the University of Rhode Island in 1972, Gordon Crane used $2,000 of his savings to launch a small natural foods distributing company in New York City. Crane's decision to start this business was based almost entirely on his assessment of the opportunity that existed in the fast growing natural food markets. After three years, he decided that this type of business was not going anywhere, particularly since he constantly had problems with labor and low margins. He found himself under capitalized, which often hindered any attempts to grow the new venture. So Crane decided to go to law school. However, financing a law degree necessitated some external sources of revenue, which eventually led him to the idea of starting a fruit juice company that would be profitable enough to finance his law degree. Hence, in 1975 using $3,000 of his savings he launched Apple & Eve. The product was apple juice pressed at a New York cider mill and shipped to Massachusetts for bottling. He sold his first case in April, 1975, and began law school in September of the same year. He soon found that law school and running a business at the same time was not feasible, so he recruited his mother to handle orders and bookkeeping, and his two brothers to manage the daily operation.

[1] See Bob Weinstein, "Liquid assets," *Entrepreneur,* October 1993, pp 144–49; Larry Jabbonsky, "Purity of essence," *Beverage World,* March 1993, pp 98–99; and Cynthia Rigg, "Innovative juice maker heats a cold war," *Crain's New York Business,* December 21, 1993, pp 3, 15.

Distribution of the unique unfiltered apple juice to supermarkets proved to be easier than expected. Large chains such as Kroger, Pathmark, Shop Rite, Grand Union, and Hills and Bohack Stores were all anxious to purchase the product to meet the growing demand for natural food products. By the end of 1976, sales reached $400,000. All of this was achieved as a part-time operation, using his parents' home as the base of the new venture's operations.

In 1978, Crane graduated from law school, and sales of Apple & Eve reached $1 million. With this kind of success, Crane changed his career plans and decided to expand Apple & Eve rather than practice law. The battle then began as Motts, Lincoln, and Seneca all introduced natural juice products to compete with Apple & Eve.

Crane believed that in order to remain competitive and continue to grow, he needed to stay ahead of his competitors with new products. His first innovation was cranberry juice that was sweetened with apple juice rather than sugar. This led to a direct confrontation with Ocean Spray, who dominated the cranberry juice market. Soon after this, Crane saw another opportunity. He learned that apple juice in glass containers was second in sales to orange juice in cartons, so he launched apple juice in cartons to the dairy sections of the supermarkets. In 1982, he packaged apple juice in the "brik-pak" juice boxes, giving him shelf space in grocery, dairy, and brik-pak sections of the supermarket.

Competition during the 80s was intense, especially from Motts, Minute Maid, and Tropicana. Despite this competition, Crane emerged victorious; in the Northeast, supermarkets now only carry two brands of apple juice in the dairy section: Tropicana and Apple & Eve.

Crane's secret to success is his attention to quality and sensitivity to the marketplace. He personally reads inquiries from consumers and often samples the product, always looking for ways to improve. He has also maintained a very small, lean company, with he and his brother Cary owning all the stock. With only 16 employees, the company depends on outside contractors for all production and thus has not had to find large sums of capital for any of its expansion.

However, the lack of capital may prove a hindrance to any future growth as the company attempts to embark on new strategies. In 1993, Crane created a single serve division to sell its new line of 20 products in the refrigerated cases of convenience stores throughout the Northeast. This endeavor may prove to be even a greater challenge than Apple & Eve's success in supermarkets since it will be difficult competing with Very Fine, Snapple, and Ocean Spray (through PepsiCo Bottling Company) who presently control this market. More resources will be necessary for distribution and promotion in order to muscle onto the overcrowded shelves.

In spite of these challenges, Crane continues to be optimistic and to maintain tight controls over his operation. In 1993, sales reached $36 million, and Crane is projecting an over 40 percent increase for 1994. Clearly, Apple & Eve is a major force in the natural juice market and will continue to find strategies and innovations to reach new heights in the future.

In this chapter, important management-decision areas are reviewed and discussed. Financial and marketing control decisions, which are recognized by entrepreneurs such as Gordon Crane as being very important during the early years, are discussed in detail.

RECORD KEEPING

Before discussing the important control issues for the new venture in its early stages, it is necessary to understand what records are necessary for the entrepreneur to maintain and what are some simple techniques for maintaining good records. It is necessary to have good records not only for effective control but also for tax purposes. Regardless of the sophistication of the record-keeping method, the entrepreneur should be comfortable and, more importantly, able to understand what is going on in the business. With the availability of new software packages that are very user friendly, much of the record keeping can be easily maintained on a personal computer. Since the long-term future of the new venture depends on profits and a positive cash flow, we can simplify the goals of a good record-keeping system by identifying key incoming and outgoing revenues that can be more effectively controlled with good records.

Sales (Incoming Revenue)

Depending on the nature of the business, it is useful to have knowledge of sales by customers both in terms of units and dollars. If you were operating a catalog business, you would find value in maintaining information about how often and how much any particular customer buys in any given time period. The types of products purchased would also be relevant, especially when and if the catalog venture wishes to notify the customer about special sale prices on items the customer has shown interest in in the past. For example, a person who has shown interest in do-it-yourself products (tools or household accessories) may want to receive flyers or special sale notices on these types of products.

For a retail store, it is more difficult, and perhaps less important than the catalog business, to know every customer's buying history or behavior. However, the entrepreneur in this type of venture should try to identify the profile of the customer who patronizes the store. This can be done by having customers fill out a short questionnaire identifying demographic information as well as their product and service interests, which could be translated into merchandise decisions for the entrepreneur. There are also occasions when retailers do like to have information on specific customers, such as when they are attempting to develop good mailing lists for sale notices or flyers. Credit card customers are easier to track since initial data on the customer would have been collected when the customer applied for the card. Credit card purchases for merchandise can be tracked for information on the type and amount of merchandise purchased.

In a service venture such as a day-care center, sales would be defined as fees for service. In this case, customers pay a monthly fee for the service. The day-care center would need to maintain records on when or if a customer had paid their monthly fee. These records are important in this type of business so that customers can be politely notified with the first late payment notice. It is also not unusual to charge a fee for any late payments, commensurate with the amount due (typically this would be 1 to 2 percent of the amount due). The existence of the late fee sometimes acts as an incentive for customers to pay their bills on time. As we will see later in this chapter, cash flow problems are probably the most significant cause of new venture failure. Thus, good records regarding customer payments are necessary to maintain sufficient incoming cash so that the entrepreneur in turn can make payments of his or her bills on time.

Record keeping of customer payments can either be handled by a simple computer software package, such as Quicken, or with a simple card file system. The software package requires the entrepreneur to enter all payments to an account with a date of payment. At any time, the entrepreneur can output the payments by customer. The software can also print out a list of nonpayees for any month at any time so that late notices can be sent out the day after payments were due. The card file works in the same fashion as the computer program but would be assumed manually by the entrepreneur. Each customer would be listed on a card file. On the card would be recorded all payments including check number and date of payment. As customers pay each month, their card would be transferred to another card file. Thus, at any time the entrepreneur would have two card files, one for customers paid and the other for customers not paid. This is a simple method of maintaining records for ventures with a fixed number of customers who are paying by the month.

If payments of customers in any business are late beyond a reasonable time, it may be necessary for the entrepreneur to hire a collection agency. This should be done as a last resort after at least two contacts have been made over the telephone and by mail. Collection agencies will usually charge a fixed fee and then may charge a percentage for all additional revenues they collect. Other agencies may charge a single fixed fee, depending on the number of delinquent accounts and amount of money. Generally, it is more cost beneficial to choose an agency that charges by the amount collected. It is also important for the entrepreneur to make sure that the agency is reliable and professional.

Expenses/Costs (Outgoing Revenue)

Records of expenses or outgoing revenue can usually be maintained quite easily through the checking account. It is good business practice for the entrepreneur to use checks as payment for all expenses in order to maintain records for tax purposes. On those occasions where cash is used, a receipt should be requested and filed for future reference.

Cancelled checks provide the entrepreneur with proof of payment and hence should be kept in order (by number and date) and then stored. The length of time they should be kept is generally a function of Internal Revenue Service requirements. Invoices that are due in a small venture can be sorted by date due. Checks can then be made once a week to maintain a clean slate with no late payments. Entrepreneurs may find it necessary in the early stages of a new venture to do everything possible to make payments on time. This establishes good credibility with suppliers and can be helpful in assuring prompt deliveries and good service.

In addition to the above items, the entrepreneur should maintain information about employees, such as address, social security number, date of birth, date hired, date fired or released, and so on. This can also be either maintained in a software program or in a card file. Also, it may be necessary to maintain records on all assets owned by the business. If there are significant assets, they should be identified with a date of purchase. This will be helpful in determining depreciation for tax purposes.

Once a good record-keeping system is in place, the entrepreneur will find it easier to maintain controls over cash, disbursements, inventory, and assets. In general, it is advised to establish a control process for financial variables such as cash, assets, and costs, and for marketing and sales goals. These areas will be discussed below.

FINANCIAL CONTROL

The financial plan, as an inherent part of the business plan, was discussed in Chapter 7. Just as we outlined how to prepare pro forma income and cash flow statements for the first three years, the entrepreneur will need some knowledge of how to provide appropriate controls to ensure that projections and goals are met. Some financial skills are thus necessary for the entrepreneur to manage the venture during these early years. Cash flows, the income statement, and the balance sheet are all of the key financial areas that will need careful management and control. Since Chapter 7 explains how to prepare these pro forma statements, the focus in this section will be controls and management of these elements.

ACCRUAL VERSUS CASH ACCOUNTING

It is important for the entrepreneur to establish an accounting procedure that will effectively enhance his or her ability to control the finances of the new venture. The accrual method is not very desirable for the new venture. It is utilized mostly by large businesses that do not have problems with short-term cash flows.

Table 12–1 compares the accrual method of accounting with the cash method. As can be seen, in the accrual method actual cash inflows and outflows are ignored. Thus, sales may have been incurred but no payments received, or it is possible that expenses have been incurred but no disbursements made.

The cash flow method is much more consistant with cash flow. Thus, the entrepreneur has a much tighter control over cash using this approach. However, even using the cash method, the entrepreneur must be sensitive to the fact that some cash

TABLE 12–1 Accrual versus Cash Basis

	Accrual Method	*Cash Method*
Sales	Accounted for when sales are made	Not counted until cash is actually received
Expenses	Accounted for when the expense is actually incurred	Not counted until cash is actually paid out

outflows are not expense items; hence, a profitable venture may not necessarily be liquid. This is evidenced when the entrepreneur has large capital expenditures in any year for equipment or has the repayment of the principal on a loan that is either not considered an expense in its entirety in the case of the equipment (depreciated over time) or that is not an expense at all in the case of the repayment of the loan.

We can see the relationship of the accrual and cash methods by using an example. Let's suppose that in August the entrepreneur sells $10,000 worth of merchandise in a clothing store. A total of $6,000 of this amount is received in cash, and the remainder is charged by the customers. An additional $2,000 that was purchased on credit in July is received in August. In the same month, the entrepreneur purchases $8,000 worth of merchandise ($2,000 from each supplier). All of this merchandise is to be paid in 30 days (September). The entrepreneur paid $10,000 in August for merchandise purchased in July. There was also $1,000 repayment of the principal on a personal loan from a family member.

Below, we can see the distinction between the two approaches. Using the cash basis, the entrepreneur has lost $2,000 in August, while the accrual basis shows a $2,000 profit. Cash flow is further affected by the repayment of the loan principal of $2,000, which is not an expense. Thus, for cash purposes the entrepreneur has a cash outflow of $12,000 and a cash inflow of only $8,000 during August. The $4,000 that has been charged in August will be included as revenue when the cash is actually received.

	Cash Basis	*Accrual*
Basis		
August		
Revenue	$8,000	$10,000
Expenses	10,000	8,000
Net Income	($2,000) loss	$2,000

The cash basis, although it may not properly reflect net income, does give the entrepreneur a better picture of the cash position. Either method is acceptable by the IRS. Control over money that is owed to the entrepreneur (accounts receivable) can be critical if cash flow becomes a problem. To balance the problem of slow receivables, the entrepreneur may try to delay payments of debts (accounts payable), but if this becomes a chronic problem, suppliers may refuse to deliver except on a cash basis.

Managing Cash Flow

Since cash outflow may exceed cash inflows, the entrepreneur should try to have an up-to-date assessment of his or her cash position. This can be accomplished by preparing monthly cash flow statements, such as that found in Figure 12–1, and comparing the bugeted or pro forma statements with the actual results. The July budgeted amounts are taken from the pro forma cash flow statement of MPP Plastics (see Figure 7–5). The entrepreneur can indicate the actual amounts next to the budgeted amounts. This will be useful for adjusting the pro forma for remaining months, as well as for providing some indication as to where cash flow problems may exist.

Figure 12–1 shows a few potential problem areas. First, sales receipts were less than anticipated. Whether this was due to nonpayment by some customers or due to an increase in credit sales needs to be assessed. If the lower amount is due to nonpayment by customers, the entrepreneur may need to try enforcing faster payment by

FIGURE 12–1

MPP PLASTICS INC.
Statement of Cash Flow
July Year 1 (000s)

	July	
	Budgeted	*Actual*
Receipts		
Sales	$ 24.0	$ 22.0
Disbursements		
Equipment	100.0	100.0
Cost of goods	20.8	22.5
Selling expenses	1.5	2.5
Salaries	6.5	6.5
Advertising	1.5	1.5
Office supplies	0.3	0.3
Rent	2.0	2.0
Utilities	0.3	0.5
Insurance	0.8	0.8
Taxes	0.8	0.8
Loan principal and interest	2.6	2.6
Total disbursements	$ 137.0	$ 140.0
Cash flow	(113.1)	(118.0)
Beginning balance	275.0	275.0
Ending balance	161.9	157.0

sending reminder letters or making telephone calls to delinquent customers. If the lower receipts are resulting from higher credit sales, the entrepreneur may need to either consider short-term financing from a bank or try to extend the terms of payment to his or her suppliers.

Cash disbursements for some items were greater than budgeted and may indicate a need for tighter cost controls. For example, cost of goods was $22,500, which was $1,700 more than budgeted. The entrepreneur may find that suppliers increased their prices, which may require a search for alternative sources or even raising the prices of the products/services offered by the new venture. If the higher cost of goods (assuming cash basis of accounting) resulted from the purchase of more supplies, then the entrepreneur should assess the inventory costs from the income statement. It is possible that the increased cost of goods resulted from the purchase of more supplies because sales were higher than expected. However, if these additional sales resulted in more credit sales, the entrepreneur may need to plan to borrow money to meet short-term cash needs. Conclusions can be made once the credit sales and inventory costs are evaluated.

The higher selling expenses may also need to be assessed. If the additional selling expenses were incurred in order to support increased sales (even if they were credit sales), then there is no immediate concern. However, if no additional sales were generated, the entrepreneur may need to review all of these expenses and perhaps institute tighter controls.

Comparison of budgeted or expected cash flows with actual cash flows can provide the entrepreneur with an important assessment of potential immediate cash needs and indicate possible problems in the management of assets or control of costs. These items are discussed further in the next sections.

Management of Assets

Figure 12–2 illustrates the balance sheet for MPP Plastics after the first three months of operation. In the asset section of the balance sheet, are items that all need to be managed carefully by the entrepreneur in the early months of the new venture. We have already discussed the importance of cash management using cash flow projections. Other items, such as the accounts receivable, inventory, and supplies, also need to be controlled to ensure maximum cash flow and effective use of funds by the new venture.

Due to the increasing use and number of credit cards, it is likely that many consumers will consider buying on credit. Some ventures may even consider providing their own credit to avoid paying fees to a credit card company. There are some trade-offs in determining whether credit cards such as MasterCard, Visa, American Express, and Discover are acceptable or whether other credit options will be made available.

If credit cards are acceptable to the new venture, the risk for accounts receivable collections will be shifted to the credit card companies. Shifting the risk, however, costs the entrepreneur a fee of about 3 to 4 percent. More often, firms are offering

FIGURE 12–2

MPP PLASTICS INC.
Balance Sheet
First Quarter Year 1

Assets		
Current assets		
Cash	$ 13,350	
Accounts receivable (40% of $60,000 in sales the previous month)	24,000	
Merchandise inventory	12,850	
Supplies	2,100	
Total fixed assets		$ 51,300
Fixed assets	$240,000	
Equipment		
Less depreciation	9,900	
Total fixed assets		$230,100
Total assets		281,400
Liabilities and Owner's Equity		
Current liabilities		
Accounts payable (20% of 40 CGS)	$ 8,000	
Current portion of L-T debt	13,600	
Total current liabilities		$ 21,600
Long-term liabilities		
Notes payable		223,200
Total liabilities		244,800
Owner's equity		
C. Peter's capital	$ 25,000	
K. Peter's capital	25,000	
Retained earnings	(13,400)	
Total owner's equity		$ 36,600
Total liablities and owner's equity		281,400

customers lower prices for cash sales. Those opting for credit cards will pay a higher price for the privilege of using their cards, thereby offsetting the fee paid by the company.

If customers are allowed to buy on internal credit, the entrepreneur will be responsible for collecting any delinquent payments. Delays in payments can also be problematic since, as we have seen in cash flow analysis, these delays can cause negative cash flows. Any nonpayment of accounts receivable will become an expense (bad debt) on the income statement at the end of the fiscal year. In any event, the entrepreneur will need to be sensitive to major changes in accounts receivable and should always compare actual with budgeted amounts (generally estimated to be a percentage of gross sales) as a means for controlling and managing this important asset.

Inventory control is also important to the entrepreneur. This is an expensive asset and requires careful balancing of just enough inventory to meet demand for finished goods. If inventory is low and the firm cannot meet demand on time, sales could be lost. On the other hand, carrying excess inventory can be costly, either because of excessive handling and storage costs or because it becomes obsolete before being sold. Growing ventures typically tie up more cash in their inventory than in any other part of the business. Skolnik Industries, a $10 million manufacturer of steel containers for storage and disposal of hazardous materials, recently developed an inventory control system that allows them to ship products to their customers within 24 to 48 hours. This was accomplished with a very lean inventory, thanks to the installation of a computerized inventory-control system that allows the firm to maintain records of inventory on a product-by-product basis. In addition to this capability, the system allows the company to monitor gross margin return on investment, inventory turnover, percentage of orders shipped on time, length of time to fill back orders, and percentage of customer complaints to shipped orders. Software to accomplish these goals are readily available and in many cases can even be modified to meet the exact needs of the business. The reports from this system are generated every two to four weeks in normal sales periods and weekly in heavy sales periods. This system not only provides Skolnik with an early warning system, but it has freed up cash normally invested in inventory, and improved the overall profitability of the firm.[2]

From an accounting point of view, the entrepreneur will need to determine the value of inventory and how it affects the cost of goods sold (income statement). For example, assume that an entrepreneur made three purchases of inventory for manufacturing a finished product. Each purchase of inventory involved a different price. The issue will be what to use as a cost of goods sold. Generally, either a FIFO (first-in, first-out) or LIFO (last-in, first-out) system will be used. Most firms use a FIFO system since it reflects truer inventory and cost of goods sold values. However, there are good arguments for using the LIFO method in times of inflation. This issue will be discussed later in this section.

We can see below the differences between using FIFO and LIFO. We can see how inventory affects cost of goods sold. Using either FIFO or LIFO, the first 800 units sold would be valued at $1. The next 600 units sold under FIFO would result in a cost of goods sold of $640—200 units sold at $1 and 400 units sold at $1.10. Under the LIFO method, the 600 units would have a cost of goods of $650. This is determined by 500 units at $1.10 and 100 units at $1. The next 950 units sold under FIFO would have a cost of goods sold of $1,037.50, or 100 units at $1.10 and 850 units at $1.15. For LIFO, cost of goods sold would be $1,092.50, which results from 950 units costed at $1.15.

		Cost of Goods	
Inventory	*Units Sold*	*FIFO*	*LIFO*
1,000 units @ $1.00	800	$ 800.00	$ 800.00
500 units @ $1.10	600	$ 640.00	$ 650.00
1,000 units @ $1.15	950	$1,037.50	$1,092.50

[2]Jill Fraser, "Hidden cash," *Inc.*, February 1991, pp 81–2.

As stated above, there are occasions where the entrepreneur might find that the LIFO method can actually increase cash flow. A case in point was the Dacor Corporation, a manufacturer of scuba diving equipment. In 1983, the venture switched from FIFO to LIFO and incurred average annual increases in cash flow of 10 percent, until 1989, when inflation increased so much that the company showed an increase of 25 percent in its cash flow. This decision was timely for Dacor and was implemented in the following manner.

First it was necessary to decide whether to group inventory into categories or to cost each item individually. These costs must also be pinpointed at the beginning of the year or at the end or must be based on an annual average. For a very large inventory, the entrepreneur should categorize or pool the inventory. For those ventures with limited product lines, each item or product can be costed individually. Because of the wide variety of products sold, Dacor chose to categorize or pool their inventory for costing purposes. These options in stage one should be assessed carefully, because once the decision is made, it is difficult to change back without incurring penalties from the IRS.

In stage two, all inventory must be costed by searching through historical records. The amount of effort required for a venture will depend again on the breadth of the product line.

Once the inventory cost has been ascertained for each category or product, an average inventory cost must be calculated. For a new venture with only one or a few products, this would be relatively easy. For Dacor, with a wide product line, this required the assistance of an accounting firm. After all the calculations are made, management must notify the IRS (Form 970) that it is converting to the LIFO method.

The decision to convert from a FIFO to a LIFO system is not simple; thus, it is important for the entrepreneur to carefully evaluate his or her goals before making any commitment. Conversion to LIFO can typically be beneficial if the following conditions exist.[3]

1. Rising labor, materials, and other production costs are anticipated.
2. The business and inventory are growing.
3. The business has some computer-assisted inventory control method capability.
4. The business is profitable. If the start-up is losing money, there is no point in converting methods.

Regardless of the inventory costing method used, it is important for the entrepreneur to keep careful records of inventory. Perpetual inventory systems can be structured using computers or a manual system. As items are sold, inventory should be reduced. To check the inventory balance, it may be necessary to physically count inventory periodically.

Fixed assets generally involve long-term commitments and large investments for the new venture. These fixed assets, such as the equipment appearing in Figure 12–2,

[3] J. Fraser, "Taking stock," *Inc.*, November 1989, pp 161–2.

will have certain costs related to them. Equipment will require servicing and insurance and will affect utility costs. The equipment will also be depreciated over time, which will be reflected in the value of the asset over time.

If the entrepreneur cannot afford to buy equipment or fixed assets, leasing could be considered as an alternative. Leasing may be a good alternative to buying depending on the terms of the lease, the type of asset to be leased, and the usage demand on the asset. For example, leases for automobiles may contain a large down payment and possible usage or mileage fees that can make the lease much more expensive than a purchase. On the other hand, lease payments represent an expense to the venture and can be used as a tax deduction. Leases are also valuable for equipment that becomes obsolete quickly. The entrepreneur can take a lease for short periods, reducing the long-term obligation to any specific asset. As with any other make or buy decision, the entrepreneur should consider all costs associated with a lease or buy decision as well as the impact on cash flows.

Long-Term versus Short-Term Debt

To finance the assets and ensure that the new venture can meet its cash needs, it may be necessary for the entrepreneur to consider borrowing funds. Generally, to finance fixed assets the entrepreneur will assume long-term debt by borrowing from a bank. The bank's collateral for such a loan will be the fixed asset itself. The alternatives to borrowing from a bank are to borrow from a family member, friend, or, in the case of a partnership, having each partner contribute more funds to the business. A corporation may sell stock to the new venture. This decision, however, may require the entrepreneur(s) to give up some equity in the business. Whatever the option chosen, the entrepreneur should consider the pros and cons of each.

Managing Costs and Profits

Although the cash flow analysis discussed earlier in the chapter can assist the entrepreneur in assessing and controlling costs, it is also useful to compute the net income for interim periods during the year. The most effective use of the interim income statement is to establish cost standards and compare the actual with the budgeted amount for that time period. Costs are budgeted based on percentages of net sales. These percentages can then be compared with actual percentages and can be assessed over time to ascertain where tighter cost controls may be necessary.

Figure 12–3 compares actual and expected (standard) percentages on MPP Plastic's income statement for its first quarter of operation. This analysis gives the entrepreneur the opportunity to manage and control costs before it is too late. Figure 12–3 shows that cost of goods sold is higher than standard. Part of this may result from the initial small purchases of inventory, which did not provide any quantity discounts. If this is not the case, the entrepreneur should consider finding other sources or raising prices.

FIGURE 12–3

MPP PLASTICS INC.
Income Statement
First Quarter Year 1 (000s)

		Actual (%)	Standard (%)
Net sales	$150.00	100	100
Less cost of goods sold	100.00	66.7	60
Gross margin	(50.0)	32.3	40
Operating expenses			
Selling expenses	11.7	7.8	8.0
Salaries	19.8	13.2	12.0
Advertising	5.2	3.5	4.0
Office supplies	1.9	1.3	1.0
Rent	6.0	4.0	3.0
Utilities	1.3	0.9	1.0
Insurance	0.6	0.4	0.5
Taxes	3.4	2.3	2.0
Interest	3.6	2.4	2.0
Depreciation	9.9	6.6	5.0
Miscellaneous	0.3	0.2	0.2
Total operating expenses	$ 66.3	42.6	38.7
Net profit (loss)	(13.3)	(9.3)	1.3

Most of the expenses appear to be reasonably close to standard or expected percentages. The entrepreneur should assess each item to determine whether these costs can be reduced or whether it will be necessary to raise prices to ensure future positive profits. As the venture begins to evolve into the second and third years of operation, the entrepreneur should also compare current actual costs with prior incurred costs. For example, in the second year of operation the entrepreneur may find it useful to look back at the selling expenses incurred in the first year of operation. Such comparisons can be done on a month-to-month basis (i.e., January of year 1 to January of year 2), or even quarterly or yearly, depending on the volatility of the costs in this particular business.

Where expenses or costs have been much higher than budgeted, it may be necessary for the entrepreneur to carefully analyze the account to determine what the exact cause of the overrun is. For example, utilities represent a single expense account yet may include a number of specific payments for such things as heat, electricity, gas, hot water, and so on. Thus, the entrepreneur should retain a running balance of all these payments so as to ascertain the cause of an unusually large utility expense. In Figure 12–1, we see that the utility expense was $500, which was $200 over the budgeted amount, or a 67 percent increase. What caused the increase? Was any particular utility responsible for the overrun, or was it a result of higher oil costs, which affected all of the utility expenses? These questions need to be resolved before the entrepreneur accepts the results and makes any needed adjustments for the next period.

Comparisons of the actual and budgeted expenses in the income statement can be misleading for those new ventures where there are multiple products or services. For financial reporting purposes to shareholders, bankers, or other investors, the income statement would summarize expenses across all products and services. This information, although helpful to get an overview of the success of the venture, does not indicate the marketing cost for each product, the performance of particular managers in controlling costs, or the most profitable product(s). For example, selling expenses for MPP Plastics Inc. (Figure 12–3) were $11,700. These selling expenses may apply to more than one product, in which case the entrepreneur would need to ascertain the amount of selling expense for each product. He or she may be tempted to prorate the expense across each product, which would not provide a realistic picture of the relative success of each product. Thus, if MPP Plastics Inc. produced three different products, the selling expense for each might be assumed to be $3,900 per product, when the actual selling expenses could be much more or less.

Some products may require more advertising, insurance, administrative time, transportation, storage, and so on, which could be misleading if the entrepreneur chooses to allocate these expenses equally across all products. In response to this problem, it is recommended that the entrepreneur allocate expenses as effectively as possible, by product. Not only is it important to evaluate these costs across each product, but it is also important to evaluate them by region, customer, distribution channel, department, and so on.[4] Arbitrary allocation of costs should be avoided in order to get a real profit perspective of every product marketed by the new venture.

Taxes

The entrepreneur will be required to withhold Federal and State taxes for his or her employees. Each month or quarter (depending on the size of the payroll), deposits or payments will need to be made to the appropriate agency for funds withheld from wages. Generally, federal taxes, state taxes, social security, and medicare are withheld from employees salaries and are deposited later. The entrepreneur should be careful not to use these funds since, if payments are late, there will be high interest and penalties assessed. In addition to withholding taxes, the new venture may be required to pay a number of other taxes, such as state and federal unemployment taxes, a matching FICA and medicare tax, and other business taxes. These taxes will need to be part of any budget since they will affect cash flow and profits. To determine the exact amount, dates due, and procedures, the unemployment agency for the federal government and the appropriate state or the IRS can be contacted.

---

[4]R. Kaplan, "Accounting critic Robert Kaplan," *Inc.*, April 1988, pp 54–67.

The federal and state government will also require the entrepreneur to file end-of-the-year returns of the business. If the venture is incorporated, there may be state corporation taxes to be paid regardless of whether the venture earned a profit. The filing periods and tax responsibilities will vary for other types of organizations. Chapter 8 provides some insight into the tax responsibilities of a proprietorship, partnership, or corporation. As stated earlier, a tax accountant should also be considered to avoid any errors and provide advice in handling these expenses. The accountant can also assist the entrepreneur in planning or budgeting appropriate funds to meet any of these expenses.

MARKETING AND SALES CONTROLS

In addition to financial controls, the early stages of the new venture will also require control over marketing and sales. These controls usually focus on key variables that reflect performance results established in the annual marketing plan. Some of these key variables might be market share, distribution, promotion, pricing, customer satisfaction, and sales.[5]

Market Share—Market share is often difficult to measure unless the market is easily defined. However, it is often possible to ascertain the total industry sales from trade publications. The entrepreneur can then determine his or her market share by taking the venture's sales as a percentage of total industry sales. Where the venture is geographically limited, it may be possible to find out sales by state or region. If that data is not available, the best option would be to try to estimate state or regional sales by population of customers in the area as a percent of the population of the entire market. For example, a new venture marketing a liquid grill cleaner to restaurants may know the number of restaurants in the United States but not in a specific state. The entrepreneur may be able to find out from a business directory the number of restaurants in a state or may simply estimate based on the state's population.

Market share control may be important when the market is new and competitors are entering the market, and when the market is growing rapidly. Thus, if a market is growing by 20 percent but the venture's sales are only growing by 10 percent, there may be cause for concern unless there are many new competitors in the market, which would dilute the shares of individual firms. In this case, other variables, such as sales, should be considered.

Sales—Where the new venture involves sales personnel, it is important to monitor sales information such as the following:

- Average sales calls per week per salesperson.
- Average dollar sales per contact per salesperson.
- Average cost per sales call and/or per sales transaction.

---

[5]P. Kotler, *Marketing Management,* 8th ed. (Englewood Cliffs, NJ: Prentice-Hall Inc., 1994), pp 742–56.

- Number of new accounts established per salesperson.
- Number of lost accounts per salesperson.
- Number of customer contacts per salesperson.
- Total selling costs.

Each of the above items can provide important information over time regarding the activity of the sales force. Changes in any of these numbers would require action by the entrepreneur and might intercept a problem that could become more serious if left unattended.

Distribution—One of the common problems for the new venture during the growth stage is being out of stock. In this case, customers will usually buy a substitute. In addition, it upsets retailers since they may lose sales to another retailer that may have more or different alternatives. The best approach besides using an effective inventory control system is to have a toll free number for the customer to call so that merchandise can be rushed to that account.

Besides inventory issues, the entrepreneur may also need to evaluate sales by retail account and by distributor, and even the increase or decrease in numbers of actual distributors and retailers carrying the product. Monitoring this information can be helpful in determining trade promotions and strategy regarding sales contacts.

Promotion—Many entrepreneurs do not monitor the effectiveness of a promotion effort. It is important to know why a customer buys. Is it because of the ad that appeared in the newspaper? advertising on television or radio? a coupon? a point of purchase display? the special low price? a yellow pages ad? This information can be collected in many different ways, such as having sales personnel ask customers where they heard about the product or service. In the case of a print ad or mailing, it is possible to include a coupon that might provide some savings to the customer. The number of coupons redeemed would thus be a useful measure of the effectiveness of the particular ad. Understanding what promotion strategies are effective is important in controlling marketing costs and enhancing the sales volume of the new venture.

Customer satisfaction—The use of marketing research described in Chapter 6 can be extremely important in ascertaining the satisfaction levels of existing customers. Information can also be obtained from a customer 800 number, from telephone complaints, or complaint letters. All complaints should be monitored and followed up on to insure that the customer is satisfied. Some firms have also found that the use of a suggestion box can be helpful in monitoring problems as well as identifying new ideas for the business.

Effective marketing and sales controls in the early stages of the operation of a new venture can help the entrepreneur to identify problems before they become too serious and to take corrective actions where appropriate to insure that marketing goals are met. Often, the entrepreneur incurs more serious marketing and sales problems when the business is in a rapid growth stage. Because of the strain on management and resources during the growth stage, it is more difficult to be aware of all of the key variables in the day-to-day operations. If everyone in the organization manages and controls their areas of responsibility, it is possible to avoid any serious problems.

RAPID GROWTH AND MANAGEMENT CONTROLS

As we saw above, when the new venture begins to reach a rapid growth phase, the entrepreneur needs to be sensitive to some of the resultant management problems. Usually, rapid growth is seen as a positive sign of success, and any attempt to establish important financial or management controls that were discussed above are abandoned for the sake of doing more and more business. However, rapid growth can quickly change the status of a new venture from profitable to bankrupt if the entrepreneur is not sensitive to certain growth issues. What are these issues? How can growth quickly turn a business into a failure? How should growth be managed? These are a few of the important questions that will be addressed in this section.[6]

First let's look at some of the growth problems that can affect the management of the new venture. These are summarized in Table 12–2. Before rapid growth occurs, the new venture is usually operating with a small staff and a limited budget. Hence, less time is spent in evaluating management, personnel planning, and cost controls because cash seems to be plentiful.

Rapid growth can also dilute the leadership abilities of the entrepreneur. Shared vision and purpose becomes difficult, as the entrepreneur has to devote so much time to the short-term growth demands on his or her time. As a result, communication begins to diminish, and more compartmentalization of goals develops. Training and development of personnel is overlooked, and eventually the entrepreneur and all of the employees begin to feel pressure and stress. The entrepreneur's unwillingness to delegate responsibility can lead to even greater delays in decision making and less emphasis on the long-term survival of the business.

The entrepreneur can avoid these problems with preparation and sensitivity about handling rapid growth when it occurs. If the entrepreneur finds that these issues cannot be internally resolved, an outside consultant should be hired to provide an objective view of how to manage the venture during this stage of the venture life cycle.

It may also be necessary to put a limit on the venture's growth. This may sound like blasphemy to a new venture, but it is important to try to stay within the capabilities of the firm. Standing back and reflecting on the goals and objectives of the venture may be an important part of the control of growth. The future financial well-being of the venture may necessitate a more controlled growth rate. The limits to the growth of any venture will depend on the availability of a market, capital, and management talent. Too rapid growth can stretch these limits and lead to serious financial problems and possible bankruptcy.

PROMOTING THE NEW VENTURE

In the early stages of a new venture, the entrepreneur should focus his or her effort on trying to develop an awareness of the products or services offered. Thus, the initial emphasis of a new venture should be to get some publicity in local media.

---

[6] M. Henricks, "The bigger the better," *Entrepreneur,* December 1990, pp 131–37.

TABLE 12–2 Problems During Rapid Growth

- It can cover up weak management, poor planning, or wasted resources.
- It dilutes effective leadership.
- It causes the venture to stray from its goals and objectives.
- It leads to communication barriers between departments and individuals.
- Training and employee development are given little attention.
- It can lead to stress and burnout.
- Delegation is avoided and control is maintained by only the founders, creating bottlenecks in management decision making.
- Quality control is not maintained.

Publicity is free advertising provided by a trade magazine, newspaper, magazine, radio, or TV program that finds it of public interest to do a story on a new venture. Local media such as newspapers, radio, or cable TV encourage entrepreneurs to participate in their programs or stories. The entrepreneur can increase the opportunity for getting this exposure by preparing a news release and sending it to as many possible media sources as he or she can.

In order to issue a news release it is important to follow these steps:[7]

1. Identify the news release as such when mailing it to the editor.
2. Begin the release with the service or product to be marketed.
3. List the features and benefits of the product or service to the customer.
4. Make the written news release about 100 to 150 words. This is especially important for print media.
5. Include a high-quality, glossy photograph of the product or of the service being performed.

For radio or TV, the entrepreneur should identify programs that may encourage local entrepreneurs to participate. A telephone call and follow up with written information enhance the opportunity to appear on any of these programs.

Free publicity can only introduce the company and its services in a general format. Advertising, however, can be focused to inform specific potential customers of the service—what they will receive, why they should buy it, where they can buy it, and how much it may cost. If the advertising program is to be effectively developed, it may be necessary to hire an advertising agency.

Selecting An Advertising Agency

An advertising agency can provide many promotional services to the entrepreneur. The advertising agency itself may even cater to new ventures or specialize in the specific market the entrepreneur is trying to target. Traditionally, the advertising

[7]R. D. Hisrich and M. P. Peters, *Marketing Decisions for New and Mature Products,* 2nd ed. (New York: Macmillan Publishing Company, 1991), pp 392–94.

agency has been perceived as an independent business organization composed of creative and business people who develop, prepare, and place advertising in media for its customers. The agency can even provide the entrepreneur with assistance in marketing research or in some of the strategy needed to market the product or service.

Before selecting an agency, it might be useful to check with friends or agencies such as the SBA to obtain recommendations. Local chambers of commerce or trade associations can also be of some assistance. In any event, regardless of what agency is considered, it is important to determine whether the agency can fulfill all of the needs of the new venture.

Table 12–3 provides a checklist of items that the entrepreneur may consider in evaluating an agency. It is especially important to meet the agency staff and to talk with some of its clients to be sure it is the right choice. All of the items in the checklist could be evaluated subjectively or by assigning some scale value (i.e., 1 to 7) in order to identify the best agency for the new venture.

The advertising agency should support the marketing program and assist the entrepreneur in getting the product or service effectively launched. The costs or budget for advertising may be small initially, but certain agencies are willing to make their investment because of the potential growth of the venture and hence the advertising budget.

TABLE 12–3 Checklist for Selecting an Advertising Agency

Item	*Value*
1. Location of agency	______
2. Organizational structure of agency	______
3. Public relations department services	______
4. Research department and facilities	______
5. Creativity of agency's staff	______
6. Education and professional qualifications of agency's top management	______
7. Media department's qualifications and experience	______
8. Qualifications and experience of account executives (if identifiable)	______
9. Interest or enthusiasm shown toward firm and new product	______
10. Copywriters' qualifications and experience	______
11. Art director's qualifications and experience	______
12. Recommendations by other clients	______
13. Experience and success with new products	______
14. Ability of agency to work with the company's advertising department	______
15. Extra services provided	______
16. Accounting and billing procedures	______
17. Overall formal presentation	______

HIRING EXPERTS

Most of this chapter involves areas such as financial and marketing analysis that may require expertise that the entrepreneur is unable to contribute. In those instances where the entrepreneur does not have the expertise, it is recommended that outside experts be hired. Trying to save money by performing these tasks alone could end up costing the entrepreneur more than the experts' fees.

There are usually accountants, or financial experts, marketing consultants, and advertising agencies who cater to new ventures and small businesses. These firms can usually be identified from local business contacts, the SBA, trade associations, or even from the yellow pages.

SUMMARY

This chapter deals with some of the key managerial areas of expertise that will be required to keep the business going in the early months and growth phases of the start-up. These areas, such as financial analysis, marketing and sales analysis, and advertising, may necessitate the hiring of outside experts if the entrepreneur cannot fulfill these managerial needs.

In the area of financial analysis, the entrepreneur must be concerned with managing cash, assets, debt, and profits. Cash flows must be monitored on a regular basis (usually monthly). Budgeted and actual cash flows should be evaluated when they vary significantly.

Assets can be managed by using the balance sheet. Besides cash, the entrepreneur will need to control accounts receivable and inventory. If accounts receivable are late or delinquent, the entrepreneur will need to tighten collection procedures. Increases in accounts receivable due to increased credit sales may require short-term financing of receivables to meet short-term cash needs.

Expenses need to be controlled in two ways. First it is important to understand that expenses should be allocated by product, region, department, and so on. Otherwise, the entrepreneur may inaccurately reflect the profitability of any product or service. Accuracy can improve the ability of the entrepreneur to understand which products or services are a problem and perhaps even to explain which department, region, or manager is responsible.

Inventory also must be controlled. Too much inventory can be costly to the venture; too little can result in fewer sales because delivery dates cannot be met. FIFO or LIFO accounting may be used to cost inventory (cost of goods). FIFO will generally provide a more realistic value of cost of goods sold unless the cost of inventory is increasing by an abnormal rate or the economy is in a cycle of inflation.

Fixed assets such as equipment may require long-term debt. Long-term debt can be obtained from bank loans; loans from friends or relatives; or, in the case of a corporation, the sale of stock. The sale of stock may require the entrepreneur to give up some equity in the business and hence must be weighed carefully.

Comparing actual costs from the income statement with standard percentages (percentages related to net sales) will be useful in managing the costs and profits of the new venture. Higher costs than anticipated should be carefully evaluated so they do not surprise the entrepreneur later.

Marketing and sales controls require careful monitoring of key market information as well as an effective reporting system by sales personnel. Key variables such as market share, sales, distribution, promotion, and customer satisfaction require monitoring to insure that marketing plan goals and objectives are being achieved. If problems are identified, corrective action can be taken before the problem becomes too serious.

Rapid growth brings a number of unique problems to the new venture. These problems usually result in weak planning, poor communication, no training or employee development, poor quality control, and a general lack of leadership. These problems can be minimized by the entrepreneur through preparedness and sensitivity about handling rapid growth when it occurs.

One of the most important problems an entrepreneur faces during the early stages of start-up is creating awareness of the venture and its products and services. Finding creative ways to take advantage of free advertising or publicity can save the entrepreneur significant amounts of money. In addition to publicity, the entrepreneur may need to consider some advertising. Generally, the decision to advertise will require the hiring of an agency unless the entrepreneur has expertise in this area.

QUESTIONS FOR DISCUSSION

1. Contrast and compare the accrural and cash basis of accounting.
2. What effect would each of the following have on a) cash flow, b) profits?
   - Repayment of $5,000 personal loan.
   - Purchased $8,000 worth of inventory payable in 30 days.
   - Purchase of equipment for $15,000.
   - Increase salaries by $4,000.
3. Why is it important to manage assets such as accounts receivable and inventory?
4. What is the effect on cash flow of FIFO and LIFO when the cost of goods is a) increasing, b) decreasing?
5. Identify important marketing control variables for a new venture that markets baby toys. Discuss how this venture might control each of these variables.
6. What is the significance of publicity to a new venture? What procedure would you recommend to take advantage of any publicity opportunities?
7. What are some of the major problems created by rapid growth of sales in the new venture?

KEY TERMS

accrual method of accounting
cash method of accounting
FIFO
LIFO
marketing and sales controls
publicity

SELECTED READINGS

Burck, C. (April 5, 1993). The real world of the entrepreneur. *Fortune,* pp 62–81.

This article reflects a several-month study conducted across the United States by the magazine, talking to over 100 new ventures. The focus of the study was to identify some of the effective strategies used by these entrepreneurs to successfully grow their businesses. Issues such as specialization, preparing employees for constant change during growth, keeping good employees, and keeping management down to earth are a few of the topics discussed.

Fraser, J. (January 1990). Plans to grow by. *Inc.,* pp 111–113.

Financial planning doesn't always involve just charts, tables, financial statements, and reams of paper. It should also include careful planning of growth that involves asking oneself some very important questions. In this article, an example provides an interesting backdrop to some critical issues that are likely to affect the efforts to successfully grow a new venture. The basic premise is that unplanned growth can be dangerous because of its strain on cash, credit, customer service, and product quality.

Jones, J., Cohen, M. B., & Coppola, V. (1988). *The Coopers & Lybrand Guide to Growing Your Business.* New York: John Wiley & Sons.

Entrepreneurs have the need for guidance during the early years of operation of a venture, especially in a changing economic environment. This book covers a wide range of topics that are important to the entrepreneur during this period. Topics include strategies for growth, asset management, accounting systems and internal controls, tax strategies, computer systems, and employee benefit plans.

Kyd, C. (December 1988). Weighing your debt load. *Inc.,* pp 151–152.

Many entrepreneurs lack the understanding of whether they are making or losing money on the cash they borrowed for growing the new venture. In this article, the author presents a number of formulas that can help the entrepreneur determine his or her return on debt. Formulas are explained with a simple example to help clarify their relevance.

Lewis, H. G. (1977). *How to Handle Your Own Public Relations.* Chicago, IL: Nelson Hall.

This is an interesting book that explains how to handle your own publicity. It is a concise how-to book that offers a step-by-step explanation of public relations. In addition there are a number of examples of businesses and P. R. projects.

Potts, A. J. (Fall 1993). Cash flow—the oil that keeps the small and family business organization running smoothly. *Journal of Small Business Strategy,* pp 69–80.

The emphasis in this paper is on the purposes and uses of the statement of cash flows. Two different methods of calculating cash flows are presented. Explanations are provided as to how to interpret cash flow, considering different outcomes of the venture.

Stodder, G. S. (April 1991). Ready or not. *Entrepreneur,* pp 87–91.

How does an entrepreneur handle the surprise of success? A number of examples are discussed in this article. Skateboard manufacturer Richard Novak (N.H.S. Inc.), ice cream gurus Jerry Greenfield and Ben Cohen (Ben & Jerry's), retailer Mark Bagelman (The Office Club), and management consultants Jim and Michelle Foy (Dynamic Alternatives) provide a wide range of examples of problems they incurred and how they were handled.

Viscione, J. Small company budgets: targets are key. (1992). In W. A. Sahlman and H. H. Stevenson. *The Entrepreneurial Venture.* Boston, MA: Harvard Business School Publications, pp 348–58.

As a new venture evolves into one that is prosperous and growing, it is important for the entrepreneur to develop a good budgeting process. Using a case model, the author illustrates what can happen if deviations from the budget occur. Setting realistic targets in the budget provide the venture with important controls during the early years.

CHAPTER

13

Managing Growth and Expansion

Chapter Objectives

1. To explain the need and methods for growth and expansion.
2. To discuss the need, benefits, and principles of time management.
3. To identify the factors affecting the growth of the venture.
4. To explain the aspects of negotiation.
5. To discuss the types of joint ventures and their uses.
6. To discuss the concepts of acquisitions and mergers.
7. To discuss the appropriateness and uses of leveraged buyouts.

Steve Jobs

Steve Jobs, the adopted son of Paul and Carla Jobs, grew up near San Francisco, California. While in junior high school, his family moved to Los Gatos, south of San Francisco, in the heart of what would be known as "Silicon Valley." From an early age, Steve showed an interest in figuring out how things worked and by high school was obsessed with electronics. He went to weekly talks given for teenagers by local Hewlett-Packard engineers. When he needed parts for a class electronics project, Steve decided to call Bill Hewlett directly. Impressed with Job's single-mindedness, the CEO gave him the necessary parts and helped arrange summer employment.

Steve's single-mindedness did not extend to academic matters, however. After graduating from high school, Steven spent one semester at Reed College in Oregon and then two years hanging out—"wandering through the labyrinths of post-adolescent mysticism and post-Woodstock culture," as he later described it. Out of money and no longer supported by his family, he returned home to find a job. Answering an ad that read "Have fun and make money," Steve became the 40th employee of a new company called Atari.

Although designing video games was "fun," and the atmosphere of Atari was relaxed, Steve couldn't fit in. Since he was an idea man, not an engineer, the other engineers thought he was brash and arrogant as he championed his visions. Eventually, Steve worked only at night to avoid them and started spending time with the Homekrew Computer Club, of which his former high school friend, Steve Wozniak, was a member. Wozniak was a calculator chip engineer at Hewlett-Packard (HP) who in his spare time had developed a video game called Breakout. Accepting a challenge from Atari's president to design a game using fewer than 50 computer chips, the two Steves modified Breakout to claim the $700 prize. Atari got what became one of its best-selling games, and the world got its first taste of the duo that would drive Apple Computer.

Wozniak had been tinkering with computer designs since his high school days. With the help of ideas obtained at the Homekrew Computer Club, he was able to design and build the first easy-to-use personal computer. HP responded to Wozniak's project by saying they were not interested in a hobby project that connected to a home TV. While Wozniak accepted their verdict, Jobs saw the potential and did not want to give away the schematics at a club meeting when they could be selling a finished product!

With Homekrew members and a local computer store showing interest, Jobs sold his Volkswagen microbus and Wozniak his HP calculator to raise $1,300 to open a primitive production line. Apple I was born. Building computers in Jobs' parents' garage out of parts hustled on credit, they sold about 200 of the primitive computers in 1976. "I didn't even know what '30 days net' meant," Jobs later admitted.

As back orders began to pile up, Jobs discovered his true calling as a wheeler-dealer, a dynamo, and an energy source. He repeatedly visited the area's top public relations specialist, Regis McKenna, until McKenna broke down and accepted Apple as a client. In attempting to raise capital, Jobs approached Don Valentine, a well-known investor in new firms; Valentine dismissed the sandals-and-jeans-clad Jobs as a "renegade from the human race." However, A. C. Markkula, a former marketing manager for Intel, pledged his expertise and $250,000 of his own money for an equal partnership. Through Mr. Markkula, Apple was able to establish a line of credit with the Bank of America and obtain financing from two venture-capital firms.

When it became apparent that the Apple I was really only a gadget, Wozniak added a typewriter-style keyboard, video terminal, disk drive, and power supply, creating the Apple II. But it was Jobs who conceptualized what the machine should be able to do and how it should look. He insisted on designing an attractive housing and writing thorough and concise operating manuals. The Apple II was an immediate success upon its introduction in 1977, essentially creating its own market.

Apple dominated the business market by default, with sales growing to over $200 million by 1980. Then two catastrophic blows occurred: the Apple III was a failure when released (14,000 had to be recalled because of serious mechanical problems), and IBM introduced its PC. Almost overnight, the IBM PC became the industry standard, and by 1984 it had almost twice the market share of Apple. The personal computer market once defined by Apple was changing without a challenge.

During the rapid growth years of the late 70s, Apple had come to depend more and more on the marketing and management skills of experts hired from other industries. Feeling that the Apple II and the IBM PC were boring and technologically clumsy machines, Jobs assembled a group of Apple employees to work on a project sometimes called his "back-to-the-garage fantasy." As chairman of the board of directors as well as project head, he got few arguments from his co-workers. The MacIntosh was introduced in late 1983 as a "computer for the rest of us." Targeted for the business market, the Mac had several drawbacks as an office machine; it was not easy to use; the internal software was complicated and slow; it could not be customized; little software was written for it; and it was not IBM-compatible. The Mac sold well to individuals but not to business customers.

Jobs' obsession with following his own vision of what a personal computer should be created problems within the company. He refused to allow Apple II to be marketed as a business computer, and insulted managers working for other divisions. Finally, in 1985, Jobs was asked to resign from the company he helped found.

Although his career at Apple was over, his computer dreams were not dead, as is indicated in an interview shortly after leaving Apple: "What I'm best at doing is finding a group of talented people and making things with them. You have to set double goals, but you still have to have a very lofty vision. You need a well-articulated vision that people can follow."

Jobs pursued a new dream partially funded from the sale of $21 million in Apple Computer stock. According to him, "Passion is what drives an entrepreneur," and his passion is a great product. "You have to go hide away with people that really understand the technology but also really care about the customers, and dream up the next breakthrough."

Jobs' second company, NeXT, Inc., is based on what they think is the next breakthrough in the computer industry: an aesthetically pleasing machine with the power of a workstation in a package the size of a PC. The target market of this new machine changed from colleges to businesses due to various factors occurring during the development of the NeXT machine. One was the price. By the time the machine was introduced, it was doubtful that colleges could afford it. Jobs now has more than just a new machine, he has a second chance to prove he can manage an established corporation.

As was the case with Steve Jobs and the turbulent growth of Apple Computer, it is frequently difficult for an entrepreneur to both manage and expand the venture created. While some entrepreneurs are able to bridge the gap and successfully grow and manage an expanding company, others cannot. An entrepreneur needs to assess his or her abilities in the management area, identifying when it is necessary to turn the reins over to someone else in order for the venture to expand, grow, and in some cases even survive. As a new venture grows, there can be a need for more and more administration. Also, at times, a new infusion of the entrepreneurial spirit that formed the venture is needed. This infusion, called *intrapreneurship* (entrepreneurship in an existing organization), is the focus of Chapter 17. Sometimes an entrepreneur forgets the basic axiom in every business: The only constant is change. An entrepreneur who understands this axiom will effectively manage change by continually adapting organizational culture, structure, procedures, strategic direction, and products. This requires, above all, effective monitoring of the environment by tracking the tasks and needs of the marketplace. But how does an entrepreneur accomplish this and effectively manage an expanding company? Are there any management methods or procedures needed for growth and expansion? This chapter looks at some of the issues in growing and managing an expanding company: time management, control, and negotiations; some of the actual techniques for expansion: joint ventures, mergers, acquisitions, and leveraged buyouts; and an important aspect of growth and expansion: valuing the company.

NEW VENTURE CREATION AND GROWTH

In the past, many have felt that large corporations had the most significant impact on economic development through job creation and new product introduction. This conventional wisdom has been challenged by research that has indicated that the small business/entrepreneurial sector is the main component of any economic unit, whether that be an area of a country or the entire country itself. Of the 20 million small firms in the United States, 25 percent are farms, 25 percent are part-time, 25 percent are self-run with no employees, and only 25 percent have employees. Revenues for these firms have a similarly skewed distribution: 12 million firms have revenues less than $25,000, 6 million firms have revenues between $25,000 to $100,000, 1.2 million have revenues from $100,000 to $1 million, and .8 million have revenues $1 million and above. Of these 20 million firms, 65,000 generate 93 percent of all net new jobs, while over 1 million new ventures are started each year. Most of these start-ups are small, part-time, or temporary businesses.

Many of these small start-up firms will also remain small due to the type of firm and/or the entrepreneur. Some entrepreneurs do not want to grow their venture, choosing instead to pursue other interests, spend more time with family, or develop other business activities.

The growth of a new entrepreneurial venture is a function of both market and management factors. The pervasive market factors are the nature and size of the target market and the window of opportunity. The window of opportunity reflects the existing competitive conditions, the degree of technological advancement, and the amount of protection in the form of patents, copyrights, and trade secrets.

The management factors affecting growth involve the ability to manage growth and the psychological propensity for growth. A useful system for looking at growth appears in Figure 13–1, where firms are classified high or low in terms of their degree of propensity and degree of ability for growth. Statistics for the United States indicate that most new entrepreneurial ventures are life-style or marginal small firms. Few firms have the ability or propensity to achieve solid growth, and several factors affect the entrepreneur's management of those that do. The first, and perhaps most important, factor is changing the job of the CEO. In the start-up phase, the entrepreneur/CEO needs to be involved in almost all areas of the venture's operation from production, marketing, finance, accounts receivable, sales, and receiving. As the venture grows, the entrepreneur's participation and primary decision making in all these areas is no longer possible. He or she must delegate decision making to others in the venture and spend more time in planning the venture's strategy and overall direction. The entrepreneur takes on more of the activities of an administrator or manager. Yet, in this new role he or she should still approach the strategic decisions of the company from the entrepreneurial, not the administrative, domain, as was discussed in Chapter 1. This can be a difficult task, as some people have problems relinquishing control over something they have created and have invested a significant amount of time and energy. Nevertheless, for a new venture to grow, the entrepreneur must delegate authority and responsibility throughout, allowing and encouraging decision making and creativity at the lowest possible decision level.

FIGURE 13–1 New Venture Classification System Based on Growth

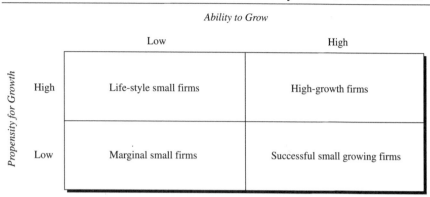

Propensity for Growth	*Ability to Grow*: Low	*Ability to Grow*: High
High	Life-style small firms	High-growth firms
Low	Marginal small firms	Successful small growing firms

This change in the job of the CEO affects the second growth management factor: change in the entrepreneur's behavioral style. Some entrepreneurs feel at ease in their new roles and are excited about stimulating entrepreneurial behavior in others. Others only reluctantly accept this new orientation. Some do not accept it at all. Companies have an easier time growing if the entrepreneur readily embraces this new behavioral pattern and encourages entrepreneurship, or more appropriately, intrapreneurship, to permeate the entire venture.

A third factor affecting growth is the difficulty of managing a more complex company. A typical start-up organization is very flat, with all the strategic decisions concentrated, short-run, and episodic in nature, as was discussed in Chapter 1. With only scarce resources available, these ventures rent necessary equipment as much as possible and make financing decisions on a sequential basis. As the small entrepreneurial venture grows, a bureaucratic, hierarchical organizational structure tends to develop. Such a structure has a developed and detailed reporting system, requiring that certain rules and procedures be followed. This bureaucratic structure can stifle the entrepreneurial spirit that helped to grow the venture.

The final factor affecting growth is the age of both the entrepreneur and the venture. As previously discussed, most entrepreneurs start their first significant venture in their 30s, and there is only so much energy available to start and grow new ventures. Some entrepreneurs find that a venture ceases to be the fun experience it once was after it has been in existence for some years. Instead of an entrepreneurial philosophy, more of a management philosophy is needed to direct and grow the venture. At this stage, many entrepreneurs leave and start new ventures offering new entrepreneurial excitement.

Several strategies are possible to successfully grow a new venture.[1] One is for the entrepreneur to immediately see the new venture as a large entity. From the beginning of the venture, the entrepreneur makes decisions that promote the eventual

[1]These and other success strategies are discussed in D. C. Hambrick & L. M. Crozier, "Stumblers and stars in the management of rapid growth," *Journal of Business Venturing,* Winter 1985, pp 31–46.

emergence of a large company. There is no small-firm philosophy guiding any management decisions. Another success strategy is for the entrepreneur to hire and train individuals in anticipation of growth. Care must be taken in implementing this strategy to avoid having costly resources without the needed sales and revenues to support them. A third strategy for successful growth is to avoid establishing a bureaucratic structure. Keeping decision making at the lowest possible level and operating units small and versatile helps to preserve the entrepreneurial spirit. This strategy is probably the easiest to implement, as it requires only minimal change from the original operation of the venture.

A final success strategy is to give employees a stake in the future performance of the company. The founding entrepreneur should realize that some of his or her motivations for starting the new venture may also exist in some employees. Giving these employees an ownership position in the company can motivate them to work even harder for the success of the company. This increased effort and initiative can help grow the venture successfully while creating a new intrapreneurial spirit.

TIME MANAGEMENT

One of the biggest problems in growing and expanding the venture is encapsulated in the phrase, "If I only had more time." While this is a common problem for all busy people, it is particularly acute for the entrepreneur in starting and growing the venture. It seems that no one has enough time. Time is the entrepreneur's most precious yet most limited resource. It is a unique quantity—an entrepreneur cannot store it, rent it, hire it, or buy it. With its supply being inelastic, it is totally perishable and irreplaceable. Everything requires it, and it passes at the same rate for everyone. While important throughout the life of the venture, time is particularly critical at start-up and during growth and expansion of the venture. No matter what an entrepreneur does, today's ration of time is 24 hours, and yesterday's time is already history.

Entrepreneurs typically spend their time (as many do) with a prodigality that would shame even the laziest individual. Few entrepreneurs use time effectively, and none of them ever reach perfection. Entrepreneurs can always make better use of their time, and the more they strive to do so, the more it will enrich their venture as well as their personal lives.

Most individuals can be three or four times more productive without ever increasing the number of working hours, which reflects the basic principle that it is more important to do the right things than to do things right. This principle implies that the key to effective time management is prioritizing the items that should be accomplished in any particular time period. Instead, an entrepreneur typically establishes priorities that reflect his or her personality and values.

How does one get more out of the time spent? How does one effectively manage time? **Time management** involves investing time to determine what you want out of life, including what you want out of the venture created. This implies that entrepreneurs have focused values about their ventures, work, family, social activities, possessions, and selves.

Why does the problem of time management exist for the entrepreneur? It is basically due to a lack of information and a lack of motivation. The entrepreneur must want to manage his or her time effectively and then spend the time necessary to acquire the information necessary to accomplish this. Effective time management starts with an understanding of some benefits that will result.

Benefits of Time Management

The entrepreneur reaps numerous benefits from effectively managing his or her time, some of which are listed in Table 13–1. One of these—increased productivity—reflects the fact that there is always enough time to accomplish the most important things. Through a conscious effort and increased focus, the entrepreneur can determine what is most important to the success and growth of the venture and focus on these rather than on less important or more enjoyable aspects; an entrepreneur must learn to focus on the majors, not the minors.

This overt action will lead to the second benefit: increased job satisfaction. Getting more important things done and being more successful in growing and developing the venture will give more job satisfaction to the entrepreneur.

There will also be an improvement in the *esprit de corps* of the venture as the entrepreneur and others in the company experiences less time pressure, better results, and more job satisfaction. While the total time the entrepreneur spends with other individuals in the company may in fact decrease, the time spent will be of better quality, allowing him or her to improve interrelations. This also makes more time available for the entrepreneur to spend with family and friends.

A fourth benefit is that the entrepreneur will experience less anxiety and tension. Worry, guilt, and other emotions tend to reduce mental effectiveness and efficiency, making decisions less effective. Effective time management reduces concerns and anxieties, allowing better and faster decisions to be made.

TABLE 13–1 Time Management for the Entrepreneur

Typical Payoffs from Time Management
Increased productivity
More job satisfaction
Improved interpersonal relations
Reduced time anxiety and tension
Better health
Basic Principles of Time Management
The Principle of Desire
The Principle of Effectiveness
The Principle of Analysis
The Principle of Teamwork
The Principle of Prioritized Planning
The Principle of Reanalysis

All of these benefits culminate in a final one for the entrepreneur: better health. Large amounts of energy and persistence are needed for the growth as well as for the start of a venture, as was discussed in Chapter 1. High energy levels and long working hours require good health, and poor management of time often leads to mental and physical fatigue, poor eating habits, and curtailment of exercise. If there is one thing an entrepreneur needs to help the venture grow, it is good health. And good health is a by-product of good time management.

Basic Principles of Time Management

How does an entrepreneur develop good time management? By first recognizing that he or she is a time waster. This insight leads the entrepreneur to value time and to change any personal attitudes and habits as needed. This is embodied in the Principle of Desire (see Table 13–1). Like effective dieting, effective time management depends on willpower and self-discipline. It requires that the entrepreneur have a real desire to optimize his or her time.

Second, the entrepreneur should adhere to the Principle of Effectiveness; that is, he or she should automatically focus on the most important issues, even when under pressure. Whenever possible, an entrepreneur should try to complete each task in a single session. This requires that enough time is set aside to accomplish the task. While quality is of course important, perfectionism is not and often leads only to procrastination. The entrepreneur must not take excessive time trying to make a small improvement in one area when time could be better spent in another.

To manage time effectively, the entrepreneur needs to know how his or her time is presently being spent. Following the Principle of Analysis will help accomplish this. Using a time sheet with 15-minute intervals, the entrepreneur should record and analyze the time spent during the past two weeks. This analysis will reveal some areas of wasted time and provide the basis for prioritizing the tasks to be accomplished. It is particularly important for the entrepreneur to develop methods for handling recurrent situations. Checklists should be developed and kept handy. Handouts on the company and its operation should be prepared for visitors and the press. Standardized forms and procedures should be developed for all recurrent events and operations.

The essence of time management is embodied in an important principle that most entrepreneurs had to employ in starting the venture: the Principle of Teamwork. During the time analysis, one thing will become very apparent to the entrepreneur: the small amount of time that is totally under his or her control. The entrepreneur needs to help members of the management team become more sensitive to the time management concept when dealing with other individuals in the company. Each member of the management team needs to employ effective time management in dealing with other team members.

The Principle of Prioritized Planning includes elements of all the previously mentioned principles of effective time management. Each day, an entrepreneur needs to list the things to be accomplished and indicate their degree of importance. One method may be a scale, such as 1 being most important, 2 somewhat important, and 3 moderately important. By indicating on a 3 × 5 card the most important items to be accomplished that day, the entrepreneur can focus on getting to the ones of lesser importance as time permits. This prioritizing, planning, and focus on the key issues is fundamental to time management, as it allows each individual to accomplish the most important tasks. Also, some entrepreneurs are most efficient in the morning, some during the afternoon, and some at night. The most efficient period of the day should be used to address the most important issues.

As with any implemented procedure, the entrepreneur should periodically review the objectives and the degree to which these have been achieved. This is the Principle of Reanalysis. Tasks should be delegated whenever possible. The clerical staff and close assistants should be well trained and encouraged to take initiative. The clerical staff should sort out all correspondence and draft routine letters for the entrepreneur's signature. The office system should be well organized with a daily diary, a card index, reminder list, operation board, and an efficient pending file. All incoming calls should be filtered and a time set for making and receiving calls except for those most critical. All meetings should be analyzed to see if they are being run effectively. If not, the person who runs the meetings should be trained in how to conduct them. Finally, any committee in the venture should be carefully scrutinized in terms of its results. Committees tend to tie up personnel, slow down decisions, and have the habit of multiplying themselves beyond their need. Through all these effects, the entrepreneur can become a timesaver, not a timeserver. This efficient use of time enables the entrepreneur to expand and grow the venture properly, increasing productivity and lessening encroachment of the venture on his or her private life.

NEGOTIATION

Growing and expanding a new enterprise requires the ability to negotiate. Even though it is important, negotiation is usually not a skill well developed by the entrepreneur. As one women entrepreneur stated, "A woman entrepreneur should develop her negotiating skills as quickly as possible. It is so important in starting and particularly in expanding a business. Women tend to be weaker in negotiating skills than men. This may reflect the level of issues typically negotiated at home versus in a business situation. These skills can be learned and then must be practiced."

What is negotiation? **Negotiation** is the process by which parties attempt to resolve a conflict by agreement. While a resolution is not always possible, the process of negotiation identifies the critical issues in the disagreement and is therefore central to business dealings. In learning and developing negotiation skills, it is important to understand the underlying motivations, the two types of negotiation (**distributive** and **integrative bargaining**), the tactics involved in each type, and the skills required.[2]

---

[2] A thorough discussion of negotiation can be found in R. E. Walton & R. B. McKersie, *A Behavioral Theory of Labor Negotiations* (New York: McGraw-Hill, 1965).

Underlying Motivation

The underlying motivation of negotiation often involves one party attempting to get another to do something the first desires. At times, this second party will not act unless obtaining something of interest in return. This motive for a return must be understood in the negotiation process, whether the negotiation is cooperative or competitive.

Another underlying motive in negotiation is habit. Many behavioral patterns can be attributed to a subconscious drive to continue to do things in the same way. Some individuals, for example, feel the need to negotiate even though they are happy with the present terms of the arrangement. This drive to negotiate just for negotiation's sake can make the process more important to the individual than the actual outcome. Some individuals develop a reputation for such behavior. The entrepreneur must be careful to avoid such negotiations as well as to avoid his or her own predictability in a negotiation process. Periodic illogical behavior ensures that predictability of behavior will not occur.

Cooperative Negotiation—Integrative Bargaining

Integrative bargaining involves **cooperative negotiation** between the negotiating parties. In this situation, the entrepreneur is willing to let the other side achieve its desired outcome while maintaining a commitment to his or her own goals. In one sense, integrative bargaining is joint problem solving based on the concept of rational decision making. A model of this process depicts the negotiation flow moving from establishing objectives, to establishing criteria, to analyzing the cause-and-effect relationships involved, to developing and evaluating alternatives, to selecting an alternative and an action plan (see Figure 13–2). To be complete, this process requires the outcomes be measured once implementation begins. The effectiveness of the decisions made through this process depends on the technical adequacy of information and the commitment of the parties involved to implement the decision reached.

The implementation of this **rational decision model** in an integrative bargaining situation involves several steps. First, the problem must be clearly identified. All parties in the negotiation must exchange views on the problem without blaming the other parties or demanding a specific outcome. Each party involved must be genuinely interested in solving the problem and understanding the underlying concerns of the others involved. Meetings need to be scheduled frequently, with each person involved having the authority to convene a meeting whenever necessary. Advance notice of each meeting must be given to allow all participants to prepare for the meeting. Each meeting should have an agenda, with a majority of the concerns having a high probability of resolution. Each agenda item should be stated to provide for open discussion and integrative bargaining to reach a mutually agreeable solution. This requires that each agenda item be stated in terms of the problem, not in terms of a proposed solution.

FIGURE 13–2 The "Rational" Model for Decision Making

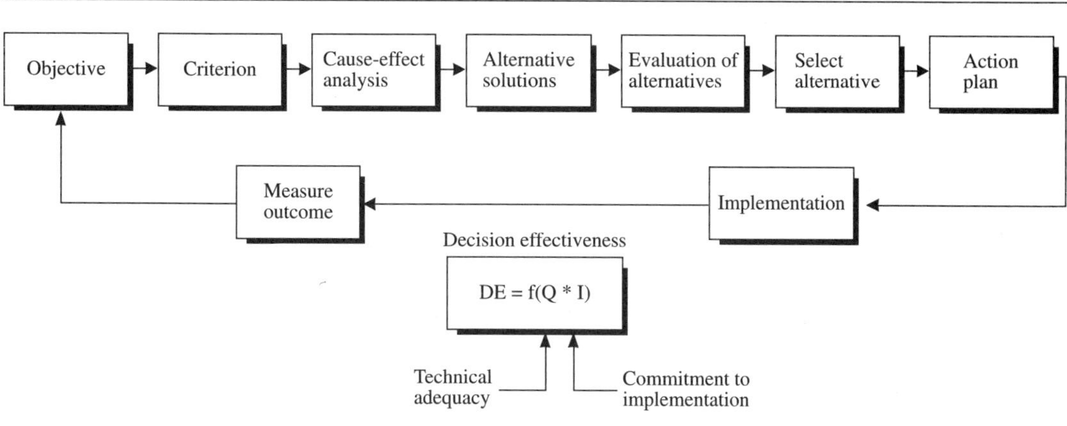

Source: C. Jackson, Working paper, University of Tulsa, October 1987.

The second step in effective integrative bargaining is searching for alternative solutions. In so doing, the entrepreneur and other parties involved should remember that it is just as important to uncover areas of agreement as to realize areas of divergence. This requires that concrete terms be used and appropriate ground rules be established. It is much easier to find a solution to a problem stated in specific terms than in general terms. Similarly, it is much easier to develop alternatives when ground rules encourage trust and respect. Through frequent preliminary discussions, all parties can air tentative solutions and ideas; these can then be refined before being formally considered. This informal, exploratory discussion of a possible solution reduces the likelihood of immediate rejection. Since a solution to one problem may affect solutions to others, all parties involved must maintain flexibility and not emphasize the order and sequencing of the items discussed. The techniques and frameworks used should differ depending on the specific problem at hand. Integrative bargaining occurs more quickly when the parties involved sense a greater likelihood of success. This requires that easier items be dealt with first, with any difficult items laid aside temporarily if an impasse is reached. On the other hand, negotiators should not follow a rigid formula in developing this atmosphere for success. Creative solutions do not come from following a systematic procedure since the creative process is unpredictable and spontaneous, as was discussed in Chapter 4.

Finally, as indicated in the model of rational decision making, the best alternative solution should be selected. This requires the establishment of an open, honest relationship that allows each party to indicate when something is wrong and to accurately report preferences and range of latitude in each problem area. This is the area most susceptible to distortion and further problems. Inadvertent distortion can be most easily avoided by using the most specific data available. Specificity not only helps eliminate selective perception but also builds an atmosphere of trust between participants. Also, it should be remembered that a problem divided into parts is more easily solved than an entire problem that is not broken down.

Competitive Negotiation—Distributive Bargaining

Even more important for the successful growth and expansion of a business is the entrepreneur's effectiveness in distributive bargaining. Distributive bargaining is essential to the successful start-up of a company as well as its expansion through joint ventures, mergers, acquisitions, and leveraged buyouts. In contrast to integrative bargaining, distributive bargaining does not allow the other party to achieve his or her goals. There is a fixed pie to be divided, which means that the larger the opponent's share, the smaller the entrepreneur's. Since there is no trust between the parties involved, a solution can be reached only through a series of modified positions of compromise and concession. In this competitive adversarial bargaining arena, the agenda items and their positioning become issues as each party tries to discover the other's goals, values, and perceptions. Some problems involve more conflicts of interest than others. The amount of conflict usually revolves around the differing economic objectives and attitudes of the parties involved. When the entrepreneur and the other party have conflicting economic objectives, distributive bargaining can be successful only if each party compromises his or her objectives to some extent. Directly competing claims on a fixed, limited economic resource (such as the amount of the 100 percent equity in the venture) require concessions in allocating the shares. Since each party brings to the table different attitudes shaped by prevailing social, economic, organizational, and technological forces, this disparity is frequently more difficult to overcome than differences in economic objectives.

The key to successful distributive bargaining is for the entrepreneur to discover the goals and perceptions of the other party through direct and/or indirect methods. Indirect methods include discussing the person with anyone who has had previous contact, such as your own employees, the party's employees, or outside individuals; carefully reviewing all previous written and verbal correspondence with the party; and walking around the party's business to get a feel of its vitality and direction. The entrepreneur should employ each of these indirect methods whenever possible to get a feel for the other party's goals and drives so that a strategy can be planned before the actual negotiation commences.

The entrepreneur should also use more direct methods to obtain some insight into the other party. Whenever possible, he or she should meet informally with representatives of the other company, probing them to determine their levels of preparation. Particular emphasis should be directed to the weakest member of the team. Frequently, insight can be obtained from this individual's responses to relaxed, almost innocent questions.

Several other direct methods employed during the negotiation process can also reveal significant clues. One of these is for the entrepreneur to exaggerate his or her level of impatience. This often forces the other party to prematurely reveal the amount of bargaining room left. Another method employs the principle of "non-sequiturization." In other words, at a crucial moment in the negotiation, the entrepreneur should take an entirely different posture than what has been employed throughout. This can be accomplished by making a sudden shift in manners, argument, or demands. For example, this shift can take the form of an attack if a laid-back approach had been adopted previously.

Whether direct or indirect methods are used, an entrepreneur skillful at negotiation attempts to determine the **settlement range** of the other party. The settlement range is the area of values in which a mutually agreeable solution can be reached. This area is between the resistance points of the parties involved and can be either positive or negative, as indicated in the example in Figure 13–3. In the positive settlement range, the resistance points of the two parties are compatible. In this situation,

FIGURE 13–3 Settlement Ranges in Distributive Bargaining

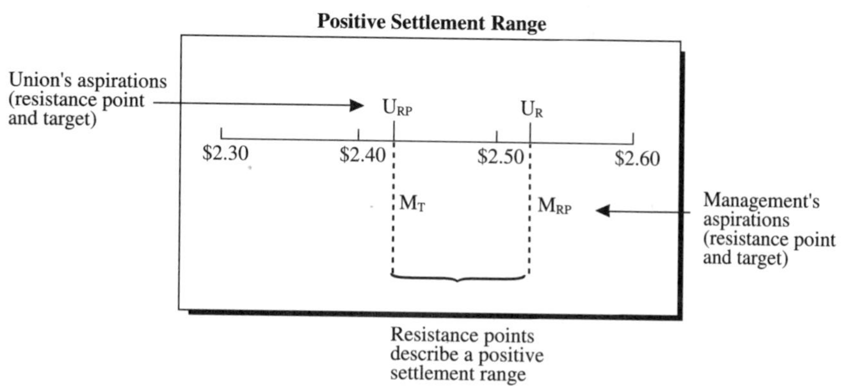

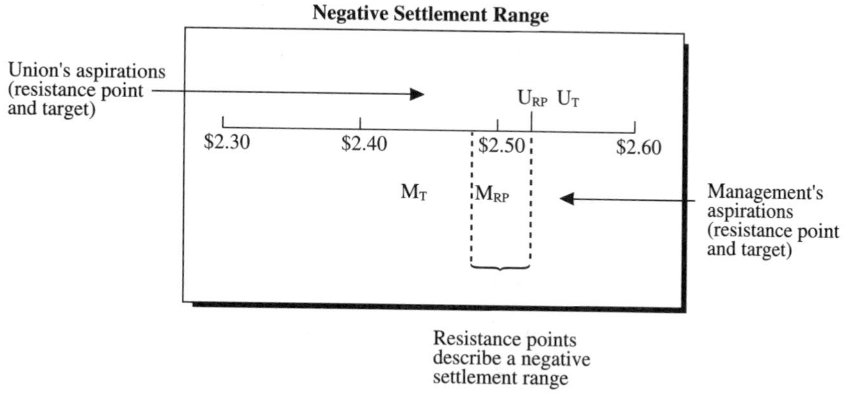

Source: R. E. Walton & R. B. McKerse, *A Behavior Theory of Labor Negotiations* (New York: McGraw-Hill, 1965), p 43.

both parties would rather be involved in the deal than have a work stoppage, as may be the case in a union settlement (Figure 13–3). The opposite is true when a negative settlement range exists. In this situation, the resistance points are not compatible. It will be difficult to reach an agreement that would be even minimally acceptable to the two parties.

The key to good negotiations lies in your ability to manipulate the other party's perception of a likely settlement point so that this point results in a more favorable position for you. This can be accomplished through several strategies. One calls for the entrepreneur to indicate higher initial demands than he or she actually desires. These high demands, along with a consistent image, can often move the other party to a different, more favorable, position. Similar results can often be achieved by the entrepreneur indicating an overly strong commitment to a particular position. This position needs to be clearly stated, usually through public statements; implied needs should also be clearly stated, again usually through public statements that also have implied threats of stopping the negotiations if this position is not achieved. Another strategy involves focusing on the other party by either minimizing their opportunity to develop a fixed position or by enabling the party to easily revise a previously committed position. The former strategy involves avoiding written documentation and media coverage and not being available for communication between formal negotiation sessions. The second tactic—making it easy for the other party to revise a previous position—can be accomplished by establishing that conditions have changed, making the present situation an entirely new one. This change in circumstances can be augmented by appealing to the public good or presenting new data.

Perhaps the best strategy for the entrepreneur is to bargain in good faith—indicating a willingness to bargain and be flexible. This will mean that the entrepreneur will make concessions throughout the negotiation process where warranted, particularly when his or her position is further away from a possible solution than the other party's. Any concessions should be linked to the other party's change or at least to an understanding that certain issues are critical in securing an agreement. This strategy often leads to obtaining a settlement point that is acceptable to both parties, completing the negotiation faster than by using other strategies.

Negotiation Approach

While many strategies can be used in negotiations, it is important that the entrepreneur select one approach. One negotiation approach that is easy to implement has eight steps: prepare, discuss, signal, propose, respond, bargain, close, and agree.[3]

Probably the most critical and yet the most often overlooked step in the process is preparation. With all the time pressures, an entrepreneur frequently fails to set aside the necessary time to define what has to be done and to develop objectives, the

[3]This process is adapted from G. Kennedy, J. Benson, & J. McMillan, *Managing Negotiations* (London: Business Books Ltd., 1980) and is discussed in R. D. Hisrich & C. G. Brush, *The Woman Entrepreneur* (Lexington, MA: Lexington Books, 1986), pp 150–55.

settlement range, and alternative strategies for accomplishing these objectives before the negotiation commences. The objectives need to be prioritized and back-off positions developed.

The second step is the initial meeting. Here, as well as throughout the negotiation process, it is critical that the entrepreneur listen carefully to the other party in order to determine its direction and goals.

Signaling is one aspect of negotiation that tests the other party's willingness to move toward a solution. Through signaling, the entrepreneur can discern real objections and assess the other party's willingness to change his or her original position. This is accomplished through using a phrase such as "I could never agree to that the way it is stated." The entrepreneur must carefully develop the art of signaling and of reading the other party's signals.

Once an agreement to move forward to a closure is reached, a proposition must be laid out for discussion. The proposition serves as the basis for developing the final agreement.

The negotiation approach involves responses to the other party's suggestions. These responses are particularly important once a proposition has been put forth. While a response should take into account the interest and limitations of the other party, it does not necessarily contain concessions. Any concessions granted should reflect the priorities and points of inflexibility of the other party.

Besides response and signaling, another difficult aspect of the negotiation approach is bargaining. In bargaining, the entrepreneur gives up something for something. At first, to help develop this ability, an entrepreneur can state all bargaining items on a conditional basis: "If I . . . then you . . ."

Every negotiation needs a closure. Closing the agreement frequently is based on a concession or on a summary. A summary is used when a multitude of issues have been discussed and resolved.

The ideal closing ends in a mutually satisfactory agreement—the ultimate goal of negotiation. Reaching an agreement is, after all, the objective of most negotiations. Any verbal agreement reached should be detailed in writing as specifically as possible.

Through negotiation, an entrepreneur can expand the original venture. The actual expansion and growth of the venture can take the form of a joint venture, merger, acquisition, or leveraged buyouts.

JOINT VENTURES

With the increase in business risks, hyper-competition, and failures, joint ventures have occurred with increased regularity, involving a wide variety of players.[4] This increase should be no great surprise since joint ventures have been used for

[4]For some different perspectives on joint ventures, see: R. D. Hisrich, "Joint Ventures: research base and use in international methods," in *The State of the Art of Entrepreneurship* (Boston: PWS-Kent Publishing Co.), pp 520–579; J. McConnell & T. J. Nantell, "Corporate combinations and common stock returns: the case of joint ventures," *Journal of Finance* 40 (June 1985), pp 519–36; "Corporate Odd Couples," *Business Week,* July 21, 1986, pp 100–14: R. Thompson, "Joint ventures with industry may solve shortage of education funds," *Modern Healthcare,* July 15, 1985, p 224.

a long time by entrepreneurial firms to expand into new businesses and to enter new markets. The frequency of this activity has increased significantly in newly industrialized areas and in international markets.

What is a joint venture? A **joint venture** is a separate entity involving two or more active participants as partners. Sometimes called strategic alliances, they involve a wide variety of partners, including universities, not-for-profit organizations, businesses, and the public sector.[5] Joint ventures have occurred between such rivals as General Motors and Toyota or General Electric and Westinghouse. They have occurred between U.S. and foreign concerns in order to penetrate an international market. As will be discussed in Chapter 18, a joint venture is a good way for an entrepreneur to enter an international market.

Historical Perspective

Joint ventures were one of the earliest ways of transacting business. Used by ancient merchants of Babylonia, Phoenicia, and Egypt, they served as a vehicle to conduct commercial trading operations. The use of joint ventures by merchants continued and was particularly prevalent in the 15th and 16th centuries; Great Britain used joint ventures to obtain the resources of distant areas, specifically in India and North America.

In the United States, joint ventures were first used for large-scale projects in mining and the railroads in the 1800s. This type of venture continued in the 1900s in shipping, oil exploration, and gold. Probably the best-known and largest joint venture in this period was the formation of ARAMCO by four oil companies to develop crude oil reserves in the Middle East. By 1959, about 345 joint ventures were being operated in the United States by some of the largest U.S. corporations.[6] Frequently, these domestic joint ventures are vertical arrangements made between competitors. A joint venture of this type (such as the sharing of a primary aluminum reduction plant as a supply facility) allowed the large economies of scale needed for cost-effective plant operation. From 1960 to 1968, the Federal Trade Commission reported that over 520 domestic joint ventures were formed, primarily in the manufacturing sector, by over 1,131 U.S. firms.[7] In the 1980s, there was an increase in the formation of joint ventures of various types, particularly on an international basis. For example, in 1983 alone, the number of joint ventures in communications systems and services exceeded the total number of previous joint ventures in that industrial sector.

The increase in the number of joint ventures particularly by smaller entrepreneurial firms has been significant in the 1990s. Regardless of the type, entrepreneurs are using joint ventures more and more frequently to grow and expand their ventures.

---

[5]For a discussion of some different types of joint ventures, see R. M. Cyert, "Establishing university-industry joint ventures," *Research Management* 28 (January–February 1985), pp 27–28; F. K. Berlew, "The joint venturer—a way into foreign markets," *Harvard Business Review*, July–August 1984, pp 48–49 and 54; and Kathryn Rudie Harrigan, *Strategies for Joint Ventures* (Lexington, MA: Lexington Books, 1985).

[6]S. E. Boyle, "The joint subsidiary: an economic appraisal," *Antitrust Bulletin* 5 (1960), pp 303–18.

[7]S. E. Boyle, "An estimate of the number and size distribution of domestic joint subsidiaries," *Antitrust Law and Economics Review* 1 (1968), pp 81–82.

Types of Joint Ventures

While there are many different types of joint venture arrangements, the most common is still between two or more private-sector companies. For example, Boeing/Mitsubishi/Fuji/Kawasaki entered into a joint venture for the production of small aircraft in order to share technology and cut costs. Agreements in order to cut costs were made between Ford and Mesasurex in the area of factory automation and General Motors and Toyota in automobiles. Other private-sector joint ventures have had different objectives, such as entering new markets (Corning and Ciba-Geigy and Kodak and Cetus), entering foreign markets (AT&T and Olivetti), and raising capital and expanding markets (U.S. Steel and Phong Iron and Steel).

New types of joint ventures are also occurring. A current trend is to form a joint venture for cooperative research. Probably the best known of these is the Microelectronics and Computer Technology Corporation (MCC), formed in 1983 in Austin, Texas. Supported by 13 major U.S. corporations, this for-profit corporation does long-range research with a yearly budget of over $75 million. Individual researchers and scientists are loaned to MCC for up to four years and then return to their competing companies to apply the results of their research activities. MCC retains title to all the resulting knowledge and patents, making them available for license by the companies participating in the program.

A different type of joint venture for research development is the Semi-Conductor Research Corporation, located in Triangle Park, North Carolina. A not-for-profit research organization, it began with the participation of 11 U.S. chip manufacturers and computer companies. The number has grown to over 35 since its inception in 1981. The goal of the corporation is to sponsor basic research and train professional scientists and engineers to be future industry leaders. The major drawback to the organization is that it has no formal mechanism for the transfer of people or technology, so the results usually end up as published research available to the general public.

Industry-university agreements for the purpose of doing research are another type of joint venture agreement that have seen increasing activity. Two major problems have kept these types of joint ventures from proliferating even faster. First, a profit corporation has the objective to obtain tangible results, such as a patent, from its research investment, and many universities also want to share in the possible financial returns from the patent. The second problem revolves around proprietary results versus knowledge dissemination. While the corporation wants the competitive edge offered by retaining all proprietary data found in the research effort, university researchers want to make the knowledge available through research papers. In spite of these problems, numerous industry-university teams have been established. In one joint venture agreement in robotics, for example, Westinghouse retains the patent rights, while Carnegie-Mellon receives a percentage of any license royalties. The university also has the right to publish the research results as long as it withholds from publication any critical information that might adversely affect the patent.

The joint venture arrangement between Celanese Corporation and Yale University for researching the composition and synthesis of enzymes took a somewhat different form. Although the agreement specifies the type of research to be accomplished, the partners share the costs. While Celanese assumes the expense of any needed supplies and equipment for the research, as well as the salaries of the post-doctoral researchers, Yale pays the salaries of the professors involved. The research results can be published only after a 45-day waiting period.

A more coordinated joint research effort was established for the study of microbiology by W. R. Grace Company and Massachusetts Institute of Technology (MIT). Under this joint venture agreement, researchers at MIT propose research projects for funding to a committee consisting of four managers from W. R. Grace and four MIT professors. While W. R. Grace established the research fund covering all the expenses, MIT, at its sole discretion, can use 20 percent of it to do research in microbiology. MIT can publish the results of the research after a review by W. R. Grace managers for proprietary information. In addition, MIT retains the patents, while W. R. Grace gets a royalty-free license on the research results. MIT, however, can license to other companies for a royalty fee.

As these examples illustrate, joint ventures between universities and corporations take on a variety of forms, depending on the parties involved and the subject of the research. These and new types of research arrangements should continue to proliferate, particularly as long as government support for university research remains at a minimum level.

International joint ventures, which will be further discussed in Chapter 18, are rapidly increasing in number due to their relative advantages. First, both companies can share in the earnings and growth, even when the venture involves sales and earnings beyond the initial technology or product. Second, the joint venture can have a low cash requirement if the knowledge or patents are capitalized as a contribution to the venture. Third, the joint venture provides ready access to new international markets that otherwise may not be easily attained. Finally, since talent and financing come from all the parties involved, an international joint venture causes less drain on a company's managerial and financial resources than a wholly owned subsidiary.

There are several drawbacks in establishing an international joint venture. First, the business objectives of the joint venture partners can be quite different, which can cause problems in the direction and growth of the new entity. In addition, cultural differences in each company can create managerial difficulties in the new joint venture. Finally, U.S. government policy sometimes can have a negative impact on the direction and operation of the international joint venture.

In spite of these problems, the benefits usually outweigh the drawbacks, as evidenced in the frequency rate of establishing international joint ventures. For example, an international joint venture between General Motors and Fanuc Ltd., a Japanese firm, was established to develop the 20,000 robots needed by GM to automate its plants. In this 50–50 joint venture partnership, GM supplied the initial design, and Fanuc supplied the engineering and technology to develop and produce the car-painting robots.

Cy/Ro is an international joint venture between Cyamid (United States) and Rochm (Germany) in the area of acrylic plastics. Cyamid supplied the distribution network and plant space for the new acrylic plastic technology of Rochm. Even though Cy/Ro has a high degree of operational autonomy, a high turnover rate has occurred, which is particularly a problem for German executives.

Another type of international joint venture was established between Dow Chemical (United States) and Asaki Chemicals (Japan) to develop and market chemicals on an international basis. While Asaki provided the raw materials and was a sole distributor, Dow provided the technology and obtained distribution in the Japanese market. The arrangement eventually dissolved because of the concerns of the Japanese government and the fundamental difference in motives between the two partners: Dow was primarily concerned with the profits of the joint venture; whereas, Asaki was primarily concerned with having a purchaser for its basic petrochemicals.

Even though there are many instances of international joint ventures dissolving, others are still being established to take advantage of production, technology, and marketing advantages of the partners involved. In any international arrangement, care should be taken to ensure that the primary objectives of the two partners are compatible and that the overall arrangement has the approval of the governments involved.

Factors in Joint Venture Success

Clearly, not all joint ventures succeed. An entrepreneur needs to assess this method of growth carefully before using it. In order to use joint venture effectively, an entrepreneur needs to understand the factors that help ensure success as well as the problems involved. One of the most critical factors for success is the accurate assessment of the parties involved and how best to manage the new entity in light of the ensuing relationships. The joint venture will be more effective if the managers involved can work well together. Without this chemistry, the joint venture has a high probability of encountering great difficulties or even failure.

A second factor for success involves the symmetry between the partners. This symmetry goes beyond chemistry to objectives and resource capabilities. When one partner feels that he or she is bringing more to the table, or one wants profits and the other product outlet (as was the case in the Asaki-Dow international joint venture), problems arise. For a joint venture to be successful, the managers in each parent company, as well as those in the new entity, must concur on the objectives of the joint venture and the level of resources that will be provided. Good relationships must be nurtured between the managers in the joint venture and those in each parent company.

A third factor for success is that the expectations of the results of the joint venture must be reasonable. Far too often, at least one of the partners feels a joint venture will be the cure-all for other corporate problems. Expectations of a joint venture must be realistic.

The final factor for the successful establishment of a joint venture is also essential for the successful start-up of any new business entity: timing. With environments constantly changing, industrial conditions being modified, and markets evolving, a particular joint venture could be a success one year and a failure the next. Intense competition provides a hostile environment and increases the risks of establishing a joint venture. Some environments are just not conducive to success. The entrepreneur must determine whether the joint venture will offer opportunities for growth or will penalize the company, for example by preventing it from entering certain markets.

A joint venture is not a panacea for expanding the entrepreneurial venture. Rather, it should be considered as one of many options for supplementing the resources of the firm and responding more quickly to competitive challenges and market opportunities. The effective use of joint ventures as a strategy for growth and expansion requires the entrepreneur to carefully appraise the situation and the potential partner(s).

Concerns in Establishing Joint Ventures

Since a joint venture allows the entrepreneur to expand the business through sharing equity, control, and risks with a partner, there is always concern that the new entity will not be able to achieve its strategic objective. The entrepreneur must evaluate whether or not to cooperate in a particular situation and, if so, what type of partner should be involved. The resource contribution of each partner is clearly a concern; perhaps even more problematical is how these resources and other contributions should be valued. The degree of autonomy for the new entity must also be established. Other strategic alternatives to the joint venture, such as acquisitions, mergers, and leveraged buyouts, should also be considered.

ACQUISITIONS

Another way the entrepreneur can expand and grow the venture is by acquiring an existing business. Acquisitions can provide the entrepreneur with an excellent way to grow a business and enter new markets or new product areas. For example, one entrepreneur acquired a chemical manufacturing company after becoming familiar with its problems and operations as a supplier of the entrepreneur's company. An **acquisition** is the purchase of a company or a part of it in such a way that the acquired company is completely absorbed and no longer exists as a business entity. An acquisition can take many forms, depending on such factors as the goals and position of the parties involved in the transaction, the amount of money involved, and the type of company.

While one of the key issues in buying a business is agreeing on a price, successful acquisition of a business actually involves much, much more. In fact, often the structure of the deal can be more important to the parties involved and the resultant success of the transaction than the actual price. One radio station was successful after being acquired by a company primarily because the previous owner loaned the money and took no principal payment (only interest) on the loan until the third year of operation.

From a strategic viewpoint, a prime concern of the entrepreneurial firm is to maintain the focus of the new venture as a whole. Whether the acquisition will become the core of the new business or represents a needed capability, such as a distribution outlet, sales force, or production facility, the entrepreneur must ensure that it fits into the overall direction and structure of the strategic plan of the present venture.

Evaluating a Firm

There are three widely used valuation approaches—asset, cash flow, and earnings—that the entrepreneur can use to determine the worth (or value) of an acquisition candidate. Some important factors helpful in the evaluation process that measure profitability, activity, and liquidity are indicated in Table 13–2. In addition, a glossary of terms used in financial analysis and evaluation is found at the end of this chapter. When using the asset valuation method, the entrepreneur is valuing the underlying worth of the business based on its assets. Four methods can be used to obtain this valuation: book value, adjusted book value, liquidation value, or replacement value. While the easiest method for assessing the value of the firm is book value, the figure obtained should only be a starting point since it reflects the accounting practices of the company. A better refinement of this figure is adjusted book value, where the stated book value is adjusted to reflect the actual market value. Another method of valuing the assets of a potential acquisition company is to determine the amount that could be realized if the assets of the company were sold or liquidated and the proceeds used to settle all liabilities. This liquidation value reflects the valuation at a specific point in time. If the company continues operations successfully, the calculated value is low compared to the contribution of the assets. If the company encounters difficulties, a subsequent liquidation would probably yield significantly less than the amount calculated. The final method for valuing assets is the replacement value—the current cost of replacing the tangible assets of the business.

Another way of evaluating a firm, which is particularly relevant for an entrepreneur who is attempting to appraise a return on investment and a return on time, is to calculate the prospective cash flow from the business. There are several different cash flows that are important to the entrepreneur: positive cash flow, negative cash flow, and terminal value. Positive cash flow is cash received from the operation of

TABLE 13–2 Key Factors in Evaluating a Firm

- One-person management
- Poor corporate communications
- Few management tools being used
- Insufficient financial controls
- Highly leveraged—thinly capitalized
- Variations and poorly prepared financial statements
- Sales growth with no increase in bottom line
- Dated and poorly managed inventory
- Aging accounts receivable
- No change in products or customers

the business including interest and salary, business-related expenses absorbed by the company, debt repayment, and dividends. Negative cash flow, signifying the company is losing money, can be a benefit to the entrepreneur and the investor in certain tax situations. Frequently the entrepreneur is not in a position to realize these benefits because of a low income; however, the tax benefits can provide substantial value to investors or those entrepreneurs in higher tax brackets. The final cash flow value—the terminal value—is a source of cash when the entrepreneur sells the business.

The last frequently used evaluation method is earnings valuation. This method capitalizes earnings of a company by multiplying the earnings by the appropriate factor (the price earnings multiple). There are two critical issues in this evaluation procedure: the earnings and the multiple. The question of earnings involves determining the appropriate earnings period as well as the type of earnings. The earnings period can be either historical earnings, future earnings under the present management and ownership, or future earnings under new management and ownership. The type of earnings used during the selected period can be earnings before interest and taxes (EBIT), operating income, profit before tax, or profit after tax. The EBIT is used more frequently, as it indicates the earning power and value of the basic business without the effects of financing.

After the time period and type of earnings have been established, the final step in earnings evaluation is to select the appropriate price earnings multiple. If the primary return from the investment will be in the form of stock sale at some future time, it is appropriate to select a price earnings multiple of a publicly traded stock similar to the company being evaluated in terms of the product, the nature of industry, the anticipated earnings, growth, and likely stage of the stock market. This can be quite difficult, but usually a value or at least a range of values can be ascertained.

Whether the valuation of assets, cash flow, or earnings is used, the valuation of a business, though difficult, is vitally important in determining the feasibility of its acquisition. There are also some other important considerations in the acquisition decision process: synergy, a specific valuation method, structuring the deal, legal considerations, and the plan for managing the acquired entity.

Synergy

"The whole is greater than the sum of the parts" is a concept that applies to the integration of an acquisition into the entrepreneur's venture. The synergy reflected in this content should occur in both the business concept—the acquisition functioning as a vehicle to move toward overall goals—and the financial performance. The acquisition should positively impact the bottom line, affecting long-term gains and future growth. Lack of synergy is one of the most frequent causes of an acquisition failing to meet the anticipated goals of the entrepreneur. An acquisition should be carefully valuated and planned with specific attention given to its integration.

An entrepreneur can no longer determine whether a company is a good candidate for acquisition by merely evaluating the company's financial statements and asking a few questions. Evaluation in today's changing environment focuses not only on management and market potential but also on the company's upside potential, downside risks, and vulnerability to changes in markets and technology. Some of the warning signs the entrepreneur should consider in evaluating an acquisition candidate include poor corporate communications, few management tools being used, poorly prepared financial statements, and a low number of new products and new markets being entered (see Table 13–2). These signs indicate the degree to which the firm is ready for the future and the amount of work that will be needed following the acquisition.

The evaluation process begins with financial analysis—analyzing the profit and loss figures, operating statements, and balance sheets for the years of the company's operation, concentrating on the more recent years. Past operating results, particularly those occurring in the last three years, indicate the potential for future performance of the company. Ratios and operating figures indicate that the company is healthy and has been well managed. Areas of weakness, such as too much leverage, too little financial control, dated and slow turning inventory, poor credit ratings and bad debts should also be carefully evaluated. A firm's financial record does not tell the entire story. Sometimes a firm with an unimpressive financial record is on the verge of a technological breakthrough that will send its sales and profits skyrocketing. Conversely, a company with a good financial record may have problems in the future due to its somewhat obsolete products in its highly competitive or shrinking markets.

In evaluating a firm's product lines, the entrepreneur should study the past, present, and future. The strengths and weaknesses of the firm's past products should be investigated, particularly in terms of design features, quality, reliability, unique differential advantage, and proprietary position. The life cycle and present market share of each of the firm's present products should also be evaluated. Is this market share diversified or concentrated among a small number of customers? How do past, present, and potential customers regard the firm's products? What is happening with the market in respect to competition, prices, and margins? The entrepreneur must carefully consider the compatibility of the firm's product lines from a marketing, engineering, and manufacturing perspective. The future of the firm's product lines must be assessed as to their rate of market growth or contraction. What are the developing trends in the number of competitors, degree of competition, number of new products being introduced, and the rate of technology? Is there any vulnerability to business cycle changes?

One method for evaluating the product line is to plot sales and margins for each product over time. Known as S or life-cycle curves, they indicate the life expectancy of the product and any developing gaps. For example, even though a firm is highly profitable today, it may not have provided for the future. The S-curve analysis could reveal that all products of this firm are at or near their period of peak profitability.

The future of the firm's products and market position is affected by its research and development. The entrepreneur should carefully probe the nature and depth of the candidate firm's research and development and engineering capability, assessing their strengths and weaknesses. How can this important yet difficult area be evaluated? Conventional wisdom says to look at the total amount of dollars spent on research and development; however, because of the inefficiencies that usually occur in these expenditures, this only indicates the amount invested and does not present a very accurate picture. The evaluation should instead determine whether the R&D expenditures and programs are directed by the firm's long-range plans and whether the firm has allocated enough money to accomplish the tasks outlined. The output and success of the new products developed should be compared with the expenditures. What is the quantity and quality of the patents produced? How much has R&D contributed to lowered break-even points by improving materials or methods? How much has R&D contributed to increased sales and profits?

Similarly, the entrepreneur should carefully evaluate the firm's entire marketing program and capabilities. While all areas of marketing should be assessed, particular care should be taken in evaluating the quality and capability of the established distribution system, sales force, and manufacturers' representatives. One entrepreneur acquired a firm primarily because of the quality of its sales force. Another acquired a firm to obtain its established distribution system, which allowed access to new markets. The entrepreneur can gain insight into the market orientation and sensitivity of the firm by looking at its marketing research efforts. Does the firm have facts about customer satisfaction, trends in the market, and the state of the art of the technology of the industry? Is this and other information forwarded to the needed managers in a timely manner? Is there a marketing information system in place?

The nature of the manufacturing process—the facilities and skills available—is also important in deciding whether to acquire a particular firm. Are the facilities obsolete? Are they flexible, and can they produce output at a quality and a price that will compete over the next three years? The increasing pace of technology requires a more careful appraisal of the manufacturing operation than ever before.

Finally, the entrepreneur should rate the management and key personnel of the candidate firm. The individuals who have contributed positively to past success in sales and profits of the firm should be identified. Will they stay once the acquisition occurs? Have they established good objectives and then implemented plans to successfully reach these objectives? By comparing previous plans, the entrepreneur can determine whether results have been directed or randomly achieved. Insight into management capability and the firm's morale can be gained through an examination of the turnover in executive ranks. Is it large or concentrated in a given area or type of individual? Has the firm implemented any executive development programs? Is there a strong management team in place?

Specific Valuation Method

In this specific valuation method, the simplifying assumptions are that (1) there is only one investor involved, (2) only one round of investment is being contemplated, (3) there is only one class of stock, and (4) the candidate company is in the second stage of development (i.e., manufacturing and shipping in commercial quantities). The valuation of the company has produced the following conclusions:

- The current revenue level (R) is $2 million.
- The expected annual rate of growth of revenue (r) is 50%.
- The expected amount of required capital (K) is $2.5 million.
- The expected number of years between now and the liquidity date (n), also called the "holding period," is five years.
- The expected after-tax profit margin at the time of liquidity (a) is 11 percent.
- The expected price/earnings ratio as of the liquidity date (P) is 15.
- The appropriate discount rate (d) for a VC investment of this stage, risk, and liquidity is 40 percent.

This information can be used to work backward from the future point of liquidity to the present value of the company, using the following sequence of steps:

Step 1—Compound the current revenue level of $2 million forward at an annual rate of 50 percent for five years to yield a revenue level at time of liquidity of $15.19 million.

Step 2—Multiply the future revenue level of $15.19 million times the expected after-tax profit margin at time of liquidity of 11 percent to produce an expected earnings level of $1.67 million as of the date of liquidity.

Step 3—Multiply the estimated earnings level of $1.67 million at time of liquidity times the expected price/earnings ratio of 15 to yield a future market valuation of the company of $25.06 million.

Step 4—To obtain a present value factor, raise the quantity 1.40 (that is, 1+ the discount rate of 40 percent) to the power of 5 (the holding period of five years), to yield a present value factor of 5.378.

Step 5—Divide the future company value of $25.06 by the present value factor of 5.378 to produce a present value of the company of $4.66 million.

Step 6—To price the deal, divide the required capital of $2.5 million by the present company value of $4.66 million to obtain a minimum ownership of 53.7 percent for the investment required.

This valuation method is represented by the following equation.

$$\text{Present value of company} = V = \frac{R\,(1 + r)^n\,a\,P}{\text{Present value factor}}$$

$$V = \frac{R\,(1 + r)^n\,a\,P}{(1 + d)^n}$$

In this simplified example, the $2 million current level of revenue is considered to grow at a constant rate of 50 percent per year. In reality, revenue growth is usually very irregular from year to year.

One problem in using this simplified method is how to treat future tax savings from net operating loss carryforward, popularly known as the value of the tax losses which most companies have at start-up. Although they are labeled "operating losses" on financial statements, they often represent investment in R&D, the most important kind of investment that a high technology company can make. Sometimes the net operating losses are applied to later profitable years and are used up before a company reaches the cash-out point, posing no problem. If, however, the tax losses are not projected to be used up at the point of cash-out, their effect on projected earnings needs to be eliminated before applying a price/earnings ratio in this method.

Structuring the Deal

Once the entrepreneur has identified a good candidate for acquisition, an appropriate deal must be structured. Many techniques are available for acquiring a firm, each having a distinct set of advantages to both the buyer and seller. The deal structure involves the parties, the assets, the payment form, and the timing of the payment. For example, all or part of the assets of one firm can be acquired by another for some combination of cash, notes, stock, and/or employment contract. This payment can be made at the time of acquisition, throughout the first year, or extended over several years.

The two most common means of acquisition are the entrepreneur's direct purchase of the firm's entire stock or assets or the bootstrap purchase of these assets. In the direct purchase of the firm, the entrepreneur obtains funds from an outside lender or the seller of the company being purchased. The money is repaid over time from the cash flow generated from the operations. While this is a relatively simple and clear transaction, it usually results in a long-term capital gain to the seller and double taxation on the funds used to repay the money borrowed to acquire the company.

In order to avoid these problems, the entrepreneur can make a bootstrap purchase, acquiring a small amount of the firm, such as 20 to 30 percent, for cash. He or she then purchases the remainder of the company by a long-term note that is paid off over time out of the acquired company's earnings. This type of deal results in more favorable tax advantages to both the buyer and seller.

Legal Considerations

The legality of a particular acquisition centers around the type of acquisition and the resulting economic impact. In terms of the legality, acquisition activities can be classified as horizontal, vertical, and conglomerate. The entrepreneur must know the legal constraints of each of these before acquiring a particular operation.

Managing the Acquired Entity

Of course, the key for success of an acquisition is its management by the entrepreneur—the planning, execution, and postacquisition integration. A profile containing acquisition criteria and prospect data can help guide the search and initial screening. For a good profile, the entrepreneur must construct a checklist that identifies a prospective company, its history, management, product (or service), finances, marketing, production, and labor relations and then briefly evaluates the prospect. Prospects can be identified through internal referrals and external sources such as accountants, brokers, investment bankers, and lawyers. Once the prospect passes the initial checklist, more rigorous analysis further evaluates the viability of the acquisition.

MERGERS

Another method for expanding a venture is through a **merger**—a transaction involving two (or more) companies in which only one company survives. Acquisitions are so similar to mergers that at times the two terms are used interchangeably. In each of the last several years, merger and acquisition activity has been at the $180 billion level in over 3,000 transactions. A key concern in any merger (or acquisition) is the legality of the purchase. The Department of Justice frequently issues guidelines for horizontal, vertical, and conglomerate mergers, such as the 1968 *Merger Guidelines.* These documents further define the interpretation that will be made in enforcing the Sherman Act and Clayton Act, while strengthening the enforcement of Section 7 of the Clayton Act. Since the guidelines are extensive and technical, the entrepreneur should secure adequate legal advice when any issues arise.

Why should an entrepreneur merge? There are both defensive and offensive strategies for a merger, as indicated in Figure 13–4. Merger motivations range from survival to protection to diversification to growth. When some technical obsolescence, market or raw material loss, or deterioration of the capital structure has occurred in the entrepreneur's venture, a merger may be the only means for survival. The merger can also protect against market encroachment, product innovation, or an unwarranted takeover. On a more offensive side, a merger can provide a great deal of diversification as well as growth in market, technology, and financial and managerial strength.[8]

How does a merger take place? It requires sound planning by the entrepreneur. The merger objectives, particularly those dealing with earnings, must be spelled out with the resulting gains for the owners of both companies delineated. Also, the entrepreneur must carefully evaluate the other company's management to ensure that if retained it would be competent in developing the growth and future of the combined entity. The value and appropriateness of the existing resources should also be determined. In essence, this involves a careful analysis of both companies to ensure that the weaknesses of one do not compound those of the other. Finally, the entrepreneur should work toward establishing a climate of mutual trust to help minimize any possible management threat or turbulence.

The same methods for valuing the entrepreneur's company can be used to determine the value of a merger candidate. This will result from assessing plant value, marketing opportunity, earnings potential, or owner's value. The process involves the entrepreneur looking at the synergistic product/market position, the new domestic or

---

[8]For a discussion of the impact of mergers, see M. Rockmore, "Life after a corporate merger," *American Way,* April 15, 1986, pp 66–69.

FIGURE 13–4 Merger Motivations

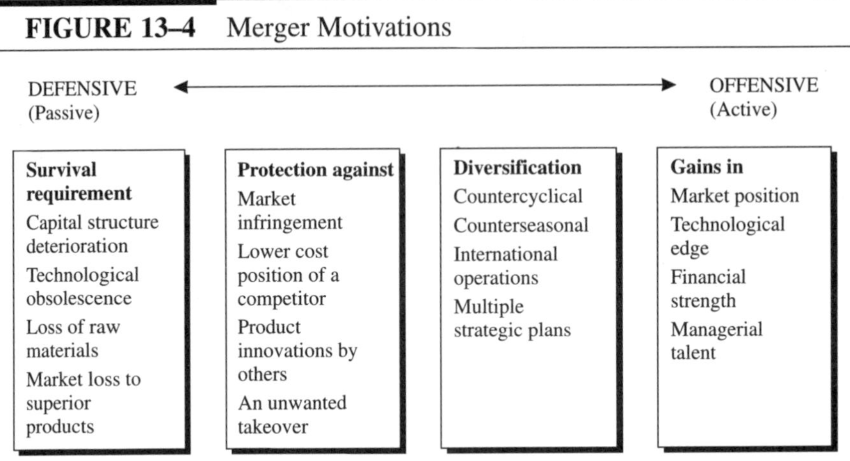

DEFENSIVE
(Passive)
OFFENSIVE
(Active)
Survival requirement
Capital structure deterioration
Technological obsolescence
Loss of raw materials
Market loss to superior products
Protection against
Market infringement
Lower cost position of a competitor
Product innovations by others
An unwanted takeover
Diversification
Countercyclical
Counterseasonal
International operations
Multiple strategic plans
Gains in
Market position
Technological edge
Financial strength
Managerial talent

Source: F. T. Haner, *Business Policy, Planning and Strategy* (Cambridge, MA: Winthrop, 1976), p 399.

international market position, any undervalued financial strength, whether or not the company is skilled in a related industry, or any underexploited company asset. A common procedure for determining value is to estimate the present value of discounted cash flows and the expected after-tax earnings attributable to the merger. This should be done on optimistic, pessimistic, and probable scenarios of cash flows and earnings using various acceptable rates of return.

HOSTILE TAKEOVERS

One form of acquisition, the hostile takeover, has received increased attention through the activities of such corporate raiders as Carl Icahn and T. Boone Pickens. Although hostile takeovers do not create wealth, as the underlying wealth is the assets of the corporation which were created by the company management, they often result in a more accurate appraisal of the company.

Three items make a hostile takeover possible: (1) a low stock evaluation versus performance, (2) a low debt/equity ratio, allowing the entrepreneur to use the assets of the company to fund the takeover, and (3) a high percentage of institutional investors holding the company's stock. Since the objective of these institutional investors is to turn a quick profit, they will frequently vote in favor of the hostile takeover due to the anticipated gain in stock price and firm evaluation.

The most effective method for the entrepreneur to acquire a company in a hostile takeover is by using a multiple-step junk bond offer. Here the raiding entrepreneur acquires a small percent of the company (around 5 percent), lines up financial backers, and makes a very attractive offer for 51 percent of the company financed through the use of junk bonds. This enables current shareholders to sell their stock and obtain their fair share of the value. If a stockholder does not tender his or her shares, that individual's stock has less value once the takeover occurs because the greater value of the company has been used to acquire 51 percent of the stock; the remaining 49 percent has less value.

An entrepreneur can also execute a hostile takeover through shareholder action by consent. This less publicized takeover format occurs when the majority of the shareholders are not pleased with the performance of the present management. They agree to back the entrepreneur in voting out the current management and electing a new management team.

As might be expected, the increase in hostile takeovers has prompted companies to use a variety of defensive measures. One defensive weapon is to stagger the terms of the board of directors by electing only one-third of the board each year. This requires the raiding entrepreneur to go through two annual elections to obtain board control. Another more direct measure is for the company to alter the corporate charter, eliminating shareholder action by consent.

A third defensive measure is for the company to institute a "**poison pill**"—a mechanism to protect values of existing shareholders. With a poison pill in place at the time of an attempted hostile takeover, existing shareholders have the right to additional values. This additional value can be in the form of a provision that automatically increases the value of a current shareholder's stock in the event of a hostile takeover bid. Tendering stock to the raiding entrepreneur would then decrease the shareholder's value.

A fourth defensive measure is to institute **covenants** governing the level of allowable debt debentures. Covenants such as this would totally prohibit or dramatically reduce additional debt that can be incurred by the company, which makes it very difficult for a raider to use the assets of the company for the leverage needed to finance the takeover.

A final defensive weapon against hostile takeovers is "**poison puts.**" These are provisions in a company's bonds that allow the bond's holders to cash in if the insurer of the bond (the company) is taken over. This provision not only discourages takeovers but also helps hold the price of the bonds, which otherwise tend to decrease in takeover activity and the accompanying lower bond ratings.

Even if an entrepreneur does not use the hostile takeover mechanism for acquiring a venture, he or she should know about the activity, particularly the defensive weapons available; such knowledge might prove useful once the entrepreneur's own venture is successful. Perhaps one or more of these defensive measures can be incorporated in the original structure of the new venture to prevent a hostile takeover later.

LEVERAGED BUYOUTS

A **leveraged buyout** occurs when an entrepreneur (or any employee group) uses borrowed funds to purchase an existing venture for cash. Most leveraged buyouts (LBOs) occur because the entrepreneur purchasing the venture believes that he or she could run the company more efficiently than the owners have done. The buyout can be from a variety of sellers: an entrepreneur or other owner who wants to retire; a large corporation desiring to divest itself of a subsidiary that is too small, that has problems, or that does not fit its long-term strategic plan; or some other group desiring to terminate its ownership position.

The purchaser needs a large amount of external funding since personal financial resources to acquire the firm directly are frequently limited. Since the issuance of additional equity to raise the needed funding is usually not possible, the capital needed is most often in the form of long-term debt financing (five years or more) with the assets of the firm being acquired serving as collateral. Who usually provides this long-term debt financing? Banks, venture capitalists, and insurance companies have been the most active providers of the debt needed in LBOs.

The actual financial package used in an LBO reflects the lender's risk-reward profile. While banks tend to use senior-debt issues, venture capitalists usually use subordinated debt issues with warrants or options. Regardless of the instrument used, the repayment plan established must be in line with the pro forma cash flows expected to be generated. The interest rates are usually variable and are consistent with the current yields of comparable risk investment.

In most leveraged buyouts, the debt capital usually exceeds the equity by 5:1, with some ratios as high as 10:1. Given this high debt load and the accompanying high level of risk, successful LBOs usually involve a financially sound and stable company. Of course, any time such a high level of borrowed funds is employed in any business transaction, there still remains a high risk of default. In a leveraged buyout, there is significantly more debt relative to equity than in a typical firm's capital structure. While this makes the financial risk great, the key to a successful LBO is not the relative debt-to-equity ratio but rather the ability of the entrepreneur taking over to cover the principal and interest payments through increased sales and profits. The ability depends on the skills of the entrepreneur and the strength and stability of the firm.

Given the importance of the characteristics of the firm in a successful leveraged buyout, it is not surprising that most LBOs involve companies with a long track record of solid earnings, a strong management team, and a strong market share position. These factors help reduce the risk of the LBO failing. This risk can be further reduced by requiring the entrepreneur to invest most of his or her personal assets in the equity of the new firm.

How does the entrepreneur determine whether a specific company is a good opportunity for a leveraged buyout? This determination can be made by following a basic evaluation procedure. First, the entrepreneur must determine whether the present owner's asking price is reasonable. Many subjective and quantitative techniques can be used in this determination. Subjective evaluations need to be made of the competitiveness of the industry and the competitive position of the firm in that industry; the uniqueness of the offering of the firm and the stage in the **product life cycle;** and the abilities of management and other key personnel remaining with the firm.

In addition to the important information gained from this evaluation, more quantitative techniques are used to evaluate the fairness of the asking price. Some useful evaluation techniques were presented earlier in this chapter. The price-earnings ratio of the LBO prospect should be calculated and compared with those of comparable companies, as well as the present value of future earnings of the prospect and its book value.

After the proposed purchase price is found to be reasonable, the entrepreneur must assess the firm's debt capacity. This is particularly critical since the entrepreneur wants to raise as much of the capital needed as possible in the form of long-term debt. How much long-term debt can a prospective LBO carry? It depends on the prospect's business risk and the stability of its future cash flows. The cash flow must cover the long-term debt required to finance the LBO. Any financial amount that cannot be secured by long-term debt, due to the inadequacy of the cash flow, will need to be in the form of equity from the entrepreneur or other investors.

Once the level of long-term debt financing that can be handled is determined, the third step takes place: developing the appropriate financial package. The financial package must meet the needs and objectives of the providers of the funds as well as the situation of the company and the entrepreneur. While each LBO financial package is tailored to the specific situation, there are usually some significant restrictions. Typical restrictions include the payment of dividends. Frequently, an LBO agreement with venture capitalists has warrants that are convertible into common stock at a later date. Also, a sinking fund repayment of the long-term debt is frequently required.

There are many instances of both successful and unsuccessful LBOs. One of the most publicized involved R. H. Macy and Co., a well-known department store chain. Macy's was not in bad condition before the merger in terms of the traditional measures of sales per square foot, profitability, and return on assets. It had experienced a significant drop in profits and was losing talented middle executives. The LBO was accomplished by some 345 executives participating and sharing a 20 percent ownership in the $4.7 billion retailer. Since the acquisition, there has been a new entrepreneurial spirit in management, which fosters more loyalty in the employees; a renewed motivation, with middle managers actually selling and earning sales floor bonuses during slack time; and a long-term planning direction for the board of directors, which meets five times a year instead of once a month—all of which indicate that this LBO will be one of the more successful.

Recently, LBOs have also made news in terms of the size and the improprieties involved, particularly in the junk bond market in 1989–90. The largest LBO by far was that led by Kohlberg Kravis Roberts in acquiring RJR Nabisco for $25 million, which was 440 percent of book value. Another large LBO during that same year was HCA-Hospital Corporation of American acquiring Hospital Corporation of America for $3.9 million, 241 percent of book value. These and numerous other LBOs occurring during this period were financed in part by junk bonds. With the discontinuance of junk bonds in 1990, LBOs will not be as numerous, and financing will be more difficult to obtain. Some LBOs will still use cash and stock for financing, such as the Wings Holdings acquisition of NW Airlines for $3.6 million in cash.

SUMMARY

There are special considerations confronting entrepreneurs in expanding their companies. Time management is important, especially during periods of growth and expansion. Effective time management increases productivity and job satisfaction, improves *esprit de corps,* reduces tension, and promotes better health. To achieve effective time management, the entrepreneur should analyze current use of time, develop efficient methods of dealing with routine tasks, and use prioritized planning. Effective use of time will improve efficiency throughout the organization.

Negotiation is another skill needed by entrepreneurs in expanding an organization. Understanding the underlying motivations is important in approaching a negotiation situation. When cooperation is possible, integrative bargaining occurs, with parties using rational decision making to solve a joint problem.

In competitive negotiation, techniques of distributive bargaining are employed. Since conflicting goals make this area of negotiation more difficult, the entrepreneur should learn as much as possible about his or her adversary. The settlement range of the other party will determine the likelihood of reaching an agreement. In any negotiation situation, the entrepreneur should follow eight steps: prepare, discuss, signal, propose, respond, bargain, close, and agree. Negotiation skills are particularly important in expansion through joint ventures, acquisitions, mergers, and leveraged buyouts.

Joint ventures are separate entities formed by two or more partners. Although the most common joint ventures are between private-sector companies, they can involve universities, other nonprofit organizations, and the public sector. Objectives include: sharing technology, cutting costs, entering new markets, and entering foreign markets. The success of joint ventures depends on the relationships of the partners, the symmetry of the partners, reasonable expectations, and timing.

Another method an entrepreneur can use in expanding the business is acquisition. An acquisition is the purchase of a company so that it is completely absorbed by the acquiring company. The acquisition process involves evaluating a candidate business and structuring a final deal. The evaluation process involves analyzing the firm's financial data, product line, research and development, marketing, manufacturing processes, and management. When a candidate passes the evaluation process, an appropriate deal needs to be structured.

A third method for expanding a company is through a merger. This transaction involves two or more companies, with only one company surviving. Motivations to engage in a merger include survival, protection, diversification, and growth.

An increasingly popular alternative for entrepreneurial expansion is the leveraged buyout. In this method, assets of the acquired company are used to finance the deal.

Entrepreneurs facing expansion require skills in time management and negotiation in order to efficiently achieve growth in the marketplace. These skills and knowledge of joint ventures, mergers, acquisition, and leveraged buyouts can result in successful growth of the venture.

QUESTIONS FOR DISCUSSION

1. Apply the techniques of time management to your current situation. Analyze your use of time for a three-day period. Discuss your findings. Identify your priority tasks.
2. Is a labor dispute more likely to involve distributive or integrative bargaining? Explain your answer.
3. In a labor dispute between management and union, press releases may be used by one or both parties. Discuss the motivation for each side to utilize or to avoid publicity.
4. Why is "good faith" an important element of bargaining?
5. Why have many different valuation techniques been developed for determining the worth of a firm? In any given situation, is there one "right answer" for a company's value? What effects do your answers to these questions have on the entrepreneur making an acquisition?
6. Discuss the problems that can occur when universities and industry form joint ventures for research purposes. How have these problems been solved by some joint ventures?
7. The Chinese government has recently been interested in encouraging joint ventures with foreign companies. As a U.S. company, what might be your advantages to forming a joint venture in China? Discuss any drawbacks to consider.
8. Why does the valuation of a candidate business in an acquisition involve such detailed analysis?
9. Discuss at least three motivations a firm might have in forming a merger.

KEY TERMS

acquisition
cooperative negotiation
covenants
distributive bargaining
industry-university agreements
integrative bargaining
joint venture
leveraged buyouts
merger
negotiation
poison pill
poison puts
product life cycle
rational decision model
settlement range
time management

GLOSSARY OF TERMS

acid-test ratio A measure of the liquidity of a company found by dividing cash, marketable securities, and accounts receivable by current liabilities. Also called "quick ratio."

after-tax cash flow The expected return from an investment project.

asset-based financing Loads or capital secured by long-term assets.

asset turnover ratio A measure of company efficiency found by dividing net sales by total assets.

average rate of return A comparison of the average net income of a company to average investment.

book value The original cost of an asset less its accumulated depreciation.

cash flow Income less receipts (a proxy for this is net income plus depreciation).

cost of capital The minimum rate of return that a company must earn on its assets to satisfy investors.

current ratio A measure of the liquidity of a company found by current liabilities.

debt-to-equity ratio The proportion of debt to equity in a firm's financial structure.

degree of financial leverage The percentage change in earnings per share resulting from a 1 percent change in earnings before interest and taxes.

earning per share A measure of profitability derived by dividing the net income of the company by the average number of shares outstanding.

equity The portion of the balance sheet representing ownership that includes capital stock, preferred stock, retained earnings, and certain other reserve or surplus accounts.

expected cash flow The most likely (or weighted average) cash flow.

factoring Sale of accounts receivable to a bank or finance company.

financial leverage The relationship between borrowed funds and shareholders' equity. (When there is a high proportion of debt-to-equity in a company it is highly leveraged, which increases the financial risk of the firm.)

financial risk The risk that a firm may not be able to meet its financial obligations.

funds flow statement A formalized statement of the funds flow cycle, incorporating all sources and uses of funds.

going concern A company whose operation is expected to continue.

golden parachute A provision to protect existing officers and directors of a company from removal in the event of a takeover. Often a large sum of money is involved on removal.

gross profit margin The difference between net sales and the cost of goods sold, expressed as a percentage of net sales.

inventory turnover ratio A ratio measuring the number of times the inventory of a company is turned (sold) each year.

investment value The theoretic intrinsic value of an asset or company.

joint venture An agreement between companies to enter into a partnership for a specific project.

leveraged buyout A buyout in which the purchaser borrows funds to buy the stock of a company and then uses the resources of the company to repay the loan.

liquidity The ability of a company to meet its current financial obligations.

market value The price investors are willing to pay for the securities of a company.

merger A combination of two or more companies in which one company survives, retaining its identity.

net present value The present value of expected cash flows discounted at the cost of capital less the investment outlay.

net profit margin The percentage of profit earned for each dollar of sales calculated by dividing net income by net sales.

operating leverage The effect that a change in sales can have on the earnings of a company due to certain fixed expenses.

operating margin A measure of return on sales of a company determined by dividing earnings from operations by net sales.

participating preferred Stock that provides stated dividends but also shares in the earnings of the company.

payback period The number of years required to return an investment outlay.

preferred stock A type of stock representing one class of ownership on a company; generally has fixed dividends.

present value The current value of dollars that will be received in the future.

price/earnings (P/E) ratio A ratio determined by dividing the market price of stock by its earnings. A high price/earnings ratio of a company indicates that investors expected good company growth.

pro forma financial statements Projected financial statements of future periods of the operations of the company.

profit margin A measure of profitability of a company determined by dividing net income by net sales.

profitability index (PI) An index measuring the value of the expected cash flow of a company discounted at the cost of capital divided by the investment outlay.

return on assets The net income divided by the assets of a company.

return on equity The net income divided by the equity of a company.

sole proprietorship An unincorporated business owned by one person.

term loan A loan from a commercial bank with a usual maturity of five years or less commonly used for plant and equipment, working capital, or debt repayment.

time value of money The principle that money received in the present is worth more than the same amount received in the future.

variable cost Expenditures that change in direct proportion to the number of units sold.

working capital The dollar amount of a company's current assets.

SELECTED READINGS

Davidson, Per. (1991). Continued Entrepreneurship: Ability, Need, and Opportunity as Determinants of Small Firm Growth. *Journal of Business Venturing.* Vol. 6, no. 6, pp 405–429.

General conclusions were reached in examining the growth and nongrowth of individual small businesses, such as objective measures of ability, need, and opportunity can explain a substantial share of the variation in actual growth rates.

El-Namak, M. S. S. (1992). Creating a Corporate Vision. *Long Range Planning.* Vol. 25, no. 6, pp 25–29.

Vision is important in strategic management and provides a challenge for the whole organization and mirrors the goals of the constituents. The corporate vision may be killed by fear of mistakes, inability to tolerate ambiguity, and lack of challenge.

Evans, K. R., Feldman, H. D., & Foster, J. (January 1990). Purchasing Motor Carrier Service: An Investigation of the Criteria Used by Small Manufacturing Firms. *Journal of Business Venturing.* pp 39–47.

Gardner, Ken, Leslie, John, & Chrisman, James J. (1991). Case: Bulldog Pizza and Spirits. *Entrepreneurship: Theory and Practice.* Vol. 15, no. 4, pp 67–83.

A case on Bulldog Pizza and Spirits describes how the owner must make changes in order to grow, particularly when the external environment changes.

Gilmore, T. N., & Kanzanjian, R. K. (January 1989). Clarifying Decision Making in High-Growth Ventures: The Use of Responsibility Charting. *Journal of Business Venturing,* pp 69–83.

Discusses the complications that may arise as a venture grows rapidly. Responsibility charting can be used to resolve problems that can no longer be solved by a single individual or team. The most powerful aspect of such a process is the allowance provided to a management team to deal with both power and authority. Using such a structure greater clarity on how decisions are to be made and accountability for those decisions can be achieved.

Golden, Peggy A., & Dollinger, Marc. (1993). Cooperative Alliances and Competitive Strategies in Small Manufacturing Firms. *Entrepreneurship: Theory and Practice.* Vol. 17, no. 4, pp 43–56.

A study of the interaction between the strategic posture of small firms and their propensity to form cooperative linkages supports game theorists who suggest that sharing resources with competitors, suppliers, trade associations, and the community provides a better outcome for all the game players.

Lant, Theresa K., & Mezics, Stephen J. (1990). Managing Discontinuous Change: A Simulation Study of Organizational Learning and Entrepreneurship. *Strategic Management Journal.* Vol. 2, no. 0143–2095, pp 147–179.

The results of this study indicate that there are important organizational implications under different levels of ambiguity.

Lengmick-Hall, Cynthia A. (1992). Strategic Configurations and Designs for Corporate Entrepreneurship: Exploring the Relationship Between Cohesiveness and Performance. *Journal of Engineering and Technology Management.* Vol. 9, no. 2, pp 127–154.

The relationship between cohesiveness and performance is surprisingly durable and is shown to have a substantial impact only for those firms whose environments require high levels of adaptability and flexibility characteristics.

McCarthy, Anne M., Krueger, David A., & Schoenecker, Timothy S. (1990). Changes in the Time Allocation Patterns of Entrepreneurship. *Entrepreneurship: Theory and Practice.* vol. 15. no. 2, pp 7–18.

Miller, Lynn E., & Simmons, Karen A. (1992). Differences in Management Practices of Founding and Nonfounding Chief Executives of Human Service Organizations. *Entrepreneurship: Theory and Practice.* Vol. 16, no. 4, pp 31–39.

The results of a survey of 37 founding and 133 nonfounding chief executives indicated that organization founders had significantly larger spans of control, smaller boards of directors, and higher proportions of board members from inside the organization than nonfounding chief executives.

Miner, John B. (1990). Entrepreneurs, High Growth Entrepreneurs, and Managers: Contrasting and Overlapping Motivational Patterns. *Journal of Business Venturing.* Vol. 5, no. 4, pp 221–234.

The study found a superiority of entrepreneurs over managers in task motivation.

Sandberg, William R. (1992). Strategic Management's Potential Contribution to a Theory of Entrepreneurship. *Entrepreneurship: Theory and Practice.* Vol. 16, no. 3, pp 73–90.

The contributions of strategic management to entrepreneurship are described specifically dealing with issues of new business creation, innovation, opportunity seeking, user assumption, top management teams, and group processes in strategic decisions.

Walters, Peter G. P., & Samiee, Saeed. (1990). A Model for Assessing Performance in Small U.S. Exporting Firms. *Entrepreneurship: Theory and Practice.* Vol. 15, no. 2, pp 33–50.

A study of small U.S. exporters found that management commitment, administrative arrangement, and strategy variables are important export success factors.

Willard, Gary E., Krueger, David A., & Fesser, Henry R. (1992). In Order to Grow, Must the Founder Go: A Comparison of Performance Between Founder and Nonfounder-Managed High Growth Manufacturing Firms. *Journal of Business Venturing.* Vol. 7, no. 3, pp 181–194.

No significant differences in performance were found between founder-managed and professionally managed firms although, on average, founder-managed firms were somewhat smaller and growing at a slightly lower rate.

CHAPTER

14

Ending the Venture

Chapter Objectives

1. To illustrate differences in alternative types of bankruptcy under the bankruptcy act of 1978 (amended in 1984).
2. To illustrate rights of creditors and entrepreneurs in different cases of bankruptcy.
3. To provide the entrepreneur with an understanding of the typical warning signs of bankruptcy.
4. To illustrate how some entrepreneurs can turn bankruptcy into a successful business.
5. To describe the succession of a business to family or nonfamily members.

J. B. Fuqua

One of the most difficult decisions for an entrepreneur is knowing when to end a venture. Bankruptcy, liquidation, selling, or downsizing a new venture are not pleasant alternatives for an entrepreneur. However, most venture ending decisions are necessary, to avoid even further financial disaster. J. B. Fuqua, the founder of Fuqua Industries, has encountered many successes and failures during his life of high risk and aggressive entrepreneurial activity.[1]

At the age of 75, J. B. Fuqua recently asked that his name be removed from Fuqua Industries. Although he had sold the business in 1989 (1.3 million shares) to Charles "Red" Scott, his name and reputation were still reflected in the business. However, he was upset with Scott and many of the poor recent business decisions he had made.

"Red" Scott had purchased Fuqua Industries with the intent of carrying on J. B.'s aggressive style of buying and selling new ventures. His beginning at the company, however, was not viewed favorably by J. B. Fuqua. Scott had used company funds to buy back 4.9 million shares of stock at a prohibitively high price; he had replaced Lawrence Klamon, one of J. B.'s former associates, with himself as CEO; and he then made a number of poor business decisions. For the Snapper Division, which had been a long-time cash cow, he decided to develop a lower priced line of lawn equipment to be sold in discount stores. He also cut back on the advertising budget. Both decisions had infuriated Snapper dealers, whom J. B. Fuqua had spent years nurturing. Scott also transferred 26 percent of Fuqua stock to Intermark Inc., a financially troubled company in which he served as chief executive. In fact, in March 1992 Intermark was ready to file Chapter 11 bankruptcy.

As the founder of Fuqua Industries, J. B. Fuqua did not appreciate what was happening to the company. To disassociate himself more completely, J. B. offered Scott $1 million to change the company name. Subsequently, the now downsized conglomerate changed its name to Actava Group Inc. Scott's intent was to shift strategy again and divest unprofitable companies and only focus on the recreational sports industry. Whatever the results of future efforts, J. B. Fuqua's name would no longer be associated with the company.

---

[1]See, S. N. Chakravarty, "Ransom," *Forbes,* July 5, 1993, pp 40–41; *New York Times,* July 22, 1993, p D4; and S. N. Chakravarty, "The Trader," *Forbes,* March 7, 1988, pp 72–3.

This recent turmoil of Fuqua Industries (now Actava) was not the only time that J. B. had been through rough times. His entrepreneurial business dealings had taken him through very good and very bad periods. Fortunately, most of his dealings were very successful, as evidenced from his present accumulated wealth of more than $200 million.

Born in 1919, John Brooks Fuqua was raised by poor parents on a tobacco farm in Virginia. Too poor to go to college, he borrowed business books by mail from Duke University. He subsequently repaid the university with a $10 million gift to the business school, which now holds his name.

Fuqua's first entrepreneurial endeavor was the purchase of a Royal Crown Bottling Plant. With a tip from a lawyer friend, he used existing harsh tax laws to his advantage to purchase the plant with no down payment. The owner of the plant would have had to pay a very high tax, plus penalties, because it had accumulated too much cash. J. B.'s offer to buy the plant was immediately accepted. His buyout allowed the owner to escape by paying only a capital gains tax instead of huge penalties. Three years later, J. B. sold the plant for $100,000 and was well on his way to a successful entrepreneural career.

In the 1960s J. B. Fuqua began building his empire with a $14 million tile business. Using stock swaps, debt, and other creative financing, he bought dozens of companies. In 1968, the stock for Fuqua Industries reached 47½.

The 1970s brought problems to Fuqua Industries because of low net margins, unprofitable companies, and a disenchanted Wall Street. So J. B. began to sell off parts of his conglomerate, eventually focusing on consumer businesses such as sporting goods, garden equipment, and film processing. Sold off were a multitude of companies in such industries as petroleum distribution, radio and TV stations, boat trailers, bicycles, movie theatres, and metal fabrication. J. B. continued his buying and selling of companies into the 1980s, depending on their success and the pulse of the economy. In 1989, he sold the company to Charles "Red" Scott.

Not all entrepreneurs can simply sell off financially troubled companies nor deal as J. B. Fuqua did. Instead, many entrepreneurs are forced to succumb to more serious consequences. This chapter focuses on some of the bankruptcy issues and alternatives that an entrepreneur may need to consider at some point in his or her career.

BANKRUPTCY—AN OVERVIEW

The above saga of J. B. Fuqua is probably not indicative of the average life of an entrepreneur. Even though more of his companies succeeded than failed, he was forced many times to sell off unprofitable companies. Fortunately, with his conglomerate, these failures were able to be absorbed by those companies that were very profitable.

EXHIBIT 14–1 Type of Bankruptcies from 1983–1993

Number of bankruptcies

700,000
600,000
500,000
400,000
300,000
200,000
100,000
0

1983 1984 1985 1986 1987 1988 1989 1990 1991 1992 1993

Year

Chapter 7
Chapter 11
Chapter 13

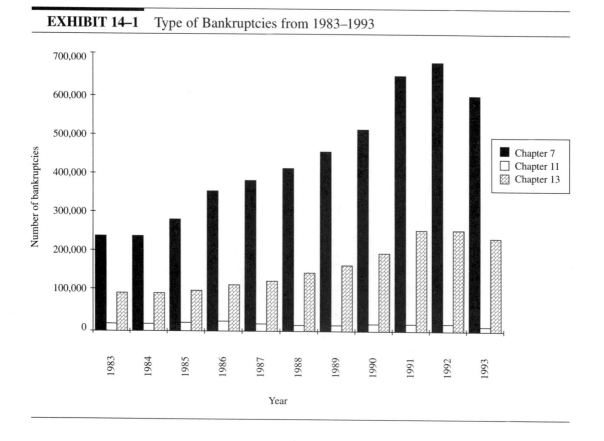

Failure is not uncommon in many new ventures. According to the Small Business Administration, about half of all new start-ups fail in their first years. The failures are personally painful for the entrepreneur and too often could have been prevented by paying more attention to certain critical factors in the business operation. Figure 14–1 compares Chapter 7, 11, and 13 bankruptcy filings (explained later in this chapter) from 1980 to 1993. It can be seen from Figure 14–1 that the number of Chapter 11 filings has declined from a high of 24,740 in 1986 to only about 3,043 in 1993. This may be indicative of the low likelihood of any venture actually being able to turn around the situation.

It appears from this data that more people are choosing to file for Chapter 13, which protects the entrepreneur from creditors and sets up a payment plan. The number of Chapter 7 filings has increased each year from 234,594 in 1983 to 681,663 in 1992. The number of Chapter 7 filings in 1993 declined to 585,264.

In 1993, the actual filings of total bankruptcies declined about 8.2 percent over the same period in 1992. This could be interpreted both positively and negatively. From a positive perspective, it may imply that the economy is improving and therefore providing more opportunities for entrepreneurs to succeed. On the other hand, it could also be interpreted negatively, that fewer start-ups are occurring, which means there are relatively fewer ventures that can fail.

Bankruptcy is a term heard too often among entrepreneurs, yet it doesn't always end the ambitions of an entrepreneur nor does it always have to result in the end of the business in question. Experiences of entrepreneurs regarding the results of bankruptcy vary from situation to situation. A few examples will illustrate. Bill Lewis, founder and CEO of Federal Refunds Inc., has filed bankruptcy twice. He now has launched a new company that assists buyers of petroleum products in recovering funds on overbilled accounts. Thus far he has not made the same mistakes he made in earlier endeavors, and his new business has remained profitable. John Koss, the founder of Koss Corp., a manufacturer of stereo headphones, filed Chapter 11 in 1984 and through a reorganization reemerged almost one year later. In 1993, sales for this venture reached $32 million.

Paul Perkins, on the other hand, is now driving a school bus after his Voyages International Travel Co. went bankrupt in 1989. He is in the process of starting another new venture. Phil Akin is presently trying to bring his Duds 'n Suds, a combination laundromat and bar, out of Chapter 11 bankruptcy. His biggest problem was out of his control—the October 19, 1987, stock market crash. It happened right when Akin was attempting a public stock offering. Following this disastrous event, he had to scramble to protect his company from venture capitalists who wanted to dismantle it. He then filed for Chapter 11 protection and is in the process of trying to reorganize and return his company to its earlier days of success. All of these entrepreneurs have indicated how much they have learned from the experiences of bankruptcy. Some of the lessons can be summarized as follows.[2]

- Many entrepreneurs spend too much time and effort trying to diversify in markets where they lack knowledge. They should focus only on known markets.
- Bankruptcy protects entrepreneurs only from the creditors, not from competitors.
- It's difficult to separate the entrepreneur from the business. They put everything into the company, including worrying about the future of their employees.
- Many entrepreneurs never think their business is going to fail until it's too late. They should file early.
- Bankruptcy is emotionally painful. Going into hiding after bankruptcy is a big mistake. Bankruptcy needs to be shared with employees and everybody else involved.

As the above examples indicate, bankruptcy is serious business and requires some important understanding of its applications. The Bankruptcy Act of 1978 (with amendments added in 1984) was designed to ensure a fair distribution of assets to creditors, to protect debtors from unfair depletion of assets, and to protect debtors

[2] See S. Barlow, "The 11th Hour," *Entrepreneur,* April 1993, pp 133–37; and T. Richman, "The Lessons of Bankruptcy," *Inc.,* December 1989, pp 29–38.

from unfair demands by creditors. The act provides three alternative provisions for a firm near or at a position of insolvency. The three alternative positions are 1) reorganization or Chapter 11 bankruptcy, 2) extended time payment or Chapter 13 bankruptcy, and 3) liquidation or Chapter 7 bankruptcy. All attempt to protect the troubled entrepreneur as well as provide a reasonable way to organize payments to debtors or to end the venture.

CHAPTER 11—REORGANIZATION

This is the least severe alternative to bankruptcy. In this situation, the courts try to give the venture time and "breathing room" to pay their debts. Usually, this situation results because the venture has cash flow problems, and creditors begin to pressure the firm with lawsuits. The entrepreneur feels that, with some time, the business can become more solvent and liquid in order to meet its debt requirements.

A major creditor or any party in interest or a group of creditors will usually present the case to the court. Then a plan for reorganization will be prepared to indicate how the business will be turned around. The plan will divide the debt and ownership interests into two groups: those who will be affected by the plan and those who will not. It then will specify whose interests will be affected and how payments will be made.

Once the plan is completed, it must be approved by the court. All bankruptcies are now handled by the U.S. Bankruptcy Court, whose powers were restructured under the Bankruptcy Amendments Act of 1984.

Approval of the plan also requires that all creditors and owners agree to comply with the reorganization plan as presented to the courts. The decisions made in the reorganization plan generally reflect one or a combination of the following:[3]

1. *Extension*—This occurs when two or more of the largest creditors agree to postpone any claims. This acts as a stimulus for smaller creditors to also agree to the plan.
2. *Substitution*—If the future potential of the venture looks promising enough, it may be possible to exchange stock or something else for the existing debt.
3. *Composition settlement*—The debt is prorated to the creditors as a settlement for any debt.

Even though only 20 to 25 percent of those firms that file for Chapter 11 bankruptcy will make it through the process, it does present an opportunity to find a cure for any business problems.[4] Some of these problems are resolvable, and without the Chapter 11 protection even these 20 to 25 percent that file would never have the opportunity to succeed.

---

[3]R. A. Anderson, I. Fox, & D. P. Turney, *Business Law: Principles Cases Legal Environment,* rev. ed. (Cincinnati, OH: South-Western Publishing, 1987), p 777.

[4]S. Barlow, p 133.

It is generally believed by experts that one of the primary reasons why companies do not successfully come out of Chapter 11 bankruptcy is because they wait too long before filing for protection. In 1990, Yield House, a successful catalog/retailer of colonial style furniture and accessories, filed for reorganization before its financial condition had become too severe. Its strategy during reorganization was to revamp the mail order operation by eliminating some products that were not profitable and adding lower-cost household furnishings, refining the mailing list, and closing unprofitable stores. Although the price points went down, the company's mailing list was directed to more upscale consumers. This strategy allowed Yield House to recently come out of bankruptcy with increased productivity and profitability.

Entrepreneurs have a tendency to ignore warning signs for bankruptcy and hold on until there is an emergency, such as running out of cash. Recognizing the signals may give an entrepreneur the opportunity to develop a strategy or plan, such as Yield House.

Surviving Bankruptcy

The most obvious way to survive bankruptcy is to avoid it altogether. However, since it is becoming such a common occurrence, it may be helpful for the entrepreneur to have a plan should he or she find it necessary to declare bankruptcy. Some of the suggestions for survival are listed below.[5]

- Bankruptcy can be used as a bargaining chip to allow the entrepreneur to voluntarily restructure and reorganize the venture.
- File before the venture runs out of cash or has no incoming revenue so that expenses not protected by bankruptcy can be paid.
- Don't file for Chapter 11 protection unless the venture has a legitimate chance of recovery.
- Be prepared to have creditors examine all financial transactions for the last 12 months, seeking possible debtor fraud.
- Maintain good records (see Chapter 12).
- Understand completely how the protection against creditors works and what is necessary in order to keep it in place.
- Any litigation in existence should be transferred to the bankruptcy court, which may be a more favorable forum for the entrepreneur.
- Focus efforts on preparing a realistic financial reorganization plan.

Following some of the above suggestions and being prepared should bankruptcy be necessary is the best advice that anyone could give to an entrepreneur. Preparation will prevent unfavorable conditions and could increase the likelihood of successfully coming out of bankruptcy.

---

[5] *Stores,* December 1992, p 59.

Prepackaged Bankruptcy

In response to the poor economic environment of the early 90s, a new type of reorganization plan has emerged, called the prepackaged bankruptcy. Basically, it's a declaration that the entrepreneur will be declaring bankruptcy in the near future. Its intent is to make a Chapter 11 filing more predictable and thus, hopefully, a more successful process.[6]

The prepackaged bankruptcy plan allows the entrepreneur to work with creditors to settle debts before legal proceedings begin. In this case, the entrepreneur presents all stakeholders (creditors, lenders, and owners) with a reorganization plan and a disclosure statement detailing all information about the venture's financial position. Negotiations then take place, and differences are resolved before the plan reaches the courts. In most cases, creditors are agreeable to this declaration because they have not had to deal with legal issues, nonpayment of debts, and expensive legal fees.

A prepackaged plan can allow a company to emerge from a bankruptcy in four to nine months rather than the more common nine months to two years via the regular route. In fact, since the process is less complicated, the entrepreneur can focus his or her attention on the business rather than on legal issues. Thus, it can save creditors and lenders significant time and money for legal fees.

However, there are shortcomings to the prepackaged bankruptcy. As soon as an entrepreneur announces a plan to reorganize, it labels the entrepreneur and the business a failure. It may thus make it difficult to sell to new customers or to contract with distributors.

Chapter 11 bankruptcy is used when there is hope that the business can resolve its financial woes and get back on track. If this is not likely, the entrepreneur may need to consider other bankruptcy options, such as Chapter 13.

CHAPTER 13—EXTENDED TIME PAYMENT PLANS

If the entrepreneur has a regular income, it is possible to file for extended time payments, as long as the unsecured debts are less than $100,000 and the secured debts are less than $350,000. This option is only available for individual proprietorships, and it is strictly a voluntary form of bankruptcy. Under this plan, the entrepreneur files a plan for the installment payment of outstanding debts. If approved by the court, it binds the creditors, even if they had not originally agreed to such installment payments.

The entrepreneur must file with the court a plan that basically budgets future income with respect to any outstanding debts. The plan must provide for the payment of all claims identified as having priority under the Bankruptcy Act. In addition, the

---

[6] See D. M. Morris and E. C. Dobbs, "A Package Deal," *Small Business Reports,* March 1992, pp 15–19; and "Prepackaged Bankruptcies: Bust Today, Back Tomorrow," *Economist,* February 15, 1992, pp 78–80.

plan will outline how much is to be paid until all payments have been completed. It also allows the entrepreneur to continue to own and operate the business while Chapter 13 is pending.

The claims to be paid are in the following order of priority: (1) secured creditors, (2) administrative expenses, (3) claims arising from operation of the business, (4) wage claims up to $2,000 per person, (5) contributions to employee benefit plans, (6) claims by consumer creditors, (7) taxes, and (8) general creditors.[7]

CHAPTER 7—LIQUIDATION

The most extreme case of bankruptcy requires the entrepreneur to liquidate, either voluntarily or involuntarily, all nonexempt assets of the business.

If the entrepreneur files a voluntary bankruptcy petition under Chapter 7, it constitutes a determination that his or her venture is bankrupt. Usually, the courts will also require a current income and expense statement.

Table 14–1 summarizes some of the key issues and requirements under the involuntary bankruptcy petition. As the table indicates, an involuntary bankruptcy can be very complicated and can take a long time to resolve. Sometimes, however, liquidation is in the best interests of the entrepreneur if there is no hope of recovering from the situation.

STRATEGY DURING REORGANIZATION

Normally, reorganization under Chapter 11 or an extended payment plan under Chapter 13 takes a significant amount of time. During this period, the entrepreneur can speed up the process by taking the initiative in preparing a plan, selling the plan to secured creditors, communicating with groups of creditors, and avoiding writing checks that are not covered.

The key to enhancing the bankruptcy process is keeping creditors abreast of how the business is doing and stressing the significance of their support during the process. Improving the entrepreneur's credibility with creditors will help the venture emerge from financial difficulties without the stigma of failure. But trying to meet directly with groups of creditors usually results in turmoil and ill will, so these meetings should be avoided.

Bankruptcy should be a last resort for the entrepreneur. Every effort should be made to avoid it and keep the business operating.

---

[7] *Business Law*, pp 785–786.

TABLE 14–1 Liquidation under Chapter 7 Involuntary Bankruptcy

Requirements	*Number and Claims of Creditors*	*Rights and Duties of Entrepreneur*	*Trustee*
Debts are not being paid as they become due.	If 12 or more creditors, at least 3 with unsecured claims totaling $5,000 must sign petition.	Damages may be recovered if creditor files in bad faith.	Elected by creditors. Interim trustee appointed by court.
Custodian appointed within 120 days prior to filing of petition.	If less than 12 creditors, 1 creditor whose unsecured claim is at least $5,000 must sign the petition.	If involuntary petition is dismissed by court, costs, fees, or damages may be awarded.	Becomes by law owner of all property considered nonexempt for liquidation.
Considered insolvent when fair value of all assets is less than debts. Called a balance sheet test.	A proof of claim must be filed within 90 days after first meeting of creditors.	Must file a list of creditors with courts. Must file a current income and expense statement.	Can set aside petitions; transfer of property to a creditor under certain conditions.

KEEPING THE VENTURE GOING

Any entrepreneur who starts a business should pay attention to, as well as learn from, the mistakes of others. There are certain requirements that can help keep a new venture going and reduce the risk of failure. We can never guarantee success, but we can learn how to avoid failure.

Table 14–2 summarizes some of the key factors that can reduce the risk of business failure. The entrepreneur should be sensitive to each of these issues regardless of the size or type of business started.

Many entrepreneurs have confidence in their abilities, which is necessary for them to be successful in their field. However, they may have excessive optimism, which can be dangerous in a new venture. Inevitably, the overly optimistic entrepreneur becomes sloppy in managing the business and often misses important signals that the business needs help.

Kenneth J. Susnjara of Thermwood Corporation illustrated how being optimistic regarding the market potential for his company's robotic paint sprayer almost led to a disaster. Susnjara left his post as CEO for three months to become a distributor for the paint sprayer. The purpose was to learn more about why the product had not been as well accepted by distributors. Susnjara had assumed that the paint sprayer would sell itself without significant promotional materials and explanation of product benefits. The time spent as a distributor gave him a completely different view of Thermwood and what was needed to promote the paint sprayer to distributors. By

TABLE 14–2 Requirements for Keeping a New Venture Afloat

- Avoid excess optimism when business appears to be successful.
- Always prepare good marketing plans with clear objectives.
- Make good cash projections and avoid capitalization.
- Keep abreast of the marketplace.
- Identify stress points that can put the business in jeopardy.

seeing his business through the eyes of his customers, Susnjara was able to get a different perspective on his business. As a result of his experience, he developed new promotional materials and strategies to more effectively meet the needs of the company's distributors, thus also increasing the product's likelihood of success.[8]

Preparing an effective marketing plan for a twelve-month period is essential for the entrepreneur. The marketing plan discussed in Chapter 6 helps the entrepreneur prepare for contingencies and controls his or her day-to-day activities.

Good cash projections are also a serious consideration for the entrepreneur. Cash flow is one of the major causes for an entrepreneur to have to declare bankruptcy. Thus, in preparing cash projections entrepreneurs should seek assistance from accountants, lawyers, or a federal agency such as the SBA. This may prevent the situation from reaching a point where it is too late for any hope for recovery.

Many entrepreneurs avoid gathering sufficient information about the market (see Chapter 5). Information is an important asset to any entrepreneur, especially regarding future market potential and forecasting the size of the immediate attainable market. Entrepreneurs will often try to guess what is happening in the market and ignore the changing marketplace. This could spell disaster, especially if competitors are reacting more positively to the market changes.

In the early stages of a new venture, it is helpful for the entrepreneur to be aware of stress points, that is, points in time at which the venture is changing in size, requiring new survival strategies. Early rapid rises in sales can be interpreted incorrectly so that the venture finds itself adding plant capacity, signing new contracts with suppliers, or increasing inventories, resulting in shrinking margins and being overleveraged. To offset this situation, prices are increased or quality weakened, leading to lower sales. This becomes a vicious circle that can lead to bankruptcy.

Stress points can be identified based on the amount of sales. For example, it may be possible to recognize that sales of $1 million, $5 million, and $25 million may represent key decision marks in terms of major capital investment and operational expenses such as hiring new key personnel. Entrepreneurs should be aware of the burden of sales levels on capital investment and operational expenses.[9]

[8]N. L. Croft, "Keeping Your Business Afloat," *Nation's Business,* February 1987, pp 16–17.

[9]Crofts, p 18.

WARNING SIGNS OF BANKRUPTCY

Entrepreneurs should be sensitive to signals in the business and the environment that may be early warnings of trouble. Often, the entrepreneur is not aware of what is going on or is not willing to accept the inevitable. Table 14–3 lists some of the key early warning signs of bankruptcy. Generally, they are interrelated and one can often lead to another.

For example, when management of the financial affairs become lax, there is a tendency to do anything to generate cash, such as reducing prices, cutting back on supplies to meet orders, or releasing important personnel such as sales representatives. A new office furniture business catering to small or medium-sized businesses illustrates how this can happen. Top management of the firm decided that moving merchandise was its top priority. Sales representatives earned standard commission on each sale, and were free to reduce prices where necessary to make the sale. Hence, without any cost or break-even awareness, sales representatives often reduced prices below direct costs. They still received their commissions when the price charged was below cost. Thus, the venture eventually lost substantial amounts of money and had to declare bankruptcy.

When an entrepreneur sees any of the warning signs in Table 14–3, he or she should immediately seek the advice of a CPA or an attorney. It may be possible to prevent bankruptcy by making immediate changes in the operation in order to improve the cash flow and profitability of the business.

STARTING OVER

Bankruptcy and liquidation does not have to be the end for the entrepreneur. History is full of examples of entrepreneurs who have failed many times before finally succeeding.

TABLE 14–3 Warning Signs of Bankruptcy

- Management of finances becomes lax, so that no one can explain how money is being spent.
- Directors cannot document or explain major transactions.
- Customers are given large discounts to enhance payments because of poor cash flow.
- Contracts are accepted below standard amounts to generate cash.
- Bank requests subordination of its loans.
- Key personnel leave company.
- Lack of materials to meet orders.
- Payroll taxes are not paid.
- Suppliers demand payment in cash.
- Increase in customers' complaints regarding service and product quality.

Gail Borden's tombstone reads "I tried and failed, and I tried again and succeeded." One of his first inventions was the Terraqueous Wagon, which was designed to travel on land or water. The invention sank on its first try. Borden also had three other inventions that failed to get patents. A fourth invention was patented but eventually wiped him out because of lack of capital and poor sales. However, Borden was persistent and committed that his vacuum condensation process, giving milk a long shelf life, would be successful. At 56, Borden had his first success with condensed milk.

Over the years, other famous entrepreneurs have also endured many failures before finally achieving success. Rowland Hussey Macy (Macy's retail stores), Ron Berger (National Video), and Thomas Edison are other examples of struggling entrepreneurs who lived through many failures.

The characteristics of entrepreneurs were discussed in Chapter 3. From that chapter, we know that entrepreneurs are likely to continue starting new ventures even after failing. There is evidence that they learn from their mistakes, and investors often look favorably on someone who has failed previously, assuming that he or she will not make the same mistakes again.[10]

Generally, entrepreneurs in endeavors after failure tend to have a better understanding and appreciation for the need for market research, more initial capitalization, and stronger business skills. Unfortunately, not all entrepreneurs learn these skills from their experiences; many tend to fail over and over again.

However, business failure does not have to be a stigma when it comes time to seek venture capital. Past records will be revealed during subsequent start-ups, but the careful entrepreneur can explain why the failure occurred and how he or she will prevent it in the future, restoring investors' confidence. As discussed in Chapter 5, the business plan will help sell the business concept to investors. It is in the business plan that the entrepreneur, even after many failures, can illustrate how this venture will be successful.

BUSINESS TURNAROUNDS

Too often we hear only about the business failures and overlook those who are able to survive bankruptcy or near bankruptcy and turn their business into a success. History provides some good examples of such turnarounds.

Many of the firms discussed below are large businesses that started small and grew through the efforts of their entrepreneurs. They demonstrate that Chapter 11 reorganization can give the entrepreneur time to resolve financial problems without pressure from creditors.

Allegheny International, a business conglomerate, filed for Chapter 11 on February 20, 1988, when it was unable to meet its debt of $500 million even after divesting

[10] L. M. Lament, What Entrepreneurs Learn from Experience. *Journal of Small Business Management,* 10 (1972), p 36.

Wilkinson Sword. As part of the reorganization, Goldman Sachs bought the firm for $655 million, and changed the company name to Sunbeam-Oster. The company emerged from Chapter 11 on September 28, 1990. However, the company still experienced losses into the early 90s.

Baldwin-United, a financial services firm, filed for Chapter 11 on September 26, 1983, with $600 million of debt. During reorganization, the company settled more than 8,300 claims. Assets decreased from $9 billion to $490 million. The company, under a new name, was then acquired by Leucadia National. On November 13, 1986, the company emerged from bankruptcy. It recently achieved revenues of $350 million and profits of $35 million.

Storage technology is a true success story. It emerged from Chapter 11 bankruptcy without being acquired by another firm. In 1984, the computer hardware firm was unable to pay its debt of $645 million, so $60 million of its assets, including a computer chip factory, were sold. The business was refocussed on computer storage, and on July 28, 1987, it emerged from Chapter 11 reorganization. In 1990 the firm had profits of $70 million on sales of $1.1 billion.[11]

Some entrepreneurs consider finding a company near bankruptcy to be a good way to start a business. Keith Martin and Chris Dunn bought KTQQ-FM, a radio station in Lake Charles, Louisiana, because it was cheaper and easier than starting from scratch. Their strategy was to acquire and turn around a country western radio station, nearly bankrupt, by making changes in programming and staffing. Revenues were increased by retraining the sales staff to be more aggressive and by keeping costs at a minimum. Projections were that the station would earn its first profit this past year after two earlier years of small losses.[12]

In 1991, there were 85,027 bankruptcy filings, up 47 percent from the previous year. Given the state of the economy, there is the belief that either the number of new ventures launched will decrease, or we will likely continue to see more bankruptcies. Thus, it seems that bankruptcy is becoming a more common strategy to protect businesses against creditors. How many of these companies will actually survive the bankruptcy is difficult to ascertain because many are acquired before the reorganization is complete. However, the stigma of being or having been in bankruptcy should not affect the entrepreneur's determination to make his or her venture successful.

If it becomes necessary to file for bankruptcy, the entrepreneur should seek the advice of attorneys, accountants, and investment bankers when appropriate. Although their fees may be high, there is often no other alternative. As stated above, with the prepackaged bankruptcy plan, the entrepreneur can minimize these fees by trying to get the creditors to preapprove any restructuring or reorganization, thus reducing the time that a firm remains under Chapter 11 and the necessity of the advisor's services.

---

[11] Kate Ballen, "Life After Chapter 11 for Six Big Survivors," *Fortune,* February 11, 1991, p 13.

[12] Jay Finegan, "Music Men," *Inc.,* January 1993, pp 80–87.

SUCCESSION OF BUSINESS

Many new ventures will be passed on to family members. If there is no one in the family interested in the business, it is important for the entrepreneur to either sell the business or train someone within the organization to take over.

Transfer to Family Members

Passing the business on to a family member can create internal problems. This often results when a son or daughter is handed the responsibility of running the business without sufficient training. A young family member can be more successful in taking over the business if he or she assumes various operational responsibilities early on. It is beneficial for the family member to rotate to different areas of the business in order to get a good perspective of the total operation. Other employees in these departments or areas will be able to assist in the training and get to know their future leader.

It is also helpful if the entrepreneur stays around for a while to act as an advisor to the successor. This can be helpful in the business decisions. Of course, it is also possible that this can result in major conflicts if the personalities involved are not compatible. In addition, employees who have been with the firm since start-up may resent the younger family member assuming control of the venture. However, while working in the organization during this transition period, the successor can help prove his or her abilities, justifying his or her future role.

Transfer to Nonfamily Member

Often a member of the family is not interested in assuming responsibility for the business. When this occurs, the entrepreneur has three choices: train a key employee and retain some equity, retain control and hire a manager, or sell the business outright.

Passing the business on to an employee ensures that the new principal is familiar with the business and the market. The experience of the employee minimizes transitional problems. In addition, the entrepreneur can take some time to make the transition smoother.

The key issue when passing the business on to an employee is ownership. If the entrepreneur plans to retain some ownership, the question of how much becomes an important area of negotiation. The new principal may prefer to have control, with the original entrepreneur remaining as a minority owner or a stockholder. The financial capacity and managerial ability of the employee will be important factors in the decision on how much ownership is transfered.

If the business has been in the family for some time and the succession to a family member may become more likely in the future, the entrepreneur may hire a manager to run the business. However, finding someone to manage the business in the same manner and with the same expertise as the entrepreneur may be difficult. If someone is found to manage the business, the likely problems are compatibility with the owners and willingness of this person to manage for any length of time without a promise of equity in the business. Executive search firms can help in the search process. It will be necessary to have a well-defined job description to assist in identifying the right person.

The last option, often referred to as **harvesting,** is to sell the business outright to either an employee or an outsider. The major considerations in this option are financial, which will likely necessitate the help of an accountant and/or lawyer. This alternative also requires that the value of the business be determined (see Chapter 11).

HARVESTING STRATEGY

There are a number of alternatives available to the entrepreneur in harvesting the venture. Some of these are straightforward and others involve more complex financial strategy. Each of these methods should be carefully considered and one selected, depending on the goals of the entrepreneur.

Direct Sale

Although this is the most common method of harvesting a venture, it does not always occur as a last resort to bankruptcy. Many entrepreneurs choose to sell so they can move on to new endeavors. Steven Rosendorf provides a good example of the considerations involved in any possible sale of the business. In 1976, his brother/partner died suddenly, leaving him alone with a $2 million costume jewelry business. At that point, Rosendorf began to plan for the eventual sale of the company. The plan included upgrading of showrooms and cost-cutting measures, including a reduction of his own salary. Within a few years, the company showed $2 million profits on sales of $13 million. Rosendorf felt it was time to sell the business, and within one year he did so, for $16 million.[13]

Unless the entrepreneur is desperate, putting a business up for sale may require time and planning, as Rosendorf's example indicates. Successful small businesses are in demand by larger firms that wish to grow by acquisition.

One of the important considerations of any business sale is the type of payment the buyer will use. Often, buyers will purchase a business using notes based on future profits. If the new owners fail in the business, the seller may receive no cash payment and possibly find him or herself taking back the company that is struggling to survive.

---

[13] Terri Thompson, "When It's Time to Sell Out," *U.S. News & World Report,* June 28, 1989, pp 62–64.

As exemplified in the Rosendorf example, preparing for a sale may necessitate serious financial reconsiderations. Many entrepreneurs give themselves big salaries and large expense accounts that obviously cut into profits. This also makes the company's earning capacity appear to be much lower than it is. Thus, if the entrepreneur must or plans to sell the business, he or she should tighten spending, avoid large personal salaries and expenses, and reinvest as much profit as possible back into the business. This formula will likely result in a much better sale agreement.

Business brokers in some instances may be helpful, since trying to actually sell a business will take time away from running it. Brokers can be discreet about a sale and may have an established network to get the word around. Brokers earn a commission from the sale of a business. Generally these commissions are based on a sliding scale starting at about 10 percent for the first $200,000.

The best way to communicate the business to potential buyers is through the business plan. A five-year comprehensive plan can provide buyers of the business with a future perspective and accountability of the value of the company (see Chapters 6 and 7).

Once the business is either sold or passed on to a family member or employee, the entrepreneur's role may depend on the sale agreement or contract with the new owner(s). Many buyers will want the seller to stay on for a short time to provide a smooth transition. Under these circumstances, the seller (entrepreneur) should negotiate an employment contract that specifies time, salary, and responsibility. If the entrepreneur is not needed in the business, it is likely that the new owner(s) will request that the entrepreneur sign an agreement not to engage in the same business for a specified number of years. These agreements vary in scope and may require a lawyer to clarify details.

An entrepreneur may also plan to only retain a business for a specified period of time, with the intent to sell it to the employees. This may entail all employees through an employee stock option plan or through a management buyout, which allows sale to occur to only certain managers of the venture.

Employee Stock Option Plan

Under a stock option plan, the business is sold to employees over a period of time. This time period may be two or three years or several years, depending on the intent of the entrepreneur in exiting the business. The employee stock option plan (ESOP) is often considered an alternative to a pension plan, particularly when the venture is too small to support a pension plan. Its purpose is to reward employees and to clarify early the succession decision of the new venture.

The ESOP has a number of advantages. First, it offers a unique incentive to employees, which can enhance their motivation to put in extra time or effort. Employees recognize that they are working for themselves and hence will focus their efforts on innovations that contribute to the long-term success of the venture. Second, it provides a mechanism to pay back those employees who have been loyal to the venture, particularly during more difficult times. Third, it allows the transfer of the business under a carefully planned written agreement.

However, in spite of its favorable attributes, the ESOP has some disadvantages. This type of stock option plan is usually quite complex to establish. It requires a complete valuation of the venture in order to establish the amount of the ESOP package. In addition, there are issues such as taxes, payout ratios, amount of equity to be transferred per year, and the amount actually invested by the employees. The agreement would also specify if the employees can buy or sell additional shares of stock once the plan has been completed. Regardless, it is clear from the complexity of this type of plan that the entrepreneur will need the advice of experts. A more simple method may be a more direct buyout by key employees of the venture.

Management Buyout

It is conceivable that the entrepreneur only wants to sell or transfer the venture to loyal, key employees. Since the ESOP described above can be rather complicated, the entrepreneur may find that a direct sale would be simpler to accomplish.

Management buyouts usually involve a direct sale of the venture for some predetermined price. This would be similar to selling one's house. To establish a price, the entrepreneur would have an appraisal of all of the assets and then determine goodwill value established from past revenue.

Sale of a venture to key employees can be for cash, or it could be financed in any number of ways. A cash sale would be unlikely if the value of the business is substantial. Financing the sale of the venture can be accomplished through a bank, or the entrepreneur could also agree to carry the note. This may be desirable to the entrepreneur in that the stream of income of the sale would be spread out over a determined period of time, enhancing cash flow and lessening the tax impact. Another method of selling the venture would be to use stock as the method of transfer. The managers buying the business may sell nonvoting or voting stock to other investors. These funds would then be used as a full or partial payment of the venture. The reason that other investors would be interested in buying stock or a bank would be interested in lending the managers money is because the business is continuing with the same management team and with its established track record.

Other methods of transferring or selling a business are through a public offering or even a merger with another business. These topics are discussed in Chapters 11 and 13.

Before determining the appropriate harvesting strategy, the entrepreneur should seek the advice of outsiders. Every circumstance is different, and the actual decision will depend on the entrepreneur's goals. Case histories of each of the above methods can also be reviewed to help determine which option is best for the given circumstances.

SUMMARY

This chapter deals with the decisions, problems, and issues involved in ending the venture. Even though the intent of all entrepreneurs is to establish a venture for a long time, many problems can cause these plans to fail. Since about one-half of all new businesses fail in their first four years of business, it is important for the entrepreneur to understand the options for either ending or salvaging a venture.

Bankruptcy offers three options for the entrepreneur. Under Chapter 11 of the Bankruptcy Act of 1978 the venture will be reorganized under a plan approved by the courts. New versions of this form of bankruptcy now allow the entrepreneur an opportunity to file a prepackaged bankruptcy plan. This plan avoids large expenses and prepares creditors in advance so that negotiations can occur before the courts become involved.

Chapter 13 provides for an extended time payment plan to cover outstanding debts. This is not involuntary and is not an alternative for partnerships or corporations. Both of these alternatives are designed to help entrepreneurs salvage the business and keep it going. Under Chapter 7, the venture will be liquidated either voluntarily or involuntarily.

Keeping the business going is the primary intent of all entrepreneurs. Avoiding excessive optimism, preparing good marketing plans, making good cash projections, keeping familiar with the market, and being sensitive to stress points in the business all can help keep the business going.

Entrepreneurs can also be sensitive to key warnings of potential problems. Lax management of finances, discounting to generate cash, loss of key personnel, lack of raw materials, nonpayment of payroll taxes, demands of suppliers to be paid in cash, and increased customer complaints about service and product quality are some of the key factors that lead to bankruptcy. If the business does fail, however, the entrepreneur should always consider starting over. Failure can be a learning process, as evidenced by the many famous inventors who succeeded after many failures.

One of the other venture-ending decisions that an entrepreneur may face is succession of the business. If the business is family owned the entrepreneur would likely seek a family member to succeed. Other options, if no family member is available or interested, include transferring some or all of the business to an employee or outsider, or hiring an outsider to manage the business. Direct sale, employees' stock option plan, or management buyout offers the entrepreneur alternatives in selling the venture.

QUESTIONS FOR DISCUSSION

1. Describe the major differences between Chapter 7, Chapter 11 and Chapter 13 bankruptcy.
2. What advantages and disadvantages are there in presenting a prepackaged bankruptcy plan to creditors?

3. The entrepreneur can play an important role in enhancing the speed at which reorganization under bankruptcy occurs. Discuss.
4. In the early stages of a new venture, certain stress points may be critical in determining future direction. Explain these stress points and how they can affect various parts of the operation.
5. Entrepreneurs should be sensitive to certain identifying signs of bankruptcy. Describe these warning signs.
6. What are some of the key issues involved in providing for the succession of the business?

KEY TERMS

Chapter 11 bankruptcy
Chapter 7 bankruptcy
Chapter 13 bankruptcy
prepackaged bankruptcy plan
harvesting
voluntary bankruptcy
involuntary bankruptcy

SELECTED READINGS

Barlow, S. (April 1933). The 11th Hour. *Entrepreneur,* pp 133–37.

Uses a case example to describe when and how an entrepreneur should file for bankruptcy protection. Ignoring the classic signs of bankruptcy usually results in a situation where it is too late to expect any positive reorganization. Also discusses issues to help someone make it through the bankruptcy process.

Brockhaus, R. H., Sr. (April, 1985). Is There Life After Death? The Impact of Unsuccessful Entrepreneurial Endeavors on the Life of the Entrepreneurs. *Proceedings,* 1985 Conference on Entrepreneurship. pp 468–81.

Provides insight into the impact of failed entrepreneurial endeavors on the lives of exentrepreneurs after the conclusion of their entrepreneurial experience. Of those studied, most remained in a career involving a rather high degree of independence. They were glad they had started their own business, but only a few would do it again.

Croft, N. L. (February 1987). Keeping Your Business Afloat, *Nation's Business,* 75, No. 2, pp 16–23.

Provides a number of case studies that show how to keep a business going. Each gives helpful hints for dealing with bankruptcy, trying to start over, and responding to danger signals. Expert opinions on specific requirements to avoid bankruptcy are discussed.

Goldstein, A. S. (1983). *How to Save Your Business.* (Enterprise Publishing, Inc.) New York, N.Y.

Provides a chapter-by-chapter how-to approach for entrepreneurs who are having problems in a new venture. Each chapter provides specific strategies and techniques that can keep the venture out of bankruptcy court and on the road to prosperity. Provides approaches to get back in business in the event insolvency does occur.

Moulton, W. N., and Howard, T. (February 1993). Bankruptcy as a Deliberate Strategy: Theoretical Considerations and Empirical Evidence. *Strategic Management Journal,* pp 125–35.

Bankruptcy reorganization has been identified as a remedy for financial distress, yet there is little agreement as to its value to managers and their firms. A review of 73 bankruptcies and subsequent reorganization efforts is discussed. Factors that contribute to the success of any reorganization are also identified.

Singleton, M. (September 1986). What's it Worth to You? *Inc.,* pp 113–15.

The first step in selling a business is to get an accurate appraisal. Describes several types of appraisals that can be done, depending on the purpose. The methods of valuation used are discussed, and some guidelines on selecting an appraiser are given.

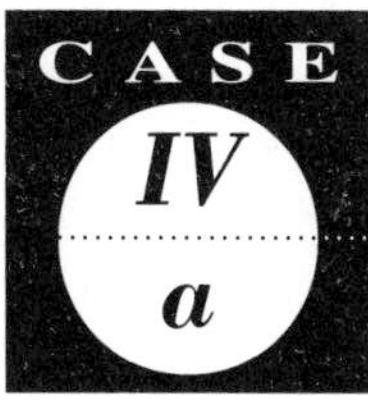

Ski Boot Buckler

Brian Sorenson, a native of Vermont and an avid skier, had always found buckling and unbuckling icy, snow-covered ski boots difficult. He felt a boot buckler that would make the irritating process effortless was much needed on the ski scene.

Finally, in the winter of 1979, Brian and his wife, Linda, decided that the manufacture and sale of such a product would be worth a try. Initial plans for both the development of the product and the financing required were laid out. Brian left his job with a major New York City bank, and Linda left her job with an investment firm to devote all of their time to the development and manufacture of the new ski boot buckler. After several start-up problems, they finally introduced a boot buckler in 1980.

From 1980 to 1982, 35,000 bucklers were produced. Yet, by 1982 only 7,000 had actually been sold. The product was used by the National Ski Patrol and had been endorsed by the U.S. Olympic Ski Team. Given those facts, the Sorensons were confident that the buckler was a good product. What they needed was a way to get the attention of the general skiing market.

INDUSTRY BACKGROUND

Sporting Goods

The sporting goods industry has always experienced extreme variability in sales. The industry comprises many diverse product areas, which seldom move in tandem. Certain goods or activities come into vogue just as others go out. Some sports, however, such as weightlifting, baseball, tennis, and skiing, have shown continuous popularity throughout the cycles that other sports have experienced.

Sporting goods are also highly dependent on the consumer's discretionary income, particularly for certain sports. For instance, golf and ski equipment appear to be especially sensitive to income changes; whereas, such items as exercise equipment are not.

Finally, some sports, especially skiing, are highly susceptible to weather conditions. Early snow is critical to ski sales because most sales occur before Christmas. If snow comes later in the winter, skiers tend to make do with their old equipment. Manufacturers, distributors, retailers, resort areas, and even ski-oriented magazines are all affected by a poor snow season. The following section explains more about the ski industry in particular.

Why they buy. Purchasing considerations varied from product to product, but durability, quality, and price were three key factors of all items of ski equipment. Comfort was the most important factor when buying boots, and safety was the most important factor for bindings.

Downhill skiers most often used ski-shop personnel, advice of other skiers, and ski publications to help them with their purchasing decisions. The average skier tended to visit approximately two stores before deciding on a particular place to make his or her purchase.

Distribution: a tumultuous history. Ski-shop owners before 1960 were primarily people who wanted to turn their love for snow skiing into profits. As a result, there were few specialty ski shops, and they usually could be found only near ski areas.

In the 1960s, specialty ski shops began springing up in metropolitan areas all over the country, experiencing a great deal of success. Recognizing this as a lucrative market, discount houses, department stores, and sporting goods "supermarkets" began offering ski products as well. Sales results for these outlets were very disappointing, however. They lacked the experience, expertise, and professionalism required to satisfy skiers' sales and service needs, and as a result manufacturers were unwilling to supply them with their high-quality lines.

In the 1970s, these same manufacturers experienced an oversupply of merchandise. They were forced to expand distribution of their quality ski supplies beyond the small specialty shops to larger retailing operations. These larger sporting goods chains grew in number but not in the total percentage of ski sales. As of 1980, independent ski shops still accounted for 88 percent of all ski sales. Industry surveys showed that they held the high-performance and high-priced segment of the market, while sporting goods chains generally served the lower-priced segment.

In 1980 and 1981, poor snow conditions resulted in a severe change in the makeup of the market as 10 million fewer skiers hit the slopes in each of those two years. Ski equipment sales fell fast. Some observers estimated that the ski industry had seen a 50 percent drop in retail sales.

Weaker, smaller retailers began disappearing, and manufacturers were hit with yet another merchandise glut. Liberal financing policies, which had always allowed retailers to postpone payments to manufacturers until after the ski season, became a thing of the past. Heavy promotion and sponsorship of big-name skiers and racing events were sharply curtailed and replaced by local promotions. Many felt that in addition to being less costly, local promotions more accurately addressed specific ski market conditions in local markets. Advertising in consumer magazines also decreased significantly.

Specialty discounters and off-price retailers, backed with heavy promotion and advertising budgets, emerged to take advantage of oversupply. Small specialty shops, who bought from wholesalers, were hit hardest by competitive pressures from these discounters.

Chain retailers, who dealt directly with manufacturers, suffered as well. Some of these retailers responded by pulling out of the ski market altogether, while others restricted their efforts to specific target markets.

In the meantime, manufacturers began making fewer model changes to enable them to carry inventory from year to year. Large manufacturers gained a large share of the market, while smaller companies merged with others in order to survive.

In sum, an estimated 200 retailers of ski equipment and an undetermined number of manufacturers declared bankruptcy by the end of the 1981 season.

Promotion. The retail trade did most of its buying in March through May. In certain areas of the country, such as in New England, retailers bought at home through company salespeople or reps. But most retail buying was done at the ski trade shows, which were usually held in the spring months.

The requirements to enter trade shows varied. The Ski Industries of America required each exhibitor at its yearly trade shows to be a member of the association. Dues varied according to the amount of ski-related business generated, but in general ran from $1,000 to $5,000 annually. In addition, exhibit fees at the trade show ran $2.75 per square foot. On the average, approximately 10,000 retailers from an estimated 4,000 shops around the country came to this trade show to do their buying.

There were also regional trade shows held two to four times a year. Membership stipulations varied here, too, but they generally involved a $500 initial membership fee, an additional annual fee of $100, plus a small exhibit fee. Approximately 1,000 to 1,500 buyers attended regional trade shows.

THE SKI BOOT BUCKLER

As noted at the beginning of the case, Brian Sorenson was no stranger to the ski scene. Having skied since the age of four, he eventually put himself through college working as a ski instructor at Killington Ski Resort in Vermont. Since graduation, both Brian and Linda had lived in New York, but both were avid skiers and continued to spend their weekends at their chalet in Killington during the ski season. The Sorensons went into the ski boot buckler business because they felt there was an unmet need in the ski market; they also felt they could fill that need as successfully as anyone.

The Product

The ski boot buckler was manufactured as a one-piece aluminum tool with a protective oxide film covering it. When the prongs of the buckler were slipped over the latch of the boot buckle, the tool formed a five-inch extension to give the skier better leverage, greatly facilitating the buckling and unbuckling of ski boots. In addition, the flat end could be used to scrape snow from the boots. The buckler was pocket-sized, weighed about 2½ ounces, was brightly colored, and was of a high quality and unique design.

The Sorensons' problems started when they introduced the first boot buckler in 1980. Almost immediately, they received complaints that it didn't work well on certain models of ski boots. The buckler was immediately recalled, and a modification in its curvature solved the problem. However, it wasn't long before another problem appeared.

Competition

There were several other bucklers on the market, and one of them claimed that the Sorensons had infringed on their patent. The Sorensons didn't feel the claim was valid, as the other manufacturer's buckler was of a different, less practical design. It was narrower and made of steel, which made it heavier and more difficult to use. Nevertheless, the Sorensons were forced to hire a lawyer who would battle the case in court. They hoped to obtain a patent on their buckler if they won the case.

Marketing

A detailed marketing strategy for product introduction had not been established during the first two years of operation. No market pretesting had been done. The current marketing program consisted of using ski manufacturers' representatives to sell to specialty ski shops in the local ski areas and to make a few personal presentations at ski shows. The Sorensons also ran some ads in ski magazines and *The Wall Street Journal.* Through direct mail distribution, the buckler had obtained some market penetration in ski areas in New Hampshire, Colorado, New York, and Iowa. Although the ads ran in other parts of the country, the Sorensons had not been successful in obtaining distribution in other ski areas.

EXHIBIT 1 Income Statement

		Year Ending 1981		*Year Ending 1982*
Sales	@3,000	$30,000	@4,000	$40,000
Cost of goods sold		3,750		5,000
Gross profit		$26,250		$35,000
Operating expenses		3,750		5,000
Net profit		$22,500		$30,000

Finance

The ski boot buckler was produced at an average cost of $1.25 and sold at retail outlets for $10 each. As the income statement in Exhibit 1 shows, the 7,000 bucklers sold in the first two years produced a profit of $55,200 before interest and taxes. However, since 35,000 bucklers had actually been produced and not sold, there was an inventory of 28,000 bucklers, representing a $35,000 investment.

Total investment to date by both the Sorensons and the two silent partners who had been with the project from the start had been $80,000. The profit margin on the ski boot bucklers that were sold was substantial and seemed to prove that the buckler could be successful. However, the number of sales in the first two years of operation was disappointing. A substantial sum of money had been invested already, and if more were needed, alternative sources of financing would be required. The Sorensons felt it would be worth it, however, and were currently looking for a new way to market the product. Key issues at this point were whether to hire a consultant to assess the market, invest more funds in promoting the product, or restructure the marketing efforts toward other markets.

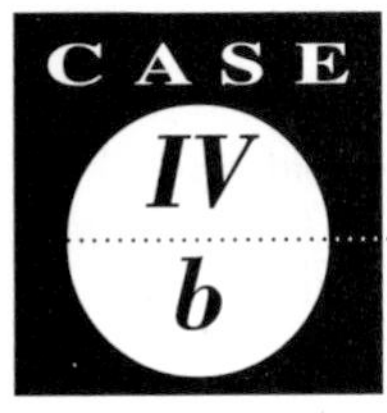

Dickens Data Systems

It was a great day for Gordon Dickens, founder of Dickens Data Systems (DDS). The Atlanta sun was shining brightly, and he was enjoying a terrific round of golf. While lining up his drive on the sixteenth hole, the young entrepreneur decided he was going to try to reach the green. He would need one of his best drives ever, but the way things were going this might not be much to ask. Unfortunately, his forceful swing gave no indication that he had only grazed the ball. It was a miserable drive. Gordon stood still for a moment in disbelief. Later that night, still frustrated by the overswing that started his game spiraling downward, he couldn't help wondering if the same thing could happen to his business. DDS was facing by far the biggest opportunity in its history. There didn't appear to be any way they could lose. Still, he wondered. Years ago it was easier to keep track, to oversee the whole company, but now it was more and more difficult to guide DDS. He realized that the rapid growth phase was different from the ones in the past. He would have to change from "doing" to "managing." Although Gordon had become a computer industry expert, his managerial experience was still limited. Could his management skills accommodate all the changes facing DDS?

BACKGROUND

Gordon Dickens received his bachelors degree in physics in 1976 from Emory University and a masters degree in nuclear engineering from Georgia Tech in 1977. This background would later aid him in software programming and in management of other engineers.

These talents, combined with his ability to manage the creative, if eccentric, genius of his engineers, help him to grow the business. In addition, Gordon Dickens possessed a great deal of business vision. His insights into the future of the computer field had served him extremely well to date. Furthermore, unlike many entrepreneurs, he desired to stay with his firm for the enjoyment of it and well beyond the point of financial independence.

This case was originally prepared by Bart Janssen, Dr. Herbert Reichsollner, and Jeff Schleger under the supervision of Dr. Richard T. Meyer, Professor of Entrepreneurship at the Emory Business School, as the basis for class discussion rather than to illustrate either effective or ineffective handling of a management situation. Financial support for the completion of this case was provided by a grant from the Center for Entrepreneurial Leadership of the Ewing Marion Kauffman Foundation.

Moreover, Gordon could be characterized as an extremely hard-working, committed person. Other character traits included his conservative nature, confidence, and sharp analytical skills. Of particular importance was the conservative business approach he brought to the Dickens Data Systems. This was powerfully exemplified by the centralizing of all equity in the top management team.

DDS was founded in 1981. Gordon's right-hand man since 1983, and a minority equity holder, was Ted Davis. Gordon felt that Ted's more liberal nature provided a necessary counterbalance to his own. Additionally, while Ted participated in virtually all facets of the business, his sales and marketing talents were a key success factor for DDS. Like Gordon, Ted was an engineer who quickly developed a clear vision as to the trends in the computer industry.

FORMATION AND GROWTH OF DICKENS DATA SYSTEMS

While still an engineering undergraduate, Gordon Dickens became fascinated by the burgeoning computer industry. He spent a good deal of his free time sharing ideas with other computer enthusiasts and investigating the latest advances in computer stores.

As his knowledge about the industry grew, he began to develop graphics packages in his spare time. His first commercial effort was the Superplotter, a set of generic graphics systems. Through the personal selling efforts made by Gordon and his wife, Melissa, as well as through the professionally produced ads they bought, the Superplotter sold in significant numbers.

It is important to note that the personal computer industry at this time was in its infancy. There were only a few microcomputer manufacturers, and software developers were equally scarce. The software publishers typically worked out of their homes, lacked slick product packaging, and designed their own ads. Therefore, one of DDS's earliest competitive advantages was its use of professionally designed ads.

By the start of 1982, Dickens Data Systems had sold over 250 Superplotters. The size of their margins, $50 per unit sold to a retailer against just $2 of product cost, encouraged the Dickens to quit their full-time jobs and focus on Dickens Data Systems. Within eight months, they had achieved a level of success that justified obtaining office space. The hiring of additional employees soon followed.

Within a year, he realized that the graphics software, which they designed and sold, did not go far enough in addressing the full package of computer needs that was frequently requested. In response, Dickens Data Systems shifted its focus towards creating turnkey solutions (primarily in accounting) for the computer needs of small businesses. This was made possible through the accounting, programming, and sales strengths possessed by Dickens' first few employees.

During this time, Dickens Data Systems developed its basic business strategy. Among the main points were: 1) emphasize "consultant selling" and meet the price/performance needs of the multi-user microcomputer segment; 2) emphasize DDS's engineering and programming capabilities for the development of products which were not available off-the-shelf; 3) emphasize the development of products that could be sold many times over and were developed with in-house R&D funds; and 4) emphasize the sale of in-house developed products through distribution to dealers, agents, and end users.[1]

DDS's business strategy had consistently been one of diversification. The owners believed that this was a significant advantage in the volatile computer industry. Surprisingly, many businesses in their field had fallen on hard times because they relied on only one, seemingly strong offering.

Another constant concern of the founders was to spot future developments in their markets. For instance, by 1983, a time when few people even knew the word *UNIX,* DDS had decided to shift from the MP/M systems to UNIX in the area of multi-user environments. Another critical decision at that time was to take on larger-scale technical projects. This move was spurred on by DDS's realization that it had grown to a size where it had the resources and manpower to provide large-scale engineering and programming services.

The year 1986 brought a turning point in DDS's activities. Gordon Dickens was contacted by "Big Blue" (IBM) to market its new UNIX-based system, the Reduced Instructions Set Computer Technology (RT). This resulted from IBM's belief that this market was too small for it. IBM proceeded to seek out DDS as a more appropriately sized firm to handle the business. DDS began to develop a strong connection with IBM. In fact, Gordon Dickens' firm worked as a vendor for IBM, as a provider of engineering and programming services, and also as a supplier of third-party products to IBM customers.

THE OPPORTUNITY

By far the largest opportunity in the history of Dickens Data Systems emerged when AT&T's UNIX operating system became the focal point for the federal government's efforts to popularize one particular system with the versatility to work with any type of software. IBM responded with the introduction of the UNIX-based RT in 1986. RISC, Reduced Instructions Set Computer technology, resulted from the findings in the mid-1970s that showed that 20 percent of computer instructions performed 80 percent of the computer's work. IBM's RT, a scientific and engineering workstation, was one of the first processors based on RISC technology.

At this juncture, IBM reversed its position on UNIX. It announced its AIX Family Definition (IBM's version of UNIX). This development of an integrated set of UNIX offerings by IBM opened up the previously untapped UNIX market and provided an alternative route for committed IBM users who had a UNIX requirement

---

[1]DDS Business Plan, 1989.

and would otherwise have had to leave the IBM fold. In addition to the AIX, the computer giant also developed Systems Application Architecture, which made it possible for many of the uses of traditional IBM operating systems to be provided by the AIX. This was in contrast to the many non-IBM architectures that were made available in IBM's proprietary systems.

W. Frank King, general manager of IBM's Advanced Engineering Systems Division, made it clear that the newly introduced RT's architectural concept was a fundamental advance and would be included in many more machines. The RT was a leap forward for IBM in terms of capacity and performance, just as was the Personal Computer (PC). At the low end of the market PC/DOS was expected to remain prevalent, but UNIX was seen as the future leading system at the workstation level.

Although IBM was very vocal in their support for the RT, the company was not likely to introduce a multiprocessor version (one that had the expansion board technology to run more than four users off a single RT) for fear of hurting sales of its more profitable systems. This limited support generated a unique opportunity for Gordon Dickens' company.

While consulting several clients on the use of the RT, Dickens Data Systems modified third-party products for effective use with the RT. Their landmark improvement, however, was an expansion board that enabled the user to run more than four workstations off the IBM system. A workstation can be defined as any microcomputer with a performance level significantly higher than a mainstream PC, and which can be configured to share data easily with other workstations. At first, the company doubled the number of workstations (to eight) that could be run. As the months went by, DDS was able to double this number again, and again, and eventually reached the 64 workstation capacity level of the RT.

This breakthrough came about because of a very wise hiring decision made early in the company's history. One summer, Gordon Dickens employed a young engineering intern from Georgia Tech. Fred Stern was no ordinary intern. He possessed the remarkable ability to remember and analyze phenomenal amounts of data. For example, he was consistently able to rattle off *pi* to fifty digits beyond the decimal point. This skill enabled him to be an extremely effective programmer, a fact not lost on Gordon. DDS took the extraordinary step of funding his education and ultimately hiring him as their chief programmer. Together with his research staff, this young man went on to do what 10 other firms had failed to accomplish despite significant R&D investment: He developed a proprietary expansion board for the RT.

At first, there was limited understanding of the huge potential for this board, as it was only built to satisfy the unique requirements of a few customers. Nonetheless, DDS quickly informed IBM of this advancement. IBM, for the reason stated above, was not interested in acquiring this improvement. However, since there seemed to be some interest from IBM's clients, the giant computer company E-mailed its worldwide network information about this enhancement. Gordon Dickens later referred to this event as an "unbelievable opportunity." He not only anticipated tremendous domestic possibilities but also international ones.

UNIX AND THE IBM RT

While Gordon Dickens was confident that the UNIX system would carve out a substantial market, various industry observers felt that its future was less secure. MIS managers continued to be confused about the UNIX operating system, mainly because of the fragmented nature of the UNIX marketing and support industry.

Most of the uncertainty about the future of UNIX was fed by unclear commitments from AT&T and IBM. Many doubted AT&T's long-term commitment to the computer industry as a whole on the basis of its tentative support for the UNIX system, a system that AT&T itself had selected to be its standard. IBM's limited involvement to date was generally viewed as a temporary interest as well.

It was clear that UNIX still had a long way to go before becoming a generally accepted standard. In fact, only a few companies were using it for significant business applications at this time. Even in the scientific environment, which was the core application field for UNIX, the operating system already experienced serious competition from more advanced systems like LISP and Prolog.

On the positive side, a few hardware manufacturers, such as Hewlett-Packard, Sperry, and Sun Microsystems, developed substantial expertise in the UNIX system and actively supported their UNIX offerings. Moreover, a number of governments had been UNIX-based from the time of its inception. Additionally, some observers estimated that well over half of the large computer system procurements specified UNIX as their base from which to operate. These successes were tied to the competitive advantages of the UNIX system. It possessed great strength as a communication tool, while its superior ability to share information across applications and users was unquestioned.

The IBM RT, as introduced in 1986, had a list price of $7,900 (1 MB RAM color monitor, 32 bit RISC CPU, 40 MB hard disk, no networking capabilities). IBM's AIX version sold for $2,295. The AIX had not been successful initially. The product experienced strong competition from offerings by Sun, Apollo, and DEC. In general, the RT and AIX combination was a notch below the other workstations in performance, graphics support, and networking. Moreover, its AIX operating systems meant a significant loss of software compatibility. The main perception was that the machine was underpowered, and that it needed a new graphics card, as well as a faster processor, to become a serious competitor in the workstation market.

MANAGING THE GROWTH

In the face of his firm's proprietary expansion board innovation, Gordon never really considered changing the basic strategy of the business, which relied on three sources of income (see Exhibit 1):[2]

---

[2]DDS Business Plan, 1987.

EXHIBIT 1

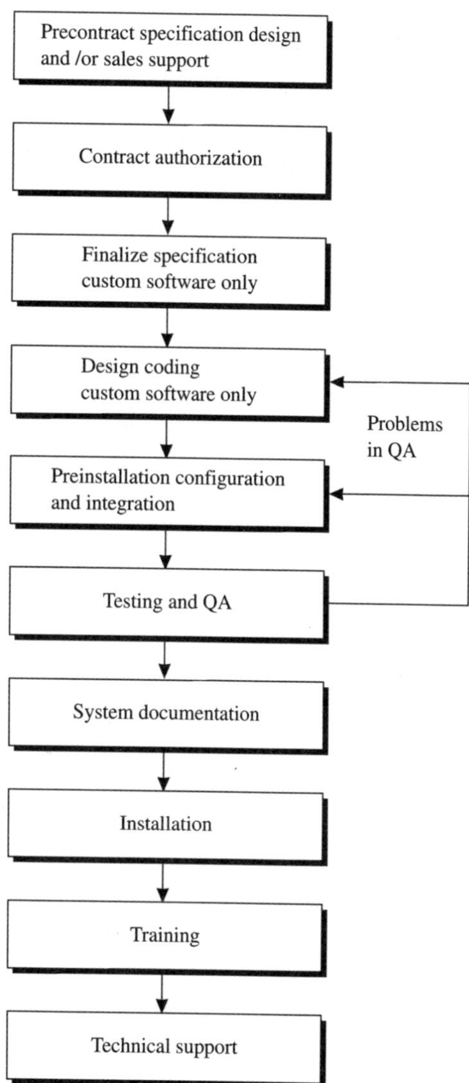

1. Consulting, management, and programming services.
2. Resale of proprietary Dickens Data Systems computer hardware and software products developed with in-house and/or contracted research and development funds.
3. Resale of off-the-shelf computer hardware and software products.

While dropping one or two lines of business could have been viewed as a coping strategy in light of the demands of the coming rapid growth phase, Gordon preferred to focus on how to juggle all of the lines at once. However, Gordon was wondering how he should deal with the fast growth that his company was about to experience. For DDS, the issue was not whether to embrace the opportunities before them but rather how to manage the inevitable changes they would bring. Furthermore, he realized that the decisions to be made would have massive effects on all aspects of the company.

Financing

To take full advantage of the emerging market, substantial capital would be necessary. However, as the following sections illustrate, there existed a wide array of optional tactics that DDS could employ. The firm's decisions regarding these tactics would greatly affect whether they would need to seek outside funding or not. Any such decision could end their historical pattern of keeping all equity in the hands of top management and/or add a substantial amount of debt to the balance sheet. Both strategies carried new risk for Gordon, Ted, and the rest of the firm. The other alternative was to grow the company in a limited way that could be financed through internally generated cash flows. Whatever specific decisions they made, Gordon was certain that he did not want to risk the company's fate on any high risk tactic (see Exhibits 2, 3, 4, and 5).

EXHIBIT 2 Historical Performance Summary and Projections

Year	*Sales ($ millions)*	*Profit ($ thousands)*	*Margin (percentage)*
Historical			
1981	0.01	1	10.00
1982	0.1	10	10.00
1983	0.2	20	10.00
1984	0.4	64	16.00
1985	0.9	59	6.56
1986	1.2	70	5.83
Forecasted			
1987	2.2	230	10.00
1988	4	400	10.00
1989	7	700	10.00
1990	10	1,000	10.00
1995	25	2,500	10.00

EXHIBIT 3

Present 1986 performance (until October)		*1987 projected*
Sales	$1,834,855	$2,486,875
Cost of goods	$848,167	$1,178,000
Net sales	$986,688	$1,308,875
Sales expense	$505,164	$621,000
Administrative expense	$346,476	$419,750
Other expense	$39,336	$1,873
R&D expense	$26,974	$34,500
Net income	$68,738	$231,752

EXHIBIT 4

Balance sheet	*1986*	*1987 (projected)*
Current assets	$304,855	$950,000
Fixed assets	$63,558	$170,000
Total assets	$368,413	$1,120,000
Current liabilities	$282,413	$660,000
Long-term liabilities	$7,826	$20,000
Total liabilities	$290,239	$680,000
Net worth	$78,174	$440,000

EXHIBIT 5 Historical Gross Profit Margins

Year	*Overall gross profit*
1984	54%
1985	55%
1986	54%

1987 quarterly projections

	1Q	2Q	3Q	4Q
Sales	$350,000	$450,000	$650,000	$775,000
Cost of goods	$160,000	$205,000	$295,000	$355,000
Net sales	$190,000	$245,000	$355,000	$420,000
Sales expense	$85,000	$110,000	$155,000	$190,000
Administrative expense	$55,000	$75,000	$110,000	$125,000
Other expense	$7,000	$9,000	$13,000	$16,000
R&D expense	$5,000	$6,000	$9,000	$10,000
Net income	$38,000	$45,000	$68,000	$79,000

Culture

In 1987, the culture at Dickens Data Systems was very informal. They had only 20 employees, most of whom had multiple roles and shared their intense work ethic. This helped make it possible for Gordon and Ted to be managers and to engage in many nonmanagerial tasks. But how would this culture change with a swift 100 percent or larger increase in the number of employees? Both entrepreneurs seemed to be captured too much by the potential of their products and by the unexpected high inflow of expansion board orders to consider the cultural implications fully. Put simply, should the informal culture be maintained, and if so, how?

Marketing and Sales

At this time, Dickens Data Systems was receiving revenues mainly from software sales and related services. Most of the software development was done on a contract basis. As soon as a new software product or an upgrade was developed, new and existing customers were approached. Ted Davis's personal efforts led to roughly 80 percent of the sales.

The sales challenge presented to Dickens Data Systems was an interesting one. Their first mover position in expansion boards and the assistance from IBM enabled orders to roll in virtually unsolicited. Having said this, DDS had other offerings and believed it might even find various synergies between its turnkey, customized, and expansion board lines. All of this would certainly require careful selling, and lots of it, to be realized fully. The firm's owners knew they would face increasing time constraints and that their historical roles in selling DDS's offerings would be threatened. The central sales-related question they faced was whether to increase the size of their sales force in the usual frugal manner or to hire many representatives immediately in order to capture all possible opportunities.

Advertisements to date were done on a limited scale. Trade magazines ads were used as a major way to update the client base about DDS's new offerings. However, such magazines might not be a suitable medium for this new highly specialized opportunity. Given the larger size of the corporate clients brought in by IBM's E-mail notification, the partners wondered if they should pursue future expansion board customers via media spending of any sort. In short, these bigger corporate customers could perhaps best be attracted by the partners' own sales calls.

A different dilemma was the pricing of the expansion board. Pricing the expansion board too high would mean that a significant share of the market would pass it up. Conversely, a very low price would "leave money on the table." They were well aware that it was common practice in the computer industry to price a product in accordance with the amount of money it saved in labor costs. Margins somewhere between 50 percent and 100 percent were normal, and frequently the take went well beyond these figures. Additional pricing techniques were also considered. For example, they could set the figure at some large percentage of the price of a minicomputer with similar strengths. This would provide a handsome margin because their expansion board was far less expensive to produce.

Another issue that would have to be addressed concerned the company's distribution channels. There were two main options. In-house selling and shipping guaranteed the largest margins but could also seriously hamper exposure to the industry. Using distributors would do the opposite.

Customer Service

There was a definite parallel between the company's sales and service situations. As the flood of orders came in and as even more would be vigorously sought out, the tiny service staff of two would be overwhelmed. There were several choices. As with the selling staff needs, the service personnel could be brought in proactively or only in response to the severely overworked existing staff. Alternatively, Dickens Data Systems had the option of striking some deal whereby the makers of the expansion boards would service the units they produced. As with so many of the decisions Dickens Data Systems grappled with during this prosperous time, the overriding concern was to make no move that had the potential to jeopardize the entire operation. And, if at all possible, the credit line was to remain greatly underutilized.

Research & Development

Upgrading this new product and supporting it was going to consume considerable amounts of the R&D staff's time. Currently, Dickens Data Systems only needed three months to bring a new product to the market. This could slow significantly without further additions to the R&D staff. Additionally, because the top researchers were critical to the success of the firm, how should their time be allocated?

Also to be resolved was the thorny issue of whether to keep focusing on the improvement of competitor's offerings or to shift towards in-house innovation. Incrementally upgrading others' work was faster, but it did not have the consistency nor the brand name enhancement potential of internal developments.

International Opportunities

The product features of DDS's offerings were top quality, customized, and highly appreciated by customers. Because the margins on goods and services sold overseas were typically larger than domestic margins, Dickens Data Systems could afford the convenience of using independent international distributors. As a result, international sales accounted for 15–20 percent of overall sales. However, IBM's announcement of DDS's proprietary expansion board opened up even greater international opportunities. Gordon and Ted wondered how they should address this aspect of their business. Should Dickens Data Systems stick with their present

EXHIBIT 6

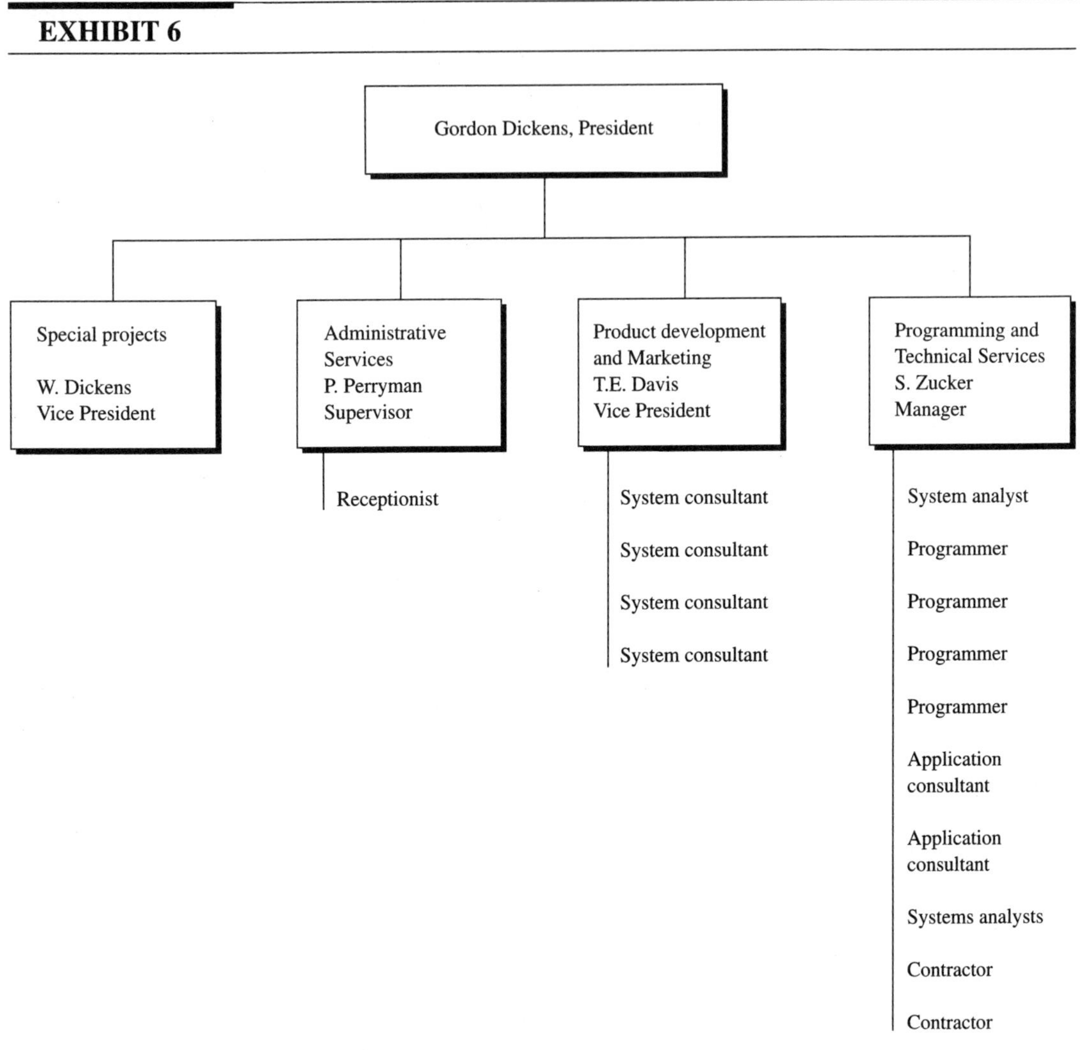

channel or consider strategic alliances, licensing agreements, or even the creation of one or more subsidiaries? This question was of particular interest because each option would involve significantly different needs for capital.

Organization and Staffing

As Dickens Data Systems faced its rapid growth phase, it employed 20 people. Besides Gordon and Ted (then vice president), there were two other managers, four programmers, six service and salespersons, two analysts, two contractors, and one receptionist (see Exhibit 6).

The Dickens Data Systems organization lacked professional managers. Even Gordon Dickens questioned his managerial skills, having only trial and error training in that function. Given this, the firm had to decide whether it wanted to promote staff to manage each function or go outside and hire professionals. They never questioned their roles as the top managers. Complicating their dilemma was the issue of what kind of professional manager they might even consider. Should corporate types be brought in or managers with an entrepreneurial background?

With the necessary influx of middle managers, the DDS partners had to settle on a strategy to handle the inevitable conflicts and power plays that would evolve. Two basic alternatives presented themselves: retain their united front approach and never let factions rattle their own rapport, or change to a more divided structure that would pit Gordon's functional underlings against Ted's. This latter approach would bring conflicts to the surface at all levels and hopefully lead to healthy dispute resolution. On the other hand, the company culture, so successful to date, would be threatened by the advent of two opposing camps.

As the rapid growth phase descended upon them, Gordon and Ted debated whether to increase the level of specialization in job responsibilities at all levels. At present, one typical worker was selling, order processing, and shipping products. Gordon Dickens himself wore many hats. He could be programming one minute, selling the next, and trying to manage others throughout. Did this situation create large numbers of flexible employees or just inefficiently use them?

Then there was the issue of how to train the fast increasing workforce. It was felt that two weeks a year was the appropriate amount of structured training each employee should receive. Should they use the one free week of dealer training offered by IBM and combine it with one reimbursed week of whatever training any employee selected or should they develop an in-house training system that would also give two weeks of training a year? The advantages of the latter method would be consistently management-selected materials and trainers, and general solidification of the corporate culture. The other alternative had the advantages of being less costly and allowing the workforce to vest themselves in the training they most valued.

It was an exciting time at Dickens Data Systems. The opportunities were numerous, but so were the pitfalls. Many a start-up had flopped in this rapid growth phase, and the two partners at Dickens Data Systems were well aware of this. A golden opportunity had been created by their efforts to date. The only question was whether they could capitalize on it.

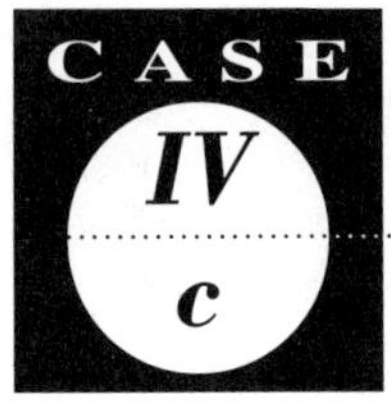

American Professional Slo-Pitch League

The American Slo-Pitch League (APSPL) was entering its fourth season in 1979. It already had teams in 12 cities across the nation and was considering opening a new franchise in the central New England area. Steve Bergstrom, a league player, was currently trying to locate a specific area in that region with both the appropriate demographic target market and a stadium that satisfied league requirements.

THE LEAGUE

Slo-pitch softball had been popular in America for years. Although an estimated 35 million Americans participated in the sport, the APSPL was the first and only professional league in the game's history. Its originators wanted to develop an organization that would "make its mark" with the other great sports leagues. They felt slo-pitch softball fans would be willing to pay to watch the game "played at its very best, in a stadium small enough to hear the chatter the way it was meant to be." Fans would also pay to park their cars, eat a couple of hot dogs, and quench their thirst with beer or soft drinks, management reasoned. The APSPL played its first game on May 30, 1975.

The slo-pitch softball season lasted four months. It began in May and lasted through August. Each team played a 32 doubleheader schedule, with 16 of those games played at home. The players were all professional or local softball stars, and many were retired baseball greats. They received an average salary of $5,000 per season, and for the most part held other jobs in the off season. Bergstrom, for example, was a teacher in Boston during the school year.

The league's marketing strategy was to create awareness of the APSPL as a reputable organization that was here to stay. The league used a proportion of the $50,000 annual membership dues paid by each franchise to provide members with materials, ideas, and guidance to successfully market their individual teams. The franchises were also expected to supplement the league's effort with a marketing campaign tailored for their specific communities. The league anticipated that future broadcasting revenues from games aired on TV would eventually help finance additional marketing expenditures.

Each franchise's home stadium had to meet specific league requirements. For instance, it had to be a certain size, have suitable seating capacity (a minimum of 6,000 seats), and have adequate lighting and parking facilities. Franchise owners either leased minor league parks in their areas or built their own parks that conformed to the league specifications.

THE NEW ENGLAND FRANCHISE

Bergstrom felt that slo-pitch softball could be successful in central New England. His goal was to create a franchise in the area that would show a profit within five years. To accomplish this, he needed a team that would create a following of 3,000 to 5,000 spectators per game. The league had projected that with a minimum of 3,000 spectators at each game, a franchise could make up to $45,000 in the second year of operation, excluding marketing costs. Exhibit 1 outlines the league's projected costs and revenues.

To determine the market potential in Massachusetts, Bergstrom first wrote to the APSPL for information about what to look for in choosing a site. Although the league had not conducted any full-scale marketing research, they were able to provide the following information.

EXHIBIT 1

AMERICAN PROFESSIONAL SLO-PITCH LEAGUE
Estimated Costs and Revenues
Second Year of Operation

Costs	
Fee to purchase membership	$ 50,000.00
Ballpark operations	10,000.00
Office, telex, secretary, supplies, etc.	25,000.00
Field manager and general manager (depends on management)	15,000.00
Public relations director	7,500.00
Ticket manager (Note: In some locations, positions of P.R. director and ticket manager can be combined)	7,500.00
Player operations, figured at 3 months	30,000.00
Team travel	15,000.00
Miscellaneous	15,000.00
Total costs	$175,000.00
Revenues (based on 16 playing dates at home)	
Sale of 3,000 season tickets, $30 each	$ 90,000.00
Sale of 2,000 general admission tickets, $2 each for 16 playing home dates	64,000.00
Concessions (based on 3,000 per-game attendance)	35,000.00
Advertising	7,500.00
Sale of items such as novelties, programs, jackets, hats, etc. (based on 3,000 per-game attendance)	24,000.00
Total revenues	220,500.00
Total costs	175,000.00
Profit	$ 45,500.00

These figures vary with different types of management. They do not include home or away games played during the short exhibition season prior to the regular schedule.

For the most part, the average fan was between 25 and 55 years old and had some type of softball background, as either a participant or a spectator. He or she was generally in the lower-middle income bracket and had a high school education.

As a result of those demographic statistics, the league had found that the most desirable communities for slo-pitch softball were those with a large working-class population and not highly cosmopolitan in nature. Also, areas with little variety of entertainment fared better because there was less competition for each entertainment dollar.

The most difficult part of starting a franchise, the league felt, was to find someone willing to finance the operation. Potential investors must be willing to take a loss for two or three years and be capable of investing enough money in marketing to establish credibility within the community. Public relations played an important role, the league said, by organizing press conferences and speaking engagements to promote the team.

Another key problem was in securing the playing facilities. Unless an owner had his own field, he was required to go through various recreation departments to rent a field with the proper facilities and location. In some cases, local recreation departments asked for improvements on the field in addition to rental fees, which could lead to costly expenditures. On the other hand, several teams had worked out agreements with local recreation departments that were beneficial to both parties.

Finally, the league felt that, to sell the team, it was of the utmost importance to obtain both the best amateur players in the area and a management team that knew how to promote them.

In addition to the above information, Bergstrom gathered data from the Bureau of Census on 12 central New England sites that he felt had the most potential. The key factors he concentrated on were total population of the area, age, education, and income of the population, and composition of the labor force. The information he compiled is presented in Exhibit 2.

On the basis of the information he obtained from these statistics plus those the league had provided him, Bergstrom had to decide whether he should pursue the establishment of a central New England slo-pitch league, and if so, which geographic areas would be the most profitable.

EXHIBIT 2 Demographics of Market Area

	Total Population	Persons 25 Years and Older	4 Years of High School or More (%)	Total Labor Force	Percent in Manufacturing	Per Capita Income	Median Family Income	No. of Families	Earned above Poverty Level but less than $15,000 (%)	$15,000–$24,999 (%)
Brockton	95,878	48,204	55.9	35,230	30.1	$4,189	$10,377	31,930	9.5	17.1
Fall River	100,430	57,301	25.6	40,416	44.6	$3,685	$ 8,286	25,521	16.1	8.1
Lawrence	67,390	38,917	40.7	28,819	45.0	$4,035	$ 9,492	16,892	12.9	14.7
Lowell	91,493	50,945	45.0	38,645	39.0	$3,959	$ 9,493	22,854	12.6	14.3
New Bedford	100,133	60,750	27.8	41,090	45.8	$3,784	$ 8,230	25,438	17.8	9.7
Newton	88,559	52,582	79.0	38,937	16.3	$7,129	$15,381	22,094	4.0	28.2
Pittsfield	54,893	32,185	58.6	22,400	39.5	$4,759	$10,678	14,716	8.7	17.9
Quincy	91,494	50,703	63.8	37,198	21.5	$5,507	$11,094	22,496	7.4	21.4
Springfield	170,790	90,867	5.1	64,527	29.7	$4,145	$ 9,609	40,462	13.9	14.2
Waltham	56,251	34,089	55.1	26,817	28.9	$4,478	$11,523	14,155	6.8	22.3
Worcester	171,566	102,313	49.8	72,150	29.9	$4,435	$10,038	43,618	10.7	16.0
Manchester	83,417	49,497	47.5	37,011	33.6	$4,192	$ 9,486	22,197	11.0	12.9

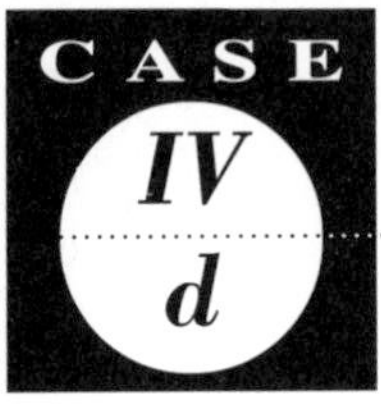

Fisher & Waterman

INTRODUCTION

Michelle Foote was recently hired as a consultant by the accounting firm of Fisher and Waterman to assist a new client with marketing and strategic planning. Although Fisher and Waterman had not usually provided such services for their clients, they had made this a trial arrangement for one who had requested help in setting up his new venture. The resulting revenue and new projects made a favorable impression on the partners of the well-established CPA firm.

Foote enjoyed working for Fisher and Waterman, and since the assignment had turned out well, she decided to approach the partners with a plan to include consulting as one of their regular services. Foote had been operating her own marketing and public relations firm for two years and felt that by combining her operations with an already established firm she could reach more clients through the accounting firm's client base.

Additionally, Foote knew that many large accounting firms offered clients business services beyond the typical accounting needs. Fisher and Waterman were already the largest independent CPA firm in the state. Their targeted clients were small, closely held firms with annual revenues of $1 million to $20 million. Foote knew that the majority of these firms needed some outside financial and marketing assistance. She felt it would be an advantage to both the client and the accounting firm if these services could be obtained from a single source.

Foote needs to convince Fisher and Waterman that the expansion of their business by hiring her as a full-time marketing consultant will be advantageous for the growth of their firm. Foote researched her market and presented her findings to Fisher and Waterman for their approval. The following is Foote's business plan.

EXECUTIVE SUMMARY

This business plan proposes the addition of marketing consulting capabilities and related business planning services to the certified public accounting firm of Fisher and Waterman. Presently, Fisher and Waterman is the largest local CPA firm, with 45 employees and an annual revenue of $2.6 million.

The addition of marketing and consulting services will enable the firm to offer a more complete range of business planning capabilities to clients and to enhance the firm's objectives to an even greater extent. Through marketing and consulting, the firm will expand its knowledge of each client's business, fulfill more needs, and expand creativity in the area of business goals.

From the firm's perspective, an additional source of revenue will be generated, particularly during the off-season of May through September. The proposal has a net present value of $130,000 and very little initial outlay. The increase in services to clients should increase a client's chargeable time and increase the client's reliance on the firm. The new services will also provide another avenue of attracting clients to the firm.

On plan adoption and accomplishment of stated goals at the end of five years, Foote proposes to negotiate an equity position as a principal.

THE PRODUCT

Marketing services will be combined with already existing financial services of the established CPA firm. Few locally based consulting firms offer strategic planning assistance, including finance, budgeting, and marketing. With the addition of marketing consulting, Fisher and Waterman will offer clients a complete approach to business planning: evaluation of strengths and weaknesses, assessment of the marketplace and environment, evaluation of competition, and definition of goals and strategies.

Specifically, the firm could develop an annual report or corporate brochure after auditing or preparing tax returns. Another example could be the development of a retirement plan and the communication of that plan to the employees. Ideally, the new practice area would encompass strategic planning and marketing sessions, pricing analysis, business plans, and break-even analysis.

The consulting area will involve a team of professionals led by a partner or manager and the marketing director. The practice will utilize the firm's CPAs for services such as break-even analyses and pricing structure. For original research necessary for marketing consulting, the firm will contract with freelancers, university students, or specialized research firms. Available secondary research on products, pricing, promotion, and distribution will be utilized.

Clients will be billed $75 per hour. Projects and services will likely use a range of professional positions within the firm whose hourly rates range from $40 to $150. The $75 per hour billing rate is sufficient to cover budgeted operating costs of $56 per hour.

INDUSTRY

Background

Fisher and Waterman has operated for 35 years by providing traditional tax, accounting, and auditing services. They provide management advisory service in the areas of computer selection, cost studies, and litigation support.

The accounting profession is a mature industry that locally has faced a declining and uncertain economy. Firms experience a slow or stagnant growth. Because of their repeat purchases, buyers are more experienced and more price-sensitive. Most local CPA firms have shrunk in size. New products are hard to justify because of increased risks. Profits are declining.

Competition

The local economy supports 45 CPA firms, but only one firm employs a professional marketing consultant. Although most firms offer business planning, they limit it to financial and accounting areas. There is therefore little competition locally for marketing services within a CPA firm. However, other firms could easily enter the market. The biggest expense is the hiring of the market consultant. Given the current economy, a competent marketing consultant could be hired at a reasonable rate. Because market planning is not traditionally an accounting-related service, clients will not instinctively turn to CPAs for it. This may be an initial disadvantage in selling the service. However, once the service is successfully integrated with financial planning, the profession's solid and respected image will help sell it.

A survey of the competition from marketing, advertising, and public relations firms showed that few firms offered comprehensive business planning. Only 9 percent of respondents claimed to offer break-even analysis. Several firms provided business plan services, but clients provided the financial analysis.

Sales Predictions

Sales predictions are based on the target market, the economic environment, and needs determined by a client survey.

The target market is closely held firms or industries within a 75-mile radius with fewer than 200 employees. Of the 2,716 firms or professionals who meet the targeted criteria, the desired market share is 76 or 2.8 percent. These firms include financial institutions and those in telecommunications, retail, manufacturing, real estate, health care, and other professions.

An analysis of the economy shows slow growth through 1991. Although this may appear to be a discouraging time, another perspective should be considered. When times are difficult, businesses need to plan more carefully, reassess markets and review costs. The services of a consultant can be especially useful for businesses as they contemplate the following options: (1) sell, liquidate, or reorganize; (2) reduce operations; (3) develop new products or markets; or (4) acquire businesses in other markets. The addition of a marketing consultant will facilitate the CPA firm in aiding clients who opt for the latter two choices.

Clients were surveyed to see if they would use marketing and financial services from the same firm. Of the clients who responded, 54 percent indicated a favorable reaction to obtaining marketing services from their CPA firms.

MARKETING

The new services will be promoted through personal contacts and civic/professional activities by the marketing consultant and by each of the 14 managers and partners in the firm. Supervisors and senior accountants will be encouraged to identify opportunities for marketing and planning consultation as they are for other management advisory services.

An initial mailing to key clients will introduce the services. There will also be promotional articles in the firm's three newsletters. The services will be included in an updated version of the firm's brochure, a new professional services directory, the "additional services" section of proposals, and the internal staff manual's inventory of services.

The staff will become familiar with the program at its monthly meeting. In addition, marketing the new service will be a topic at a business planning training session for management and supervisory personnel.

FINANCIAL

Projected income statements, break-even analysis, and sources and uses of funds statements are indicated in Exhibits 1, 2, and 3, respectively.

MANAGEMENT

Presently, the Fisher and Waterman firm does not formally provide for consulting in the organizational chart. This plan proposes to create a formal department with both staff and line responsibilities. Foote will be marketing director and report to the administrative accounting partner, but she will work directly with other partners as needed by their clients. She will be directly responsible for new clients she obtains in marketing engagements.

EXHIBIT 1

F&W MARKETING, CONSULTING, AND BUSINESS PLANNING
Income Statements
FY 1988–1992

Fiscal Years	*1988*	*1989*	*1990*	*1991*	*1992*	*Totals*
Fee income						
Marketing director*	$ 4,500	$ 6,000	$24,000	$ 42,500	$ 63,000	$140,000
Accounting professionals†	20,000	31,500	44,100	57,881	72,930	226,412
Commissions on third-party fees	750	1,200	1,500	1,800	2,250	7,500
Total fee income	$25,250	$38,700	$69,600	$102,181	$138,180	$373,912
Incremental operating Expenses						
Salaries‡	$ 3,000	$ 4,185	$15,512	$ 19,800	$ 25,403	$ 67,900
Dues and memberships	300	325	450	500	525	2,100
Microcomputers, software			2,000			$2,000
Miscellaneous, contingency	300	300	300	300	300	1,500
Professional development	1,500	1,300	1,400	1,500	1,800	7,500
Subscriptions	100	100	100	100	100	500
Promotion (brochure)	1,000		1,500		1,500	4,000
Total operating expenses	$ 6,200	$ 6,210	$21,262	$ 22,200	$ 29,628	$ 85,500
Operating income	$19,050	$32,490	$48,338	$ 79,982	$108,552	$288,412
Income tax (34%)	6,477	11,047	16,435	27,194	36,908	98,060
Net income	$12,573	$21,443	$31,903	$ 52,788	$ 71,645	$190,350

Present Value of Proposed Consulting Venture

Net income, discounted at 10% borrowing rate		$133,662			
*Marketing director's fee income is based on the following: Chargeable time, % of total	3.00%	4.00%	15.00%	25.00%	35.00%
Number of available hours	2,000	2,000	2,000	2,000	2,000
Hourly rate, mktg. director	$ 75	$ 57	$ 80	$ 85	$ 90
†Additional salaries based on:					
Salary under proposed plan	$34,500	$37,260	$20,241	$ 22,165	$ 48,691
Current salary w/5% raise	$31,500	$33,075	$34,719	$ 36,465	$ 38,288
Incremental mktg. director salary	$ 3,000	$ 4,185	$ 5,512	$ 7,800	$ 10,403
Add'l staff salary, tax, and benefits	$ 0	$ 0	$10,000	$ 12,000	$ 15,000
‡Accounting fee income is based on the following:					
Average fee per engagement	$ 2,000	$ 2,100	$ 2,205	$ 2,315	$ 2,431
Number of engagements	10	15	20	25	30
Total accounting fee income	$20,000	$31,500	$44,100	$ 57,881	$ 72,930
Average chargeable hours/job	22	23	24	25	26
Chargeable hours—accounting	220	345	480	625	780
Chargeable hours—marketing	60	80	300	500	700
Total chargeable hours	302	448	804	1,150	1,506

EXHIBIT 2 Break-Even Analysis*

Total sales (for income statements)	$373,911
Gross profit (total operating income)	288,412
Fixed expenses (total operating expenses)	$$ 85,500
Gross profit as % of sales*	77.13%
Break-even (in dollars of revenue)†	$110,846

Thus, break-even would be reached during the first half of Year 3, although positive income streams begin in Year 1.

*Gross profit divided by sales.
†Fixed expenses divided by gross profit as % of sales.

EXHIBIT 3 Sources and Uses of Funds

Sources	
Retained earnings	$85,500
Uses	
Salaries	67,900
Equipment	2,000
Promotion	4,000
Operating expenses	2,600
Training and development	7,500
Contingency	1,500
Total	$85,500

PART V

Special Issues for the Entrepreneur

CHAPTER

15

Legal Issues for the Entrepreneur

Chapter Objectives

1. To understand the nature of a patent and the rights it provides to the entrepreneur.
2. To recognize the differences between utility and design patents.
3. To illustrate the process for filing a patent.
4. To understand the purpose of a trademark and the procedure for filing.
5. To learn the purpose of a copyright and how to file for one.
6. To understand the value of licensing to either expand a business or to start a new venture.
7. To understand important issues related to product safety and liability.
8. To explain how to hire a lawyer.

Edwin H. Land

Edwin Land has been called one of the greatest living inventors and entrepreneurs. As a 22-year-old Harvard dropout living in New York, he used to sneak into the Columbia University labs to conduct research on an idea he had for polarizing light. Needing capital to start a business and continue research on his concept, he obtained $375,000 in capital from investors such as W. Averill Harriman, James P. Warburg, and several others. With this money, he started Polaroid Corporation.

Initially, Land was intent on directing Polaroid's research effort at finding a solution for glare in automobile headlights by means of a polarizing lens. Unfortunately, the auto manufacturers were not interested in the lens, so Land turned to optic lenses, which were in demand during World War II.

After the war the optic lens market dried up, and Polaroid was on the verge of bankruptcy. Edwin Land then announced that he had discovered a near-magic process that would permit a camera to take a picture, develop it inside the camera, and produce a photo print in minutes.

In 1948, Polaroid Corporation unveiled the first sepia print instant camera. It had been the idea of Edwin Land after one of his children had asked why the picture could not be seen immediately after it was taken. Land then spent the next few years developing the process until he was able to effectively master it. For the next 30 years Land and Polaroid produced innovation after innovation, each one carefully protected by patents. Each innovation seemed to improve on the previous discovery and pushed photographic technology beyond the bounds of the average person's comprehension. By 1980, with the help of his many inventions, Land had built the company into a $1.4 billion business. At that point, at age 70, he retired from the company.

Patents were very important to Polaroid because the company was so dependent on this single technology. Any failure to be at the leading edge of this technology could have bankrupted the company. Over the years, Land and Polaroid continued to pioneer development in this field. With the innovation and development of many processes and products, the company successfully obtained nearly 2,000 patents. Edwin Land personally has his name on 537 U.S. patents, second only to Thomas Edison's 1,093.

Yet Polaroid's existence under the direction of Edwin Land was not without its problems. A number of product failures, such as Polavision, as well as continued improvement in 35-mm cameras and processing, diminished the significance of instant photography to the ultimate user. Market activity restricted to the amateur market and a single-product line also caused some doubts as to the future of his company. Even threats from competitors such as Kodak caused concern over Polaroid's future.

One of Polaroid's major legal battles over patent rights was with Eastman Kodak, which introduced an instant camera to compete with Polaroid. With Kodak's strong distribution, film manufacturing capability, and image, Polaroid was believed to be in serious trouble. However, Edwin Land was not about to give up his success to anyone. Polaroid filed a patent infringement suit against Eastman Kodak, which shocked the photography industry.

In October 1985, after nine years of litigation, a federal court judge ruled that Eastman Kodak was guilty of infringement on 7 of 10 patents named in the lawsuit. In the lawsuit, Polaroid claimed that Kodak had copied patents from its popular SX-70 camera introduced in 1972. Kodak, which had sold 16.5 million cameras and captured 25 percent of the instant market, was ordered to cease production on cameras and film. The problem Kodak then faced was how to cushion the blow for its customers. To address this problem, Kodak offered trade-ins, a hot line, and brochures outlining the options for customers.

The actual litigation of damage determination to Polaroid from the patent infringement took a total of 14 years and was finally settled in late 1990, when a Boston court ruled that Kodak would have to pay Polaroid $985 million. This was the largest damage award ever won by a company in a patent litigation. Polaroid has been able to use the money awarded to reduce long-term debt and to retire preferred stock held by an investment banking firm that had rescued Polaroid from an earlier takeover bid by Shamrock Holdings.

With Kodak's market share dropping and consumer interest diminishing, the ruling by the courts seemed to be a blessing in disguise. The future of instant photography does not appear favorable because of the new 35-mm technology, fast photo services, improved video technology, and simple boredom with a process that is no longer unique. These trends have forced Polaroid to refocus their marketing strategy on special market niches, particularly in commercial markets. For example, recently real estate and insurance agents have been two of the largest buyers of the instant photography system. New laser imaging slated for medical applications with ultrasound, CAT scanners, and nuclear medicines also offer favorable market potential.[1]

We can see from the Polaroid-Kodak case that patents can be an important means of protecting a new technology, process, and so on for an entrepreneur. Unfortunately, the 14 years of litigation incurred by Polaroid and Kodak would not have been possible for a new venture. However, legal issues like patents are important concerns in any new venture. Good advice can save money, the entrepreneur's reputation, and the future existence of the business. This chapter provides some insight for the entrepreneur on such issues as patents, copyrights, trademarks, product liability, and insurance.

---

[1] See "Polaroid vs. Kodak: The Decisive Round," *Business Week,* January 13, 1986. p 37; "Instant Getaway," *Time,* January 20, 1986, p 43; and J. Palmer, "Spending Kodak's Money," *Barron's,* October 7, 1991, pp 16–18.

NEED FOR A LAWYER

Since all business is regulated by law, the entrepreneur needs to be aware of any regulations that may affect his or her new venture. At different stages of the start-up, the entrepreneur will need legal advice. It is also likely that the legal expertise required will vary, based on such factors as whether the new venture is a franchise, an independent start-up, or a buyout, produces a consumer versus an industrial product, is nonprofit, or involves exporting or importing.

Most lawyers have developed special expertise; the entrepreneur should carefully evaluate his or her needs before hiring one. Awareness and sensitivity to legal questions are also important for the entrepreneur. This chapter provides some insight into the areas that will probably require legal assistance. The form of organization, as well as franchise agreements, are discussed in Chapters 8 and 16, and will not be addressed here. Legal advice for these agreements (i.e., partnership, franchise, or articles of incorporation) is necessary to ensure that the most appropriate decisions have been made.

By being aware of when and what legal advice is required, the entrepreneur can save much time and money. In addition, the chapter concludes with some advice on how to select a lawyer and where to get legal advice and information regarding legal issues.

PATENTS

A patent is a contract between the government and an inventor. In exchange for disclosure of the invention, the government grants the inventor exclusivity regarding the invention for a specified amount of time. At the end of this time, the government publishes the invention, and it becomes part of the public domain.[2]

Basically, the patent gives the owners a negative right, because it prevents anyone else from making, using, or selling the defined invention. Moreover, even if an inventor has been granted a patent, in the process of producing or marketing the invention he or she may find that it infringes on the patent rights of others. The inventor also should recognize the distinction between utility and design patents.

- *Utility Patents*—When speaking about patents, most people are referring to utility patents. A utility patent has a term of 17 years, beginning on the date the Patent and Trademark Office (PTO) issues it. It grants the owner protection from anyone else making, using, and/or selling the identified invention and generally reflects protection of new, useful, and unobvious processes such as film

[2] See, *Patents,* U.S. Department of Commerce, Patent and Trademark Office (U.S. Government Printing Office: Washington, D.C., 1992) and M. Mann and P. Canary, "Protecting Innovation Through Patents," *Business and Economic Review,* Jan–Mar 1993, pp 25–27.

developing; machines such as photocopiers; compositions of matter such as chemical compounds or mixtures of ingredients; and articles of manufacture such as the toothpaste pump.

- *Design Patents*—Covering new, original, ornamental, and unobvious designs for articles of manufacture, a design patent reflects the appearance of an object. These patents are granted for a 14-year term and, like the utility patent, provide the inventor with a negative right excluding others from making, using, or selling an article having the ornamental appearance given in the drawings included in the patent.
- *Plant Patents*—These are issued for 17 years on new varieties of plants. Very few of these types of patents are issued.

Patents are issued by the Patent and Trademark Office (PTO). In addition to patents, this office administers other programs. One of these is the Disclosure Document Program, whereby the inventor files disclosure of the invention, giving recognition that he or she was the first to develop or invent the idea. In most cases, the inventor will subsequently patent the idea. A second program is the Defensive Publication Program. This gives the inventor the opportunity to protect an idea for which he or she does not wish to obtain a patent. It prevents anyone else from patenting this idea, but gives the public access to the invention.

The Disclosure Document

It is recommended that the entrepreneur first file a disclosure document to establish the date of conception of the invention. This document can be important when two entrepreneurs are filing for patents on similar inventions. In that instance, the entrepreneur who can show that he or she was the first one to conceive of the invention will be given the rights to the patent.

To file a disclosure document, the entrepreneur must prepare a clear and concise description of the invention. In addition to the written material, photographs may be included. A cover letter and a duplicate are included with the description of the invention. Upon receipt of the information, the PTO will stamp and return the duplicate copy of the letter to the entrepreneur, thus establishing evidence of conception. There is also a fee for this filing, which can be determined by telephoning the PTO.

The disclosure document is not a patent application. Before actually applying for the patent, it is advisable to retain a patent attorney to conduct a patent search. After the attorney completes the search, a decision can be made as to the patentability of the invention.

The Patent Application

The patent application must contain a complete history and description of the invention as well as claims for its usefulness. In general, the application will be divided into the following three sections:

- *Introduction*—This section should contain the background and advantages of the invention and the nature of the problems it overcomes. It should clearly state how the invention differs from existing offerings.
- *Description of Invention*—Next the application should contain a brief description of the drawings that accompany it. These drawings must comply with PTO requirements. Following this would be a detailed description of the invention, which may include engineering specifications, materials, components, and so on that are vital to the actual making of the invention.
- *Claims*—This is probably the most difficult section of the application to prepare since claims are the criteria by which any infringements will be determined. They serve to specify what the entrepreneur is trying to patent. Essential parts of the invention should be described in broad terms so as to prevent others from getting around the patent. At the same time, the claims must not be so general that they hide the invention's uniqueness and advantages. This balance is difficult and should be discussed and debated with the patent attorney.

In addition to the above sections, the application should contain a declaration or oath that is signed by the inventor or inventors. This form will be supplied by an attorney. The completed application is then ready to be sent to the PTO, at which time the status of the invention becomes patent pending. This status is important to the entrepreneur because it now provides complete confidential protection until the application is approved. At that time, the patent is published and thus becomes accessible to the public for review.

A carefully written patent should provide protection and prevent competitors from working around it. However, once granted, it is also an invitation to sue or be sued if there is any infringement.

The fees for filing an application will vary, depending on the patent search and on claims made in the application. Attorney fees are also a factor in completing the patent application. The average cost of a patent seems to be about $1,500.

Patent Infringement

To this point, we have discussed the importance of and the procedure for filing for a patent. It is also extremely important for the entrepreneur to be sensitive about whether he or she is infringing on someone else's patent.

The fact that someone else already has a patent does not mean the end of any illusions of starting a business. Many businesses, inventions, or innovations are the result of improvements or modifications of existing products. Copying and improving on a product may be perfectly legal (no patent infringement) and actually good business strategy. If it is impossible to copy and improve the product to avoid patent infringement, the entrepreneur may try to license the product from the patent holder. Figure 15–1 illustrates the steps that an entrepreneur should follow as he or she considers marketing a product that may infringe on an existing patent. Each step is discussed in the following paragraphs.

FIGURE 15–1 Options to Avoid Infringement

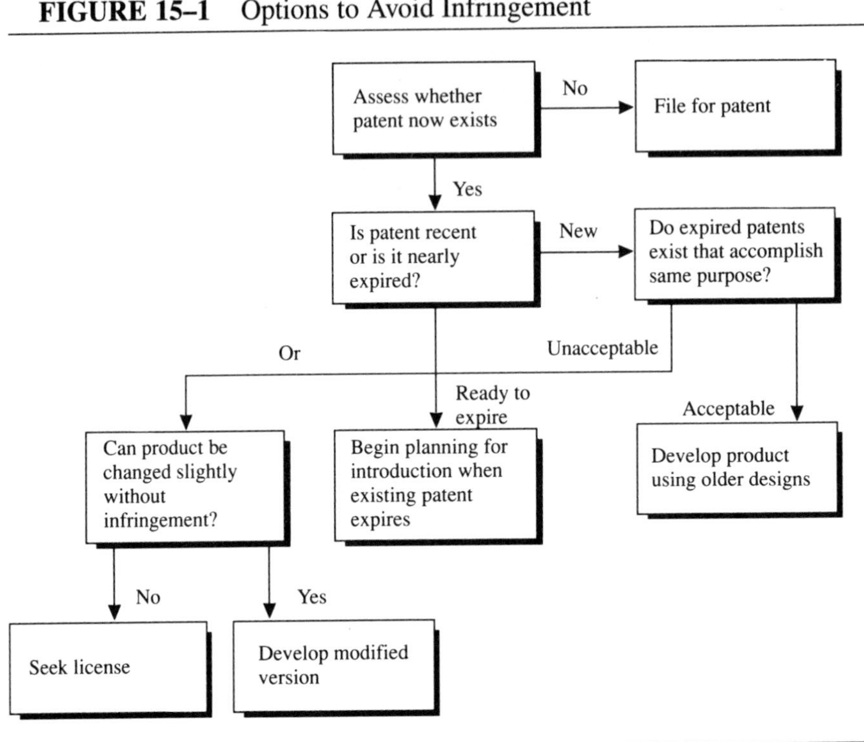

Source: Adapted from H. D. Coleman and J. D. Vandenberg, "How to Follow the Leader," *Inc.*, July 1988, pp 81–82.

First, an entrepreneur should confirm the existence of a patent. This can usually be accomplished by reviewing information on the company's package. Even if a patent is known to exist, the entrepreneur should find out exactly what it entails. If there is some doubt, a patent search may be necessary. Computer software is also available to provide the entrepreneur with information on existing patents that are in the same product category. If all else fails, the entrepreneur should consider hiring a patent attorney to perform a more thorough search.

Once the patent is found, it should be ascertained if it is new or is ready to expire. If it is new, the entrepreneur has two options: to try to modify the product without infringement of an existing patent or to identify older designs of a similar product, whose patents have expired. If older designs are unacceptable or unavailable, it may be possible to modify the existing patented product without infringement. If modification is not possible, the entrepreneur may consider licensing, or offering the patent holder a proposal that would benefit both parties. Licensing is discussed later in this chapter.

If the original patent held by a competitor is ready to expire, the entrepreneur may either try to modify it or plan for the time when it can be legally copied. Once a patent has been granted, it becomes public information, which can be to the entrepreneur's advantage when considering the introduction of a similar product. In fact, a review of the proceedings that led to the granting of a patent can often suggest ways to modify the product to avoid infringement.

TRADEMARKS

A trademark may be a word, symbol, design, or some combination of such, or it could be a slogan or even a particular sound that identifies the source or sponsorship of certain goods or services. Unlike the patent, a trademark can last indefinitely, as long as the mark continues to perform its indicated function. The trademark is given an initial 20-year registration with 20-year renewable terms. In the fifth to sixth year, the registrant is required to file an affidavit with the PTO indicating that the mark is currently in commercial use. If no affidavit is filed, the registration is canceled.

Prior to 1989, before filing an application for a trademark, the entrepreneur must have actually used the mark on goods that were shipped or sold or on services rendered. The law today allows the filing of a trademark solely on the intent to use the trademark in interstate or foreign commerce. The filing date then becomes the first date use of the mark. This does not imply that the entrepreneur cannot file after the mark has already been in use. In fact, there are benefits to registering a mark that has already been in use. For example, if the business is not yet national in scope, the filing for a mark already in use on a regional basis will provide freedom to expand nationally under the same name.[3]

The protection awarded is dependent on the character of the mark itself. There are four categories of trademarks: (1) coined marks denote no relationship between the mark and the goods or services (e.g., Polaroid, Kodak) and afford the possibility of expansion to a wide range of products; (2) an arbitrary mark is one that has another meaning in our language (e.g., Shell) and is applied to a product or service; (3) a suggestive mark is used to suggest certain features, qualities, ingredients, or characteristics of a product or service (e.g., Halo shampoo). It differs from an arbitrary mark in that it tends to suggest some describable attribute of the product or services. Finally, (4) a descriptive mark must have become distinctive over a significant period of time and gained consumer recognition before it can be registered. The mark then is considered to have secondary meaning, that is, it is descriptive of a particular product or service (e.g., Rubberoid as applied to roofing materials that contain rubber).[4]

Registering a trademark can offer significant advantages or benefits to the entrepreneur. Figure 15–2 summarizes some of these benefits.

---

[3] A. Baum, "Overlooking the Basics Causes Disaster for Clients: How to Choose, Search for and Register a Trademark," *New York Law Journal,* April 12, 1993, p 4.

[4] D. A. Burge, *Patent and Trademark Tactics and Practice,* 2nd ed. (New York: John Wiley and Sons, 1984) pp 124–25.

FIGURE 15–2 Benefits of a Registered Trademark

- It provides notice to everyone that you have exclusive rights to the use of the mark throughout the territorial limits of the United States.
- It entitles you to sue in federal court for trademark infringement, which can result in recovery of profits, damages, and costs.
- It establishes incontestable rights regarding the commercial use of the mark.
- It establishes the right to deposit registration with customs to prevent importation of goods with similar mark.
- It entitles you to use the notice of registration ®.
- It provides a basis for filing trademark application in foreign countries.

Registering the Trademark

As indicated earlier, the PTO is responsible for the federal registration of trademarks. To file an application, the entrepreneur must complete the form illustrated in Figure 15–3. The application varies only in the address and applicant name if the business is a partnership or a corporation. For a partnership, names of all partners are included. In the case of a corporation, the corporation's name and address, and the state of incorporation would be given.

Filing of the trademark registration must meet four requirements: (1) completion of the written form, (2) a drawing of the mark, (3) five specimens showing actual use of the mark, and (4) the fee. Each trademark must be applied for separately. Upon receipt of this information, the PTO assigns a serial number to the application and sends a filing receipt to the applicant.

The next step in the registering process is a determination by the examining attorney at the PTO as to whether the mark is suitable for registration. Within about three months, an initial determination is made as to its suitability. Any objections by the entrepreneur must be raised within six months, or the application is considered abandoned. If the trademark is refused, the entrepreneur still has the right to appeal to the PTO.

Once accepted, the trademark is published in the *Trademark Official Gazette* to allow any party 30 days to oppose or request an extension to oppose. If no opposition is filed, the registration is issued. This entire procedure usually takes about 13 months from the initial filing.

COPYRIGHTS

A copyright protects original works of authorship. The protection in a copyright does not protect the idea itself, and thus it allows someone else to use the idea or concept in a different manner.

The copyright law has become especially relevant to computer software companies. In 1980, The Computer Software Copyright Act was added to the Federal Code of Copyright Laws. It provided explanation of the nature of software protection under

FIGURE 15–3

TRADEMARK APPLICATION, PRINCIPAL REGISTER, WITH DECLARATION (Individual)	MARK *(identify the mark)*
	CLASS NO. *(if known)*

TO THE COMMISSIONER OF PATENTS AND TRADEMARKS:

NAME OF APPLICANT, AND BUSINESS TRADE NAME, IF ANY

BUSINESS ADDRESS

RESIDENCE ADDRESS

CITIZENSHIP OF APPLICANT

The above identified applicant has adopted and is using the trademark shown in the accompanying drawing for the following

goods: ________________________________

____

and requests that said mark be registered in the United States Patent and Trademark Office on the Principal Register established by the Act of July 5, 1946.

The trademark was first used on the goods on ____________ *(date)* ; was first used on the goods in ____________ *(type of commerce)* commerce on ____________ *(date)* ; and is now in use in such commerce.

The mark is used by applying it to ________________________________

____

and five specimens showing the mark as actually used are presented herewith.

____

(name of applicant)

being hereby warned that willful false statements and the like so made are punishable by fine or imprisonment, or both, under Section 1001 of Title 18 of the United States Code and that such willful false statements may jeopardize the validity of the application or any registration resulting therefrom, declares that he/she believes himself/herself to be the owner of the trademark sought to be registered; to the best of his/her knowledge and belief no other person, firm, corporation, or association has the right to use said mark in commerce, either in the identical form or in such near resemblance thereto as may be likely, when applied to the goods of such other person, to cause confusion, or to cause mistake, or to deceive; the facts set forth in this application are true; and all statements made of his/her own knowledge are true and all statements made on information and belief are believed to be true.

____

(signature of applicant)

____

(date)

FORM PTO-1476FB (REV. 4-87) U.S. DEPARTMENT OF COMMERCE/Patent and Trademark Office

the copyright laws. Authors or publishers of software are protected similarly to creators of artistic works. The idea of the software (e.g., spreadsheets) is not eligible for protection, but the actual program to produce the spreadsheet is eligible.

Copyrights are registered with the Library of Congress and will not usually require an attorney. All that is necessary is that the form, illustrated in Figure 15–4, two copies of the work, and the appropriate fee is sent to the Register of Copyrights. The term of copyright is the life of the author plus 50 years. If the author is an institution, the term of the copyright is 75 years from publication.

Besides computer software, copyrights are desirable for such things as books, scripts, articles, poems, songs, sculptures, models, maps, blueprints, collages, printed material on board games, data, and music. In some instances, several forms of protection may be available. For example, the name of a board game may be protected by a trademark, the game itself protected by a utility patent, the printed matter or the board protected by a copyright, and the playing pieces covered by a design patent.[5]

TRADE SECRETS

In certain instances, the entrepreneur may prefer to maintain an idea or process as confidential and sell or license it as a trade secret. The trade secret will have a life as long as the idea or process remains a secret.

A trade secret is not covered by any federal law but is recognized under a governing body of common laws in each state. Employees involved in working with an idea or process may be asked to first sign a confidential information agreement that will protect against their giving out the trade secret either while employees or after leaving the organization. The entrepreneur should hire an attorney to help draw up any such agreement. The holder of the trade secret has the right to sue any signee who breaches such an agreement.

What or how much information to give to employees is difficult to judge and is often determined by the entrepreneur's judgement. Historically, entrepreneurs tended to protect sensitive or confidential company information from anyone else by simply not making them privy to this information. Today, there is a tendency to take the opposite view, that the more information entrusted to employees the more effective and creative employees can be. The argument is that employees cannot be creative unless they have a complete understanding of what is going on in the business.[6]

Most entrepreneurs have limited resources, so they choose not to find means to protect their ideas, products, or services. This could become a serious problem in the future, since obtaining competitive information legally is so easy, unless the entrepreneur takes the proper precautions. For example, it is often easy to obtain competitive information through such means as trade shows, transient employees, or media

---

[5] T. Husch, "Protecting Your Ideas," *Nation's Business,* September 1991, p 62.

[6] A. Bauman, "Strictly Confidential," *Entrepreneur,* October 1992, pp 126–31.

FIGURE 15–4

Filling Out Application Form TX

Detach and read these instructions before completing this form. Make sure all applicable spaces have been filled in before you return this form.

BASIC INFORMATION

When to Use This Form: Use Form TX for registration of published or unpublished non-dramatic literary works, excluding periodicals or serial issues. This class includes a wide variety of works: fiction, non-fiction, poetry, textbooks, reference works, directories, catalogs, advertising copy, compilations of information, and computer programs. For periodicals and serials, use Form SE.

Deposit to Accompany Application: An application for copyright registration must be accompanied by a deposit consisting of copies or phonorecords representing the entire work for which registration is to be made. The following are the general deposit requirements as set forth in the statute:

Unpublished Work: Deposit one complete copy (or phonorecord).

Published Work: Deposit two complete copies (or phonorecords) of the best edition.

Work First Published Outside the United States: Deposit one complete copy (or phonorecord) of the first foreign edition.

Contribution to a Collective Work: Deposit one complete copy (or phonorecord) of the best edition of the collective work.

The Copyright Notice: For published works, the law provides that a copyright notice in a specified form "shall be placed on all publicly distributed copies from which the work can be visually perceived." Use of the copyright notice is the responsibility of the copyright owner and does not require advance permission from the Copyright Office. The required form of the notice for copies generally consists of three elements: (1) the symbol "©", or the word "Copyright," or the abbreviation "Copr."; (2) the year of first publication; and (3) the name of the owner of copyright. For example: "© 1981 Constance Porter." The notice is to be affixed to the copies "in such manner and location as to give reasonable notice of the claim of copyright."

For further information about copyright registration, notice, or special questions relating to copyright problems, write:

Information and Publications Section, LM-455
Copyright Office
Library of Congress
Washington, D.C. 20559

PRIVACY ACT ADVISORY STATEMENT
Required by the Privacy Act of 1974 (Public Law 93-579)

AUTHORITY FOR REQUESTING THIS INFORMATION
- Title 17, U.S.C., Secs. 409 and 410

FURNISHING THE REQUESTED INFORMATION IS
- Voluntary

BUT IF THE INFORMATION IS NOT FURNISHED
- It may be necessary to delay or refuse registration
- You may not be entitled to certain relief, remedies, and benefits provided in chapters 4 and 5 of title 17, U.S.C.

PRINCIPAL USES OF REQUESTED INFORMATION
- Establishment and maintenance of a public record
- Examination of the application for compliance with legal requirements

OTHER ROUTINE USES
- Public inspection and copying
- Preparation of public indexes
- Preparation of public catalogs of copyright registrations
- Preparation of search reports upon request

NOTE
- No other advisory statement will be given you in connection with this application
- Please keep this statement and refer to it if we communicate with you regarding this application

LINE-BY-LINE INSTRUCTIONS

1 SPACE 1: Title

Title of This Work: Every work submitted for copyright registration must be given a title to identify that particular work. If the copies or phonorecords of the work bear a title (or an identifying phrase that could serve as a title), transcribe that wording *completely* and *exactly* on the application. Indexing of the registration and future identification of the work will depend on the information you give here.

Previous or Alternative Titles: Complete this space if there are any additional titles for the work under which someone searching for the registration might be likely to look, or under which a document pertaining to the work might be recorded.

Publication as a Contribution: If the work being registered is a contribution to a periodical, serial, or collection, give the title of the contribution in the "Title of this Work" space. Then, in the line headed "Publication as a Contribution," give information about the collective work in which the contribution appeared.

2 SPACE 2: Author(s)

General Instructions: After reading these instructions, decide who are the "authors" of this work for copyright purposes. Then, unless the work is a "collective work," give the requested information about every "author" who contributed any appreciable amount of copyrightable matter to this version of the work. If you need further space, request additional Continuation sheets. In the case of a collective work, such as an anthology, collection of essays, or encyclopedia, give information about the author of the collective work as a whole.

Name of Author: The fullest form of the author's name should be given. Unless the work was "made for hire," the individual who actually created the work is its "author." In the case of a work made for hire, the statute provides that "the employer or other person for whom the work was prepared is considered the author."

What is a "Work Made for Hire"? A "work made for hire" is defined as: (1) "a work prepared by an employee within the scope of his or her employment"; or (2) "a work specially ordered or commissioned for use as a contribution to a collective work, as a part of a motion picture or other audiovisual work, as a translation, as a supplementary work, as a compilation, as an instructional text, as a test, as answer material for a test, or as an atlas, if the parties expressly agree in a written instrument signed by them that the work shall be considered a work made for hire." If you have checked "Yes" to indicate that the work was "made for hire," you must give the full legal name of the employer (or other person for whom the work was prepared). You may also include the name of the employee along with the name of the employer (for example: "Elster Publishing Co., employer for hire of John Ferguson").

"Anonymous" or "Pseudonymous" Work: An author's contribution to a work is "anonymous" if that author is not identified on the copies or phonorecords of the work. An author's contribution to a work is "pseudonymous" if that author is identified on the copies or phonorecords under a fictitious name. If the work is "anonymous" you may: (1) leave the line blank; or (2) state "anonymous" on the line; or (3) reveal the author's identity. If the work is "pseudonymous" you may: (1) leave the line blank; or (2) give the pseudonym and identify it as such (for example: "Huntley Haverstock, pseudonym"); or (3) reveal the author's name, making clear which is the real name and which is the pseudonym (for example: "Judith Barton, whose pseudonym is Madeline Elster"). However, the citizenship or domicile of the author **must** be given in all cases.

Dates of Birth and Death: If the author is dead, the statute requires that the year of death be included in the application unless the work is anonymous or pseudonymous. The author's birth date is optional, but is useful as a form of identification. Leave this space blank if the author's contribution was a "work made for hire."

Author's Nationality or Domicile: Give the country of which the author is a citizen, or the country in which the author is domiciled. Nationality or domicile **must** be given in all cases.

Nature of Authorship: After the words "Nature of Authorship" give a brief general statement of the nature of this particular author's contribution to the work. Examples: "Entire text"; "Coauthor of entire text"; "Chapters 11-14"; "Editorial revisions"; "Compilation and English translation"; "New text."

FIGURE 15–4 (*continued*)

3 SPACE 3: Creation and Publication

General Instructions: Do not confuse "creation" with "publication." Every application for copyright registration must state "the year in which creation of the work was completed." Give the date and nation of first publication only if the work has been published.

Creation: Under the statute, a work is "created" when it is fixed in a copy or phonorecord for the first time. Where a work has been prepared over a period of time, the part of the work existing in fixed form on a particular date constitutes the created work on that date. The date you give here should be the year in which the author completed the particular version for which registration is now being sought, even if other versions exist or if further changes or additions are planned.

Publication: The statute defines "publication" as "the distribution of copies or phonorecords of a work to the public by sale or other transfer of ownership, or by rental, lease, or lending"; a work is also "published" if there has been an "offering to distribute copies or phonorecords to a group of persons for purposes of further distribution, public performance, or pubiic display." Give the full date (month, day, year) when, and the country where, publication first occurred. If first publication took place simultaneously in the United States and other countries, it is sufficient to state "U.S.A."

4 SPACE 4: Claimant(s)

Name(s) and Address(es) of Copyright Claimant(s): Give the name(s) and address(es) of the copyright claimant(s) in this work even if the claimant is the same as the author. Copyright in a work belongs initially to the author of the work (including, in the case of a work made for hire, the employer or other person for whom the work was prepared). The copyright claimant is either the author of the work or a person or organization to whom the copyright initially belonging to the author has been transferred.

Transfer: The statute provides that, if the copyright claimant is not the author, the application for registration must contain "a brief statement of how the claimant obtained ownership of the copyright." If any copyright claimant named in space 4 is not an author named in space 2, give a brief, general statement summarizing the means by which that claimant obtained ownership of the copyright. Examples: "By written contract"; "Transfer of all rights by author"; "Assignment"; "By will." Do not attach transfer documents or other attachments or riders.

5 SPACE 5: Previous Registration

General Instructions: The questions in space 5 are intended to find out whether an earlier registration has been made for this work and, if so, whether there is any basis for a new registration. As a general rule, only one basic copyright registration can be made for the same version of a particular work.

Same Version: If this version is substantially the same as the work covered by a previous registration, a second registration is not generally possible unless: (1) the work has been registered in unpublished form and a second registration is now being sought to cover this first published edition; or (2) someone other than the author is identified as copyright claimant in the earlier registration, and the author is now seeking registration in his or her own name. If either of these two exceptions apply, check the appropriate box and give the earlier registration number and date. Oth. rwise, do not submit Form TX; instead, write the Copyright Office for information about supplementary registration or recordation of transfers of copyright ownership.

Changed Version: If the work has been changed, and you are now seeking registration to cover the additions or revisions, check the last box in space 5, give the earlier registration number and date, and complete both parts of space 6 in accordance with the instructions below.

Previous Registration Number and Date: If more than one previous registration has been made for the work, give the number and date of the latest registration.

6 SPACE 6: Derivative Work or Compilation

General Instructions: Complete space 6 if this work is a "changed version," "compilation," or "derivative work," and if it incorporates one or more earlier works that have already been published or registered for copyright, or that have fallen into the public domain. A "compilation" is defined as "a work formed by the collection and assembling of preexisting materials or of data that are selected, coordinated, or arranged in such a way that the resulting work as a whole constitutes an original work of authorship." A "derivative work" is "a work based on one or more preexisting works." Examples of derivative works include translations, fictionalizations, abridgments, condensations, or "any other form in which a work may be recast, transformed, or adapted." Derivative works also include works "consisting of editorial revisions, annotations, or other modifications" if these changes, as a whole, represent an original work of authorship.

Preexisting Material (space 6a): For derivative works, complete this space **and** space 6b. In space 6a identify the preexisting work that has been recast, transformed, or adapted. An example of preexisting material might be: "Russian version of Goncharov's 'Oblomov'." Do not complete space 6a for compilations.

Material Added to This Work (space 6b): Give a brief, general statement of the new material covered by the copyright claim for which registration is sought. **Derivative work** examples include: "Foreword, editing, critical annotations"; "Translation"; "Chapters 11-17." If the work is a **compilation**, describe both the compilation itself and the material that has been compiled. Example: "Compilation of certain 1917 Speeches by Woodrow Wilson." A work may be both a derivative work and compilation, in which case a sample statement might be: "Compilation and additional new material."

7 SPACE 7: Manufacturing Provisions

General Instructions: The copyright statute currently provides, as a general rule, that the copies of a published work "consisting preponderantly of nondramatic literary material in the English language" be manufactured in the United States or Canada in order to be lawfully imported and publicly distributed in the United States. If the work being registered is unpublished or not in English, leave this space blank. Complete this space if registration is sought for a published work "consisting preponderantly of nondramatic literary material that is in the English language." Identify those who manufactured the copies and where those manufacturing processes were performed. As an exception to the manufacturing provisions, the statute prescribes that, where manufacture has taken place outside the United States or Canada, a maximum of 2000 copies of the foreign edition may be imported into the United States without affecting the copyright owners' rights. For this purpose, the Copyright Office will issue an Import Statement upon request and payment of a fee of $3 at the time of registration or at any later time. For further information about import statements, write for Form IS.

8 SPACE 8: Reproduction for Use of Blind or Physically Handicapped Individuals

General Instructions: One of the major programs of the Library of Congress is to provide Braille editions and special recordings of works for the exclusive use of the blind and physically handicapped. In an effort to simplify and speed up the copyright licensing procedures that are a necessary part of this program, section 710 of the copyright statute provides for the establishment of a voluntary licensing system to be tied in with copyright registration. Copyright Office regulations provide that you may grant a license for such reproduction and distribution solely for the use of persons who are certified by competent authority as unable to read normal printed material as a result of physical limitations. The license is entirely voluntary, nonexclusive, and may be terminated upon 90 days notice.

How to Grant the License: If you wish to grant it, check one of the three boxes in space 8. Your check in one of these boxes, together with your signature in space 10, will mean that the Library of Congress can proceed to reproduce and distribute under the license without further paperwork. For further information, write for Circular R63.

9,10,11 SPACE 9, 10, 11: Fee, Correspondence, Certification, Return Address

Deposit Account: If you maintain a Deposit Account in the Copyright Office, identify it in space 9. Otherwise leave the space blank and send the fee of $10 with your application and deposit.

Correspondence (space 9): This space should contain the name, address, area code, and telephone number of the person to be consulted if correspondence about this application becomes necessary.

Certification (space 10): The application can not be accepted unless it bears the date and the **handwritten signature** of the author or other copyright claimant, or of the owner of exclusive right(s), or of the duly authorized agent of author, claimant, or owner of exclusive right(s).

Address for Return of Certificate (space 11): The address box must be completed legibi,v since the certificate will be returned in a window envelope.

FIGURE 15–4 (*continued*)

FORM TX
UNITED STATES COPYRIGHT OFFICE

REGISTRATION NUMBER

TX TXU

EFFECTIVE DATE OF REGISTRATION

Month Day Year

DO NOT WRITE ABOVE THIS LINE. IF YOU NEED MORE SPACE, USE A SEPARATE CONTINUATION SHEET.

1

TITLE OF THIS WORK ▼

PREVIOUS OR ALTERNATIVE TITLES ▼

PUBLICATION AS A CONTRIBUTION If this work was published as a contribution to a periodical, serial, or collection, give information about the collective work in which the contribution appeared. **Title of Collective Work ▼**

If published in a periodical or serial give: **Volume ▼** **Number ▼** **Issue Date ▼** **On Pages ▼**

2

a **NAME OF AUTHOR ▼** **DATES OF BIRTH AND DEATH** Year Born ▼ Year Died ▼

Was this contribution to the work a "work made for hire"? ☐ Yes ☐ No

AUTHOR'S NATIONALITY OR DOMICILE Name of Country OR { Citizen of ▶ ______ Domiciled in ▶ ______

WAS THIS AUTHOR'S CONTRIBUTION TO THE WORK Anonymous? ☐ Yes ☐ No Pseudonymous? ☐ Yes ☐ No If the answer to either of these questions is "Yes," see detailed instructions.

NATURE OF AUTHORSHIP Briefly describe nature of the material created by this author in which copyright is claimed. ▼

b **NAME OF AUTHOR ▼** **DATES OF BIRTH AND DEATH** Year Born ▼ Year Died ▼

Was this contribution to the work a "work made for hire"? ☐ Yes ☐ No

AUTHOR'S NATIONALITY OR DOMICILE Name of country OR { Citizen of ▶ ______ Domiciled in ▶ ______

WAS THIS AUTHOR'S CONTRIBUTION TO THE WORK Anonymous? ☐ Yes ☐ No Pseudonymous? ☐ Yes ☐ No If the answer to either of these questions is "Yes," see detailed instructions.

NATURE OF AUTHORSHIP Briefly describe nature of the material created by this author in which copyright is claimed. ▼

c **NAME OF AUTHOR ▼** **DATES OF BIRTH AND DEATH** Year Born ▼ Year Died ▼

Was this contribution to the work a "work made for hire"? ☐ Yes ☐ No

AUTHOR'S NATIONALITY OR DOMICILE Name of Country OR { Citizen of ▶ ______ Domiciled in ▶ ______

WAS THIS AUTHOR'S CONTRIBUTION TO THE WORK Anonymous? ☐ Yes ☐ No Pseudonymous? ☐ Yes ☐ No If the answer to either of these questions is "Yes," see detailed instructions.

NATURE OF AUTHORSHIP Briefly describe nature of the material created by this author in which copyright is claimed. ▼

NOTE

Under the law, the "author" of a "work made for hire" is generally the employer, not the employee (see instructions). For any part of this work that was "made for hire" check "Yes" in the space provided, give the employer (or other person for whom the work was prepared) as "Author" of that part, and leave the space for dates of birth and death blank.

3

YEAR IN WHICH CREATION OF THIS WORK WAS COMPLETED **This information must be given in all cases.** ______ ◀ Year

DATE AND NATION OF FIRST PUBLICATION OF THIS PARTICULAR WORK **Complete this information ONLY if this work has been published.** Month ▶ ______ Day ▶ ______ Year ▶ ______ ______ ◀ Nation

4

COPYRIGHT CLAIMANT(S) Name and address must be given even if the claimant is the same as the author given in space 2.▼

See instructions before completing this space.

TRANSFER If the claimant(s) named here in space 4 are different from the author(s) named in space 2, give a brief statement of how the claimant(s) obtained ownership of the copyright.▼

DO NOT WRITE HERE OFFICE USE ONLY
APPLICATION RECEIVED
ONE DEPOSIT RECEIVED
TWO DEPOSITS RECEIVED
REMITTANCE NUMBER AND DATE

MORE ON BACK ▶ • Complete all applicable spaces (numbers 5-11) on the reverse side of this page. • See detailed instructions. • Sign the form at line 10.

DO NOT WRITE HERE

Page 1 of ______ pages

FIGURE 15–4 *(concluded)*

EXAMINED BY

FORM TX

CHECKED BY

☐ CORRESPONDENCE Yes

☐ DEPOSIT ACCOUNT FUNDS USED

FOR COPYRIGHT OFFICE USE ONLY

DO NOT WRITE ABOVE THIS LINE. IF YOU NEED MORE SPACE, USE A SEPARATE CONTINUATION SHEET.

5

PREVIOUS REGISTRATION Has registration for this work, or for an earlier version of this work, already been made in the Copyright Office?
☐ **Yes** ☐ **No** If your answer is "Yes," why is another registration being sought? (Check appropriate box) ▼
☐ This is the first published edition of a work previously registered in unpublished form.
☐ This is the first application submitted by this author as copyright claimant.
☐ This is a changed version of the work, as shown by space 6 on this application.
If your answer is "Yes," give: **Previous Registration Number ▼** **Year of Registration ▼**

6

DERIVATIVE WORK OR COMPILATION Complete both space 6a & 6b for a derivative work; complete only 6b for a compilation.
a. Preexisting Material Identify any preexisting work or works that this work is based on or incorporates. ▼

b. Material Added to This Work Give a brief, general statement of the material that has been added to this work and in which copyright is claimed. ▼

See instructions before completing this space

7

MANUFACTURERS AND LOCATIONS If this is a published work consisting preponderantly of nondramatic literary material in English, the law may require that the copies be manufactured in the United States or Canada for full protection. If so, the names of the manufacturers who performed certain processes, and the places where these processes were performed **must** be given. See instructions for details.
Names of Manufacturers ▼ **Places of Manufacture ▼**

8

REPRODUCTION FOR USE OF BLIND OR PHYSICALLY HANDICAPPED INDIVIDUALS A signature on this form at space 10, and a check in one of the boxes here in space 8, constitutes a non-exclusive grant of permission to the Library of Congress to reproduce and distribute solely for the blind and physically handicapped and under the conditions and limitations prescribed by the regulations of the Copyright Office: (1) copies of the work identified in space 1 of this application in Braille (or similar tactile symbols); or (2) phonorecords embodying a fixation of a reading of that work; or (3) both.
a ☐ Copies and Phonorecords **b** ☐ Copies Only **c** ☐ Phonorecords Only

See instructions

9

DEPOSIT ACCOUNT If the registration fee is to be charged to a Deposit Account established in the Copyright Office, give name and number of Account.
Name ▼ **Account Number ▼**

CORRESPONDENCE Give name and address to which correspondence about this application should be sent. Name/Address/Apt/City/State/Zip ▼

Area Code & Telephone Number ▶

Be sure to give your daytime phone ◀ number

10

CERTIFICATION* I, the undersigned, hereby certify that I am the
Check one ▶
☐ author
☐ other copyright claimant
☐ owner of exclusive right(s)
☐ authorized agent of
Name of author or other copyright claimant, or owner of exclusive right(s) ▲

of the work identified in this application and that the statements made by me in this application are correct to the best of my knowledge.

Typed or printed name and date ▼ If this is a published work, this date must be the same as or later than the date of publication given in space 3.

date ▶

Handwritten signature (X) ▼

11

MAIL CERTIFICATE TO

Certificate will be mailed in window envelope

Name ▼

Number/Street/Apartment Number ▼

City/State/ZIP ▼

Have you:
- Completed all necessary spaces?
- Signed your application in space 10?
- Enclosed check or money order for $10 payable to *Register of Copyrights*?
- Enclosed your deposit material with the application and fee?

MAIL TO: Register of Copyrights, Library of Congress, Washington, D.C. 20559

* 17 U.S.C. § 506(e): Any person who knowingly makes a false representation of a material fact in the application for copyright registration provided for by section 409, or in any written statement filed in connection with the application, shall be fined not more than $2,500.

U.S. GOVERNMENT PRINTING OFFICE: 1985: 491-560/20,011

December 1985—200,000

interviews or announcements. In all three instances, overzealous employees are the problem. To try to control this problem, entrepreneurs should consider some of the ideas listed below:

- Train employees to refer sensitive questions to one person.
- Provide escorts for all office visitors.
- Avoid discussing business in public places.
- Keep important travel plans secret.
- Control information that might be presented by employees at conferences or published in journals.
- Use simple security such as locked file cabinets, passwords on computers, and shredders where necessary.
- Have employees and consultants sign nondisclosure agreements.
- Debrief departing employees on any confidential information.
- Avoid faxing any sensitive information.
- Mark documents *confidential* when necessary.

Unfortunately, protection against leaking of trade secrets is difficult to enforce. And legal action can be taken only *after* the secret has been revealed. It is not necessary, however, for the entrepreneur to worry extensively about every document or piece of information. As long as minimal precautions are taken, most problems can be avoided, primarily because leaks usually occur inadvertently.

LICENSING

Licensing may be defined as an arrangement between two parties, where one party has proprietary rights over some information, process, or technology protected by a patent, trademark, or copyright. This arrangement, specified in a contract (discussed later in this chapter), requires the licensee to pay a royalty or some other specified sum to the holder of the proprietary rights (licensor) in return for permission to copy the patent, trademark, or copyright.

Thus, licensing has significant value as a marketing strategy to holders of patents, trademarks, or copyrights to grow their business in new markets, when they lack resources or experience in those markets. It is also an important marketing strategy for entrepreneurs who wish to start a new venture but need permission to copy or incorporate the patent, trademark, or copyright with their idea.

A patent license agreement specifies how the licensee would have access to the patent. For example, the licensor may still manufacture the product but give the licensee the rights to market it under their label in a noncompetitive market (i.e., a foreign market). In other instances, the licensee may actually manufacture and market the patented product under their own label. This agreement must be carefully worded and should involve a lawyer, to insure the protection of all parties.

Licensing a trademark generally involves a franchising agreement. The entrepreneur operates a business using the trademark and agrees to pay a fixed sum for use of the trademark, pay a royalty based on sales volume, buy supplies from the franchisor (examples would be Shell, Exxon, Dunkin Donuts, Pepsi Cola or Coca Cola bottlers, or Midas Muffler shops), or some combination of these. Chapter 16 discusses franchising as an option for the entrepreneur to start a new business.

Copyrights are another popular licensed property. They involve rights to use or copy books, software, music, photographs, and plays, to name a few. In the late 1970s, computer games were designed using licenses from arcade games and movies. Television programs have also licensed their names for board games or computer games. Celebrities will often license the right to use his or her name, likeness, or image in a product (i.e., Andre Agassi tennis clothing, Elvis Presley memorabilia, or Mickey Mouse lunch boxes). This is actually analogous to a trademark license. A good example of this occurred in 1990 when Eagle Eyewear was granted a license by Yoko Ono to affix John Lennon's signature to a line of eyewear that reflected the John Lennon look. In addition, the license gave Eagle Eyewear the right to use John Lennon's likeness in promotional materials.[7]

The licensing agreement between Eagle Eyewear and Bag One Arts (the licensing arm of Lennon's estate) consisted of 28 pages of comprehensive documentation establishing the scope, duration, geographic coverage, key terms, performance standards, and compensation. Additional stipulations included such areas as reporting requirements, training and support, indemnifications, guarantees and warranties, taxes, and dispute resolutions.

Hit movies can also result in new products. The movie *Who Framed Roger Rabbit* resulted in a licensing agreement with Hasbro to produce a line of plush dolls, and with McDonald's to offer Roger Rabbit drinking glasses. In fact, the success of the movie resulted in nearly 50 license agreements.[8] Other movies, such as *Rambo, Willow,* and *Crocodile Dundee,* have also resulted in numerous licensing agreements providing opportunities for entrepreneurs and as a means to extend the profit potential of the movie company. Licensing is also popular around special sporting events, such as the Olympics, marathons, bowl games, and tournaments. Licenses to sell t-shirts, clothing, and other accessories require written permission in the form of a license agreement before sales are allowed.

Rose Evangelista's toy company, Just Toys, is an example of a new venture that has been very successful through using licensing for her toys and dolls. In 1990, she manufactured 50,000 Little Mermaid Ariel dolls in anticipation of the video release of the movie. However, the market was soft and she was almost ready to give up her effort when suddenly the demand for the rubber figurines began to soar. By the time the demand had peaked, her firm had sold two million dolls. The Teenage Mutant Ninja Turtles trend has accounted for over $2 billion in licensing. Most of the firms that made Turtles' products were small entrepreneurial ventures.[9]

---

[7] T. Owens, "A Contractual Approach to Partnering," *Small Business Reports,* July 1991, pp 29–40.

[8] "Hit Movies Spark Licensing Tie-ins," *Playthings,* August 1988, pp 56–57.

[9] A. Hornaday, "Cashing In on the Little Green Turtles," *Working Woman,* February 1992, pp 48–53.

Licensing can be particularly valuable for a high-technology firm lacking the resources to conduct R&D to develop a product. Technology licensing usually entails a contractual agreement by which a firm (licensee) acquires the rights to product, process, and/or management technology from another firm (licensor) for a lump sum payment and/or royalties. According to recent research, technology licensing is becoming extremely popular among small ventures as a means to develop new products. This research indicated that the two most important reasons for licensing were to gain competitive advantage and to improve the venture's technical skills. Firms participating in the study found that licensing technology reduced their R&D costs, lowered marketing and legislative risks, and enhanced the speed of market entry.[10]

Before entering a license agreement, the entrepreneur should ask the following questions:

- Will the customer recognize the licensed property?
- How well does the licensed property complement my products or services?
- How much experience do I have with the licensed property?
- What is the long-term outlook for the licensed property? (For example, the loss of popularity of a celebrity can also result in an end to a business involving that celebrity's name.)
- What kind of protection does the licensing agreement provide?
- What commitment do I have to payment of royalties, sales quotas, and so on?
- Are renewal options possible and under what terms?

Licensing is an excellent option for the entrepreneur to increase revenues, without the risk and costly start-up investment. To be able to license requires the entrepreneur to have something to license, which is why it is so important to seek protection for any product, information, name and so on with a patent, trademark, or copyright. On the other hand, licensing can also be a way to start a new venture when the idea may infringe on someone else's patent, trademark, or copyright. In this instance, the entrepreneur has nothing to lose by trying to seek a license agreement from the holder of the property.

Licensing continues to be a powerful marketing tool. With the advice of a lawyer, entrepreneurs may find that licensing opportunities are a way to minimize risk, expand a business, or complement an existing product line.

PRODUCT SAFETY AND LIABILITY

It is very important for the entrepreneur to assess whether any product that is to be marketed in the new venture is subject to any regulations under the Consumer Product Safety Act. The act, which was passed in 1972, created a five-member commission that has the power to prescribe safety standards for more than 10,000 products.

---

[10]K. Atuahene-Gima, "Buying Technology for Product Development in Smaller Firms," *Industrial Marketing Management,* August 1993, pp 223–32.

In addition to setting standards for products, the commission also has a great deal of responsibility and power to identify what it considers to be substantial hazards and to bar products it considers unsafe. It is especially active in recognizing whether possible product defects may be hazardous to consumers. When this is the case, the commission will request the manufacturer, in writing, to take corrective action.

The act was amended in 1990 and signed into law by President Bush. The amended law establishes stricter guidelines for reporting product defects and any injury or death resulting from such defects. Manufacturers could be subject to fines of $1.25 million for failing to report product liability settlements or court awards. Manufacturers have presented their concerns to the Consumer Product Safety Commission about information in these reports becoming public prematurely. This information could prove damaging even when the Commission may subsequently find that the firm was not negligent.[11]

Any new product that is responsible for the entrepreneur's entry into a business should be assessed to ascertain whether it falls under the Consumer Product Safety Act. If it does, the entrepreneur will have to follow the appropriate procedures to ensure that he or she has met all the necessary requirements.

Product liability problems are complex and continue to be an important consideration for entrepreneurs. Increases in insurance premiums, legal fees, and the number of liability cases all seem to indicate that the entrepreneur must be sensitive to this possibility and should consult with an attorney and insurance agent to provide satisfactory coverage and protection.

Claims regarding product liability usually fall under one of the following categories:

1. *Negligence*—Extending to all parts of the production and marketing process, this involves being negligent in the way a product is presented to a client, such as using deficient labels, false advertising, and so on.
2. *Warranty*—Consumers may sue if advertising or information overstates the benefits of a product or the product does not perform as stated.
3. *Strict Liability*—In this action, a consumer sues on the basis that the product in question was defective prior to its receipt.
4. *Misrepresentation*—This occurs when advertising, labels, or other information misrepresent material facts concerning the character or quality of the product.

The best protection against product liability is to produce safe products and to warn consumers of any potential hazards. It is impossible to expect zero defects, so entrepreneurs should be sensitive to what kinds of product liability problems may occur.

[11] C. Johnson, "Product Liability Payouts to be Told to Federal Agency," *Business Insurance,* January 14, 1991, pp 3, 47.

INSURANCE

Some of the problems relating to product liability were discussed in the previous section. Besides being cautious, it is also in the best interests of the entrepreneur to purchase insurance in the event that problems do occur. Service-related businesses such as day care centers, amusement parks, shopping centers, and so on have had significant increases in the number of lawsuits.

In general, most firms should consider coverage for those situations described in Figure 15–5. Each of these types of insurance provides a means of managing risk in the new business. The main problem is that the entrepreneur usually has limited resources in the beginning. Thus, it is important for the entrepreneur to determine not only what kind of insurance to purchase but also how much to purchase and from what company. The total insurance cost represents an important financial planning factor, and the entrepreneur needs to consider increasing premiums in cost projections.

Skyrocketing medical costs have probably had the most significant impact on insurance premiums. This is especially true for workers' compensation premiums, which for some entrepreneurs have doubled or tripled in the last few years. Steve

FIGURE 15–5 Types of Insurance and Possible Coverage

Type of Insurance	*Coverage Possible*
Property	• Fire insurance to cover losses to goods and premises resulting from fire and lightning. Can extend coverage to include risks associated with explosion, riot, vehicle damage, windstorm, hail, and smoke. • Burglary and robbery to cover small losses for stolen property in cases of forced entry (burglary) or if force or threat of violence was involved (robbery). • Business interruption will pay net profits and expenses when a business is shut down because of fire or other insured cause.
Casualty	• General liability covers the costs of defense and judgments obtained against the company resulting from bodily injury or property damage. This coverage can also be extended to cover product liability. • Automobile liability is needed when employees use their own cars for company business.
Life	• Life insurance protects the continuity of the business (especially a partnership). It can also provide financial protection for survivors of a sole proprietorship or for loss of a key corporate executive.
Workers' compensation	• May be mandatory in some states. Provides benefits to employees in case of work-related injury.
Bonding	• This shifts responsibility for employee or performance of a job. It protects company in case of employee theft of funds or protects contractor if subcontractor fails to complete a job within agreed-upon time.

Cole, owner and founder of Cafe Allegro in 1984, has seen his workers' compensation premiums reach nearly $15,000 per year for 30 full- and part-time employees. This increase was incurred without any serious claims, but instead reflects a trend in certain industries, such as restaurants. With only three states—New Jersey, Texas, and South Carolina—still not requiring employers to carry workers' compensation insurance, it has become a serious problem for entrepreneurs.[12]

Insurance companies calculate the premium for workers' compensation as a percentage of payroll, the type of business, and the number of prior claims. Given the problems with fraudulant or suspicious claims, some states are beginning to undertake reforms in the coverage. Even before reforms are enacted, the entrepreneur can take some action to control the premiums by paying attention to details, such as promoting safety through comprehensive guidelines that are communicated to every staff member. Being personally involved with safety can, in the long run, significantly control workers' compensation premiums.

Seeking advice from an insurance agent is often difficult because the agent is trying to sell insurance. However, there are specialists at universities or the Small Business Administration who can provide this advice at little or no cost.

CONTRACTS

The entrepreneur, in starting a new venture, will be involved in a number of negotiations and contracts with vendors, landlords, and clients. It is very important for the entrepreneur to understand some of the fundamental issues related to contracts, while also recognizing the need for a lawyer in many of these negotiations.

Often, business deals are concluded with a handshake. Ordering supplies, lining up financing, reaching an agreement with a partner, and so on are common situations in which a handshake consummates the deal. Usually, when things are operating smoothly this procedure is sufficient. However, if there are disagreements, the entrepreneur may find that there is no deal and that he or she may be liable for something never intended. The courts generally provide some guidelines based on precedence of cases. One rule is to never rely on a handshake if the deal cannot be completed within one year. For example, a company that trains salespeople asked another firm to produce videotapes used in the training. The training firm was asked to promise to use the tapes only for its own salesforce and not to sell the tapes to others. Some time after the tapes were produced, this firm began to produce and sell the tapes under a newly formed company. The original developer of the tapes brought suit, and the courts ruled that an oral agreement for more than one year is not enforceable. The only way this could have been prevented was if the copying firm had signed a contract.

[12] S. Barlow, "Crisis Proportions," *Entrepreneur,* March 1993, pp 103–6.

In addition to the one-year rule of thumb, the courts insist that a written contract exist for all transactions over $500. Even a quote on a specified number of parts from a manufacturer may not be considered a legal contract. For example, if an entrepreneur asked for and received a quote for 10 items and then only ordered one item, the seller would not have to sell that item at the original quoted price unless a written contract existed. If the items totaled over $500, even the quoted price could be changed without a written contract.

Most sellers would not want to try to avoid their obligations in the above example. However, unusual circumstances may arise that force the seller to change his or her mind. Thus, the safest way to conduct business deals is with a written contract, especially if the amount of the deal is over $500 and is likely to extend beyond one year.

Any deal involving real estate must be in writing to be valid. Leases, rentals, and purchases all necessitate some type of written agreement.

Although a lawyer might be necessary in very complicated or large transactions, the entrepreneur cannot always afford one. Therefore, it is helpful for the entrepreneur to understand the four essential items in an agreement to provide the best legal protection.[13]

1. All of the parties involved should be named and their specific roles in the transaction specified (e.g., buyer, seller, consultant, client, etc.).
2. The transaction should be described in detail (e.g., exact location of land, dates, units, place of delivery, payor for transportation etc.).
3. The exact value of the transaction should be specified (e.g., installment payment with finance charges).
4. Obtain signature(s) of the person(s) involved in the deal.

HOW TO SELECT A LAWYER

Lawyers, like many other professionals, are specialists not just in the law but in specific areas of the law. The entrepreneur does not usually have the expertise or know-how to handle possible risks associated with the many difficult laws and regulations. A competent attorney is in a better position to understand all of the possible circumstances and outcomes related to any legal action.

In today's environment, lawyers are much more up-front with their fees. In fact, in some cases these fees, if for standard services, may even be advertised. In general, the lawyer may work on a retainer basis (stated amount per month or year) by which he or she provides office and consulting time. This does not include court time or other legal fees related to the action. This gives the entrepreneur the opportunity to call an attorney as the need arises without incurring high hourly visit fees.

[13] M. Manley, "Let's Shake on That," *Inc.*, June 1986, pp 131–32.

In some instances, the lawyer may be hired for a one-time fee. For example, a patent attorney may be hired as a specialist to help the entrepreneur obtain a patent. Once the patent is obtained, this lawyer would not be needed, except perhaps if there were litigation regarding the patent. Other specialists for setting up the organization or for purchase of real estate may also be paid on a service-performed basis. Whatever the fee basis, the entrepreneur should confront the cost issue initially so no questions arise in the future.

Choosing a lawyer is like hiring an employee. The lawyer you work with should be someone you can relate to personally. In a large law firm, it is possible that an associate or junior partner would be assigned to the new venture. The entrepreneur should ask to meet with this person to ensure that there is compatibility.

A good working relationship with a lawyer will ease some of the risk in starting a new business and will give the entrepreneur necessary confidence. When resources are very limited, the entrepreneur may consider offering the lawyer stock in exchange for his or her services. The lawyer then will have a vested interest in the business and will likely provide more personalized services. However, in making such a major decision, the entrepreneur must consider any possible loss of control of the business.

SUMMARY

This chapter explores some of the major legal concerns in starting a new venture. It is important for the entrepreneur to seek legal advice in making all of the legal decisions required in the new venture. Lawyers have specialties that can provide the entrepreneur with the most appropriate advice under the circumstances.

A patent requires a patent attorney, who assists the entrepreneur in completing an application to the Patent and Trademark Office with the history and description of the invention, as well as claims for its usefulness. Patent fees will vary but in general will cost about $1,500. An assessment of the existing patent(s) will help to ascertain whether infringement is likely and to evaluate the possibilities of modifying the patented product or licensing the rights from the holder of the patent.

Trademarks may be a word, symbol, design, or some combination, or a slogan or sound that identifies the source of certain goods or services. Trademarks give the entrepreneur certain benefits as long as the following four requirements are met: (1) completion of the written application form, (2) submission of a drawing of the mark, (3) submission of five specimens showing actual use of the mark, and (4) payment of the required fee.

Copyrights protect original works of authorship. Copyrights are registered with the Library of Congress and do not usually require an attorney. Copyrights have become especially relevant to computer software firms.

Licensing is a viable means of starting a business using someone else's product, name, information, and so on. It is also an important strategy that the entrepreneur can use to expand the business without extensive risk or large investments.

The entrepreneur also should be sensitive to possible product safety and liability requirements. Careful scrutiny of possible product problems, as well as insurance, can reduce the risk. Other risks relating to property insurance, life insurance, workers' compensation, and bonding should be evaluated to ascertain any insurance needs. Workers' compensation premiums have been a serious concern of many states. Entrepreneurs can also play a role in controlling these premiums by establishing and communicating good safety policies.

Contracts are an important part of the transactions the entrepreneur will make. As a rule of thumb, oral agreements are invalid for deals over one year and over $500. In addition, all real estate transactions must be in writing to be valid. It is important in a written agreement to identify all the parties and their respective roles, to describe the transaction in detail, to specify the value of the deal, and to obtain the signatures of the persons with whom you are doing business.

QUESTIONS FOR DISCUSSION

1. Patents are often imitated, thus raising a much-debated issue as to their relevance. What can an entrepreneur do to protect his or her product? What procedures must be followed to file for a patent?
2. Discuss the appropriateness of a disclosure document.
3. Using examples, discuss the difference between the four categories of trademarks. What are the benefits of a trademark to an entrepreneur?
4. Under what conditions would a license be considered?
5. What are the essential ingredients of an acceptable written contract?
6. What procedure would you recommend for hiring a lawyer?

KEY TERMS

contract
copyright
disclosure document
license
patent
product safety and liability
trademark
trade secret

SELECTED READINGS

Bauman, A. (October 1992). Strictly confidential. *Entrepreneur.* pp 126–31.
The decision of whether to confide in employees with sensitive information can be difficult for an entrepreneur. Letting employees in on sensitive information can be a boon to

the venture, yet opens the door to possible problems. Safeguards that can minimize these problems are presented and discussed.

Burge, D. A. (1984). *Patent and Trademark Tactics and Practice* (2nd ed.). New York: John Wiley and Sons.

This is probably the most comprehensive source on patents, trademarks, and copyrights. It takes the reader through a step-by-step procedure to register for any of the above items. A clear explanation of the options for the entrepreneur is also presented.

Manley, M. (June 1986). Let's shake on that. *Inc.* 8, no 6, pp 131–132.

Courts are usually unwilling to enforce oral agreements. Thus, as the article points out, it is important to get something in writing even if it is a note, telegram, letter, or receipt. The written item should include the names of the parties, a description of the transaction, value of the deal, and signatures.

Morgan, F. (Summer 1982). Marketing and product liability: A review and update. *Journal of Marketing* 46, pp 69–78.

There is considerable controversy regarding the relevance of product liability. An overview of the problem and possible types of lawsuits that may be made by the consumer are described in detail. A complete overview and summary of the trends in litigation is also provided.

Patent and Trademark Office, U.S. Department of Commerce. (May 1992). *General Information Concerning Patents.*

Provides a general overview of the operations of the Patent and Trademark Office and the process required to file for a patent. Useful to inventors, students, and others who may be interested in learning how the system functions.

Sheeran, L. R. (April 1986). Copycat and mouse. *Inc.* 8, no 4, pp 123–124.

This article discusses the risks in filing a patent infringement suit. It's a good idea, states the author, for entrepreneurs to carefully consider all of the alternatives before beginning a lawsuit. There are no precedents regarding lawsuits, so the decision must be made carefully.

Soter, T. (November 1992). At the movies: marketing lessons from tinseltown. *Management Review,* pp 10–15.

Hollywood represents one of the largest sources of licensing deals. These deals represent excellent models for an entrepreneur who is considering a license opportunity. The article discusses a number of factors and criteria that can be applied to any licensing arrangement.

CHAPTER

16

Starting A New Venture Through Franchising or Acquisition

Chapter Objectives

1. To present the advantages and disadvantages of franchising to franchisor and franchisee.
2. To contrast and compare the different types of franchises.
3. To explain the risks in investing in a franchise.
4. To identify the steps in evaluating a franchise opportunity.
5. To understand the franchise agreement.
6. To understand the alternative option of entering a new venture through acquisition.
7. To identify where acquisition opportunities can be located.
8. To understand how to evaluate acquisition alternatives.

Fred DeLuca

Franchising represents an opportunity for an entrepreneur to enter into a business with less risk, and without experience and knowledge of the business. It is also an important strategy by which an entrepreneur can grow an existing business without excessive capital.

Fred DeLuca represents one of the most successful entrepreneurs in the franchising field since Ray Kroc developed McDonald's. Although still growing in number of franchises, DeLuca's Subway sandwich shops outnumber McDonald's in southern parts of Florida and California. Having achieved the honor of the number one franchise by *Entrepreneur* magazine four times, DeLuca continues to seek new opportunities for expanding Subway and Cajun Joe's, which was founded in 1985.[1]

Fred DeLuca initiated his first endeavor in 1965 at age 17. Up to that point, his only work experience was as a stock boy. He borrowed $1,000 from his partner Pete Buck and opened a sandwich shop in Connecticut called Pete's Submarines. After opening this store, DeLuca and his partner found that the name of their restaurant was often confused with a competitor's restaurant called Pizza Marines, so they first changed the name of their shop to Pete's Subways and then shortly thereafter to Subway Sandwiches.

The early success of the business led DeLuca to consider franchising. In 1974, he began to franchise Subway with a unique franchise strategy based on small stores, low overhead, and a simple menu. He wanted the franchise to appeal to individuals with very little start-up capital, so his plan was to set a franchise fee of $10,000 for the first store and $2,500 for the second. Franchises would be required to spend about $65,000 on construction and new equipment for each store or alternatively $40,000 for construction and an equipment leasing program through Subway. With the low start-up costs, DeLuca believed that the franchisee would be willing to pay an 8 percent royalty on gross sales and a 2.5 percent contribution to the advertising fund. The royalty is at least 2 percent higher and in some cases double what most competitors charge for a franchise fee. DeLuca, however, believed that with the lower start-up costs, good training, procurement channels, and store management systems, he would attract a large number of interested entrepreneurs.

---

[1] See E. Kotite, "Earl of Sandwich," *Entrepreneur,* January 1994, pp 111–12; J. Birmingham, "What Now?" *Restaurant Business,* July 20, 1992, pp 80–8; and P. Keegan, "FTC Drops Subway Investigation," *Nation's Restaurant News,* December 20, 1993, pp 3 and 107.

The results of DeLuca's franchising strategy have been phenomenal. As of the end of 1993, he had 8,300 stores worldwide and an additional 600 stores in construction. Total sales were about $2 billion. Average store sales were up 5 percent from one year earlier, at a time when many restaurants were struggling to survive. The low start-up costs and high royalty strategy actually helped drive expansion because many franchisees felt they could own more than one Subway store.

DeLuca's simplified approval to the business in terms of organization and store size has kept costs at a minimum. Labor costs range from 18 percent to 22 percent of sales, and profits range from 15 percent to 18 percent. Expansion has also been enhanced by local development agents employed by the franchisor. These individuals are responsible for selling franchises and receive a very lucrative percentage of the royalties from every franchise they sell.

DeLuca has now begun to find nontraditional outlets for the Subway stores in rural towns with small populations, truck stops, sports arenas, and as add-ons to convenience stores. In 1988, he acquired controlling interest of Cajun Joe's, a chicken franchise operation, to which he has introduced many of the Subway concepts.

In 1991, Subway launched its first national advertising campaign, developed by a group of franchisees. The campaign is expected to increase store traffic in a time when competitors are adding sandwiches to their menus.

Recently DeLuca's strategy to grow the business as rapidly as possible has come under criticism. The FTC initiated a probe regarding whether the sandwich chain illegally misled franchisees about potential earnings. At the close of 1993, the FTC ended its nine-month investigation because of a lack of sufficient evidence about any of the charges made by disenchanted franchisees.

We can see that franchising proved to be an excellent option for DeLuca to grow his business without huge amounts of capital. His strategy provided opportunities for thousands of entrepreneurs to enter into a business venture with low risk by using the Subway name and reputation. We also see from the lawsuits that no matter how favorable a franchise investment looks, there is still risk; the entrepreneur needs to gather information and to carefully assess both the opportunity and the risks.

UNDERSTANDING FRANCHISING

As we saw from the discussion of Subway, franchising represents an opportunity for an entrepreneur to enter into business with the benefit of experience, knowledge, and support from the franchisor. Often, the entrepreneur is beginning a new venture with little assurance that it will succeed. With a franchise, the entrepreneur will be trained and supported in the marketing of the business and will be using a name that has an established image.

Franchising is also an alternative strategy for an entrepreneur to expand his or her business by having others pay for the use of the name, process, product, service, and so on. In January 1980, Jim Fowler decided to franchise his housecleaning venture, Merry Maids. The concept of a housecleaning service provided on a weekly or bi-weekly basis was difficult for the public to understand. Through franchising, Fowler believes that the venture achieved more credibility, which helped to facilitate franchise sales. Now operating in 48 states and in a number of foreign countries, Merry Maids has grown into a 560 location, $80 million business. Concentration on image with uniforms, quality training for franchisees, and a line of pretested cleaning products, the franchisor has been able to expand a simple housecleaning business and to also offer opportunities for entrepreneurs to become successful business men and women.[2] This example reflects how franchising represents two opportunities, one to the franchisor as a means of growing a business, and the second to an entrepreneur as an opportunity to become a business owner as a franchisee.

During recent years, franchising businesses have been expanding rapidly and have found new areas of application. By 1993, there were about 3,000 business-format franchise companies representing nearly 500,000 franchises. These business-format franchises accounted for more than $260 billion in sales and employed more than 8 million people in more than 60 major businesses.[3]

Any person who has the urge to own his or her own business may feel that a franchise is an easy solution. There are, however, some important risks involved that will be discussed later in this chapter. The important thing is that the entrepreneur should have a clear understanding of what a franchise is, its advantages, and potential risks.

Definition of Franchising

Franchising may be defined as "an arrangement whereby the manufacturer or sole distributor of a trademarked product or service gives exclusive rights of local distribution to independent retailers in return for their payment of royalties and conformance to standardized operating procedures."[4] The person offering the franchise is known as the **franchisor.** He or she probably has many years of experience in the business and knowledge of what is and is not successful. The **franchisee** is the person who purchases the franchise and is given the opportunity to enter a new business with a good chance to succeed. However, there is risk in any new business, and there are some good franchise opportunities and some that are much less desirable.

---

[2] J. Huber, "Respect," *Entrepreneur,* January 1992, pp 117-23.

[3] See, E. Kotite, "Franchising Comes Alive," *Entrepreneur,* April 1991, pp 99–101 and J. Huber, "Brave New World," *Entrepreneur,* January 1994, pp 72–76.

[4] D. D. Seltz, *The Complete Handbook of Franchising* (Reading, MA: Addison-Wesley Publishing Co., 1982), p 1.

TABLE 16–1 What You May Buy in a Franchise

1. A product or service with established market and favorable image
2. A patented formula or design
3. Trade names or trademarks
4. A financial management system for controlling the financial revenues
5. Managerial advice from experts in the field
6. Economies of scale for advertising and purchasing
7. Head office services
8. A tested business concept

Advantages of Franchising—To the Franchisee

One of the most important advantages of buying a franchise is that the entrepreneur does not have to incur all the same risks that are often associated with starting a business from scratch. Table 16–1 summarizes the important advantages of owning a franchise. Typically, the areas that entrepreneurs have problems with in starting a new venture are product acceptance, management expertise, meeting capital requirements, knowledge of the market, and operating and structural controls. These problem areas create risk for the entrepreneur and are often the cause for failure. In franchising, these risks are minimized through the franchise relationship. Each of these advantages is briefly discussed below.

Product acceptance. The franchisee, as stated above, usually enters into a business that has an accepted name, product, or service. In the case of Subway, any person buying a franchise will be using the Subway name, which is well-known and established throughout the United States. The franchisee does not have to spend resources trying to establish the credibility of the business. That credibility already exists based on the years of existence of the franchise. Subway has also spent millions of dollars advertising its shops, thus building a favorable image of the products and services offered. An entrepreneur who tries to start a sandwich shop would be unknown to the potential customers and would require significant effort and resources to build credibility and a reputation in the market.

Management expertise. Another important advantage to the franchisee is the managerial assistance provided by the franchisor. Each new franchisee is usually required to enter into a training program that will educate the new owner in all aspects of operating the franchise. This training could include classes in accounting, personnel management, marketing, and production. McDonald's, for example, requires all of its franchisees to spend time at their school, where everyone takes classes in the above mentioned areas. In addition, some franchisors require their new franchisees to actually work with an existing franchise owner or at a company owned store or facility to get on-the-job training. Once the franchise has been started, most franchisors will offer managerial assistance on a need basis. For example, most franchisors have follow-up training programs for franchisees that may reflect new concepts in effectively managing the business. Toll free numbers are also available so that the franchisee can ask questions at any time about any part of the franchise operation. Local sales offices for the larger franchises are continually visiting the local franchises to offer advice and keep owners informed of new developments.

The training and education offered is actually an important criterion that the entrepreneur should consider in evaluating any franchise opportunity. If the assistance in start-up is poor, the entrepreneur should probably look elsewhere for opportunities unless he or she already has extensive experience in the field.

Capital requirements. As we've seen in the previous chapters, starting a new venture can be costly both in terms of time and money. The franchise offers an opportunity to start a new venture with less start-up capital and with up-front support that would save the entrepreneur significant time. For example, franchisors will conduct location analysis and market research of the area that might include an assessment of traffic, demographics, business conditions, and competition. All of this information would be used in assessing the location and projecting sales and profit potential. In many cases, the franchisor will also finance the initial investment to start the franchise operation. The initial capital required to purchase a franchise generally reflects a fee for the franchise, construction costs, and the purchase of equipment.

The layout of the facility, control of stock and inventory, as well as the potential buying power of the entire franchise operation can save the entrepreneur significant funds. The size of the parent company can be advantageous in the purchase of health care and business insurance since the entrepreneur would be considered a participant of the entire franchise organization. Savings in start-up are also reflected in the pooling of monies by individual franchisees for advertising and sales promotion. The contribution by each franchisee is usually a function of the volume and of the number of franchises owned. This allows advertising on both a local and national scale to enhance the image and credibility of the business, something that would be impossible for a single operation.

Knowledge of the market. Any established franchise business, such as Subway, offers the entrepreneur years of experience in the business and knowledge of the market. This knowledge is usually reflected in a plan offered to the franchisee that details the profile of the target customer and the strategies that should be implemented once the operation has begun. This is particularly important because of regional and local differences in markets. Competition, media effectiveness, and tastes can vary widely from one market to another. Given their experience, franchisors can provide advice and assistance to accommodate any of these differences.

Most franchisors will be constantly evaluating market conditions and determining the most effective strategies to be communicated to the franchisees. Newsletters and other sources of publication that reflect new ideas and developments in the overall market are continually sent to franchisees. Local ideas will often come from the regional office or from the development representative employed by the corporate office.

Operating and structural controls. Two problems that many entrepreneurs have in starting a new venture is maintaining quality control of products and services and establishing effective managerial controls. The franchisor, particularly in the food business, will identify purveyors and suppliers who meet the quality standards established. In some instances, the supplies are actually provided by the franchisor, such as in the Merry Maids example described earlier in this chapter. Standardization in the supplies, products, and services provided help ensure that the entrepreneur will maintain quality standards that are so important in many types of businesses. Standardization also supports a consistent image that the franchise business depends on for expansion.

Administrative controls usually involve financial decisions relating to costs, inventory, and cash flow, and personnel issues such as criteria for hiring/firing, scheduling, and training to ensure consistent service to the customer. These controls will usually be outlined in a manual supplied to the franchisee upon completion of the franchise deal.

Although all of the above are advantages to the franchisee, they also represent important strategic considerations for an entrepreneur who is considering growing the business by selling franchises. Since there are so many franchise options for an entrepreneur, the franchisor will need to offer all of the above services in order to succeed in the sale of franchises. One of the reasons for the success of such franchises as McDonald's, Burger King, KFC, Boston Chicken, Subway, Midas, Jiffy Lube, Holiday Inn, Mail Boxes, etc., and Merry Maids is that these firms have established an excellent franchise system that effectively provides the necessary services to the franchisee.

Advantages of Franchising—To the Franchisor

The advantages of franchising to the franchisor are mostly related to expansion risk, capital requirements, and cost advantages due to extensive buying power. It is clear from the Subway example that Fred DeLuca would have not been able to achieve the size and scope of his business without franchising. However, in order to consider franchising, the franchisor must have established value and credibility that someone else is willing to buy.

Expansion risk. The most obvious advantage of franchising for an entrepreneur is that you can expand a venture quickly, with little capital. This advantage is significant when we reflect on the problems and issues that an entrepreneur faces in trying to manage and grow a new venture (see Chapter 12). A franchisor can expand a business nationally and even internationally by authorizing and selling franchises in selected locations. The capital necessary for this expansion is much less than it would be without franchising. Just think of the capital needed by DeLuca to build 8,300 Subway sandwich shops.

The value of the franchise depends on the to-date track record of the franchisor and on the services offered to the entrepreneur or franchisee. Subway's low franchise fee has enhanced expansion opportunities because more people can afford it. At the same time, quality training and site management also contribute to a high probability of success of the franchise. Other franchise companies charge higher franchise fees and lower royalties. The entrepreneur needs to evaluate each opportunity carefully. This investigation process is discussed later in this chapter.

Operating a franchised business requires fewer employees than if the business were not franchised. Headquarters and regional offices can be lightly staffed to primarily support the needs of the franchisees. This allows the franchisor to maintain low payrolls, and it minimizes personnel issues and problems.

The franchised business can be an attractive public company and can thus raise larger sums of money than if the business were not franchised. Recall earlier that we discussed the Boston Chicken public offering that was so successful in raising large amounts of funds for expansion into new businesses. The expansion thus occurs more quickly and with less funds from the founders.

Cost advantages. The mere size of a franchised company offers many advantages to the franchisees. The franchisor can purchase supplies in large quantities, thus achieving economies of scale that would not have been possible otherwise. Many franchise businesses produce parts, accessories, packaging, raw materials, and so on in large quantities and then in turn sell these to the franchisees. The franchisee would usually be required to purchase these items as part of the franchise agreement. However, because they are provided directly to the franchisee and they are produced in large quantities, the franchisee benefits from lower prices. In turn, the large designated market provides large profits to the franchisor.

One of the biggest cost advantages of franchising a business is the ability to commit larger sums of money to advertising. Each franchisee contributes a percentage of sales (1 to 2 percent) to an advertising pool. This pooling of resources allows the franchisor to conduct advertising in major media across a wide geographic area. If the business had not been franchised, the founder would have had to provide funds for the entire advertising budget.

Disadvantages of Franchising

Franchising is not always the best option for an entrepreneur. Anyone investing in a franchise should investigate the opportunity thoroughly. What should be involved in such an investigation is discussed later in this chapter.

Problems between franchisor and franchisee are common and have recently begun to receive much attention from the government and the trade associations. It is likely that some of these conflicts will result in new legislation.

The disadvantages to the franchisee usually center on the inability of the franchisor to provide services, advertising, and location. When promises that are made in the franchise agreement are not kept, the franchisee may be left without any support in important areas. A good example of this was when Curtis Bean bought a dozen franchises in Checkers of America Inc., which provides auto inspection services. After losing $200,000, Bean and other franchisees filed a lawsuit in which they claimed that the franchisor had misrepresented advertising costs and had made false claims that no experience was necessary to own a franchise.[5] Thus, broken promises about support services and hidden costs are probably the two most significant disadvantages or risks of buying a franchise.

The franchisee may also face the risk or disadvantage of a franchisor that fails or is bought out by another company. No one knows this experience better than Vincent Niagra, an owner of three Window Works franchises. Niagra had invested about $1 million in these franchises when the franchise was sold in 1988 to Apogee Enterprises and then resold in 1992 to a group of investors. Since that time, franchises have been failing rapidly with the total now at 50 franchises. Failed franchises have made it difficult for Niagra to continue because customers are apprehensive about doing business with him for fear that he will also go out of business. No support services that were promised are available and the future looks bleak. Niagra and about 30 franchisees are preparing a possible lawsuit for breach of franchise obligations.[6]

As a franchisee, there is sometimes little flexibility for developing new products or in expanding a business in a specific location. The franchisee in this case is bound by the franchise agreement, which can hinder creativity.

The franchisor also incurs certain risks and disadvantages in choosing this alternative rather than a traditional business. In some cases, the franchisor may find it is very difficult to find quality franchisees. Poor management, in spite of all the training and controls, can still lead to individual franchise failures, which could reflect negatively on the entire franchise system. As the number of franchises increases, the ability to maintain tight controls becomes more and more difficult.

Whether an entrepreneur chooses to buy a franchise or to use franchising as a method of expanding a business, the possible advantages and disadvantages of each option should be thoroughly investigated before entering into an agreement. Advice from a lawyer or specialist in franchising can be extremely useful in determining the most effective strategy for an entrepreneur.

Types of Franchises

Basically, there are three types of franchises available.[7] Variations may also exist as new innovations in franchising are developed. One type of franchise is dealerships, with many found in the automobile industry. Here, manufacturers use franchises to distribute their product lines. These dealerships act as the retail stores for the

[5] L. Bongiorno, "Franchise Fracas," *Business Week,* March 22, 1993, pp 68–71.

[6] F. Huffman, "Under New Ownership," *Entrepreneur,* January 1993, pp 101–105.

[7] W. Siegel, *Franchising* (New York: John Wiley & Sons, 1983), p 9.

automobile manufacturers. In some instances, they are required to meet quotas set by the manufacturers, but as does any franchise, they benefit from the advertising and management support provided by the franchisor.

The most common type of franchise is the type that offers a name, image, method of doing business, and so on, such as McDonald's, Subway, KFC, Midas, Dunkin Donuts and Holiday Inns. There are many of these types of franchises and their listing, with information, can be found in various sources.[8]

A third type of franchise offers services, such as personnel agencies, income tax preparation companies, and realtors. These services offer established names and reputations and methods of doing business. In some instances, such as real estate, the franchisee has actually been operating a business and then applies to become a member of the franchise.

Recent franchising opportunities have evolved because of important changes in the environment. Some of the important trends that have contributed to the development of new franchises are as follows:[9]

- *Good health*—Today people are eating healthier food and spending more time keeping fit. Many new franchises have developed in response to this trend. For example, Bassett's Original Turkey was created in 1983 in response to consumer interest in eating foods lower in cholesterol. Frozen yogurt franchises, such as TCBY in New England and Nibble-Lo's in Florida, have also been very successful. In Los Angeles, a unique restaurant, The Health Express, offers its customers a 100 percent vegetarian menu.
- *Time saving or convenience*—More and more consumers are finding they prefer to have things brought to them rather than having to go out of their way to buy them. In fact, many food stores now offer home delivery services. In 1990, Auto Critic of America Inc. was started as a mobile car inspection service. About the same time, Ronald Tosh started Tubs To Go, which offers the delivery of a jacuzzi to almost any location for an average of $100 to $200 per night.
- *Environmental consciousness*—Radon testing service franchises have grown as a response to consumers' need to protect themselves and their families from dangerous radon gas. In 1987, Ecology House, a gift store, began to add consumer products such as water-saving devices, rechargeable batteries, and energy saving light fixtures.
- *The second baby boom*—Today's baby boomers are having babies themselves, which has resulted in a number of child-related service franchises. Child-care franchises such as Kinder Care and Living and Learning are thriving. In 1989, two attorneys, David Pickus and Lee Sandoloski, decided to open Jungle Jim's

---

[8]*Directory of Franchising Organizations* (Babylon, NY: Pilot Industries, 1985).

[9]K. Rosenberg, "Franchising, American Style," *Entrepreneur,* January 1991, pp 86–93.

Playland. This is an indoor amusement park with small-scale rides in a 20,000 to 27,000 square-foot facility. One franchise, Computertots, teaches classes on computers to preschoolers. This franchise has spread to 25 locations in 15 states.

INVESTING IN A FRANCHISE

As we've seen in the earlier discussion on the advantages and disadvantages of franchising, it involves many potential risks to an entrepreneur. We hear of the success of McDonald's or Burger King, yet for every one of the successes there are many failures. Franchising, like any other venture, is not for the passive person. It requires effort, as any business does, since business such as hiring, scheduling, buying, accounting, and so on, are still the franchisee's responsibility. In many cases, long hours are required to ensure that the business operates effectively.

Certain steps can be taken to lower or minimize the risks in investing in a franchise. Each of these is discussed below.

Conduct A Self-Evaluation

The entrepreneur should conduct a self-evaluation to be sure that entering a franchise venture is right for him or her. Answering the following questions can help a person determine if this is the correct decision.

- Are you a self-starter?
- Do you enjoy working with other people?
- Do you have the ability to provide leadership to those who will work for you?
- Are you able to organize your time?
- Can you take risks and make good business decisions?
- Do you have the initiative to continue the business during its ups and downs?
- Are you in good health?

If you answered yes or maybe to most of the above questions, chances are you are making the right decision to enter a new franchise venture.

Investigate the Franchise

Not every franchise is right for every entrepreneur. He or she must evaluate the franchise alternatives (it is valuable to look at more than one) to decide which one is most appropriate. A number of factors should be assessed before making the final decision.

1. *Unproven versus proven franchise*—There are some trade-offs when investing in a proven or unproven franchise business. An unproven franchise will be less expensive as an investment. However, the lower investment is offset by a

substantial amount of risk. In an unproven franchise, the franchisor is likely to make mistakes as the business grows. These mistakes could inevitably lead to failure. Constant reorganization of a new franchise can result in confusion and mismanagement. On the favorable side, a new and unproven franchise can offer more excitement and challenge and can lead to significant opportunities for large profits should the business grow rapidly.

A proven franchise offers lower risk of failure but requires a substantial financial investment. However, there's always some risk, even in a mature franchise business.

2. *Financial stability of franchise*—The purchase of a franchise by an entrepreneur should entail an assessment of the financial stability of the franchisor. There are a number of factors that will help the entrepreneur ascertain the long-term stability and profitability of the franchise organization. The potential franchisee should ask the franchisor the following questions or should ascertain the answers from alternative sources:

- How many franchises are in the organization?
- How successful is each of the members of the franchise organization?
- Are most of the profits of the franchise a function of fees from sale of franchises or from royalties based on profits of franchisees?
- Does the franchisor have management expertise in production, finance, and marketing?

Some of the above information can be obtained from profit-and-loss statements of the franchise organization. Face-to-face contact with the franchisor can also reveal a strong sense of the success of the organization. It may also be worthwhile to contact some of the franchisees directly to determine their success and to identify any problems that have occurred. If the entrepreneur cannot effectively evaluate the financial statements, he or she should hire an accountant to provide this assessment. If financial information of the franchisor is unavailable, the entrepreneur may purchase a financial rating from a source such as Dun & Bradstreet. Generally, the following are good external sources of information:

- Franchise association
- Other franchisees
- Government
- Accountants and lawyers
- Libraries
- Franchise directories and journals
- Business exhibitions

3. *Potential market for the new franchise*—It is important for the entrepreneur to evaluate the market area from which customers will be attracted to the new franchise. One simple starting point is to take a map of the community or local area and try to evaluate the traffic flow and demographics of the residents in the area. Traffic flow information may be observed by visiting the area. Direction of traffic flow, ease of entry to business, and amount of traffic (pedestrian

and automobile) may be estimated by observation. The demographics of the area can be determined from census data, which can be obtained from local libraries or the town hall. It can also be advantageous to locate competitors on the map to determine their potential effect on the franchise business.

If the franchisor is willing or if financing is available, marketing research in the market area is helpful. Attitudes and interest in the new business can be assessed in the marketing research. If the resources are not available for a market research study, the entrepreneur may consider using local colleges or universities as part of a student project. In some instances, the franchisor will conduct a market study as a selling point to the franchisee.

4. *Profit potential for new franchise*—As in any start-up business, it is important to develop pro forma income, balance sheets, and cash flow statements. The franchisor should provide projections in order to calculate the needed information. Again, the entrepreneur may need assistance from an accountant to develop these statements. See Chapter 7 for specific information on how to prepare these statements.

In general, most of the above information should be provided in the disclosure statement or the prospectus. In 1979, the Federal Trade Commission's Franchise Rule became law. It requires franchisors to make full presale disclosure in a document that provides information about 20 separate aspects of a franchise offering.[10] The information required in this disclosure is summarized in Table 16–2. However, even though such a statement is required by law, it is often not made available until a few days before the signing of the franchise agreement. Thus, it is usually necessary for the entrepreneur to seek out much of the information, as described above. The alternative is to request a disclosure agreement at the beginning of the negotiations. It is also important to realize that some of the information will be well written and comprehensive and some will be poorly written and sketchy. There are always weaknesses that must be evaluated prior to making a commitment. The disclosure statement represents a good resource, but it is also important to evaluate the other services mentioned earlier in this chapter. If in doubt, a lawyer and/or accountant may help.

The entrepreneur should never make the decision to buy a franchise on a gut feeling or after a slick presentation without significant study and research. All of the information that is gathered in the evaluation process should be retained in organized folders and be clearly labeled. All of the information should be read carefully. If there is any doubt about the agreement or the risk, the appropriate questions should be asked of the franchisor to get the necessary information. If the franchisor is unwilling to respond to reasonable questions, it is likely they are trying to hide something.[11]

---

[10] D. J. Kaufmann & D. E. Robbins, "Now Read This," *Entrepreneur,* January 1991, pp 100–105.

[11] A. Caffey, "Know It All," *Entrepreneur,* January 1994, pp 85–88.

TABLE 16–2 Information Required in Disclosure Statement

1. Identification of the franchisor and its affiliates and their business experience.
2. The business experience of each of the franchisor's officers, directors, and management personnel responsible for franchise services, training, and other aspects of the franchise programs.
3. The lawsuits in which the franchisor and its officers, directors, and management personnel have been involved.
4. Any previous bankruptcies in which the franchisor and its officers, directors, and management personnel have been involved.
5. The initial franchise fee and other initial payments that are required to obtain the franchise.
6. The continuing payments that franchisees are required to make after the franchise opens.
7. Any restrictions on the quality of goods and services used in the franchise and where they may be purchased, including restrictions requiring purchases from the franchisor or its affiliates.
8. Any assistance available from the franchisor or its affiliates in financing the purchase of the franchise.
9. Restrictions on the goods or services franchises are permitted to sell.
10. Any restrictions on the customers with whom franchises may deal.
11. Any territorial protection that will be granted to the franchisee.
12. The conditions under which the franchise may be repurchased or refused renewal by the franchisor, transferred to a third party by the franchisee, and terminated or modified by either party.
13. The training programs provided to franchisees.
14. The involvement of any celebrities or public figures in the franchise.
15. Any assistance in selecting a site for the franchise that will be provided by the franchisor.
16. Statistical information about the present number of franchises; the number of franchises projected for the future; and the number of franchises terminated, the number the franchisor has decided not to renew, and the number repurchased in the past.
17. The financial statement of the franchisor.
18. The extent to which the franchisees must personally participate in the operation of the franchise.
19. A complete statement of the basis of any earning claims made to the franchisee, including the percentage of existing franchises that have actually achieved the results that are claimed.
20. A list of the names and addresses of other franchises.

As all of the information is assessed, the entrepreneur will eliminate some of the franchise alternatives. It is often useful at this point for the entrepreneur to work in one or more of the franchises to get a better sense of whether he or she is well suited to this business. Front-end procedure fees, royalty payments, expenses, and so on should be compared to those of franchises in the same field, as well as in different business areas.

If one franchise looks good as an investment, the entrepreneur may request a franchise package from the franchiser. It should contain a draft franchise agreement or contract. Generally, this package will require a deposit of $300 to $500. The entrepreneur should not pay any more than this for the package and should be sure that the deposit is fully refundable.

THE FRANCHISE AGREEMENT

The contract or franchise agreement is the final stage in becoming a franchisee. At this stage, a lawyer experienced in franchising is needed. The franchise agreement contains all of the specific requirements and obligations of the franchisee. Things such as the exclusivity of territory coverage will protect against the franchisor's granting another franchise within a certain radius of the business. The renewable terms will indicate the length of the contract and the requirements for renewing it. Financial requirements will stipulate the initial price for the franchise, the schedule of payments, the royalties to be paid, and so on. Termination of franchise requirements should indicate the terms for ending the agreement with the franchisor. The terms should indicate what will happen if the franchisee becomes disabled or dies and what provisions are made for the family. Terminating a franchise generally results in more lawsuits than any other issue in franchising. These terms should also provide for the franchisee to obtain fair market value should the franchise be sold.

All of these items are important and require the assistance of a lawyer. Even though the agreement may be standard, the franchisee should try to negotiate important items in a manner that can reduce the investment risk.

As can be seen, the franchise can offer the entrepreneur an easier alternative to starting a new business than beginning from point zero. There are still risks but, given a careful assessment of the issues discussed in this chapter, an informed decision can be made.

ACQUISITIONS

In Chapter 13, we considered acquisition as a means of expanding an established business. Factors such as finances, product lines, research and development, marketing strategy, and management were considered in the discussion of acquisition. In this chapter, we will focus on the reasons for acquisition, where to locate candidates, and the evaluation process in an acquisition, as another low-risk alternative to franchising for an entrepreneur to enter into a new venture.

Why an Acquisition?

Just as in the acquisition of a franchise, the entrepreneur needs to conduct a self-evaluation before entering into a venture through acquisition. Consideration should include an evaluation of the pros and cons of acquisition, buying a franchise, or starting from scratch. We've already discussed the issues in buying a franchise and starting from scratch, so we will now focus on the pros and cons of acquiring an existing business.

Advantages of an Acquisition

There are many advantages to acquiring an existing business for an entrepreneur. These advantages can be considered in relationship to other options such as buying a franchise or starting a business from scratch.

1. *Established Business*—The most significant advantage in acquiring an existing business is that the acquired firm has an established image and track record. Assuming through evaluation of tax records that this firm has been profitable, the entrepreneur would only need to continue the existing strategy to be successful. There would be an established customer base that could be easily contacted to identify the new ownership and to insure that the new owners are committed to operating the business the same as in the past. Neither the franchise nor the start-up can reflect this advantage.
2. *Location*—Although the franchisor usually provides location and site research and planning, there is still always the question of customer response. In the case of acquiring an existing business, this is not a question since the entrepreneur will already know how customers respond to the location. In the case of a start-up and a franchise, construction always raises questions as to timing and costs. With an existing facility, this is not a problem and hence an advantage of acquisition.
3. *Established Marketing Structure*—One of the most important factors that affects the value of an acquired firm is its existing channel and sales structure. Known suppliers, wholesalers, retailers, and manufacturers' reps are important assets to an entrepreneur. With this structure already in place, the entrepreneur can concentrate on improving or expanding to new target markets. One of the most difficult tasks for a start-up is trying to establish the channel of distribution. Since most start-ups involve a single product, the ability to attract channel members is quite difficult.
4. *Cost*—The actual total cost of acquiring a business could be lower than trying to buy a franchise or starting from scratch. In the case of a franchise, the entrepreneur may have to pay a franchise fee, construction costs for a new facility, and royalty and advertising fees. Even though the entrepreneur may have to pay for goodwill created by an existing business, the total cost may be less than a

franchise. In a start-up there is no cost for goodwill, but the entrepreneur would have to invest significant resources in trying to establish the business. Thus, the option of acquiring a business can actually be the least costly.

5. *Existing Employees*—The employees of an existing business can be an important asset in the acquisition process. They know how to run the business and can help assure that the business will continue in its successful mode. They already have established relationships with customers, suppliers, and channel members and can reassure these groups when a new owner takes over the business. For a franchisee or start-up, all the hiring decisions have to be made before beginning the operation.
6. *More Opportunity to be Creative*—Since the entrepreneur does not have to be concerned with finding suppliers, channel members, hiring new employees, or creating customer awareness, more time can be spent assessing opportunities to expand or strengthen the existing business. There are many details that have to be considered in a start up or a franchise that are already in place when an acquisition is made.

Disadvantages of an Acquisition

Although we can see that there are many advantages of acquiring an existing business, there are also disadvantages. The importance of each of the advantages and disadvantages should be weighed carefully with any other options, such as a franchise or starting a venture from scratch.

1. *Marginal Success Record*—Most ventures that are for sale have an erratic, marginally successful, or even unprofitable track record. This does not mean the choice should not be considered, but it makes the choice more difficult, especially when other options such as a franchise or starting up are available. What is important is a comprehensive review of the records as well as meetings or interviews with important constituents involved in the business to ascertain information that will allow for an assessment of the marginal record with the future potential. For example, if the store layout is poor, this factor can be rectified. On the other hand, if the location is poor, the entrepreneur would be better off buying a franchise or starting a new venture. A negative customer image may be possible to change if the reason for the problem can be identified. A more serious negative image may take significant resources to change and thus would dissuade an entrepreneur from buying the firm.
2. *Overconfidence in Ability*—Often, an entrepreneur may assume that he or she can succeed where others have failed. This is why a self-evaluation is so important before entering into any purchase agreement. The fact that others who also have the expertise and ability have failed does not give much hope that a new owner can succeed. Even though the entrepreneur brings new ideas and management qualities, the venture may never be successful for reasons that are not possible to resolve.

3. *Key Employee Loss*—Often, when a business changes hands, key employees also leave. Key employee loss can be devastating to an entrepreneur who is acquiring a business, since the value of the business is often a reflection of the efforts of the employees. This is particularly evident in a service business where it is difficult to separate the actual service from the person who performs it. In the acquisition negotiations, it is helpful for the entrepreneur to speak to each employee to get some assurance of their intentions as well as to inform them of how important they will be to the future of the business. Incentives can sometimes be used to assure that key employees will remain with the business.
4. *Overevaluated*—It is possible that the actual purchase price can be inflated because of the established image, customer base, channel members, suppliers, and so on. If the entrepreneur has to pay too much for a business, it is possible that the return on his or her investment will be unacceptable. It is important to look at the investment required in purchasing a business and at the potential profit. The entrepreneur will need to establish a reasonable payback to justify the investment.

After balancing the pros and cons of the acquisition, the entrepreneur should try to determine a fair price for the business.

Determining the Price for an Acquisition

In Chapter 10 we discussed how to value a company. The same criteria that are used to value a company can be used to determine a fair price for a venture. Some of the key factors used in determining price are earnings (past and future potential), assets, owner's equity, stock value, customer base, strength of distribution network, personnel, and image. Some of these factors are difficult to put value on, so it is recommended that the entrepreneur get outside help in this process. Most important is that, whatever the price paid, there should be opportunity to get a reasonable payback and good return on the investment. For more information on how to value a company see Chapter 10.

Locating Acquisition Candidates

If an entrepreneur is seriously seeking to buy a business, there are some good sources of assistance. There are professional business brokers that operate similarly to a real estate broker. They represent the seller and will sometimes aggressively find buyers either through referrals, advertising, or direct sales. Because these brokers would be paid a commission on the sale, they often expend more effort on their best deals. Marginal firms are more difficult to sell and are therefore a less desirable addition to their portfolio of businesses for sale. Since these business brokers represent the seller and are interested in earning a commission, it is important for the entrepreneur to use advisors or consultants to represent their best interests.

Accountants, attorneys, bankers, business associates, and consultants may also be aware of good acquisition candidates. Many of these professionals may have a good working knowledge of the business, which can be helpful in the negotiations.

It is also possible to find business opportunities in the classified sections of the newspaper or in a trade magazine. Since these listings are usually completely unknown, they may involve more risk. On the other hand, an entrepreneur who has expertise in some of these businesses may find that the costs attached to these businesses are much lower.

Determining the best option for an entrepreneur involves significant time and effort. Quick, uninformed, and emotional decisions to enter into an acquisition or purchase of a franchise is not wise. The entrepreneur should gather as much information as possible, read it carefully, consult with advisors and experts, consider his or her own situation, and then make a constructive decision.

SUMMARY

In this chapter we have discussed two very important options for the entrepreneur to start a new business: franchising and acquisition. Both offer opportunities that should be considered with the other possibility of starting a business from scratch.

In starting a franchise, the entrepreneur has the advantage of the experience of the franchisor to help in getting the business underway. An established name, advertising strength, and management advice all help to reduce the risk in the new venture.

Before entering a franchise agreement, the entrepreneur should conduct a self-evaluation to be sure that the franchise form of business is right for him or her. In addition, it is important to investigate the franchise carefully, especially if it is unproven. The financial stability, market potential, and profit potential should all be considered in the investigation. After investigating the franchise, an agreement will be signed. At this point, the entrepreneur should consult a lawyer to avoid any future legal problems.

Acquiring a business can be advantageous, particularly if the business being purchased has a successful history. In this case, the entrepreneur will be entering a business with important strengths, such as a quality product or service reputation, a large customer base, quality personnel, good suppliers, and efficient channels of distribution. An acquisition can be less expensive than a franchise or starting from scratch if the construction, site development, franchising fees, and marketing costs are prohibitive.

Acquisitions can also be risky, particularly when the business is marginally profitable or even losing money. There is also the risk that employees could leave when a new owner enters the picture. Sometimes entrepreneurs feel they can succeed where others fail. This type of emotional justification should be left out of any decision to acquire another business.

Business brokers, accountants, lawyers, consultants, bankers, and business associates are a few sources who can provide leads to businesses for sale. In any case, the entrepreneur should seek outside advice when investing in a new business opportunity either through franchising or acquiring an existing venture.

QUESTIONS FOR DISCUSSION

1. What are the major advantages and disadvantages of franchising compared with an acquisition?
2. Identify a local franchise in your area and determine where the competitors are located and where other franchises from the same company are located. Evaluate the existing potential for the franchise.
3. Why is it important for the entrepreneur to conduct a self-evaluation before entering a franchise operation?
4. If you were evaluating a franchise opportunity, what would you look for and why?
5. What are the advantages and disadvantages of an acquisition and starting a business from scratch?

KEY TERMS

broker
franchise
franchise agreement
franchisee
franchisor

SELECTED READINGS

Caffey, A. (January 1994). Know it all. *Entrepreneur,* pp 85–89.
When considering a franchise purchase, the entrepreneur should follow an approach that is organized and rational. The article discusses nine steps in this process.

Case, J. (February 1991). Buy now avoid the rush. *Inc.,* pp 36–45.
Entrepreneurs in the 1990s are looking to buy companies instead of starting them. Sales in the middle market $1 million to $50 million are doing well, while small ventures and megadeals are not.

Coriell, J. (January 1994). One day at a time. *Entrepreneur,* pp 90–95.
An entrepreneur discusses step-by-step his story of buying a franchise and how he survived the experience. The lessons he learned are valuable advice for anyone considering a franchise.

Kreisman, R. (September 1986). How start-up franchisors fail. *Inc.,* pp 106–18.

The root of growth through franchising is explored, with suggestions given on how to best carry out such a plan. Support of franchisees, the use of consultants, the need of competent legal advice, and acquiring capital are all covered.

Mandell, M. (May 1993). Corporate castaways. *Small Business Reports,* pp 50–60.

In recent years, the larger corporations have been divesting divisions, subsidiaries, and even products that don't meet the firms' financial criteria. These castaways offer entrepreneurs an opportunity for entering a new business at reasonable prices. Examples of these acquisitions are provided.

Matusky, G. (September 1992). Only the fittest survive. *Success,* pp 60–67.

In order to quickly expand franchise sales, some franchisors are turning to subfranchising. Regional franchisees or development agents are given the responsibility to sell franchises in a region and to provide all of the services normally provided by the franchisor. This allows faster expansion and with less capital since the only cost is sharing some of the franchising royalties with the subfranchisor.

Russel, S. (September 1985). A formula that works. *Venture,* pp 36–38.

The growth and profit potential of various successful franchises are discussed. An overview of the franchise experience is given, highlighting the importance of understanding the business deal offered by the franchisor.

Seltz, D. D. (1982). *The Complete Handbook of Franchising.* Reading, MA: Addison-Wesley.

This is probably the most complete book on the procedure for setting up a franchise. Guidelines, information, data, and various supporting agreements and forms that are needed in a franchise business are presented.

CHAPTER

17

Intrapreneurship

Chapter Objectives

1. To identify the reasons for the interest in intrapreneurship.
2. To explain the organizational environment conducive for intrapreneurship.
3. To discuss the differences between corporate and intrapreneurial cultures.
4. To identify the general characteristics of an intrapreneur.
5. To explain the process of establishing intrapreneurship in an organization.

Ewing Marion Kauffman

Born on a farm in Garden City, Missouri, Ewing Marion Kauffman moved to Kansas City with his family when he was eight years old. A critical event in his life occurred several years later when a doctor diagnosed leakage of the heart. His prescription was one year lying in bed; he was not even allowed to sit up. Ewing Kauffman's mother, a college graduate, came up with a solution to keep an active eleven year old lying in bed—reading. According to Ewing Kauffman, "I sure read! Because nothing else would do, I read as many as 40 and 50 books every month. When you read that much, you read anything. So I read the biographies of all the presidents, the frontiersmen, and I read the Bible twice and that's pretty rough reading."

Another early childhood experience centered around selling. Since his family did not have a lot of money, Ewing Kauffman would sell door-to-door 36 dozen eggs sent from the farm. He would also sell door-to-door cleaned and dressed fish that he and his father caught. His mother was a great encourager during these formative school years telling Ewing each day, "There may be some who have more money in their pockets but Ewing, there is nobody better than you."

During his youth, Ewing Kauffman also worked as a laundry delivery person and was a Boy Scout. In addition to passing all the requirements to become an Eagle Scout and a Sea Scout, he sold twice as many tickets as anyone else in Kansas City to the Boy Scout Roundup, enabling him to go free to a two-week scout summer camp that his parents would not otherwise have been able to afford. According to Ewing Kauffman, "This experience gave me some of the sales techniques which came into play when subsequently I went into the pharmaceutical business."

Then, Ewing Kauffman went to junior college from eight to twelve in the morning, then walked two miles to the laundry where he worked until seven at night. Upon graduation, he went to work at the laundry full-time for Mr. R. A. Long, who eventually became one of his role models. His job as route foreman involved being in charge of 18–20 route drivers where he would set up sales contest such as one where he would challenge the other drivers to get more customers on a particular route than he could. Ewing says, "I got practice in selling and that proved to be beneficial later in life." R. A. Long not only made money at the laundry business but also on patents such as a form fit for the collar of a shirt that would hold the shape of the shirt. He showed his young protege that one could make money not only with brawn but also with the brain. Kauffman commented, "He was quite a man and had quite an influence on my life."

Ewing Kauffman's sales ability was also useful when he joined the Navy after Pearl Harbor on January 11, 1942. When designated as an apprentice seaman, which paid $21 per month, he responded, "I'm better than an apprentice seaman because I have been a sea scout. I've sailed ships and I've ridden in whale boats." His selling ability convinced the Navy that he should instead start as a seaman first class with a $54 monthly salary. Assigned to the Admiral's staff, he was the best signalman (transmitting messages from ship to ship) in part because he was able to read messages better than anyone due to his previous intensive reading. Encouraged by the Admiral, he took a correspondence navigator's course and was given a deck commission and made a navigation officer.

After the war was over in 1947, Ewing Kauffman began his career as a pharmaceutical salesperson, having done better on an aptitude test than 50 other applicants. The job involved selling supplies of vitamin and liver shots to doctors. Working on straight commission, without expenses or benefits, his pay was higher than the president's salary by the end of the second year. The president, not liking this, cut the commission. Eventually, Ewing Kauffman was made Midwest sales manager, where he made 3 percent of everything his salespeople sold and again continually made more money than the president. When his territory was cut, he eventually quit and in 1950 started his own company—Marion Laboratories. (Marion is his middle name.)

When reflecting on founding the new company, Ewing Kauffman commented, "It was easier than it sounds because I had doctors whom I had been selling office supplies to for several years. Before I made the break, I went to three of them and said, I'm thinking of starting my own company. May I count on you to give me your orders if I can give you the same? These three were my biggest accounts and each one of them agreed to because they liked me and were happy to do business with me."

Marion Laboratories started by marketing injectable products manufactured by another company under their label. The company expanded to other accounts and other products, such as tablets, and then developed its first prescription product—Vicam—a vitamin product. The second pharmaceutical product—oyster shell calcium—also sold well and had sales of $25 million in 1992.

In order to expand the company, Kauffman borrowed $5,000 from the Commerce Trust Company. He repaid the loan, and the company continued to grow. After several years, outside investors could buy $1,000 worth of common stock, if they would loan the company $1,000 to be paid back in five years at $1,250, without any intermittent interest. This initial $1,000 investment, if held to 1993, would have been worth $21 million.

Marion Laboratories continued to grow from its founding in June 1950 and reached over a billion a year in sales due primarily to the relationship between Mr. Kauffman and the people in the company—who were called associates, not employees. "They are all stockholders, they build this company, and they mean so much to us," said Kauffman. The concept of associates was also a part of the two basic philosophies of the company: those who produce should share in the results or the profits and treat others as you would like to be treated.

The company went public through Smith Barney on August 16, 1965, at $21 per share. The stock jumped to $28 per share immediately and has never dropped below that level, sometimes selling at a 50 to 60 price earnings multiple. The associates of the company were offered a profit sharing plan where each could own stock in the company. When Marion Laboratories merged with Merrill Dow in 1989, there were 3,400 associates, 300 of whom became millionaires as a result of the merger. The new company, Marion Merrell Dow, Inc., now has over 9,000 associates and sales over $3.0 billion in 1993.

Ewing Marion Kauffman's philosophies of associates, rewarding those who produce, and allowing decision making throughout the organization are the fundamental concepts underlying what is now called intrapreneurship in a company. He went even further and illustrated his belief in entrepreneurship and the spirit of giving back when he established the Kauffman Foundation. When fully funded, the foundation will have assets over $1.2 billion and will equally support programs in two areas: youth development and entrepreneurship. Truly a remarkable entrepreneur, Mr. K, as he is affectionately referred to, will now produce many more successful "associate entrepreneurs."

CAUSES FOR RECENT INTEREST

The interest in intrapreneurship shown by existing organizations has resulted from a variety of events occurring in the United States on social, cultural, and business levels. On a social level, there is an increasing interest in "doing your own thing" and doing it on one's own terms. Individuals who believe strongly in their own talents frequently desire to create something of their own. They want responsibility and have a strong drive for individual expression and more freedom in their present organizational structure. When this freedom is not forthcoming, frustration can develop that can lead to the individual becoming less productive or even leaving the organization to achieve self-actualization elsewhere. This new search for meaning, and the impatience involved, has recently caused more discontent in structured organizations than ever before. When meaning is not provided within the organization, individuals often search for an institution that will provide it. Intrapreneurship is one method for stimulating and then capitalizing on individuals in an organization who think that something can be done differently and better.

Most people think of a large bureaucratic Fortune 100 company when they think of Xerox. While this may in part be true of the $15 billion giant company, Xerox has done something unique in trying to ensure that its creative employees do not leave like Steve Jobs did to form Apple Computer, Inc. In 1989, Xerox set up Xerox Technology Ventures (XTV) for the purpose of generating profits by investing in the promising technologies of the company, many of which would have otherwise been overlooked.[1] Xerox hopes to avoid mistakes of the past by having "a system to prevent technology from leaking out of the company," according to Robert V. Adams, President of XTV.

The $30 million fund has funded a dozen start-ups thus far, only two of which have failed. XTV is run as a classic venture-capital operation, providing seed-capital and finding outside investors when needed. The story of the 12 companies is much like that of Quad Mark, the brainchild of Dennis Stemmle, a Xerox employee for 25 years. Stemmle's idea was to make a battery-operated, plain paper copier that would fit in a briefcase along with a laptop computer. For 10 years, the idea was shot down by Xerox's operating committee. The idea was funded by XTV and Taiwan's Advanced Scientific Corporation, which has 20 percent of the company for its $3.5 million investments, and the company Quad Mark was born. As occurs with all the companies funded by XTV, 20 percent of each company is owned by the founder and key employees. This provides an incentive for people like Dennis Stemmle to take the risk, leave Xerox, and form a new technology-based venture.

The payoffs can be enormous, as was the case with the first company funded by XTV: Advanced Workstations Products, Inc. The company developed the idea of its founder Tony Domit—an add-in circuit board that inside an inexpensive IBM personal computer allowed the PC to perform like a $10,000 Xerox workstation. Xerox decided it needed to buy back this most successful company for $15 million (of which the company's founders and employees received $2 million) and market the product itself. While this is a rare case involving a parent company buy back, Dennis Stemmle is hopeful that his new product will be so well received at the 1994 Consumer Electronics Show in Las Vegas that he will reap similar monetary returns, perhaps by taking his company public.

XTV provides both financial and nonfinancial benefits to its parent, Xerox. The funded companies will return profits for the parent company as well as the founders and employees when they go public or are bought out by other companies. Some of the nonfinancial benefits have already been realized, as Xerox managers now more carefully watch employees' ideas and the internal technologies. The company's technologists are similarly affected in that they know a good idea will not be stonewalled but could become the next company funded by XTV.

Is XTV a success? Apparently so, if replication is any indication. The XTV concept has the element of risk in that Xerox employees forming new ventures are not guaranteed a management position if the new venture fails. This makes XTV different from most intrapreneurship ventures in companies. This aspect of risk and no guaranteed employment is the basis for AT&T Ventures, a two-year old fund modeled on XTV.

What Xerox recognized is what hundreds of executives are also becoming aware of in their own organizations: It is important to keep or instill the entrepreneurial spirit in an organization in order to innovate and grow. This realization is promising

---

[1]For a discussion of XTV, see: Larry Armstrong, "Nurturing an Employee's Brainchild," *Business Week/Enterprise 1993,* p 196.

to revolutionize American management and economic thinking. In a large organization, problems often occur that thwart creativity and innovation, particularly in activities not directly related to the organization's main mission. When an organization finally recognizes the importance of these secondary activities, it frequently takes too long to plan and implement them, in part because the established plans lack the needed flexibility. The growth and diversification that can result from this flexibility is particularly critical since large, vertically integrated, diversified corporations are often more efficient in a competitive market than are smaller firms. Internally administered coordination in a large corporation can often be more effective than the coordination achieved through market mechanisms.[2]

The resistance against flexibility, growth, and diversification can, in part, be overcome by developing a spirit of entrepreneurship within the existing organization. This spirit, called **intrapreneurship,** is discussed in terms of its causes, new venture creation and the necessary management transition, differences between corporate cultures, environment for intrapreneurship, characteristics of the intrapreneur, procedures for implementing intrapreneurship in an organization, and intrapreneurial strategy and strategy guidelines.

In addition to the increase in the social and cultural pressures for intrapreneurship, there has been an increase in business pressures caused by severe competition. Hypercompetition both at home and abroad have forced U.S. companies to have an increased interest in such areas as new product development, diversification, and increased productivity. The increased productivity has caused some reductions in the company's labor force. During a recent five-year period, employment in Fortune 500 companies decreased by 2.2 million people. Yet, these and new individuals are being absorbed in the work force. Where has this employment occurred? Basically, in small businesses, particularly start-up efforts. In 1985, almost 700,000 new companies were formed, compared to 200,000 in 1965 and only 90,000 in 1950.[3] In addition to these 700,000 there were about 400,000 new partnerships and 300,000 newly self-employed people. These 1.4 million new entities correspond to the average annual 1.4 million new private-sector jobs created each year in the economy.

In 1989, there were about 20 million new private firms in the United States: 25 percent of these were farms, 25 percent solo self-employed, 25 percent part-time, and 25 percent companies with employees. These 20 millions firms varied greatly in terms of revenue: 6 million firms generated between $25,000 and $100,000 in revenue; 1.2 million firms generated between $100,000 and $1 million in revenue; and only .8 million firms generated revenues greater than $1 million.

This increasing shift away from large corporations to small or decentralized ones is indicated by comparing the real growth in gross national product (GNP) with the number of new incorporations each year. Since 1975, an increasing number of businesses have become involved in increasing the GNP of the United States. An analysis of the net change in firms entering and exiting versus the growth in GNP reveals that

---

[2]These concepts are developed in D. Chandler, *The Visible Hand: The Managerial Revolution in American Business,* (Cambridge: Harvard University Press, 1977) and O. E. Williamson, *Markets and Hierarchies: Analysis and Antitrust Information* (New York: The Free Press, 1979).

[3]D. L. Birch, "The Atomization of America," *Inc.,* March 1987, p 21.

the higher the net change in firms entering versus exiting, the higher the growth in GNP. Since exit rates remain about the same, this increase in growth in GNP is due to the increase in the number of new businesses being started.

VENTURE GROWTH AND MANAGEMENT TRANSITION

As the statistics on the size of the businesses within the United States indicate, most firms are not growing, and few are growing at a high growth rate of more than 25 percent per year. The ability to grow is affected by many factors such as the degree of competitiveness in the industry, the nature and geographical location of the company and its initial market, the degree of the company's success, the company's protectability, the universality of the product and its unique selling proposition, the company's financial capability, and the desire and capabilities of the entrepreneur and the management team. Not all companies are able or willing to grow, but this does not necessarily mean failure. While growth is not automatic for a new venture, when it does occur it goes through various stages: start-up, rapid growth, competitive turbulence, and decline. The **growth patterns** of new ventures are indicated in Figure 17–1. While these growth patterns generally occur across all industries, deviations do occur. The few firms that have high start-up and high growth are those that achieve $25 million in sales in the first year and increase sales at least $1 million per year. Their growth mainly depends on two factors: (1) market factors, particularly size of the market and the window of opportunity and (2) management factors, such as the desire and drive for growth and the ability to manage it. Classifying firms on these two management factors—the propensity and ability to grow—yields four types of firms. Marginal small firms have a low propensity for growth yet a high ability to manage it. High-growth firms have both a high propensity to grow and a high ability to manage it. High-growth firms can have either a slow or fast start.

A flexible, capable entrepreneur and management team is required to successfully grow a venture. In addition, several success themes for growth have been identified.[4]

CORPORATE VERSUS INTRAPRENEURIAL CULTURE

Business and sociological conditions have given rise to a new era in American business: the era of the entrepreneur. The positive media exposure and success of entrepreneurs is threatening to some established corporations, as these smaller, aggressive, entrepreneurially driven firms are developing more new products and becoming dominant in certain markets. Recognizing the positive results that occur when employees of other large corporations catch the "entrepreneurial fever," many companies are now attempting to create the same spirit, culture, challenges, and

[4] A study indicating these success themes is D. C. Hambrick and L. M. Crozier, "Stumblers and Stars in the Management of Rapid Growth," *Journal of Business Venturing* 1 (Winter 1985), pp 31–46.

FIGURE 17–1 Possible Growth Patterns of New Businesses

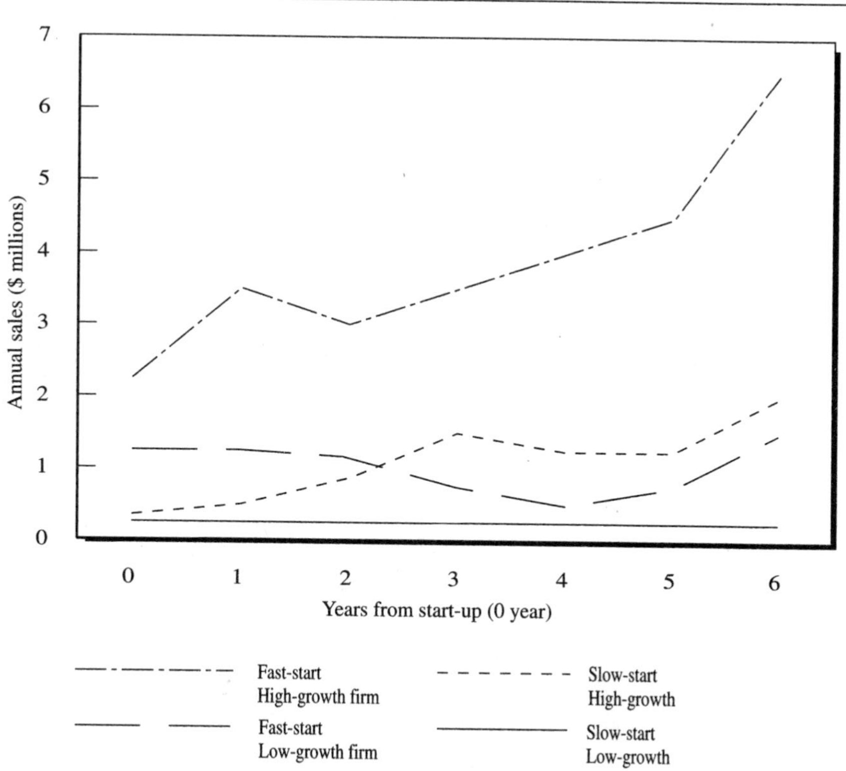

rewards of entrepreneurship in their organizations. What are the differences between corporate and entrepreneurial cultures? Between managers, entrepreneurs, and intrapreneurs?

The typical **corporate culture** has a climate and reward system that favors conservative decision making. Emphasis is on gathering large amounts of data as the basis for a rational decision and to use to justify the decision should the intended results not occur. Risky decisions are often postponed until enough hard facts can be gathered or a consultant hired to "illuminate the unknown." Frequently, there are so many sign-offs and approvals required for a large-scale project that no individual feels personally responsible.[5]

The traditional corporate culture differs significantly from an **intrapreneurial culture.** The guiding principles in a traditional corporate culture are: follow the instructions given; do not make any mistakes; do not fail; do not take initiative but wait

[5]For a discussion of this aspect, see N. Fast, "A Visit to the New Venture Graveyard," *Research Management* 22 (March 1979), pp 18–22.

for instructions; and stay within your turf and protect your backside. This restrictive environment is, of course, not conducive to creativity, flexibility, independence, and risk taking—the guiding principles of intrapreneurs. The aspects of an intrapreneurial culture are quite different: develop visions, goals, and action plans; be rewarded for actions taken; suggest, try, and experiment; create and develop regardless of the area; and take responsibility and ownership. This environment supports individuals in their efforts to create something new.

There are also differences in the shared values and norms of the two cultures. The traditional corporation is hierarchical in nature, with established procedures, reporting systems, lines of authority and responsibility, instructions, mandates, standardized hours, and control mechanisms. These support the present corporate climate and inhibit new-venture creation. The culture of an intrapreneurial firm is in stark contrast to this. Instead of a hierarchial structure with all the accompanying problems, an intrapreneurial climate has a flat organizational structure with networking, teamwork, sponsors, and mentors abounding. Close working relationships help establish an atmosphere of trust and counsel that facilitates the accomplishment of visions and objectives. Tasks are viewed as fun events, not chores, with participants gladly putting in the number of hours necessary to get the job done. Instead of building barriers to protect turfs, individuals make suggestions within and across functional areas and divisions, resulting in a cross-fertilization of ideas.

As would be expected, these two different cultures produce different types of individuals and management styles. A comparison of traditional managers, entrepreneurs, and intrapreneurs reveals these differences (see Table 17–1). While **traditional managers** are motivated primarily by promotion and typical corporate rewards, entrepreneurs and intrapreneurs thrive on independence and the ability to create. The intrapreneurs expect their performance to be suitably rewarded.

The differences are also reflected in the time orientation of the three groups, with managers emphasizing the short run, entrepreneurs the long run, and intrapreneurs somewhere in between. Similarly, the primary mode of activity of intrapreneurs falls between the delegation activity of managers and the direct involvement of entrepreneurs. While intraprenuers and entrepreneurs are moderate risk takers, managers are much more cautious about taking any risks. Protecting one's backside and turf is a way of life for many traditional managers. These managers attempt to avoid mistakes and failures at almost any cost. On the other hand, most entrepreneurs usually fail at least once, and intrapreneurs learn to conceal risky projects from management until the last possible moment.

While the traditional managers tend to serve those at a higher level in the organization, entrepreneurs serve self and customers, and intrapreneurs add sponsors to these two entrepreneur categories. This reflects the respective backgrounds of the three individuals. Managers tend to come from families who have worked for large organizations, while intrapreneurs and entrepreneurs come from entrepreneurial or professional families. Instead of building strong relationships with those around them, the way entrepreneurs and intrapreneurs do, managers tend to follow the relationships outlined in the organizational chart.

TABLE 17–1 Comparison of Entrepreneurs, Intrapreneurs, and Traditional Managers

	Traditional Managers	*Entrepreneurs*	*Intrapreneurs*
Primary motives	Promotion and other traditional corporate rewards, such as office, staff, and power	Independence, opportunity to create, and money	Independence and ability to advance in the corporate rewards
Time orientation	Short-term—meeting quotas and budgets, weekly, monthly, quarterly, and the annual planning horizons	Survival and achieving 5–10-year growth of business	Between entrepreneurial and traditional managers, depending on urgency to meet self-imposed and corporate timetable
Activity	Delegates and supervises more than direct involvement	Direct involvement	Direct involvement more than delegation
Risk	Careful	Moderate risk taker	Moderate risk taker
Status	Concerned about status symbols	No concern about status symbols	Not concerned about traditional corporate status symbols—desires independence
Failure and mistakes	Tries to avoid mistakes and surprises	Deals with mistakes and failures	Attempts to hide risky projects from view until ready
Decisions	Usually agrees with those in upper management positions	Follows dream with decisions	Able to get others to agree to help achieve dream
Who serves	Others	Self and customers	Self, customers, and sponsors
Family history	Family members worked for large organizations	Entrepreneurial small-business, professional, or farm background	Entrepreneurial small-business, professional, or farm background
Relationship with others	Hierarchy as basic relationship	Transactions and deal making as basic relationship	Transactions within hierarchy

Source: An extensively modified version of table in G. Pinchot, *Intrapreneuring* (New York: Harper & Row, 1985) pp 54–6.

CLIMATE FOR INTRAPRENEURSHIP

How can the climate for intrapreneurship be established in an organization? In establishing an intrapreneurial environment, certain factors and leadership characteristics need to be operant.[6] The overall characteristics of a good intrapreneurial environment

[6]For a thorough discussion of the factors important in intrapreneurship, see R. M. Kanter, *The Change Masters* (New York: Simon & Schuster, 1983) and G. Pinchot III, *Intrapreneuring* (New York: Harper & Row, 1985).

are summarized in Table 17–2. The first of these is that the organization operates on the frontiers of technology. Since research and development are key sources for successful new product ideas, the firm must operate on the cutting edge of the industry's technology, encouraging and supporting new ideas instead of discouraging them, as frequently occurs in firms that require rapid return on investment and high sales volume.

Second, experimentation—trial and error—is encouraged. Successful new products or services usually do not appear fully developed; instead, they evolve. It took time and some product failures before the first marketable computer appeared. A company wanting to establish an intrapreneurial spirit has to establish an environment that allows mistakes and failures in developing new innovative products. While this is in direct opposition to the established career and promotion system of the traditional organization, without the opportunity to fail in an organization, few, if any, corporate intrapreneurial ventures will be developed. Almost every entrepreneur has experienced at least one failure in establishing a successful venture.

Third, an organization should make sure that there are no initial **opportunity parameters** inhibiting creativity in new product development. Frequently in an organization, various "turfs" are protected, frustrating attempts by potential intrapreneurs to establish new ventures. In one Fortune 500 company, an attempt to establish an intrapreneurial environment ran into problems and eventually failed when the potential intrapreneurs were informed that a proposed new product and venture was not possible because it was the domain of another division.

Fourth, the resources of the firm need to be available and easily accessible. As one intrapreneur stated, "If my company really wants me to take the time, effort, and career risks to establish a new venture, then it needs to put money and people resources on the line." Often, insufficient funds are allocated to the task of creating something new, with available resources being committed instead to solving problems that have an immediate effect on the bottom line. Some companies like Xerox and AT&T have recognized this problem and have established separate venture

TABLE 17–2 Intrapreneurial Environment

- Organization operates on frontiers of technology
- New ideas encouraged
- Trial and error encouraged
- Failures allowed
- No opportunity parameters
- Resources available and accessible
- Multidiscipline teamwork approach
- Long time horizon
- Volunteer program
- Appropriate reward system
- Sponsors and champions available
- Support of top management

capital areas for funding new internal ventures. When resources are available, all too often the reporting requirements become obstacles to obtaining them, causing frustration and dissatisfaction.

Fifth, a multidiscipline team approach needs to be encouraged. This open approach, with participation by needed individuals regardless of area, is the antithesis of the corporate organizational structure and theory. An evaluation of successful cases of intrapreneurship indicated that one key to success was the existence of "skunkworks" involving key people. Some companies can facilitate internal venturing by legitimizing and formalizing the skunkworks already occurring. Developing the needed teamwork for a new venture is further complicated by the fact that a team member's promotion and overall career within the corporation is related to his or her job performance in the current position, not to his or her contribution to the new venture being created.

Besides encouraging teamwork, the corporate environment must establish a long time horizon for evaluating the success of the overall program as well as the success of each individual venture. If a company is not willing to invest money with no guarantee of return for 5 to 10 years, it should not attempt to create an intrapreneurial environment. This patient attitude toward money in the corporate setting is no different than the investment/return time horizon used by venture capitalists and others in the risk-capital market when investing in an entrepreneurial effort.

Sixth, the spirit of intrapreneurship cannot be forced on individuals; it must be on a volunteer basis. There is a difference between corporate thinking and intrapreneurial thinking, with individuals performing much better on the latter side of the continuum. Most managers in a corporation are not capable of being successful intrapreneurs. Those who do emerge from this self-selection process must be allowed the latitude to carry a project through to completion. This is not consistent with most corporate procedures for new product introduction, where different departments and individuals are involved in each stage of the development process. An individual willing to spend the excess hours and effort to create a new venture needs the opportunity and the accompanying reward of carrying the project through to completion. An intrapreneur falls in love with the newly created internal venture and will do almost anything to help ensure its success.

The seventh characteristic is a **reward system.** The intrapreneur needs to be appropriately rewarded for all the energy and effort expended in the creation of the new venture. These rewards should be based on the attainment of established performance goals. An equity position in the new venture is one of the best methods for motivating and eliciting the amount of activity and effort needed for success.

Eighth, a corporate environment favorable for intrapreneurship has sponsors and champions throughout the organization who not only support the creative activity and resulting failures but also have the planning flexibility to establish new objectives and directions as needed. As one intrapreneur stated, "For a new business venture to succeed, the intrapreneur needs to be able to alter plans at will and not be concerned about how close they come to achieving the previously stated objectives." Corporate structures frequently measure managers on their ability to come close to objectives, regardless of the quality of performance reflected in this accomplishment.

Finally, and perhaps most important, the intrapreneurial activity must be wholeheartedly supported and embraced by top management, both by physical presence and by making sure that the personnel and the financial resources are readily and easily available. Without top management support, a successful intrapreneurial environment cannot be created.

INTRAPRENEURIAL LEADERSHIP CHARACTERISTICS

Within this overall corporate environment, there are certain individual characteristics needed for a person to be a successful intrapreneur. As summarized in Table 17–3, these include understanding the environment, being visionary and flexible, creating management options, encouraging teamwork while employing a multidisciplined approach, encouraging open discussion, building a coalition of supporters, and persisting.

An entrepreneur needs to understand all aspects of the environment. Part of this ability is reflected in the individual's level of creativity. Creativity, perhaps at its lowest level in large organizations, generally tends to decrease with age and education. To successfully establish a successful intrapreneurial venture, the individual must be creative and have a broad understanding of the internal and external environments of the corporation.

The person who is going to establish a successful new intrapreneurial venture must also be a visionary leader—a person who dreams great dreams. Although there are many definitions of leadership, the one that best describes that needed for intrapreneurship is: "A leader is like a gardener. When you want a tomato, you take a seed, put it in fertile soil, and carefully water under tender care. You don't manufacture tomatoes, you grow them." Another good definition is that "leadership is the ability to dream great things and communicate these in such a way that people say yes to being a part of the dream." Martin Luther King, Jr., said "I have a dream" and thousands followed, in spite of overwhelming obstacles. To establish a successful new venture, the intrapreneurial leader must have a dream and overcome all the obstacles to achieve it by selling the dream to others.

The third needed characteristic is that the intrapreneur be flexible and create management options. An intrapreneur does not "mind the store," as is frequently taught in many business schools, but is playful and a bit irreverent. By challenging the beliefs and assumptions of the corporation, an intrapreneur has the opportunity to create something new in the largely bureaucratic organizational structure.

The intrapreneur must possess a fourth characteristic: the ability to encourage teamwork and use a multidisciplined approach. This also violates the organizational practices and structures taught in most business schools and apparent in established corporate plans. Every new company formation requires a broad range of business skills: engineering, production, marketing, and finance. In forming a new venture, recruiting those in the organization usually requires crossing established departmental structure and reporting systems. To minimize the negative effect of any disruption caused, the intrapreneur must be a good diplomat.

TABLE 17–3 Intrapreneurial Leadership Characteristics

- Understands the environment
- Visionary and flexible
- Creates management options
- Encourages teamwork
- Encourages open discussion
- Builds a coalition of supporters
- Persists

Open discussion must be encouraged to develop a good team for creating something new. Many corporate managers have forgotten the frank, open discussion and disagreements that were a part of their educational process. Instead, they spend time building protective barriers and insulating themselves in their corporate empires. A successful new intrapreneurial venture can be formed only when the team involved feels the freedom to disagree and to critique an idea in an effort to reach the best solution. The degree of openness among the team depends on the degree of openness of the intrapreneur.

Openness leads also to the establishment of a strong coalition of supporters and encouragers. The intrapreneur must encourage and affirm each team member, particularly during difficult times. This encouragement is very important, as the usual motivators of career paths and job security are not operational in establishing a new intrapreneurial venture. A good intrapreneur makes everyone a hero.

Last, but not least, is persistence. Throughout the establishment of any new intrapreneurial venture, frustration and obstacles will occur. Only through the intrapreneur's persistence will a new venture be created and successful commercialization result.

ESTABLISHING INTRAPRENEURSHIP IN THE ORGANIZATION

An organization desiring to establish an intrapreneurial environment must implement a procedure for its establishment. Although this can be done by its employees, frequently an organization finds it easier to use an outside consultant to facilitate the process. This is particularly true when the organization's environment is very traditional and has a record of little change and few new products being introduced.

The first step in this process is to secure a commitment to intrapreneurship in the organization by top, upper, and middle management levels. Without **top management commitment,** the organization will never be able to go through all the cultural climate changes necessary for implementation. Once the top management of the organization has committed to intrapreneurship for a sufficient period of time (1–3 years), the concept is introduced throughout the organization. This is accomplished most effectively through seminars, where the aspects of intrapreneurship are introduced and strategies are developed to transform the organizational culture into an intrapreneurial one. General guidelines need to be established for intrapreneurial venture development. Once the initial framework is established and the concept embraced, intrapreneurial leaders need to be identified, selected, and trained. This training needs to focus on obtaining resources within the organization, identifying viable opportunities and their markets, and developing the appropriate business plan.

Second, ideas and general areas that top management are interested in supporting should be identified, along with the amount of risk money that is available to develop the concept further. Also, overall program expectations and the target results of each intrapreneurial venture should be established. As much as possible, these should specify the time frame, volume and profitability requirements for the new venture, and the impact on the organization. Along with the intrapreneurial training, a mentor/sponsor system needs to be established. Without sponsors or champions, there is little hope that the culture of the organization can be transformed into an intrapreneurial one.

Third, a company needs to use technology to make itself faster and more flexible. Technology has been used successfully for the past decade by small companies that act like they are big ones.[7] How else could a small firm like Value Quest Ltd. compete against very large money management firms except through a 486 personal computer and access to large data banks? Similarly, large companies can use technology to make themselves responsive and flexible like a smaller firm (see Table 17–4). Four areas are particularly important in this change: desktop computers, networks and communications, computerized information, and manufacturing.

Manufacturing is a critical area for change if intrapreneurship is to flourish. Until the last decade, the rule of manufacturing has been to achieve economies of large-scale production. Today flexibility, just-in-time delivery, and quality have become more important. This change has resulted in the new buzz words *agile manufacturing, computer-integrated manufacturing,* and the *virtual factory.*[8] There is a trend today to simplify shop-floor operations, break down the factory walls, and electronically link the plant floor with all aspects of the company, thus creating a dynamically responsive environment. This has resulted in the responsive factory having such characteristics as: concurrent everything, fast development cycles, flexible production, quick response, and commitment to life-long quality (see Table 17–5). These can totally transform a company's manufacturing operations as evidenced recently when a computer at Ford Motor Company sent a design for a car's connecting rod to a computer at a supplying company—Allied Signal. This computer transformed the design into instructions that were fed to a machine tool on the factory floor.

Fourth, the organization can firmly establish an intrapreneurial culture by using a group of interested managers to train and share their experiences with other members. The training sessions should be conducted one day per month for eight months.

[7]For a discussion of this aspect, see Peter Coy, "Start with Some High-Tech Magic . . .", *Business Week/Enterprise 1993,* pp 24, 25, 28, and 32.

[8]This and the need for a change in manufacturing is well presented in Otis Port, "The Responsive Factory," *Business Week/Enterprise 1993,* pp 48, 49, 52, and 53.

TABLE 17–4 Technologies Allowing Big Companies to Act Small

Desktop Computers	*Networks and Communications*	*Computerized Information*	*Manufacturing*
Cheaper machines and advanced software let small companies do jobs such as computer-aided design that used to require specialists.	Intercompany electronics networks help small, niche concerns round out their skills through partnerships with each other or with larger companies.	Small companies don't need their own well-stocked business libraries. Commercial databases, a phone line away, put a vast store of facts at their disposal.	Computer controls on machine tools and electronic exchange of data help small companies provide quality equal to that of giant manufacturers.
Personal computers can give big-company drones the power to become decision makers by setting them free from the corporate computing center.	By making it easier to share information and insights, networks break down the walls inside companies. Even widely dispersed workers can form problem-solving teams.	Corporate giants can sift through their customers' purchasing records by computer, getting to know their wants and needs as well as the local merchant does.	Manufacturing methods that produce cost-effective small lots let big factories offer the sort of customized products once available only from little guys.

Source: Peter Coy, "Start with Some High-Tech Magic . . ." *Business Week/Enterprise 1993,* pp 24–25.

Informational items about intrapreneurship in general and about the specifics of the company's activities in developing ideas into marketable products or services that are the basis of new business venture units should be well publicized. This will require the intrapreneurial team to develop a business plan, obtain customer reaction and some initial intentions to buy, and learn how to coexist within the organizational structure.

Fifth, the organization needs to develop ways to get closer to its customers.[9] This can be done by tapping the data base, hiring from smaller rivals, and helping the retailer (see Table 17–6). Pepsi Co. Inc. is spending about $20 million to create electronic profiles of about 9 million Pizza Hut customers. Dannon is sharing its research with retailers and tailoring much of its marketing effort to the individual chains.

Sixth, an organization that wants to become more entrepreneurial must learn to be more productive with fewer resources.[10] This has already occurred in many companies that have severely cut back the number of managers. Top-heavy organizations are out-of-date in today's hypercompetitive environment. Some company

[9]This is discussed in Christopher Power, "How to Get Closer to Your Customers," *Business Week/Enterprise 1993,* pp 42, 44, and 45.

[10]For a good discussion of this aspect, see John A. Byrne, "Tightening the Smart Way," *Business Week/Enterprise 1993,* pp 34, 35, and 38.

TABLE 17–5 Characteristics of the Responsive Factory

Concurrent everything	Enterprise-wide computer integration, with electronic links to customers and suppliers, means that transactions occur mostly between computers, which will automatically route information to all the proper departments or operations.
Fast development cycles	A real-time data base will unite the distributed-processing computers used by design, engineering, production, logistics, marketing, and customer service—whether the work is done in-house or outsourced. All parties will have instant access to the latest information, eliminating the rework now caused by delays in shuffling paper.
Flexible production	Flexibility will be built into all levels of manufacturing, from the controls on each machine to the computers that coordinate work cells and factory-wide systems. Products can thus be turned out in greater variety and customized easily, with no cost penalty for small production runs.
Quick response	Dynamic factory-scheduling systems will put production "on call" and thus pare inventories to the bone. Production will begin only after a customer places an order.
Commitment to lifelong quality	Ongoing quality programs will lead to continuous improvement of both processes and products. A primary focus will be to make products easier to recycle or dispose of in environmentally sound ways.

Source: Otis Port, "The Responsive Factory," *Business Week/Enterprise 1993,* p 49

characteristics and their analysis are indicated in Table 17–7. To accommodate the large cutbacks in middle management, much more control had to be given up to subordinates at all levels in the organization. Not surprisingly, the span of control has risen to as high as 30 to 1 in divisions of such companies as Ameritech. The concept of lean and mean is the buzz word if intrapreneurship is to prevail.

Seventh, the organization needs to establish a strong support structure for intrapreneurship. This is particularly important since intrapreneurship is usually a secondary activity in the organization, not the primary one. Since intrapreneurial activities do not immediately affect the bottom line, they can be easily overlooked and receive little funding and support. To be successful, these ventures require flexible, innovative behavior, with the intrapreneurs having total authority over expenditures and access to sufficient funds. When the intrapreneur has to justify expenses on a daily basis, it is really not a new internal venture but merely an operational extension of the funding source.[11]

[11]For a discussion of this aspect, see R. Peterson & D. Berger, "Entrepreneurship in Organizations," *Administrative Science Quarterly* 16 (August 1971), pp 97–106; and D. Miller and P. Friesen, "Innovation in Conservative and Entrepreneurial Firms: Two Models of Strategic Momentum," *Strategic Management Journal* 3 (May 1982), pp 1–25.

TABLE 17–6 Methods for Getting Closer to the Customer

How Big Marketers Can Act as Deftly as Small Companies . . .	
Tap the data base	Use purchase data to customize incentives and direct-mail based on demographics, location, product preference, and price.
Hire from smaller rivals	They excel at "guerrilla marketing"—using local promotions to get close to customers and break through advertising clutter.
Help your retailer	Creating store-specific marketing programs—as Dannon does for retailers setting its yogurt—will win retailer loyalty, differentiate your product, and build local sales.
. . . and Small Marketers Can Outwit the Giants	
Find the missed opportunities	Small marketers can often focus on a relatively neglected product—such as duct tape or dental floss—and take share from a bigger player or increase sales in a tired category.
Apply the personal touch	Smaller marketers can get a big payoff when top executives pay personal attention to customers' letters, retailers' queries, and sales staff's suggestions.
Embrace technology	The cost of database technology is dropping, making direct-mail marketing a viable tactic for small marketers with tight budgets.

Source: Christopher Power, "How to Get Closer to your Customers," *Business Week/Enterprise 1993,* p 45

Eighth, the support must also involve tying the rewards to the performance of the intrapreneurial unit. This encourages the team members to work harder and compete more effectively since they will benefit directly from their efforts. Because the intrapreneurial venture is a part of the larger organization and not a totally independent unit, the equity portion of the compensation will be difficult to administer along with the salary. Incentives should also be established to reward cooperation with other areas of the company.

Finally, the organization needs to implement an evaluation system that allows successful intrapreneurial units to expand and unsuccessful ones to be eliminated. Just as occurs in an entrepreneurial firm, when a good job is done, an intrapreneurial unit should be allowed to expand to fill market demands as warranted. The organization can establish constraints to ensure that this expansion does not run contrary to the corporate mission statement. Similarly, inefficient intrapreneurial venture units should not be allowed to exist just because of vested interests in perpetuating them. To have a successful intrapreneurial environment, the organization must allow some ventures to fail even as it allows more successful ones to expand. However, some ventures may be continued, even if unprofitable, if the venture is subsidizing some other part of the larger organization, blocking some competitive entrance, or laying the groundwork for entering a new strategic business area.

TABLE 17–7 Determining the Need to Downsize

Company Characteristic	*Analysis*
Layers of management between CEO and the shop floor	Some companies, such as Ameritech, now have as few as 4 or 5 where as many as 12 had been common. More than 6 is most likely too many.
Number of employees managed by the typical executive	At lean companies, spans of control range up to one manager to 30 staffers. A ratio of lower than 1:10 is a warning of arterial sclerosis.
Amount of work cut out by your downsizing	Eliminating jobs without cutting out work can bring disaster. A downsizing should be accompanied by at least a 25% reduction in the number of tasks performed. Some lean companies have hit 50%.
Skill levels of the surviving management group	Managers must learn to accept more responsibility and to eliminate unneeded work. Have you taught them how?
Size of your largest profit center by number of employees	Break down large operating units into smaller profit centers—fewer than 500 employees is a popular cutoff—to gain the economies of entrepreneurship and offset the burdens of scale.
Post-downsizing size of staff at corporate headquarters	The largest layoffs, on a percentage basis, should be at corporate headquarters. It is often the most overstaffed—and the most removed from customers.

Source: John A. Byrne, "Belt-Tightening the Smart Way," *Business Week/Enterprise 1993,* p 35.

PROBLEMS AND SUCCESSFUL EFFORTS

Intrapreneurship, or what is alternatively called corporate venturing, is not without its problems. One study found that new ventures started within a corporation performed worse than those started independently by entrepreneurs.[12] The reasons cited were the corporation's difficulty in maintaining a long-term commitment, a lack of freedom to make autonomous decisions, and a constrained environment. (These findings were supported by another study which found similar obstacles for establishing joint ventures.[13] Although joint ventures are not without their own obstacles, they have fewer problems and provide the opportunity to gain experience in different development processes before attempting a new-venture creation. Companies tend to become more adept at overcoming the obstacles, but this frequently does not occur until the fourth attempt at creating a new internal venture.

[12] N. Fast, "Pitfalls of Corporate Venturing," *Research Management,* March 1981, pp 21–24.

[13] I. C. MacMillan, Z. Block, & P. N. Subba Narasimha, "Obstacles and Experience in Corporate Venturing," *Proceedings,* Babson Research Conference (April 1984), pp 341–63.

Given the many obstacles, high failure rate, and learning curve necessary for successful intrapreneurship to occur, an organization should consider all alternative growth strategies before selecting intrapreneurship. These include joint venturing, acquisitions, and internal product development using the established corporate procedures. As was the case with joint venturing, independent, venture-capital-based start-ups by entrepreneurs tend to outperform corporate start-ups significantly. On average, not only did the independents become profitable twice as fast, they ended up twice as profitable.[14]

However, these findings should not deter organizations committed to intrapreneurship from starting the process. There are numerous examples of companies that, having understood the environmental and intrapreneurial characteristics necessary, have adopted their own version of the implementation process previously discussed to successfully launch new ventures. One of the best known of these firms is Minnesota Mining and Manufacturing (3M). Having had many successful intrapreneurial efforts, 3M in effect allows employees to devote 15 percent of their time to independent projects. This enables the divisions of the company to meet an important goal: that a significant percent of sales come from new products introduced within the last five years. One of the most successful of these intrapreneurial activities was the development of Post-it Notes by intrapreneur Arthur Fry. This effort developed out of Fry's annoyance that pieces of paper marking his church hymnal constantly fell out while he was singing. As a 3M chemical engineer, Fry knew about the discovery by a scientist, Spencer Silver, of a very low sticking-power adhesive, which to the company was a poor product characteristic. However, this characteristic was perfect for Fry's problem; a marker with lightly sticking adhesive that is easy to remove provided a good solution. But Fry had to obtain approval to commercialize the idea. This proved to be a monumental task until the samples made and distributed to secretaries within 3M, as well as other companies, created such a demand that the company eventually began selling the product under the name Post-it. Sales have reached more than $500 million.

Another firm committed to the concept of intrapreneurship is Hewlett-Packard. After failing to recognize the potential of Steven Wozniak's proposal for a personal computer (which was the basis for the intrapreneurial venture called Apple Computer Inc.), Hewlett-Packard has taken steps to ensure that it will be recognized as a leader in innovation and not miss future opportunities. However, the road to commercialization at HP is not always an easy one. This was the case for Charles House, an engineer who went far beyond his intrapreneurial duty when he ignored an order from David Packard to stop working on a high-quality video monitor. The monitor, once developed, was used in NASA's manned moon landings and in heart transplants. Although projected to achieve sales of no more than 30 units, more than 17,000 of these large-screen displays (about $35 million in sales) have already been sold.

---

[14]For complete information on the relative performance, see R. Biggadike, "The Risky Business of Diversification," *Harvard Business Review,* May–June 1979, pp 103–11; L. E. Weiss, "Start-up Business: A Comparison of Performances," *Sloan Management Review,* Fall 1981, pp 37–53; and N. D. Fast and S. E. Pratt, "Individual Entrepreneurship and the Large Corporation," *Proceedings,* Babson Research Conference (April 1984), pp 443–50.

Even the computer giant, IBM, decided seven years ago that intrapreneurship would help spur corporate growth. The company developed the independent business unit concept in which each unit is a separate organization with its own mini-board of directors and autonomous decision-making authority on many manufacturing and marketing issues. The more than 11 business units have developed such products as the automatic teller machine for banks, industrial robots, and the IBM Personal Computer. The latter business unit was given a blank check with a mandate to get IBM into the personal computer market. Intrapreneur Philip Estridge led his group to develop and market the PCs, through both IBM's sales force and the retail market, breaking some of the most binding operational rules of IBM at that time. This independent business unit has grown into a division with more than 10,000 employees and yearly sales exceeding $5 billion.

These and other success stories indicate that the problems of intrapreneurship are not insurmountable and that the concept can lead to new products, growth, and the development of an entirely new corporate environment and culture.

SUMMARY

Social and business pressures have caused an increase in new venture creation both outside and inside existing corporate structures. Within existing corporate structures, this entrepreneurial spirit and effort is called intrapreneurship.

To develop successful innovation, a corporation should establish a conducive organizational procedure. This will differ greatly from the traditional corporate climate. Traditional managers tend to adhere more strictly to established hierarchical structures, to be less risk-oriented, and to emphasize short-term results. This tends to inhibit the creativity, flexibility, and risk required for new ventures. Organizations desiring an intrapreneurial climate need to encourage new ideas and experimental efforts, eliminate opportunity parameters, make resources available, promote a teamwork approach and voluntary intrapreneurship, and enlist top management's support.

The intrapreneur must also have appropriate leadership characteristics. In addition to being creative, visionary, and flexible, the intrapreneur must be able to work within the corporate structure. Intrapreneurs need to encourage teamwork and work diplomatically across established structures. Open discussion and strong support of team members is also required. Finally, the intrapreneur must be persistent in order to overcome the inevitable obstacles.

The process of establishing intrapreneurship within an existing organization requires the commitment of management, particularly top management. The organization must carefully choose intrapreneurial leaders, develop general guidelines for ventures, and delineate expectations of the program before the intrapreneurial program begins. Training sessions are an important part of the process. As role models and intrapreneurial ventures are introduced, the organization must establish a strong organizational support system, along with a system of incentives and rewards to encourage team members. Finally, it should establish a system to expand successful ventures and to eliminate unsuccessful ones.

Intrapreneurship can be fraught with perils. Studies have cited problems with corporate ventures due to lack of commitment, lack of freedom, and constrained environments. For companies not willing to commit to intrapreneurship, joint ventures offer an alternative for growth and diversification. However, the numerous examples of successful intrapreneurial ventures prove that the concept is indeed successful. Intrapreneurship is becoming a recognized component for growth and innovation within established corporations in response to the new challenges and hypercompetitive environment confronting American business.

QUESTIONS FOR DISCUSSION

1. Discuss business pressures that have led to intrapreneurship.
2. Explain why traditional corporate management has not been conducive to intrapreneurship.
3. Discuss the characteristics necessary for a successful intrapreneur. In what ways do these characteristics differ from those of an entrepreneur?

KEY TERMS

corporate culture
growth patterns
intrapreneurial culture
intrapreneurship
opportunity parameters
reward system
top management commitment
traditional managers

SELECTED READINGS

Bailey, J. E. (April 1984). Intrapreneurship—Source of High Growth Startups or Passing Fad? *Proceedings,* 1984 Conference on Entrepreneurship, pp 358–67.

Intrapreneurship development programs have emerged in the past few years in Scandinavia and the United States. This paper provides an overview of the types of programs being provided and attempts to evaluate their effectiveness as generators of high-growth business start-ups.

Cascio, Wayne F. (1993). Downsizing: What Do We Know? What Have We Learned? *Academy of Management Executive.* vol. 7, no. 1, pp 95–104.

For any long-term sustained improvements in efficiency, reductions in head count need to clone as a part of a process of continuous improvement that includes organization redesign coupled with systematic changes designed to eliminate redundancies, waste, and inefficiency.

Fulop, Liz. (1991). Middle Managers: Victims or Vanguards of the Entrepreneurial Movement? *Journal of Management Studies,* vol. 28, no. 1, pp 25–44.

Three approaches to corporate entrepreneurship are identified: (1) the approach in which entrepreneurship is made synonymous with rationalizations in labor, technology, and management structures; (2) the innovation process model approach; and (3) the resource mobilization approach.

Jones, Gareth, & Butler, John E. Managing Internal Corporate Entrepreneurship. *Journal of Management.* vol. 18, no. 4, pp 733–49.

This article explores the relationship between internal corporate and external entrepreneurship and examines the organizational factors that cause agency problems.

Kanter, Rosabeth Moss, Quinn, Gina, & North, Jeffrey. (1992). Engines of Progress vs. NEES Energy, Inc. *Journal of Business Venturing.* vol. 7, no. 1, pp 73–89.

The case study describes a fifth model for stimulating and managing entrepreneurship within established firms: the standalone new venture that serves as an entrepreneurship laboratory.

Kanter, Rosabeth Moss, & Richardson, Lisa. (1991). Engines of Progress: Designing and Running Entrepreneurial Vehicles in Established Companies—The Enterprise Program of Ohio Bell, 1985–1990. *Journal of Business Venturing.* vol. 6, no. 3, pp 209–29.

Four generic types of entrepreneurial vehicles are identified: the pure venture capital model, the new venture development incubator, the idea creation and transfer center, and the employee project model.

Kamm, Judith, B., & Nurick, Aaron J. (1993). The Stages of Team Venture Formation: A Decision Making Model. *Entrepreneurship: Theory and Practice.* vol. 17, no. 2, pp 17–27.

A model of multifounder organizational formation assumes that the organization emerges in the following way: the idea stage, the implementation of decisions such as who will supply resources, what inducements will be used, and how will the team be kept together.

Kamm, Judith B., Shuman, Jeffrey C., Seeger, John A., & Nurlick, Aaron J. (1990). Entrepreneurial Teams in New Venture Creation: A Research Agenda. *Entrepreneurship: Theory and Practice.* vol. 14, no. 1, pp 7–17.

The objectives of all research on entrepreneurial teams should be to address the research gap on venture teams and provide information that will help to form and maintain effective venture teams.

Kobayashi, Yotaro. (1990). Sustaining Entrepreneurship in the Large Organizations of Fuji Xerox. *Management Japan.* vol. 23, no. 1, pp 3–10.

The company's new Work Way Program encourages individual thinking from all the employees of the company and has been the foundation for new venture creation within the company.

Kuratko, Donald F., Hornsby, Jeffrey S., Naffziger, Douglas W., & Montagno, Ray U. (1993). Implementing Entrepreneurial Thinking in Established Organizations. *SAM Advanced Management Journal.* vol. 59, no. 1, pp 28–33.

The key to creating an entrepreneurial environment within an established organization is to develop and articulate a specific strategy for encouraging innovative activity and establishing the necessary climate within the organization.

Oliver, Carol, Pass, Sandra, Taylor, Jane & Taylor, Pam. (1991). Entrepreneurship and Entrepreneurship Amongst MBA Graduates. *Management Decision,* vol. 29, no. 5, pp 8–11.

The study found that intrapreneurial activities require an organizational structure that promotes an innovative climate and has the support of top management.

Pinchot, G. III. (1985). *Intrapreneuring.* New York: Harper & Row.

Argues that intrapreneuring is not a new phenomenon, but one that has been functioning despite the past and present corporate system. Formulates some basic rules and strategies for executives who want to nurture the intrapreneurial spirit in themselves and others in their company.

Stevenson, Howard H., & Jurillo, J. Carlos. (1990). A Paradigm of Entrepreneurship: Entrepreneurial Management. *Strategic Management Journal.* vol. 11, no. 0143–2095, pp 17–27.

Six specific propositions are defined concerning corporate entrepreneurship research, and three elements of the corporate entrepreneurship process are discussed.

Stevenson, Howard, & Harmeling, Susan. (1990). Entrepreneurial Management's Need for a More Chaotic Theory. *Journal of Business Venturing.* vol. 5, no. 1, pp. 1–14.

With societal and individual forces for change, it is doubtful that a theory based on searching for repetitive outputs would develop insight into the dynamics of corporate entrepreneurship. This theory, instead, should be built on a theory of change.

Zahra, Shaker A. (1991). Predictors and Financial Outcomes of Corporate Entrepreneurship: An Exploratory Study. *Journal of Business Venturing.* vol. 6, no. 4, pp 259–285.

The results of a study of 119 of the Fortune 500 firms found that environmental dynamism, hostility, and heterogeneity intensify corporate entrepreneurship as do growth-oriented strategies and the scanning, formal communications, and integration components of organizational structure.

CHAPTER

18

International Entrepreneurship: Opportunities and Problems

Chapter Objectives

1. To identify the aspects of international entrepreneurship and its importance to economics and firms.
2. To identify the important strategic issues in international entrepreneurship.
3. To identify the available options for entering international markets.
4. To discuss the recent research on international entrepreneurship.
5. To discuss the problems and barriers to international entrepreneurship.

Bernard Tapie and Wang Yong Xian

No one knows better that entrepreneurship, and particularly international entrepreneurship, is a risky business than Bernard Tapie, a Frenchman who runs, among other things, his own holding company, Bernard Tapie Finance, S.A.[1] Raised in a working-class neighborhood in a suburb of Paris, Tapie is native to a culture that is among the most risk-averse in Europe. The social stigma associated with bankruptcy and business failure is so strong that most French citizens choose to work for someone else rather than take the risks and reap the rewards of starting their own business.

Not so for Tapie, who began his career at age 18 as a door-to-door television salesman. Even while working as a business consultant in the 1960s, he was convinced he had the skills to run his own company. Tapie's debut as an entrepreneur, however, ended in a business reversal and a conviction for false advertising. Although the conviction was retracted on appeal, the negative publicity from the affair made for a less than auspicious beginning.

Since 1977, Tapie has been in the business of buying and revitalizing well-known companies that find themselves in difficulty. "Group Tapie" is composed of 45 firms, including Wonder-Mazda, a battery maker; Look, a company that was until recently in the sports industry; Terraillon, a maker of scales for personal kitchen uses; and La Vie Claire, a chain of health food stores.[2]

The billion dollar holding company Tapie created has brought him more than financial success; his high profile in the media has made him a cultural hero for the nation's young and a symbol of individual success. This has resulted in his hosting a quarterly television show called "Ambitions" that addresses the special issues of business start-up.[3]

Business success is not the only element contributing to Bernard Tapie's celebrity status. In 1986, Tapie owned the Marseille Soccer Team—"Le Club

---

[1]For more in-depth information on this company and the founder, see P. Sherrid, J. P. Shapiro, M. Wechsler, & M. Lord, "America's Hottest New Export," *U.S. News and World Report,* July 27,1987, pp 39–40.

[2]A. Cressatti, "Bernard Tapie a la Rescousse d'Adidas," *Journal Francais d'Amerique* 12, no. 16 (July 27–August 23, 1990), p 8.

[3]R. I. Kirkland Jr., "Europe's New Entrepreneurs," *Fortune,* April 27, 1987, p 258.

Olympique de Marseille" (OM)—which he bought when the team was floundering. The team soon became a heavyweight team in France and is almost always a yearly contender for the European championship.[4]

Tapie has also become involved in France's political arena. Elected to Parliament in 1988 and seated among the socialists in the National Assembly, he has taken on many challenging issues including the support for the far-right in southern France, a region beset by a host of problems associated with immigration. Tapie's tough stance on racism and his bold, confrontational way with leaders of the far-right such as Jean Marie LePen have won him favor and respect in much of France.[5]

Tapie also closed a deal with Adidas, giving him 80 percent ownership of the German sporting-goods concern. Financing for the purchase was arranged using a combination of short-term loans and stock and bond issues.[6] Following the death of Chairman Horst Dassler in 1987, Adidas lost its grip on the number one spot in the world of sports footwear, reporting a loss for 1989 amounting to 120 million marks, or $72 million, on 4.6 billion marks in sales.[7] Of course, Tapie has plans to change all that.

Tapie is one of a growing number of people who are making entrepreneurship work in a variety of cultures and contexts throughout the world. Since 1973, there have been over 1 million new jobs created yearly in the United States, largely due to the growth of small businesses. Other nations, witnessing the growth and dynamism of the U.S. economy, are turning to entrepreneurship as a solution for old economic solutions.

In contrast to the life-style of Tapie in France is Wang Yong Xian, who, in his blue denim Mao jacket and trousers, does not look out of place on Canton's busy streets. A 49-year-old plant manager of a shipyard, Xian has worked his way up from a mechanic's position. Xian said that during China's Cultural Revolution, "No one bothered me because I was only a junior manager." In 1974, while in Peking at the Sixth Ministry of Machine Building, which supervises shipyards, Xian helped negotiate the contract for a container plant. He then became its manager.

Xian initiated a work bonus plan by first seeking his employees' advice. The employees developed a plan based on individual contributions to increasing productivity. Xian refined the plan and established quotas that needed to be surpassed if the employees are to earn extra money. His workers get an average $25 bonus each month in addition to their regular pay of $31 to $48. In theory, the bonus system will allow some to double their normal earnings, receiving as much as Xian—about $75 a month. Xian himself is not eligible for a bonus.

---

[4]H. Haget, "Voyage au Coeur de l'OM, *L'Express*, September 14, 1990, p 36.

[5]D. de Montvalon, "Tapie Peut-il Briser Le Pen? *L'Express*, June 22, 1990, pp 24–30.

[6]E. S. Browning, "Tapie Discloses Loan Package to Raise $289 Million to Buy 80% of Adidas AG," *Wall Street Journal*, July 18, 1990, p A6.

[7]V. Beaufils, "Comment Reussir a Perdre Adidas," *L'Express*, August 3, 1990, p 17.

Xian also makes sure that the government helps the shipyard attain the self-sufficiency needed in a Chinese factory such as the container plant, which has been equipped to make its own machine parts, carpenters' aprons, and even ice-cream bars.

In addition to government and employee intervention, Xian willingly adopts other good suggestions. For example, when one engineer pointed out that many employees lingered outside the plant after their lunch break, Xian had a gong installed to summon them back to work promptly. Xian's managerial style is surprising. When an office employee had nowhere to leave her 19-month old child, Xian spent part of the day cheerfully bouncing the toddler on his lap. Immediately after that, he was a tough negotiator in a business meeting.

As these vignettes suggest, the area of international business and entrepreneurship is becoming increasingly important. Entrepreneurs in developed countries like the United States, Japan, Great Britain, and Germany must sell their products in a variety of new and different market areas early on in the development of their firms.

Never before in the history of the world has there been such interesting and exciting international business opportunities. The opening of the once-controlled economies of Eastern and Central Europe, the former USSR, and the People's Republic of China to market-oriented enterprise provides a myriad of possibilities for individual entrepreneurs wanting to start in a foreign market as well as for existing entrepreneurial firms desiring to expand their business.

As more and more countries become market oriented and developed, the distinction between foreign and domestic markets becomes less pronounced. What was once only produced domestically is now produced internationally. For example, Yamaha pianos are now manufactured in the United States. Digital Equipment Company has plants in Puerto Rico. Nestle's chocolate is made in Europe. This blurring of national identities will continue to accelerate as more and more products are introduced outside domestic boundaries at an earlier stage in the development of entrepreneurial firms.

THE NATURE OF INTERNATIONAL ENTREPRENEURSHIP

Simply stated, **international entrepreneurship** is the process of an entrepreneur conducting business activities across national boundaries. It is exporting, licensing, opening a sales office in another country, or something as simple as placing a classified advertisement in the Paris edition of the *Herald Tribune*. The activities necessary for ascertaining and satisfying the needs and wants of target consumers often take place in more than one country. When an entrepreneur executes his or her business in more than one country, international entrepreneurship occurs.

With a commercial history of only 300 years, the United States is a relative newcomer to the international business arena. As soon as settlements were established in the "New World," the new Americans began an active international trade with Europe. Foreign investors helped build much of the early industrial trade with Europe as well as much of the early industrial base of the United States. The future commercial strength of the United States will similarly depend on the ability of U.S. entrepreneurs and established U.S. companies to take advantage of markets outside its borders.

THE IMPORTANCE OF INTERNATIONAL BUSINESS TO THE FIRM

International business has become increasingly important to firms of all sizes. No longer are international sales only important for the survival and growth of some of the largest U.S. firms. Each firm is now competing in a global economy.

There can be little doubt that today's entrepreneur must be able to move in the world of international business. The successful entrepreneur will be someone who fully understands how international business differs from purely domestic business and is able to act accordingly. The entrepreneur considering entering the international market should answer the following questions:

Is managing international business different from managing domestic business?

What are the strategic issues to be resolved in international business management?

What are the options available for engaging in international business?

How should one assess the decision to enter into an international market?

INTERNATIONAL VERSUS DOMESTIC ENTREPRENEURSHIP

Whether international or domestic, an entrepreneur is concerned about the same basic issues: sales, costs, and profits. What differentiates domestic from international entrepreneurship is the variation in the relative importance of the factors being considered in each decision. International entrepreneurial decisions are more complex due to the effect of such uncontrollable factors as economics, politics, culture, and technology.

Economics

When an entrepreneur designs a domestic business strategy, a single country at a specified level of economic development is the focus. The different regions of this country are affected by the same international factors, such as currency valuation and the balance of payments. The entire country is almost always organized under a single economic system. Creating a business strategy for a multicountry area means dealing with different levels of economic development, varying degrees of balance of payments problems, and possibly vastly different economic marketing and distribution systems. These differences manifest themselves in each aspect of the entrepreneur's international business plan.

Stage of Economic Development

The United States is an industrially developed nation with regional variances of relative income, but no region would be classified as less developed or developing. While needing to adjust the business plan according to regional differences, an entrepreneur doing business only in the United States does not have to worry about the lack of such infrastructure as roads, electricity, communication systems, banking facilities, adequate educational systems, a well-developed legal system, and established business ethics and norms.

Balance of Payments

With the switch to a system of flexible exchange rates, a country's **balance of payments** (the difference between the value of a country's imports and exports over time) is reflected in the value of its currency. The automobile industry provides an example of how an economic variable will affect an international business program. At one time, Italy's chronic balance of payments deficit led to a radical depreciation in the value of the lira, the currency of Italy. Fiat responded to this by offering significant rebates on cars sold in the United States. These rebates cost Fiat very little because fewer dollars purchased many more lira due to the depreciation in value of the lira.

Type of System

Pepsi-Cola began considering the possibility of marketing in the former U.S.S.R. as early as the 1959 visit of then Vice President Nixon to the country. When Premier Nikita Khrushchev expressed his approval of Pepsi's taste, the slow wheels of East-West trade began moving, with Pepsi entering the former U.S.S.R. 13 years later. Instead of using its traditional type of franchise bottler in this entry, Pepsi used a barter-type arrangement that satisfied both the Soviet socialized system of the former U.S.S.R. and the U.S. capitalist system. In return for receiving technology and syrup from Pepsi, the former U.S.S.R. provided the company with Soviet vodka and the right to distribute it in the United States. Many such **barter** or **third-party arrangements** have been used to increase the amount of business activity with the former U.S.S.R. and Eastern and Central European countries. Now direct foreign investments and joint ventures are used, with some or all of the profits being taken out in the form of currency.

There are still many difficulties in establishing joint ventures in Eastern and Central Europe and the Commonwealth of Independent States, the former U.S.S.R. In the Commonwealth of Independent States, only 10–12 percent of the 1,400 registered joint ventures are actively operating. Some of the reasons are the gaps in the basic knowledge of the Western system regarding business plans, product promotion, marketing, and profits; widely variable rates of return; nonconvertibility of the ruble, which necessitates finding a countertrade item; differences in the accounting system; and nightmarish communications.[8]

Political-Legal Environment

The multiplicity of political and legal environments in the international market create vastly different business problems, opening some market opportunities for entrepreneurs and eliminating others. For example, U.S. environmental standards have eliminated the possibility of entrepreneurs establishing ventures to import several models of European cars. In addition, as part of a political agreement, Japanese entrepreneurs and companies have agreed to reduce the volume of their exports to the United States. Perhaps the most significant events in the political-legal environment involve the price fluctuations in oil, reflecting the previous oil embargo, overproduction of oil, the Iraqi invasion of Kuwait, and the breakdown in the strength of the Middle East oil cartel.

Each element of the business strategy of an international entrepreneur has the potential to be affected by the multiplicity of legal environments. Pricing decisions in a country that has a value-added tax are different from those decisions made by the same entrepreneur in a country with no value-added tax. Advertising strategy can be affected by the limitations and variations of what can be said in the copy or by the support needed for advertising claims, which vary dramatically between countries. Production decisions are affected by legal requirements on labeling, ingredients, and packaging. Type of ownership and organizational forms vary widely throughout the world. The laws governing these business arrangements also vary greatly in the over 150 different legal systems and operant sets of national laws.

Cultural Environment

The impact of culture on entrepreneurs and strategies is also significant. Entrepreneurs must make sure that each element in the business plan has some degree of congruence with the local culture. For example, in some countries, point of purchase displays are not allowed in retail stores as they are in United States.

[8] R. Cooper, "Much Ventured, Little Gained," *Euromoney*, February 1990, pp 21–3.

Respect for the local culture is most necessary when the entrepreneur develops worldwide strategies and plans. The entire debate over the degree of adaptation and standardization in worldwide plans revolves around the concept of culture, and this is an important issue that must be resolved by each entrepreneur doing international business.

Technological Environment

Technology, like culture, varies significantly across countries. The variations and availability of technology are often surprising, particularly to an entrepreneur from a developed country. Many Americans, for example, have a difficult time understanding how a technologically advanced military economy like the former U.S.S.R. could have shortages of food and consumer goods and an almost Third World communication system, while U.S. firms produce mostly standardized, relatively uniform products that can be sorted to meet industry standards; this is not the case in many countries, making it more difficult to achieve consistency in the final product.

New products in a country are often created on the basis of self-referential criteria and assumptions about technology or its related output. For example, U.S. car designers can assume wide roads and less expensive gasoline than can European designers. When these same designers had to work on transportation vehicles for other parts of the world, they had to alter their assumptions significantly.[9]

Strategic Issues

Four strategic issues are of paramount importance to the international entrepreneur or an entrepreneur thinking about going international: (1) the allocation of responsibility between the U.S. and foreign operations; (2) the nature of the planning, reporting, and control systems to be used throughout the international operations; (3) the appropriate organizational structure for conducting international operations; and (4) the degree of standardization possible.

The problems of allocation of responsibility between headquarters and subsidiary essentially concern the degree of decentralization that can be tolerated. As entrepreneurs move through their experience with international operations, they tend to change their approach to the allocation of responsibility. This frequently occurs in the following progression:

- *Stage 1*— When making his or her first moves into international business, an entrepreneur typically follows a highly centralized decision-making process. Since the entrepreneur generally has limited numbers of, if any, individuals with

[9] J. A. Lee, "Cultural Analysis in Overseas Operations," *Harvard Business Review*, March–April 1966, pp 106–14.

international experience, a centralized decision-making network is usually used. The attitude is often: "What do those people from another country know about our product and its needs? We'd better do it all from here."

- *Stage 2*—When success occurs, the entrepreneur finds it is no longer possible to use a completely centralized decision-making process. The multiplicity of environments become far too complex to handle from a central headquarters. In response, an entrepreneur often goes to the other extreme and decentralizes the entire international operation. The philosophy at this point can be summed up as follows: "There's no way I am ever going to be able to understand the differences between all of those markets. Let them make their own decisions."
- *Stage 3*—The process of decentralization carried out in Stage 2 becomes intolerable once further success is attained. Business operations in the different countries end up in conflict with each other. The U.S. headquarters is often the last to receive information about problems in which they should be actively involved. When this occurs, limited amounts of power, authority, and responsibility are pulled back to the U.S. base of operations. A balance between the U.S. headquarters having reasonably tight control on major strategic marketing decisions and the in-country operating unit having the responsibility for the tactical implementation of corporate strategy is usually achieved. Planning, reporting, and control systems become very important aspects of international success at this stage. They allow the entrepreneur to identify and evaluate the worth of markets, to monitor the company's performance in those markets already entered, and to make any necessary changes in the operations.

To understand what is required for effective planning, reporting, and control, the entrepreneur should consider the following questions.

Environmental Analysis

1. What are the unique characteristics of each national market? What characteristics does each market have in common with other national markets?
2. Can any national markets be clustered together for operating and/or planning purposes? What dimensions of markets should be used to cluster markets?

Strategic Planning

3. Who should be involved in marketing decisions?
4. What are the major assumptions about target markets? Are these valid?
5. What needs are satisfied by the company's products in the target markets?
6. What customer benefits are provided by the product in the target markets?
7. What are the conditions under which the products are used in the target markets?
8. How great is the ability to buy our products in the target markets?
9. What are the company's major strengths and weaknesses relative to existing and potential competition in the target markets?

10. Should the company extend, adapt, or invent products, prices, advertising, and promotion programs for target markets?
11. What are the balance-of-payments and currency situations in the target markets? Will the company be able to remit earnings? Is the political climate acceptable?
12. What are the company's objectives, given the alternatives available and the assessment of opportunity, risk, and company capability?

Structure

13. How should the organization be structured to optimally achieve the established objectives, given the company's skills and resources? What is the responsibility of each organizational level?

Operational Planning

14. Given the objectives, structure, and assessment of the market environment, how can effective operational marketing plans be implemented? What products should be marketed, at what prices, through what channels, with what communications, and to which target markets?

Controlling the Marketing Program

15. How does the company measure and monitor the plan's performance? What steps should be taken to ensure that marketing objectives are met?[10]

One key to successful marketing planning is an appreciation of the market phase. Questions 1 and 2 in the preceding list of 15 questions focus on this dimension of the planning process. The first step in identifying markets and clustering countries is to analyze data on each country of interest along the following six vectors.

1. Market Characteristics
   - *a.* Size of market: rate of growth
   - *b.* Stage of development
   - *c.* Stage of product life cycle; saturation levels
   - *d.* Buyer behavior characteristics
   - *e.* Social/cultural factors
   - *f.* Physical environment
2. Marketing Institutions
   - *a.* Distribution systems
   - *b.* Communication media
   - *c.* Marketing services (advertising and research)
3. Industry Conditions
   - *a.* Competitive size and practices
   - *b.* Technical development

[10] W. J. Keegan, "A Conceptual Framework for Multinational Marketing," *Journal of World Business,* November–December 1972, p 75.

4. Legal Environment
   (laws, regulations, codes, tariffs, and taxes)
5. Resources
   a. Personnel (availability, skill, potential, and cost)
   b. Money (availability and cost)
6. Political Environment
   a. Current government policies and attitudes
   b. Long-range political environment

ENTREPRENEURIAL ENTRY INTO INTERNATIONAL BUSINESS

A wide range of choices are available to an entrepreneur who wants to get into international business and market products internationally. The choice of entry method or the mode of operating overseas is very much dependent on the goals of the entrepreneur and the company's strengths and weaknesses. The modes of entering or engaging in international business can be divided into three categories: exporting, nonequity arrangements, and direct foreign investment.

Exporting

As a general rule, an entrepreneur starts doing international business through exporting. **Exporting** normally involves the sale and shipping of products manufactured in one country to a customer located in another country. Since there are many different methods of exporting, it is helpful to divide them into two categories, direct and indirect.

Indirect exporting. **Indirect exporting** involves having a foreign purchaser in the local market or using an export management firm. For certain commodities and manufactured goods, foreign buyers actively seek out sources of supply and have purchasing offices in markets throughout the world. An entrepreneur wanting to sell into one of these overseas markets can deal with one of these buyers. In this way, the entire transaction is handled as though it were a domestic transaction, but the entrepreneur knows that the goods are going to be shipped out of the country. This method of entering exporting involves the least amount of risk for the entrepreneur.

Export management firms, another method for indirect exporting, are located in almost every commercial center. For a fee, these firms will provide representation in foreign markets. Typically, they have a group of noncompeting manufacturers from the same country who have no interest in becoming directly involved in exporting. The management firm handles all of the selling tasks, including marketing and delivery and any technical problems involved in the export process.

Direct exporting. If the entrepreneur wants more involvement without any financial commitment, **direct exporting** through independent distributors or his or her own overseas sales office is a way to get involved in international business. Independent foreign distributors usually handle products for firms seeking relatively rapid entry into a large number of foreign markets. This independent distributor directly contacts foreign customers and potential customers and takes care of all the technicalities of arranging for export documentation, financing, and delivery for an established commission rate.

Entrepreneurs who do not wish to give up control over their marketing efforts, as occurs when using independent distributors, can open their own overseas sales offices and hire their own salespeople to provide market representation. In starting out, the entrepreneur may send a U.S. or domestic salesperson to be a representative in the foreign market. As more business is done in the overseas sales in the foreign market, warehouses are usually opened, followed by a local assembly process when sales reach a level high enough to warrant the operation. The assembly operation can eventually evolve into establishment of manufacturing operations in the foreign markets. Entrepreneurs then export the output from these manufacturing operations to many other markets.

Nonequity Arrangements

If market and financial conditions warrant, an entrepreneur can enter into international business by one of three types of nonequity arrangements: licensing, turn-key projects, and management contracts. Each of these ways of engaging in international business allows the entrepreneur to enter a market and obtain sales and profits without direct equity investment in the foreign market. Entrepreneurs who either cannot export or make direct investments or who simply choose not to engage in those activities still have the possibility of doing international business through nonequity arrangements.

Licensing. **Licensing** involves a entrepreneur who is a manufacturer (licensee) giving a foreign manufacturer (licensor) the right to use a patent, trademark, technology, production process, or product in return for the payment of a royalty. The licensing arrangement is most appropriate when the entrepreneur has no immediate intention of entering a particular market on his or her own through exporting or direct investment. Since the process is usually low risk and an easy way to generate incremental income, a licensing arrangement can be a very beneficial way for the entrepreneur to become involved in international business. Unfortunately, some entrepreneurs have entered into these arrangements without careful analysis and have later found they have licensed their largest competitor into business or that they are investing large sums of time and money in helping the licensor to adopt the technology or know-how being licensed.

Wolverine World Wide Inc. opened a Hush Puppies store in Sofia, Bulgaria, in the summer of 1988, through a licensing agreement with Pikin, a combine. Similar arrangements were made a year later in the former U.S.S.R. with Kirov, a shoe combine.[11] The stores have done well through the two arrangements.

---

[11] J. A. Cohen, "Footwear and the Jet Set," *Management Review,* March 1990, pp. 42–5.

Turn-key projects. Another method by which the entrepreneur can gain some international business experience without risk is to be involved in **turn-key projects.** The underdeveloped or lesser developed countries of the world have recognized their need for manufacturing technology and infrastructure and yet do not want to turn over substantial portions of their economy to foreign ownership. The solution to this dilemma has been to have a foreign entrepreneur build a factory or other facility, train the workers to operate the equipment, and train the management to run the installation. Once the operation is on line, the operation is turned over to its local owners, hence the name turn-key operation.

Entrepreneurs who might otherwise have been unable to enter a particular foreign market have found the turn-key project an attractive alternative. Initial profits can be made from the turn-key project. (The initial project can be a major stimulus to follow-up export sales that can provide cash flow throughout the entire project.) Financing is often provided by the local company or the government, and periodic payments are made over the entire period of construction and training.

Management contracts. A final method the entrepreneur can use to enter into international business in a nonequity arrangement is using a **management contract.** Several entrepreneurs have successfully entered international business by contracting their management techniques and managerial skills. These contracts sometimes follow a turn-key project where the foreign owner wants to maintain the management of the turn-key supplier.

The management contract allows the purchasing country to gain foreign expertise without turning ownership of its resources over to a foreigner. For the entrepreneur, the management contract is another way of entering foreign markets that would otherwise be closed and of obtaining a profit without a large equity investment.

Direct Foreign Investment

The wholly owned foreign subsidiary has been the preferred mode of ownership for entrepreneurs using a direct foreign investment to international markets. Joint ventures and minority and majority equity positions are also methods for making direct foreign investments. The percentage of ownership obtained in the foreign venture by the entrepreneur is related to his or her nationality, the amount of his or her overseas experience, the nature of the industry, and the rules of the host government.

Minority interests. Japanese companies have been frequent users of the minority equity position in direct foreign investment. The **minority interest** provides the firm with either a source of raw materials or a relatively captive market for its products. Entrepreneurs have used minority positions to gain a foothold or experience in a market before making a major commitment. When the minority shareholder has something of value to offer the organization, the ability to influence its decision-making process is often far in excess of the shareholding.

Joint ventures. Another direct foreign investment method used by entrepreneurs to enter foreign markets is the **joint venture.** The joint venture can take on many forms. In its most traditional form, two firms (for example, one U.S. firm and one German firm) get together and form a third company in which they share the equity. Another mode is for an entrepreneur to purchase 50 percent of the equity in a foreign firm.

Joint ventures have been used by entrepreneurs most often in two situations: (1) when the entrepreneur wants to purchase local knowledge and an already established marketing or manufacturing facility, and (2) when rapid entry into a market is needed. Sometimes joint ventures are dissolved, with the entrepreneur taking over 100 percent ownership to control the marketing program.

Even though using a joint venture to enter a foreign market is a key strategic decision, the keys to its success have not been well understood, and the reasons for forming a joint venture today are different than those in the past. In the past, joint ventures were viewed as partnerships, and often involved firms whose stock was owned by several other firms. Originally, joint ventures were used for trading purposes and were one of the oldest ways of transacting business. Merchants of ancient Babylonia, Egypt, and Phoenicia used joint ventures to conduct large trading operations. This use continued through the 15th and 16th centuries when merchants in Great Britain used joint venturing to trade all over the world, particularly in the Americas and India.

Joint ventures in the United States took a somewhat different form, being used by mining concerns and railroads as early as 1850. The use of joint ventures, mostly vertical joint ventures, increased significantly during the 1950s. Through the vertical joint venture two firms could absorb the large volume of output where neither one could handle it alone or afford the diseconomies associated with a smaller plant. This use continued to accelerate up through the 90s.

What has caused this significant increase in the use of joint ventures, particularly since not all of them have worked well? The studies of success and failure rates of joint ventures have revealed many different motives for their formation.

One of the most frequent reasons an entrepreneur forms a joint venture is to share the costs and risks of a very uncertain project. Projects where new costly technology is involved frequently need resource sharing, allowing each firm to concentrate on its strengths. This can be particularly beneficial when the entrepreneur does not have the financial resources to engage in capital intensive activities.

Another reason for an entrepreneur forming a joint venture is the **synergy** between the firms. **Synergy** is the qualitative effect on the rates of return of the acquiring firm brought about by complimentary factors inherent in the firm being acquired. This synergy may be in the form of people, inventory, plant, or equipment and provides leverage for each firm in the market. The degree of the synergy determines how beneficial the joint venture will be for both companies involved. This synergy frequently provides for a reduction in inventory or an increase in the information available.

Another reason for forming a joint venture is to obtain a competitive advantage. A joint venture can preempt competitors, allowing an entrepreneur to access new customers and to expand its market base. It can also result in an entity that is more effectively competitive than the original company, since hybrids of companies tend to possess the strength of each of the joint venture partners and tend to be, therefore, stronger than either one alone.

Joint ventures are frequently used by entrepreneurs to enter markets and economies that pose entrance difficulties. This has been the case for the former countries of Eastern Europe and the U.S.S.R. The rules and strategic aspects of joint ventures in these countries vary greatly. For example, it is easier to establish a joint venture in Hungary than in other Eastern European countries because of fewer registration requirements.

Majority interest. Another equity method for the entrepreneur to enter international markets is by purchasing a majority interest in a foreign business. In a technical sense, anything over 50 percent of the equity in a firm is a **majority interest.** The majority interest allows the entrepreneur to obtain managerial control, while minimizing the capital outlay. This method also allows the firm to maintain its local identity. Entrepreneurs who have initially taken small majority positions when entering an international market have a tendency to increase the ownership to 100 percent as sales and profits occur. At times, this reflects the tight regulation in many countries concerning the rights of minority shareholders. The move to 100 percent ownership also reduces any possible conflict with the local owner.

100 Percent ownership. An entrepreneur using 100 percent ownership to engage in international business assures complete control. U.S. entrepreneurs have the tendency to desire complete ownership and control over their foreign investments. This eliminates the need for a foreign partner. If the entrepreneur has the capital, technology, and marketing skills required for successful entry into a market, there may be no reason to share ownership.

One form of 100 percent ownership that has been used significantly in international business as well as within the United States is mergers and acquisitions. Mergers and acquisitions have varied in use as a strategic option by entrepreneurs. During periods of intense merger activity, entrepreneurs may spend significant time searching for a firm to acquire and developing the appropriate deal for the transaction. The deal itself should reflect basic principles of any capital investment decision and should make a net contribution to shareholders' wealth. The merits for a particular merger are often difficult to determine. Not only must the benefits and cost of a merger be determined, but special accounting, legal, and tax issues must be addressed. Also, the entrepreneur needs to have a general understanding of the benefits and problems of mergers as a strategic option and of the complexity of integrating an entire company into present operations.

There are five basic types of mergers: horizontal, vertical, product extension, market extension, and diversified activity. A **horizontal merger** is the combination of two firms that produce one or more of the same or closely related products in the same geographical area. They are motivated by economies of scale in marketing, production, or sales, such as occurred with 7-Eleven Convenience Stores acquiring Southland Stores.

A **vertical merger** is the combination of two or more firms in successive stages of production that often involve a buyer-seller relationship. This form of merger stabilizes supply and production and offers more control of these critical areas. Examples are McDonald's Corporation acquiring their store franchises, and Phillips Petroleum acquiring their gas station franchises, making these outlets company-owned stores.

A **product extension merger** occurs when acquiring and acquired companies have related production and/or distribution activities but do not have products that compete directly with each other. Examples are Miller Brewing being acquired by Phillip Morris; and Western Publishing, a publisher of children's books, being acquired by Mattel Toy Company.

A **market extension merger** is when the two firms produce the same products but sell them in different geographic markets. The motivation is that the acquiring firm can economically combine its management skills, production, and marketing with that of the acquired firm. An example is Dayton Hudson (a Minneapolis retailer) acquiring Diamond Chain (a West Coast retailer).

The final type of merger is a **diversified activity merger.** This is a conglomerate merger involving the consolidation of two essentially unrelated firms with as limited a transfer of skills and activities as possible. Usually, the acquiring firm is not interested in actively running and managing the acquired company. An example is Hillenbrand Industries (a caskets and hospital furniture manufacturer) acquiring American Tourister (a luggage manufacturer).

Mergers are a sound strategic option for an entrepreneur when synergy is present. What makes two firms worth more together than apart? Several factors cause synergy to occur, increasing the value of the two-firm combination to more than the value of the separate entities.

The first factor, economics of scale, is probably the most prevalent reason for mergers. Economies of scale can occur in production, coordination and administration, sharing central services such as office management and accounting, financial control, and upper level management. Economies of scale increase operating, financial, and management efficiency, resulting in better earnings.

The second factor is taxation or, more specifically, unused tax shields. Sometimes a firm has a loss but not enough profits to take tax advantage of the loss. Corporate income tax regulations allow the net operating losses of one company to reduce the taxable income of another when they are combined. By combining a firm with a loss with one with a profit, the tax-loss carryover can be used.

The final important factor for mergers is the benefits received in combining complementary resources. Many entrepreneurs will merge with other firms to ensure a source of supply for key ingredients, to obtain new technology, or to keep the other firm's product from being a competitive threat. It often is quicker and easier for a firm to merge with another that already has a new technology developed, combining the innovation with the acquiring firm's engineering and sales talent, than to develop the technology from scratch.

BARRIERS TO INTERNATIONAL TRADE

Until recently, there has been a generally positive attitude throughout the world concerning free trade. This attitude started around 1947 with the development of general trade agreements and the reduction of trade, particularly tariff, barriers.

General Agreement on Tariffs and Trade (GATT)

The positive attitude toward free and open trade is probably best exemplified by the General Agreement on Tariffs and Trade (GATT), which was established in 1947 with U.S. leadership. GATT is a multilateral agreement with the objective of liberalizing trade by eliminating or reducing tariffs, subsidies, and import quotas. GATT membership now includes over 100 nations and has had eight rounds of tariff reductions, the most recent, the Uruguay Round, lasting from 1986–1993. In each round, mutual tariff reductions are negotiated between member nations. These negotiated tariffs are enhanced by a mutual monitoring mechanism. If a member country feels that a violation has occurred, it can ask for an investigation by the Geneva-based administrators of GATT. If the investigation uncovers a violation, member countries can be asked to pressure the violating country to change its policy and conform to the agreed tariffs and agreements. Usually, this pressure has not been sufficient to get an offending country to change. While GATT has assisted in developing more unrestricted trade, its voluntary membership gives it very little authority in ensuring this type of trade will occur.

Increasing Protectionist Attitudes

In the latter part of the 1970s the strong support of free trade and GATT began to wane. The support increased significantly in the 1980s, however, due to the rise in protectionist pressures in many industrialized countries. This renewed support reflected three major events. First, the world trading system was strained by the persistent trade deficit of the United States, the world's largest economy. This trade deficit has been occurring since the early 1980s, peaking in 1987 at over $170 billion. The U.S. deficit has caused adjustments in such industries as automobiles, semiconductors, steel, and textiles. Unemployment resulting from the loss in sales and in market share has spurred a U.S. interest in protectionism. Second, the economic success of a country perceived as not playing by the rules (e.g., Japan) has also strained the world's trading systems. In ruins when GATT was created, Japan has grown to become the world's second largest economy and largest trader. Japan's success and the perception that its internal markets are, in effect, closed to imports and foreign investment have caused problems. The third reason for the change in attitude has resulted from the previous two reasons. In response to the pressures created by the trade and payment deficit of the United States and the trade surplus and barriers of Japan, many countries have established bilateral voluntary export restraints to circumvent GATT.

Trade Blocs and Free Trade Areas

Around the world, groups of nations are banding together to increase trade and investment between nations in the group and exclude those nations outside the group. One less well-known agreement is between the United States and Israel. This agreement, signed in 1985, establishes a Free Trade Area (FTA) between the two nations, gradually, over a 10-year period. At the end of the 10 years, all tariffs and quotas except on certain agricultural products will have been phased out. In 1989, an FTA went into effect between Canada and the United States that will phase out tariffs and quotas between the two countries, who are each other's largest trading partners.

Many trading alliances have evolved in the Americas. In 1991, the United States signed a framework trade agreement with Argentina, Brazil, Paraguay, and Uruguay for the development of more liberal trade relations. The United States has also signed bilateral trade agreements with Bolivia, Chile, Colombia, Costa Rica, Ecuador, El Salvador, Honduras, Peru, and Venezuela. And a more-publicized agreement is the North American Free Trade Agreement (NAFTA) between the United States, Canada, and Mexico. This agreement will reduce trade barriers and quotas and encourage investment between the three countries, creating the most significant trading bloc in the world.

Similarly, the Americas, Argentina, Brazil, Paraguay, and Uruguay have the Treaty of Asuncion, which created the Mercosul trade zone, a free trade zone between the countries.

Another important trading bloc has been developed by the European Community (EC). The EC and the European Free Trade Association have created the European Economic Area (EEA), one of the most affluent and largest trading areas in the world.

Entrepreneur's Strategy and Trade Barriers

Clearly, **trade barriers** post problems for the entrepreneur who wants to become involved in international business. First, trade barriers increase the costs of an entrepreneur exporting products or semi-finished products to a country. If the increased cost puts the entrepreneur at a competitive disadvantage with respect to indigenous competitive products, he or she may find it economical to establish production facilities in the country. Second, voluntary export restraints may limit an entrepreneur's ability to sell products in a country from production facilities outside the country.

These may also cause the entrepreneur to establish production facilities in the country in order to compete. Finally, an entrepreneur may have to locate assembly or production facilities in a country to conform to the local content regulations of the country.

ENTREPRENEURIAL PARTNERING

One of the best methods for an entrepreneur to enter an international market is to partner with an entrepreneur in that country. These foreign entrepreneurs know the country and its culture and therefore can facilitate business being done in the country while keeping the entrepreneur current on business, economic, and political conditions. This partnering is facilitated by understanding the nature of entrepreneurship in the country. Three areas of particular interest to U.S. entrepreneurs are Europe, the Far East, and once-controlled economies.

Europe

Europe has only recently become interested in the growth of entrepreneurship. Risk taking in general is discouraged by most European cultures, and business failure is considered a social disgrace. Recently however, several changes in the social and political climate have conspired to change this traditional, security conscious culture. Successful entrepreneurs, some of whom have become cultural heroes, are breaking through the stigma associated with striking out on one's own. In the political arena, in spite of the overregulation, new tax laws are providing incentives to would-be entrepreneurs.[12]

One group that exemplifies these newcomers are academics, especially scientists and engineers. Many European academic circles dislike the practical world of commerce. Even for those scientists and engineers working in commercial enterprises, entrepreneurship is not very enticing, as private corporations and public research organizations where they are presently employed offered secure, well-paid, risk-free careers. This makes it difficult for small European entrepreneurs to attract people with a knowledge of innovative management techniques and the know-how to launch high-technology products. Yet, today individuals are emerging in both academic circles and large companies who are looking for a challenge and are finding it in entrepreneurship. New government policies are making it easier to raise money for starting up businesses.[13] Britain and France are the European leaders in entrepreneurship with an abundance of venture capital; in West Germany and Italy, entrepreneurs are faced with limited access to bank credit for financing growth.[14]

---

[12] R. I. Kirkland Jr., "Europe's New Entrepreneurs," *Fortune,* April 27, 1987, p 253.

[13] D. Dickson, "An Entrepreneurial Tree Sprouts in Europe," *Science* 245 (September 8, 1989), pp 1,038–40.

[14] C. Gaffney, "Hot Start-ups from Hong Kong to Hamburg," *Business Week,* May 23, 1988, p 135.

In 1983, the United Kingdom government created the Business Expansion Scheme (BES) to provide external capital to new and small business ventures. Investors in the BES receive a tax break on their investments in "unquoted" enterprises.[15]

While the French government is also trying to develop entrepreneurial enterprises as part of an overall strategy to stimulate their economy, several economic and social factors in France create difficulties for aspiring entrepreneurs. In the first place, French venture capital is managed by bankers who are risk averse and have little understanding of the needs of small businesses and little regard for new venture creation. A second major hurdle for entrepreneurs is the French contempt for both failure and success. Inherited fortunes are respected, but created wealth is generally considered unsavory, regardless of the money's origin.[16]

Significant research in Ireland has produced a general profile of entrepreneurs based on the results of a survey of 272 entrepreneurs. The average age of the enterprises was seven years. The industry with the largest percentage of firms was manufacturing (31 percent); 45 percent of the businesses surveyed did not export, but among those that did, exporting accounted for 20 percent of total business.

In-depth personal interviews with a sample of the entrepreneurs from this survey indicated that the typical entrepreneur is a 40-year-old man who was the first born in his middle-class family. He is married, with three children. Although his parents are not educated, he typically completed high school and has experience in the field in which he is operating. This individual tends to be independent, energetic, goal-oriented, competitive, and flexible.[17]

One 1988 study of Northern Ireland entrepreneurs supports these findings. The United Kingdom allocates about $1 billion per year for the education and financial support of entrepreneurs in Northern Ireland. Yet, despite this and other efforts made by the Industrial Development Board and the Northern Ireland Economic Council, entrepreneurship has not taken roots. Many people are hesitant to start new businesses because, in addition to a volatile political situation, they must contend with high taxes, the high cost of capital, and customs regulations.[18]

In Sweden, a 1980 national survey of 1,500 female entrepreneurs and 300 male entrepreneurs broke down the population of entrepreneurs into three subclasses: single women (16 percent), married women (37 percent), and coentrepreneurs, or husband and wife teams (47 percent). While female entrepreneurs, ranging in age from 19 to 65, were found in almost every line of business and in every geographic location, they tended to be more active than men in areas of retail, restaurants, and service, and were found less in the manufacturing, construction, and transportation industries.[19]

---

[15] R. T. Harrison and C. M. Mason, "Risk Finance, the Equity Gap and New Venture Formation in the United Kingdom: The Impact of the Business Expansion Scheme," *Frontiers of Entrepreneurship Research,* 1988, pp 595–611.

[16] Jean-Louise Gassee, "The French Connection," *Across the Board* 24 (July–August 1987), p 35.

[17] R. D. Hisrich, and B. O'Cinneide, "The Irish Entrepreneur: Characteristics, Problems and Future Success," *Frontiers of Entrepreneurship Research,* 1986, pp 66–75.

[18] R. D. Hisrich, "The Entrepreneur in North Ireland: Characteristics, Problems and Recommendations for the Future," *Journal of Small Business Management,* pp 32–9.

[19] C. Holmquist and E. Sundin, "Women as Entrepreneurs in Sweden: Conclusions from a Survey," *Frontiers of Entrepreneurship Research* 1988, pp 626–42.

A comparison study of high-technology firms with retail, manufacturing, and repair industries in Sweden was conducted through 15-minute telephone interviews with 540 firms. Typically, the high-technology firms were found to be younger than the others, with their managers having a higher level of formal education. There were no entrepreneurial role models in the personal history of the entrepreneur.[20]

Another research study of more than 400 Swedish concerns with 2 to 20 employees in the same industries found that entrepreneurs' willingness to let their businesses grow is influenced by an anticipated loss of control over the enterprise (deterrent), increased independence as a result of growth (motivator), and financial gains (motivator).[21]

The Far East

The success of the entrepreneur in some Asian countries has been significant because of the culture and the political and economic systems in place. While Malaysia and Singapore are very close geographically and share some common history, both, once a part of the British Empire, have evolved in very different ways.

The people of the Malaysia peninsula converted to Islam in the 15th century, not long before the advent of a European rule that lasted more than 400 years. The natives traditionally lived in rural areas, leaving the cities to the dominant foreign powers, which delayed industrialization. There is still a lack of social mobility in this country. While the government established the Malaysian Industrial Development Authority to promote and coordinate efforts to eradicate poverty and to restructure the social environment through economic development and stability, the agency has not accomplished much.

The roots of entrepreneurship in Singapore reach as far back as the 14th century. In 1819, Sir Stamford Raffles bought the island and transformed it into a refuge for entrepreneurs, establishing a free port open to merchants of any ethnic background. When Singapore claimed its independence from Malaysia in 1965, the island once again became ethnically pluralistic, wrote secularism into its constitution, and gave tax incentives to entrepreneurs. In 1985, the Small Enterprise Bureau of Singapore was established to provide information and guidance to entrepreneurs in starting and expanding their enterprises. Social mobility is high, and entrepreneurial success is greatly esteemed.[22]

Japan is a country whose social structure does not encourage entrepreneurship. Large corporations have dominated the economy for some time, and most Japanese

---

[20] P. Davidsson and K. Brynell, "Small High-Tech Firms and Conventional Small Firms—Similarities and Differences," Paper presented at Second Workshop on Recent Research and Entrepreneurship in Europe, IASM, Vienna, December 5–6, 1988.

[21] P. Davidsson, "Entrepreneurship—and After? A Study of Growth Willingness in Small Firms," *Journal of Business Venturing* 4 (May 1989), pp 211–26.

[22] L. P. Dana, "Entrepreneurship and Venture Creation—An Entrepreneurial Comparison of Five Commonwealth Nations," *Frontiers of Entrepreneurship Research,* 1987, pp 573–89.

entrepreneurial activity is limited to service and information-technology industries.[23] Even though these giant organizations encourage innovation and invention in their employees, research findings indicate that the five most important motivators for starting a high-technology firm in Japan were all centered on desires for self-actualization and creativity,[24] a need not addressed by this consensus-oriented society. Trailblazers like Wataru Ohashi and Kazuhiko Nishi are starting to break down the psychological barriers necessary to encourage entrepreneurship. Ohashi began a parcel-delivery service in 1981 that has since evolved into an enterprise that directly markets luxury items. The company makes over half of its earnings from the sales of items like melons, fresh salmon, caviar, and furs.[25]

At age 20, Nishi left the highly acclaimed Waseda University to start his own company, eventually teaming up with William Gates of Microsoft. Within a few years, Nishi's company, ASCII, became the biggest PC software supplier in Japan.[26]

By contrast, Hong Kong is a hotbed of entrepreneurial activity. Many of the present entrepreneurs were previously managers of large companies before they broke away to start their own businesses.[27] As a center for venture capital, Hong Kong has produced some of the wealthiest men in the world. Sir Yu Pao, driven out by Chinese communists in 1948, worked initially to establish his family in the import/export business. In the mid-1980s, he bought his first ship, a coal-burning steamer. Since that time, Pao has built his fleet to become the world's largest private/independent shipowner and has amassed a personal fortune of over $1 billion. Kuang-Piu Chao is another refugee of communist China who left in the 1950s. Chao runs one of Hong Kong's largest textile operations, which, in 1987, claimed a 4 percent share of Hong Kong's knitwear exports market. Li Ka-Shing arrived in Hong Kong with his parents at age 12. When his father died two years later, Li became the family breadwinner. By 20, Li was factory manager at the plastics factory where he first went to work, and several years later he had enough money to start his own plastic flower factory. With an estimated net worth of over $230 million, Li has a controlling interest in companies that are valued over $1 billion.[28]

Controlled or Once-Controlled Economies

While China's centralized, planned economy has not openly encouraged entrepreneurship, there still has been a great deal of entrepreneurial activity taking place under the communist umbrella. Guau Guarymei, a worker from Benxi, is a case in

---

[23]C. Gaffney, 1988, p 135.

[24]D. M. Ray, "Factors Influencing Entrepreneurial Events in Japanese High-Technology Venture Business," *Frontiers of Entrepreneurial Research,* 1987, pp 557–72.

[25]T. Holden, "Deliverymen Who Always Ring Twice," *Business Week,* May 23, 1988, p 135.

[26]S. M. Dabrot, "Tensaiji: Whiz Kid Wins Business—Even in Japan," *Scientific American,* January 1990, p 104.

[27]C. Gaffney, 1988, p 135.

[28]"Hong Kong's Entrepreneurs on a Winning Streak," *Euromoney,* November 1987, pp 44, 46, and 48.

point. Guarymei leased eight government-run shops in 1985 and rapidly changed them from businesses operating at a loss to profitable enterprises. How did she do it? Guarymei reduced the managerial staff by 50 percent, devised a method of pay that made wages a function of performance, and instituted a system of fines for those who broke discipline. Controversy occurred over the amount of Guarymei's income as it was 20 times the wage of an average salesperson. This income level stands in opposition to the egalitarian socialistic system in which every person enjoys equal benefits, regardless of the amount and quality of his or her contribution. These old values are slowly giving way to the idea of a socialist society that rewards those making contributions.[29]

Guau Guarymei is an example of the rising number of woman entrepreneurs in China. A study of 50 woman entrepreneurs indicated that Chinese woman entrepreneurs are mainly in the textile and clothing industries (48 percent) and have enterprises that have been operating for 10 or more years. While 64 percent of the entrepreneurs are from the coastal area of China, 36 percent are from the interior. The majority of the woman entrepreneurs are between the ages of 40 and 50 (60 percent), with most having run their businesses less than 15 years (56 percent). Sixty percent of the women surveyed had received secondary technical training or higher education and 96 percent were members of the Communist party.[30]

Although the educational level of woman entrepreneurs in China is lower than their counterparts in other countries, the problems they encounter are much the same. Capital is lacking. There is a need for training and education in management, administration, and coordination of personnel. Finally, the needs for reform and implementation of countrywide policies are concerns shared with entrepreneurs in other countries with controlled economies, such as the former U.S.S.R. and those in former Eastern and Central Europe.

In Poland, the transitional upheaval and lack of adequate reform has led to a thriving black market, particularly in hard currency. One man who saw an opportunity was Bogdan Chosna, a 36-year-old Polish manager and co-owner of Promotor, a trading company based in Warsaw. In the 1980s, Chosna made a fortune by using investors' stashes of hard Western currency to buy cheap personal computers from Taiwan and Singapore. He then sold them to businesses at a premium in zloty, the local currency. Chosna gave his clients something to buy with the zloty, circumventing the slow-moving official channels. He exchanged the vast profits in zlotys for dollars on the black market.

Another successful entrepreneur is Leonid Melamed from Riga, Latvia, in the former U.S.S.R. Melamed began his professional life as a military lawyer, but since the advent of perestroika, he has established 15 businesses—among them three newspapers, a stainless steel cutlery operation, and a women's lingerie business.

---

[29] L. Delysin, "The Case of an Entrepreneur," *World Press Review,* January 1988, pp 23–4.

[30] R. D. Hisrich and Zhang Fan, "Women Entrepreneurs in the People's Republic of China: An Exploratory Study," *Journal of Managerial Psychology* 6, no.1 (March/April, 1991).

When the government began allowing joint ventures, Melamed promptly reinvested four million rubles of his earnings in a joint venture with a Polish company and later found other partners in West Germany and the United States.

The economic reforms taking place in both once-controlled and less-developed economies have been supported by the Overseas Private Investment Corporation (OPIC) of the U.S. government. OPIC provides a number of services, such as: (1) selling political risk insurance that covers currency inconvertibility, appropriation, and political violence (long-term policies, up to 20 years); (2) offering direct loans—up to $6 million to individuals with a total outlay of $20 million; (3) providing loan guarantees up to $200 million; (4) organizing overseas missions through which U.S. business people can explore investment possibilities; and (5) providing investor information services.

One country becoming more entrepreneurial due in part to OPIC is Hungary. The reforms in this country have supported decentralization, private initiative, and market-orientation of the economy. Hungary has a large number of joint ventures, which reflects its very favorable joint venture conditions. One major advantage Hungary has in the establishment of joint ventures is the relative ease in obtaining government permission. A survey of 46 Hungarian entrepreneurs found that most of them were between the ages of 30 and 50, and equally divided among three educational levels: craftsman school, high school, and university. There were a variety of motivations for starting the new venture: to put their experience to work, to gain financial independence, or simply to work for themselves. Most of the entrepreneurs are operating in the service sector, with firm size being generally small, although the number of employees ranges from 1 to 300.[31]

SUMMARY

International business is becoming important to more and more entrepreneurs and to their country's economy. International entrepreneurship—an entrepreneur conducting business activities across national boundaries—is occurring much earlier in the growth of new ventures as opportunities open up in the hypercompetitive global arena. Several factors (economics, stage of economic development, balance of payments, type of system, political-legal environment, cultural environment, and technological environment) usually make decisions in international entrepreneurship more complex than those in domestic entrepreneurship.

Four strategic issues are important for an entrepreneur to consider before going international: the allocation of responsibility between the U.S. and foreign operation; the type of planning, reporting, and control system to be used; the appropriate organizational structure; and the degree of standardization possible.

[31] J. Vecsenyi and R. D. Hisrich, "Entrepreneurship and the Hungarian Transformation: An Entrepreneurial Perspective," *Journal of Managerial Psychology* 5 (1990), pp 11–16.

If the entrepreneur decides to be involved in international business once these key issues have been considered, there are three general modes of market entry: exporting, nonequity arrangements, and equity arrangements. Each mode has several alternatives providing varying degrees of risk, control, and ownership.

Entrepreneurs in the United States can find their counterparts in a wide variety of economies. Entrepreneurship is thriving from Dublin to Hong Kong, providing new products and new jobs, and thereby stimulating the countries' economies.

QUESTIONS FOR DISCUSSION

1. Why is international business so important to an entrepreneur and the United States specifically?
2. What are the similarities and differences between international and domestic business management?
3. Discuss the various options for entrepreneurs to enter into international business and the advantages and disadvantages of each.
4. Discuss the use of joint ventures as a method for entering such markets as Hungary, the Russian Federation, Thailand, and Iran.
5. What are the similarities and differences between entrepreneurs in the United States, Europe, and the Far East, and areas with controlled economies?

KEY TERMS

balance of payments
barter
direct exporting
diversified activity merger
exporting
horizontal merger
indirect exporting
international entrepreneurship
joint venture
licensing
majority interest
management contracts
market extension merger
minority interests
nonequity arrangements
product extension merger
third-party arrangements
trade barriers
turn-key projects
synergy
vertical merger

SELECTED READINGS

Abetti, Pier A. (1992). Planning and Building the Infrastructure for Technical Entrepreneurship. *International Journal of Technology Management.* vol. 7, nos. 1–3, pp. 129–39.

A comparison of the entrepreneur programs in Sud-Oise in France, the Capital Business District in New York, and Cuernavaca in Mexico indicates that entrepreneurs and principals of technological companies planning to locate in a given area should make certain that all the elements for success are present or under active development in the area.

Brenner, Reuven. (1992). Entrepreneurship and Business Ventures in the New Commonwealth. *Journal of Business Venturing,* vol. 7, no. 6, pp. 431–39.

The obstacles to entrepreneurship and business ventures in Russia's New Commonwealth are not due to a lack of entrepreneurial talent but rather a lack of significant advances in legal and institutional reforms and expectations of the monetization of the government's deficits.

Brunner, Hans-Peter. (1993). Entrepreneurship in Eastern Europe: Neither Magic nor Mirage. A Preliminary Investigation. *Journal of Economic Issues.* vol. 27, no. 2, pp. 505–13.

Four stylized strategies (the capital strategy, privatization of state enterprises strategy, the nucleus strategy, and the evolutionary strategy) are used to compare and discuss Eastern Europe's entrepreneurial potential.

Buss, Terry F., & Vaughn, Robert J. (1993). Local Economic Development in Hungary: From Communism to Democracy. *Economic Development Review.* vol. 2, no. 2, pp. 51–56.

A comparison of the economic development strategies of four of Hungary's largest cities indicates that entrepreneurship is intended to become the driving force of the economy of each city.

Chang, Wein, & MacMillan, Ian C. (1991). A Review of Entrepreneurial Development in the People's Republic of China. *Journal of Business Venturing.* vol. 6, no. 6, pp. 375–79.

This article examines the recent history of entrepreneurship in the People's Republic of China and concludes that the pursuit of entrepreneurship exists and will continue to exist in the country because the Chinese people are increasingly aware that starting their own business is the best way to assure their own survival and the survival of their nation.

Dana, Leo Paul. (1992). A Look at Small Business in Austria. *Journal of Small Business Management.* vol. 30, no. 4, pp. 126–30.

Central to the Austrian economy is a multitude of small, non-high tech businesses which are not capital-intensive in such areas as services, tourism, crafts, shops, and agriculture.

Deshponde, Rohit, Farley, John U., & Webster, Frederick E., Jr. (1993). Corporate Culture, Customer Orientation, and Innovativeness in Japanese Firms: A Quadrad Analysis. *Journal of Marketing.* vol. 57, no.1, pp. 23–37.

A study of Japanese firms and their vendors found business performance positively correlated with the customer's evaluation of the company's customer orientation. Japanese companies with corporate cultures stressing competitiveness outperformed others without these characteristics.

Erramilli, M. Krishna, & D'Souza, Derrick, E. (1993). Venturing into Foreign Markets: The Case of the Small Service Firm. *Entrepreneurship: Theory and Practice,* vol. 17, no. 4, pp. 29–41.

The results of a study of 54 small and 87 larger service firms indicated that small service firms are as likely as their larger counterparts to enter culturally distant markets and to choose foreign direct investment modes reflecting the low level of capital intensity of the industry.

Hawking, Del I. (1993). New Business Entrepreneurship in the Japanese Economy. *Journal of Business Venturing.* vol. 8, no. 2, pp. 137–50.

New business entrepreneurship plays a significant role in the Japanese economy as over 99 percent of all Japanese enterprises are categorized as small or medium and these firms provide over 80 percent of all Japanese employment.

Hensley, Mathes L., & White, Edward P. (1993). The Privatization Experience in Malaysia. *Columbia Journal of World Business.* vol. 28, no. 1, pp. 70–82.

Some techniques used in the very ambitious Malaysian privatization program are: private sale, public offering, joint venture, and concession on build-operate-transfer.

Hisrich, Robert D., & Fuldop, Gyula. (1993). Women Entrepreneurs in Controlled Economies—A Hungarian Perspective. *Proceedings 1993 Conference on Entrepreneurship,* pp. 25–40.

The results of a survey of women entrepreneurs in Hungary indicate that they possess many similar attributes to their U.S. counterparts and are playing an important role in the market transformation occurring in the country.

Hisrich, Robert D., & Grachev, Mikhail. (1993). The Russian Entrepreneur. *Journal of Business Venturing.* vol. 8, no. 6, pp. 487–97.

The historical background of entrepreneurship in Russia is discussed along with scenarios of three present-day entrepreneurial firms—a high-tech company, a Russian brokerage company, and an educational organization.

Hisrich, Robert D., & Vecsenyi, Janos. (1990). Entrepreneurship and the Hungarian Economic Transformation. *Journal of Managerial Psychology.* vol. 5, no. 5, pp. 11–16.

Characteristics of entrepreneurs and their businesses were presented as well as the changes suggested to support new venture creation such as education, business, infrastructure, and government policy initiatives.

Kuratko, Donald F. (1993). Family Business Succession in Korean and U.S. Firms. *Journal of Small Business Management.* vol. 31, no. 2, pp. 132–36.

Differences and similarities existing between U.S. and South Korean family businesses are discussed. The patterns of preferred and expected succession are similar in the two countries.

Reginer, Phillipp. (1992). Small Business and Industrialization in South Korea. *Asia Pacific Journal of Management.* vol. 9, no. 1, pp. 107–17.

The promotion of small business is being done through reinforced measures of public assistance and the promotion of an economic climate more conducive to spontaneous entrepreneurship.

Siu, Wai-sum, & Martin, Robert G. (1992). Successful Entrepreneurship in Hong Kong. *Long Range Planning.* vol. 25, no. 6, pp. 87–93.

In Hong Kong, such factors as the free open market, voluntary exchange, blocked upward mobility in political channels, and a need for personal achievement, power, and influence significantly encourage business success and entrepreneurship.

Zolton, Roman. (1991). Entrepreneurship and Small Business: The Hungarian Trajectory. *Journal of Business Venturing.* vol. 6, no. 6, pp. 447–65.

This article examines four initiatives in Hungary: (1) the birth and flourishing of the second economy; (2) the rise and fall of the new intrapreneurial groups; (3) the turn from toleration to promotion of private small business; and (4) the art of the divestiture.

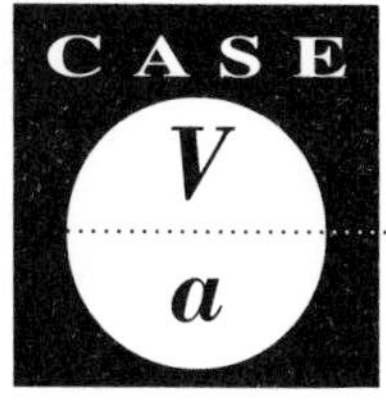

Infotechnology Corporation

In the board room at Infotechnology hung a framed poster espousing the words

> We can't direct the wind,
> But we can adjust the sails.

These words seemed extremely apropos to the firm's current situation. A mere six months earlier, Technology Systems's Paul Arnold had purchased 20 percent of Infotechnology, providing the company the capital to redesign its software products to be compatible with the IBM AS/400 system. This move would allow Infotechnology to build on its past success and expand the firm into a market leadership position. Today however, it is apparent that the winds have shifted, leaving the firm headed for the shoals of bankruptcy. It is truly time for Infotechnology to adjust its sails.

THE ENTREPRENEUR

John Stevens had over 30 years of business experience, including positions in research, sales, production, data processing, marketing, and general management. Having worked for Motorola for over 20 years in Canada, Great Britain, and the United States, John had worked his way through the corporate system and up to president of an operating subsidiary by the age of 38. When the firm encountered financial difficulties, John put together a team of former managers and executed a leveraged buyout of the subsidiary, Infotechnology, in 1980. Three years after the LBO, he sold the firm in three pieces. The largest piece was sold to ABA, a Houston-based computer software firm. As a result of these sales, Stevens received a 750 percent return on the original investment.

Stevens joined ABA as a vice president, where he continued to manage the former Infotechnology as a division of ABA. Originally planning only to spend one-and-a-half years with ABA, Stevens eventually left the organization in 1988.

> Every time I tried to leave the firm, they gave me a more challenging position. Of course, it didn't hurt that the pay was pretty good too. Eventually, I was running Infotechnology

---

This case was originally prepared by Richard Barnard, Won Ill Lee, and Scott Morrison, under the supervision of Dr. Richard T. Meyer, Professor of Entrepreneurship at the Emory Business School, as the basis for class discussion rather than to illustrate either effective or ineffective handling of a management situation. Financial support for the completion of this case was provided by a grant from the Center for Entrepreneurial Leadership of the Ewing Marion Kauffman Foundation.

> as an autonomous division of the firm. However, when I realized that the President of ABA was attempting to consolidate the various divisions into one for the purpose of selling the company, I could see the writing on the wall.

In 1988, Stevens and some of his key managerial staff left ABA to reform Infotechnology.

FORMATION AND GROWTH OF THE COMPANY

Infotechnology was founded anew in February 1989 by a group of four partners who had previously worked together at ABA, Inc. Recognizing the niche of providing application software with increased functionality on midrange computers to the public sector market, the partners of Infotechnology underwent an extensive search for established products or companies for market entry. The partners found a 13-year-old software company based in Nashua, New Hampshire, named Comprehensive Data Corp. (CDC).

CDC's software, an accounting product line that ran on the DEC VAX machine, had proven acceptability in the market. Combined with Infotechnology's enhancements, CDC's software would be the most feature-rich product available on the market. In addition, a purchase, as opposed to in-house development, would provide Infotechnology with immediate access to the market and provide first-mover advantage.

In addition to product enhancements, Infotechnology could also provide added-value in terms of marketing ability. CDC, because of a previous 10-year association with a company where CDC existed only as the development and support arm, did not have the established marketing skills to compete in the public sector market.

A licensing agreement between CDC and Infotechnology was struck. Infotechnology would receive exclusive marketing and distribution rights to the CDC product line. CDC would receive a 50 percent royalty on software sales and provide technical support.

With the licensing agreement in place, the business strategy for Infotechnology was to market the CDC product line to VAX users. The resulting sales would find an interim program of creating product line enhancements as well as porting the product line to the IBM AS/400 and to the UNIX operating system. Eventually, with these enhancements and the portability of the CDC product line, Infotechnology would be best positioned to take advantage of the identified niche in the public sector.

With a firm strategy implemented, Infotechnology received its first source of outside funding of $1 million in May 1989. The financing was provided by a Boston venture capital company named Venture Holdings, Inc. The terms of the financing agreement were an initial $500 thousand for a 20 percent equity share and $500 thousand for an additional 10 percent equity share, given that certain sales and cash collection objectives were met.

EXHIBIT A–1

Infotechnology Corporation
Balance Sheet
October 31, 1992

Assets	
Current assets	
Cash	2,141
Accounts receivable	595,836
Bad debt allowance	(50,000)
Prepaids	41,135
Total current assets	589,112
Property and equipment	208,309
Other assets	5,513
Total assets	802,934
Liabilities and capital	
Current liabilities	
Accounts payable	31,376
Interest payable	4,685
S-T leases payable	13,454
Consulting/support payable	47,995
Contract programming payable	31,462
Royalties payable	308,377
Other	(8,746)
Total current liabilities	428,603
Long-term liabilities	
Notes payable	490,602
Deferred income	85,180
Other	49,850
Total long-term liabilities	625,632
Total liabilities	1,054,235
Capital	
Common stock (par)	1,030
Preferred stock (par)	4,583
Preferred stock (surplus)	491,890
APIC common	218,979
APIC preferred	945,077
Retained earnings	(1,464,685)
Current earnings	(448,175)
Total capital	(251,301)
Total liabilities and capital	802,934

EXHIBIT A–2

Infotechnology Corporation
Income Statements

	Fiscal Years Ending:			*8 Months*
	2/28/90	*2/28/91*	*2/28/92*	*10/31/92*
Sales				
Software licenses	211,913	1,685,870	786,500	250,000
Consulting	14,022	359,503	922,928	436,439
Maintenance			50,000	56,281
Interest income				3,011
Total revenue	225,935	2,045,373	1,759,428	745,731
Cost of goods sold				
Royalties	84,544	673,604	393,250	139,300
Contracted services	0	0	215,000	57,834
Cost of sales	84,544	673,604	608,250	197,134
Gross margin	141,391	1,371,769	1,151,178	548,596
Expenses				
Payroll/benefits	617,713	877,276	1,081,754	615,248
Commissions/ bonuses	0	59,518	0	5,099
Travel/entertainment	249,907	124,015	67,708	45,224
Leases	35,925	44,792	46,758	37,209
Depreciation	24,331	36,755	38,000	52,053
Telephone/Fax	20,985	36,885	41,900	25,927
Office supplies	2,949	17,357	32,138	4,201
Sales promotions	31,270	5,411	22,000	3,710
Professional services	53,014	40,954	26,999	26,562
Other	47,453	66,785	31,675	181,538
Total expenses	1,083,547	1,309,748	1,388,932	996,771
Income from operations	(942,156)	62,021	(237,754)	(448,175)

Revenues increased from $226,000 in the first year of operations to $2.0 million in the second year of operations, and net income increased from a loss of $942,000 to a profit of $62,000 (see Exhibit A). As a result of the positive financial results, and in line with the original agreement, Venture Holdings advanced an additional $500 thousand to Infotechnology. Later, in April 1990, Infotechnology and Venture Holdings were selected as the "Best Venture Deal of 1989" by the *Boston Business Chronicle* and the accounting firm of Deloitte & Touche.

In early 1992, after a reversal in fiscal year 1991 revenue and net income to $1.8 million and ($238,000) respectively, Infotechnology started searching for an additional $500,000 in equity capital in order to accomplish its initial strategic plan.

EXHIBIT A–3

	Infotechnology Corporation Statement of Cash Flows *Current Month*	*8 Months*
	October 31, 1992	
Net income	(66,185)	(448,175)
Adjustments:		
Accumulated depreciation	1,989	13,963
Accumulated amortization	4,188	33,506
Accounts receivable—billed	58,732	108,008
Accounts receivable—unbilled	0	53,536
Prepaid support/consulting	13,982	(34,646)
Accounts payable	13,982	(57,776)
Interest payable	0	(5,572)
Accrued commissions	(1,181)	3,633
Suspense—clearing account	(7,191)	(4,641)
Leases payable	(738)	2,514
Consulting/support payable	0	47,995
Contract programming payable	0	(62,049)
Royalties payable	0	(51,871)
Other	(6,068)	(11,404)
Total adjustments	77,695	35,196
Net cash provided by operations	11,509	(412,978)
Cash flow from investing activities		
Furniture & fixtures	0	(16,293)
Office equipment	0	(46,246)
Deposits—leases	0	(2,274)
Net cash investing	0	(64,814)
Cash from financing		
Long-term debt	0	24,661
Deferred income	5,292	139,053
Deferred rent	387	6,102
Notes payable		(45,000)
Deferred income	(10,753)	(138,363)
Customer deposits	0	(2,125)
Net cash from financing	5,074	(15,546)
Net increase/decrease in cash	6,436	(493,339)

Moreover, because of an unexpected lack of technical support from CDC, Infotechnology began to build an in-house technical support group that would develop product enhancements and the portability of the product line to the IBM AS/400 and UNIX system. The additional equity capital would fund the new, in-house technical support group as well as expand the sales force. With equity financing in place and the strategic plan back on course, Infotechnology projected fiscal year 1993 revenue to be $4 million and net income to be $561,000.

In April 1992, John Stevens met Paul Arnold (CEO of Technology Systems, an established $45 million revenue company in Atlanta) at a new venture conference in Atlanta. Technology Systems had established a successful history of buying and selling software companies, and the prospects of Infotechnology enticed Arnold. In June 1992, Technology Systems advanced $500,000 for a 20 percent equity share of Infotechnology.

THE PRODUCTS

Infotechnology provides specialized products and services to the public sector, i.e., state and local governments, education, and other not-for-profit organizations where fund accounting, commitment and encumbrance controls, and sponsored program management are required. Essentially, Infotechnology offers products focused on major financial and administrative applications: general ledger (fund accounting in accordance with GASB standards), budgeting, accounts payable, purchasing, inventory, fixed assets, accounts receivable, and forecasting. Some of the product highlights include (see Exhibit B):

- Highly adaptable 35 character account code with up to 15 dimensions for added security.
- Users are able to define summary accounts and reporting structures.
- The system allows for multiple fiscal years, multiple budgets, unlimited years of transactions and balance history, and multiple statistics.
- The ability to do concurrent full-accrual, modified-accrual, and cash basis accounting.
- Project tracking.

THE MARKETS

The selection of the public sector market was based on several factors. Recognizing the difficulties of selling to the public sector, i.e., long sales cycles and general bureaucracy, the firm anticipated little competition in this market. In addition, the firms active in this sector were generally small and financially weak.

The government and education market was made up of several similar submarkets that have a common not-for-profit mission, public accountability, restrictive purchasing and contract regulations and laws, and special accounting-standards setting bodies (GASB for governments and school boards, NACUBO for colleges and universities).

Government and education administrators tended to be risk-adverse, as their actions were subject to public scrutiny. This resulted in the frequent use of consultants to advise in systems selection. Requests for proposals were responded to under formal rules that made it difficult to sell directly to the decision maker.

EXHIBIT B

EDGE TECHNOLOGY FOR THE PUBLIC SECTOR

PROVEN LEADING —

INFOTECHNOLOGY FUND ACCOUNTING SYSTEM MODULES

BUDGET AND FINANCE General Ledger/Fund Accounting (GAAFR, GASB, AICPA)
- **Budget Preparation**
- **Budget Control**
- **Cost Allocation**
- **Accounting Treatment**

Forecasting and Modeling
- **Budget PC Transfer**

Accounts Payable
Accounts Receivable
Fixed Assets
Job Cost Accounting

MATERIALS AND SERVICES
- **Purchasing** • **Inventory**

HUMAN RESOURCES
- **Payroll** • **Personnel**
- **Position Control**

REPORTING
- **Report Writer**

SECURITY
- **Policy and Security Manager**

APPLICATION DEVELOPMENT
- **SCOPE Video Forms Manager**
- **Clone Application Porting**
- **OmniTrac Information Tracking**

The modular design of the Infotechnology Fund Accounting System enables the customer to select only those modules needed immediately.

ADAPTABLE TO UNIQUE REQUIREMENTS AND CONTROLS

▲ Highly adaptable thirty-five-character account code with up to fifteen dimensions (elements or segments)

▲ Users can define summary accounts and reporting structures

▲ Highly adaptable budgetary controls

SYSTEMS HIGHLIGHST

Integrated planning, execution and control

Handles complex accounting requirements

▲ Multiple fiscal years, multiple budgets, unlimited years of transactions and balance history and multiple statistics

▲ Concurrent full-accrual, modified-accrual, and cash basis accounting

▲ Grant accounting and management

▲ Cost allocation

INFOTECHNOLOGY, INC.

Infotechnology, Inc. provides its Fund Accounting System to state and local governments, school districts, higher education institutions and other not-for-profit organizations. Infotechnology is distinctive because the staff includes professionals who are former public administrators from federal, state and local governments and higher education. Infotechnology's experience in public sector finance, administration and information systems is crucial to understanding the customer's special requirements of fund accounting and budgetary control.

Infotechnology has worked with numerous public sector organizations to improve the productivity of their financial and administration systems, and has the understanding and experience required to make implementations successful as well as making integrated financial software productive for public sector organizations.

Generally, a matrix was used by which bidders were rated on such items as functionality, price, technical ability of system, strength of the vendor, and so on.

According to Infotechnology's business plan, the successful vendor in such a market saw these apparent problems as an opportunity. The key was to identify target clients and get to know them before a formal evaluation process began. Infotechnology believed that because its management team was composed of former government systems and administrative executives, the firm had an advantage. They knew how to deal with organizations such as the Government Finance Officers Association, the National Association of State Auditors, and so on. By maintaining a high profile in market-related organizations, the firm could ensure the opportunity to compete for business from a position of strength and trust.

Within the public sector, Stevens's group identified three market segments for both products and customers: mainframe, midrange, and micro/personal computers. The characteristics of these markets were as follows.

Mainframe

Large-scale computer applications were targeted to Fortune 1000 companies, large governments, and other large organizations. These systems were generally associated with expensive set-up, operation, and maintenance costs, were generally user-unfriendly, and had slow response times to user needs. Producers of mainframes are fairly concentrated in a handful of large producers, such as IBM and Digital. These firms were believed to have little interest in the midrange market, especially the public sector segment. Conversely, the midrange segment appeared to have little interest in mainframes due to the high level of expense and limited software applications.

Midrange

This market typically involved medium to small business applications. The public sector was believed to be 8 to 10 years behind the private sector in this segment in terms of accepting packaged software. This segment represented the bulk of the total market, with 81,000 potential customers. With no dominant vendor, this market was fragmented and characterized by functionally weak products that were technically outdated. These systems had recently benefited from significant price performance advancements encouraging mainframe users to switch to the easier-to-use midrange systems.

Micro

Personal computer applications were for home, business, and other organizations of all sizes. Usually this market implied single-user oriented although local area networks and other enhancements were making more sophisticated applications possible. Generally this market was not considered viable for Infotechnology nor was it a threat to its target market.

INFOTECHNOLOGY'S MARKET

Infotechnology was developed to serve the midrange customer. Stevens pointed to several factors that supported this decision:

- While with ABA, Stevens noted the shift among users from large, expensive mainframes to more flexible midrange systems.
- IBM's introduction of the AS/400 system and the trend toward using packaged software were stimulating interest in this segment. The tremendous growth in usage of the AS/400 enhanced Infotechnology's own market share as a compatible product.
- Various studies done by consulting firms such as Touche/Ross had determined that 80 percent of the public sector used in-house-developed automated account systems.
- Only three firms competed for the remaining 20 percent of the market.
- The increasing cost of maintenance of the old applications, the changing technology, and the growing influence of the Government Accounting Standards Board were expected to encourage municipalities strongly to upgrade their accounting systems, switching from home-grown systems to price-efficient packaged software systems within the next five years.
- The projected market for the services such as Infotechnology offered was estimated to be 81,000 users. Of these, one-third of those surveyed planned to replace their current finance systems within two years.
- Industry analysts anticipated an annual market growth rate of 20 percent for the foreseeable future.
- The founders of Infotechnology believed that a group of a mere 500 clients would produce a profitable organization.

INFOTECHNOLOGY'S MARKET STRATEGY

- Infotechnology opted to develop a multiplatform product, i.e., one that would operate on both the VAX and the AS/400, to allow for maximum market penetration.

- The firm specifically chose these mainstream platforms to ensure its accessibility to the vast majority of users.
- The firm preferred developing long-term, presale/preproposal relationships with potential customers to facilitate sales and used a limited amount of advertising in specialty journals.
- Infotechnology's staff included former public administrators, to enhance relationships with customers.

DISTRIBUTION

The typical and only appropriate distribution channel for midrange application software was a direct sales force. The decisions were major ones, and the sales were consultative in nature, involving many people. Postsales support was critical to building a reference base and maintaining a close working relationship with the client. Some vendors had tried distributing through "Big Six" consulting firms, but with generally poor results.

COMPETITION

The current competitors in the government software market were numerous. Yet each one had significant limitation in the midrange market. Again, competitive threats may be divided into two areas: mainframe vendors and midrange vendors.

Mainframe Vendors

Mainframe vendors are large national companies such as D&B Software. D&B and American Management Systems had approximately 14 percent of the mainframe government finance and administrative applications. Six percent was held by a number of smaller firms. The remaining 80 percent of the market consisted of in-house-developed systems. This market was considered relatively immature. Consequently, vendors were expected to continue to focus on these products.

Midrange Vendors

Midrange competitors were typically small regional or local companies that either did not focus specifically on government or did not offer packages as an adjunct to their consulting or turn-key business. Most of them either specialized in a particular vertical application, such as police or courts, and had a good product or offered a wide range of applications characterized by weak products and obsolete technology. There was no dominant midrange vendor. Some of the large vendors in the mainframe market did, however, compete in the midrange arena. Andrews

Software, a company with $100 million in sales, for example, had recently recognized the potential of the government market and had hired some government-experienced people. Their software was considered to be inferior to Infotechnology's, however.

INFOTECHNOLOGY AFTER APRIL 1992

As planned, Infotechnology used the capital infusion from Technology Systems to port its products to the AS/400 system. However, much to everyone's surprise, sales did not expand at the rate expected. John Gifford, Vice President of Finance at Technology Systems (the Atlanta investing company) explained.

> In retail, everyone talks about location, location, location. In new ventures, the thing we look at is management, management, management. Infotechnology has a great management team, and that is specifically why we invested in them. (See Exhibit C). But almost as soon as they changed the platform on their products, a number of things changed. Suddenly sales that we thought were done deals fell through. The sales process in the public sector is a long, drawn-out process where each firm is reviewed on a matrix. The matrix consists of things such as functionality, price, size and financial strength of the vendor, number of minorities in the vendor's firm, etc. Infotechnology was winning the functionality portion of the bids hands down. No one can produce as good a product as they can. But suddenly competitors were bidding literally half as much for the contract. When our bid is $400,000 and a competitor comes in at $195,000, functionality just goes out the window.
>
> Furthermore, Infotechnology is a small company. One of its competitors is a $100 million company which has been around for 30 years. It will never be perceived to be as stable as that firm. We see its competitors to be divided into two groups. There are the really big companies that sell the expensive high-end products. These companies are like the one just described, established with a long list of installations and solid financials. At the other extreme is a group of firms which sell what we call "shrink-wrap" software. Their products have about 90 percent of the functionality of Infotechnology's but at about 10 percent of the price. How can a government agency in the midst of budget deficits justify buying a $300,000 system when it can get a system, which doesn't do it all but does a lot, for $30,000? Then there is Infotechnology, caught right in the middle.

John Stevens, Infotechnology's president, gave a slightly different explanation.

> I think the economy has a lot to do with our current situation. When we got into the public sector, there really were no competitors. However, once the software market started to go bad, everyone started to scramble for any piece of business that was available. People who never would have even attempted to sell in the public sector, people who really don't even understand this market, are walking in with extremely low bids. In virtually every case, we're told that our product was clearly superior. Our contacts really wanted our system, but they just couldn't justify the price. We go in thinking that we're placing a competitive bid only to find that our competitor has underbid us by as much as $200,000. What do you do in that situation? Should we give away the software to get the service contract and hope the revenues are there to support us?

EXHIBIT C

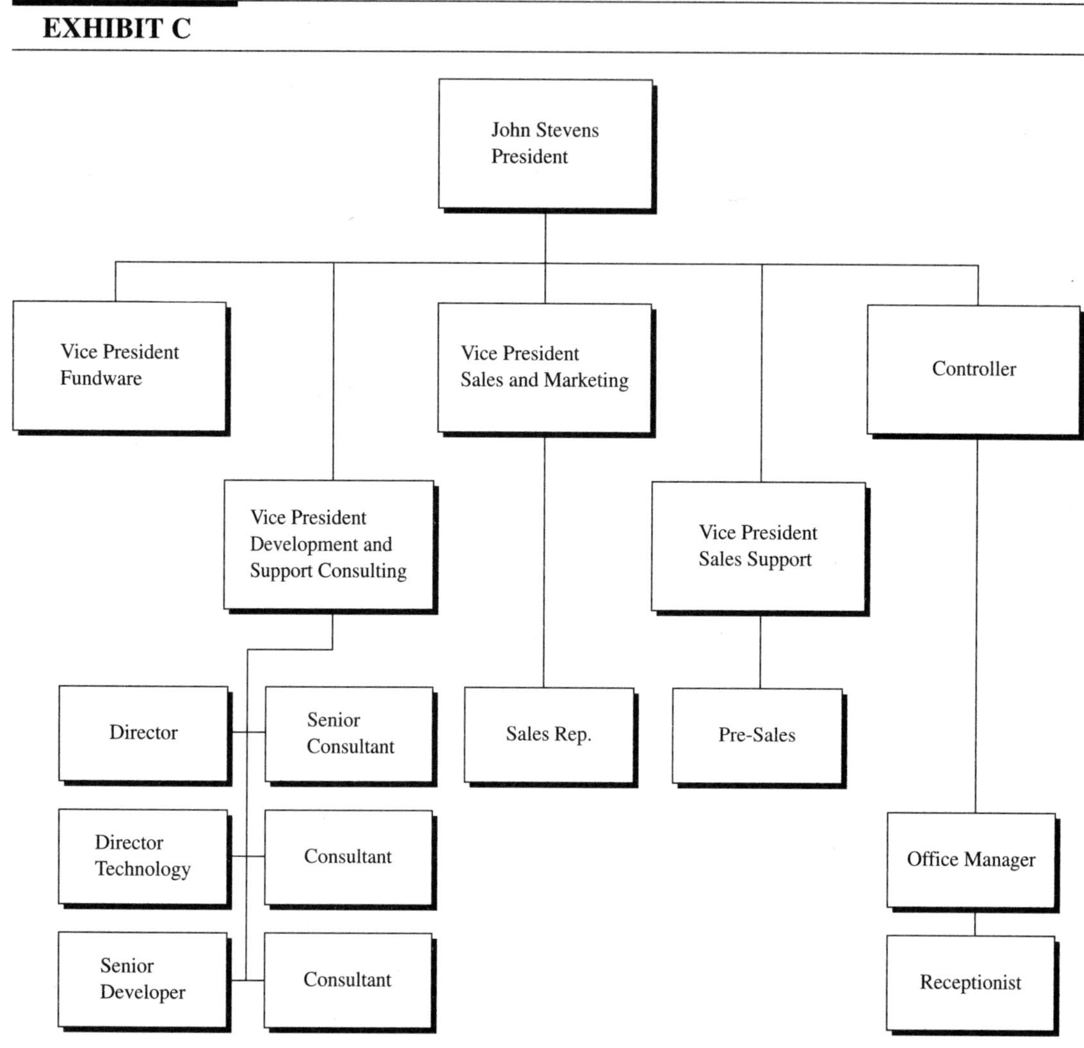

In addition to the added competition in the public sector, is the issue of budget deficits. A lot of municipalities that we expected to upgrade from "home-grown" systems have not invested in new systems. This is largely due to budget constraints. The changes in the accounting requirements also didn't have the impact we thought they would.

Another issue that we didn't expect was the inability of the market to recognize the value of our systems. The AS/400 was designed as a cost-efficient way of gaining the advantages of a mainframe system without having to invest in a mainframe. Although we missed part of the wave as it was introduced years before we could get our product ported, we still caught a good portion of the wave. The real problem is that a lot of the

> current AS/400 purchasers are former PC users. These people were used to the software prices normally associated with PCs. That software is nowhere near what we charge for a program.

In addition to the above problems, Stevens estimated that it cost his firm an average of $30,000 to bid on a project (the cost of proposals, demos, travel, etc.). This cost was particularly important when considering the pricing structure. Stevens mentioned the difficulty in justifying a selling price of $30 or $40 thousand given the $30,000 cost per bid. "What happens when we lose two or three bids to win one?" In addition, there was the licensing agreement with CDC. By contract, Infotechnology had to remit 50 percent of software revenues to CDC. If prices were cut, the impact on CDC had to be considered. Nevertheless, even though CDC does not benefit from the revenues associated with other Infotechnology services (i.e., consulting), CDC had been fairly cooperative with the firm on the pricing issue.

Cooperation by CDC, however, may not have been out of pure benevolence. Stevens mentioned some difficulties encountered with CDC. The original agreement had been designed with the intent of making Infotechnology an independent sales and marketing firm for CDC, which would provide the basic product under license and the necessary customer service support. However, due to financial difficulties and modifications made by Infotechnology, CDC was unable to provide satisfactory service support. As a result, Infotechnology had found it necessary to hire its own consulting and service staff. In addition, the alliance with CDC was supposed to provide the image of an established operation. The fact that CDC currently bordered on bankruptcy severely undermined this image.

AN OUTSIDE VIEW

Kirk Wilhelm, CEO of Palmetto Software and a member of the Infotechnology Board of Directors, asserted his diagnosis of the situation.

> The situation at Infotechnology has a lot to do with how they market the product. They have a customer which is represented by several individuals, all of whom have expertise in certain areas. The decision to purchase any new system is based on the aggregate opinions of all these individuals. Most of these people have a tremendous fear of making the wrong decision and, therefore, tend to be very conservative in their decision making. As they say, 'No one ever got fired by buying IBM equipment.'
>
> Infotechnology is never going to be able to compete on financial stability; their competitors are just too large and established. But they do have a superior product. They need to seek out the functionality expert and get that individual to champion their product to the other decision makers. That is what their competitors are doing to them. Their competitors are finding the people responsible for looking at the number of installations and financial stability and pointing out Infotechnology's shortcomings in those areas. Infotechnology is presenting a bid and then throwing its hands up and saying 'You can't influence these people; it's a matrix purchase decision. Here is our bid; let us know if you want to buy.' They just aren't aggressive enough.

BACKED AGAINST THE WALL

Whatever the reasons for the problems, the firm needed a solution soon, as the situation was becoming critical. John Stevens realized that the company he had formed less than three years ago was at a crisis point. Infotechnology had to cover approximately $50 to $75 thousand in monthly cash expenses just to stay in business. Although Infotechnology's monthly revenues from its service and consulting business generated $50 thousand, Infotechnology still had to sell $50 thousand in software in order to stay above water. Of that $50 thousand, $25 thousand would go to CDC. But while staff members were consulting, they weren't selling new systems. Thus, the pipeline was bound to dry up without new sales.

Stevens commented that the early success of the firm was largely due to the staff's ability to focus on sales. They had relied on CDC to service and were, therefore, able to generate a lot of new business. Having to focus on both sales and service was significantly impeding their long-term performance. Compounding this was the reduction in service revenues. "We've had to release about half of our staff or more because we just didn't have the work to support them. Basically, we're living month to month trying to get enough revenue in to cover our expenses."

Stevens knew that software sales in the short-term were unlikely. Although there were currently three deals in the works, only one deal in Virginia seemed probable. Still, given the matrix purchasing system, even the Virginia deal couldn't be counted on. After all, Infotechnology had lost many deals in the past which were thought to be "in the bag."

By Stevens's calculations, if no software sales were made within the next 60 to 90 days, Infotechnology would have to fold. Given this dismal outlook, Stevens had to convince his investors to fund Infotechnology in the short-term in order to benefit from possible opportunities in the long-term. In other words, Stevens needed to identify both a feasible and enticing long-term option. Stevens had to bring to the table an option that would overcome the investors' negative perceptions of Infotechnology's recent performance.

THE OPTIONS

Stevens had to move quickly. He called a meeting of his senior management for the following week. Here, Stevens would present four long-term options. Hopefully, Stevens thought, the management team would identify the most feasible of the four options or would come up with either some sort of a combination of options or a completely new option. One option would be presented to the investors shortly thereafter.

In preparation for next week's meeting, Stevens began to write out each strategic option:

(1) *Align with Johnson Corporation (a payroll provider)*
Stevens has been intermittently speaking with Johnson Corporation over the past year about creating a merger or an alliance. Johnson Corporation was an established provider of payroll software in the commercial market and supported annual revenues of over $6 million.

The alliance would make sense in that Johnson's payroll software package was somewhat of a natural addition to Infotechnology's accounting software. Also, the alliance would give each company access to the other's market (private and public). For Infotechnology, this could make strategic sense, given that most of Infotechnology's larger competitors offered payroll software and also had marketing channels in both private and public markets. The downside of such an alliance was the question of synergy between the two companies, which had two different products serving two different markets. Also, there was the question of whether Infotechnology, in its current financial straits, could negotiate an advantageous merger or alliance agreement.

(2) *Sell Infotechnology to one of the larger competitors*
One of the industry's largest competitors had once expressed an interest in purchasing Infotechnology. The experience of Infotechnology's staff combined with the functionality of the software could make a valuable addition to such a company and, at the same time, lessen competition. Stevens, however, was not too enthusiastic about such an option. After all, he had started Infotechnology in order to break away from ABA. By selling Infotechnology and his talents to another larger company, Stevens would effectively be right back where he started.

(3) *Reorganize Infotechnology to a service/consulting company*
Such an option would eliminate the focus of selling CDC software in the unpredictable public market, and Infotechnology could focus on a more stable and less costly revenue stream. The downside to this option was that it might not be that appealing to investors. The return might not be significant enough to permit additional investment.

(4) *Break out on own*
CDC had not performed as agreed in the software licensing arrangement. As a result, Infotechnology had to build its own consulting and service staff. Therefore, Infotechnology could simply break the licensing agreement and continue its present operations without having to remit 50 percent of the revenues to CDC. However, such an option could have uncertain legal ramifications. Moreover, even if such an option were undertaken, Infotechnology would still have to develop a feasible long-term market strategy to convince investors.

Stevens sat back in his chair and looked over his list of options. Which option would be best for him and the company yet convince the investors to fund the company in the short-term? Were there any other options?

EPILOGUE

The fall of 1992 was the worst possible time that John Stevens and Infotechnology had ever experienced. Cash flow remained extremely bad as the company struggled from payday to payday. Worst yet, none of the four options actually became available then or during 1993. Although Stevens's first choice was the alignment with the Johnson Corporation and negotiations were pursued, a satisfactory alliance was not consummated. His next choice was to sell Infotechnology to a larger company; however, he was not able to generate any interest among his competitors. Stevens's third choice was to break the deal with CDC, but that required additional capital which he did not have or have access to; in addition, he would end up with the old CDC technology, which was becoming less competitive. Reorganizing Infotechnology into a service/consulting company was his last choice and was not pursued.

In order to meet the company's dire need for cash to make payroll, Stevens arranged for an infusion of $150,000 from his existing stockholders—each investing in proportion to his ownership percentage. That infusion kept the company going until it received its first contract in January-February 1993. Achieving that contract had required a very aggressive bid by Infotechnology against several other bidders. The bidding war continued and Stevens won a second contract shortly thereafter, followed by two major contracts later in 1993. The latter contracts provided Infotechnology with the necessary cash flow to operate and to continue its internal development of new software.

The recovery of Infotechnology was greatly assisted by Stevens's hiring of an IBM retiree who was an expert in sales to governmental clients. Bill Jones had 27 years of public sector experience; he knew the selling side of the business and was himself a good businessman. Stevens had become acquainted with Jones a year or two earlier when IBM and Infotechnology were associated in a selling activity to a client. Stevens had offered him a job upon his retirement from IBM, but Jones wanted a year off to travel.

Stevens was able to save Infotechnology by taking drastic measures, cutting expenses to the bone. A major move was the reduction of employees across the board; according to Stevens: "I had no choice!" Staff was cut from 23 employees in mid-1992 to 12 persons in the early fall of 1993. As a consequence of staff reduction and increased sales by two to three times, Infotechnology experience a turnaround and achieved profitability in 1993.

The turnaround in the general economy in 1993 was also beneficial to Infotechnology. The natures of both clients and competitors changed. The large software companies that had invaded the public sector market backed off and returned to their private sector client base. But more smaller software competitors entered the public sector market and started introducing "client server software," to which Infotechnology had to respond. According to Stevens, each bid process involved different competitors. At the same time, client requirements and their budgets loosened up somewhat such that the pricing competition was not as bad as in 1992.

For Infotechnology, the public sector remains its best customer prospect because small software companies can still play in that market. The larger companies once again primarily bid for the larger deals of the private sector market. For all types of software products, the public sector consists of approximately 43,000 potential buyers—ranging from large cities like New York to small municipalities. At average product prices of $50,000 to $75,000, this market size is billions of dollars.

According to Stevens, there are approximately 2,000 users of large mainframe systems and 38,000 prospects for smaller systems. The midrange user group consists of 6,000 to 8,000 prospects, which are the targets for Infotechnology's products. Many of the former mainframe users have shifted down to the midrange (e.g. the AS/400) and these are now customer prospects. Yet many of the former midrange users have shifted down to the PC. As a consequence, there has developed considerable turmoil in both suppliers and users; the software companies are, therefore, aligning themselves to both the midrange and the PC hardware.

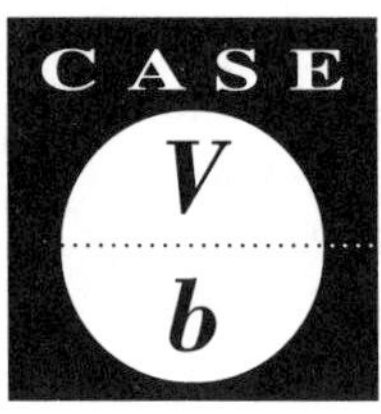

Dual Pane Company

John Grayson had been in the housing restoration business for 15 years when, in 1984, he designed a machine that could remove old windows from their frames without destroying the wooden panes around the glass known as muntins and mullions (See Exhibit 1). One of the big advantages of the tool is that it was built around a routing drill piece that moved on a three-dimensional plane. This allowed Grayson to replace windows that up until then could not be serviced. Once the small panes were removed, they would be replaced by one large pane of double glass. The muntins and mullions would be inserted over the window to give it the same look as before.

He applied for a patent as soon as he realized his machine was unique, and it was granted in August 1985. He has been operating the business since that time under the name of Dual Pane Company. He and his wife Elizabeth are the sole owners and employees of the company. She oversees the advertising and promotional aspects, and John does the actual installing. They both engage in the selling process, particularly in the colder months when the actual installation business is slower. Their current geographic market is the Boston area, although they have done business outside it. They generally have concentrated on the residential market, although they have had a couple of commercial jobs.

The restoration market is affected by several factors, such as the state of the overall economy, employment, and disposable income. Since the company began operations, the economy has been favorable. The GNP has been increasing, real disposable income has risen moderately, and there has been a decrease in unemployment in the Boston area. The restoration of windows is a relatively large expense, costing between $3,000 and $7,000, depending on the number of windows installed in the house. Homeowners are more likely to invest in this type of restoration when their level of net disposable income is greater and when the economy is good. Today, there is a trend toward less saving on the part of many Americans, and consumers are tending to borrow for expenditures like housing restorations. Therefore, the level of interest rates affects Dual Pane's business. Fortunately, interest rates have been low recently, so consumers have been able to afford such restorations.

Another factor that affects the restoration market is the cost of energy. In the late 1970s, the energy crisis forced many people to see energy as a limited resource. Since that time, people have generally tried to conserve energy. Consumers are faced with finding alternative sources of energy to heat and cool their homes and offices. This concern with conservation gives Dual Pane an advantage in that they are replacing single-pane noninsulated windows with energy-efficient dual-pane insulated windows.

EXHIBIT 1

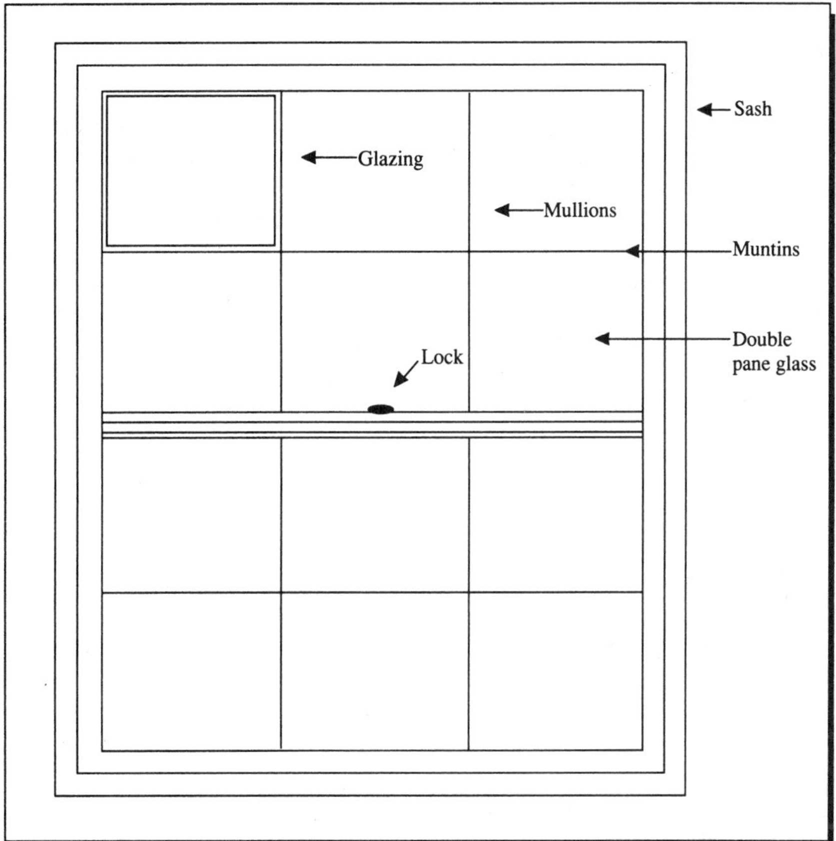

Because of the favorable economy and Dual Pane's unique method of installing double-pane glass, the Graysons have had more business than they can handle. They have advertised in the Yellow Pages and have sent direct mail to the subscribers of a regional home improvement magazine. Their customers have referred their friends to the Graysons, so business has expanded considerably. John has two ideas on how to handle his growing business. He could hire and train a staff of salespeople and installers, or he could franchise his business. He enjoyed the selling and the actual installing of the windows, but neither he nor his wife were interested in managing a staff of workers. Therefore, franchising was more appealing to him. He felt that one of Dual Pane's big advantages was the patented cutting tool, and he could bring the name Dual Pane to more customers if he franchised the business. Several contractors he contacted had expressed an interest in the Dual Pane machine and wondered if he intended to franchise the business.

John's goal was to franchise the business. There were three groups of people he could contact regarding franchising. First, he could sell the rights of the product to contractors who were in the business of restoring residential homes or commercial offices. He felt that their reach with consumers could help to broaden the exposure of the Dual Pane name. He also thought that glass companies in the Boston area might be interested in a Dual Pane franchise. Since his tool could cut odd-shaped glass, it had an advantage over existing methods, which glass companies would benefit from. Elizabeth mentioned that individuals who wanted to get into the restoration business might also be potential targets for franchising.

John needed to know how to go about franchising the business. What kind of legalities were involved? He knew that he had patent protection on the machine, but what kind of procedures should he follow in terms of setting up guidelines for owning a Dual Pane franchise? Which group should he target for franchising? How much should the franchise cost? He wanted to sell his franchise to the group or groups that would give the Dual Pane name the most exposure and continue to emphasize the quality of the work. How should he proceed?

Auto Fresh, Inc.

Two businessmen, Tom Duncan and Carl Bont, purchased both Auto Fresh Inc. and Car Wash Supplies and Accessories Inc. in 1982. The company sells coin-operated fragrance dispensers and fragrances to the car wash industry.

So far, the business has been operating at a loss. The dispenser costs $430 to manufacture and sells to the car wash owner for $1,300. Duncan and Bont feel that the company could do better and are interested in expanding its sales in order to make a profit. They feel that fragrances can be sold at twice their cost to the car wash owner. The owners feel the key to financial success is expanding sales.

Duncan and Bont would also like to market their product at gasoline stations and convenience stores and need to know how the expanded costs of production and marketing will affect projected revenues. The following is the business plan they prepared for Auto Fresh.

EXECUTIVE SUMMARY

Car Wash Supplies and Accessories, Inc. is a manufacturer of coin-operated fragrance dispensers. Auto Fresh, Inc. is a marketing and sales organization that is responsible for distributing the coin-operated fragrance dispensers and fragrances to dispenser owners. Both corporations are owned and operated by two businessmen and veterinarians in Muskogee, Oklahoma, who purchased the business from its founder in 1982. Although they are two separate companies, the business was set up so that Car Wash Supplies and Accessories manufactured the machines and then sold them to Auto Fresh, which was then responsible for marketing and selling them. In theory, these two operations were viewed by the owners as one enterprise.

Currently, they manufacture one dispenser model, which for 50 or 75 cents allows the customer a selection of four fragrances to perfume the interior of his or her auto. The sale price of the dispenser is $1,000 to the distributor and about $1,300 to the car wash owner. The same dispenser costs about $430 to manufacture. Fragrance cost is about $7.50 per gallon to Auto Fresh and sells to the car wash owner for $15. This will allow 512 applications.

Working through a network of distributors, Auto Fresh sells nationwide. They currently have concentrated on the car wash industry as the primary market. Looking ahead, the management hopes to expand the market to include gasoline stations and convenience stores. With this move, they are considering adding other vending equipment to complement their line.

THE PRODUCT

As one half of its business Auto Fresh sells a coin-operated vending machine that dispenses fragrances for use in cars. It is a relatively simple device with four fragrance selections and a fluorescent-lighted bubbler display. The applicator gun is made of steel and aluminum and is meant to withstand abuse such as cars and trucks running over it. It is designed to be weather resistant, tamper resistant, and reliable.

The second half of Auto Fresh's product line is a full line of oil-based fragrances.

Manufacturing and Packaging

The dispensers require few technological and capital resources. Production is more of an assembly operation than a manufacturing operation. The simple technology and limited capital expenditure make it an easy industry to enter. The fragrances require minimal investment due to a short delivery time.

Future Growth

Currently under consideration is the expansion of the product line into combination units; for example, fragrance/water machines or fragrance/air machines.

THE INDUSTRY

The fragrance dispenser industry began about a decade ago when three men came up with the idea. Each went on to establish a business that would manufacture and distribute coin-operated fragrance dispensers. All three of the businesses remain today, but two are under new management. One of those is Auto Fresh.

Typically, fragrance dispensers are sold to and associated with the car wash industry. They are sold as an additional profit center for the already established car wash. Many car washes are unattended, or "Mom and Pop" type operations. The car wash owners want equipment that works. Another segment of the fragrance market is the commercial application in detail shops or large car washes. The fragrance is applied by an employee of the car wash for a fee, at the customer's request.

The 1985 International Car Wash Association/National Car Wash Council Member Directory lists 86 manufacturers, suppliers, and distributors of air freshener/scent dispensers, including Auto Fresh and Car Wash Supplies and Accessories. According to the management of Auto Fresh, very few of the 86 listed are true manufacturers of coin-operated dispensers. In fact, it appears that Car Wash Supplies and Accessories is one of only three manufacturers of coin-operated fragrances in the United States.

Competition

Auto Fresh's competition in the fragrance industry is two similar companies, Aquarius Industries, Inc., and Car Fresh Manufacturing.

Car Fresh, located in Pine Bluff, Arkansas, is Auto Fresh's primary competitor. Car Fresh operates at the top end of the market. Generally, the company prices its machines higher than both Auto Fresh and Aquarius. It dispenses a water-based substance, giving the customer a choice of two fragrances. Like the machine, the fragrance Car Fresh sells is more expensive than that of its competitors. The management stresses the quality of the product in all aspects of their marketing plan.

No competitor has branched out of the industry's traditional market of car washes. Accordingly, if Auto Fresh chooses to seek additional markets, the competition from other companies will be minimal.

Sales Predictions

Traditionally, the fragrance industry and Auto Fresh have limited the fragrance market to car wash establishments. However, because of the nature of the product, it can be installed in any parking lot. Some obvious possibilities are gasoline stations, shopping centers, and convenience stores. The magnitude of the market potential is staggering.

According to the 1982 Census of Service Industries, the United States had a surprising 5,446 car washes in that year, with total receipts of $856 million. These car washes had an average annual dollar receipt of $157,000.

These figures differ substantially from the estimate of the International Car Wash Association/National Car Wash Council (ICA/NCC), which estimates that there are 22,000 car washes in the United States. The actual figure, no doubt, falls somewhere in the middle. The large discrepancy is due to the definition of car wash. (By the census definition, only businesses whose primary function is washing cars are included.)

A second market is the gasoline service station. In 1982, there were 116,000 service stations in the United States, compared to 148,000 in 1977. This represented a 21 percent drop in the number of stations. Just as dramatic was the huge increase in revenue over that same period—from $54 billion in 1977 to $95 billion in 1982. Although this tremendous gain in receipts is due primarily to an increase in fuel prices, hidden in the numbers is the remarkable increase in revenue from car washes. Car wash revenue increased from $90 million in 1972 to $190 million in 1982.

Other nonfuel product sales have also prospered over the same period. This confirms what all gasoline consumers can see: Each station has struggled to maintain margins as the refined products industry experienced large swings through the 70s. Each gasoline jobber has been forced to search for a wide variety of high-margin products to be sold along with gasoline, a perfect fit for Auto Fresh. Exhibit 1 calculates the market potential of including sales to service stations.

EXHIBIT 1 Calculated Market Potential

Market potential = Car washes + Service stations (dispensers)
514,398 = (5,466 + 166,000) × 3 bays*
154,319 = 30% market share × 514,398
$154 million = $1,000/unit × 154,319

Market potential = Car wash receipts + Car wash receipts
(Fragrance) (Car washes) (Service stations)
$1,046 billion = $856 million + $190 million
(Total annual income)
$10.46 million = 10% of total annual income
$3.138 million = 30% market share

*Estimate

MARKETING

Distribution

Effective distribution through a group of quality representatives will be an important factor in Auto Fresh's success. Currently, Auto Fresh works through 14 distributors, some active and some inactive. Proper compensation and communication will enhance these representatives' efforts. Encouragement of bulk sales through incentives should be considered.

Sales Strategy

The sales network of quality representatives will be of foremost importance.

Trade magazines and trade shows will continue to be used to increase potential customers' awareness of the product.

Quality of the product must be maintained, and Auto Fresh will back its product accordingly.

Machines need to be placed where they can feed off the traffic of an existing business and where the customer, whose car is an important asset, will travel.

FINANCIAL PROJECTIONS

The following financial package addresses two key issues: cash flow and profitability. It begins with a combined break-even analysis (see Exhibit 2). The first break-even is before interest costs. The break-even in units is 258, indicating that 21.5 units per month must be sold to cover all estimated expenses, before interest. This figure excludes the revenue from the sale of any fragrance.

EXHIBIT 2 Auto Fresh—Car Wash Supplies and Accessories—Combined Break-Even Analysis

	Annual	*Annual*	*Monthly*	*Monthly*
Break-even before interest				
Dispensers only (units)	258	$258,000	21.50	$21,500
Fragrance only (gallons)	21,757	326,355	1,813.00	27,196
75% dispensers	194	194,000	16.16	16,166
25% fragrance	5,434	81,585	452.83	6,798
		$275,585		$21,964
Break-even after interest				
Dispensers only (units)	291	$291,000	24.25	$24,250
Fragrance only (gallons)	24,582	368,000	2,048.50	30,728
75% dispensers	218	218,000	18.16	18,167
25% fragrance	6,154	92,000	512.83	7,667
		$310,000		$25,834
Cash break-even				
Dispensers only (units)	279	$279,000	23.25	$23,250
Fragrance only (gallons)	23,510	176,325	1,959.00	14,693
75% dispensers	209	209,000	17.40	17,417
25% fragrance	5,878	44,081	489.90	3,673
		$253,081		$21,090

Assumptions:
—Sales price per dispenser $1,000, gross profit $632
—Sales price per gallon of fragrance $15.00, gross profit $7.50
—Interest cost 13% on $163,000
—Combined operating expenses $163,176
—Depreciation $8,040

The next exhibits indicate both cash flow and profitability. The "Pro Forma Income and Cash Flow" statements break Auto Fresh and Car Wash Supplies and Accessories into two entities. The division of costs between the two is derived from estimates by the companies' management based on historical information. Exhibit 3 is the pro forma income statement for Car Wash Supplies and Accessories, and Exhibit 4 is the pro forma income statement for Auto Fresh. These are summarized in Exhibit 5, by including interest expenses and debt payments.

The gross profit on the dispensers is split somewhat arbitrarily. Car Wash can produce each dispenser for $368 (material cost). These units are sold to Auto Fresh for $715. Auto Fresh sells each dispenser for $1,000. Fragrance sales are found on the Auto Fresh income statement only.

The sources and uses of cash are obtained by calculating inventory, accounts receivable, and accounts payable levels for each month end. Forty dispensers were on hand January 1, 1986. Accounts receivable and accounts payable were assumed to be zero. Specifics concerning operating expenses are indicated in Exhibit 6, salaries in Exhibit 7, and bulk sales in Exhibit 8.

EXHIBIT 3

CAR WASH SUPPLIES AND ACCESSORIES
Pro Forma Income and Cash Flow Statement

	1986			*FYE 1985*
	January 1 mo.	*February 1 mo.*	*March 1 mo.*	*March 31 3 mos.*
Sales—machines	$ 7,150	$10,725	$10,725	$28,600
Material cost	3,680	5,520	5,520	14,720
Gross profit	3,470	5,205	5,205	13,880
Operating expenses	7,477	7,477	7,477	22,431
Operating income	(4,007)	(2,272)	(2,272)	(8,551)
Sources of cash				
Decrease in accounts receivable	0	0	0	0
Decrease in inventory	3,680	5,520	5,520	14,720
Increase in accounts payable	4,906	0	2,862	7,768
Depreciation	650	650	650	1,950
Total cash in	5,229	3,898	9,032	18,159
Uses of cash				
Increase accounts receivable	9,533	2,383	795	12,711
Increase inventory	0	0	0	0
Decrease accounts payable	0	1,298	0	1,298
Capital expenditures	0	0	0	0
Total cash out	9,533	3,681	795	14,009
Change in cash	(4,304)	217	8,237	4,150
Dispensers sold	10	15	15	40
Accounts receivable	9,533	11,916	17,777	17,777
Inventory—dispensers	14,400	9,200	3,680	3,680
Accounts payable	4,906	3,680	6,542	6,542

	First Quarter 1986		
	April 1 mo.	*May 1 mo.*	*June 1 mo.*
Sales—machines	$17,875	$25,025	$32,175
Material cost	9,200	12,880	16,560
Gross profit	8,675	12,145	15,615
Operating expenses	8,477	7,476	7,476
Operating income	198	4,669	8,139
Sources of cash			
Decrease in accounts receivable	0	2,450	0
Decrease in inventory	0	0	0
Increase in accounts payable	1,431	3,067	2,323
Depreciation	650	650	650
Total cash in	2,081	10,926	11,112
Uses of cash			
Increase accounts receivable	3,230	0	3,962
Increase inventory	3,450	2,070	2,323
Decrease accounts payable	0	0	0
Capital expenditures	0	0	0

EXHIBIT 3 *(continued)*

CAR WASH SUPPLIES AND ACCESSORIES
Pro Forma Income and Cash Flow Statement
First Quarter 1986

	April *1 mo.*	*May* *1 mo.*	*June* *1 mo.*
Total cash out	6,680	2,070	6,285
Change in cash	(4,401)	8,856	4,827
Dispensers sold	25	35	45
Accounts receivable	21,666	19,126	23,088
Inventory—dispensers	8,970	11,040	13,363
Accounts payable	7,973	9,813	11,872

Second Quarter 1986

	July *1 mo.*	*August* *1 mo.*	*September* *1 mo.*
Sales—machines	$35,750	$39,325	$42,900
Material cost	18,400	20,240	22,080
Gross profit	17,350	19,085	20,820
Operating expenses	7,476	8,676	8,676
Operating income	9,874	10,406	12,144
Sources of cash			
Decrease in accounts receivable	0	0	0
Decrease in inventory	0	0	0
Increase in accounts payable	1,809	1,662	1,566
Depreciation	650	650	650
Total cash in	12,333	12,713	14,360
Uses of cash			
Increase accounts receivable	3,512	3,229	3,041
Increase inventory	33	3,870	1,762
Decrease accounts payable	0	0	0
Capital expenditures	1,000	0	0
Total cash out	4,545	7,099	4,803
Change in cash	7,788	5,574	9,557
Dispensers sold	50	55	60
Accounts receivable	26,600	29,829	32,870
Inventory—dispensers	13,396	17,266	19,028
Accounts payable	13,686	15,348	16,914

Third Quarter 1986

	October *1 mo.*	*November* *1 mo.*	*December* *1 mo.*
Sales—machines	$46,475	$50,050	$53,625
Material cost	23,920	25,760	27,600
Gross profit	22,555	24,290	26,025
Operating expenses	8,676	8,676	8,676

EXHIBIT 3 *(continued)*

CAR WASH SUPPLIES AND ACCESSORIES
Pro Forma Income and Cash Flow Statement
Third Quarter 1986

	October 1 mo.	*November 1 mo.*	*December 1 mo.*
Operating income	13,879	15,614	17,349
Sources of cash			
Decrease in accounts receivable	0	0	0
Decrease in inventory	0	0	646
Increase in accounts payable	1,498	3,435	0
Depreciation	650	650	650
Total cash in	16,027	19,695	18,645
Uses of cash			
Increase accounts receivable	3,000	2,874	2,737
Increase inventory	1,685	3,864	0
Decrease accounts payable	0	0	575
Capital expenditures	0	0	1,000
Total cash out	4,685	6,738	4,312
Change in cash	11,342	12,961	14,333
Dispensers sold	65	70	75
Accounts receivable	35,780	38,654	41,391
Inventory—dispensers	20,713	24,577	23,931
Accounts payable	18,412	21,847	21,272

Fourth Quarter 1986

	January 1 mo.	*February 1 mo.*	*March 1 mo.*	*FYE 1986 March 31, 1987 3 mos.*
Sales—machines	$57,200	$60,775	$64,350	$525,025
Material cost	29,440	31,280	33,120	270,480
Gross profit	27,760	29,495	31,230	254,545
Operating expenses	8,676	8,676	8,676	100,313
Operating income	19,084	20,819	22,554	154,232
Sources of cash				
Decrease in accounts receivable	0	0	0	2,540
Decrease in inventory	0	0	0	0
Increase in accounts payable	8,579	0	1,179	26,549
Depreciation	650	650	650	7,800
Total cash in	28,313	21,469	24,383	191,121
Uses of cash				
Increase accounts receivable	2,633	2,690	2,606	33,514
Increase inventory	1,344	4,503	1,327	26,231
Decrease accounts payable	0	3,382	0	3,382
Capital expenditures	0	0	0	2,000
Total cash out	3,977	10,575	3,933	65,127
Change in cash	24,336	10,894	20,450	125,994

EXHIBIT 3 *(concluded)*

CAR WASH SUPPLIES AND ACCESSORIES
Pro Forma Income and Cash Flow Statement

	1986			*FYE*
	January 1 mo.	*February 1 mo.*	*March 1 mo.*	*1986 March 31, 1987 3 mos.*
Dispensers sold	80	85	90	735
Accounts receivable	44,024	46,714	49,320	49,320
Inventory—dispensers	24,275	29,778	31,105	31,105
Accounts payable	29,851	26,469	27,648	6,542

On the basis of these numbers, it is clear that these operations have sufficient margins to become very profitable. Sales and the ability to finance these are the keys.

ORGANIZATION

Auto Fresh and Car Wash Supplies and Accessories are corporations, with ownership being split evenly between Tom Duncan and Carl Bont. While Auto Fresh is basically a marketing company handling the sale of dispensers and fragrances, Car Wash Supplies and Accessories manufactures the fragrance dispensers and purchases all the fragrances used by Auto Fresh.

Despite these two corporations' functional differences, facilities, employees, and responsibilities are shared. From a practical standpoint, the key organization is Auto Fresh, which has the responsibility of selling and marketing the product line.

As a closely held company, the owners have ultimate responsibility and decision-making power. Generally, they handle strategic planning and financial control. The financial control of the business includes daily monitoring of cash as well as making banking decisions and arrangements. Strategic planning responsibilities include company direction as well as specific product/market decisions. The general manager and the business manager report to the owners.

The general manager, J. Lawrence Kotz, assumes daily operational control. This includes employee matters, manufacturing, outside sales, purchasing decisions, promotion, and research and development. The general manager has a production manager and six employees on staff.

Correspondingly, the business manager, Donna Reans, handles bookkeeping, receivables, payables, office management, and inside sales. She has one employee on staff. Because these two entities are so interrelated, much of the employees' time is split between the two companies.

EXHIBIT 4

AUTO FRESH, INC.
Pro Forma Income and Cash Flow Statement

	1986			*FYE 1985*
	January 1 mo.	*February 1 mo.*	*March 1 mo.*	*March 31 3 mos.*
Sales—machines	$ 10,000	$15,000	$15,000	$ 40,000
Machine cost	7,150	10,725	10,725	28,600
Gross profit	2,850	4,275	4,275	11,400
Sales—fragrances	3,000	3,000	6,000	12,000
Fragrance cost	1,500	1,500	3,000	6,000
Gross profit	1,500	1,500	3,000	6,000
Operating expenses	15,121	5,121	5,121	25,363
Operating income	(10,771)	654	2,154	(7,963)
Sources of cash				
Decrease in accounts receivable	0	0	0	0
Decrease in fragrance	0	0	0	0
Increase in accounts payable	$ 11,533	$ 2,383	$ 1,461	$ 15,377
Depreciation	20	20	20	60
Total cash in	782	3,057	3,635	5,974
Uses of cash				
Increase accounts receivable	17,333	3,333	2,445	23,111
Increase fragrance	500	0	166	666
Decrease accounts payable	0	0	0	0
Capital expenditures	0	0	0	0
Total cash out	17,833	3,333	2,611	23,777
Change in cash	(17,051)	(276)	(1,024)	(17,803)
Dispensers sold	10	15	15	40
Accounts receivable	17,333	20,660	23,111	23,111
Inventory—fragrance	500	500	666	666
Accounts payable	11,533	15,816	15,377	15,377

First Quarter 1986

	April 1 mo.	*May 1 mo.*	*June 1 mo.*
Sales—machines	$25,000	$35,000	$45,000
Machine costs	17,875	25,025	32,175
Gross profit	7,125	9,975	12,825
Sales—fragrances	7,500	8,000	8,500
Fragrance cost	3,750	4,000	4,250
Gross profit	3,750	4,000	4,250
Operating expenses	6,121	5,121	5,121
Operating income	4,754	8,854	11,954
Sources of cash			
Decrease in accounts receivable	0	0	0
Decrease fragrance	0	0	0
Increase in accounts payable	1,281	4,008	4,272

EXHIBIT 4 *(continued)*

	First Quarter 1986 *April* *1 mo.*	*May* *1 mo.*	*June* *1 mo.*
Depreciation	20	20	20
Total cash in	6,055	12,882	16,246
Uses of cash			
Increase accounts receivable	5,085	6,834	6,222
Increase fragrance	125	110	86
Decrease accounts payable	0	0	0
Capital expenditures	0	0	0
Total cash out	$ 5,210	$ 6,944	$ 6,308
Change in cash	845	5,938	9,938
Dispensers sold	25	35	45
Accounts receivable	28,166	34,000	40,222
Inventory—fragrance	791	900	986
Accounts payable	18,658	22,666	26,938

	Second Quarter 1986 *July* *1 mo.*	*August* *1 mo.*	*September* *1 mo.*
Sales—machines	$50,000	$55,000	$60,000
Machine costs	35,750	39,325	42,900
Gross profit	14,250	15,675	17,100
Sales—fragrances	9,000	9,500	10,000
Fragrance cost	4,500	4,750	5,000
Gross profit	4,500	4,750	5,000
Operating expenses	5,121	6,621	6,121
Operating income	13,629	13,804	15,479
Sources of cash			
Decrease in accounts receivable	0	0	0
Decrease fragrance	0	0	0
Increase in accounts payable	3,857	5,036	3,286
Depreciation	20	20	20
Total cash in	17,506	18,860	18,785
Uses of cash			
Increase accounts receivable	5,492	5,036	4,731
Increase fragrance	73	76	68
Decrease accounts payable	0	0	0
Capital expenditures	1,000	0	0
Total cash out	$ 6,565	$ 5,112	$ 4,799
Change in cash	10,941	13,748	13,986
Dispensers sold	50	55	60
Accounts receivable	45,714	50,750	55,481
Inventory—fragrance	1,057	1,135	1,203
Accounts payable	30,795	34,291	37,577

EXHIBIT 4 *(continued)*

	Third Quarter 1986 *October 1 mo.*	*November 1 mo.*	*December 1 mo.*
Sales—machines	$65,000	$70,000	$75,000
Machine costs	46,475	50,050	53,625
Gross profit	18,525	19,950	21,375
Sales—fragrances	10,500	11,000	11,500
Fragrance cost	5,250	5,500	5,750
Gross profit	5,250	5,500	5,750
Operating expenses	6,621	6,621	6,621
Operating income	17,154	18,829	20,504
Sources of cash			
Decrease in accounts receivable	0	0	0
Decrease fragrance	0	0	0
Increase in accounts payable	3,139	3,032	2,952
Depreciation	20	20	20
Total cash in	20,313	21,881	23,476
Uses of cash			
Increase accounts receivable	4,519	4,363	4,248
Increase fragrance	55	37	52
Decrease accounts payable	0	0	0
Capital expenditures	0	0	0
Total cash out	4,574	4,400	4,300
Change in cash	15,739	17,481	19,176
Dispensers sold	65	70	75
Accounts receivable	60,000	64,363	68,611
Inventory—fragrance	1,258	1,295	1,347
Accounts payable	40,716	43,748	46,700

	Fourth Quarter 1987 *January 1 mo.*	*February 1 mo.*	*March 1 mo.*	*FYE 1986 March 31, 1987 12 mos.*
Sales—machines	$80,000	$85,000	$90,000	$735,000
Machine costs	57,200	60,775	64,350	525,525
Gross profit	22,800	24,225	25,650	209,475
Sales—fragrances	12,000	12,500	13,000	123,000
Fragrance cost	6,000	6,250	6,500	61,500
Gross profit	6,000	6,250	6,500	61,500
Operating expenses	6,621	7,121	7,121	75,452
Operating income	22,179	23,354	25,029	195,523
Sources of cash				
Decrease in accounts receivable	0	0	0	0
Decrease fragrance	0	0	0	0
Increase in accounts payable	2,889	2,841	2,892	39,485
Depreciation	20	20	20	240
Total cash in	25,088	26,215	27,941	235,248

EXHIBIT 4 (*concluded*)

	Fourth Quarter 1987			
	January 1 mo.	*February 1 mo.*	*March 1 mo.*	*FYE 1986 March 31, 1987 12 mos.*
Uses of cash				
Increase accounts receivable	4,158	4,088	4,031	58,807
Increase fragrance	50	49	70	851
Decrease accounts payable	0	0	0	0
Capital expenditures	0	0	0	1,000
Total cash out	4,208	4,137	4,101	60,658
Change in cash	20,880	22,078	23,840	174,590
Dispensers sold	80	85	90	735
Accounts receivable	72,769	76,857	80,888	80,888
Inventory—fragrance	1,397	1,446	1,516	1,516
Accounts payable	49,589	52,430	55,322	55,322

EXHIBIT 5 Summary of Cash Flow, Debt Structure, and Interest Payments by Quarter

	3 Months, Ended 3/31/86	*3 Months, Ended 6/30/86*	*3 Months, Ended 9/30/86*	*3 Months, Ended 12/31/86*	*3 Months, Ended 3/31/87*
Auto Fresh	$ (17,803)	$ 16,721	$ 38,675	$ 52,936	$ 66,840
Car Wash Supplies	4,150	9,282	22,919	38,636	55,680
Interest payment	(5,298)	(5,193)	(5,260)	(3,429)	(565)
Net cash flow	(18,951)	20,090	56,334	88,142	121,954
Beginning debt	163,000	181,951	161,861	105,527	17,384
Change in debt	18,951	(20,090)	(56,334)	(88,142)	(17,384)
Ending debt	181,951	161,861	105,527	17,384	0
Excess cash	0	0	0	0	104,570

EXHIBIT 6 Monthly Operating Expenses

	Auto Fresh	*Car Wash Accessories and Supplies*
Advertising	$1,300.00	$ 0.00*
Bank charges	12.50	22.50
Depreciation	20.00	650.00
Dues and subscriptions	10.00	0.00
Equipment rental	137.50	0.00
Freight	100.00	400.00
Insurance	50.00	50.00
Labor	1,476.00	4,454.00†
Office supplies	45.00	20.00
Postage	80.00	20.00
Professional fees	190.00	190.00‡
Rent	500.00	500.00
Repairs	50.00	50.00
Small tools	0.00	0.00
Telephone	300.00	300.00
Travel	300.00	70.00
Utilities	150.00	150.00
Miscellaneous	400.00	400.00
	$5,121.00	$7,476.50

*January 1985 increase of $10,000 for Auto Fresh for new sales brochures.

†August and February increases for Auto Fresh $1,500 and $1,000, respectively. Purpose is additional office personnel.

August $1,000 increase for Car Wash. Purpose, additional personnel.

‡April 1986 increase of $1,000 for Auto Fresh and Car Wash Supplies for year-end tax work.

EXHIBIT 7 Salary Detail

	AF Tax	*AF Salary*	*C/W Tax*	*C/W Salary*
Production manager (900/mo.)	$ 46.08	$ 178.94	$138.18	$ 536.82
Office manager (1,000/mo.)	96.70	403.30	96.70	403.30
Office clerk (4.00/hr.)	25.53	126.47	76.56	379.44
General manager (1,280/mo.)	86.85	512.00	130.27	768.00
Shop	0	0	134.48	573.52
Shop	0	0	99.33	490.67
Shop	0	0	106.18	520.07
	$255.14	$1,220.71	$781.70	$3,671.82
Total				
Auto Fresh		1,475.85 = 1,476.00		
Car Wash Supplies and Accessories		4,453.52 = 4,454.00		

EXHIBIT 8 Bulk Sales Pro Forma

	Income Statement
Revenue	$40,000
Costs of goods sold	23,250
Gross profit	16,750
Administration and installation	5,000
Net income	11,750

	Cash Flow Statement			
	Month 1	*Month 2*	*Month 3*	*Total*
Revenue	20,000			
Expenses				
Labor	2,500	2,500		
Material	0	18,250		
Administration and installation	2,500	2,500		
Net cash flow	15,000	(23,250)	20,000	11,750

Assumes the same of 50 units at $800 each. Cost is $465 for material and labor. Fifty percent is to be paid by the purchaser at the time of the order. This assumes 60 days for manufacturing and installation. The remaining 50 percent is to be paid 30 days from the final installation.

The Artisan's Haven

THE DECISION TO GO INTO BUSINESS

John and Katie Owen were confronted with a serious problem in 1973. John was fired from his job with a large chemical company in Trenton, New Jersey, for which he had worked for 33 years. The Arab oil embargo had caused a recession in the U.S. economy, and the nation was bracing itself for anticipated high inflation. After working for one company for so long and giving the firm his best years, John was emotionally upset over his dismissal. It was not as though he had made a big mistake or that he had done anything wrong. He was simply one of the older employees whom the company wanted to replace with younger, more energetic people. The recession gave the firm the opportunity it needed to make wholesale changes in personnel.

Finding a job during a recession is not easy, and for a 55-year-old man whose experience is limited to one industry, it is almost impossible. John felt helpless. He did not know what to do, and his frustration turned into anger as he realized for the first time in his working life that he was just a pawn in a great game of corporation chess. After several weeks of fear, anxiety, and doubt, John reached a major turning point in his life. He knew that he never wanted to work for anyone or any firm again.

The decision not to work for others was a major one, but John still did not know what to do. Should he retire? If he did, it would not be a comfortable retirement. Should he start his own business? If so, what kind of business should it be? He knew that he did not want to be involved with chemicals. Even before he was fired, John had begun to have reservations about producing dangerous chemicals and dumping waste into rivers. But his pay was good, and he did not have the time or the inclination to think about these deep questions too seriously. It was more important to John to pay his bills, to take nice vacations, and, in general, to have fun.

Although John likes to take credit for the idea, Katie is the one who suggested that he consider opening a store to sell arts and crafts. John's hobby for many years had been making gold jewelry, and he had become a very good goldsmith. Katie was an amateur interior designer, and she also enjoyed doing cross-stitch and making dried floral arrangements. Starting a business to sell something they enjoyed

 This case was written by Neil H. Snyder of the McIntire School of Commerce at the University of Virginia and Brooke Garret, a graduate of the McIntire School, who is now with Signet Bank.

making and knew something about seemed like a very good idea. In addition, John and Katie could work together in this kind of business, and Katie had always wanted to spend more time with John.

In 1974, they opened their first store in Trenton, New Jersey, and it was very successful. Their location was excellent, and their merchandise was high quality. Everything they did just seemed to work, and by 1980 the Owens owned six stores in New Jersey and Pennsylvania.

In 1980, John and Katie were both 62 years old, and they were more secure financially than they had ever been. When John lost his job with the chemical company, his net worth had been about $150,000, and almost all of it was tied up in his house and furnishings. His income at the time was comfortable but not great. Now, his net worth was in excess of $1 million and John and Katie could do many things they had always dreamed of doing. One thing they had dreamed of doing was retiring to a nice southern town and enjoying life.

At age 62, John and Katie decided to sell their stores in New Jersey and Pennsylvania and move to Athens, Georgia. A couple with whom they were very close had moved to Athens several years before, and John and Katie had visited them several times. They liked the town, they liked the University of Georgia, they liked the people, and they liked the climate. The move seemed like the right thing to do.

MOVING TO ATHENS, GEORGIA

John and Katie settled into their new way of life in Athens very quickly. They joined a local church that consumed a fair amount of their time. Katie became actively involved in the Christian Women's Club. John joined the Lion's Club and was able to contribute a great deal of time to many of its projects.

However, one thing was missing. While they were in business, John and Katie enjoyed making decisions and watching the bottom line of their income statement change to reflect the quality of their judgment. None of their activities in Athens provided the same sense of excitement and satisfaction that owning and operating a business had provided. After a year, John asked Katie about opening a business in Athens, and Katie agreed.

STARTING OVER AGAIN

In the fall of 1981, the Owens opened The Artisan's Haven in downtown Athens, directly across the street from the University of Georgia, and the community responded enthusiastically. The store sold handmade gold and silver jewelry, pottery, dried floral arrangements, woodcrafts, and various other handmade objects. Upon entering the store, customers were overwhelmed by the quality of the merchandise. It looked like it could have come out of a magazine like *Country Living* or *Southern Living*. All of the merchandise was made with great care and attention to detail.

Part of the immediate success of the new store was due to the popularity of arts and crafts at the time. But the Owens themselves were the main attraction. John and Katie seemed to be more relaxed about life, and the rapport they developed with their customers was nothing short of amazing. They offered classes to teach their customers how to make many of the items sold in the store. Katie became an interior decorator whose advice was sought by many prominent and influential people in the community. John organized the artists and craftspeople in the northeast Georgia area into a guild. As a result of their work, the Owens developed a large, wealthy customer base and an excellent supply of high-quality goods to sell.

DEMOGRAPHICS OF ATHENS

The population of Athens and Clarke County, the county surrounding Athens, is approximately 83,000 people. Twenty-one percent of the residents are professionals, and almost a third of them are students at the University of Georgia. A recent study of household incomes in Athens revealed the following:

Household Income*	Number of Households*
Greater than $50,000	4,719
$35,000–$49,999	6,426
$25,000–$34,999	7,691

*An average household in Athens is composed of 2.5 people.

COMPETITION

The Artisan's Haven had no direct competition in Athens. Traditionally, few residents in the community have shown much interest in high-quality goods and services. Cultural events such as plays and musical shows are occasional attractions. Until very recently, the best restaurants in town were steak houses that catered primarily to students, fast food chains, and small, locally owned operations. Big events in Athens that set it apart from other communities in the area are University of Georgia football games and fraternity and sorority parties.

However, things in Athens are changing, and the wealthier residents in the community are beginning to pay attention to their quality of life. The only stores selling products that compete with the Artisan's Haven include jewelry stores, department store chains, and a few lower-end specialty shops. These stores are not considered direct competitors because the quality of their merchandise is inferior to that sold in The Artisan's Haven. The store's closest direct competitors are in Atlanta, the state capital about 70 miles away, and many of Athens' wealthier residents go there routinely to shop.

MANAGEMENT AND PERSONNEL

John and Katie own and operate their store. In addition, they make many of the products they sell. Fortunately, they got to know two retired, upper-middle income women who were looking for opportunities to stay busy doing things they enjoy. These two women work part-time for the Owens for nominal wages. Besides being excellent employees, their friends visit them in the store, and many of them have become regular customers.

The Owens' most important employee is Rachel Thompson. She is 57 years old. They first met her when she was a customer in the store. After they got to know her, they discovered that Rachel's hobby was interior decorating and that most of what she bought was for friends' homes. She was not paid for any of this work. When she was approached by the Owens, Rachel was more than delighted to accept their offer of employment. Rachel's primary responsibility is to work with Katie on interior decorating jobs and to wait on customers in the store. She works about 20 hours a week.

Madeline Murray lives next door to the Owens. She is 53 years old and a very skillful craftswoman who developed her talent by doing the needlework in her home and the homes of her children, relatives, and many friends. The Owens first bought needlework from her by the piece, because it was impossible for Katie to do all of the cross stitching and to wait on customers all day. After it became obvious to the Owens that Madeline enjoyed working with and being around them and that they enjoyed her, they invited her to join them at the store. Her job was to do needlework for sale in the store and to work with customers who wanted custom-designed needlework made for their homes. Madeline also works about 20 hours a week.

Rachel and Madeline are like part of the family. Customers frequenting The Artisan's Haven sense the warmth and friendliness of everyone in the store, and they tell John and Katie regularly how enjoyable it is to shop there.

MARKETING

When the Owens first opened the store in Athens, their marketing efforts targeted local residents, tourists, and students. They used radio and newspaper advertising primarily. After several months of operation, they surveyed their customers to evaluate the effectiveness of their promotion effort. Not surprisingly, they learned that word-of-mouth and the Owens themselves were by far the most effective forms of advertising. Additionally, they learned that students were not attracted to their store in large numbers because of the prices of the goods sold and because they were not furnishing homes in which they intended to live for lengthy periods. Tourists did not flock to the store either, because Athens is not known as a tourist attraction.

The Owens decided early on that The Artisan's Haven did not need extensive print or broadcast media support. However, they did continue to run an occasional radio spot or ad in the local newspaper.

ORGANIZATION

The Owens incorporated The Artisan's Haven in the beginning, because they wanted to limit their liability. They were not certain about their options in this area, so they contacted an attorney who helped them make a choice about how to incorporate. They learned that there are major differences between a Subchapter C corporation and a Subchapter S corporation. Both offer several important features, such as continuity of life, centralization of management, limited liability, and easy transferability of interest. The S corporation is usually preferred by small-business owners because it is treated like a partnership for tax purposes.

Although the Owens could have incorporated The Artisan's Haven as an S corporation, they chose the C corporation. The C corporation allowed the Owens to deduct certain fringe benefits, like medical and health insurance, and to shelter earnings for later use. Because of their age, these were important issues to them.

The major disadvantage of a C corporation is double taxation. The Owens were not as concerned about this issue as the others because they were able to pay themselves attractive salaries, which were tax-deductible expenditures.

FINANCE

Exhibits 1, 2, and 3 contain pertinent financial information for The Artisan's Haven. The income statement shown in Exhibit 1 indicates that the largest expenses for the Owens are wages, travel, and rent. The 1981 data are a little misleading, because the store was in operation for only half a year. Travel is a major budget item because the Owens travel a great deal to visit craftspeople and art shows. Advertising in 1981 was a large expense item because the Owens were establishing their name and reputation.

A MAJOR DECISION POINT

In July 1987, John Owens suffered a massive heart attack, and he was told by his doctors to restrict his activities significantly. Before the heart attack, John and Katie had discussed the possibility of selling the business. Now Katie was certain that she wanted to sell it.

In March 1987, a local entrepreneur named Don Lassiter, who was in the business of buying and selling businesses, approached the Owens about selling The Artisan's Haven. They told him no. At the time, the Owens were in no hurry to act, but John's physical condition had caused Katie to become very anxious. She was concerned that John would want to keep the business and literally work himself to death. Also, she was worried that she could not take the pressure of running the business and watching after John. She wanted to sell the business, and the sooner the better. When she raised the issue with John, he agreed with her.

EXHIBIT 1

ARTISAN'S HAVEN
Consolidated Income Statements
As of January 31, 1986

	1981	*1982*	*1983*	*1984*	*1985*	*1986*
Sales	$ 16,610	$55,673	$78,736	$105,928	$123,683	$153,186
Cost of sales	8,305	27,837	35,968	43,441	60,201	75,806
Gross profit	8,305	27,836	42,768	62,487	63,482	77,380
Expenses						
Rent	3,900	7,800	7,800	7,800	7,800	7,800
Wages to officers	10,000	11,000	15,500	20,000	25,000	50,000
Other salaries	0	0	0	4,526	9,688	10,803
Utilities	434	612	712	862	1,002	1,165
Advertising	35,000	2,000	2,000	2,000	2,000	2,000
Travel	391	774	933	1,171	1,394	1,654
Supplies	649	835	971	1,175	1,366	1,589
Insurance	145	560	560	560	560	560
Depreciation	168	535	535	535	535	535
Interest	0	278	278	278	409	409
Total expenses	$ 50,687	$24,394	$29,289	$ 38,907	$ 49,754	$ 76,515
Profit before tax	(42,382)	3,442	13,479	23,580	13,728	865
Tax	0	1,687	6,604	11,554	6,727	423
Net income	(42,382)	1,755	6,875	12,026	7,001	442

Once they decided to sell The Artisan's Haven, John and Katie had to determine how much the business was worth and if Don Lassiter still wanted to buy it. There were other issues to be considered, too. For example, Mr. Lassiter might not be the only potential buyer. How would they contact other people who might be interested in their business?

The more they thought about it, the more they realized that they had to make a multitude of decisions. John told Katie that any buyer would require them to sign an agreement not to compete. Neither of them had any problem with this condition. Also, there was a question about how much, if any, time John and Katie were willing to work with the new owner(s) after the business was sold and in what capacity. Both of them were uncertain about how to approach this question.

How many more questions would they need to answer? John and Katie did not know.

EXHIBIT 2

ARTISAN'S HAVEN
Consolidated Balance Sheets
As of January 31, 1986
Assets

	1981	*1982*	*1983*	*1984*	*1985*	*1986*
Cash	0	$ 68	$ 5,823	$16,532	$22,018	$20,996
Inventory	$18,000	26,262	30,651	35,398	40,782	62,168
Prepaid expenses	2,089	1,973	1,862	2,239	2,355	2,451
Total current assets	$20,089	$28,303	$38,336	$54,169	$65,155	$85,615
Long-term assets						
Equipment	4,675	4,675	4,675	5,752	5,752	7,860
Furniture	3,897	3,897	3,897	3,897	3,897	4,623
Less accumulated depreciation	168	703	1,238	1,773	2,308	2,843
Total P, P&E	8,404	7,869	7,334	7,876	7,341	9,640
Total assets	$28,493	$36,172	$45,670	$62,045	$72,496	$95,255
Liabilities and Stockholders' Equity						
Current maturities	$ 278	$ 278	$ 278	$ 278	$ 278	$ 597
Accounts payable	2,122	7,899	10,211	14,447	17,901	21,870
Accrued expenses	1,093	1,240	1,829	1,942	2,068	2,189
Total current liabilities	$ 3,493	$ 9,417	$12,318	$16,667	$20,247	$24,656
Long-term debt	5,000	5,000	4,722	4,722	4,592	12,500
Total liabilities	$ 8,493	$14,417	$17,040	$21,389	$24,839	$37,156
Stockholders' equity						
Common stock	$20,000	$20,000	$20,000	$20,000	$20,000	$30,000
Retained earnings		1,755	8,630	20,656	27,657	28,099
Total equity	$20,000	$21,755	$28,630	$40,656	$47,657	$58,099
Total liabilities & equity	28,493	36,172	45,670	62,045	72,496	95,255

EXHIBIT 3 Sales by Quarter

Year	*Quarter*	*Sales by Quarter*	*Total Sales*
1981	3	$ 3,246	$ 16,610
	4	13,364	
1982	1	3,080	55,673
	2	10,397	
	3	4,512	
	4	37,684	
1983	1	5,511	78,736
	2	17,321	
	3	8,663	
	4	47,241	
1984	1	9,533	105,928
	2	25,422	
	3	10,595	
	4	60,378	
1985	1	10,021	123,683
	2	32,033	
	3	14,841	
	4	66,788	
1986	1	12,195	153,186
	2	44,906	
	3	17,961	
	4	78,124	

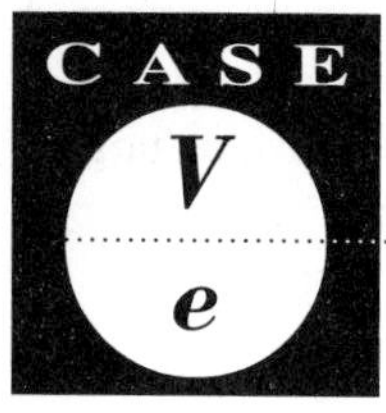

The Executive Woman

INTRODUCTION

Another frustrating Saturday spent shopping for working clothes left Susan Kenworthy wondering how professional women were supposed to put together a wardrobe with the limited time at their disposal. The specialty shops she had browsed through were too trendy for her office attire. The department stores had seemed promising with their larger variety of merchandise, but she had quickly become frustrated with the lack of help from the salespeople in trying to coordinate two outfits. She tried to envision the perfect shopping environment for the working professional women: a store with quality merchandise geared to a conservative business appearance and helpful salespeople who could design a wardrobe suited to the client.

If only such a store existed! Kenworthy wondered if this might be the market niche she had always dreamed of finding. Determined to follow through on her idea, she diligently researched the possibilities. After careful consideration, she produced the following business plan.

EXECUTIVE SUMMARY

The Executive Woman is a retail establishment serving the needs of middle-class, white-collar working women by providing a large selection of business apparel.

The product line will focus on a large selection of business suits. Emphasis will be on high-quality merchandise at competitive prices. The store will offer superior service in sales and selection. Personnel will act as wardrobe consultants to customers. A high-traffic location will be essential to the success of the business. This will mitigate the risks associated with high inventory levels.

The venture will be a limited partnership. Funding is sought in 10 equity units of $10,000 each. The present general partner plans to purchase 3 of the 10 units. This represents a substantial portion of her personal resources.

Three stores are planned. The first store will be opened in 1988, the second in 1990, and the third in 1992. Objectives are to capture 4 percent of the served market by 1992.

PRODUCT

The product is quality women's apparel with a conservative business fashion target. The inventory will include suits, dresses, separates, blouses, sweaters, coats, dress shoes, lingerie, and accessories. A variety of price ranges will be offered, with emphasis initially on the medium-price range. A shift toward higher-priced items is anticipated. A critical factor in selling the product will be wardrobe consultants to help the customer make selections.

Business merchandise will be emphasized, with suits accounting for 40 percent of the total annual sales. The large selection of suits will give a competitive advantage over department stores. The merchandise mix is projected to be approximately 44 percent suits, 11 percent dresses, and 21 percent separates. Blouses, coats, sweaters, shoes, lingerie, and accessories will make up the remaining merchandise.

The first store will open at Woodland Hills Mall. This will satisfy the requirement for high traffic and will also be conveniently located for the target market. Two other stores are planned; they will open at two-year intervals following the first store. With the success of the initial three stores, future expansion will include opening stores in other locations and possible franchises.

INDUSTRY

An analysis of the women's retail clothing stores in the Tulsa area yields five possible competitors for women's suits and business apparel. In-depth analysis shows that three of the five offer the customer little or no help in fashion selection. The stores that offer help are either limited to high-priced merchandise or poorer quality and trendy styles.

The Executive Woman will find a niche in the market and provide a competitive alternative for the consumer by using the following strategies: wider price range, large selection, quality merchandise for a focused market, and quality help.

Sales projections are to capture 0.5 percent of the target market share in the first year and increase to 4.0 percent by the end of the fifth year. Total sales should increase from $180,000 to $1,753,000 over the five-year period.

MARKET SEGMENT

Target customers are business and professional women who desire a conservative look found in an office setting. This woman wears business suits about 60 percent of the time, dresses 30 percent of the time, and separates 10 percent of the time. She desires a convenient location and quality service with a wide selection.

EXHIBIT 1

THE EXECUTIVE WOMAN
Business Plan for 1988–1992
Balance Sheet ($000s)
Assets

	1988	*1989*	*1990*	*1991*	*1992*
Current assets					
Cash	$10	$10	$10	$10	$10
Accounts receivable (net)	5	5	10	10	15
Merchandise inventory	100	100	200	200	300
Supplies	10	10	10	10	10
Prepaid expenses	2	2	2	2	2
Total current assets	$127	$127	$232	$232	$337
Fixed assets					
Fixtures	$3	$3	$6	$6	$9
Equipment	1	1	2	2	3
Total fixed assets	$4	$4	$8	$8	$12
Total assets	$131	$131	$240	$240	$349
Liabilities and Net Worth					
Current liabilities					
Accounts payable	$20	$20	$40	$40	$60
Current portion LTD					
Other	30	30	60	60	90
Total current liabilities	$50	$50	$100	$100	$150
Long-term liabilities					
Notes payable					
Bank loan payable					
Other loans payable					
Total long-term liabilities	$0	$0	$0	$0	$0
Total liabilities	$50	$50	$100	$100	$150
Net worth: owner's equity	81	81	140	140	199
Total liabilities and net worth	$131	$131	$240	$240	$349

In 1985, labor force participation by women reached 54.5 percent. The greatest increase was in ages 20 to 54. A market analysis of the Tulsa metropolitan area shows a total of approximately 150,000 female workers. Of course, approximately 73,000 have occupations in the target market: executive, managerial, professional, sales, or administrative support. In the first year of operation, the Executive Woman plans to capture 0.5 percent of the market share. By the fifth year of operation, projections indicate a 4 percent market share. These sales figures are reflected in the pro forma statements indicated in Exhibits 1 and 2.

Promotion of the stores will be through advertisements in local newspapers. There will also be target periodicals in Tulsa that cater to business people. Channels of communication will include direct mail advertising to past customers and women's professional and college organizations.

EXHIBIT 2

THE EXECUTIVE WOMAN
Business Plan for 1988–1992
Break-Even Analysis

	1988	*1989*	*1990*	*1991*	*1992*
Sales	$180,000	$536,000	$800,000	$1,181,000	$1,753,000
Cost of goods sold	106,560	317,312	473,600	699,152	1,037,776
Gross profit	73,440	218,688	326,400	481,848	715,224
Fixed expenses					
Management payroll	33,000	66,000	81,000	96,000	126,000
Rent	22,500	45,000	67,500	90,000	135,000
Depreciation	400	400	800	800	1,200
Total fixed expenses	$55,900	$111,400	$149,300	$186,800	$262,200
Gross profit as % of sales	40.80%	40.80%	40.80%	40.80%	40.80%
Break-even	76.12%	50.94%	45.74%	38.77%	36.66%

MANAGEMENT

The general partner manager will serve as business manager with responsibilities in inventory control, cash flow, budgeting, and various financial, marketing, and accounting projects. Each store will also have a manager experienced in the retail business. The first manager hired for store one will have extensive experience in women's apparel. This person may serve in a managerial capacity over the other stores if performance warrants.

Each store will have two full-time wardrobe consultants. In addition, part-time help will be hired.

Discount Medical Accessories, Inc.

In January 1988, William Carlisle, a veteran of 30 years in the medical supplies industry, began to market X-ray protection wear and accessories using a unique marketing approach for this industry—direct mail. The idea had come to Carlisle while employed as a salesman for a large medical products and accessories company. He found that many of his customers were complaining about the prices of protective wear items he carried and that many of the extras for these items, such as variety of colors, styling, monogramming, and so on, were costly and unnecessary.

As an example, Carlisle's firm offered X-ray lab aprons in four colors, three different styles, and with the name or logo of the buyer monogrammed on each product. Carlisle realized that his customers were paying a premium for these extras and that many felt they were unnecessary. Although some of his customers desired these extras, Carlisle believed that there was a significant price-sensitive market for these items. Carlisle also felt that many of his customers could order the more standard items, such as X-ray accessories, by mail because little personal selling was necessary. He believed that about 65 percent of the $50 million market for these products was price sensitive.

Carlisle's 30 years in the industry also provided many contacts. While considering his idea of a discounted medical accessories company, he approached a few manufacturers to identify a source for such products. Initially, he felt that he would offer X-ray protective wear and accessories such as lab aprons and goggles. One manufacturer agreed to produce the products and to ship directly to the customers, who would place their orders directly with Discount Medical Accessories, Inc. (DMA). This would also help to maintain low overhead, which would support the low pricing strategy. All products would meet the necessary industry standards for quality and protection.

During the summer of 1987, Carlisle began working with a friend in the advertising field to develop a catalog that could be mailed to potential customers of X-ray protection wear and accessory products. Since the mission of the firm was to be a discount catalog operation, his friend recommended that the brochure be simple and in black and white. This would help reflect the image of the firm as a discount direct mail operation. Carlisle then rented some office space in a small professional building, where customers' orders would be processed. Customers, after receiving the catalog, would call an 800 toll-free number to place their order. The order would be sent to the manufacturer and then shipped directly to the customer via UPS.

EXHIBIT 1

	BM Medical	*Med Ray*	*X-Ray Accessories*	*DMA*
Apron	$118.00	$ 79.99	$126.00	$ 69.95
Vest and skirt	295.00	130.00	140.00	110.00
Special procedure apron	295.00	235.00	275.00	210.00
Quick drop OR apron	118.00	118.00	140.00	110.00
Thyroid collar	28.00	23.00	27.00	20.00

COMPETITION

There were a number of large firms in the X-ray protective wear market. Many offered these products as a complement to their medical products and equipment. Personal selling to hospitals, clinics, HMOs, and even doctors' offices was standard practice of these firms. On a sales call, a salesperson would leave a very elaborate catalog with the customers, from which orders would be placed. None of these firms could be described as discounters and thus were not felt to be competitors by Carlisle. However, one firm, Med Ray, did offer their X-ray protective wear products at a low price. Since their main product line was X-ray equipment, they tried to create some customer goodwill by lowering the price on their X-ray protective wear. Exhibit 1 illustrates the price comparison for the major competitors in this market.

COSTS

Carlisle assumed that start-up costs would be about $15,000 to cover catalogs, mailings, office supplies, telephone expenses, and legal/accounting fees. Additional costs such as salaries, rent, utilities, and so on would be about $48,000 in the first year of operation. The firm would also incur a cost of goods that would average about 75 percent of sales. This gross margin of 25 percent would be satisfactory, according to Carlisle, to cover fixed costs and still earn a profit.

The critical decisions, according to Carlisle, were the mailings and pricing of the products. The direct-mail pieces had to reach the appropriate target market with an attractive price. It was also important to keep costs down to maintain the price advantage.

GLOSSARY

accrual method of accounting An accounting method that records income and expenses when incurred, not when cash is received, thereby ignoring cash inflows and outflows.

acquisition financing Financing used for such activities as traditional acquisitions, leveraged buyouts, and going private.

acquisitions The purchase of an entire company or part of it so that the acquired entity is completely absorbed by the acquiring company and no longer exists as a separate business.

aftermarket support The managing underwriter's readiness to purchase or sell the stock to stabilize the market, helping to prevent the price from going below that of the initial public offering.

assets Everything of value owned by the business. Value is based on the actual cost or amount expended for the asset. Assets are categorized as fixed or current, based on the length of time they will be used.

asset base for loans The entity of value pledged against the loan, ensuring a reasonable expectation of repayment. Usually the loan is based on accounts receivable, inventory, equipment, or real estate.

balance of payments The difference between the value of the goods and services imported into a country and those exported, which is reflected in the value of the country's currency.

barter Trading of goods or services without the exchange of money.

birth order A concept that the relative position of one sibling versus another in a family affects the entrepreneurial tendency of an individual.

blue sky laws The securities of a company going public must be qualified under the laws of each state in which they will be offered for sale.

book value Acquisition cost minus liabilities.

break-even The point in the operation where total revenue equals total costs. Each additional unit sold after break-even results in a profit equal to the difference between the selling price and variable cost per unit.

breakthrough innovations The few innovations that, if successful, will either radically change an existing industry or create an entirely new one.

business angels An "invisible" group of individual, informal investors who are looking for equity-type investment opportunities. They provide funds needed in all stages of financing.

business plan A concise, written document prepared by the entrepreneur, describing the present venture and market situation, future directions, and implementation strategies. The major purposes of the plan are supporting the financing needs for the entrepreneur and guiding the future direction of the venture.

cash method of accounting An accounting method where income and expenses are recorded only when cash is received or disbursed, making the results more consistent with cash flow.

C corporation This is the typical corporation, where the owners are the stockholders. Unlike the proprietorship and partnership, it is treated as a separate legal entity for tax and liability purposes.

competitive negotiation A situation involving directly competing claims on a fixed, limited economic resource. It requires concessions in allocating shares in order for a settlement to be reached.

contract A written, legally binding agreement specifying the parties, their roles, and value of transaction.

controlled economies Centralized, planned economies that are the opposite of a competitive market economy.

conventional bank loans Business loans such as lines of credit, installment loans, straight commercial loans, long-term loans, and character loans.

cooperative negotiation A situation where two parties bargain by working with each other to obtain a mutually beneficial solution.

copyright A protection of the original works of authorship for a term of the life of the author plus 50 years, or if an institution, 75 years from the date of publication.

deal structure The terms of the transaction between the entrepreneur and the funding source.

deficiency letter A letter informing the company that the preliminary prospectus covering the information contained in the final prospectus needs some modifications before being approved.

departure point The time when dissatisfaction and frustration with his or her present job causes the entrepreneur to consider leaving to form a new venture.

description of venture The part of the business plan that discusses the product/service, business location, plan and equipment, and qualifications of entrepreneurs.

desirability of new venture formation The desire to form a new venture resulting from an individual's culture, subculture, family, teachers, and peers.

developmental financing The second basic financing type in which capitalists play an active role in providing funds.

direct exporting Exporting through the use of Independent Foreign Distributor and Overseas Sales Offices.

direct foreign investment A foreign company buying assets in any economy, usually in the form of putting money or its equivalent in a company in a foreign economy.

direct marketing Seller's use of one or more media for the purposes of soliciting a response by phone, mail, or personal visit.

disclosure document The document sent to the Patent and Trademark Office to establish a date of conception of an invention. Used to prove that the inventor was the first to conceive of the invention.

distributive bargaining A situation where one party is not allowed to achieve his or her goals; therefore, there is no trust between the two parties, and a solution can only be reached through a series of modified positions of compromise and concessions.

diversified activity merger A conglomerate merger involving the consolidation of two essentially unrelated firms with as limited a transfer of skills and activities as possible.

due diligence Assessing the upside potential and downside risk as well as the markets, the industry, financial analysis, customers, and management capability before making an investment.

early-stage financing Two types of financing occur during this difficult stage for raising capital: seed capital and start-up.

earnings approach The most widely used method of valuing a company, as it provides the potential investor with the best estimate of the probable return on investment.

entrepreneur as an innovator To reform or revolutionize a present pattern by opening a new source of supply or new outlets, reorganizing a new industry, or undertaking some other innovative activity.

entrepreneur decision process The decision to leave a present career or life-style because the entrepreneurial venture being considered is desirable, and external and internal factors make the venture possible.

entrepreneurial career Dynamic stages in the life of an entrepreneur, with each stage reflecting and interacting with other stages and events in the individual's life.

entrepreneurial domain Pressures on a business to manage in a looser entrepreneurial manner caused by such factors as diminishing opportunity streams and rapidly changing technology, consumer economics, social values, and political rules.

entrepreneurial process The four distinct phases of creating a new venture: (1) identifying and evaluating the opportunity, (2) developing the business plan, (3) determining the resources required, and (4) managing the resulting entity.

entrepreneurship The process of creating a new venture of value. Involves devoting the necessary time and effort, assuming the accompanying financial, psychic, and social risks, and receiving the resulting rewards of monetary and personal satisfaction.

equity participation Having an ownership position in an organization as a result of contributing some resource, usually money.

equity pool A sum of money accumulated for investing in various situations.

exporting The sale and shipping of products manufactured in one country to a customer located in another country.

external funds Money obtained outside the company. It is usually one of two types: debt financing or equity financing.

factor approach An approach used to determine the value of a venture using one of three major factors: earnings, dividend-paying capacity, and book value.

factors in valuating a business Eight factors that indicate the importance of using the value of other corporations engaged in the same or similar line of business in valuing the business venture at hand.

FIFO Method of inventory costing called first-in-first-out. As an item is sold, the cost of goods is based on the cost of producing the oldest item in inventory.

financial plan A plan involving pro forma statements for cash flow, income, and balance sheet. Indicates the potential investment and possible sources of funds.

firm growth pattern Each industry has established track records by which a firm grows.

form S–1 A registration form used in an initial public offering. Provides information to purchasers to assess the company's cash flow from internal and external sources.

form S–18 The appropriate registration form for a small initial public offering.

foundation companies Firms created from research and development that lay the foundation for a new industry.

franchise Arrangement whereby manufacturer or sole distributor of a trademarked product or service gives exclusive rights to an entrepreneur in return for payment of royalties and conformance to standard operating procedures.

franchise agreement Written document that contains all of the specific requirements and obligations of the franchise.

franchisee The person or entrepreneur who purchases the right to use, manufacture, or sell any trademark, copyright, or patent.

franchisor The seller of a franchise. Has ownership of trademark, patent, or copyright that is offered to someone in return for royalties.

full disclosure Making sure that all pertinent facts and figures about a company are made public.

general valuation method One approach an entrepreneur can use to determine how much of the company a venture capitalist will want for a given investment.

general partner The sponsoring company that secures the needed limited partners to develop the technology.

going public The transformation of a closely held corporation into one where the general public has a proprietary interest.

government as innovator One method for commercializing the results of the interaction between a social need and technology.

high-potential venture The type of new company that receives the greatest investment interest and publicity. It frequently goes public or is purchased by a larger company.

horizontal merger A merger of two firms that produce one or more of the same or closely related products in the same geographical area.

indirect exporting Exporting through the use of a foreign purchaser in a local market and export management firm.

industry analysis An assessment of historical achievements, trends, major competitors and their strategies, market segments, and future forecasts of a particular industry.

industry–university agreement A type of joint venture agreement for the purpose of doing research. It takes on a variety of forms, depending on the parties involved and the subject of the research.

informal risk-capital market One type of risk capital that is composed of a virtually invisible group of investors who are looking for equity-type investment opportunities in a wide variety of entrepreneurial ventures.

initial public offering The first stock offering of a once privately owned company.

integrative bargaining A form of negotiation involving cooperation between the parties negotiating.

internal funds Money generated from the operations of a company. Includes profits, sale of assets, reduction in working capital, credit from suppliers, and accounts receivable.

international business The process of conducting business activities across national boundaries.

intrapreneurial culture Instilling the entrepreneurial spirit in an existing organization in order to innovate and grow.

intrapreneurial leadership characteristics These include understanding the environment, being visionary and flexible, creating management options, encouraging teamwork, encouraging open discussion, building a coalition of supporters, and persistence.

intrapreneurship Entrepreneurship within an existing business structure.

inventor A person who has family, education, and occupational experiences that contribute to creative development and free thinking; a problem solver who loves to create new things.

job description It should specify the details of the work to be performed by the person holding the position.

job specifications These identify the requirements needed by the person applying for a job. Included might be skills, experience, education, and so on.

joint venture A separate entity involving two or more active participants as partners.

leverage The ability to borrow enough money to provide the additional equity needed for the acquisition.

leveraged buyout Occurs when the assets of the acquired company are used as collateral to finance the deal.

leveraged buyout financing The money involved in acquiring a company, with the assets of the acquired company being used as collateral.

liabilities The amount a company owes to creditors. They are categorized as current or long term, depending on whether they are due within a year or longer.

license An arrangement between two parties, where one party had proprietary rights based on a patent, trademark, or copyright. Licenses are formed by contract, with a royalty or fixed sum being paid in return for permission to use the patent, trademark, or copyright.

life-cycle approach A conceptualization of entrepreneurial careers in seven major categories: educational environment, individual personalities, childhood family environment, employment history, current work situation, the individual's current perspective, and the current family situation.

life-style firm A privately held firm achieving only modest growth. It primarily supports the owners and has little opportunity for significant growth and expansion.

LIFO Method of inventory costing called last-in-first-out. As an item is sold, the cost of goods would be based on the cost of producing the most recent item in inventory.

limited partner A partner having limited liability yet not a totally taxable entity.

liquidation covenant A provision in an agreement allowing the investor to require registration, sale, or other disposition of the securities given certain conditions occur.

liquidation value The amount that would be received if the corporation liquidated.

locus of control The internal-external control dimension of an individual.

majority interests Having a large enough ownership position in a firm to have control. This usually means owning over 50 percent.

management contract A method allowing the purchasing country to gain foreign expertise without acquiring ownership of the company's resources; this allows a profit to be obtained without the need of a large equity investment.

managerial (administrative) domain Pressures on a business to manage in a more hierarchical fashion caused by such factors as power, status, financial rewards, performance measurement criteria, risk reduction, inertia, organizational culture, and planning systems.

managing underwriter The lead firm in forming the underwriting syndicate for the issuance of stocks or bonds of a company.

market extension merger An agreement reached between acquiring and acquired firms that produce the same products but sell them in different geographic markets.

marketing goals and objectives Written statements in the marketing plan that describe where the company is going in the next 12 months.

marketing mix The interaction of four major controllable variables in the marketing system: product/service, pricing, distribution, and promotion.

marketing-oriented organization This is an organization where the management philosophy is to determine the consumer's needs and then develop and deliver products and services that will effectively meet them.

marketing plan A written guide within the business plan, usually for a 12-month period, which describes the market, industry, competition, and the plan to be implemented to achieve future sales and profits. Describes how the product(s) or service(s) will be distributed, priced, and promoted, with specific forecasts and projected profitability.

marketing system A description of the interrelationships between the external and internal environment with decisions on product, pricing, distribution, and promotion.

merger A transaction involving two or more companies in which only one survives.

minority interest Having a small investment in a company to gain a foothold or experience in a market before making a major commitment.

moral-support network A cheering squad of family and friends that provides advice, encouragement, understanding, and even assistance to the entrepreneur.

motivation The drives and desires to become an entrepreneur.

need for achievement An individual's desire for responsibility in solving problems, setting goals, and reaching goals.

need for independence An individual's desire to do things in his or her own way and time. Such a person may have a difficult time working for someone else.

negotiation approach The approach by which parties attempt to resolve a conflict by agreement. If a resolution is not possible, the critical issues in the disagreement are identified. This is done in eight steps: prepare, discuss, signal, propose, respond, bargain, close, and agree.

nonequity arrangements These are agreements that involve no financial commitment. The three most popular forms are licensing, turn-key projects, and management contracts.

opportunity identification After formulating a general idea about the type of company desired, entrepreneurs use informal and formal mechanisms for identifying the best opportunity to become involved in.

opportunity parameters Boundaries of creativity in a new product development.

ordinary innovation New products or services with little uniqueness or technology.

organization culture The atmosphere and working environment of a particular organization.

organizational plan A part of the business plan describing the venture's form of ownership, terms of agreement, management team, roles and responsibilities of the team, and compensation for each member.

owner equity The excess of all assets over all liabilities. It is the net worth of the business.

partnership In this legal form of business, there is more than one owner, each with responsibility for the operation of the venture. The partnership agreement stipulates the responsibility of the owners and their liability. A partnership may have general or limited partners.

patent A contract between the government and an inventor whereby the government grants the inventor exclusivity on the material presented for a specified amount of time.

possibility of new venture formation The factors that contribute to the creation of a new venture, such as governments, background, marketing, role models, and finances.

preliminary screening An investigation of the economy of the industry. Includes an assessment of the appropriateness of the knowledge and ability of the venture capitalist.

present value of future cash flow A method of valuation that adjusts the value of the cash flow of the business for the time value of money and the business and economic risks.

pricing amendment The information contained in the final prospectus made available before the effective date. Includes offering price, underwriters' commission, and amount of proceeds.

primary data New unpublished information collected for a specific need or purpose. It usually involves the development of a market research study to collect the data.

private offering A formalized approach for obtaining funds from private investors that is faster and less costly than other approaches.

private placement A method for obtaining money from private investors, who may be family and friends or wealthy individuals.

private venture capital firm One type of venture capital firm usually involving a general operating partner and limited partners who have supplied the capital.

production plan A part of the business plan that describes the manufacturing process and its costs, any subcontractors used, machinery and equipment needed, raw materials needed, potential sources of supplies, and layout of plant and manufacturing process.

product/market opportunity A unique growing market opportunity where the company's offering has a differential advantage.

product evolution process The process through which an innovation is developed and commercialized through entrepreneurial activity stimulating economic growth.

product-extension merger An agreement between the acquiring and acquired companies having related production and/or distribution activities that do not compete directly with each other.

Product Safety and Liability Commission Empowered under the Consumer Product Safety Act, a five-member commission prescribes safety standards for more than 10,000 products. This commission identifies products considered substantial hazards and, where appropriate, will request the manufacturer to take corrective action.

professional-support network Advice obtained from a mentor, business associates, trade associations, or personal affiliations.

pro forma balance sheet Forecasts the asset, liability, and owner equity balance of a venture based on the pro forma income and cash flow statements.

pro forma cash flow Projection of cash balance sheet at the end of a specific time period based on projected cash receipts and cash disbursements from the income statement.

pro forma income statement Projection of a venture's earnings and expenses from operations. It should be prepared on a monthly basis for the first year and on an annual basis thereafter.

pro forma sources and applications of funds Projects the disposition of earnings from operations and from other financing. Indicates how the money for operation of a company will be obtained.

proprietorship The simplest form of business. The owner is the individual who starts the business and has full responsibility for its operations.

prospectus A legal offering document normally prepared as a brochure or booklet for distribution to prospective buyers.

publicity This is free advertising in which a trade magazine, newspaper, magazine, radio, or TV program finds it of public interest to do a story on the new venture.

quiet period The period of time from when the decision to go public is made to 90 days following the date of becoming effective.

rational decision model The type of negotiation flow that moves from establishing objectives, to establishing criteria, to analyzing cause-and-effect relationships involved, to developing and evaluating alternatives, and then to selecting an alternative and an action plan. The final step must be the measuring of the outcomes upon implementation.

red herring The preliminary prospectus. Its purpose is to show how income was used to increase assets or pay off debt.

referral sources Information on potential deals from such sources as business associates, friends, active personal research, investment bankers, and business brokers.

registration statement Supplemental information to the prospectus, which is available for public inspection at the office of the SEC.

Regulation D Contains a number of broad provisions designed to simplify the private offering.

replacement value A valuation method used for insurance purposes or in unique circumstances, whereby the valuation of the venture is based on the amount of money it would take to replace that asset.

reporting requirements One of the negative aspects of going public. The company must carefully observe each requirement since mistakes can have significant negative consequences.

research and development limited partnership An agreement that the sponsoring company will develop the technology and the limited partnership will provide the funds.

restrictive covenant Section of an investment agreement that protects the investor and allows the investment to be profitably liquidated at a later date.

reward system Ensures that an intrapreneur receives rewards for attaining established performance goals.

risk assessment A section of the business plan that identifies the potential risks in the venture and strategies that might be implemented to deal with them.

risk-capital market The market where financing can be obtained for new and growing companies. It has three primary parts: the informal risk capital industry, the formal venture capital industry, and the public stock market.

risk taking of an entrepreneur A calculated risk that an entrepreneur takes in order to make a profit by establishing a new venture.

role models Parents, brothers, sisters, other relatives, successful entrepreneurs in the surrounding community, or nationally touted entrepreneurs whom entrepreneurs emulate to varying extents.

S corporation This is a special type of corporation, where the income (and losses) are declared as personal income by the shareholders. There are restrictions on who can elect this form of business.

secondary data Information that already exists in a published form. It may be purchased from an outside source, or it may be available in a library.

settlement range The area of values in a negotiation procedure where a mutually agreeable decision can be reached.

situation analysis A description of the historical perspective of the new venture, including background on the entrepreneur, the product/service, and the industry. It answers the question, Where have we been?

Small Business Innovation Research (SBIR) grants An opportunity for small business to obtain research and development money through a uniform method by which each participating agency solicits, evaluates, and selects the research proposals for funding.

Small Business Investment Company (SBIC) firms The first firms that started the formal venture-capital industry.

social status The status placed on an individual or family by society, which is reflected in their behavior and value systems.

stage of economic development The different stages of economic development a country goes through, from being very undeveloped to very developed and achieving a better standard of living.

state-sponsored venture-capital firm A venture-capital firm sponsored by a state. The size and investment thrust varies from state to state. Each firm is required to invest a certain percentage of the funds in companies in the particular state.

strong management team A good team of managers having solid experience and background, commitment to the company, capabilities in their specific areas of expertise, the ability to merge challenges, and flexibility.

synergy Any situation where the whole is greater than the sum of the parts and therefore worth joining together. A particularly important characteristic for a successful joint venture.

target market A subset of the total market identified by the entrepreneur as having the greatest opportunity for success.

technological innovation A new product or service having advances in science and technology.

third-party payments Payments to a party other than the ones directly involved in the transaction.

time management Managing your time effectively by focusing on the areas most important in accomplishing the goal.

top management commitment The first step in the process of establishing intrapreneurship in an organization is to secure commitment by top management. Without this commitment, the organization will never be able to go through all the cultural climate changes necessary for implementation.

trademark A word, symbol, design, or some combination of such, or a slogan or sound that identifies the source or sponsorship of certain goods and services. It is granted by the Patent and Trademark Office for renewable 20-year periods. In the sixth year, an affidavit is filed to prove that the mark is in use.

trade secret The protection available when the entrepreneur prefers to maintain an idea or process as confidential and not copyright or patent it. Not covered by any federal law, but is recognized under a governing body of common laws in each state.

traditional managers Motivated primarily by promotion and typical corporate rewards. They tend to adhere strictly to established hierarchical structures, to be less risk-oriented, and to emphasize short-term results.

turn-key projects A company built by a foreign company that trains the workers and managers and then turns the operation over to the local owners.

underwriting syndicate A group of investors who have gotten together to issue the stock or bonds of a company.

venture-capital decision process The process by which the typical venture-capital firm decides to invest in a particular investment opportunity.

venture-capital market One of the three types of risk capital that has formal companies making investment decisions in a variety of business areas.

vertical merger A merger of two or more firms in successive stages of production that often involve a buyer-seller relationship. This stabilizes supply and production and offers more control of these critical areas.

windows of opportunity The length of time a market is available for a new product or service idea.

work history The documentation of an individual's jobs and accomplishments over time. This is an important aspect in obtaining external financing.

INDEX

C

M

Q

R